The following 4 pages contain a map which folded out in the original volume. In order to incorporate it in this reproduction without impairing the legibility, it was broken into four sections, which are arranged as follows: A (Left), B (Left Middle), C (Right Middle), and D (Right).

A   B   C   D

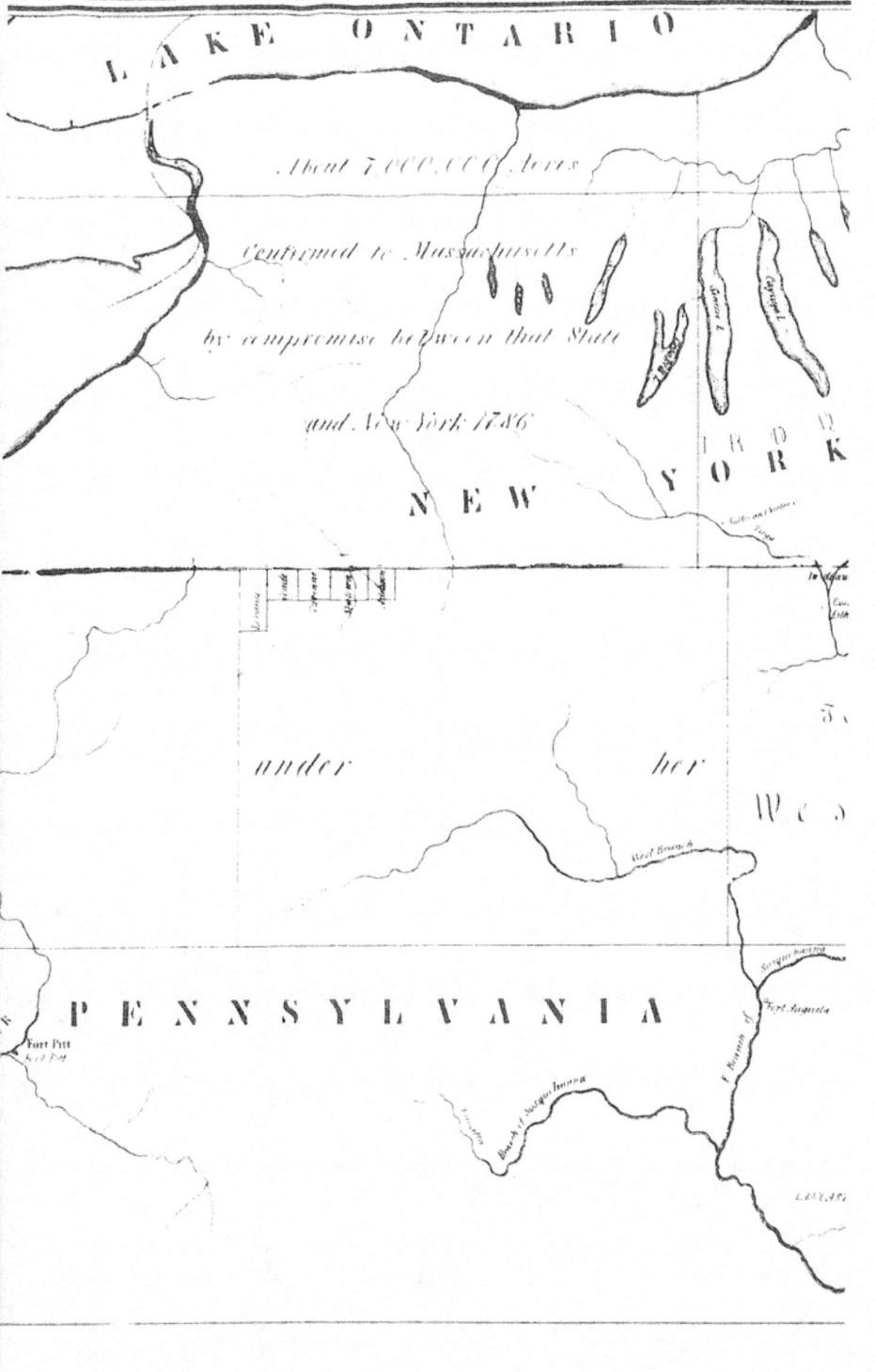

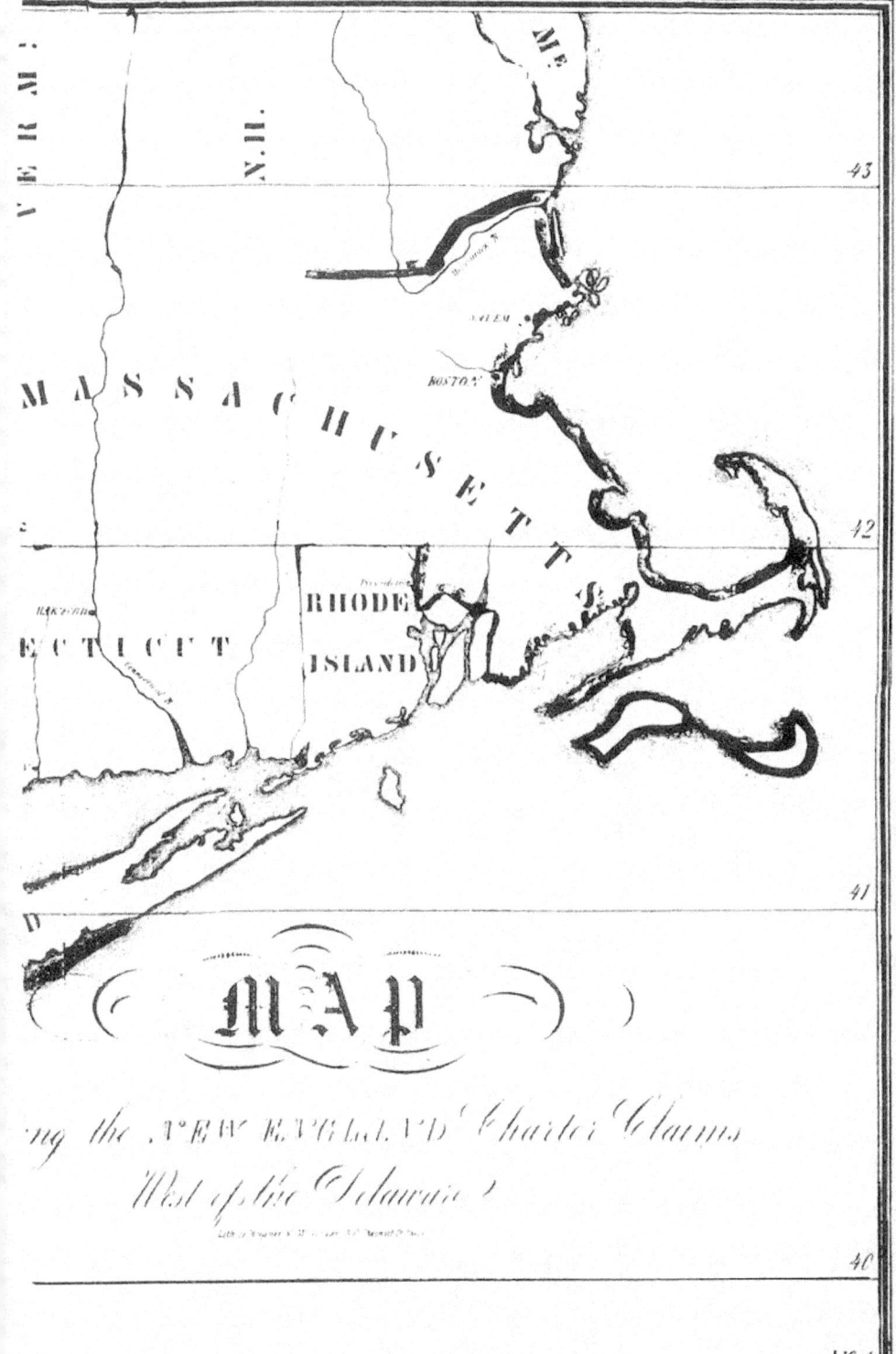

History of WYOMING

[*Wyoming Valley, Pennsylvania*]

IN A SERIES OF LETTERS
FROM
Charles Minor
TO
HIS SON
William Penn Miner, Esq.

....

"Diligence and accuracy are the only merits which a Historical writer may ascribe to himself."

"I have carefully examined all the original materials that could illustrate the subject I had under taken to treat."

....

HERITAGE BOOKS
2011

HERITAGE BOOKS
AN IMPRINT OF HERITAGE BOOKS, INC.

Books, CDs, and more—Worldwide

For our listing of thousands of titles see our website
at
www.HeritageBooks.com

A Facsimile Reprint
Published 2011 by
HERITAGE BOOKS, INC.
Publishing Division
100 Railroad Ave. #104
Westminster, Maryland 21157

Entered according to the Act of Congress, in the year 1845, by
Charles Miner,
In the Clerk's Office of the District Court
of the Eastern District of Pennsylvania.

Originally published by J. Crissy:
No. 4 Minor Street
Philadelphia
1845

— Publisher's Notice —
In reprints such as this, it is often not possible to remove blemishes from the original. We feel the contents of this book warrant its reissue despite these blemishes and hope you will agree and read it with pleasure.

International Standard Book Numbers
Paperbound: 978-1-55613-455-5
Clothbound: 978-0-7884-8638-8

INTRODUCTION.

The History of Wyoming remains to be written. The book of Mr. Chapman is certainly valuable, so far as it extends. A man of talents, research and industry;—had his life been prolonged, he would have produced a work worthy of the subject, and his own fame. Cut off in mid-life, his manuscript was the first rude essay—the mere outline of what he must have intended to accomplish. The eagerness with which the volume was sought after and read, shows the lively interest which the public mind possesses in respect to the subject.

Col. Stone's popular book, "The Poetry and History of Wyoming," deserves commendation. His polished pen has thrown a charm around the narrative, easier to admire than imitate. But the fact that he was obliged to reprint Campbell's Gertrude, with Irving's Biography of the Author, shows that, in his view, the materials of interest relating to the subject were either too few, or too remotely accessible, to form the ground-work for a respectable volume. Most of the more striking facts, and many of the more touching personal incidents, he has wrought up with a master hand, and given with all the sparkling raciness which genius imparts to an interesting subject.

I came to Pennsylvania in 1799, a settler under the Connecticut claim. The grounds of that claim, connected as they were with the early hopes of the writer, were then examined with care. Editor of a Paper, at Wilkesbarre, for thirteen years, including the period of the sharp conflicts under the Intrusion Law, the claim of Connecticut was discussed—the services and sufferings of the early settlers were inquired into, until the whole subject became one of absorbing concern, interwoven with the most interesting associations of my life. When Judge Marshall published his first edition of the Life of Washington, I took the liberty of writing to him, stating that the account of the Wyoming Massacre was exceedingly erroneous, and gave him a version of the affair, derived from the best sources. I beg leave to remark, that no important subject was ever before involved in such embarrassing contradictions. The reason I take it is this: On the invasion by Butler and his Indians, most of the leading men were slain, and the rest of the inhabitants scattered in the wildest state of alarm. Rumour brought to every flying group a tale of seven-fold horror, and these, repeated by the fugitives, wherever they fled, were told and received as historic truth. Hence the exaggerated account published at Poughkeepsie a few weeks after the massacre, which was, without doubt, the ground-work, probably the sole authority, of Gordon and Ramsay, as they were the sources from which Marshall derived materials for his first edition. Black with cruelty, and crimsoned with blood, sufficient to harrow up the soul with horror, is the simple narrative, attested by truth, which displays the ferocity of demons—the malignity of fiends. The false account was immeasurably worse. It may excite inquiry, Why the oft published error was not earlier corrected? It is obvious that the false statement which took its published form at Poughkeepsie, and was thence circulated, not only in the United Colonies, but throughout every Nation in Europe, was calculated to arouse the most powerful emotions of the human soul—pity for American suffering—detestation of blackest perfidy—and horror at unheard of cruelty on the part of Great Britain and her Savage allies: and hence to strengthen our cause, by bringing popular sentiment to bear in our favour both at home and abroad.

With motives so powerful to allow the published story to run its course, it may be doubted even if the truth was known whether any American would at the time have felt it his duty to hunt up the evidence, and publish a new version of the matter. After the war, Wyoming was, from her remote, reduced and harrassed state, too much engaged in more immediately pressing concerns, to leave her people free to study her early annals, and correct the errors of the Historian.

In 1832 I returned to Wyoming from Chester County, where I had resided fifteen years, and commenced farming. Much excluded by local position from society, I sought relaxation from labour, with more than usual pleasure, in my books. Four volumes of the Journal of Congress, during the Revolution, were upon the shelf, presenting in their details slight attraction, as I had thought, and of little use, except for occasional reference: but the leisure now afforded led me to examine them with more care, and I presently found, scattered through a mass of interesting matter, much that related to Wyoming. Communicating some facts which I had discovered, that seemed of particular interest, Gen. William Ross mentioned to me, that a bound volume containing the old Westmoreland Records was in the possession of a person in the Borough, who had used the blank leaves. A treasure to the antiquarian of themselves, they came to me with the increased charm that their contents harmonized with early and cherished studies. Every page opened new views to me. Light broke in upon the deep gloom that had heretofore, in an especial manner, enshrouded the *Civil* History of Wyoming. From the facts obtained in these precious records, and those elicited by the perusal of the Journals of Congress, I formed the conclusion that the old sufferers had endured grievous and unredressed wrongs, from their own Country as well as from the Briton and Savage. Two or three numbers, setting forth, though very imperfectly, the grounds of their claim to redress, I published in the Wilkesbarre papers, when Chester Butler, Esq., in whose prudence and judgment I had, and have, the utmost confidence, came to me, and said, "Mr. Miner, the case you are stating seems to me a very strong one, indeed almost irresistible;" and he immediately, with the greatest kindness, offered me the use of the papers of Col. Zebulon Butler, his grandfather. Mr. Anderson Dana also placed in my hands some very interesting papers belonging to his father. Thus excited and cheered, I resolved to lose not a moment in obtaining all the facts which obliterating time, and relentless death had spared, relating to the History of Wyoming. To this end I folded up little books of blank paper, for convenient carriage, took pens and ink, and accompanied by my daughter Sarah, (who though blind is, I think it not inappropriate here to say, besides being a most cheerful and agreeable companion, quick to hear, ready to understand, sound to judge, retentive of memory, and like myself, deeply interested in the subject,) we visited thirty or forty of the ancient people, who were here at the time of the expulsion. "We have come to inquire about old Wyoming, pray tell us all you know. We wish an exact picture, such as the valley presented sixty odd years ago. Give us the lights and shadows, its joys and its sorrows." In every instance we were treated with courtesy and kindness—communications, full and free, were made, not only with patience, but cheerfulness. This is said, as many of the statements, being combined of matters within the personal knowledge of the one examined, and things learned from others, our inquiries were often almost tediously minute. At night on returning home, I read over to Sarah what I had taken down, and carefully corrected any error into which the pen had fallen. If in examining several persons I found a material fact stated differently, they were revisited, the subject considered again, and new sources of information sought until we were satisfied of having arrived at a correct conclusion. This particular care was the more necessary, since, from the cause stated, multitudinous errors prevailed in respect to numerous details, in the minds of many intelligent persons.

With a view at once to communicate and elicit information, I made from time to time, publications of what we had learned, under the name of the "*Hazelton Travellers*." The title pre-supposed that two gentlemen were traveling from Hazelton through Wyoming. One, perfectly acquainted with the valley, its people and history, the other, eager to learn every thing that concerned them. The communications of one to the other in their passing conversation constituted these numbers which have excited so much public attention, and have been liberally used by Col. Stone in his recent work. I wish here distinctly to say, that the censure cast upon Col. Stone for making use of those materials, because he was aware that I was collecting the facts for my intended history, was wholly unmerited on his part. They were before the world in a newspaper—this would have been sufficient. But moreover, that gentleman had my most full and unreserved assent to his using them at his pleasure.

Interesting as are the incidents growing out of the Revolutionary war, other matters of scarcely less moment will claim the reader's attention. For nine years Wyoming, or Westmoreland, was under the jurisdiction of Connecticut—derived its laws from that State—and sent Representatives to her Assembly.

For seven years, Civil war prevailed or raged, between Wyoming and Pennsylvania. The events attendant on those unhappy conflicts demand from the historic pen a faithful record.

I have chosen to give the subject the form of familiar letters to my son, because, besides being indebted to him for aid and many valuable suggestions, it must be obvious that a variety of minute details necessary to be preserved to present a perfect picture of life, manners and events, among a plain people, in a new and rude settlement, requires an easier style and freer scope of pencil, than might be deemed fitting to the grave Delineator of the fate of Nations, or to the Historian who records the revolutions, the rise and the fall of Empires.

INTRODUCTION. vii

Thanks are in the first place due to the Hon. Edward Everett, our minister at the Court of St. James: With characteristic kindness, on my soliciting his good offices, he applied to Lord Aberdeen, who gave directions that access should be had to such documents in the State paper office as might with propriety be copied: whereupon Col. J. R. Brodhead voluntarily took upon himself the trouble of making the necessary searches, and of transcribing whatever related to Wyoming. I feel very sensibly my indebtedness to Col. Brodhead, and acknowledge it with pleasure.

The Hon. John N. Conyngham with partial kindness has inquired for and obtained for me, while in the northern portion of his circuit, various facts, from old settlers, whom I could not conveniently see, and more especially several ancient manuscripts of much value.

Senator Kidder and Mr. Speaker Wright, for their attention and politeness in obtaining, by vote of the Assembly, the ancient Susquehanna Company's Records, are desired to accept my most respectful thanks.

Wm. S. Derrick, Esq., in the State department, Washington, responded with his accustomed kindness to my inquiries, and furnished me the ancient map, and other valuable papers.

Among the persons visited, and to whom I am indebted for information, are Samuel Carey,* Mrs. Carey, Thomas Williams, Cornelius Courtright, Esq., Mrs. Cooper, Stephen Abbott, Anderson Dana, Rufus Bennett,* Mrs. Bennett, Elisha Blackman,* Eleazer Blackman, Mrs. Blackman, Nathan Beach, Esq., Alexander Jameson, Esq., Mrs. Jenkins, and several members of her family, Mrs. Myers, Rev. Mr. Bidlack, Mrs. Bidlack, Col. John Butler, George M. Hollenback, Joseph Slocum, Col. G. P. Ransom, Jose Rogers, Col. Benjamin Dorrance, Col. Edward Inman, Samuel Finch,* Elisha Harding, Esq., Mrs. Young, David Perkins, Esq., Aaron Perkins, John Carey, Comfort Carey, Mrs. Carey, Rev. Mr. Dana, Gen. Wm. Ross, Wm. Swetland, Esq., Col. Erastus Hill, Mrs. Ives, Mrs. Town, Mrs. Davis. The four whose names are designated by a star were in the battle. With one or two exceptions, the others were inhabitants of Wyoming, at the time of the massacre and expulsion, and most of them of an age to remember distinctly the events that then took place.

To Col. Joseph Kingsbury, I take pleasure in making my acknowledgments, for anecdotes of Col. Franklin, and more especially, for a journal kept by that gentleman, for several years, during the contest with the Pennsylvania land claimants. In an especial manner, I beg leave to make my grateful acknowledgments to C. L. Ward, Esq. That gentleman had been gathering materials for a History of Wyoming, and had copied from the archives at Harrisburg numerous documents bearing on the subject, several of which were new to me, and of great interest. On the unfortunate destruction, by fire of what he had written, with various papers obtained from Col. Franklin, he sent me those documents, and placed them at my disposal.

To Henry R. Strong, Esq., State Librarian, I am indebted for valuable extracts from books and documents at Harrisburg, furnished with so much promptitude as greatly to enhance the obligation. Thanks are due to Redmond Conyngham, Esq., whose thorough knowledge of our ancient history has enabled him to throw light upon numerous passages regarding the Indians. I cannot but express the hope that he will gather into a volume and publish the garnered treasures of his antiquarian researches: Thomas Elder, Esq., of Harrisburg (whose father the Rev. John Elder, at once a minister of the gospel, and Colonel of a regiment, who used, surrounded by blood seeking savages, to ascend the pulpit with his bible in one hand, and rifle in the other, and fought and prayed with Puritan courage and zeal) with the utmost kindness and confidence, sent me numerous family papers, bearing especially on incidents of the old French and Indian war. Extremely valuable, I cannot withhold my earnest wish that the facts they contain may be embodied in a volume. Few of them come within the scope of a work so local and isolated as this in which I am engaged; but such have been selected with care. Miner S. Blackman, Esq., visiting Harrisburg, with his accustomed politeness copied for my use several valuable documents.

Thus prepared with materials, I venture upon the arduous, but pleasing task of writing

THE HISTORY OF WYOMING.

P. S. *Philadelphia, August 2, 1845.*

To Mr. J. Jordan, Jr., of Philadelphia, Member of the Historical Society, I make, with pleasure, my very best acknowledgments, not only for numerous acts of kindness connected with the publication of this work, but for a number of interesting facts and documents, which his antiquarian researches and taste had enabled him to gather and preserve.

I hardly know how to express my deep sense of the considerate kindness shown, and unremitting aid afforded me by Joseph R. Chandler, Esq., during the protracted and perplexing negotiations for the printing and publishing this History. The generous confidence advanced by a gentleman of his established literary reputation, led the way to a most satisfactory arrangement; and I hope he will pardon me for saying that his efforts, so far transcending the claims of friendship, could only have proceeded from his characteristic love of doing good. My most grateful acknowledgments wait upon him.

PRELIMINARY CHAPTER,

CONTAINING A BRIEF DESCRIPTION OF WYOMING.

Wyoming, in its more limited signification, is the name given to a valley on the Susquehanna river, about twenty miles in length from northeast to southwest, and from three to four miles in width; but in its more enlarged sense, it is used to designate the part of the country within the limits of Pennsylvania, embraced within the 42d degree of north latitude, claimed by Connecticut, and partially settled by a colony sent forth under her auspices. Thus the inhabitants of Salem, Huntington, Providence, Exeter, and other townships, though not within the limits of the valley, have always been designated as "Wyoming Settlers."*

The general aspect of the territory, out of the valley, is hilly, and no inconsiderable portion of it mountainous—ridge after ridge, and peak after peak, rising one above another in sublime elevation, wherein are interspersed extensive bodies of hill and vale, rough but fertile land, yielding to laborious culture remunerating returns. The Susquehanna river rising in lake Otsego, running southerly, crosses the line dividing the 42d and 43d degrees of latitude; thence courses its way, westerly, about twenty miles, when turning to the northwest it recrosses the line, and pursuing its westerly course about forty miles, again turns to the south, and presently receives the Chemung, at Tioga Point, when it bears away southeasterly in a deep chasm, closely bounded by hills and mountains, rising precipitously, from five hundred to a thousand feet; the rock-bound shore relieved, occasionally by patches of rich intervale, until it comes to latitude

---

* In July, 1753, on the formation of the Susquehanna Company, at Windham, Connecticut, a committee was sent out to explore "A certain tract of land, lying on Susquehanna river, at or near a place called *Chiwaumuck*, an island in said river," presumed to be the Minocasy.

41 and about 20 minutes, when it breaks through its lofty barriers. Meeting the Lackawanna, it again changes its course and glides in a bright, broad and beautiful stream to the southwest. Easterly, within the great bend of the river, the land (comprising parts of Wyoming, Bradford, and the whole of Susquehanna counties) though used as hunting ground, was impervious to Indian labour, and remained until long after the revolutionary war, untouched by the axe of the white man—majestic in the extent, the depth and the loftiness of its forests—sublime as it came from the hand of the Creator. A solitary Indian path from the Lackawanna to Oquago, marked the chord of the arc, being about forty miles, while following the bow of the river, the distance exceeded one hundred and thirty miles. But we are now in the valley; lovely as ever enthusiast dreamed of, or poet sung. Standing on the bank of the river, a little below the mouth of the Lackawanna, and looking northward, it appears as if by some power, little short of Omnipotent, the solid rock had been cloven down near a thousand feet to open a passage for the water.* Being on the river bank, twelve years ago, with the able and lamented Mr. Packer, then chairman of the senatorial committee, to view the coal region of Luzerne, he pointed to a huge mass of broken and contorted rock, evidently out of place, which now lies at Pittston Ferry, between the canal and river, and expressed the decided and not improbable, opinion, that in the convulsion of nature, which separated the mountain above us, this mass must have been torn away, and borne by the rushing flood, to its present resting place. Twenty miles below, where the Susquehanna takes leave of the plains, the mountains are equally lofty and precipitous. In many places the rocks distinctly exhibit the abrasion of water, many feet above the highest pitch to which the river has ever been known to rise, going to show, that at some very remote period, this had been a lake, and indicating that there had been a chain of lakes, probably along the whole line of the stream. Banks of sand, hills covered with rounded stone, manifestly worn smooth by attrition, similar stones being found wherever wells are sunk, tend to confirm the opinion. The soil is chiefly alluvial, and the whole depth and surface, so far as examined, show great changes by the violent action of water.

---

* Near the summit of the northeastern cliff, the naked stone presents to the eye a grey crescent, which, precisely at twelve, receives the direct rays of the sun, and hence is called "Dial Rock,"--giving notice to the labouring husbandman, that it is time to turn out his team, and reposing under the shade of elm or walnut, to take his noontide repast.

The geological structure of Wyoming affords to the inquirer a matter of lively interest. Were I able to do the subject justice, this would not, perhaps, be deemed the fitting place. The richness and beauty of the coal formation, however, at least demand a moment's notice. On the top of the southern, or second range of mountains, strata of rocks make their appearance. The red-shale, for instance, lined by the pebbly conglomerate, (which is the cradle or bed in which the lower stratum of anthracite reposes,) with other accompanying rocks, are apparent, and easily traceable. On the opposite, the northwestern, or second mountain, the same rocks appear, though less distinctly, marking the outer limits of the coal basin, in that direction. Within the valley sixteen strata of coal, varying in thickness from four to twenty-six feet, have been clearly ascertained. The quality of this mineral is unsurpassed in purity; several veins, in an especial manner, being particularly excellent for the fusion of ores and the working of iron. During the war of the revolution, several boat-loads were taken down the Susquehanna, it is supposed, by Capt. Daniel Gore, for the use of the armory forges at Carlisle.

Bog ores exist in limited extent; argillaceous ores are known to prevail in near proximity with veins of coal, and an extensive stratum of mountain ore is now being wrought on one of the hills south of the Lackawanna.* These brief preliminary notices of the coal and ore of Wyoming have been made, that the distant reader may receive, at least, a partial idea of its slumbering wealth. The subject may be adverted to more in detail hereafter, if our limits shall permit.

The valley, itself, is diversified by hill and dale, upland and intervale. Its character of extreme richness is derived from the extensive flats, or river bottoms, which in some places extend from one to two miles back from the stream, unrivalled in expansive beauty; unsurpassed in luxuriant fertility. Though now generally cleared and cultivated, to protect the soil from floods, a fringe of trees is left along each bank of the river:—the sycamore, the elm, and more especially the black-walnut, while here and there scattered through the fields, a huge shellbark yields its summer shade to the weary laborer, and its autumn fruit to the black and gray squirrel, or the

---

* Sufficient proof exists to show that this rich vein of iron ore extends throughout the whole valley; beneath, and not far below, the red shale, at Solomon's creek, in Hanover, fifteen miles southwest from the mine so successfully worked by the Messrs Scrantons & Co., in Lackawanna, the vein is exposed by the deep cuttings of the Mauch Chunk Company's Railroad, and is expected soon to be wrought by Mr. Hibler, the fortunate owner.

rival plough-boy. Pure streams of water come leaping from the mountains, imparting health and pleasure in their course; all of them abounding with the delicious trout. Along those brooks and in the swales, scattered through the uplands, grow the wild plum and the butternut, while, wherever the hand of the white man has spared it, the native grape may be gathered in unlimited profusion. I have seen a grapevine bending beneath its purple clusters, one branch climbing a butternut, loaded with fruit; another branch resting on a wild plum, red with its delicious burden; the while growing in their shade, the hazlenut was ripening its rounded kernel.

Such were common scenes when the white people first came to **Wyoming**, which seems to have been formed by nature, a perfect Indian paradise. Game, of every sort, was abundant. The quail whistled in the meadow; the pheasant rustled in its leafy covert; the wild duck reared her brood, and bent the reed in every inlet; the red deer fed upon the hills, while in the deep forests, within a few hours walk, was found the stately elk. Several persons, now living, delight to relate their hunting prowess, in bringing down this noblest of our forest inhabitants. The river yielded, at all seasons, a supply of fish. The yellow perch, the pike, the catfish, the bass, the roach, and in the spring season, myriads of shad.*

From various points, the valley may be seen to advantage. Prospect Rock, on the eastern mountain, near the turnpike, affords a very fine, though rather distant, view. From Ross's Hill, on the Kingston side, looking up the river, Monockasy island, seeming to repose so sweetly, on the glassy bosom of the Susquehanna, is a landscape worthy the ablest pencil. But from Inman's Hill, the eye embracing part of Hanover, and the broad expanse of the Wilkesbarre and Kingston meadows, the prospect is eminently picturesque; presenting a scene rich in a single aspect, but in detail, studded with innumerable beauties.

* The fact is worth recording that this fish, excellent as it was justly esteemed, caught in the Chesapeake bay, or at the mouth of the river, attained to a superior size and flavour when taken so far up as Wyoming. In point of fatness and excellence, there could be no comparison. Probably, only the largest and strongest could stem the current for so great a distance; but a better reason, I apprehend, is to be found in a favorable change in quantity and quality of congenial food. In 1798 a haul was made, at Nanticoke, of uncounted thousands. The fishermen threw ashore while purchasers could be found, and then gave to those who were unable to buy. The supply of salt being exhausted, the seine was raised, and the rest allowed to escape. The Wilkesbarre Gazette announced, at the time, in an exulting paragraph, such was the multitude, "That Bonaparte (then playing the conqueror in Italy,) and all his army was captured!"

The name Wyoming was long supposed to mean, being interpreted, " A Field of Blood ;" but Mr. Heckewelder, perfectly versed in Indian language, to the inquiry of Mr. Chapman, replied : "Wyoming is a corruption of Maughwauwama, by which it was designated by the Delaware Indians, being a compound of *maughwau*, meaning *large*, and *wama*, signifying *plains*, so that it may be translated " THE LARGE PLAINS."

LETTER I.

Native inhabitants of Wyoming—Six Nations—Great head, or Council Fire, at Onondago. Mohawks.

To WILLIAM PENN MINER, ESQ.

My Dear Son,

HAVING presented you with a brief sketch of Wyoming, I proceed to trace the history of its earliest inhabitants. Speculations upon the origin of the Indians, whether they are derivations from one stock—whether this continent was peopled from Asia, the colonists landing on the northwest coast—whether the lost Tribe of Israel may have been removed and planted in America by some miraculous interposition of Providence, pleasant as they may prove to the learned antiquarian, or the ingenious idler, give little promise of solving the perplexing question. Indeed, with advancing knowledge and increasing research, doubts, instead of being dissipated, thicken around us. The recent and most wonderful discoveries in Central America, Mexico and Yucatan, the remains of vast cities, temples of hewn stone, rivaling, in grandeur of design and magnificence of execution, the noblest ruins of Egypt,—the varied and finished sculpture, speak of population and wealth—arts and arms, at a period so remote, as to render it a problem which is the old world and which the new. Nor would those disquisitions be regarded as exactly in place in a limited work like the present; but so deeply interwoven is the early history of Wyoming with that of the Indians, a few pages in reference to those tribes which governed, or inhabited here, sufficient to fix attention without fatiguing it, may be regarded as proper.

By those most deeply versed in the subject it is supposed that there were three distinct Nations in North America, radically differing in their languages. Of this opinion was the Rev. Mr. Heckewelder, certainly authority in a high degree entitled to consideration.

He enumerates the Leni-Lenape, or Delawares. The Mengwe, or Iroquois, and the Algonquins. Of these the Leni-Lenape and Iroquois were the principal inhabitants, east of the Mississippi, and south of the great lakes—But these were divided and subdivided into innumerable tribes, with most unutterable names, many of them speaking dialects so little resembling the parent language, as to create doubts of their common origin. Mr. Jefferson speaks of tribes on the Potomac and James' river, who could not converse but through an interpreter. Without pursuing this point further, I proceed directly to the matter which concerns our immediate subject.

As early after the first settlements made by Europeans in Virginia, Plymouth, and New York, as Savage policy and power could be at all comprehended, they found the Iroquois or Mengwe, five united nations of Indians, situated north of the blue mountains, amidst the lesser lakes, and on the head waters of the Hudson, the Delaware, and the Susquehanna, claiming empire and exacting homage through an extent of territory, equal to the old Thirteen States. Their names were Mohawks, Senecas, Onondagos, Oneidas, Cayugas, to which was afterwards added the Tuscaroras, constituting the well known and long dreaded confederacy of the Six Nations. Proud, ambitious, warlike, Rome in the zenith of her power, did not exercise dominion as empress of the earth, with more dictatorial and absolute sway.

This valley having been, for centuries, subject to their authority, and here having been exhibited the last dread scene in the fearful drama of their national existence, I shall endeavour to give a sketch of their history, policy, and power, so far as such exposition may tend to illustrate the annals of Wyoming. It does not appear to me that any writer has set forth, distinctly, in sufficiently bold relief—their extent of dominion—their absolute sovereignty—their profound policy—their imperial sway.

In unraveling the tangled web of Indian history, we found ourselves in the outset extremely embarrassed, especially when reading the pages of Heckewelder, and other writers of the United brethren. The removal of tribes, or parts of tribes, to the valley; their remaining a brief period, and then emigrating to some other place, without any apparent motive, founded in personal convenience, consistency, or wisdom, perplexed us exceedingly, as we doubt not it has others. The domineering spirit of the Six Nations is spoken of, and incidents are related showing their assumption of power over the surrounding tribes; but Mr. Heckewelder will not admit that the

Delawares, his beloved Leni-Lenape, were a conquered people; the vassals of the Six Nations. Yet such was unquestionably the fact, as were most of the surrounding nations; and when this truth is once admitted, what was before doubtful, becomes perfectly clear or easily explicable.

In treating this matter, I feel a lively assurance, that old facts will be presented in such new aspects and relations, and so much of novelty will be introduced, as to repay the best learned in Indian story the labour of perusal.

Whether the conjecture be well founded, which I venture to suggest, namely;—That the Empire was divided for easier government, into three provinces, the Mohawks taking the country east of the Delaware, and along the St. Lawrence—the Cayugas having administration westerly, south of the great lakes, along the Ohio, and generally beyond the Alleghany mountains to the Mississippi:— The Senecas and Oneidas governing the country west of the Delaware, east of the Alleghany, and indefinitely south, perhaps to the Saluda Gap, thence to the Mississippi: while the Onondagos were eminent as counsellors, distinguished for eloquence, perhaps revered like the tribe of Levi as the Priesthood of the confederacy, to whose care was committed the keeping, or kindling, the sacred *Fire* around which their most solemn deliberations were held—the critical reader will determine, after the facts which bear on the case are fully exhibited.

But this must be kept constantly in mind, that the "*Great Head*," or council at Onondago, was *supreme*;—that whatever was done, every material transaction, no matter by which nation, tribe or division undertaken, was the result of united councils at that Federal Congress.

With these preliminary remarks, I proceed to sketch the Iroquois in the eastern division of their empire, under the more immediate administration of the Mohawks.

In 1669 there was war between the Mohawks and Massachusetts Indians. It had raged for several years. Six or seven hundred warriors under the command of a great chief, Chikataubutt, a wise and stout man, were led out two hundred miles to attack a Mohawk fort. They were repelled and ambushed on their retreat, and a great fight ensued. "What was *most calamitous* in this *disastrous* expedition, (says the Historian) was the loss of the great chief Chikataubutt, who, after performing prodigies of valour, was killed in repelling the Mohawks in their last attack, with almost all his captains." I copy from Drake's multitudinous collection of facts, connected with Indian story; and *he* from collections of the Mass. Hist. Soc: The authority adds:—" The Mohawks considered themselves *their masters*, and although peace was brought about between them, by the mediation of the English and Dutch, yet the Massachusetts, and others, often suffered from their incursions."

The overthrow of these 6 or 700 warriors was manifestly total. One European nation was not sufficient,—the English and Dutch were obliged to unite their powerful mediation to restrain these terrible barbarians. It is evident that long before this period (1669) the Mohawk power had been established, probably for centuries. No date has ever been given when the neighbouring nations were finally subdued. The Mohawks claimed, *not* that *now* they had conquered the Massachusetts, but that, for an indefinite period, these had been their vassals. In the history of the New England Indians, at a period thirty years previous to the defeat and death of Chikataubutt, we have an account of a great sachem of the Narragansetts, who was slain by the Mohawks. "In the beginning of July 1676, those Indians who were known by the name of Mauguawogs, or Mohawks, i. e. man-eaters, had lately fallen on Philip [the renowned Narragansett chief, whose Indian name was Pometacom]—and killed forty of his men."*

About this time the Mohawks sent a threat that they would destroy all the Indians from Uncas and Mount-Hope, to the eastward as far as Pegypscot.

The New York Historian, Smith, sets forth; "When the Dutch began the settlement of New York, all the Indians on Long Island, and the northern shore of the Sound, on the banks of the Connecticut, Hudson, Delaware, and Susquehanna rivers, were in subjection to the Five Nations."—The same author asserts that, within the

---

* The Governor of New Hampshire, in 1685, received a letter written by a distinguished Sagamore, and signed by fifteen Chiefs, of which the following is an extract.

"May 15, 1685. Honor Governor, my friend, you my friend, I desire your worship and your power, because I hope you can do some great matters this one. I am poor and naked, and have no men at my place, because I afraid always Mohago he will kill me every day and night. If your worship when please pray help me you no let Mohago kill me at my place at Malamake (Merrimack) river, called Panukkog, and Natukkog, I will submit your worship and your power."

By Mohago, the Mohawks were clearly indidated. So far east as the Merrimack were their arms a source of terror.

memory of persons then living, a small tribe on the Hudson paid an annual tribute of twenty pounds to the Mohawks.

In August, 1689, the Iroquois sent out an army of 1200 warriors, who attacked Montreal, burnt the houses, sacked the plantations, and slew great numbers of the French.

Smith further says, in 1756, " These Indians (Iroquois) universally concur in the claim of all the lands not sold to the English, from the mouth of Sorel river, on the south side of lakes Erie and Ontario, on both sides of the Mississippi, and on the north side of those lakes," &c.

An extract from "Remarks on the Policy and Practice of the United States and Great Britain, in their treatment of the Indians," by Gov. Cass, published in the North American Review, April 1827, (a paper pregnant with important matter, and written with extraordinary power,) will illustrate the view I have taken. (See p. 50.)

"Charlevoix, long since described the Wyandots, as the nation of all Canada, the most remarkable for its defects and virtues. When Jacques Cartier ascended the St. Lawrence he found them established near Hockelega, now Montreal; and when Champlain entered the same river their war with the Iroquois had already commenced, and that enterprizing officer accompanied one of their parties in a hostile expedition against their enemies. *The events of the war were most disastrous, and they were driven from their country to the northern shore of lake Huron. But distance afforded no security, and the Iroquois pursued them with relentless fury.* Famine, disease and war made frightful havoc among them, and the account of their sufferings given by the old Missionaries, who witnessed and shared them, almost tasks the belief of the reader." " *They were literally hunted from their resting place, and the feeble remnant of this once powerful and haughty tribe owed their preservation to the protection of the Sioux, in whose country, west of lake Superior, they found safety and tranquillity.*" Surely that nation must have been tremendous in its power, as terrible in its wrath, that could thus nearly exterminate a powerful tribe, hunting them through twenty degrees of longitude! Nor can it be doubted that the western Indians, to lake Superior, must have been their obedient allies or trembling vassals.

I should deem myself unpardonable if I withheld the following interesting paper; for to a large proportion of the readers of this volume it probably will be new.

AN INDIAN TRADITION,

CONCERNING THE ORIGIN OF THE FIVE NATIONS.

The following is the account given by old Cannassatego, of the manner in which his country was made and peopled.

"When our good Manitta raised Akanishionegy* out of the great waters, he said to his brethren, how fine a country is this! I will make Red† men, the best of men, to enjoy it. Then with five handfuls of red seeds, like the eggs of flies, did he strow the fertile fields of Onondago. Little worms came out of the seeds, and penetrated the earth, when the spirits, who had never yet seen the light, entered into and united with them. Manitta watered the earth with his rain, the sun warmed it, the worms, with the spirits in them, grew, putting forth little arms and legs, and moved the light earth that covered them. After nine moons they came forth perfect boys and girls. Manitta covered them with his mantle of warm, purple cloud, and nourished them with milk from his fingers ends. Nine summers did he nurse them, and nine summers more did he instruct them how to live. In the mean time he had made for their use, trees, plants, and animals, of various kinds. Akanishionegy was covered with woods and filled with creatures. Then he assembled his children together and said, " Ye are Five Nations, for ye sprang each from a different handful of the seed I sowed; but ye are all brethren; and I am your father, for I made ye all; I have nursed and brought you up: Mohocks, I have made you bold and valiant, and see, I give you corn for your food: Oneidas, I have made you patient of pain and of hunger, the nuts and fruits of the trees are yours. Senekas, I have made you industrious and active, beans do I give you for nourishment: Cayugas, I have made you strong, friendly and generous, ground nuts and every root shall refresh you. Onondagos, I have made you wise, just and eloquent; squashes and grapes have I given you to eat, and tobacco to smoke in Council. The beasts, birds and fishes have I given to you all, in common. As I have loved and taken care of you all, so do you love and take care of one another. Communicate freely to each other the good things I have given you, and learn to imitate each other's virtues. I have made you the best

---

* The country of the Five Nations.

† They thus distinguished themselves from white men and black men. But their complexion is not properly red. It is rather the color of copper, or mahogany.

people in the world, and I give you the best country. You will defend it from the invasions of other nations, from the children of other Manittas, and keep possession of it for yourselves, while the sun and moon give light, and the waters run in the rivers. This you shall do if you observe my words. Spirits, I am now about to leave you. The bodies I have given you will in time grow old, and wear out, so that you will be weary of them; or from various accidents they may become unfit for your habitation, and you will leave them. I cannot remain here always to give you new ones. I have great affairs to mind, in distant places, and I cannot again attend so long to the nursing of children. I have enabled you therefore among yourselves to produce new bodies, to supply the place of old ones, that every one of you, when he parts with his old habitation, may in due time find a new one, and never wander longer than he chose under the earth, deprived of the light of the sun. Nourish and instruct your children, as I have nourished and instructed you. Be just to all men and kind to strangers, that come among you. So shall you be happy and be loved by all: and I myself will sometimes visit and assist you." "Saying this, he wrapped himself in a bright cloud and went like a swift arrow to the sun, where his brethren rejoiced at his return. From thence he often looked at Akanishionegy, and pointing, showed with pleasure, to his brothers, the country he had formed, and the nations he had produced to inhabit it."

Is it not beautiful? And does it not in some degree warrant the opinion I have suggested, that the Onondagos were regarded as the wisest, perhaps, the Sacred Nation?"

LETTER II.

Massawamees of Wyoming—Senecas and Oneidas—Indian Fortifications—Medal of George I.—Burying Places—Exhumation of an Indian King—Probable likeness of Queen Anne—Spirit, power and dominion of the Iroquois, or Great Confederacy.

THESE previously related facts make sufficiently plain the extent and spirit of dominion claimed and exercised in the eastern and northern portions of the Continent by this tremendously formidable power. We now turn to the southern Province, west of the Delaware, east of the Alleghany mountains; and southerly from the head waters of the Susquehanna, administered by the Senecas and Oneidas: and as in this territory Wyoming is included, we hope to throw more incident into our narrative, and impart greater interest to the subject.

Mr. Jefferson, after describing the numerous tribes in lower Virginia, in which the Powhattan confederacy is estimated at 8000, says: "Westward of all these tribes, beyond the mountains, and extending to the great lakes, were the Massawamees, a *most powerful confederacy*, who harrassed *unremittingly* the Powhattans, and Manahoacs. These were probably the ancestors of tribes known at present as the Six Nations." I am strongly of opinion that, at an early period, Wyoming was the head quarters of one or two of those nations, though not the scite of their great Council fire;—that was at Onondago. They were then known by the name of *Massawamees*. Is not the inference fair that the name they then bore was derived from these extensive plains? The reader will bear in mind that Indian names are not arbitrary selections of fancy, but uniformly are given as descriptive of the thing named.

Massachusetts was thus called from the blue hills, says Roger Williams. The Rev. John Cotton defines Massachusetts, in his vocabulary of Indian words, "An hill in the form of an arrow head." The name of the terrible foes of the Powhattans, then, was formed of the two words, *Massa-Hills—Waughmees*, plains—meaning A *people among the hills, seated upon extensive plains*—an exact description of Wyoming.

I have purposely left a notice of Indian fortifications, found in the valley, for this connexion, because the aspect they present strengthens the conclusion, that Wyoming was the residence of several chiefs and tribes of this gigantic empire. Mr. Chapman has given a clear description of the fort remaining on the west, or Kingston side of the river.

"In the valley of Wyoming, there exists some remains of ancient fortifications, which appear to have been constructed by a race of people very different in their habits from those who occupied the place when first discovered by the whites. Most of these ruins have been so much obliterated by the operations of agriculture, that their forms cannot now be distinctly ascertained. That which remains the most entire, was examined by the writer during the summer of 1817, and its dimensions carefully ascertained; although from frequent ploughing, its form had become almost destroyed. It is situated in the township of Kingston, upon a level plain on the north side of Toby's creek, about one hundred and fifty feet from its bank, and about half a mile from its confluence with the Susquehanna. It is of an oval or elliptical form, having its longest diameter from the northwest to the southeast, at right angles to the creek, three hundred and thirty-seven feet, and its shortest diameter from the northeast to the southwest, two hundred and seventy-two feet. On the southwest side, appears to have been a gateway about twelve feet wide, opening toward the great eddy of the river, into which the creek falls. From present appearances, it consisted, probably, of only one mound or rampart, which, in height and thickness, appears to have been the same on all sides, and was constructed of earth; the plain on which it stands, not abounding in stone. On the outside of the rampart, is an entrenchment or ditch formed, probably, by removing the earth of which it is composed, and which appears never to have been walled. The creek, on which it stands, is bounded by a high steep bank on that side, and at ordinary times, is sufficiently deep to admit canoes to ascend from the river to the fortification. When the first settlers came to Wyoming, this plain was covered with its native forests, consisting principally of oak and yellow pine; and the trees which grew in the rampart and in the entrenchment, are said to have been as large as those in any other part of the valley; one large oak particularly, upon being cut down, was ascertained to be seven hundred years old. The Indians had no tradition concerning these fortifications, neither did they appear to have any knowledge of the purposes for which they were constructed. They were, perhaps, erected about the same time with those upon the waters of the Ohio, and, probably by a simliar people, and for similar purposes."

I am happy to be able to add some very interesting facts to this description of my lamented friend. Another fortification existed on Jacob's Plains, or the upper flats, in Wilkesbarre. Its situation is the highest part of the low grounds, so that only in extraordinary floods, is the spot covered with water. Looking over the flats, in ordinarily high freshes, the site of the fort presents to the eye an island in the vast sea of waters. The eastern extremity is near the line dividing the farms of Mr. John Searle and Mr. James Hancock, where, from its safety from inundation, a fence has long since been placed; and to this circumstance is to be attributed the preservation of the embankment and ditch. In the open field, so entirely is the work levelled, that the eye cannot trace it; but the extent west, is known, " for it reached through the meadow lot of Capt. Gore," (said Cornelius Courtright, Esq., to me, when visiting the ground several years ago) " and came on to my lot one or two rods." The lot of Capt. Gore was seventeen perches in width. Taking then these two hundred and eighty feet, add the distance it extended eastwardly on the Searle lot, and the extension, westerly, on the lot of Esq. Courtright, we have the length of that measured by Mr. Chapman, so very nearly, as to render the inference almost certain, that both were of the same size and dimensions. Huge trees were growing out of the embankment when the white people began to clear the flats for cultivation. This, too, in Wilkesbarre, is oval, as is still manifest from the segment exhibited on the upper part, formed by the remaining rampart and fosse, the chord of the arc being the division fence. A circle is easily made, the elliptical form much more difficult for an untutored mind to trace. Trifling as these circumstances may appear, the exact coincidence in size and shape, and that shape difficult to form, they appeared to me worthy of a distinct notice. The Wilkesbarre fortification is about eighty rods from the river, towards which a gate opened, and the ancient people concur in stating that a well existed in the interior, near the southern line. On the bank of the river there is an Indian burying place, not a barrow or hill, such as is described by Mr. Jefferson, but where graves have been dug, and the deceased laid, horizontally, in regular rows. In excavating the canal, cutting through the bank that borders the flats, perhaps thirty rods south from the fort, was another

Copy of the Medal.

Page 27.

burying place disclosed, evidently more ancient; for the bones almost immediately crumbled to dust, on exposure to the air; and the deposits were far more numerous than in that near the river. By the representation of James Stark, Esq., the skeletons were countless, and the deceased had been buried in a sitting posture. In a considerable portion of the bank, though scarcely a bone remained of sufficient firmness to be lifted up, the closeness and position of the buried, were apparent by the discoloration of the earth. In this place of deposite, no beads were found, while they were common in that near the river.

In 1814, I visited this fortification in company with the present Chief Justice Gibson, and Jacob Cist, Esqs. The whole line, although it had been ploughed for more than thirty years, was then distinctly traceable by the eye. Fortune was unexpectedly propitious to our search, for we found a medal bearing on one side the impress of King George the First, dated 1714, (the year he commenced his reign,) on the other, an Indian chief. It was awarded to Mr. Cist, as the most curious and careful in such matters, and by him was deposited with the Philadelphia Historical Society.*

Three years ago, an ice flood passed over the flats, and left several skeletons exposed. Mr. Hancock politely sent for me, but being absent, I did not visit the spot until the next day. A profusion of blue beads remained; a skull or two, and some well preserved bones were taken by Dr Boyd: but all were regretting that I had not seen a picture of a lady, found upon the breast, worn as a locket, of, from this, the beads and other ornaments, it was supposed a great chief. Various were the conjectures who it could have been. Some supposed a European officer had presented the chief with a miniature of his mistress; this I thought improbable. The likeness was not painted on ivory, but a print pasted on an oval piece of glass, about four inches the longest way. Taken in connexion with the medal of George the First, I expressed the conviction that the picture must have been that of Queen Anne. What greatly strengthens this opinion is the fact, that in 1710, in the reign of that Queen, a deputation of chiefs of the Five Nations visited England, where they were received with marked distinction. Clothed like tragedy kings, by tailors of the theatre; taken in the coaches of state, they were waited upon by Sir Charles Cotterell, and on the 19th of April,

---

* Should it not be placed with the Indian relics in a Museum to be formed in Wilkesbarre?

introduced to her Majesty by the Duke of Shrewsbury. They were entertained by many noble persons, particularly the great Duke of Ormond,* who regaled them with a review of the life-guards. Their portraits were taken, and are now in the British Museum.

Their visit is noticed by Sir Richard Steele, in the "Tattler," of May 13, 1710.

The delegation consisted of five chiefs, of whom, the names of four are preserved :—1. Te-Yee-Neen-Ho-Ga-Prow ; 2. Sa-Ga-Yean-Qua-Peah-Ton ; 3. Elow-Oh-Koam, and 4. Oh-Nee-Yeath-Ton-No-Prow—the two last named being River Indians.†

It seems, then, probable, that the skeleton found with the picture on his breast, was one of the two latter chiefs, who had visited the Court of Queen Anne, received her likeness, pasted on glass, which was worn as a badge of honour, and was buried with him.

Mr. Jefferson further states, that the Tuscaroras became united with the Iroquois, in 1712, thus making the confederacy Six Nations. Of course, when the delegation visited England in 1710, two years before, the confederacy was constituted of, as it was called, the Five Nations. Five chiefs went to England. The inference is quite probable, nay, almost certain, that a distinguished sachem went from each nation. One died in England, leaving four, whose names we have mentioned. They were spoken of at the time as kings, and treated with great distinction. Two of these are stated to have been River Indians. We have given our reasons for believing that one of those kings died at the Indian fort at Jacob's Plains, Wilkesbarre, and that it was his skeleton which the flood washed out, of which I have spoken. He, then, was one of the River Indians. But there was another. Our inference is, that he occupied the fortification described by Mr. Chapman, on the west side of the river; that Wyoming, therefore, must have been, so late as 1715, and for a time indefinitely previous, the occasional residence of the kings of two of the Five Nations. Depending on hunting and fishing for subsistence, the tribes would, for the sake of plenty, be located some distance apart, however close their alliance; and Wyoming, from its superabundance of game and fish, would not be overlooked or neglected. What

---

* The Duke of Ormond's family name, was Butler. I throw out the conjecture, that the ancestors of Col. John Butler, the intimate friend of Sir William Johnson, and leader of the Indians, may, probably at this time, have received an appointment from his relative and namesake, to return with these chiefs to America, and act as agent of the British Government.

† For this information, my acknowledgments are due to Drake's "Book of the Indians."

two nations, then, inhabited the valley? Not the Mohawks; they were located the farthest east, as we have seen, and gave or received their name from the Mohawk river. Not the Onondagos, for they, I take it, were a distinguished or favored tribe, to whom was committed the preservation of the Sacred Council Fire; the "Great Head," or Congress, ever holding their sessions within the limits of that nation. Whether there are additional facts to warrant such an inference, I am not prepared to assert; but the Great Shikellamus, the Vice Roy over the Pennsylvania Indians, being an Onondago, might lead to the conjecture, that the more elevated civil offices of authority and honour, were exercised by that tribe. Not a fact presents itself, in my research, to lead me to suppose that the Cayugas had ever any special interest or influence here. But the Senecas and Oneidas acted so conspicuous a part in the affairs of Wyoming, that I incline strongly to the opinion, they were the nations who occupied the two fortifications described. A Seneca chief, Gi-en-gwah-toh, commanded in the battle. A delegation of Senecas, attempted and executed the impudent deception upon Congress.*

These, then, were probably the two nations whose kings kept their court in the valley. When the Moravian Indians were struck, it is stated to have been done by the Oneidas, the war party coming from *Wyoming*, showing *this* to have been within the special jurisdiction of those two nations. I offer another conjecture, which the unbiassed mind will readily receive as true: namely, That these were the Massawamees, who so incessantly harrassed the Powhattans of Virginia; struck the Catawbas of South Carolina, and took scalps and prisoners from the Cherokees on the Mississippi. The nations most southwesterly located would, naturally, be best acquainted with the southwest country and nations—know the war paths, and be best able to strike an effective blow in their own quarter. And although acting as one of, and by orders from, THE GREAT HEAD, at Onon-

---

* Without anticipating events, which will be related in the sequel, illustrative of the point in question, I may here relate, that Mary Jemison was taken prisoner, from the lower part of Pennsylvania, in 1755, by a band of Senecas. Many years afterwards she married Hiokatoo, an Indian warrior, in the Seneca tribe, "that inhabited the banks of the Susquehanna." Her husband commanded the Indians in the battle, near Northumberland, in 1779. Relating to her the events of his youth, Hiokatoo stated, that " in 1730, then aged about twenty, he was appointed a runner to collect an army to go against the Catawbas, Cherokees and other southern Indians." He told of a battle in which twelve hundred of the enemy were slain, spoke of adventures on the Mobile, and of being two years upon one expedition; constantly professing an unextinguishable hostility to the Cherokees—incidents which go far to corroborate the opinion expressed.

dago, their enemies would be apt to designate their foes by the name of the particular nation, whose warriors reached them.

A portion of the Wyandots, situate near Detroit, (having been permitted, probably, to return,) were claimed by the Iroquois as their cousins. Mr. Jefferson speaks of a tribe of Mingoes, on the Sciota, having eighty warriors. The former, probably, were confederates, or in close alliance with the Six Nations; subservient, but politically treated as if not subjugated; too remote to be admitted to an equality and free participation of power, at the Council Fire, at Onondago; and yet trusted, and used to extend and perpetuate the power of the confederacy in the west, while the Mingoes mentioned, were the more immediate agents sent out by the Iroquois, to the waters of the Ohio, as Roman legions, under her pro-consuls, were marched to Egypt or Gaul.

"In war concerns," says Heckewelder, speaking of the Iroquois, "they assumed an authority over *many* other nations, so that *they only had to dictate*, and others to obey. Not only those inhabiting Pennsylvania, but those dwelling within the limits of other provinces, and the adjacent country, *together with the Western or Lake Indians*, were called upon by the Six Nations to join the conflict, and such among them as were averse to war, were threatened with *destruction* if they did not join them."

Growing jealousy of the English, who were rapidly peopling the ocean-shore; increasing attachment to the French, whose less haughty, but more attractive manners, as well as their advancing power on the north, may have been one motive with the confederacy to concentrate the residence of their chiefs, and to fix on a more northern location, nearer to their preferred allies. The position they now assumed, it must be confessed, if less attractive in beauty, was not less fitted for the seat of extended empire, embracing, particularly, the upper branches of the great rivers, the Mohawk, the Delaware and the Susquehanna, and the lesser lakes. They had settlements at Aughquago, Owego, Tioga and Chenango. The banks of the Cayuga and Seneca lakes were spotted with their villages.* Though still in the acme of power and pride of dominion, the hour of inevitable decline was approaching with the approach of the arts and arms of the white man—whether French or English.

The Leni-Lenape, or Delaware Indians, had long before been sub-

---

* A powerful branch of the Seneca nation, the most numerous, it is believed, of the confederacy, had a location, in 1724, near lake Ontario.

jugated by the Iroquois. "We have made you women; we have placed petticoats on you," was the uniformly insulting language of the victors. Cowering with fear under the hand of their oppressors, yet possessing an Indian's pride, his passions and love of independence, the numerous and wide spread tribes of the Delawares are supposed to have given the white men a less jealous reception than their masters, hoping to find in their increasing power, protection, if not the means of revenge. Hence, the Delawares lingered in the neighborhood of the whites—sought their society—opened their ears more readily to the instruction of missionaries, than those red men who were engaged in wars, intent on conquest and fired by ambition. These considerations are deemed important as affording a key to what, otherwise, would be perplexing difficulties.

A few further facts, showing the extent and spirit of the power exercised, and authority claimed, by the Six Nations, demand notice. The quotation from Mr. Jefferson, showing the incessant and harassing attacks of the Six Nations, on the Indians of Virginia, occupies a preceding page.

Mr. Heckewelder, in his narrative, says, " The Six Nations, under a pretence that they had once conquered the Delawares, asserted that *thereby the whole country had become theirs*, and, therefore, assumed the power of dictating who should, and who should not be permitted to dwell therein."

Again:—" The intention was of settling certain Delawares at Wyoming; but they objected, on the ground that this place lay in the road of the warriors going to and coming from the *Catawbas*."

Catawbas, a river then peopled by a tribe of Indians, in South Carolina, full a thousand miles, by any accessible route, from the Council Fire of the Iroquois! This single fact is worth dwelling on a moment, as at once illustrative of the extent of dominion claimed, as also the character of that wonderful people. A band of warriors, armed, taking in a leathern bag a preparation of Indian corn, parched, and pounded with maple sugar, (called by the Mohegans *Yokeag*,) set out on a war path, to strike an enemy, and take a scalp, a thousand miles distant. Courage, fortitude, ambition; the lofty aspirations of Alexander or Napoleon were here. Nor were these all; for the geography of an extensive country must have been understood; the position and power of all the neighboring nations, comprehended by them. Books they knew not, but ignorant, it were false to deem them. It is clear, an enemy would not be sought so far, if the nearer tribes had not been previously subjugated.

Mr. H. adds another objection of the emigrating Delawares, namely, that Wyoming "*abounded* with Indians whom they mistrusted." So that the valley was then numerously peopled.

The Iroquois, it is well known, in the old French war, took part with that nation against the English. Though the intelligent Moravian Missionaries passed freely through their country, yet such was their cautious concealment that—says Heckewelder, "they kept their designs *a profound secret*, and it was not until those Indians made a sally, and murdered fourteen white people within five miles of Shamokin, where the Brethren had a small mission, that they were aware of danger." He adds:—"It became evident that a cruel Indian war would be the result of the influence the French had acquired among the Indians; and especially those of the Six Nations, who *long since on all occasions*, and particularly in war concerns, assumed an authority over *many* other nations, so that *they only had to dictate*, and *others to obey*."

This reluctant admission, from the friend and patron of the Delawares, shows that the Six Nations were indeed conquerors, and over a vast territory supreme.

When peace came, Mr. Heckewelder says:—" And the Iroquois, the Six Nations being reconciled, they caused the other nations to lay down the hatchet." 1764.

By whatever name the confederacy should be styled: a Republic, an Empire, or an Oligarchy, we behold these United people, with the 'Great Head' or Council at Onondago, clothed with dominion, and enthroned in power. Certainly from the Lakes to the Ocean, they were as absolute as a nation could be without forts, or standing armies. With the left hand they lighted up consuming fires on the St. Lawrence, even in the strong holds of the warlike French; hunted their broken enemies two thousand miles into desolate regions beyond lake Superior, brandished the tomahawk over trembling vassals eastwardly to the Merrimack, while with the right they smote the Catawbas on the southern coast of Carolina, and brought home scalps as trophies from the remote Cherokees, on the distant banks of the Mississippi.

LETTER III.

Union, pride and policy of the Confederate Nations—Subjugated tribes, removed to Wyoming—Grand Council in Philadelphia—Canassatego—Count Zinzendorf visits Wyoming—Remarkable incident—Moravians—Mission from Wyoming to Gnadenhutten.

HAVING presented a general view of the Six Nations, we now proceed to speak more particularly of them as connected with the Delaware, Shawanese, and other Indians, the principal inhabitants, not only of Wyoming, but of Pennsylvania.

So many years, perhaps ages, had elapsed since their independence was lost, that time and misfortune had obliterated the record of their greatness, or their fall. Several centuries previous to 1600, had probably seen them in their degraded state. Formerly they claimed to have been powerful in numbers, valiant warriors, and great conquerors; possibly not an idle boast, but every fact in their history, after their acquaintance with the Europeans, shows at once their subserviency and terror, when they heard the voice of their imperious masters.

On the appearance of the English, the expansion of their settlements, and the development of their power, hope seems to have entered the minds of the Lenape, that from the new people they might derive protection, or what would be dearer still, to an Indian heart, the means of revenge.—Hence their welcome to the whites,—hence their lingering around the new settlements,—hence their reluctance to retire when ordered, into the interior.

The 'Christian Library,' detailing the Moravian Missions in North America, says, [1750] speaking of the Delawares,—" They had not only a kind of tax imposed upon them, to show their dependence upon the Iroquois; but the following very singular message was sent them:—The Great Head, that is, the *Council in Onondago,* speak the truth, and lie not:—they rejoice that some of the believing

Indians had removed to Wayomick; but now they lift up the remaining Mohickans and Delawares, and set them down in Wayomick, for there a fire is kindled for them, and there they may plant and think on God: but if they will not hear, the Great Head will come and clean their ears with a red-hot iron." To this lordly threat we shall again recur.

The Historian adds—"It was soon discovered, that this proposal did not originate in the Great Council at Onondago, but with the Oneida tribe, and the warlike Mohicans and Delawares." Let the reader examine all the authorities, and he will be satisfied—that neither of the Six Nations took any important step, without consultation and the consent of the Great Head, or Council, at Onondago.

Perfect union—and harmonious Councils were the foundation of their power; as secrecy in regard to their intentions, and vigour in carrying them into effect, were characteristic of their policy. By leave obtained, the Moravian Missionaries passed freely through the settlements of the Six Nations, associating unreservedly with chiefs and people, immediately preceding hostilities that commenced the French war; yet not a word escaped from any lip—not a whisper came to the ear of any one of them, not a suspicion even was awakened in the minds of those intelligent, quick discerning white men.

Similar to our own Federal Government, the Six Nations, like the several states, attended each to whatever strictly related to its own local concerns; but in every matter affecting war, peace, their external relations, or general interests, the Great Head, or united chiefs, assembled at the Council fire, at Onondago, was supreme. The government also possessed the most marked characteristics of the feudal system. Lands, for residence, or hunting grounds, were apportioned out by the chief power—taxes and tribute were collected, and military service demanded. Hence the warlike Mohicans, Delawares, Shawanese, and others spoken of, it is evident, were the soldiers of the Iroquois, bound to implicit obedience. If at any time they seemed to act independently, it was to effect some sinister political purpose of their profound and most sagacious masters. A Shawanese,—a tributary—a dependent, was sent upon the arrogant and ungracious errand to the Christian Indians near Bethlehem. Those to whom it was delivered, comprehended it well, for general consternation spread through Gnadenhutten." A *Shawanese* carried the message. It *might* become politic, on the part of the Iroquois, to disavow it.

But the Delawares had their kings. Tedeuscung, we are told, was elected king of the Delawares! Most true. It would be a gross error to suppose the Six Nations who had conquered, and held in vassalage so extensive an empire, were a rude rabble of ignorant Indians. Letters and the arts of civilized life they had not; nor had Attila or Ghengis Khan, but they were profoundly versed in all the wiles of diplomacy, the subtlest stratagems of war, and all the arts of Savage Government, which they made subservient to the gratification of an ambition as lofty and insatiable as that of the greatest conquerors, civilized or barbarian, we read of in story. Napoleon was not more proud to be king of kings, emperor supreme over, nominally, independent kingdoms; but mark the sequel, when we come to speak of Tedeuscung's fate.

The Iroquois had, too, like Rome, their pro-consuls, to preside over distant Provinces. Thus we find Shikellimus whom Loskiel designates " first magistrate and head chief of all the Iroquois Indians living on the banks of the Susquehanna," had his residence at Conestoga. In 1742, with other chiefs, and warriors of the Six Nations, he attended a great Council in Philadelphia. At a subsequent period he was stationed at Shamokin :—" to transact," says Heckewelder, "in the capacity of agent, the business between the Six Nations, and the Government of Pennsylvania."

After the removal to the lakes of the Oneida and Seneca Indians, who occupied Wyoming at the commencement of the last century, the valley was appropriated to the residence of such tribes, or parts of tribes, as claimed protection of the Six Nations, or portions of their refractory subjects, whom they desired to place more immediately under their inspection. A tribe of Nanticokes, formerly inhabitants of Maryland, was divided, part placed at Chenango,—Choconut, and Owego—and a portion was settled on the east side of the river, in the lower part of the Wyoming valley. The Shawanese*

---

* Gov. Cass thus speaks of the Shawanese. " Their history is involved in much obscurity. Their language is Algonquin, and closely allied to the Kickapoo, and other dialects spoken by tribes who have lived for ages north of the Ohio. But they are known to have recently emigrated from the South, where they were surrounded by a family of tribes, Creeks, Cherokees, Choctaws, &c., with whose language their own had no affinity. Their traditions assign to them a foreign origin, and a wild story has come down to them of a solemn procession, in the midst of the ocean, and of a miraculous passage through the great deep. That they were closely connected with the Kickapoos, the actual identity of language furnishes irrefragable proof, and the incidents of the separation yet live in the oral history of each tribe. We are strongly inclined to believe, that not long before the arrival of the French upon these great lakes, the Kickapoos and Shawanese composed the tribe known as the Erie; living on

tribe was also divided, a portion having their residence on the Sioto, and a large number were permitted, or directed, to erect their wigwams on the extensive and luxuriant flats on the west side of the Susquehanna, now Plymouth, but more popularly designated Shawney. The Delawares at this time occupied the country below the blue mountains, between the Susquehanna and Delaware, from whom purchases of land had been made by the Governors of Pennsylvania, but from which the occupants refused to remove. Learning that the Six Nations claimed to be the owners of the country, they were conciliated by proper means, and a grand Council was held in the summer of 1742, in the city of Philadelphia, to adjust all matters in dispute. More than two hundred chiefs and warroirs of the Six Nations attended, who were met by all the chief Sachems of the Delaware tribe. A general Council was opened in presence of the officers of the Colonial Government, and a large concourse of citizens, in the great hall of the Council house.

The Governor, by means of an interpreter, opened the Conference on the part of the Proprietaries in a *long talk*, which set forth, that the proprietaries of Pennsylvania had purchased the lands in the forks of Delaware several years before, of the Delaware tribes who then possessed them. That they had afterwards received information that the same lands were claimed by the Six Nations, and a purchase was also made of them—that in both these purchases the proprietaries had paid the stipulated price; but the Delaware Indians had nevertheless refused to give up possession; and as the Six Nations claimed authority over their country, it had been thought proper to hold a Council of all parties, that justice might be done. The chiefs of the Six Nations were then informed, that as they had on all occasions required the Government of Pennsylvania to remove any whites that settled upon their lands, so now the Government of

---

the eastern shore of the lake, to which they have given their name. *It is said that this tribe was exterminated by the victorious Iroquois.* But it is more probable, that a series of disasters divided them into two parties, one of which, under the name of Kickapoos, sought refuge from their enemies in the immense prairies between the Illinois and Mississippi; and the other, under the name of Shawanese, fled into the Cherokee country, and thence farther south. Father Segard, in 1632, called the Eries the "*nation du chat,*"* or the racoon, on account of the magnitude of these animals in their country; and *that* is the *soubriquet*, which, to this day, is applied by the Canadians to the Shawanese."

The reader will thank, rather than censure us, for this note, long as it is; because the Shawanese, not only were long residents at Wyoming, but gave an enduring name to one of its richest and most delightful locations.

* Clan Chattan ?

Pennsylvania expected that the Six Nations would cause these Indians to remove from the lands which it had purchased. The deeds from the Indians, and drafts of the disputed lands were then produced, and the whole submitted to the consideration of the Council. After some deliberation among the different chiefs, *Canassatego*, a venerable chieftain, arose in the name of all the deputies, and informed the Governor, "That they saw the Delawares had been an unruly people, and were altogether in the wrong, and that they had concluded to remove them." And addressing himself to the Delawares, in a violent manner, he said:—"You deserve to be taken by the hair of your heads, and shaken till you recover your senses, and become sober. We have seen a deed signed by nine of your chiefs above fifty years ago, for this very land. But how came you to take upon yourselves to sell lands at all? We conquered you—we made women of you; you know you are women, and can no more sell lands than women. Nor is it fit you should have the power of selling lands, since you would abuse it. You have been furnished with clothes, meat, and drink, by the goods paid you for it, and now you want it again like children as you are. But what makes you sell lands in the dark? Did you ever tell us that you had sold this land? Did we ever receive any part, even the value of a pipe shank for it? You have told us a blind story that you sent a messenger to us, to inform us of the sale, but he never came amongst us, nor have we ever heard anything about it. But we find you are none of our blood, you act a dishonest part, not only in this, but in other matters. Your ears are ever open to slanderous reports about your brethren. For all these reasons, we charge you to remove instantly; we dont give you liberty to think about it. You are women; take the advice of a wise man, and remove instantly. You may return to the other side of the Delaware where you came from, but we do not know whether, considering how you have demeaned yourselves, you will be permitted to live there, or whether you have not swallowed that land down your throats as well as the lands on this side. We therefore assign you two places to go to, either to *Wyoming*, or *Shamokin*. You may go to either of these places, and then we shall have you more under our eye, and shall see how you behave. Dont deliberate, but remove away, and take this belt of wampum."

He then commanded them to leave the Council, as he had business to do with the English.

This, it will be admitted, is the language, not of equals, but of masters, to the most abject of slaves. A Roman General would hardly have dared thus to address the fallen Jews, after the destruction of their city by Titus. The imperious command was obeyed; part removed to Shamokin, and a still larger portion to Wyoming, who established themselves on the east side of the river, occupying the flats below the present town of Wilkesbarre.

New and interesting personages now appear upon the scene. Zeal for the propagation of the Gospel caused the foot of the first white man to tread the soil of Wyoming. Long the residence of kings, it may not be improper to *relate*, that the first white visiter, should have been of noble birth,—and of kingly extraction. So admirably is the event *related* by Mr. Chapman, that I copy his original and well authenticated narrative entire.

"Such was the origin of the Indian town of Wyoming. Soon after the arrival of the Delawares, and during the same season, the (summer of the year 1742,) a distinguished foreigner, Count Zinzendorf, of Saxony, arrived in the valley on a religious mission to the Indians. This nobleman is believed to have been the first white person that ever visited Wyoming. He was the revivor of the ancient church of the United Brethren, and had given protection in his dominions to the persecuted Protestants who had emigrated from Moravia, thence taking the name of *Moravians*, and who, two years before had made their first settlement in Pennsylvania.

" Upon his arrival in America, Count Zinzendorf manifested a great anxiety to have the Gospel preached to the Indians; and although he had heard much of the ferocity of the Shawanese, formed a resolution to visit them.—With this view he repaired to *Tulpehocken*, the residence of Conrad Weiser, a celebrated interpreter and Indian agent for the Government, whom he wished to engage in the cause, and to accompany him to the Shawanese town. Weiser was too much occupied in business to go immediately to Wyoming, but he furnished the Count with letters to a Missionary of the name of Mack, and the latter, accompanied by his wife, who could speak the Indian language, proceeded immediately with Zinzendorf on the projected mission.

"The Shawanese appeared to be alarmed on the arrival of the strangers, who pitched their tents on the banks of the river a little below the town, and a Council of the chiefs having assembled, the declared purpose of Zinzendorf was deliberately considered. To these unlettered children of the wilderness it appeared altogether improbable that a stranger should have braved the dangers of a boisterous ocean three thousand miles broad, for the sole purpose of instructing them in the means of obtaining happiness *after death*, and that too without requiring any compensation for his trouble and expense; and as they had observed the anxiety of the white people to purchase land of the Indians, they naturally concluded that the real object of Zinzendorf was either to procure from them the lands at Wyoming for his own use, to search for hidden treasures, or to examine the country with a view to future conquest. It was accordingly resolved to assassinate him, and to do it privately, lest the knowledge of the transaction should produce a war with the English, who were settling the country below the mountains.

"Zinzendorf was alone in his tent, seated upon a bundle of dry weeds which composed his bed, and engaged in writing, when the assassins approached to execute their bloody commission. It was night, and the cool air of September had rendered a small fire necessary to his comfort and convenience. A curtain, formed of a blanket, and hung upon pins, was the only guard to the entrance of his tent.

"The heat of his fire had aroused a large rattlesnake which lay in the weeds, not far from it; and the reptile to enjoy it more effectually crawled slowly into the tent, and passed over one of his legs undiscovered. Without, all was still and quiet, except the gentle murmur of the river at the rapids about a mile below. At this moment the Indians softly approached the door of his tent, and slightly removing the curtain, contemplated the venerable man, too deeply engaged in the subject of his thoughts to notice either their approach, or the snake which lay extended before him. At a sight like this, even the heart of the savage shrunk from the idea of committing so horrid an act, and quitting the spot, they hastily returned to the town, and informed their companions that the *Great Spirit* protected the white man, for they had found him with no door but a blanket, and had seen a large rattlesnake crawl over his legs without attempting to injure him. This circumstance, together with the arrival soon afterwards of Conrad Weiser, procured Zinzendorf the friendship and confidence of the Indians, and probably contributed essentially towards inducing many of them, at a subsequent period, to embrace the Christian Religion. The Count having spent twenty days at Wyoming, returned to Bethlehem, a town then building by his christian brethren on the north bank of the Lehigh, about eleven miles from its junction with the Delaware."

Count Zinzendorf, learning the supremacy claimed and exercised by the Six Nations, applied to their chiefs for leave to visit the

Indian villages, and instruct the natives in the doctrines of repentance and salvation, through the merits of the Saviour.

He could not have been received and replied to with more politeness, at the most refined court in Europe. The answer is so beautiful in its simple, yet dignified eloquence, that I take pleasure in transcribing it.

"Brother, you have made a long journey over the seas to preach the Gospel to the white people and to the Indians. You did not know that we were here, and we knew nothing of you. *This proceeds from above.* Come therefore to us, both you and your brethren. We bid you welcome among us. Take this fathom of wampum, in confirmation of the truth of our words.."

The Moravians who had established themselves at Bethlehem, were indefatigable in their labour of love to Christianize the Indians. Neither the heats of summer, winter's storms, the dangers of the entangled forests, nor the toil in ascending precipitous mountains, could check the holy enthusiasm of the missionaries. Eight or ten made themselves masters of the Indian languages, with their kindred dialects, that they might be understood. Two bishops, Cammerhoff and De Watteville traversed the wilderness on foot, visited the various tribes and settlements along the Susquehanna, preaching the Saviour and exhorting to repentance; the former sacrificing his life, by exposure, to the behests of duty. So that in Wyoming, the earliest European accents that were heard, were accents of peace and love, breathing of grace, and redolent of mercy. It is now about an hundred years since these pious missionaries penetrated to this, then remote valley, and for thirty years afterwards, uncultivated wilderness.

There is pleasure in casting the eye of imagination back, and beholding the learned bishops, with the zeal and eloquence of Paul, at Athens, (How different the scene!) proclaiming to the children of Nature, "The unknown God, whom ye ignorantly worship. Him, declare I unto you."

A large number of converts, whom persecution had compelled to fly from their homes, removed from the eastern borders of New York to be near the Brethren, who had purchased land, and made an establishment for them, above the water-gap of the Lehigh, at the confluence of the Mahony and that stream, opposite to Fort Allen. The name given the place, was Gnadenhutten, or Huts of Mercy. Except the erection of the fort, this was the first settlement in a north direction, in Pennsylvania, above the Kittatinny Ridge or Blue

Mountain. The village was eighteen miles above Bethlehem, and on the warrior's path, about forty miles, southerly, through a most inhospitable wilderness, from Wyoming. For several years the settlement flourished. Agriculture opened to them the stores of plenty; while moral culture and religious hope imparted cheerfulness; and the whole seemed to be pervaded by the "sunshine of the breast." In 1752, the Huts of Mercy numbered five hundred souls. In the midst of these pleasing scenes of present peace and anticipated enjoyment, they were visited by a deputation of Nanticokes and other Indians, from Wyoming, consisting of more than a hundred persons, ostensibly on a mission of peace, with whom a solemn league of mutual friendship was entered into, after which their numerous, perhaps not very welcome visiters, returned to the valley. Doubtless, they were spies, sent by the Iroquois; their large number, with exquisite art, concealing the purpose of the journey. The way traveled, being the warrior's path, thirty or forty young savages, before ignorant of the route, might unsuspectedly attend such an embassy, apparently of friendship, and on the passage receive the instruction of the old braves, who must have led the party, preparatory to being sent themselves, on expeditions against the inhabitants below.

In consequence of this mission, (and probable message) about eighty of the Christian Indians, under Tedeuscung, a Delaware chief, already of some note, and destined to appear more conspicuously on another page, accompanied the party back to the Susquehanna, and established their lodges at Wyoming.

This step was taken as a preparatory measure to the old French war. The sequel is full of stirring and painful events.

LETTER IV.

Old French War—Influence upon Wyoming—Paxinos—Second Mission to Moravian Christian Indians, at Gnadenhutten—Evasive answer—Terrible threat—Paxinos' Queen converted—Massacre at Fort Augusta—Melancholy massacre of Moravians—Cunning and success of Iroquois at Fort Allen—Kings Tadame and Tedeuscung—Grand Council at Easton—Murder of the Governor's messenger, Charles Thompson—Second Congress at Easton—Peace agreed upon.

WITH the movements of France and England, the two chief maritime nations of Europe, the destinies of this distant and secluded valley were, for many years, so intimately blended, that a rapid exposition of their policy, on this continent, may not be regarded as foreign to the purpose of these pages. In 1603, France granted a charter for a large portion of North America. Two years afterward, charters of extensive limits were granted by England. At a very early period, France commenced settlements upon the northeastern coast, on the waters of the St. Lawrence, and on the Mississippi; while England began to plant colonies on the whole line of the Atlantic shore, from the St. Croix to St. Mary's. Sharp collisions arose. Each endeavoured to enlist the Indians in their respective quarrels. To the keen encounter of opposing interests, was added the exciting rivalry of towering ambition, national pride, hereditary hate, and personal revenge. Increasing knowledge of the dormant wealth, and extensive resources of America, gave tenfold impulse to all their passions.

While the centre was rapidly peopling under the auspices of England, France, actuated by a policy vast as her ambition, pursued with a vigour worthy of her power, was endeavouring to limit and overawe the British settlements by a cordon of forts, from Quebec, along the St. Lawrence, at Montreal, Oswego, Niagara, Detroit, Du Quesne, on the Ohio, and onward, embracing the most defensible points to the delta of the Mississippi. The design was grand—the execution spirited. The savages, formerly in amity with the British, but now favorably disposed to the French, who had promised to restore the country taken from them by the English, were excited by the defeat of Braddock, in 1754, to enter with redoubled zeal into the war against the colonies. The hatchet was unburied—the war knife was unsheathed, and the remorseless furies of Indian war were let loose along a thousand miles of defenceless frontier. The mighty genius of Pitt guided the destinies of England; but the rising glories of his administration had not yet dawned upon this continent, and the Iroquois, confident in their own prowess, and reposing implicit faith in the power, if not the promises of the French, pushed the war with unceasing vigilance along the whole line of their widely extended empire. Contracting our view to the limited range of our appropriate subject, we proceed with our narrative.

The spring following the first visit to the Christian Indians, at Gnadenhutten, (i. e. 1753,) to their great consternation, there came a second band from Wyoming, consisting of twenty-three persons, under the chief command of Paxinos, a Shawanese chief, or king, of some distinction, accompanied by *three Iroquois ambassadors*, who *desired* the whole settlement at Gnadenhutten to remove to Wyoming. Not only were they indisposed to yield obedience to the unreasonable mandate, but relying, probably, on the promises and power of the Brethren, and the contiguity of Fort Allen, for protection against their ancient conquerors and detested tyrants, several ventured to make replies, little calculated to conciliate their haughty masters.

"What can the chiefs of the Six Nations give me in exchange for my soul?" said one. "They never consider how that will fare!" "God who made and saved me, can protect me," replied another. "I am not afraid of the wrath of man, for not one hair of my head can fall to the ground without his will!"—Another, with still greater confidence, declared to the ambassadors, "If even one of them should lift up his hatchet against me, and say, "Depart from the Lord and the Brethren, I would not do it." Somewhat tart, if not taunting replies. These decisive, and especially the latter peremptory refusal, roused the chiefs to anger, when the terrible answer, before quoted, was given. "The *Great Head*, i. e. the Council at Onondago, speak the truth and lie not. They rejoice that some believing Indians had moved to Wayomick; but now they lift up the remaining Mohickans and Delawares, and set them down also in Wayomick; for there a fire is kindled for them, and where they may plant and think on God. *But if they will not hear, the Great Head will come and clean their ears with a red hot poker.*"*

Paxinos, who delivered this message, then turned to the missionaries, and in a grave and solemn manner, *earnestly demanded of them*, says the Historian, " not to hinder their converts from removing to Wayomick."

The wife of Paxinos had accompanied him, and either through the Divine Power, or, what in this instance is more probable, the subtle policy of the Iroquois, and the command of her husband, was, or affected to become converted, was baptised, and admitted a member of the congregation. A Shawanese queen might be presumed to have great influence in inducing the Christian Indians to yield to the earnest wishes of the Six Nations, and return under their authority and protection!

The first blow struck by the savages, sufficiently near to be connected with Wyoming, was in the neighborhood of Shamokin, (afterwards Fort Augusta, now Sunbury.) The Moravians had a small mission there; and as it was ever a rule of action of that excellent people to do all the good in their power, they had sent out with the minister, a blacksmith with his tools. Thus religion and the useful arts, advanced hand in hand together. None of the Moravians were injured;† but fourteen white persons were murdered and scalped. The date is not precisely stated, but it was after Braddock's defeat, in 1754, and previous to November, 1755, probably in the summer of the last named year.

Hostilities commenced, the reader cannot doubt but the settlement at Gnadenhutten was marked for vengeance. " Late in the evening of the 24th November, 1755," we copy from the Christian Library, " while the missionaries were at supper, their attention was suddenly aroused by the continual barking of dogs, which was followed by the report of a gun. On opening the door of the mission house, they

---

* It is stated that this order did not originate with the Great Council, at Onondago, but with the Oneida tribe, and warlike Mohicans and Delawares. A total misconception. The Mohicans and Delawares were slaves. It is probable, that to the Oneidas was assigned the duty; for that nation, as we have seen, formerly had their head-quarters at Wyoming: and from policy, they may have made the Mohicans and Delawares, the agents to do their will. But nothing was done that had not the sanction of the confederacy.

† Let it not be supposed the savages struck at random. The war party had, doubtless, their precise orders. The Moravians had probably conciliated the friendship of the great chief Shikellimus, the Vice Roy of the Iroquois, while resident of Shamokin. Indeed their settlement at that place had been made by his express desire. Learning the situation of the Brethren, Paxinos sent from Wyoming his two sons to conduct them in safety to Bethlehem.

observed a party of hostile Indians standing before the house, with their pieces pointed towards the door. On its being opened, they immediately fired, and Martin Nitschman was killed on the spot. His wife and some others were wounded, but ran up stairs into the garret, and barricaded the door with bedsteads. Hither the savages pursued them; but, not being able to force open the door, they set fire to the house, which was soon enveloped in flames. Two of the brethren had previously made their escape, by jumping out of the back window; and a boy leaped down from the flaming roof, though not till one of his cheeks had been grazed by a ball, and his hand much burned. Sister Partsch, whose husband had escaped out of the window, likewise ventured to leap down from the burning roof. Unobserved by the enemy, she hid herself behind a tree, on rising ground, from whence she had a full view of the tragical scene. Brother Fabricious, in attempting to make his escape in the same manner, was perceived by the Indians, and instantly wounded by two balls. They then seized him, and having despatched him with their hatchets, took his scalp, and left him dead on the ground. Eleven persons, belonging to the mission, were burned alive; among whom, was a child only fifteen months old. Sister Senseman, already surrounded by the flames, was heard to exclaim: "*'Tis all well, dear Saviour! I expected nothing else.*" The murderers now set fire to the barns and stables, by which all the corn, hay, and cattle were consumed; and, having made a hearty meal, they departed."

"This melancholy occurrence proved the deliverance of the Christian Indians; for, upon hearing the report of guns, seeing the flames, and learning the dreadful cause from those who escaped, they offered to attack the enemy without delay; but, being advised to the contrary, they all fled into the woods, and the settlement was thus in a few minutes cleared of its inhabitants. By the exertions and persuasions of the missionary, Shebosh, who, alone, remained at Gnadenhutten, most of the fugitive converts returned the next day. They now hoped to remain in safety, as, in consequence of a petition presented by the Brethren, at Bethlehem, the Governor of Pennsylvania sent a party of soldiers into these parts for the protection of the Christian Indians and the country in general. But, on New Year's day, 1756, the savages attacked these troops, set fire to the settlement, and laid waste all the plantations, by which both the congregation and the missionaries were reduced to the greatest poverty."

We add a few anecdotes, gleaned from various sources. The troops sent up by the Government, of course, occupied Fort Allen; and for recreation, amused themselves with skating. It is no part of savage warfare to attack ramparts of stone, defended by ordnance; but in the stratagems of war, the soldiers were no match for the trained and wily Iroquois. Thus one or two Indians were, for some time, seen unguardedly skating too, on the frozen bosom of the Lehigh, but at a distance. At length a party left the Fort to surprise them; when, with seeming carelessness, they would first approach, and then extend their playful race, further and further. Thus, by degrees, drawing the party of whites beyond the reach of protection or retreat.—The scheme succeeded. Suddenly, from an ambush, cracked the deadly rifle—a yell arose—a large party rushed forth to seize the scalps of the slain,—scarcely one returned to the fort unhurt. Then, as if satisfied with their trophies, they gave the garrison to understand, (probably by a wounded prisoner, released on purpose,) that they were about to retire, threatening to return the next year, and skate with them again. Taking up their march on the war path, they left a strongly marked trail, as far as their enemies would be apt to pursue; when, returning by another unfrequented route, they again lay in ambush, waiting patiently, enduring the extremity of cold, rather than hazard exposure by kindling fires. At length, confidence being restored, the garrison went out and in, hunting or hauling wood, as if no enemy were within an hundred miles. Fatal security! The Indians again fell upon them, and made such slaughter, that the troops abandoned their fort, and fled below the mountains for safety, leaving a rich prize of booty to their eminently superior enemy.

War was formally proclaimed by Great Britain against France, in 1756, when, if possible, a renewed impulse was given to savage ferocity. As our purpose is only to record those events which are more immediately connected with Wyoming, we commend the bloody narrative of desolation, in Western Pennsylvania, to some abler hand. The writer should visit each interesting location, and gather from the children of the sufferers, every particular which tradition has handed down, and faithful memory preserved.

On the death of Tadame, treacherously murdered, but by whom, or for what cause, we find no record, Tedeuscung was elected king of the Delawares, at Wyoming; " a lusty, rawboned man," says Major Parsons, " but haughty, and very desirous of respect and command. He was born near Trenton, in 1705, and was now about fifty years old."

The Pennsylvania Government, anxious to conciliate the Indians, invited the various nations to a council, which was accordingly held at Easton, commencing on the 8th of November, 1756. Imposing ceremonies, both for state and security, were kept up throughout the negotiations. At three o'clock, Governor Dennie marched from his lodgings, to the place of Conference, guarded by a party of the royal Americans, in front and on the flanks, and a detachment of Col. Weiser's Provincials, in subdivisions in the rear, with colours flying, drums beating, and music playing; which order was always observed in going to the place where the Council was held.

Tedeuscung, who had been accompanied from Wyoming, by most of his principal warriors, performed the part of chief speaker on this occasion, for all the tribes present, as he had done at the preceding conferences. He is represented to have supported the rights and claims of the Indians in a dignified and spirited manner. Tedeuscung, in his talk before the Council, said in substance as follows:—
" There are many reasons why the Indians have ceased to be the friends of the English. They had never been satisfied with the conduct of the English after the treaty of 1737, when their fathers, *Tishekunk* and *Nutimus*, sold them the lands upon the Delaware: that although the rights of the purchase were to extend " *as far as a man can go in a day and a half*," from Neshamony creek, yet the man who was appointed to go over the ground, did not walk, but ran; and it was also expected he would go along the bank of the river, which he did not, but went in a straight line; and because they had been unwilling to give up the land to the English, as far as the walk extended, the Governor who then had the command in Pennsylvania, sent for their cousins, the Six Nations, who had always been hard masters to them, to come down and drive them from the land.—That when the Six Nations did come down, they met them at the Governor's house, in Philadelphia, in 1742, with the view of explaining, why they did not give up the land; but the English made so many presents to the Six Nations, that they would hear no explanation from the Delawares, and the Chief of the Council of the Six Nations (Canassatego,) abused them, and called them women. The Six Nations had, however, given to them and the Shawanese, the country upon the Juniata, for a hunting ground, and had so informed the Governor; but notwithstanding this, the latter permitted the whites to go and

settle upon those lands. That two years before, the Governor had been to Albany, to buy more of the lands of the Six Nations, and had described their purchase by *points of compass*, which they did not understand, including not only the Juniata, but also the West Branch of the Susquehanna, which the Indians did not intend to sell; and when all these things were known, they declared they would no longer be friends to the English, who were trying to get all their country from them.

He assured the Council, that they were glad to meet their old friends, the English, to smoke the pipe of peace with them, and hoped that justice would be done to them, for all the injuries they had received. This Conference continued nine days, during which time, all matters of difference were considered, and the Shawanese and Delawares, the two principal tribes, became reconciled to the English, with whom they concluded a treaty of peace."

Tedeuscung, you will perceive, bore at this Council a conspicuous part. Treaties of friendship were entered into with the Shawanese and Delawares—presents were received—smoke from the calumet ascended to the skies to bear aloft the record of reconciliation; and the vain and flattered king returned in proud triumph to the valley. It was his day of glory—bright but brief. In my view of the vassalage of these nations, the treaty, of course, I regard as nugatory, except so far as it might operate to awaken hopes of Independence, and tend to detach the Delawares from their conquerors. The contract needed the approbation of the "Gread Head at Onondago." We incline to believe the measure had been adopted, independently of their wishes, they being then, with their warriors, extremely engaged, if not severely pressed, in other quarters. What strengthens this opinion, are the facts, that almost immediately after the treaty, murders were committed below the Blue Mountains, which the Wyoming Indians solemnly disavowed; and when the Governor sent Mr. Hill on a message to Tedeuscung, he was waylaid on his journey from Minisink to the valley, by the Iroquois, and murdered. Indeed, Heckewelder states that the Delawares assured him those murders were committed by the Six Nations, to prevent the effects of the treaty. Charles Thompson, then a respected, since, a most venerable name, was present, and acted as one of the Secretaries during the negotiations. The fact he stated to the writer, at Lancaster, in 1808, where Mr. Thompson, being on business pending before the Assembly, spent part of the winter, and boarded at the same house. He further related, that Tedeuscung, pleased with what he considered as the candour and fairness of Mr. T., adopted him as a member of the Delaware nation, and gave him a name, signifying, "He who speaks the Truth." After the breaking up of Council, Mr. Thompson, in compliance with the wishes of the Government, and an invitation from the king, accompanied him to Wyoming. When, pursuing the Indian path, (near the route of the present turnpike) they came to the top of the first mountain which overlooks the valley, the king expressed fears lest there might be danger below, (dreading, I apprehend, a visit from the Iroquois.) Mr. Thompson, and all the train, but one or two, who accompanied the king, turned down southwesterly from the path, and sought repose for the night, while the cautious chief went in, to reconnoitre; but he returned early the next morning, reporting that all was well. Mr. T. spoke of the valley as a delightful spot. "He did not wonder at the contest waged for its possession." In respect to the subsequent massacre of the first settlers, he gave me a fact, and an opinion, which, not being recorded at the time, though indelibly imprinted on my memory, I think it more prudent to omit than to tell.

But the Government of Pennsylvania knew too well the importance of having the assent of the Six Nations, to rest satisfied with the treaty as made.

The influence of Sir William Johnson, agent for Indian affairs, was invoked to bring the Six Nations to a new Congress. Neither presents nor promises were spared, and in October 1758, there was opened at Easton, one of the most imposing assemblages ever beheld in Pennsylvania. Chiefs from the Six Nations were there, namely, Mohawks, Oneidas, Onondagos, Cayugas, Senecas, and Tuscaroras. There were also present ambassadors from the tributary tribes of Nanticokes, Canoys, Tuteloes, Chenangoes, Delawares, Unamies, Minisinks, Mohicans, Wapingers, and Shawanese. Both the Governors of Pennsylvania and New Jersey, attended; with Sir William Johnson, and George Crogan, Esq., sub-Indian agent, a deputation from the Provincial Assembly at New Jersey, and a large concourse of eminent citizens from Philadelphia, and the neighboring counties. All the military pomp and parade exhibited at the previous treaty, were here renewed with additional ceremonies; and our intelligent neighbours of that flourishing town, should cause a splendid historical painting to be executed commemorative of an event so imposing, and so important in their annals.

Tedeuscung, on the way to the Conference, having fallen in company with the chief who had commanded the expedition against

Gnadenhutten and Fort Allen, high words arose between them, when the king raised his tomahawk and laid the chief dead at his feet. From this moment, though vengeance might slumber, he was a doomed man, a sacrifice alike to policy and revenge.

At the Congress, Tedeuscung, eloquent, and of imposing address, took at first a decided lead in the debates. But one of the chiefs of the Six Nations, says Chapman, "on the other hand expressed in strong language his resentment against the British Colonists, who had killed and imprisoned some of his tribe, and he, as well as other chiefs of those Nations, took great umbrage at the importance assumed by Tedeuscung, whom, as one of the Delawares, they considered in some degree subject to their authority. Tedeuscung, however, supported the high station which he held, with dignity and firmness, and the different Indian tribes at length became reconciled to each other. The Conference having continued eighteen days, and all causes of misunderstanding between the English and Indians being removed, a general peace was concluded on the twenty-sixth day of October. At this treaty the boundaries of the different purchases made from the Indians were more particularly described, and they received an additional compensation for their lands, consisting of knives, hats, caps, looking glasses, tobacco-boxes, shears, gun locks, combs, clothes, shoes, stockings, blankets, and several suits of laced clothes for their chieftains, and when the business of the treaty was completed, the stores of rum were opened, and distributed to the Indians, who soon exhibited a scene of brutal intoxication."

Great offence, it appears, was given to the ambassadors of the Six Nations at the consequence assumed, and the forward part taken by Tedeuscung; and yet no immediate measures were adopted to chastise his supposed contumacy. A solution of what might otherwise seem difficult, both in his more bold, independent conduct, and the forbearance of the Iroquois, may be found in the fact, that the power of their allies was already sensibly shaken, and Great Britain was preparing with unexampled vigour to drive the French from this continent. Fort William was taken in 1757; Louisburg surrendered to their victorious arms in the summer of 1758; and far more important to the Iroquois, as it was almost in the heart of the dominions claimed by them, the shame of Braddock's defeat was washed out, and Fort Du Quesne, (afterwards named Fort Pitt,) had surrendered to the English the February preceding the October of 1758, when the Conferences at Easton were holden. That event was a fatal blow to the widely extended claim of power on the part of the confederacy; although the Council fire at Onondago was for many years after numerously surrounded by bold and ambitious chiefs and renowned warriors.*

* The Six Nations, with instinctive sagacity seeing the rapid extinction of French power, withdrew, as we have noted, from the contest. War between England and France still raged, the colonies performing for the mother country, all that zeal, hardihood and courage could accomplish. As our story is little further connected with the French war, we may here, though in advance of our dates, state;—That Quebec was taken Sept. 13, 1759. The battle on Abraham's plains, between Wolf and Montcalm, is perhaps rendered more familiar to the American reader than any other event of the contest, by the popular song,

"In a mouldering cave, where the wretched retreat," &c.

Niagara, Ticonderoga, and Crown Point, surrendered the same year. Montreal in 1760. The Moro Castle, in 1762. In this hazardous, but successful enterprise, a company of provincials, commanded by Capt. Z. Butler, shared the danger and glory. Peace was concluded in 1763; France yielding all the northern part of the continent to the victorious arms and councils of Great Britain, guided by Pitt.

LETTER V.

Renewed efforts to Christianize Wyoming Indians—Pleasing success—Wyalusing—Murder of King Tedeuscung—First Connecticut Settlement—Their massacre and expulsion—Expedition under Col. Boyd to Wyoming—John and Emanuel Hoover—Removal of Christian Indians to the Ohio—Exposition of an important matter.

THE peace concluded at Easton, allows us but a moment's respite from the record of war and crime. Turning to more congenial themes, we seize the moment and trace with pleasure, the progress of the Moravians in propagating the Gospel among the Indians. A large number of the Delaware nation were established in the valley. Waughwawame, their principal town, being situated not far below the site now occupied by Wilkesbarre. Though suffering many privations, the zeal of the missionaries did not cool; neither did their faith waver, nor their efforts relax: their souls seemed to glow with a divine ardour; success crowned their labours; several hundred Indians received the rite of baptism. Nor was it a mere formal profession on their part, for their lives were wholly changed, and the moral precepts of the Gospel regulated their conduct, while their hearts yielded assent to its doctrines. At Wyalusing, or as it is written by the German missionaries, Machwihilusing, a number of Christian Indians had united together, without a teacher, for purposes of worship, and thither the Rev. David Zeisberger repaired, and became their pastor. Under his wise direction, the settlement soon assumed a very pleasing aspect. Order, industry and neatness were established; lands were cleared and fenced. Grain, cattle, horses, poultry, every sort of useful stock were introduced, and schools were opened for the education of Indian children. A bell, the first, probably, ever heard in Pennsylvania, north of the Kittatinny mountains, sounded from the chapel, calling the Indians to worship. Methinks, as its tones, loud and clear, vibrated on the undulating air, and were borne by the breeze beyond the hills, to the strange Indian, roaming the forest or approaching the place, the sound must have come like a spirit's voice, a death knell to his race, awakening special wonder.

Three years thus passed, the settlement flourishing; a rose in a desert, and giving the highest promise of future usefulness, when the sudden outbreak of Indian war reached their ears, and created the utmost alarm. It had been a delusive hour of sunshine in the midst of a gathering storm. Strange as it may appear, though near the Iroquois, and in daily intercourse with them, the missionaries had not the least intimation of their purposes against the white settlements. When hostilities commenced, Mr. Zeisberger, and the other preachers, were left unmolested. But imminent danger threatening the Christian Indians, near Bethlehem, occasioned the recall of the pious missionary, and he attended them from that place to Philadelphia, whither they were sent for safety from the fury of the exasperated frontier inhabitants, who had been led to believe, notwithstanding their religious professions, that the Moravian Indians were guilty of the cruel murders perpetrated upon their friends.

In the mean time, Wyoming was the theatre of highly interesting events. In a previous letter, I have stated the belief that king Tedeuscung was doomed, sooner or later, to destruction. Indian revenge may sleep, but never dies; the hour may be postponed for months or years, but at last will come as sure as fate. Tedeuscung, besides the independent airs assumed at Easton, had slain with his own hand the chief who commanded the Iroquois war party in their devastation of Gnadenhutten. War upon the whites being now renewed, it is not improbable that the king may have declined to lead his tribe to battle. Certain, however, it is, that for some time several of the Six Nations had been visiting at Wyoming, without any ostensible object, mingling, socially, with the Delawares, and appearing on friendly terms with the old chief. Whiskey had been obtained, which, when in his power, the Indian propensity was too strong to be resisted, and he drank until inebriation overpowered his senses, and he lay sleeping in his wigwam, scarcely conscious of life, and wholly unsuspicious of danger. In the dead of the night, on the 19th of April, 1763, the hut of Tedeuscung, and twenty of the surrounding dwellings burst, almost at the same moment, into flames, and thus the great Delaware king miserably perished.

Indian cunning ascribed the murder to the New England people, who were just commencing settlements in the valley.

It is sufficient to say, in the absence of the slightest evidence, that such a measure on their part would have been a compound of wickedness and folly, so stupid and base, that it cannot be supposed true, for a moment. Surrounded by Savages, far removed from the whites, their policy was too obvious to be mistaken, namely, to conciliate the Indians, by every fair means. The charge was made in far deeper malevolence than mere wanton mischief, for the destruction of the Connecticut settlers had also been resolved upon by the Six Nations.

The preceding year, that is, in 1762, a considerable number of emigrants had arrived in the valley from Connecticut. After sowing grain, they returned to their families, with whom, early the following Spring, they came back, prepared to establish themselves permanently, bringing their stock, household furniture, indeed, it is most probable, all they possessed on earth. Strange to say, although my inquiries have been faithfully pursued, wherever the least prospect existed of obtaining information, they have proved fruitless, and I am unable to state from what towns in Connecticut they came, or who were their principal leaders. Their town was built nearer the river than the Indian village of Maughwawame, on the flats, below Wilkesbarre. The season had been favorable; their various crops on those fertile plains had proved abundant, and they were looking forward, with hope, to scenes of prosperity and happiness; but suddenly, without the least warning, on the 15th of October, a large party of savages raised the war whoop, and attacked them with fury. Unprepared for resistance, about twenty men fell, and were scalped; the residue, men, women and children fled, in wild disorder, to the mountains. Language cannot describe the sufferings of the fugitives, as they traversed the wilderness, destitute of food or clothing, on their way to their former homes.

Mr. Chapman states, that Col. James Boyd, ordered by Gov. Hamilton, repaired to Wyoming, found the valley abandoned by the Indians, who had scalped those whom they had killed, and carried away their captives and plunder. The bodies of the slain lay strewed upon the field, and Col. Boyd having caused them to be decently interred, withdrew with his detachment down the river. I am not able to reconcile this with certain information derived from the Rev. Mr. Elder's correspondence with Gov. Hamilton.

Extract of a letter from John Elder to the Governor, dated Paxton, 30th September, 1763.

"As a number of volunteers from this county, on the return of Col. Armstrong, design to scout a little way into the enemy's country, our troops would gladly join the volunteers, if it's agreeable to your Honour; and as that favour, they imagine has been granted the troops on the other side of the Susquehanna, they flatter themselves it will not be refused these two companies. Their principal view is to destroy the immense quantities of corn *left* by the New England men at Wyoming, which, if not consumed, will be a considerable magazine to the enemy, and enable them, with more ease, to distress the inhabitants, etc." How the corn of the New England settlers could be spoken of September '63, as "*left*," those people being then in undisturbed possession, I cannot conceive, unless it was a delicate mode of covering their purpose, by cutting off their means of subsistence, to expel them.

Lieut. Gov. Hamilton, under date, Philadelphia, October 5th, '63, answers:—

"With regard to what you mention, touching an expedition into the Indian's country, I could have no objection to their scouting as far as Wyoming, and destroying the corn, if any *left* there," etc.; but positively prohibits the troops destroying the Indian Wyalusing settlement, which was contemplated.

Another letter from Gov. Hamilton, is dated, Oct. 10th, 1763:—

"Having wrote to you a few days ago, I should not have any thing to add at this time, but for a letter the Commissioners and I have received from Mr. Robert Callender, acquainting us that Major Clayton has applied to him to furnish provisions for two hundred men, for twenty days, by which it is conceived that he hath an intention of going upon some expedition against the Indians, without having communicated the same to me, and received my approbation. A step I can by no means approve in an officer bearing the king's commission," etc.

On the 17th October, Commander Elder, writes:—

"Your favour of the 10th, I received last night, and am sorry to find that our proceedings are any way disagreeable to the Legislature. Our two companies, fired with resentment, on hearing the barbarities committed by the savages, and willing to serve their country to the utmost of their power, signified to me their strong desire to join in any expedition that might be undertaken against the common enemy. And encouraged by your acquainting me that, ' you had no objection against our destroying the corn *left* at Wyoming, I ordered them to proceed on that service; strictly prohibiting them, in obedience to your Honour's command, to make any attack on Wialusing. The party, though small, set out from Hunter's, last Tuesday, in high spirits; so that it is impossible to suspend the expedition now, as the troops are, by this time, advanced, I doubt not, as far as Wyoming. What success they may have, I know not; but if they destroy the corn and improvements made there, by the New England men, to the great displeasure of the Indians, and in contempt of your Honour's authority, and can happily intercept the murdering party on their return from Northampton, I presume it will be of considerable service."

Commander Elder again writes to the Governor, under date, Paxton, 25th October, 1763.

"I acquainted your Honour, the 17th instant, that it was impossible to suspend the Wyoming expedition; the party is now returned, and I shall not trouble your Honour with any account of their proceedings, as Major Clayton informs me he transmitted to you, from Fort Augusta, a particular account of all their transactions, from their setting out from Hunter's, till they returned to Augusta. The mangled carcasses of those unhappy creatures, who had settled there, presented to our troops a most melancholy scene, which had been acted not above two days before their arrival; and by the way the savages came to Wyoming, it appears they were the same party that committed the ravages in Northampton county," etc.

Thus it would seem the expedition of Col. Clayton to Wyoming, was principally intended to destroy the grain "*left*" by the New England people, and also, their improvements. The Indians, two days before, had effectually prevented any resistance. The corn and buildings left, were now given up to destruction.*

Did not Col. Clayton bury the dead? It is impossible to believe otherwise of a gallant soldier!

---

* *From the Pennsylvania Gazette, Nov.* 1763.

Extract of a letter from Paxton, in Lancaster County, dated Oct. 23d.—" Our party, under Capt. Clayton, has returned from Wyoming, where they met with no Indians, but found the New Englanders, who had been killed, and scalped a day or two before they got there. They buried the dead, nine men and a woman, who had been most cruelly butchered; the woman was roasted, and had two hinges in her hands, supposed to be put in red hot, and several of the men had awls thrust into their eyes; and spears, arrows, pitchforks, etc., sticking in their bodies. They burnt what houses the Indians had left, and destroyed a quantity of Indian corn. The enemy's tracks were up the river, towards Wighaloasing."

[I am indebted for this Extract, to my friend Mr. Jordan. The cruel torture might have been inferred; but before, was unknown to me.]

Was Col. Boyd with him? There could not have been two Colonels, with two hundred men!

Capt. Lazarus Stewart was, probably, in command of one of the companies. It is not a little curious to anticipate. Col. Clayton and Capt. Stewart once more met at Wyoming, nearly ten years afterwards; the former, again, on an expedition to destroy the Yankee settlement—while Stewart was defending them.

Col. Stone supposes this deed to have been perpetrated by the Delawares, in revenge for the death of Tedeuscung, while our convictions are clear, that it was the work of the same hands that slew the king. Two men, named John and Emanuel Hoover, were at work upon a chimney, being built in a house on the flats, when they were made prisoners by the Indians, who had already another captive with them. The Indians immediately took the path northward, and ascending the hill, near where the Plains School House stands, in Wilkesbarre, they met a man coming down, thoughtless of danger, carrying a small bundle in his hand. Instantly surrounding him, they drew their spears, and before he had time to beg for life, or cry, "God have mercy on my soul," thrust him through, and he fell, covered with wounds; after scalping him they marched on. They took their prisoners to near where Geneva now stands, in the settlements of the Six Nations; from whence John Hoover and the other prisoner, whose name we do not know, attempted to make their escape;*—the latter found his way to the white settlement at

---

* The following is from Mr. Stone's Work, p. 135:—" Among the individual incidents marking this singular tragedy, was the following:—Some of the fugitives were pursued for a time, by a portion of the Indians; and among them was a settler named Noah Hopkins, a wealthy man, from the county of Dutchess, in the state of New York, bordering upon Connecticut. He had disposed of a handsome patrimony in his native town, Armenia, and invested the proceeds, as a shareholder of the Susquehanna Company, and in making preparations for moving to the new colony. Finding, by the sounds, that the Indians were upon his trail, after running a long distance, he fortunately discovered the trunk of a large hollow tree, upon the ground, into which he crept. After lying there several hours, his apprehensions of danger were greatly quickened by the tread of footsteps. They approached, and in a few moments two or three savages were actually seated upon the log, in consultation. He heard the bullets rattle loosely in their pouches. They actually looked into the hollow trunk, suspecting that he might be there; but the examination must have been slight, as they discovered no traces of his presence. The object of their search, however, in after life, attributed his escape to the labours of a busy spider, which, after he had crawled into the log, had been industriously engaged in weaving a web over the entrance. Perceiving this, the Indians supposed, as a matter of course, that the fugitive could not have entered there. This is rather a *fine spun* theory of his escape; but it was enough for him that he was not discovered. After remaining in his place of concealment as long as nature could endure the confinement, Hopkins crept forth, wandering in the wilderness, without food, until he was on

Shamokin, and afterwards published, in the state of New York, a pamphlet, containing an account of his captivity and sufferings; a copy was in the valley in 1785, but cannot be found. Some time after his escape the body of John Hoover was found in the woods, he having, it was not doubted, died of fatigue and hunger. His brother Emanuel visited Wyoming after the revolutionary war, and related the circumstances to Cornelius Courtright, Esq., to whom I am indebted for nearly all I have been able to learn of the massacre of 1763. From these facts it is plain that the mischief was perpetrated, not by the Delawares, but by the Six Nations.

After the murder of Tedeuscung, the Christian Indians fled to Bethlehem, but upon the restoration of quiet, they returned in 1765 to the Susquehanna, and made their resting place again at Wyalusing. The people of that now highly cultivated and populous place, we cannot doubt, will be pleased to see the description of the Moravian Indian settlement. "Having, after many toilsome wanderings, reached the Susquehanna, they got a few boats, some sailing up the river, and others traveling along its banks, and arrived at Machwihilusing, on the 9th of May, after a journey of five weeks.

"Having fixed on a convenient spot for a settlement, they immediately began to erect a town, which, when completed, consisted of thirteen Indian huts, and upwards of forty houses built of wood, in the European manner, besides a dwelling for the missionaries. In the middle of the street, which was eighty feet broad, stood a large and neat chapel. The adjoining grounds were laid out into neat gardens; and between the town and the river, about two hundred

---

the point of famishing. In this situation, knowing that he could but die, he cautiously stole down into the valley again, whence, five days before, he had fled. All was desolation there. The crops were destroyed, the cattle gone, and the smouldering brands and embers were all that remained of the houses. The Indians had retired, and the stillness of death prevailed. He roamed about for hours, in search of something to satisfy the cravings of nature, fording or swimming the river twice, in his search. At length he discovered the carcass of a wild turkey which had been shot on the morning of the massacre, but which had been left in the flight. He quickly stripped the bird of its feathers, although it had become somewhat offensive by lying in the sun, dressed and washed it in the river, and the first meal he made therefrom, was ever afterwards pronounced the sweetest of his life. Upon the strength of this turkey, with such roots and herbs as he could gather in his way, he traveled until, after incredible hardships, his clothes being torn from his limbs in the thickets he was obliged to encounter, and his body badly lacerated—he once more found himself among the dwellings of civilized men."

"The facts of this little incidental narrative, were communicated to the author, by Mr. G. F. Hopkins, the printer of this present volume, and a nephew of the sufferer, who died at Pittsfield, Massachusetts, at a very advanced age, about thirty years ago. He was a very respectable man."

and fifty acres were divided into regular plantations of Indian corn. The burying ground was situated at some distance back of the buildings. Each family had its own boat. To this place, they gave the name of Friedenshuetten, (meaning " Huts of Peace.") This new settlement soon assumed a very flourishing appearance. The inhabitants were industrious, and dwelt together in peace and unity. Many Indians visited the town, admiring the fine situation and good order maintained in the place," etc.—*Christ. Library.*

At Sheshequin, or as it is written by the Moravians, Tschechshequaunink, there was a large settlement of Indians, many of whom became converts, and the missionary, Rothe, attended to their spiritual wants, with pious zeal.

For six years, those two congregations under the guidance of the Moravians, continued to flourish in peace; but many causes now combined to render them uneasy in their respective situations. The Six Nations had sold the land on which they lived without consulting them, to the Connecticut people. Neighboring white settlers persisted in tempting the weaker brethren with spirituous liquors; and more than either, the Delawares on the Ohio were anxious they should emigrate and join their religious brethren in the West. In consultation with Zeisberger and Heckewelder, at Wyalusing in 1770, the final decision to remove was adopted, and the succeeding year, about 250 Indians from that place set out on their way to Ohio, divided into two parties. One chiefly of men, with eighty oxen, and other stock in proportion, went through the wilderness, suffering great privations and hardships. Another party, with the women and children, descended the river in canoes, spent a day at their beloved Wyoming, shed a tear over the graves of their buried friends, and then departed from their almost worshipped Susquehanna, to return no more forever. The fate of these poor creatures, at nearly the close of the Revolutionary war, I am happy it is not my painful duty to record.*

* In his general view of the subject, Col. Stone has expressed, with sufficient distinctness, indeed with emphasis, the fact of the mastery, absolute and unqualified, of the Six Nations over the Delawares, and neighboring tribes; but in his details, it appears to me, of the policy and conduct of those tribes, a volition and independence is described, incompatible with the idea of subserviency and coerced obedience. Hence, like every author who has written in relation to those Indians, he leaves the mind perplexed by the statement of unquestionable facts, involving inexplicable contradiction.

Admit for a moment, the Delawares yet a great people, retaining their political organization, electing their own kings, allowed to enter into council, to unite in the negotiation of treaties; their braves courted, flattered, trusted, sent upon the war path; and yet subordinate, the high and imperious tone of indignation and contempt towards them, only used by their masters upon rare occasions, when they had presumed too far in affected independence, and needed to be checked, you will, we think, perceive their true condition. This view is illustrated by King Paxinos of the Shawanese, being sent on the responsible mission to the Christian Indians at Gnadenhutten; the return of Tedeuscung in obedience to the message sent him, his being forthwith elevated to the station of King of his Nation; and when, in scriptural language, "he waxed fat and kicked," assuming a tone of independence, the offence taken by the Iroquois, and their terrible vengeance wrought upon him. The same remark is applicable to the speech of Canassatego at the Treaty in Philadelphia in respect to the misconduct of the Delawares, in refusing to remove from land they had sold.

The Confederation of the Rhine was composed of sovereign states, independent communities, Kings who held their court in gorgeous state, free to do their own will—except that Napoleon was their master. So too, the French Senate and Senators were independent; they met, deliberated; the Emperor frequently attending consultations, arguing different questions, and sometimes yielding his own opinion, yet the anecdote is familiar; one of the members pressed with earnestness some point against Napoleon's wishes, until he became impatient. "Stop, stop," said he with suppressed emotion, "do not oblige me to speak with more decision." The Iroquois, if less learned than the French Chief, were as profound statesmen, and as perfect adepts in the arts of Government as the Emperor; and he, holding Poland in his fist, with power to throw her into the lap of Russia or Austria, yet by policy bound the Polish Lancers so closely to his standard and person, that they would rush into the stream at his bidding, and the last expiring cry, when swallowed by the flood, was "Vive la Napoleon." So too, I take it, the subject nations of the Iroquois were held in bondage by the ties of policy, as well as by the rod of power; until that Confederacy, wounded, yet not slain; broken, though not crushed, with instinctive perception of the true condition of affairs, they began more and more, and with bolder tone, to rear the crest, and speak the language of freemen.

Again, Col. Stone, while he speaks of the Six Nations, the A quanuschionis, meaning the "United People," leaves the impression that they were disunited in council, divided in action, some of the Confederacy taking part with the French, and others with the English. Such view of the matter, the reader is aware is at variance with the opinions we have constantly expressed in this work, and sincerely entertain. Such separation and division, I think, was rather apparent than real. The Iroquois were neither deluded by the French nor the English, to adopt any system of policy they did not deem for their own peculiar interest. They were *Iroquois*, proud of their long continued national existence and supremacy; fond, to enthusiasm of their country; ambitious of power; desirous of renown; avaricious of dominion. They watched the daily augmenting strength of both England and France, with bitter jealousy and inextinguishable hate. No moment had existed since their purposes and power had been developed, so that fears for their own independence had been awakened, but the Indians would have been rejoiced if the whole white race had but one neck, and that submitted to their exterminating hatchet. Like every other people they were compelled to yield to circumstances. The French were favored in former years because they erected trading houses, bought furs, and made little encroachment on their lands, while the British colonies awakened greater jealousy by the dreaded invasion of the woodman's axe, and the hated encroachment of the farmer's plough; yet they wavered with the vicissitudes of war, and their policy varied with the shifting success of the rival parties, meaning on the issue, if possible, to be on good terms with the strongest.

"But at least for a part of the war the Mohawks and Onondagos, sided with the British, being under the influence of Sir William Johnson."

Say rather, Sir William Johnson was the subservient agent of their policy. With the rising star of British ascendancy the apparent influence of Sir William increased. Had the French continued victorious; had not Fort William, Louisburgh, Oswego, Du Quesne, fallen, rely on it, the influence of Sir William Johnson would have been lighter with them than the down of the thistle. But Sir William took to his bed a Mohawk maiden, the sister of a great chief. Say rather the sister of a Mohawk chief was permitted, or directed to become the partner of Sir William Johnson. However profound his policy, it was at least equally wise and effective on the part of the Indians. If Napoleon wedded a daughter of Hapsburg, remember, a daughter of Hapsburg, it was hoped, would prove a powerful ally; and minister in the court of the Emperor, to defend and sustain her father's failing fortunes, even perhaps to reveal to him the secrets of her husband.

The union of those two tribes with English interests, I regard as a deep stroke of policy; painful, perhaps humiliating, but the Iroquois were now between two fires, hard pressed and obliged to resort to every wile to preserve their tottering existence. The Mohawks were nearest the English, being within striking distance of the settlements on the Hudson. How manifest the policy that these should *seem* to side with the English, do just enough to preserve themselves from attack, and serve as a shield and barrier to their confederate nations, who thereby could put forth their whole force on other points in favor of the French. What was it, but a new edition of the old policy practised in England for hundreds of years, in civil wars, for families to divide, so that whichever party might prevail the estates should be preserved from confiscation. Every step of apparent division, as well as united action, I am persuaded was the result of cool deliberation, full consultation, mature councils, and unanimous consent. United certainly they were before the war—still we find them united, acting in perfect harmony in 1758, at the treaty held in Easton, which would have been inconceivable if they had been really at variance with each other a few months before. In our Revolution the same game of apparent neutrality or disunion of the nation was attempted to be played.

A brief note was all I intended, but lo! this exposition has swollen to half the limits of a letter.

LETTER VI.

Brief outline of controversy between Pennsylvania and Connecticut—Earliest Charters of France and England—Great Plymouth Council incorporated—Massachusetts carved out of the Plymouth Patent—Warwick's Charter—Colony of Connecticut—Charter of King Charles, 1662—Extent of claim under Connecticut Charter, included Wyoming—Purchase of Indian right by Susquehanna Company—Incidental matters—Delaware Company's Purchase—First attempt to settle the lands—Adverse claims of Penn set forth—Charter to Wm. Penn, 1681.

HAVING brought down the history of Wyoming to 1763, including the murder of Tedeuscung, the massacre and expulsion of the first Connecticut settlers, and the general removal of Indians from the Valley, other matters of weighty interest call for our consideration.

For many years the public mind has been made familiar with the fact that a dispute long existed between Pennsylvania and Connecticut, for the jurisdiction and soil over a large extent of territory, within which the valley of Wyoming is included. So many important events trace their origin to this controversy, that it becomes necessary to set forth the grounds thereof somewhat in detail. Indeed, we cannot doubt but a fair and candid exhibition of the claims of the respective parties, will be acceptable not only to the general reader, but particularly so to every intelligent person resident within the contested limits. In an especial manner may it be desirable to the numerous descendants of those who first removed from New England, to make their home in this, then savage and inhospitable wilderness. The Connecticut Claim is at rest; dead and buried. Pennsylvania, so far from being regarded as an unkind step-mother, extending reluctant protection to the New England people, and their children, is universally esteemed as a kind parent, entitled to the warmest affection of every good citizen, who has the happiness to live within her borders, among whom the population on the old Susquehanna Claim, are second to none in true allegiance, veneration and love.

Were it conceded that the claim of Connecticut was a baseless speculation, merited reproach would necessarily attach to all those numerous settlers, who came to this debated land, with a view to its possession. Nor would the parent colony, or State, escape severe censure. With the two-fold view, therefore, of imparting information to those who wish to understand the ancient grounds of controversy, and to vindicate the State, and the early colonists from being reckless and unprincipled invaders of the property of others, we shall proceed to show—not that the Connecticut claim was absolutely just, but that there were at the time, with the lights before them, such grounds to believe in its justice, as to warrant the adoption of all proper measures to secure its possession.

Early after 1600, a contest commenced between France and England for the possession of North America. In November, 1603, Henry IV. of France, (a name that awakens all that is chivalrous in war, gallant in love, or romantic in incident,) granted to Sieur de Monts, American Territory, under the name of Acadia, extending from the 40th to the 46th degree of latitude. Aroused by this measure king James of England, three years afterwards, that is, in 1606, divided that part of North America lying between the 34th and 45th degrees of latitude, into two nearly equal parts; the northern half, namely, the country between the 38th and 45th degrees of latitude, he granted by patent to Thomas Hanham and others, principally inhabitants of Plymouth and Bristol. Out of this grant, as we shall trace it step by step, grew the Connecticut claim.

Subsequently the King, by letters patent dated November 3, 1620, incorporated the Great Plymouth Council, and granted "all that circuit, continent, and limits in America, in breadth, from 40 degrees of northerly latitude, from the equinoxial line to 48 degrees of said northerly latitude, and in length, by all the breadth throughout the main land from sea to sea, with all the rivers, seas, &c., within the same degrees of latitude and longitude; and incorporated the Duke of Lenox, and divers other persons, by the name of the council established at Plymouth, in the county of Devon, for the planting, ruling, ordering and governing of New England in America; and to them and their successors grants all the lands, &c., viz: that aforesaid part of America, lying and being in breadth from 40 degrees of northerly latitude, from the equinoxial line, to 48 degrees of the said northerly latitude, inclusively, and in length, of and within all the breadth aforesaid throughout the main lands, from sea to sea, together also with all the firm lands, soils, grounds, &c., and all and singular other commodities, jurisdictions, royalties, privileges, franchises and pre-eminences, both within the said tract, upon the land, upon the main, and also within the said islands, and seas adjoining: Provided always, that the said islands, or any of the premises hereinbefore mentioned, and by these presents intended and meant to be granted, were not actually possessed or inhabited by other Christian prince or state, nor within the bounds, limits or territories, of that southern colony heretofore by us granted, to be planted by divers of our loving subjects in the south part. And did further command and authorize the said Council and their successors, or the major part of them, to distribute, convey, assign, and set over such particular portions of said lands, tenements and hereditaments, to such subjects, adventurers and planters, as they should think proper."

You will observe not only, that authority is given, but the charge is expressly made, that the Plymouth Council " shall distribute, assign, and set over," to others, such portions of the territory as might be deemed politic and proper. Accordingly, Massachusetts was carved out of the Plymouth patent in 1628.—The grant for that purpose to Sir Henry Rosswell and others, runs thus: " All that part of New England in America aforesaid, which lies and extends between a great river there, commonly called Monomack, alias Merrimack, and a certain other river there, called Charles river, being in the bottom of a bay called Massachusetts, alias Mattachusetts, alias Mattattusetts bay, and all and singular, the lands and hereditaments whatsoever, lying within the space of three English miles, on the south part of said Charles river, or of any or every part thereof; and all and singular, the lands and hereditaments whatsoever, lying and being within the space of three English miles to the southward of the southernmost part of the said bay; and also, all those lands and hereditaments whatsoever, which lie and be within the space of three English miles to the northward of the said river, called Monomack, alias Merrimack, and to the northward of any and every part thereof; and all lands and hereditaments whatsoever, lying within the limits aforesaid, north and south in latitude and in breadth, and in length and longitude, of and within all the breadth aforesaid, *throughout the main lands there, from the Atlantic and western sea and ocean on the east part, to the south sea on the west part;* and all the lands, and grounds." etc.,

King Charles confirmed this charter in 1629. It will attract particular attention that the words are clear, the language explicit in the description, that the grant extends, "throughout the main lands from the *western ocean* to the *south sea.*"

Next in order we come to the Connecticut charter. In 1630 the Earl of Warwick, president of the Plymouth council, received a grant of a large tract of land, which he conveyed to Lord Say and Seal, Lord Brook and others, after having obtained the king's charter of confirmation. His deed is dated March 19, 1631, and the following is a copy of the descriptive part: "All that part of New England in America, which lies and extends itself from a river, there called Narragansett river, the space of forty leagues upon a straight line near the shore, towards the southwest, west and by south, or west, as the coast lieth, towards Virginia, accounting three English miles to the league; and also, all and singular the lands and hereditaments whatsoever, lying and being within the lands aforesaid, north and south in latitude and breadth, and in length and longitude, *of and within all the breadth aforesaid, throughout the main lands there, from the western ocean to the south sea,* and all lands and grounds, place and places, soil, wood and woods, grounds and havens, ports, creeks and rivers, waters, fishings and hereditaments whatsoever, lying within the said space, and every part and parcel thereof; and also all islands lying in America aforesaid, in the said seas, or either of them, on the western or eastern coasts, or parts of the said tracts of lands, by these presents mentioned to be given, granted," etc.

Again it will be observed that the words of description expressly include " the main lands from the western ocean to the south sea."

This grant having been partially settled, an association, under the name of the colony of Connecticut, purchased out the right of Lord Say and Seal, Lord Brook, and others, for 16,000 pounds sterling. In 1662, April 20, king Charles the 2nd renewed and confirmed the charter, distinctly recognizing the territory as part and parcel of the old Plymouth grant, set off and allotted according to national policy and the royal will. As this is the Connecticut charter proper, we quote the descriptive words.—" To the Governor and company of the English colony of Connecticut, in New England, in America," with certain privileges and powers of government; and "granted and confirmed to the said Governor and company, and their successors, all that part of our dominions in New England, in America, bounded on the east by Narragansett river, commonly called Narragansett bay, where the said river falleth into the sea; and on the north, by the line of the Massachusetts Plantation; and on the south, by the sea; and in longitude, as the Massachusetts colony, running from east to west, that is to say, from the said Narragansett bay, on the east, to the south sea, on the west part, with the islands thereunto adjoining, together with all firm lands, soils, grounds, havens, ports, rivers, waters, fishings, mines, minerals, precious stones, quarries, and all and singular other commodities, jurisdictions, royalties, privileges, franchises, pre-eminences, and hereditaments whatsoever, within the said tract, bounds, lands, and islands aforesaid, or to them or any of them belonging: To have and to hold the same unto the said Governor and company, their successors and assigns, forever, upon trust; and for the use and benefit of themselves and their associates, freemen of the said colony, their heirs and assigns."

A third time it will strike the reader, the descriptive words distinctly mention, "from the said Narragansett bay on the east, to the *south sea* on the west." More particularly is attention directed to the repetition of those words, because Mr. Stone quotes a somewhat recent opinion of Col. Pickering, "that in early times the continent was (probably) supposed to be of comparatively little breadth." In respect to an opinion from authority so respectable we may observe, 1st. That several of the Southern colonial charters were also bounded westerly by the south sea. 2nd. A boundary used and repeated many times, for more than fifty years, by a government so intelligent in maritime affairs, and consequently of the position of the ocean's shores, it would be an unwarrantable presumption to suppose them ignorant of. 3rd. That Col. Pickering having removed to Wyoming, as a Pennsylvanian, and suffered violence from the Connecticut settlers, would be little apt to form an impartial opinion on any point connected with the dispute. 4th. And more important, the great extent of those early grants, was matter of profound policy, thereby to appropriate as much of the continent as possible, a settlement on one part of the grant being claimed as possession of the whole, by such means strengthening the claim of England against that of France, or any other nation. It is moreover asserted by Avery, I know not on what authority, that at the time of the Connecticut charter, the distance from the Atlantic ocean to the south sea was spoken of in public documents as about three thousand miles.

A grave question here presents itself. Why, on each new grant growing out of the Plymouth Company's charter, did the Crown renew the conveyance, and issue a new charter? was it claimed or admitted that the crown could resume its grants at pleasure?—Certainly not. All the rights of soil and property passed by grants from the proprietors; but the powers of government were considered of a nature so sacred, that they could only be derived directly from the king. It was held, that to assign the powers of government was to relinquish them.

Hence the uniform opinion existed, where mere territory was sold, that a deed from the proprietors was sufficient. Where a new colony, with powers of government was to be established, a release was made to the crown, and a new charter granted, yet expressly recognizing the rights of, and confirming the conveyance from those who had derived title from the old Plymouth Company.

In the Connecticut Charter, it will be noted that no exception in terms is made of lands "actually possessed or inhabited by any other christian power or State," yet the exception in the patent, or old Plymouth Charter was supposed sufficient, and held to govern in all grants growing out of it. The descriptive words of the charter, east, north and west, are clear and explicit—Narragansett river on the east; on the north by the Massachusetts Plantation—a well established boundary; being the ending of the 42nd, and beginning of the 43rd degree of latitude—on the west the *south sea*." It will be seen hereafter that good use was made by England in her negotiations with France, of these extensive charter boundaries, as prescient sagacity contemplated, when the grants were originally made. How far south the southern line would have run if accurately defined, it is not necessary here to inquire. A degree of latitude was claimed.—That these boundaries included Wyoming, has never, that we are aware of, been controverted.

The colony of Connecticut then, claimed west of Delaware river the forty-second degree of latitude, west, until bounded by the south sea. The territory east of the Delaware within that parallel of latitude to the line dividing New York and Connecticut, being in possession of the Dutch when her charter was granted, was of course excepted out of the grant.

In that part of America claimed by England, three requisites were demanded to render title to lands perfect.—First,—a grant or charter from the king;—Secondly,—a purchase of the soil from the Indians;—Thirdly, possession. Having exhibited the Connecticut claim by charter, we proceed briefly to examine their title by purchase of the natives.

In 1754 a Congress of Delegates, from a number of the British colonies was called, with the approbation of the Crown, to assemble at Albany, to hold a conference with the Six Nations of Indians, and consult together of the general welfare. That Pennsylvania was fully and ably represented, will be seen when we state that her delegation consisted of John Penn, Isaac Norris, Benjamin Franklin, and Richard Peters.

The preceding year, 1753, a number of persons had united, with a view to purchase the Indian title, within the charter limits of the colony of Connecticut, on the waters of the Susquehanna.

The persons so uniting were styled "The Connecticut Susquehanna Company," and consisted, at first, of eight hundred and forty persons, including a large proportion of the leading men of the colony. Afterwards the number of proprietors was augmented to twelve hundred. It may be regarded as an unofficial popular movement of the colony itself.—Meaning fairly, they proceeded openly. That a time should have been selected for the negotiation and purchase, when so large an assembly of delegates had convened, would seem to evince consciousness of right and fairness of purpose. In error they might have been; ignorant or stupid they were not; and yet to suppose they selected the time of such a public meeting, to make clandestinely a fraudulent Treaty with the Six Nations of Indians, would be the imputation of unexampled folly.

During the session of this Congress, under the eye of the Pennsylvania Delegation, a treaty with the Indians, the acknowledged proprietors of the territory, was executed, dated July 11, 1754, and a purchase of land made. "After describing the grantors, and their right and authority, as 'chiefs, sachems and heads of the Five Nations,' and the native proprietors of the land, and that the same lies within the limits of the Royal Charter to Connecticut; mentioning the application of the grantees being subjects of king George the Second, and inhabitants of Connecticut, and expressing the good understanding which had mutually subsisted between the parties, their wish for its continuance, and the benefits which would result from a settlement on the premises, the deed contains these words:— 'Now, thereupon, for and in consideration thereof, and for the further, full and ample consideration of the sum of two thousand pounds of current money, of the province of New York, to us, to our full satisfaction, before the ensealing hereof, contented and paid, the receipt whereof, to our full content, we do hereby acknowledge; thereupon do give, grant, bargain, sell, convey, and confirm to,' etc. (Here follow the names of the grantees, etc.) "Which said given and granted tract of land is butted, bounded and described as followeth, viz.—Beginning from the one and fortieth degree of north latitute, at ten miles distance east of Susquehanna river, and from thence, with a northerly line ten miles east of the river, to the forty-second, or beginning of the forty-third degree of north latitude, and to extend west two degrees of longitude, one hundred and twenty miles, and from thence south to the beginning of the forty-second degree, and from thence east to the aforementioned bounds, which is ten miles east of the Susquehanna river, together with all and every the mines, etc., and all other the hereditaments, etc., to have and to hold the above granted and bargained premises, etc., to them and to their heirs and assigns forever," etc. There are also the usual covenants of seizin and warranty."

The deed was signed by eighteen chief sachems of the Six Nations. It is stated that the consideration money was counted out in the stoop of Col. Lydius, agent and interpreter for the Company, taken by the Indians in a blanket, in open day, into an orchard, and there divided among them. The Rev. Mr. Heckewelder states, that one principal reason given by the Christian Indians, at Wyalusing, for wishing to remove to the Ohio was, that the Six Nations had sold the lands they resided on, to the New England people. The Rev. Samuel Kirkland, a missionary to the Six Nations, in an affidavit taken on the subject, some years after; " deposeth, that soon after he came to reside among the five confederate nations of Indians, which was in 1765, an Indian chief with whom he resided near two years in the Seneca country, told him that the Five Nations (or Six Nations as they were then styled,) had sold a large tract of land on the Susquehanna, or Wyoming, to the New England people, and had received a large sum of money for it; and that one Lydius, of Albany, was concerned in the purchase, as interpreter or principal agent. This information, with many other transactions of a similar nature, the said deponent received from the Indians, at their own voluntary motion, while they were giving him an historical account of their country, and various negotiations of the white people. The same account of the Susquehanna purchase, and others similar to it, the deponent has frequently heard related by different Indians of the Five Nations, having resided in their territory for near thirty years, and scarce ever absent from them more than three months at a time, during that term; and never, to his remembrance, heard any of the said Indians complain of said purchase."

Subsequently to the Susquehanna Company's purchase; a second association of persons took place in Connecticut, styled " The Delaware Company," who bought with less formality, the Indian title, from certain chiefs, of all the land. bounded east by Delaware river, within the forty-second degree of latitude, west to the line of the Susquehanna purchase, to wit, ten miles east of that river.

"In May, 1755, a committee of the Susquehanna Company, consisting of Phineas Lyman and others, petitioned the Assembly of Connecticut, reciting their purchase aforesaid of the Indians, and praying the acquiescence of the Assembly, and their consent for an application to his Majesty, to erect them into a new colony or plantation. Whereupon it was, among other things, resolved by the Assembly, that, '*they accordingly hereby manifest their ready acquiescence therein*,' etc. During the same year, the Company sent surveyors to begin the laying out of the land; but the war with the French prevented any actual settlements."

Two of the three requisites for the acquisition of a perfect title, having, as alleged, been obtained, namely, the Charter Right and Indian Title, the Proprietors next proceeded to add the third, by taking possession of the soil.

So early as 1757, a settlement was commenced by the Delaware Company at Coshutunk, to establish a colony on the Delaware river, which flourished for several years, having in 1760, thirty dwelling houses, a block-house for defence, with a grist-mill and saw-mill. A previous attempt to establish a colony, made by people of Connecticut, in 1670, at the Minissinks, was almost immediately abandoned, the Indian title not having been extinguished; and the fact is thought worthy of preservation, chiefly as it proves the opinion, then existing, that the Charter, passing over New York, was in full force west of that province.

We have, before, recorded the attempted settlement in 1762, at Wyoming, and the massacre the year following. In 1769, the settlement was renewed, and with various interruptions, rendered permanent.

The adverse claim of Pennsylvania we shall endeavour to set forth with equal precision and fairness. To do so, we copy "The Statement and Representation" of Messrs. Bradford, Reed, Wilson, and Sargeant, agents, on the part of the State, at the Trenton trial.

"To the Honorable the Commissioners and Judges, appointed to hear and finally determine the controversy subsisting between the State of Pennsylvania and the State of Connecticut. The Agents of the State of Pennsylvania beg leave, humbly, to state and represent in behalf of the said State,

"1st. That king Charles the Second, then king of Great Britain, on the 4th day of March, in the year of our Lord, 1681, by his letters patent, dated on the same day and year aforesaid, did grant to William Penn, the first proprietary and governor of Pennsylvania, his heirs and assigns, 'all that tract or part of land in America, with the islands therein contained, as the same is bounded on the east by Delaware river, from twelve miles distance northward of Newcastle town, unto the three and fortieth degree of northern latitude, if the said river doth extend so far northward; but if the said river shall not extend so far northward, then by the said river so far as it doth extend, and from the head of the said river the eastern bounds are to be determined by a meridian line to be drawn from the head of the said river unto the said forty-third degree; the said land to extend westward five degrees in longitude, to be computed from the said eastern bounds; and the said lands to be bounded on the north by the beginning of the three and fortieth degree of northern latitude, and on the south by a circle drawn at twelve miles distance from Newcastle, northward and westward unto the beginning of the fortieth degree of northern latitude, and then by a straight line westward to the limits of longitude above mentioned.' By which letters patent the jurisdiction and right of government within the limits aforesaid, and also the right of soil were conveyed, and under which Pennsylvania hath been held, settled and possessed.

"2d. That the said William Penn, and the succeeding proprietaries of Pennsylvania, at different periods, purchased from the native Indians their right of soil within different districts of the limits aforesaid, and received deeds of them for the same, and particularly on the 25th day of October, in the year of our Lord, 1736, the said Indians conveyed to Thomas Penn and Richard Penn, the then proprietaries of Pennsylvania, the full and absolute right of pre-emption of, and in all the lands not before sold by them to the said proprietaries, within the limits aforesaid.

"3d. That the southern bounds of Pennsylvania, so far as the same adjoins on Maryland, have been long since settled; and the same, so far as the State adjoins upon Virginia, have also been settled by a line, called Mason and Dixon's line, continued to the end of five degrees of longitude from the river Delaware; that the northern bounds have always been deemed to extend to the end of the forty-second degree, where the figures 42 are marked on the map, the river Delaware being found to extend so far north, and farther; that the said river, pursuing the east or main branch thereof above the forks at Easton, hath ever been deemed to be one boundary of Pennsylvania, from twelve miles above Newcastle, on the said river, to the said end of the forty-second degree, and that a straight line, from thence to the place where the same shall intersect another straight line, drawn from the end of the said southern line of boundary of Pennsylvania, commonly called Mason and Dixon's line, continued to the extent of five degrees of longitude from the river Delaware, is another boundary of the said State of Pennsylvania.

"4th. That the late province of Pennsylvania, on the 4th day of July, in the year of our Lord, 1776, did join with the other twelve late provinces, now States, in the declaration of independence, and soon after established a Constitution and Government, founded on the authority of the people, which they continue still to exercise and enjoy; and they did also join in the Articles of Confederation of the United States; and that being so independent and sovereign, on the 27th day of November, in the year of our Lord, 1779, they did by an act of their Legislature, consisting of the representatives of the freemen of the said Commonwealth of Pennsylvania, in General Assembly met, duly made and passed according to the directions of their frame of government, vest the right of soil and estate of the late proprietaries of Pennsylvania in the said Commonwealth; and that by means thereof, and of the several matters and things herein before set forth, the said Commonwealth, or State of Pennsylvania, is entitled to the right of jurisdiction, and right of soil, within all the limits aforesaid."

The charter of Pennsylvania, was, therefore, in 1681, nineteen years after that to Connecticut. It would hence appear, that both cover the controverted territory.

The Pennsylvania Agents do not set forth a conveyance of the land from the Natives; but a deed of pre-emption, or the promise to convey at some future time.

No settlement or possession is alleged.

From this fair and candid statement of the facts in the case, we infer, confidently, and claim for Connecticut, and the early settlers, this verdict:—That, without deciding the nice question of absolute right, the reasons of the case were so strong in favour of Connecticut, that intelligent and honorable men may have regarded her title so far just—that the Susquehanna and Delaware Companies, and the settlers under them, may have felt warranted in taking possession of the lands, and defending them by all fair and lawful means, until legally dispossessed by a solemn judicial decision.

So much for the outline. In our next we shall proceed to more minute, but we trust, not uninteresting particulars.

LETTER VII.

A more detailed view of the controversy—Objections to the Connecticut Claim by Charter—Intervening settlements of the Dutch—Dividing line between New York and Connecticut—Letter of King Charles—Final adjustment of that line, and plausible inference—Gov. Penn—Pratt (British Attorney General's) opinion—Col. Dyer sent to England—Counter opinions of Wedderburne, Thurlow, Jackson and Dunning—Powerful argument of a known, but nameless American—Rev. Dr. Smith—Tench Coxe Esq.

In the preceding letter we have endeavored to present a brief but clear exhibit of the titles respectively of Pennsylvania and Connecticut. The cursory reader, seeking amusement and studious of novelty, may deem such general view sufficient. But as almost every interesting event in the history of Wyoming, had its origin in these conflicting claims, it seems fitting that a more full and detailed statement should be made of them, than has been attempted by any recent historian.

For half a century the subject occupied no inconsiderable share of public attention; engaged the pens of many a ready writer, and enlisted on one side or the other, both in England and America, the best talent and the ablest counsel that a popular controversy, embracing millions in value, or liberal retaining fees could command. Every weapon of party warfare was employed with zeal. The newspaper paragraph, the eloquent debate, the Legislative protest, elaborate essays, and numerous pamphlets now before me, show the interest and ability which the contest awakened. If the matter itself be regarded as dry and forbidding, we can promise some relief from enlivening incident, more from studied brevity, and most from the assurance that this and the succeeding letter, are indispensable to a just comprehension of the subject.

Shaking then from these multitudinous papers, the venerable dust with which antiquity had shrouded them, we proceed with cheerful alacrity to our task.

It was objected: 1st. That the Crown must have been deceived, and the Connecticut Charter could never have been intended to cover so vast an extent of territory as was claimed under it.

In reply it was said—that it embraced no more than the Charter of Massachusetts: That those grants were, for state reasons, purposely extensive. That being made to a numerous company, it was less comparatively than that to Mr. Penn, an individual. That the Colonial Congress at Albany, in 1754, acting in reference to conflicting English and French claims, made a report containing this express recognition, viz: "The ancient colonies of the Massachusetts Bay and Connecticut, were by their respective charters made to extend to the south sea," which was transmitted by Messrs. Penn, Peters, Norris and Franklin, to the Government in Philadelphia, and entered on the records.

It was objected—2d. That in establishing the county of Litchfield, the act declares it located in the north-west corner of the colony; acknowledging, therefore, that the charter extended no further west; or that, if before the charter had greater limits, this was a waver of all claim beyond the bounds assigned to Litchfield.

In answer it was said: That the relinquishment of so important an interest could not, by any fairness, be predicated upon an expression, so manifestly in relation to the great question of charter bounds, inconsiderate and inapplicable. That if a farmer had a plantation half a mile wide, east and west, and two miles long, north and south—100 acres on one end in cultivated fields—the rest a wilderness—were he, in a lease, to speak of the most distant cleared field adjoining the forest, as the outer limits of his farm, no one would assume it as an abandonment of what lay beyond, being four-fifths of his whole estate. The construction would be forced and unnatural. And indeed it was maintained that the absurdity of such plea was evidence that no sufficiently valid objection existed, or one so preposterous would not be urged.

3d. A far more grave and weighty objection next presents itself for consideration; which was carried up before the king in council, and engaged the first talents on the stage of action at that period, distinguished for eminent legal abilities. Platt, afterwards Earl Camden; Wedderburne, afterwards Lord Loughborough, Thurlow, Dunning and Jackson, gave opinions upon the point.

The early settlements upon Hudson river by the Dutch from New York to Albany, are presumed to be familiar to the reader. On the west, the claims of the Dutch were clearly defined, the Delaware river being the boundary; but east and north, their limits were extremely indefinite. Hence the most spirited contests arose between them and the adjoining colony of Connecticut, in respect to the division line between the two Provinces. Irving, in the delightful pages of his Knickerbocker, has found in that dispute materials for more than one of his most pleasing chapters. For a time civil war raged, the Dutch pressing their eastern boundary towards Connecticut river, to which they claimed; the people of that colony, with a zeal and pertinacity in no way inferior, urging their limits west towards the Hudson. At length, in 1650, "Articles of agreement were made and concluded at Hartford, on Connecticut river, betwixt the delegates of the honored commissioners of the United Colonies (of Hartford and New Haven,) and the delegates of Peter Stuyvesant, Governor of the New Netherlands:" We quote so much as is germain to the matter in hand.

"Concerning the bounds and limits betwixt the English United Colonies, and the Dutch province of New Netherlands, we agree as followeth:—

"The bounds upon the main to begin at the west side of Greenwich Bay, being about four miles from Stamford, and so to run a northerly line, twenty miles up into the country; and after as it shall be agreed by the two governments, of the Dutch and New Haven, provided the said line come not within ten miles of Hudson's river. And it is agreed that the Dutch shall not, at any time hereafter, build any house or habitation within six miles of said line. The inhabitants of Greenwich to remain, (till further consideration thereof be had,) under the government of the Dutch."

This was the first amicable essay towards a settlement of the disputed line. "This agreement," says an able writer, whose work was printed nearly fifty years ago, "does not appear to have been ratified, or the terms satisfactorily observed. New difficulties succeeded; new complaints were made, and new claims advanced. In this state matters continued till the charter of 1662, which comprehended both the New Haven and Connecticut Plantations, and until the conquest of the Dutch in 1664. Their territory, with all its appendages, had been transferred to the Duke of York, by a royal patent or charter, dated March 12th, 1664. On the 26th day of April, a commission had been given to Col. Richard Nichols, to dispossess the Dutch, and put the Duke in possession, which the Colonel accomplished in August; whereupon it became necessary to settle the extent of the Dutch plantations eastward, and thereby to ascertain the divisionary bounds of the Duke's patent, and the patent of Connecticut. For the last mentioned being the earliest, the other could not effectually convey any part of what was before conveyed from the crown. Though the Duke's charter contained within its premises, all the land between Connecticut river and the Delaware, yet the colony contended that a part of the land thus granted to him, was theirs by their older charter. But how much of it was vested in them, so as not to pass to him, or, in other words, where the division line ought to be, was still an unsettled question, the former settlement not being satisfactory or conclusive. Here was a direct interference between the Dutch claim, to which the Duke had now succeeded, and that of the colony. Each party insisted on Long Island, and the tract between Connecticut river and a line a few miles east of Hudson's river.

As the colony of Connecticut had now a prince of the blood royal, and the presumptive heir of the crown, to contend with, it became a serious object with them, to obtain as early and as favorable an adjustment of the line as possible. Commissioners had come over with extensive powers to adjust disputed questions, at issue between the colonies. New York was now the property of the king's brother, who was anxious he should hold it in peace, and especially that all contests should cease in respect to the boundary claimed by him. King Charles by his commissioners, transmitted a letter to the Connecticut colony, full of gracious expressions. As it is not long, we will give the letter entire:—

" Charles R.

Trusty and well beloved, we greet you well, having according to the resolution we declared to Mr. John Winthrop, at the time when we renewed your charter, now sent these persons of known abilities and affection to us, that is to say, Col. Richard Nichols, &c., our commissioners, to visit these our several colonies and plantations in New England, to the end that we may be the better informed of the state and welfare of our good subjects, whose prosperity is very dear to us. We can make no question but that they shall find that reception from you, which may testify your respect to us, from whom they are sent for your good. *We need not tell you how careful we are of your liberties and privileges, whether ecclesiastical or civil, which we will not suffer to be violated in the least degree;* and that they may not be is the principal business of our said commissioners, as likewise to take care that the bounds and jurisdiction of our several colonies there, may be clearly agreed upon; that every one may enjoy what of right belongeth unto them, without strife or contention; and especially that the natives of that country, who are willing to live peaceably and neighbourly with our English subjects, may receive such justice and civil treatment from them, as may make them the more in love with their religion and manners; so, not doubting of your full compliance and submission to our desire, we bid you farewell. Given at our court, at Whitehall, the 23d day of April, 1664, in the 16th year of our reign. By his Majesty's command.

HENRY BENNET."

The colony of Connecticut, more than ever desirous to have the disputed line finally settled, immediately, that is, Oct. 13, 1664, appointed a committee, consisting of Mr. Allen, Mr. Gould, Mr. Richards, and Mr. Winthrop, to repair to New York, to bear the congratulations of the colony to the Royal commissioners; for the period was eminently distinguished by ceremonial politeness; and the committee were expressly authorized, if possible, *to issue the bounds between the Duke's patent and ours."*

A second adjustment of boundary grew out of this mission. Long Island was adjudged to New York, and the contested line was established thus.

"*Determination of his Majesty's commissioners, respecting the boundaries of His Royal Highness the Duke of York's patent, and the colony of Connecticut.*

"By virtue of his Majesty's commission, we have heard the differences about the bounds of the patents granted to his Royal Highness, the Duke of York, and his Majesty's colony of Connecticut; and, having deliberately considered all the reasons alleged by Mr. Allen, Secretary, Mr. Gould, Mr. Richards, and Capt. Winthrop, appointed by the assembly held at Hartford, the 13th day of October, 1664, to accompany John Winthrop, Esq., Governor of his Majesty's colony of Connecticut, to New York, and by Mr. Howell and Capt. Young, of Long Island, why the said Long Island should be under the government of Connecticut, which are too long here to be recited; We do declare and order, that the southern bounds of his Majesty's colony of Connecticut is the sea; and that Long Island is to be under the government of his Royal Highness the Duke of York; as is expressed by plain words in the said patents respectively. And also by virtue of his Majesty's commission, and by the consent of both the Governor and the gentlemen above named, we also order and declare, that the creek, or river, called Mamaroneck, which is reputed to be about twelve miles to the east of West Chester, and a line drawn from the east point, or side, where the fresh water falls into the salt, at high water mark, north-northwest to the line of Massachusetts, *be the western bounds of the said colony of Connecticut;* and the plantations lying westward of that creek, and line so drawn, to be under his Royal Highness's government; and all plantations lying eastward of that creek and line, to be under the government of Connecticut.

Given under our hands at Fort James, in New York, on Manhattan's Island, this 30th day of November, 1664.

RICHARD NICHOLS," etc.

The assent of the agents was expressed as follows, viz:

"We, underwritten, on behalf of the colony of Connecticut, have assented unto this determination of his Majesty's commissioners, in relation to the bounds and limits of his Royal Highness, the Duke's patent, and the patent of Connecticut.

JOHN WINTHROP, etc.

November 30, 1664."

The plantation of New Haven, though included in the charter to Connecticut, had nevertheless maintained their own separate government, and refused to join with the other colony, until after this determination of his Majesty's commissioners; so that they were not as yet parties to the settlement. After much correspondence and negotiation, however, they concluded to unite under the charter; and accordingly, on the 5th of January, 1665, communicated their final acquiescence, in a letter, in which (among other things not directly pertinent to this point,) they say, "We now signify, that having seen the copy of his Majesty's commissioners' determination, (*deciding the bounds betwixt his Highness the Duke of York, and Connecticut Charter,*) we do declare submission thereunto."

Scarcely had the lines been settled, when the vicissitudes of war again threw the colony of New York into the hands of the Dutch, which they retained until 1674, when, by the Treaty of Peace, it was finally restored to the British Crown. A new charter, with precisely the former boundaries, was forthwith issued to the Duke of York, and the ancient dispute with Connecticut revived.

Col. Dungan having been appointed Governor of New York, Connecticut, in 1683, appointed commissioners to repair to that place, to bear the congratulations of the colony on his arrival, and to adjust, if practicable, for the third time, the contested boundary. Accordingly, the Governor, Major Gould, Capt. Allyn, and Mr. Wm. Pitkin, were designated, and set forth on their mission. A new line was fixed upon, which constitutes the present limits between Connecticut and New York.

The whole of this long contest is so far detailed, and regarded important in relation to the Wyoming History, because it is asserted to have been a relinquishment on the part of Connecticut of all claim west of New York. It was declared, that the line fixed upon "*shall be the western bounds of the said colony of Connecticut,* and the plantations lying westward of that creek, and line so drawn, to be under his Royal Highness's government; and all plantations eastward of that creek and line, to be under the government of Connecticut." It is said these expressions are clear and unequivocal, and whatever rights Connecticut might have previously had to the Susquehanna lands, that declaration was a waver, or relinquishment of them, for ever.

Governor Penn sets forth this view of the case with marked emphasis. "The uncertainty," says he, "in the bounds and extent of the Connecticut Charter, as well as of other of the New England grants, occasioned a Royal commission to issue, so early as within two years after the date of that charter, for the declared purpose of settling the bounds and limits of their several charters and jurisdictions; in consequence of which, a north-northwest line, drawn from Mamaroneck river to the line of Massachusetts, was declared, and expressly fixed and established to be the western bounds of the colony of Connecticut, which boundary was then solemnly assented to, ratified and confirmed, by the Governor and Commissioners of the colony."

Still more full, authoritative and emphatic, was the opinion of the Attorney General of the Crown, Mr. Pratt, given in 1761, in answer to the following query by the Proprietary Government, to wit: "Whether the people of Connecticut have any colour or pretence under their charter to set up this right to this tract of land westward of New Jersey through Pennsylvania, as far as the south sea; and what is most advisable for the proprietaries to do in case the Government of Connecticut persist in their claim?

"If all the colonies in North America," says Mr. Pratt "were to remain at this day bounded in point of right as they are described in the original grant of each, I do not believe there is one settlement in that part of the globe that has not been encroached upon, or else usurped upon its neighbour, so that if the grants were of themselves the only rule between the contending plantations, there never would be an end to the dispute, without unsettling large tracts of land where the inhabitants have no better title to produce than either possession or posterior grants, which in point of law would be suspended by prior charters. Hence I conceive that many other circumstances must be taken into consideration besides the parchment boundary, for that may at this day be extended or narrowed by possession, acquiescence, or agreement, by the situation and condition of the territory at the time of the grant, as well as by various other matters with respect to the present dispute. The western boundary of Connecticut was barred at the time of the original grant, by the Dutch settlements, and the *Crown* was deceived when they were prevailed upon to convey a territory which belonged to another State then in amity with the Crown of England. Besides this objection, the settlement of the new boundary under the king's commission in 1664, and what is still stronger, the new line marked out by agreement between this Province and New York, has now conclusively precluded Connecticut from advancing one foot beyond those limits. It was absolutely necessary for the Crown, after the cession of the New Netherlands, to decide the clashing rights of the Duke of York and the adjoining colonies; and therefore all that was done by virtue of the commission then awarded for that purpose must at this day be decreed valid, as the nations have ever since that time submitted to those determinations, and the colonies of New York and New Jersey subsist only upon the authority of those acts. I am of opinion therefore that the colony of Connecticut has no right *to resume* its ancient boundary by overleaping the Province of New York so as to encroach upon the Pennsylvania grant, which was not made until after the Connecticut boundary had been reduced by new confines, *which restored the land beyond those settlements westward, to the Crown, and laid them open to a new grant.* The state of the country in dispute is a *material state reason* why the Crown ought to interfere in the present case, and put a stop to this growing mischief. But I doubt this business cannot be adjusted very soon, because Mr. Penn must apply to the Crown for relief, which method of proceeding will necessarily take up time, as the province of Connecticut must have notice, and be heard."

This seems justly to have been regarded as a most impregnable fortress to the Pennsylvania claim. But the Attorney General admits, that the Connecticut Charter did originally cover the lands west of the Delaware; for he says, "I am of opinion that the colony of Connecticut *has no right to resume its ancient boundary*, by overleaping the province of New York;" thus distinctly recognizing the fact that the "*ancient boundary*" did overlap New York.

The reader, we are sure, will be anxious to see the authorities on the other side, and weigh the objections which truth or ingenuity may have marshalled in opposition to this formidable, if not conclusive array of fact, and opinion.

Questions in respect to the contested lands having been made before the king in council, the Susquehanna company despatched Col. Eliphalet Dyer, as their agent, to England. This gentleman, a native of Wyndham, was one of the most eminent lawyers of Connecticut: His name will frequently occur in the subsequent pages of this work, accompanied with some amusing anecdotes.* Of good form, of pleasing address, an ardent advocate of the Connecticut claim; a more suitable selection could not have been made. A countryman hearing him plead before the court, went away and said—"No man need ever speak again"—meaning he could not be surpassed.—On an occasion when in the Connecticut assembly, he was endeavoring to awaken the house to strenuous efforts in behalf of their Wyoming settlement, a wit penned this impromptu:

> "Canaan of old, as we are told,
> Where it did rain down Manna;
> Wa'nt half so good, for heavenly food,
> As Dyer makes Susquehanna."

His voice was a fine tenor, which he modulated with art, and he was an agreeable and effective debater. But this is a digression.

Mr. Pratt having given his opinion in favour of Mr. Penn, the Connecticut agent propounded the following questions to the gentlemen whose names are subscribed to the answer.

"Have not the said Governor and company of the colony of Connecticut, the right of pre-emption, and the title under the Crown to the lands aforesaid, within the limits and bounds of their patent aforesaid, lying westward of the province of New York, and not included in the patent of king Charles the second to the Duke of York, notwithstanding the several settlements of boundaries, between the colony on the east, and the Province on the west, made as well by

---

* There are few New England people who have not read, and laughed at, the story of the Frogs in the Willimantic, connected with the name of "Col. Dyer—Elderkin too."

agreement between the parties, as under the royal authority, and notwithstanding the subsequent charter to Sir William Penn?

To which they unanimously answered, " The agreement between the colony of Connecticut and the province of New York, can extend no farther than to settle the boundaries between the respective parties, and has no effect upon other claims that either of them had in other parts; and as the charter to Connecticut was granted but eighteen years before that to Sir William Penn, there is no good ground to contend, that the crown could, at that period, make an effectual grant to him of that country, which had been so recently granted to others. But if the country had been actually settled under the latter grant, it would now be a matter of considerable doubt, whether the right of the occupiers, or the title under which they hold, could be impeached by a prior grant without actual settlement.

(Signed)   E. Thurlow,
M. Wedderburne,
Rd. Jackson,
Jn. Dunning."

With regard to the circumstance mentioned in the latter clause of their answer, the reader will please to recollect, that the land now in dispute, was first actually settled under the former grant, and not the latter.

Here then we have weighty opinions, against opinions of equal weight. Legal gentlemen who may honor these pages with a perusal, will probably agree with me in sentiment, that the learned council in each case, gave opinions agreeable to the wishes of their respective employers; and if they had happened to be retained on directly opposite sides, their opinions would have been exactly reversed.

It will be then but fitting and fair, that we examine the question, and decide impartially for ourselves. Such examination is deemed more important, because I regard the whole matter mainly to rest on the point of charter right; for surely, if the Connecticut charter did not embrace the territory, it would be little short of absurdity to maintain that the people of that colony had any right to come within Mr. Penn's charter to buy lands of the Indians. Charter rights, in my opinion, give, as matter of course, the pre-emption or right of Indian purchase.

The pride of authorship would naturally lead me, after thoroughly comprehending the reasoning of different writers, to remould them in my own language, adding whatever might appear pertinent or illustrative. But an argument lies before me so neat, perspicuous, and effective, that it would be inexcusable to change a word or syllable, as for a common mason to alter a finished piece of Grecian sculpture. It would be deemed, perhaps, too much to aver, that there is but one man now living who could improve the piece. A strong motive for presenting it entire, arises from the wish to exhibit to the reader an evidence that if the talents of chancellors and attorneys general in England were engaged on the question, abilities, if less distinguished, certainly not less powerful, discussed the point on this side the Atlantic. We have been assured that the able penman was endowed with powers of elocution fitted to give persuasive utterance to the conceptions of his strong understanding and well disciplined mind. In the brightness of mid-day usefulness and fame, a cloud gathered round his brow. A whirlwind swept him from the scenes of his early triumphs, and his rising glory—scattering his fortune, his honors and his hopes to the scorn of an unfeeling world; the malignant triumphs of envious foes, and the deeper wounding pity of a thousand friends. A false and fatal step, involving a question of integrity, sent him to die an exile in a foreign land.

> "No further seek his merits to disclose,
> Or draw his frailties from their dread abode;
> There they alike in trembling hope repose,
> The bosom of his father and his God."

But to the argument.

"The reader being presented with a particular statement of all the requisite facts and documents, is now prepared to judge whether anything in this whole transaction, can operate as a bar of the Connecticut claim to the Susquehanna lands. What conclusion does the mind naturally draw from all these premises? Is it not this, that the settlement in 1650, by the arbitration of the commissioners of the United Colonies; that in 1664, through the intervention of the royal commissioners; that in 1683, and all the succeeding settlements, were only different adjustments of the same dispute, and respected merely the divisionary line between New Netherlands, afterwards New York, and Connecticut, without the remotest relation to the question whether the charter gave Connecticut any lands west of the Delaware? If the determination of 1664 bars the right of Connecticut to the western lands, its validity must be founded either upon the authority of the commissioners, derived from the crown, or upon the consent of Connecticut, expressed by her agents. Let us examine the amount of each. The commissioners had no authority to reduce the limits of the charter. 1st. The king could give them no such power; for he had none himself, especially after having solemnly stipulated in this charter, that it should be good and effectual in law, to all intents and purposes whatever, and receive such construction, as should be most favorable to the grantees. A charter is sacred and inviolable in its nature. It is not an act which may be reversed at pleasure; but a solemn compact, to which there are two parties, whose joint consent is necessary to the revocation or alteration of it. The royal, or rather ministerial attempts to alter and abridge the colonial charters were considered illegal and unconstitutional stretches of prerogative. The American revolution occasioned by them, is a standing memorial of the light in which they ought to be viewed. 2d. The commission to Nichols and others, imports no such authority. The objects of the commission are expressed in the preamble. So far as relates to this point, there appear to be certain complaints that there were differences about interfering claims of limits, by reason whereof all the colonies did not enjoy the liberties and privileges granted to them by their several charters, " upon confidence and assurance of which, they transported themselves and their estates, into these parts." Here it is plain, that the intent of this commission was not to give or take away, not to enlarge or curtail, any charter rights; but only to adjust the existing disputes about such rights, and to see that every one enjoyed his own peaceably and fully. 3d. This is made, if possible, still more evident, by the letter which the commissioners brought over from the king, to the colony of Connecticut, in which his Majesty says, " Your liberties and privileges we will not suffer to be violated in the least degree; and that they may not be, is the principal business of our said commissioners, as likewise to take care that the bounds and jurisdictions of our several colonies there, may be more clearly agreed upon; that every one may enjoy what of right belongeth unto them, without strife or contention." Their authority, we see, extended only to the protection of charter rights, and the adjustment of disputes respecting such rights. Now there were in fact, no opposite or adversary claims, as to the western land, covered by the Connecticut charter. No foreign nation had any pretensions to it. The Duke did not and could not claim it, the Delaware being expressly made his western limit. The king advanced no claim to it, and gave no intimation that he was dissatisfied with his own grant of it to Connecticut. In short, there was no manner of dispute or contention about it. The commissioners therefore, according to the tenor of their commission, had nothing in the world to do or determine respecting it. If they did undertake to decide with regard to it, and to reduce the Connecticut grant, they exceeded their jurisdiction; and their acts so far forth, were consequently void, unless sanctioned by the consent of Connecticut. Let us then see how far the colony consented. The Hartford or Connecticut plantation, which then acted by itself, expressed their assent by their agents, which could bind the colony no farther than these agents were authorized. A stream cannot rise higher than its fountain. The acts of agents must be so construed, as to be consistent with their commission; for beyond that they are of no force. Now the whole amount of power delegated in this case, was merely "*to issue the bounds between the Duke's patent, and that of the colony.*" As to the question, whether the charter did, or did not, give a title to the land west of the Duke's patent, that is, west of the Delaware river, the agents had not the smallest particle of authority to agree or to treat. The assent of the colony therefore, is confined solely to issuing the bounds between New York and Connecticut, that is, to settling the partitionary line. The same limitation qualified the assent of the New Haven jurisdiction, when they acceded to the united government, and to this settlement. They say, "having seen a copy of his Majesty's commissioners' determination, (*deciding the bounds betwixt his Highness, the Duke of York, and Connecticut charter*) we do declare submission thereunto."

"Now can it be pretended with any color of reason, that this amounts to either a surrender of the land west of the Delaware to the crown, or a transfer of it to the Duke, or an authoritative determination, that no such land was included within the charter of 1662? Had these documents been well attended to, I am persuaded no man in his senses, would ever have contended for such a wild and monstrous conclusion.

"The determination itself, taken altogether, neither expresses nor implies any such thing. In the first place, nothing is expressed with regard to the western land. It is not so much as mentioned. And surely a positive grant, which was to be reputed and construed in the most favorable sense for the grantees, was not to be taken away by doubtful construction and implication. 2d. The subject matter, which is easily learned from the circumstances of the times, is also stated in the preamble, or recital of the instrument of determination, in which the commissioners say, "We have heard the differences about the bounds of the patents granted to his Royal Highness, the Duke of York, and his Majesty's colony of Connecticut,' etc. What they heard, and undertook to determine, was evidently nothing more or less than disputes existing between the Duke (who had now succeeded to the Dutch claims and pretensions) and Connecticut, respecting the bounds of their patents. These disputes, which appear to be all that was submitted to them, had no reference to any land, to which the Duke made no claim. The only interfering claims respected the land which was included in the Duke's patent, as well as that of Connecticut. Unless the determination therefore, is to operate upon a subject not submitted or heard, it can have no effect, but upon Long Island, and the land between Hudson and Connecticut rivers.

"If this settlement is to be viewed in the light of a judicial adjudication, or award of arbitrators, it was only of a controversy, or controversies, subsisting between the Duke and the colony. They were the only parties, and were present by their respective representatives. If we consider it rather as an agreement, it was still between the same, and no other parties. And can a judgment, or an agreement between any two parties, respecting their mutual demands, be conclusive, as to the claims or disputes, which may then exist, or afterwards arise, between either of them and another party? Common sense and common law answer in the negative.

"Though the terms 'western bounds of the colony of Connecticut,' are used in the report, they are certainly to be understood with reference to the subject matter, about which they are so used, and in connection with the whole instrument.—They are explained and limited by the words which immediately follow—" *And the plantations lying westward of that creek and line, so drawn, to be under his Royal Highness's government, and all plantations lying eastward of that creek and line, to be under the government of Connecticut.*" How far eastward is the country here adjudged to Connecticut? The expression is not limited, unless it be by the limits of the commissioners' authority, or the subject of this their determination. Could Connecticut, by virtue of it, claim Rhode Island, for example, because it lies eastward of that creek and line, though it was not within the submission? Or, to take an instance exactly in point, could this determination be pleaded in bar against the claim of the Duke to the tract of country at St. Croix, or Nantucket, or Martha's

Vineyard, which was granted to him, by his charter, because that tract is situated eastward of the line here specified? If not, then neither can the expression " western bounds of the colony of Connecticut," be a bar to the claim of Connecticut, to land lying west of the Duke's patent, and covered by their charter. This conclusion appears, to my mind, to be irresistible. The whole determination must be interpreted in the same limited or unlimited sense.

"But the only true, natural, and legal construction of the settlement, is, that it was, and was understood and intended to be, co-extensive with the dispute submitted, which was relative merely to Long Island, and the tract of country east of Hudson's river, and west of Connecticut river; or, if viewed in the utmost extent, east of Delaware and west of Narragansett, beyond which the claims of the two parties did not, and could not interfere. Mamaroneck creek, and a north north-west line drawn from thence to Massachusetts, was determined and consented to be the line of division, that is, the eastern bounds of New York, and the western bounds of Connecticut; as to the controverted territory, so much of which as lay east of that line, was to be considered as belonging to that colony, and so much of it as lay west, to the Duke, and that according to the true intent of the two charters taken together. As to Nantucket, Martha's Vineyard, St. Croix, or any plantation or place, which lay east of the claim of Connecticut, this determination has no operation, notwithstanding the generality of the phrase, that, "all plantations eastward of that line were to be under Connecticut." With regard to those plantations, the Duke's claim was left, to be afterwards controverted and decided on its original merits. So, likewise, notwithstanding the generality of the phrase, " the western bounds of the colony of Connecticut," any lands west of the Duke's claim, and within the limits of the Connecticut charter, were entirely out of this determination, and the title to them consequently was left to be disputed and determined upon its own original merits.

"This is the sense in which a Judge or a Juror, a Lawyer or a man unacquainted with law, would understand it.—For the truth of the remark, I appeal to the candid reader; and would confidently risk the whole controversy upon the appeal."

The most conspicuous and able writers on behalf of the Pennsylvania claim, were the Rev. Dr. Smith, and Tench Coxe, Esq. The former, distinguished for learning, eloquence and eccentricity, lent his pen to the subject before the Revolution; the latter, highly intelligent, indefatigable in whatever cause he engaged, entered into the controversy with a zeal that left no source of information unexplored, and with an ability that gave to his facts the most powerful impression. All the proceedings of the government of Connecticut were very fairly scrutinized for matter to show a waver on the part of that colony, of any right west of New York. Two points made by those gentlemen, and regarded as important, especially demand attention.

First,—That in reply to a message sent by Mr. John Armstrong,* by Gov. Hamilton of Pennsylvania, Gov. Wolcott of Connecticut, in a letter dated Windsor, March 13, 1754, wrote thus: " Some of our inhabitants hearing of this land at Susquehanna, and that it was north of the grant made to Mr. Penn, and that to Virginia, are upon a design of making a purchase of the Indians, and hope to obtain a grant of it from the Crown. This appearing a design to promote his Majesty's interests and render the country more defensible we were all wishers to it. But Mr. Armstrong informs me that this is certainly within Mr. Penn's grant. If so, I dont suppose our people had any purpose to quarrel with Pennsylvanians."

A tart sarcasm on the supposed folly of this epistle, is all we find in the ardent pages of the advocate for the Connecticut claim. May it not be regarded a stroke of policy, to lull the jealousy of Mr. Penn's government? There is nothing so very explicit in its wording as to be taken as a formal abjuration of claim.—" I dont suppose our people had any purpose to quarrel with Pennsylvanians!"

Second,—That in 1761, in reply to certain inquiries sent out from the king to the Governors of the several colonies, one of which was to ascertain the extent of their respective boundaries. Gov. Fitch of Connecticut answered—" That the colony was bounded west by New York!"—It was therefore assumed, and powerfully urged, that this was either an acknowledgment that the charter limits never extended beyond the Delaware; or was to be regarded as a solemn relinquishment of such claims.

Mr. Avery, who treats this point more fully than any other writer, on behalf of Connecticut, sets forth,—

" That the Committee of Assembly drew the reply stating, as was the usual answer, that the colony was bounded by their charter, to which they referred:—that so worded, the report was adopted. That the subject was then handed over to the Executive, to receive pro-

---

* The name of John Armstrong will appear frequently in these pages, and his character more fully developed hereafter.

per form, and be forwarded in reply. That Governor Fitch, without authority, of his own mere motion, so changed the matter as to declare, "That the colony was bounded on the west by New York." That when discovered, a universal burst of censure pervaded the colony. Gov. Fitch was left out at the next election, Mr. Pitkin being chosen in his place; and that from this fall he never recovered." Mr. Avery adds, but gives no authority for the opinion, that Gov. F. was supposed to have received a bribe of twelve hundred dollars for this abjuration of claim west of New York. In the absence of any proof, this imputation we should deem unfounded. Who would have given a sum so considerable for an opinion which could weigh so little in a solemn adjudication of the question? It seems much more probable that Gov. Fitch supposed the inquiries related to the settled parts of the colony; as a man, when asked the size of his plantation, answers two hundred acres, not thinking it pertinent to the inquiry to speak of unimproved out lots of one thousand acres, which he may possess.

Justice demands of us to record some further objections, made by Dr. Smith and Mr. Coxe, to which the replies of adverse writers furnish so little of interest to detain the reader, that a brief remark will be sufficient to dispose of each.

Objection first. That the Susquehanna Company never had a formal grant from the colony of Connecticut.

Second. That the colony of Connecticut received nothing from the Company as a consideration for those lands.

Third. That the Company made their purchase of the Indians, contrary to the laws of Connecticut.

Fourth. That the king, in 1763, forbid the settling this territory.

In reply to the first three objections, it may be said to be matter exclusively between the Susquehanna Company and the colony, or State. The whole proceedings of the Company having, again and again, received the most full and explicit recognition and confirmation from the Connecticut government.

In reply to the fourth, it may be asked, after the king had granted the lands by charter, what authority had he reserved to forbid the settlement?

In conclusion. The Connecticut charter was granted in 1662. That to William Penn, in 1681—nineteen years afterwards.

LETTER VIII.

Susquehanna Company's Indian Purchase—Runs the gauntlet—Keenly assailed—Spiritedly defended—Proceedings in Council—Peter Hendrick's Speech—Letters from Gov. Morris and Richard Peters, Esq.—Purchase of Pennsylvania at Fort Stanwix—Fierce assaults on that Deed, by Connecticut claimants—Close of Documentary testimony.

The Susquehanna Company's purchase, and their Indian Deed, has now to run the gauntlet through a long array of intelligent, well disciplined, and eager controversialists.

My best efforts have been directed to simplify and arrange. Thus a general outline of the Indian history has been given by itself, down to 1770, embracing events in which the whites were concerned, so far only as seemed indispensable.

Then we have set forth a clear *general* view of the Pennsylvania and Connecticut claims.

Thirdly, We have taken up, in detail, the Connecticut Claim. First, by Charter, and considered the objections thereto. Keeping separate the consideration of the title by purchase of the Indians, we now proceed to that interesting topic.

In our opening, we have stated that the Susquehanna Company claim to have purchased of eighteen chief sachems, representing the Six Nations, in open treaty, at the colonial Congress, held at Albany, in July, 1753, the disputed territory on the Susquehanna.

The purchase awakened the greatest alarm in the Proprietary Government, and steps were immediately taken to counteract the effects of a measure so pernicious, if not fatal, to their interests. Some facts of unquestionable authenticity, are, at this time, wholly inexplicable. The Susquehanna Company advanced to their object, not in secret, but openly avowing their purpose. Indeed, their being eight hundred original proprietors, each of whom must be taxed to raise the requisite funds, all notions of secrecy, even, if ever thought politic, must have been deemed impossible. The letter of Governor

Hamilton, sent by Armstrong, to Gov. Wolcott, previously quoted, shows that the Government of Pennsylvania was fully apprised of the purpose of the Connecticut people. Why then was not the Treaty of Albany prevented? If done in opposition to the wishes of the Six Nations, there assembled in full council, why did not those nations, on the remonstrance of the respectable Pennsylvania Delegation, disavow the Deed, and inflict condign punishment on those Indians, who had presumed to speak and act in the name of the whole Confederacy, and to dispose of one hundred and twenty miles, by seventy, of the territory, embracing nearly five millions of acres?

In truth the Delegates from Pennsylvania were neither faithless nor idle. The utmost efforts were made to prevent the sale to the Susquehanna Company, and to purchase the lands for the Proprietary Government. In their report, made the 6th of August, after their return to Philadelphia, is the following sentence:—" The Commissioners of Pennsylvania, having held a private treaty with the Six Nations, whilst at Albany, for the purchase of lands," etc. Their Report was read, and ordered to be entered on the minutes. Efforts, it appears, were made July 4th and 5th, to induce the chiefs to sell them the Wyoming lands, to which they steadily refused to accede.

There were two chiefs of the Mohawks by the Dutch name of Hendrick; one of whom signed the Susquehanna Deed; the other, Peter Hendrick, an eloquent sachem, and warrior of great note, being in the Proprietary interest, made the following reply to the urgent application of the Commissioners;—" We have heard, since we came here that our brother *Onas*, (Sir Wm. Penn having received that name on first landing, it meaning, in the Indian language, a *quill* or *pen*,) and our brothers of New England, have had some dispute about the lands of Susquehanna, a dispute of the same kind as that of the Governor of Canada and Assaragoah; but we desire you would not differ with one another about it, for neither shall have it. We will not part with it to either of you—we will reserve it for our western Indians to live on."

From this declaration, placed on record, opposing advocates draw different conclusions. On behalf of the Proprietaries, it is claimed as evidence that the head chiefs of the Six Nations refused to sell, and could not, therefore, have concurred in Lydius's purchase.

On the Connecticut side, it is said:—" This was not in open Council, but in secret Treaty. Peter Hendrick had been won over to Pennsylvania's interest, but went alone. It does not appear that any other chief concurred with him. The declaration that they would keep Wyoming for their western Indians, a matter too improbable to be worth a moments consideration, showing that Hendrick meant nothing, or more probably did not know what he meant.

But at those *secret* conferences, the Commissioners made a purchase of lands, between the Blue Mountains, and the Forks of the Susquehanna, (at Fort Augusta, Sunbury,) of course below the tract sold to the Connecticut people.

"Behold," says Avery, "This purchase made in the dark, is unquestioned, and unquestionable—good beyond doubt—fair beyond all controversy! while the openly obtained Deed of the Susquehanna Company, is a nullity, forsooth!"

Sir William Johnson, principal Agent of the king, for Indian affairs, lent the whole weight of his influence to render nugatory the Susquehanna Company's Deed. A letter from the Governor of Pennsylvania, dated Nov. 15th, 1754, requested him "to induce the Indians, if possible, to deny the regularity of the contract," and to this end, by all means, "to win over, effectually, Peter Hendrick to his interest, and prevail on him to visit Philadelphia." Gov. Morris wrote, himself, to Hendrick. The letter is too important to be omitted.

"Some matters of great moment to this Government, as well as to the Indians of the Six Nations, having lately fallen out, which makes it necessary for me to have a private conference with you, before I can proceed to give public notice to them of my arrival here; and as you was so good as to promise to the Commissioners, when at Albany, that you would, at the request of Goverment, come at any time to Philadelphia and give your sentiments on any thing that might be proposed for the public service, I now earnestly desire that you would favour us with a visit, in order to consult on some affairs, in which the safety of the Indians, and His Majesty's colonies are very much concerned, that cannot be done by message, but must first be communicated to you in personal conference. If you should incline to take with you one or two of your best friends, it will be the more agreeable. Mr. Daniel Clause is well acquainted with the nearest and best roads to this city, and he has my directions to accompany you, furnish the necessaries, and make every thing as agreeable to you as possible."

"Behold!" says the Connecticut Advocate; "A single chief is invited to Philadelphia—Heaven and earth are to moved! The aid of Sir Wm. Johnson is invoked! Hendrick is requested to bring *one* or *two* of his best friends; not more!—Daniel Clause will *furnish the necessaries!* He will make *every thing* as agreeable as possible!"

Sir Wm. Johnson in his reply to the Governor, says :—" I have been honored with yours of the 15th ultimo, by Mr. Daniel Clause, whom I immediately sent to call Hendrick to my house. Upon his arrival, I delivered and interpreted your Honour's letter, or instructions to him, and urged his waiting on you immediately, which when he agreed to, I spoke to him concerning the affair as far as I judged necessary; and I flatter myself it will have a good effect, he having faithfully promised me to exert himself, and use his utmost endeavours for the interest of the Proprietaries against the Connecticut attempt. After my expatiating some time on the injustice of their proceedings, more especially so, after what had passed at Albany, last June, Hendrick then, with some warmth, disapproved of them, as well as the weakness of those of his brethren who were seduced by Lydius, and promised to do all he could to make them revoke or retract what they had so shamefully done."

" Mark!" say the Connecticut advocates, " the means used, and the influences brought to bear, to destroy the effect of a miscalled deed, clandestinely obtained of a few drunken Indians !"

Measures being adopted in Connecticut, to commence a settlement at Wyoming, Mr. John Armstrong was again sent as an agent to that colony to gather all the information in his power. He was also the bearer of a letter from Governor Morris to the Governor of Connecticut, in which the former again refers to the deed from the Six Nations to William Penn, dated October 11, 1736, and to the engagement then made by the Indians to sell all the lands in Pennsylvania to William Penn, and to no one else; after which he proceeds to say :—

" You will give me leave further to observe to you, that the Six Nations at the late Congress at Albany, in open council mentioned an application then made to them by agents from Connecticut for the purchase of some of the Susquehanna lands, and that they had absolutely refused to give any ear to such proposal, telling the several governments then present by their commissioners, that they were determined the lands at a place called Wyomink on the Susquehanna, should not be settled, but reserved for a place of retreat."

He further observes: " Notwithstanding which, I am informed that Mr. John Lydius, who is known to be a Roman Catholic, and in the French interest, has been since employed by some people of your province, to purchase from the Indians some lands within this government: that he has in a clandestine manner, by every unfair means, prevailed on some few Indians to whom he secretly applied, to sign a deed for a considerable part of the lands of this province, including those at Wyomink. And as we stand engaged to the Six Nations by treaty, neither to settle the lands at Wyomink, or suffer them to be settled, this government thought it proper (among other things) to inform the Indians that those people were not authorized or even countenanced by this government, and their attempts were disavowed by the government of Connecticut, and were to be looked upon as a lawless set of people, for whose conduct no government is accountable."

On the return of Mr. Armstrong, he communicated the information obtained, and among other things curious, and worthy to be known, which we have found no where else so fully stated—That "there were formerly five hundred subscribers to the Susquehanna Company at seven dollars each, to which are now added three hundred at nine dollars each." The aggregate would be 6200 dollars. The consideration in the Indian deed was stated to be two thousand pounds, New York currency—or five thousand dollars; which, from this exhibition of the funds of the company, seems probable—leaving twelve hundred dollars for contingent expenses.

Letters from Conrad Weiser, a celebrated Indian interpreter, much employed by the Proprietaries, written to the Governor, dated the 16th, and 27th October, 1754, and entered by order of council on the records, are too important to be passed over without notice. The following are extracts:—

"As to the Connecticut affair, I am clear of opinion, that, by order of the Governor, you should write to Hendrick, putting him in mind of his promise he made to the commissioners of this province in Albany, when he said he would come down to us upon any occasion, to advise with the Governor, as in the presence of the Most High. That the Governor wants to see him in this critical time about matters of moment. Daniel Clause might come with him. He knows the way by land. If Hendrick refuses to come, he may be suspected to have a hand in it; and we must then act by Shickalamy and Jonathan, and as secret as possible, otherwise Lydius, and that wicked priest at Canojoharry, will defeat our designs. I would advise in the mean time, to have belts of wampum provided, and two or three large belts all black. You will want a couple to send to the south before long, and one must be made use of to demolish Lydius's proceedings. Mr. Clause must be ordered to keep every thing relating to this affair as a secret, and to search very diligently whether Henry had any hand in signing the deed to the Connecticut people. If he had not, we shall succeed without doubt. He must have liberty to bring one or more Indians with him. If all wont do, and that Hendrick will not come, we must send to Onondago next spring, &c.

According to the invitation so pressingly given, Hendrick and ten other Indians came to Philadelphia.

"In Council, *January* 15, 1755. The council advised the Governor, that after thanking Hendrick and the Indians accompanying him, for this undertaking, etc., to mention these several points, viz: to state sundry matters relative to the grant of Pennsylvania, their deed from Governor Dungan, their deed or promise of the right of pre-emption, 1736, etc., and lastly, of the deed to the Connecticut people from the Six Nations, that it is incumbent on them to represent this matter to the government of Connecticut, and to insist that the deed be delivered up by Lydius, by order of that Government, as a fraud and imposition."

"*Extract of Hendrick's Speech, January* 15, 1755. We have considered what you said to us about the deceitful deed which John Lydius inveigled some of us to sign. We agree with you that the deed should be destroyed. We agree with you that it is a false proceeding. We will give you our assistance; but you know that we cannot destroy the deed ourselves. That would be another mistake. It would be to do as bad as they have done. It must be the act of the Council of the Six Nations. We will think of the proper means. We advise the Governor to send for two deputies from each, or of every nation, to meet here, or at Albany, to kindle a council fire, to find out a way to oblige Connecticut to discountenance the deed," etc.

"In Council, *January* 17, 1755. The Governor, Mr. Peters, and Mr. Weiser, had many conferences with the Indians, in which it was considered, what might be the proper methods for the Indians to take, in order to invalidate the deed of Lydius, etc. Among other things, it was proposed, that at the Council of Onondago, this affair should be mentioned, and Lydius's deed declared to be no deed of the Six Nations; and to prevent this, and other like attempts, that it should be proposed by the Council of Onondago, to convey to the Proprietaries, by a formal deed, the lands lying within the province of Pennsylvania, etc. The Indians consented to this, and engaged to confer with Col. Johnson first, and to settle everything with him, of which he should acquaint the Governor; and when the matter should be brought to effect, then Mr. Weiser and Mr. Peters might come to Col. Johnson," etc.

Extract of a letter from Gov. Morris to Col. Johnson, dated Philadelphia, January 22, 1755.

"Sir,—I am favored with yours by Hendrick, and heartily thank you for the part you have been so good as to take in the Connecticut affair. Hendrick has been very explicit on the subject; and I have entertained him and his companions in the best manner I could. You will give me leave to refer you to a letter you will receive with this, from Mr. Peters, for the particulars that have passed here, and for the plan that we have agreed to prosecute, to put an end to this affair; in which I hope for the continuance of your friendly offices. You will observe, we propose that the Six Nations should be invited to send deputies to your house early in the spring, with full powers to treat and agree upon this matter, relative to the purchase of Lydius, and to prevent the like for the future, when I shall send commissioners to meet them, and it will give me particular pleasure, if you will permit me to name you in the commission."

Extract of a Letter from Richard Peters to Col. Johnson, dated January 23, 1755.

"He (speaking of Hendrick) told me you had made him a hearty friend to this Province, and would join with and support him in any measures, which the Government of Pennsylvania should advise, to get rid of this Connecticut Deed.—I heartily thank you for this singular kindness. In consideration of this hearty concurrence of yours and the Mohock, his Honour, the Governor, gave Hendrick a belt, with a string of wampum tied to it. By the belt he was asked to undertake, along with you, the breaking of the Connecticut Deed. And for that purpose, *and because there is no other way in the world to get rid of it,* he was further desired to consider with you, what will be the best method to procure the meeting of a Council at your house, as soon as possible, to consist of two or three Deputies from each nation, and no more, in order to consult together of the most effectual manner how to do it. And by the string you are desired to convene such a Council.

"We further intimated to Hendrick, and now inform you, that to get rid of this Deed, we cannot devise any other method that will be effectual, unless the Six Nations in Council, will execute a conveyance to the Proprietaries, of all the lands lying within their grant, on such conditions, and in such manner, as shall be agreed on, at your house. And to show the Indians, and yourself their just intentions, they propose to name you one of the Commissioners, with Mr. Penn and myself.

"Hendrick seems to approve much of this proposal; and I believe the more you think of the matter, the more you will be persuaded that no other way can do the thing effectually. If it meets with your approbation, which I hope it will do, the Governor begs the favour of you to summon a Council, at your house, and leaves it to you to fix the time, and to take such measures with the Indians previous to the meeting, as you and Hendrick shall think proper. It is thought that more than three deputies need not come from any one nation; but that there should be three from each."

The purpose so sedulously pursued was not finally accomplished until Nov. 5th, 1768, when at a treaty held at Fort Stanwix, the Proprietaries obtained a deed from the Six Nations, of the Susquehanna lands, being the same previously claimed to have been conveyed to the Susquehanna Company.

Pennsylvania was no longer in pursuit. She had carried off the prize. Victory perched on her standard: And forthwith all concerned in the Connecticut claim, opened in full cry to run down the Indian Deed of Fort Stanwix. "That wicked Priest of Canojoharry," as he is termed by Mr. Weiser, the Rev. Jacob Johnson, appears first upon the tapis, and makes the following affidavit:—
"That some time in the month of November, 1768, he was present at a Treaty, held at Fort Stanwix, with the Indians of the Six Nations, and that Sir William Johnson, Superintendant of the Six Nations, John Penn, Governor of Pennsylvania, Gov. Franklin, of New Jersey, Col. Elizur Fitch, of Windham, and the chiefs of the Six Nations, Seguanathua, a Tuscarora chief, and chief speaker, and many other persons were present—that the business of the treaty was to settle a division line between the claims of the King and the Indians, and to distribute a donation sent by the King, as Sir William Johnson informed the deponent, by letter and express—that this deponent was at that time a missionary to the Indians of the Six Nations, and resided at the Oneida Upper Castle—that Gov. John Penn, at this time, by the agency of Sir William Johnson, endeavored to obtain from the Indians a deed of the lands on the Susquehanna—that several private consultations were had with the said chiefs, from which this deponent was excluded, and that there was no agent present at said treaty, to represent the State of Connecticut or the Susquehanna Company. That this deponent, during the treaty, was

informed by several of the Indians present, that Gov. Penn wanted the Indians present to give him a deed of the lands on the Susquehanna, and they replied that they had given the New England white people, a deed of the same lands, and had received their pay for the same, and could not sell the same again. But they said they had agreed to give Gov. Penn, a deed of the same land, because Sir William Johnson had told them that their former conveyance to the New England white people was unlawful—that they had no right to purchase that land, which was within Penn's Charter, and Penn alone had the right of purchasing the same—that near the end of the treaty the deponent well recollects to have heard Seguanathua, chief speaker, in a public speech declare the same reasons as above said—for selling the land a second time, which was publicly interpreted by Sir William Johnson."

Col. Elizur Fitch, of Windham, was present in the Penn interest. I am not able to learn whether this gentleman was the Governor of Connecticut, of that name, who, in 1761, had bounded that colony, west, by New York, or a relative. If either, the fact may throw a ray of light on that transaction.

The Rev. Mr. Kirkland, an Indian missionary, also deposeth—"That he attended the Treaty with the Five Nations, held at Fort Stanwix, in the year 1768, for several of the last days of the treaty, and that on his arrival on the ground, the Rev. Jacob Johnson, then a missionary to the Oneida's, told the deponent that he had been forbid by Sir William Johnson to sit in Council with the Indians, and that Col. Butler, and several others had given him the same information—that several Indian chiefs told the deponent, at that time, that they had sold the Susquehanna land to the Pennsylvanians, and that they were finally induced to do it, by the council and advice of the Commissioners, urging that the Connecticut people had done wrong in coming over the line of Pennsylvania, to buy land of the Indians—that it was, however, not effected without great difficulty. At the close of the business, the Indians were called upon to execute the writings, which were not publicly read in the English language, but one of the Mohock chiefs gave a brief statement of their general purport in the Indian language; and the deponent further saith, that one of the Christian Indians, of the Oneida nation, by name, Theondintha, or Thomas, some months after said treaty, voluntarily and of his own mere motion, told the deponent that some undue influence had been made use of, at said treaty, respecting said land; that he, himself, namely, Thomas, had been the subject of this undue influence, and nine or ten more Indian chiefs were in the same predicament, and that he felt much troubled in his mind about it."

One of the fairest and ablest writers in favour of the Susquehanna company, observes:—' Conscious that the purchase at Fort Stanwix was radically defective, they resolved to make one more effort, to procure from the Indians a public disavowal of the Connecticut deed, and an acknowledgment of their own. In 1775 a treaty was held at Albany, with those Indians, under the authority of Congress, by Messieurs Woolcot, Schuyler, Edwards, Francis and Dow, to explain to them the causes of the American war. Col. Francis was a Pennsylvanian, a claimant of large tracts of the contested land, a leader of the opposition to the Connecticut settlers, and a principal agent of Penn. Notwithstanding, the Commissioners, by their interpreter, had told the Indians that nothing was to be said or done at the treaty, concerning lands, yet Col. Francis, towards the close of it, sent for Tegohagwanda and two other Onondago chiefs, to his lodgings at Mr. Bloodgood's, together with Thomas Fulmer, the Interpreter employed by the Commissioners. Mr. Fulmer, in his affidavit, swears, that after some preleminary conversation about the Susquehanna lands, "Col. Francis said, did you not sell those lands to the Pennsylvanians, and receive a Beaver skin full of dollars for them? To this one of the chiefs made answer, and said, no, we sold them to the Westernlonians (that is Bostonians, the name by which the New England provinces were called among the Five Nations) and we received the Beaver skin full of dollars from them. There was not any person present at this private meeting but Col. Francis, this deponent, and the three Indian chiefs before named. At the close of this meeting Col. Francis enjoined it upon the Indians, and the deponent likewise, not to tell any one that he had said this to them about the Susquehanna lands," The said Fulmer, in another place, swears further, concerning this interview, "that they smoked and discoursed together for some time, until the Indians appeared to this deponent to be considerably in liquor, when Col. Francis told them Gov. Penn had requested him to ask the Onondagos, who had first bought the lands called Wywamick, the said Gov. Penn, or the New England people? that the said Indian chief thereupon answered, that he had heard, from his uncle, that Gov. Penn had bought the lands on the east side of the Susquehanna, and that he did not know whether the New England people had bought any lands or not. That the said Col. Francis further asked the said Indian chief, if he did not know how many dollars Gov. Penn had paid at Fort Stanwix, for said lands? The said Indian answered that he had not seen all the money, yet he had heard that he paid 10,000 dollars.—That the said Col. Francis thereupon asked the said Indian whether he would on the following day, in the public conference, when the other business was done, declare the same in public, but not mention his name? Which the said Indian promised to do.—Whereupon Col. Francis told him, if he did that, he and Gov. Penn would make a present to the Onondago Indians. Which said discourse, at the request of Col Francis, was interpreted between them by this deponent. That when the Indians left his lodgings, he presented them with a bottle of rum. And this deponent further saith, that on the following day, in the public conference, the said Onondago chief made mention of the sale of these lands; but this deponent hath understood from the other Indians that it was without their knowledge."

"The Rev. Mr. Kirkland, in his affidavit, respecting this speech or declaration of the Indian chief, deposeth, that it was received with many marks of disapprobation and some degree of resentment, expressed by many Indians, of the best character in said nation, saying it was entirely foreign to the business of the treaty, and known beforehand only to a few individuals, and several Indians soon told the deponent, that upon their complaining to their chief speaker Tegohagwanda, and his chief Black Cap, of the impropriety of such a piece of conduct, at that time, they replied that the Indians were not to blame—that it originated wholly from the white people, and they were importuned and pressed hard to make the speech. A few hours after Thomas Fulmer, interpreter at said treaty, told the deponent that Col. Francis sent for him to his lodgings, the evening before, and had a private conference with the Onondago chiefs upon the subject, and prevailed upon them to make the speech."

Here closes the documentary evidence respecting those two adverse and conflicting Indian deeds, too important to be omitted; and which cannot fail from the interesting facts disclosed, amply to repay a careful perusal.

It addition, it is proper to say—that on the part of Pennsylvania, it is strenuously contended that the right of pre-emption before mentioned, granted by the Six Nations in 1736, of all lands within their charter, precluded them from selling, and making a valid conveyance to the Susquehanna Company. So strongly was this pre-emption right relied on, that in the exhibition of claim at Trenton, it was alone mentioned, of her Indian grounds of claim—the subsequent deed of 1768 not being adverted to.

To this it is replied—that the Indians then, and long after, supposed the claim of Mr. Penn not to extend above the Blue Mountains in a direction towards Wyoming.

On the part of Pennsylvania it was contended that Governor Dungan of New York, had obtained a pre-emption right to those lands, and sold the same to the Pennsylvania Proprietaries.

That the descriptive part of the Susquehanna deed was written on an erasure.

To this it was answered: The alteration took place before signing, at the desire of the Indians; that it lessened, instead of increasing the boundaries. That the deed was left by Col. Dyer in the hands of an agent in England, from whom it was, as is alleged, unfairly obtained by the opposite party, who had it in possession in Philadelphia in 1782, and could, and would have produced it at the Trenton trial, if it had been vitiated by interlineation; and that as they did not, the presumptions were all in favour of its fairness.

Surprise having been expressed, that the Six Nations should so readily have made (or, if you please, permitted to be made in their name,) a deed for the contested territory, against the remonstrance of the Pennsylvania commissioners; and the still more powerful influence of urgent solicitations to sell to them; we beg leave to advert to a suggestion previously made, viz: that the Pennsylvania Proprietaries were not favorites of the Six Nations, for the reason that they had declined to recognize the Delawares as their subjects, but had persisted in regarding them as an independent people, and as such making treaties, and purchasing lands of them. Pride, jealousy, revenge, the strongest motives that sway the savage breast, would lead them to thwart the wishes, and counteract the policy of the Proprietaries, and throw themselves into the embrace of the subtle Yankees.

The Six Nations being admitted by both parties to have been the original owners of the land, the public or a jury of the country will decide, which of the two deeds was valid, and conveyed the soil, that at Albany of July 11, 1754, to the Susquehanna Company, or that of November 5, 1768, at Fort Stanwix, to the Pennsylvania Proprietaries. The reader will remember that, as a historian, meaning to be as impartial as early convictions, and long cherished prejudice will admit, I only claim, that there were such reasoable grounds to believe the Connecticut title just, as that very honest men might have given their assent thereto, and be justified in taking every legal means to assert and defend it, until the question could be legally adjudicated.

The great trial at Trenton will be fully considered in due chronological order; when unimpeachable facts will be presented, leading to irresistible conclusions, which will create astonishment throughout both Connecticut and Pennsylvania.

Note.—The letter of Mr. Peters to Col. Johnson is entitled to special consideration. Hendrick enters thoroughly into the wishes of the Proprietary Government. He had been " made a hearty friend." He would join with Col. Johnson, and support him in any measures which the Government of Pennsylvania should advise, to get rid of the Connecticut deed." "Because *there was no other way in the world to get rid of it*, he was further desired to consider with you what will be the best method to procure the meeting of a council." What council? Look back to Hendrick's speech, January 15, 1755. " We agree with you that the deed should be destroyed. We agree with you that it is a false proceeding. We will give you our assistance, but you know that we cannot destroy the deed ourselves. That would be another mistake. It would be to do as bad as they have done. It must be the act of the Council of the Six Nations."

The remarks are too obvious to escape attention, and they weigh on the mind with too much force to be suppressed. That if the deed had been fraudulent, if it had been without adequate consideration—if it had been agreed upon not " at any public council, but of little knots of unauthorized chiefs," no such difficulties would have interposed themselves to its instant, indignant abjuration.

It may be instructive as well as amusing to contrast the 2000 pounds paid by the Susquehanna Company, with the consideration paid the Indians for land below the mountains.

The deed to William Penn, to which we in particular refer, was given in 1685, and ran thus :—

"This Indenture witnesseth, that We, Packenah, Jarckham, Sikals, Partquesott, Jervis, Essepenauk, Felktroy, Heckellappan, Econus, Machloha, Mettheonga, Wissa, Powey, Indian Kings, Sachemakers, right owners of all lands, from Quingquingus, called Duck Creek, unto Upland, called Chester Creek, all along by the west side of Delaware river, and so between the said creeks backwards *as far as a man can ride in two days with a horse,* for and in consideration of these following goods to us in hand paid, and secured to be paid by *William Penn,* Proprietary and Governor of the province of Pennsylvania and territories thereof, viz: 20 guns, 20 fathoms match-coat, 20 fathoms Stroudwater, 20 blankets, 20 kettles, 20 pounds powder, 100 bars of lead, 40 tomahawks, 100 knives, 40 pairs of stockings, 1 barrel of beer, 20 pounds red lead, 100 fathoms wampum, 30 glass bottles, 30 pewter spoons, 100 awl blades, 300 tobacco pipes, 100 hands of tobacco, 20 tobacco tongs, 20 steels, 300 flints, 30 pair of scissors, 30 combs, 60 looking glasses, 200 needles, one skipple of salt, 30 pounds sugar, 5 gallons molasses, 20 tobacco boxes, 100 jewsharps, 20 hoes, 30 gimblets, 30 wooden screw boxes, 100 string of beads.—Do hereby acknowledge, etc., given under our hands, &c., at New Castle, second day of the eighth month, 1685."

LETTER IX.

Commencement of Settlement, 1769—First Pennymite War—Conspicuous men of the two parties marshalled for the field—Capt. Zebulon Butler, Col. John Durkee—Denison, the Gores, M'Dowell, Shoemaker, Stewart and others, on the part of the Yankees. Capt. Amos Ogden; John Jennings, Esq., Charles Stewart, with Clayton, Francis, Dick, Morris, Ledlie and Craig, on the part of Mr. Penn—Capt. Ogden invested in Block-house at mouth of Mill Creek—A parley—Yankees outwitted—Taken prisoners and sent to Easton Jail—Liberated, return and take possession of Wyoming—Fort Durkee built—Expedition of Col. Francis—Mission of Col. Dyer and Elderkin to Philadelphia—Capt. Ogden returns—The four-pounder—Durkee taken prisoner and sent to Philadelphia—The Fort surrenders—Second expulsion of the Yankees.

The Susquehanna Company having completed their purchase of the soil, proceeded to make arrangements for establishing settlements at Wyoming, possession only being necessary, in their estimation, to render their title complete. Their purpose, unquestionably was, to do, as all the previous companies, cut out of the original Plymouth Charter, had done, namely, to obtain a confirmatory charter from the King, and establish at Susquehanna, an independent colony. From all the lights before us, we regard the proceedings as a spontaneous unofficial movement of the people of Connecticut. Perfect unanimity was not to be expected. The nature and history of man; reason and experience, preclude the idea. But we are confident in the opinion, that a people, generally, were never less divided upon any point of magnitude, than those of Connecticut on this subject. One thing more was demanded to satisfy the law. An assent, previous or subsequent to an Indian purchase within the limits of the colony, was required to render such purchase valid. Accordingly in May, 1755, on the petition of Phineas Lyman, and others, a Committee of the Susquehanna Company, reciting their purchase of the Indians, and praying the acquiescence of the Assembly, and their consent for an application to His Majesty, to erect them into a new colony, or plantation, it was among other things, Resolved, that,

" They (the Legislature) hereby, accordingly, manifest their ready acquiescence therein," etc.

Subsequently, to wit : In 1782, the Agents of Connecticut in setting forth their claim before the Court at Trenton, distinctly declare, That the purchase of the Susquehanna adventurers had the approbation of the Assembly.

An attempt to establish a colony at Wyoming, in 1762 ; the massacre of twenty of the settlers, and the expulsion of the remainder, the subsequent year, has been already noticed. The purchase of the soil from the Indians by the Pennsylvania Government, in 1768, has been mentioned. And now commenced the strife, foot to foot, and hand to hand, of the conflicting parties for the possession of this beautiful valley. Gallant spirits, with a will to do, and courage to dare, met spirits equally gallant and determined. We approach the contest, still known in the common parlance of the country, as " *The First Pennymite War.*"* In the bosom of the wilderness, far removed from any civilized settlement, extensive plains, beautiful as Persian groves, or Eden's bowers, the prize to crown and reward the victor. Though widely separated by rugged hills, and deep-tangled forests, from the busy mart, or the church-warning bell, yet were the combatants fully aware that the eyes of anxious multitudes were upon them. All Connecticut was on tiptoe to watch, to cheer, and to sustain her adventurous colony at Wyoming. Philadelphia, the first city on the continent—abounding in wealth, distinguished for talents, with such portions of the surrounding country as was more especially within the circle of her influence, gazing with anxious suspense, were equally eager, and not less zealously determined to stand by the party that had nobly volunteered to defend the honour and maintain the rights of Pennsylvania. The respective combatants, in no inconsiderable degree resembling the Roundheads and Cavaliers of the civil wars, the preceding century.

Before the charge is sounded, and the battle begins, each party must be traced in its march to the field of action.

First, then, of the Susquehanna Company.—Preparatory to a recommencement of their settlement, a meeting was convened at Hartford, in 1768, at which it was resolved, That five townships, five miles square, should be surveyed and granted, each to forty settlers, being Proprietors, on condition that those settlers should remain upon the ground, " man their rights" as was the phrase, and defend them-

---

* "Pennymite" and "Yankee" being the terms by which the parties were generally designated at the time ; and are used by us in no invidious " sense."

selves, and each other, from the intrusion of all rival claimants. Forty were to set forth without delay; the others, to the amount in all, of two hundred, were to follow the succeeding Spring. As further encouragement, a sum of two hundred pounds, Connecticut currency, i. e. six hundred and sixty-seven dollars, was appropriated to provide implements of husbandry and provisions, (including, probably, arms and ammunition,) for those who might require assistance. To those two hundred who emigrated on settling rights, must be added all those other proprietors of the Susquehanna purchase, who chose to take possession of their western property. Among the forty who obtained land on settlement rights, were no inconsiderable number of substantial farmers, who by this means, added to their other claims as proprietors, the choice of some of the most desirable lots, embracing the inviting river bottoms, unequalled in fertility. Five townships in the heart of the valley, were allotted for those adventurers, to wit:—Wilkesbarre, Hanover, Kingston, Plymouth, and Pittston.

Subsequently, three other townships, to be located on the west branch of the Susquehanna, were appropriated to forty settlers each.

Among the emigrants from the east, several bore parts so prominent in the scenes which transpired as to demand a particular introduction to the notice of the reader. The "Old French War," then recent, had developed the talent, and called into action the energies of a large number of young men in the colonies of New England. Connecticut furnished her full complement for that war. Capt. Zebulon Butler, of Lyme, after sharing in the campaign at Ticonderoga and Crown Point, in 1758, commanded a company, and earned reputation at the taking of the Havanna, 1762. A brave and vigilant officer, his superior manners and address at once commanded general respect, and conciliated the attachment of his soldiers. This gentleman, if not clothed with official power, was, by common consent, regarded as the leader of the Connecticut train. Captains Durkee and Ransom, both of whom had seen honorable service in the French war, accompanied, and rallied under their old companion in arms. Full of enterprise, never doubting the entire justice of the Connecticut claim, tired of the piping songs of peace, they sought action, honour and independence in the stirring scenes, opening on the Susquehanna. Obadiah Gore, Esq., with his seven sons (who will figure conspicuously in the succeeding pages,) were among the early emigrants. Nathan Denison, from Stonington, a descendant of Capt. Denison, distinguished in the old Pequot wars, mild yet firm, grave yet active, constituted one of the number. Nor was the wise policy neglected, of obtaining friends and adherents within the limits of Pennsylvania. How effected, no account remains; but above the Blue Mountains, on the Delaware, a settlement existed near by, or embracing Stroudsburg, the present seat of justice of Monroe county, whereof a number of the principal inhabitants united with the Connecticut people, and entered heart and hand into their cause. The aid afforded by these Pennsylvania allies, was of the utmost importance to the new colony. Benjamin Shoemaker, one of the Executive Committee, was from this settlement. John M'Dowell, a wealthy, high-toned Cameronian Scotchman, became a true friend to the Yankees. With Highland zeal, he espoused their cause. His granaries and purse were ever tendered to the suffererers with a "Highland Welcome."*

Other and efficient aid was found in the Stewarts, Young, with other bold and daring leaders from Hanover, near the Susquehanna, then in Lancaster county, now in Dauphin, who will presently appear among the armed combatants upon the field of action.

On the other hand, the Proprietaries of Pennsylvania designated their leaders, and marshalled their forces for the contest. Charles Stewart, a surveyor, trained, like Washington and Wayne, in the hardships and dangers of a forest-life, to lead in the paths of glory, stands forth most conspicuously. He was afterwards a popular and efficient officer of the Pennsylvania line, and for some time an aid to General Washington. With him was associated Capt. Amos Ogden, and John Jennings, Esq., Ogden uniting to the truest courage, and untiring activity, an intuitive perception of all the arts and stratagems of war, was the indefatigable military leader. John Jennings, Esq., High Sheriff of Northampton county, was the civil magistrate. These three constituted the Chief Executive Directory, to conduct the Proprietaries' affairs at Wyoming. To these, a lease had been executed for a hundred acres of land for seven years, upon condition that they should establish an Indian trading house thereon, and defend the valley from encroachment.†

* When Death's dark stream I ferry o'er,
 A time that surely will come;
 In Heaven itself, I ask no more,
  Than just a *Highland welcome.*—BURNS.

† "I have seen," says Col. Pickering, "March 2, 1798, among the Proprietaries' papers, a list of forty or fifty who purchased on the express condition of defending, in arms, the possession of these lands from the Connecticut claimants." So that the plan of *manning their rights*, was common to both parties.

The names of several gentlemen of distinction, besides Ogden, appeared in this war, at the head of armed companies. Asher Clayton, Turbot Francis, Joseph Morris, John Dick, Andrew Ledlie, and Thomas Craig, were among the best officers of the Province. The latter, by the merit of perfect discipline, and tried bravery, rose to be a colonel in the continental service, during the revolutionary war, and was afterwards major-general of the militia. In declining age, when I knew him, his manners were highly polished, but he told me the habits of the soldier had become so fixed in him, that for thirty years he had not slept on a bed. At night, a blanket or two spread upon a table, constituted his most welcome couch. Col. Clayton had held a commission in 1763, in the Paxton Rangers, and was probably progenitor of the distinguished senator, of that name, from Delaware. The son of Capt. Dick, full of wit, who loved his jest, his bottle, and his friend, though residing in Northampton, afterwards practised law in Luzerne, a general favorite, and successful advocate.

It will, at a glance, be seen that such parties did not meet, though the prize at issue was great, in mere mercenary contention.

Stewart, Ogden, and Jennings, were first upon the ground, having arrived in January, 1769. It was winter, and the stillness of death brooded over the valley. A block-house and a number of huts, near the confluence of Mill Creek with the Susquehanna, a mile above the present town of Wilkesbarre, left by the massacred, or expelled settlers of 1763, were easily fitted up, and afforded shelter for their men. The first step was to lay off two manors, embracing a considerable portion of the finest lands on each side of the river.

Having selected the heart for themselves, the Proprietaries left the remainder to reward the enterprise of such friends as might be able to render assistance in meeting with defiance, and resisting with effect, the "moss trooping" Yankees from the east.

Seventeen hundred and sixty nine, was an eventful year in Wyoming history. On the 8th of February, the first *forty*, the pioneer detachment of Yankees appeared on the ground. Finding their expected shelter in the possession of an enemy, they forthwith invested the block-house of Ogden, cutting off all communication with the surrounding country, so that the besieged could neither obtain fuel nor venison; and demanded in the name of Connecticut the surrender of the garrison, and peaceable possession of the valley. Expected reinforcements anxiously looked for, not arriving, Captain Ogden equally ready, for fair, open fight, or the subtle wiles of diplomacy, as might be best adapted to his condition, or calculated to effect his purpose—having only ten men able to bear arms, one fourth only of his invading foe, determined to have recourse to negociation. A very polite and conciliatory note was addressed to the commander of the *forty*, an interview respectfully solicited, and a friendly conference asked on the subject of the respective titles. Ogden proved himself an accomplished angler. The bait was too tempting. Propose to a Yankee to talk over a matter, especially which he has studied, and believes to be right, and you touch the most susceptible chord that vibrates in his heart. That they could out talk the Pennymites, and convince them the Susquehanna title was good, not one of the forty doubted. Three of the chief men were deputed to argue the matter, viz: Isaac Tripp and Benjamin Follett, two of the executive committee, accompanied by Mr. Vine Elderkin. No sooner were they within the block-house, than Sheriff Jennings clapped a writ on their shoulders. "Gentlemen, in the name of the Commonwealth of Pennsylvania, you are my prisoners!" "Laugh where we must, be candid where we can." The Yankees were decidedly outwitted. By common consent the prisoners were transported to Easton jail, guarded by Captain Ogden; but accompanied in no hostile manner by the thirty-seven remnants of the forty. Here the advantage of having friends in Pennsylvania was made manifest. No sooner was the key turned than bail was entered for their appearance, the prisoners were set at liberty, and returned immediately to Wyoming.

This was the first scene of the first act, of the Pennymite and Yankee war. So far, some ill temper may have arisen, but the deep feelings of revenge, and thirst for blood had been on neither side awakened. Important events now trod closely on the heels of each other. Ogden had gained nothing by victory—the Yankees had lost nothing by defeat; nay, they had attained their object, and were, without any act of violence on their part, in peaceable possession of Wyoming.

Mortified at the result, aroused by pride, stimulated by the Proprietaries, Sheriff Jennings raised the posse of Northampton county, and accompanied by several magistrates, repaired to Wyoming, stormed the fortified house in which the Yankees had entrenched themselves, and captured nearly the whole party. Trained as the New England men had been to an almost superstitious reverence for the civil law, a magistrate's writ served by a sheriff, had something too awful in its character to be resisted. Forthwith about thirty in number were marched to Easton, and all committed to prison, and almost immediately liberated on bail. This was in the month of March. All these changes of fortune had transpired within ninety days of the arrival of Captain Ogden, and within less than sixty from the appearance of the forty at Wyoming. Twice captured and sent to jail, a distance of sixty miles, through a dreary wilderness, in the depth of winter too, it might well be imagined would have cooled the ardor of the most impassioned zealots. They must have travelled going and coming twice, two hundred and forty miles. Yankee perseverance and enterprize were rarely ever more conspicuously exhibited under deeply discouraging circumstances. And this may be regarded the second scene of the first act in the drama.

The additional quotas for the other four townships, of forty each, making one hundred and sixty, arrived in April. These, with the first forty returned from prison, and a considerable number of adventurers who held shares in the Susquehanna Company, constituting two hundred and seventy or eighty able bodied men in all, assembled on the river banks, where Wilkesbarre now stands, on the 10th of April. The block-house at Mill creek was too remote from the flats near the old town of Wywamick, where large fields, long since cleared, invited cultivators. A new fortification, called Fort Durkee, after the new commander, was therefore erected on the banks of the river at Fish's eddy, (near the lower line of the borough) and twenty or thirty huts built in its immediate vicinity.

Forts, or fortifications, and block-houses are so often mentioned in this and the succeeding war, that I cannot doubt but the reader will be pleased with a brief description of one of each, which will answer for all. The block-house is generally a square building of heavy hewn logs. When raised to the height of one story, the timber used for joists or beams, are projected over every side six or eight feet. The second story is built up of lighter logs, placed on the ends of these projecting timbers, the whole roofed of course with boards, shingles or bark. Loop-holes are formed through which to fire on an approaching enemy. The purpose of making the upper story larger than the lower, is to enable those who defend the block-house, to throw down stones (gathered for the purpose,) or boiling water, or other missiles, on the heads of assailants who should attempt to force the door, or set fire to the building.

Forts, or fortifications, are built thus. The ground being fixed on, near to water, a square, or paralellogram is traced out, of a size proportioned to the number to be sheltered and defended. That built subsequently, at Mill creek, was supposed to contain half an acre. A ditch three feet deep is dug, in which hewn logs, eighteen feet long, are placed on end, close together all round, except at the four corners, where flanking towers are projected. A ditch several feet wide is then dug four feet from the upright timbers, and the dirt thrown up against them. Sometimes, double rows of timbers are placed round so as to break joints. Usually there are two gateways, or entrances, opposite each other, strongly barricaded. Around the inside, against the wall of timbers, huts are erected for the accommodation of families, or messes. Loop-holes at proper distances for firing rifles or small arms, finish the work within. Sometimes a covered way is dug to the water; and not unfrequently wells are sunk in the enclosure.

Having now complete possession, the Connecticut people entered with alacrity upon their agricultural pursuits, while their surveyors were employed in running out the five townships allotted to the actual settlers. But no one supposed that peace and security were finally yielded them by their alert and powerful opponents. Every breeze from the southern mountain awakened fears of an approaching enemy. Capt. Ogden with the civil magistrate, Sheriff Jennings, though absent, had not been idle, but having recruited their forces, appeared on the plains on the 20th of May. After reconnoitering the position of the Yankees, finding it too strong, and their number too large to be attacked with a rational prospect of success, they withdrew to Easton; and Sheriff Jennings, in his report, informed the Governor that the intruders mustered three hundred able bodied men, and it was not in his power to collect sufficient force in Northampton to dislodge them. In the delightful season of Spring, nature unfolding her richest robes of leaf and flower, the Susquehanna yielding boundless stores of delicious shad, a brief hour of repose seemed only to wed the Yankee emigrants more strongly to the valley. The beautiful low lands, where scarcely a stone impeded the plough, contrasted with the iron bound shores of New England, and her rock covered fields, was a prospect as inviting as the plains of Italy of old to its northern invaders. But another force was threading the paths of the wilderness to attack them. Col. Turbot Francis, commanding a fine company from the city, in full military array, with colours streaming, and martial music, descended into the plain, and sat down before Fort Durkee, about the 20th of June; but finding the Yankees too strongly fortified, returned to await reinforcements below the mountains.

Knowing the value of time in strengthening and consolidating their settlements, for every day that accounts of the richness of those western lands reached Connecticut, new bodies of emigrants set forth for Wyoming; the Susquehanna Company resolved to disarm the energies of the Proprietaries by entering into negotiations. That the object was to amuse and create delay till the summer should have passed, we infer from the fact that the colony of Connecticut did not officially move in the matter, and the great improbability that the Government of Pennsylvania could be induced to make either concession or compromise with agents merely of the Susquehanna Company. But the step was dictated by sound policy, and has not the less merit that it did not succeed.

Early in the summer two distinguished personages, agents of the Susquehanna Company, viz: Col. Eliphalet Dyer, and Major Jedediah Elderkin, clothed with full power to open a negotiation with the Proprietary Government for a settlement of the controversy respecting the Wyoming lands, appeared in Philadelphia. They were met with the courtesy that ever has distinguished the manners of that city of polished gentlemen of the old school. The Hon. Benjamin Chew was appointed to confer with Messrs. Dyer and Elderkin. But to their propositions, to submit the question at issue to a court of law, or to arbitration, a respectful but decided negative was returned in answer. Nor did the Pennsylvania authorities for a moment intermit the vigorous prosecution of measures that were in train to throw upon the disputed ground a force decisively overwhelming.

The brave and indefatigable Ogden was to have the chief military command; yet as the whole bore the name, if not the character of a civil movement, Sheriff Jennings of Northampton, was clothed ostensibly with the direction, and to him the Governor issued his orders. They conclude thus: "It is however, warmly recommended to you, to exercise on this unhappy occasion, the utmost discretion and prudence, to avoid the effusion of blood; and that neither you nor your party strike, fire at, or wound the offenders, unless you are at first stricken, fired at, or wounded."

Sheriff Jennings commenced his march with about two hundred men, well armed and equipped for battle, in the beginning of September. To enable him to comply more effectually with his peaceful instructions, an artillery company constituted part of his force. An iron four pound cannon, with a supply of cartridge and ball—the first piece of ordnance that ever was at Wyoming, had been brought up from Fort Augusta, (Sunbury) in a boat, by Captain Alexander Patterson, an active partizan officer, the most effective of Ogden's subordinates. In a more elevated station, and a wider field of action, this gentleman will again be presented to the reader.

As Jennings approached the valley, Captain Ogden, who was already on the ground with fifty armed men, by a vigorous and well timed movement seized Captain Durkee,* commander of the Yankees. Too valuable a prize to be risked at Easton, for greater safety the prisoner was sent in irons under a safe escort to Philadelphia, and there closely incarcerated in prison. Immediately after this successful enterprise Sheriff Jennings, and his pacific cohort, descended from the passes of the mountain, and displayed in formidable array on the plains before Fort Durkee. Their commander captured, menaced by a force so imposing, above all, that terrible four pounder destroying every hope of victory, quelled all disposition to resistance. Being summoned to surrender, articles of capitulation were entered into. Three or four leading men were detained as prisoners. Seventeen men were to remain of the Connecticut people, to gather the ripening harvest; all the others, without exception, were to leave the valley immediately; the property being private, was to be respected. Taking up their melancholy march, sad as the exiles from Paradise; men, their wives and little ones, with such of their flocks and herds as could be collected, with aching hearts took leave of the fair plains of Wyoming.†

It is with pain we record the fact that so gallant an officer as Ogden, should sully his fair fame by acts of injustice and oppression. No sooner had the mass of settlers been expelled, than in violation of the articles of capitulation, he commenced the plunder of all the property remaining. Cattle, horses and sheep, were driven to markets on the Delaware, and the seventeen left without means to sustain themselves, were compelled to follow their exiled friends on their

---

* John Durkee, afterwards Colonel in the Continental army.

† Durkee and his companions were not forgotten in their captivity. A meeting of the executive committee of the Susquehanna Company held at Windham, voted that fifty pounds be immediately raised, and forwarded for their relief. Thirty-four pounds to Captain Durkee; the remaining sixteen to be appropriated to the use of Simeon Draper, Daniel Gore, Asa Ludington and Thomas Bennett, six pounds each. It was further voted—that Ebenezer Backus, Captain Silas Parke, Wm. Hurlbut, Esq., Capt. Ebenezer Baldwin, Mr. Wm. Gallup, Increase Mosely, Esq., Major Eleazer Talcott, Capt. Joseph Eaton, Capt. Robert Durkee, Capt. Zebulon Butler, John Jenkins, John Pitkin, Ezra Buel, Nathaniel Landon, Jeremiah Angel, Jonathan Pettibone, Gad Stanley, John Smith, Esqs., and Capt. Obadiah Gore, be a committee to collect and forward the money.

journey to Connecticut. No life having been lost, not a wound having been received by either side; the campaign closed, the Yankees having been three times expelled, leaving the valley in undisputed possession of Ogden, Jennings, and their victorious forces. Thus closed 1769, the first year of the far-famed Pennymite and Yankee war for the possession of Wyoming. But bolder spirits were on the way, and scenes of deeper interest were soon to be presented on the stage.

LETTER X.

1770.——Sudden descent. Wyoming—Reinstatement of the Yankees—Captain Ogden returns and resumes his old quarters at Mill Creek—A fortunate omen—His Fort invested by the Yankees—Battle—William Stager killed—The Connecticut party defeated—Reinforced and in possession of the four pounder, the Yankees renew the siege—Stirring incidents—Gov. Penn's application to Gen. Gage for aid—Surrender of Fort Ogden—Proclamations of the Governor—Captain Ogden returns—Masterly address—Impetuous assault—Fort Durkee taken—The Yankees for the third time expelled—Vicissitudes—With a "Hurrah for King George" the Connecticut claimants repossess themselves of the Valley.

The year 1770 now dawns upon our view. It is the depth of winter. We look down on the valley of Wyoming, the past season so animated by contending factions; smoke from a single chimney is the only indication that it is tenanted by a human being. So perfect had been the conquest over the intruding Yankees, their expulsion so complete, and so great the distance of their former homes to which they had gone, no immediate difficulty was apprehended from their return. Indeed, when the losses they had sustained, and the evidences exhibited to them of the power and determination of Pennsylvania to maintain her territorial rights, were considered, it was scarcely doubted that so prudent and calculating a people would desist from any further attempt to establish a colony on the Susquehanna. Captain Ogden therefore, leaving a garrison of ten men to keep possession, and take charge of the property, marched his victorious troops below the mountains, where they were disbanded, while he and his able civil coadjutor, the spirited and efficient sheriff, Jennings, repaired to Philadelphia to spend a part of the winter, display their laurels, and enjoy the well-earned honours of victory.*

* A city distinguished for hospitality would not fail to welcome to their sumptuous tables, gentlemen who had served so faithfully, and accomplished so much for the public interest and their own. The high toned Allen—the courteous Chew—the proud Willing—the witty, but profound Peters—doubtless vied with each other who should render the entertainment of

Late in February there came the astounding tidings to Captain Ogden, suddenly arresting the flowing tide of hilarity and enjoyment, that his garrison had been surprised and expelled by a superior force. Prompt, alert, he was instantly in motion; gathering a few tried followers, he hastened with all possible celerity to the field of action. Captain Lazarus Stewart, from Hanover, in Lancaster county, with "*forty*" settlers, who had accepted from the Susquehanna Company, a township, to be named after their parent town, having with him ten Connecticut people, appeared in the valley the beginning of February, ousted the few men left by Ogden, from their comfortable quarters at Fort Durkee, but did not attempt to arrest or keep them as prisoners.

The dread cannon, the formidable four pounder, was the first object of concern. It had been carefully housed, with ammunition a good store, in the fortress at Mill Creek, from whence it was taken, and with emotions of pride at the capture, and a pleasing sense of security from the possession, transported in safety to Fort Durkee.

It is difficult at this distant time to determine which should be regarded as most extraordinary, the facility with which the Yankees were taken to prison, or the certainty and ease with which they escaped. Our story left Captain Durkee confined in the Philadelphia jail; by what means he obtained his freedom, I have sought information in vain; but we find him now, with unabated vigor and increased zeal at the head of the Connecticut forces.

Sheriff Jennings could not accompany his friend Ogden, but the latter, according to settled policy, choosing to be attended by, and to act professedly under the orders of a civil magistrate, took with him a deputy sheriff from Northampton. On arriving upon the ground, Fort Durkee being in possession of the Yankees, strengthened in its defences and well garrisoned, Captain Ogden with fifty men, entered upon his old quarters at Mill Creek, which he put in the best posture of defence. His policy was obvious and instantly adopted, his numbers being unknown, to keep them concealed as much as possible, to appear diffident, not venturing out, risking nothing, but seeming busy, as if adding to the strength of his fortress, so as to induce his enemy to suppose him weak and waiting for reinforce-

---

the protectors of Wyoming from Yankee intrusion, most acceptable. Pure wine flowed—healths to the victors were quaffed—the joke passed, and Ogden, truly a most capital soldier, assured them in those moments of hilarity that the work was accomplished—the four pounder, superior to "if" was the true peace-maker; and he was confident that never another Yankee would dare to place his intruding foot upon the Susquehanna. ?

ments, by this means leading them from too much confidence into some rash act that might expose them to capture.

A fortunate omen had already occurred to inspire hopes, and stimulate the ardor of his men. The Yankees, to avoid awakening suspicion, were to come into the valley in small detachments; one of these, consisting of ten or twelve men, who had learned the success of Stewart, but were not apprised of the arrival of a Pennsylvania force, appeared cold and hungry, before the gate at the Mill Creek fortress, not doubting a cordial welcome from expecting friends. Very readily were they admitted, but instantly arrested by the deputy sheriff as prisoners, and so closely confined that escape was impossible, and their arrival and capture was unknown to their friends at Fort Durkee.

The policy of Captain Ogden produced its desired effect, (as afterwards the affected caution of Napoleon at Austerlitz, rendered presumptuous the Russian and Austrian generals, and terminated in their discomfiture.) Major Durkee and his officers, after full consultation, resolved to capture Ogden while he was yet weak, and before reinforcements should enable him to bid them defiance. Heretofore the Connecticut people had acted merely as civil citizens united for mutual protection; they now assumed a more martial aspect, and marched out with the Connecticut flag flying, to the inspiring music of the fife and drum.

However much this display may have imparted confidence, and inspired courage among the Yankees, Captain Ogden was the last man in whom it could occasion despondence, or create the slightest alarm. A negotiation was opened immediately after the besiegers had drawn up before the Mill Creek fortress. Ogden, to reconnoiter, came out with a flag to demand their purpose, and estimate their numbers. Finding their strength not greatly superior to his own, he retired. Placing the deputy sheriff on duty, he suddenly rushed out with all his men armed, ordered the sheriff's officer to arrest the whole Yankee array, in the name, and by authority of Pennsylvania. A sharp conflict ensued; the Connecticut people were defeated with the loss of one man, William Stager, who was shot dead on the spot, and several were wounded. This was the first blood shed in those memorable Pennymite and Yankee wars for the possession of Wyoming.

Controversy arose as to which party was responsible for firing the first gun, and occasioning the first effusion of blood. Such an inquiry on this occasion, would seem to be useless, as regards the general question, as unavailing in this particular case. The Yankees here marched forth in military array, with martial music, their guns loaded with ball, to capture Ogden. By every rule of honorable war he had a right to consider them as enemies, and would have been justified in opening a fire upon them from his fortification, without notice or parley. The manner in which they came, was a declaration of war. War was meant. And it was justifiable to answer war with war. But the first man who fell was one of the Connecticut party, and it roused into more fiery action those deep and deadly passions, which the events of the preceding summer were calculated to awaken into bitterness. But there is another reflection which, in justice, should be recorded in association with that just expressed. Was this the commencement of the contest? Had not the Connecticut people been expelled by an armed force, in full military array, with artillery as well as small arms, pointed for their destruction? Was not this in fact, the earliest decided belligerent demonstration; an unequivocal act of war? Leaving the decision of this point to an abler casuist, or a less partial judge, I advance to the siege of Fort Ogden.

In possession of the cannon, it was resolved to bring its power to bear on the enemy. A neighboring hill overlooked the Fort, and completely commanded the position But the Yankees, with a respectful caution highly complimentary to Capt. Ogden's prowess, did not choose to risk the piece within reach of a sortie of their intrepid enemy. A slight redoubt was therefore thrown up on the western river bank, directly opposite the fortification. The cannon was transported across, and mounted ready for action. The piece had to be elevated, for the fort was not less that fifty feet above the level of the gun. The distance between the two points was about sixty rods. Little skilled in the science of projectiles, it would not be expected that the Yankee farmers could manage their artillery so as to produce a very powerful effect. But on the 15th of April, they opened their fire. Never, before, had echoes of those mountains been disturbed by, and answered to a voice so tremendous. Shot after shot was sent booming across the Susquehanna; day after day, roar succeeded roar, but to the astonishment of all, without doing the least possible execution. Time was too precious to be thus wasted. Reinforcements might arrive. The cannon was removed to the eastern shore, and Major Durkee, having received an accession to his forces, marched up a second time in military array to invest the fort. Dividing his men into three divisions, each, with all possible despatch, erected a breast-work; the cannon was mounted in the one under his immediate command. A spirited fire was opened on the stockade. The siege gave rise to a gallant act on the part of the Yankees. A storehouse adjoining the fort, strong and well manned, was stormed, set on fire, and burnt to the ground, by which most of the valuable articles for peace or war, belonging the Pennsylvania party, were entirely consumed.

Capt. Ogden had failed in no part of the duty of an able officer. Immediately after his attack, in March, he had despatched a trusty messenger to the Governor, stating his situation, urging the necessity of immediate aid, and saying he would defend his position to the utmost extremity, or while there was hope of relief.

Governor Penn was in no condition to comply with the request. A dark cloud, portending a storm, lowered in another quarter. The disputes between the colonies and the mother country seemed rapidly festering into an open contest. The massacre at Boston had taken place on the 5th of the month, and lurid flames of threatening war shot up from every point of the surrounding horizon. He, therefore, applied to Gen. Gage, commander-in-chief of his Majesty's forces in North America, whose head-quarters were then at New York, for assistance to suppress what was considered the lawless and unprincipled invasion by the Connecticut people, of the peaceful and assured territory of Pennsylvania. Such, it seems, Gen. Gage did not regard it. His reply is important, not only as it shows his own, but, probably, as it exhibits the general opinion of the country in regard to the contest.

" New York, April 15, 1770.—The troops in all the provinces have orders, in general, to assist the civil power, when they shall be legally called upon; but the affair in question seems to be a dispute concerning property, in which I cannot but think it would be *highly improper* for the King's troops to interfere."

No aid arriving, and the siege being pressed with vigour, a flag sent in by Major Durkee, led to negotiations which terminated in the surrender of the fort. Articles of capitulation were entered into on the 29th of April. Capt. Ogden was to retire from the valley, with all his forces, in three days, except that to take care of his property, which was to be respected, six men were to be left in possession of one of the houses. To the surprise of the besiegers, and the delight of the captives, the party of Yankee prisoners were discovered and released, after more than a month's confinement, so rigorous, that they had not been able to give their friends the least intimation of their captivity.

The nicer laws, which tend so much to soften the asperities and relieve the distresses of war, unhappily were but too slightly regarded on either side. Justifying his conduct by that of Capt. Ogden himself, to the seventeen Connecticut people, left to keep possession, by the articles of capitulation the previous Autumn, Major Durkee proceeded, very unceremoniously, to expel the six as very unwelcome neighbours, indeed, as spies on his proceedings, and according to established usage on both sides, or in the homely adage of the time, "tit for tat," he relieved them from the charge of what property had been left under their care. This, however, was not all demanded by prudence, and justified by the laws of war. The fort was strong—the adjacent buildings comfortable. With the force then under his command, to spare a suitable detachment to garrison the place was impossible. If left, it was apprehended that the Pennsylvania party would retake possession, perhaps with more ordnance, and greater numbers, and bid defiance to all the power of the Yankees to dispossess him. After full consultation it was resolved to set fire to the fort, and level the whole establishment with the earth. Eight years previous, the first habitations of white men had been erected on this spot by the unfortunate settlers of 1762, which had been preserved by the Savages, when they massacred or expelled the Connecticut people from the Valley. The aspiring flames were a grand but melancholy sight, awakening sad recollections of the past, and gloomy forbodings for the future. But the position was too admirably chosen to be long neglected.

Reader, as we turn from this scene of destruction, I beg leave to remind you that we shall look in upon it again, ere long, under more pleasing auspices.

No sooner had the news reached Philadelphia, than the Executive published a proclamation, denouncing what he conceived the highhanded, and outrageous conduct of the intruders.

Writs were issued by the Supreme Court for the arrest of several of the Yankee leaders, for whose capture a large reward was offered; under the authority of which Lazarus Stewart was made prisoner while on a visit below the mountains. By the aid of partizans, with some violence to the officer, he succeeded to make his escape.

Planting time had come. Peace reigned. Wyoming was in the undisturbed possession of the Yankees. The luscious shad again came up in countless myriads, inviting the toil-worn emigrants from the dangers of the field, to the sports of the stream,* from the half famished abstinence of the camp, to feast on the richest of nature's dainties. Hope, and joy, and confidence began to prevail. Every new detachment of adventurous settlers, and especially one under the command of Capt. Butler, whose presence had been anxiously looked for, was hailed with shouts of welcome. Settlements commenced on the west side of the river, were prosecuted with spirit. Old Forty fort, so celebrated in the future history of Wyoming, was begun. More distant positions were explored, David Mead and Christopher Hurlbut, Esqs., the principal surveyors on behalf of the Susquehanna Company, with untiring assiduity again followed the compass over hill and dale, in locating and lotting the several townships set off for actual settlers.

Spring passed away without the appearance of an enemy; summer followed, and not a foe had disturbed their repose. Rich harvests were ripening to crown their labours, and a feeling of security would have pervaded the breasts of the most timid, were it not for the recollection of the untoward events of the preceding fall.

Disappointed in his application for assistance from Gen. Gage, Governor Penn viewed the aspect of affairs at the north, with the extremest embarrassment, almost amounting to despair. But the arrival of Capt. Ogden, his faithful military commander, reanimated his desponding hopes, and he resolved to make a vigorous effort to regain possession of the disputed ground.—Moral as well as physical force was brought into action.—On the 28th of June a proclamation was issued, referring to the events which had recently transpired at Wyoming, and forbidding, under severest penalties, any person from making a settlement there, unless by the authority of the proprietaries, or their lessees, Stewart, Ogden, and Jennings. The utmost force that could be assembled for the occasion, was raised, and placed under the orders of Capt. Ogden, with directions to repair to the scene of action, and dispossess the Yankees if in his power. Again, with characteristic consistency, the military was marched under the ostensible auspices of the civil authority. The official term of Sheriff Jennings had expired, and Aaron Van Campen, Esq., a magistrate, whose zeal had previously led him to take an active part in the controversy, was selected to accompany the commander on his expedition.

---

* Mrs. Young states that the first rude nets were made of willow boughs, woven in meshes together. Ropes were made of bark of trees, or long grape vines. But so abundant were the fish, a boundless profusion was taken by those seines.

So difficult had it become to raise recruits, that it was late in September before he arrived on the eastern mountain that overlooks the valley.

Surprise will naturally be excited, that the powerful province of Pennsylvania did not at once raise and maintain a force of sufficient strength to expel the Connecticut people, and to build, arm, and garrison two or more forts, in suitable positions, effectually to put an end to all hope of making a permanent settlement at Wyoming. A popular government in a cause deemed just, possessing the wealth, the numbers, and the resources of Pennsylvania, could have crushed, like an egg shell in the hand of a giant, all the power which the Susquehanna Company had yet been able to concentrate on the Susquehanna; for the colony of Connecticut, biding its time, cautiously watching events, had as yet neither committed itself by a direct recognition of, nor lent the least official aid to the measures adopted for the settlement of Wyoming, further than to express their assent to the formation of the company, the purchase of the Indians, and the proposed application to the king for a charter to the new colony. Had the Proprietary Government aroused itself with becoming spirit, and put forth at once, with decisive energy, all the strength the occasion demanded, Connecticut would probably have postponed the avowal of her claim to jurisdiction until a more inviting season.

Doubtless the inefficient movements on the part of the Proprietary Government are to be ascribed, principally, to its own unpopularity. It is sufficient that we advert to the long existing contention between the people of the province and the proprietaries, in respect to taxation chiefly, and the jealousy existing because of their immense, and as it was deemed, unreasonable land monopoly, connected with numerous other points of lesser magnitude, exciting feelings of mutual distrust and enmity, paralyzing almost every effort of the Governor, either for good or evil. The contest at Wyoming was a dispute respecting the soil. The best part of the valley it was known, had been surveyed, and appropriated to the proprietaries themselves. Without scrutinizing very closely the origin of titles, the people sympathised very generally with the Wyoming *settlers*, and no inconsiderable number wished success to their cause.

We have before stated that there were three paths (roads they could not be called,) to Wyoming. The old warrior's path, by way of the Lehi water gap and Fort Allen, coming into the valley a mile below Solomon's Creek, in Hanover; the path from the Delaware at

Coshutunk, (where was a small Yankee settlement,) which came in through Cob's Gap to the Lackawana, at Capouse meadows,—the other from Easton, through the Wind Gap, near the line of the present turnpike. By the latter way, all the military expeditions had heretofore invaded the valley, and that alone was watched by the Yankee sentinels. Aware of this fact, with far more tact than was displayed by his adversaries, Captain Ogden took the old warrior path, marched with celerity and secrecy, and on the 21st of September[*] encamped on the head waters of Solomon's Creek. Kindling no fire, creating no smoke, giving no alarm, early the next morning this gallant leader took a position from which, with his telescope, he could bring the greater part of the valley under his eye. All was quiet; the settlers were unconcernedly engaged in their usual occupations. The husbandmen repaired each to his own field, with his hands. The population was thus divided into little parties of from three to six, through the flats, and along the meadows. Ready to conceive, and prompt to execute, this most able commander instantly divided his force, consisting of one hundred and forty men, into detachments of ten, each under an approved leader, and directed them to hasten noiselessly and secretly to the fields, and seize upon the laborers. The plan succeeded to admiration. A considerable portion of the settlement fell into his power, and were immediately sent to Easton jail, while the remainder fled for refuge to Fort Durkee. Captain Ogden withdrew to his bivouac of the preceding night on the mountain, but in a way that left no suspicion that he had not entered by the usual route. The night was one of unexampled gloom and confusion in Fort Durkee. The position and number of their invaders were unknown, but it was presumed to be powerful; for it could not be supposed that the enemy was unapprized of the accession of numbers, who had emigrated during the summer from Connecticut, or that they would attempt to dislodge them without adequate preparation. A large number of their men the Yankees knew were made prisoners, and immediate assistance was deemed necessary. Four men were therefore selected to carry tidings of their disaster to the friendly settlement at Coshutunk, and solicit all the forces in their power to muster. A step so probable, the Yankees imagined the enemy would not fail to foresee and counteract. Taking it for granted that the passes by the usual Minisink road, and the generally traveled central way would be guarded, the Yankee

[*] Mr. Chapman.

messengers, as directed, sought to evade the vigilance of the foe by taking the much neglected warrior's path. Scarcely had they ascended the mountain, when they found themselves prisoners in the presence of Captain Ogden. The confused state of Fort Durkee was no sooner learned from the reluctant captives, than with a promptitude that would have done honour to Bonaparte, in his early Italian campaigns, Captain Ogden put his men in motion—stormed the Fort with such an impetuous rush, that Captain Craig, who led the van, gave the first alarm by springing into the midst of the astonished multitude. But the armed men did not yield without a short, but severe struggle. Several lives were lost, and Captain Butler was only saved from a bayonet aimed at his breast, by the noble humanity and timely interposition of Craig.* Severely hurt, Captain B. was taken into the hut of Mr. Beach, and had his wounds dressed. Ten years afterwards these two gallant officers, and Major John Durkee, making a third, found themselves each in the command of a regiment, in their country's service, efficient supporters of the cause of Independence, respected and beloved. Captain Butler, Mr. Spalding, and a few of the most prominent of the Yankee leaders were honored with the distinction of being sent to Philadelphia for imprisonment, while the others were escorted to the jail at Easton.

All the Connecticut possessions were now, as on the preceding autumn, abandoned, and the whole labor of the summer fell into the hands of their Pennymite foes. Mr. Beach and family started down the river in a canoe; tarrying a night at what is now Beach Grove, they liked the place, and made a settlement. The property lost was by no means inconsiderable, and the soldiers of the successful party were richly rewarded with the plunder.

Again Ogden retired from this fourth effectual expulsion of the Connecticut people, not doubting now, after this signal overthrow,

* Captain Thomas Craig was a native of Allentown, Northampton county. On this invasion he commanded a company under Ogden. Leading the storming party he stepped lightly in advance of his men and speaking low to the sentinel, as a friend, threw him off his guard, knocked him down and entered the fort as stated. Early in the Revolutionary war, Captain Craig led a company into service under Washington, and rose to the command of a regiment. Not only was he brave, but constitutionally impetuous. He was at Quebec, in the battles of Germantown and Monmouth, and at the taking of Lord Cornwallis.

His intrepid and humane conduct in storming the fort, and preserving the prisoners from slaughter, entitle him to our esteem. Though brave as either, in his social walks he resembled Marc Antony rather than Scipio. Having quit the tented field, he sought excitement and pleasure, amid the lilies and the roses, with the blond and the brunette beauties of the stream and hill, in old Northampton. Colonel Craig lived to the very advanced age of 93 years, having departed this life in January 1832.

that the contest was at an end, and the Proprietaries secured in the peaceful possession of the valley forever.

A small garrison of twenty men was left as before, to take charge of the property, until the lessees should come out early in the spring, to resume their engagement to erect a suitable house and open a trade with the Indians.

But the Susquehanna Company's forces were like the Arab cavalry, or the far sweeping hurrah of the Cossacs of the Don; however often forced to retreat, they renewed the struggle again and again, with tenfold vigor. Though the middle of December was passed, the second year of the Pennymite and Yankee war had not terminated. On the 18th of that month, suddenly, without the slightest previous notice, a " Hurrah for King George !" started the sleeping garrison, too confidently secure even to keep a sentinel on duty, and Captain Lazarus Stewart with thirty men, took possession of the fort in behalf of the colony of Connecticut. Six of the garrison escaped nearly naked to the mountains; the others were as unceremoniously expelled as had been the previous Yankee tenants. The fugitives hastened to give information to Captain Ogden, who in the midst of festal enjoyment, and the sweetest of all adulation to the ambitious mind, that of plaudits to a victorious chief, was once more astounded with the heart-sickening annunciation, that his thrice conquered Wyoming was lost, and the audacious Yankees were again in full possession.

Thus closed 1770, an ever memorable year in our interesting annals.

LETTER XI.

1771.——Capt. Ogden with increased force returns—Summons Fort Durkee to surrender—Builds Fort Wyoming—Battle—Nathan Ogden mortally wounded—Fort Durkee abandoned—A reward offered for Capt Stewart—Fort Wyoming invested by Capt. Butler—The four-pounder brought into action—Pepperage Log Cannon—Remarkable feat of courage and conduct on the part of Capt. Ogden—He escapes to the City—Captains Dick, Morris, Clayton, Ledlie and Ogden, hasten with their companies to the relief of Fort Wyoming—Soldierly conduct of Capt. Butler—Ambush and victory—Captains Dick and Ogden, with loss of provisions, forced into the starving garrison—Fierce War—Ogden wounded—Redyard killed—Fort surrenders—Capitulation—The Pennsylvania troops withdrawn—Close of hostilities—Negotiation between the authorities of Connecticut and Pennsylvania.

OUR letter commences with the opening year, and we find ourselves at the beginning of 1771, in the midst of the Pennymite and Yankee war, already of two full years duration. At the close of 1770, we have recorded that Capt. Stewart and his followers descended like a whirlwind on the garrison left by Capt. Ogden, expelled them from the valley, and held undivided sway over Wyoming.

On learning the fact of the arrest and violent release of Stewart, together with his subsequent descent and victory upon the disputed lands, a new warrant was issued by Judge Willing for his apprehension, and a larger sum offered as a bounty for his capture and safe delivery in prison. Peter Hacklein, Esq., was now sheriff of Northampton, in place of Jennings, who has figured so conspicuously in our preceding pages, and with whom we cannot part without the proffer of our testimony to his merits as a vigilant and enterprising officer, who performed his whole duty as a faithful magistrate of Pennsylvania.

Capt. Amos Ogden was again placed at the head of the military, and acted as before, the undisputed leader of the expedition, although ostensibly under the direction of the civil magistrate: He was accompanied by a brother, Nathan Ogden. So far as we can learn, his first campaign, probably a young man whose ambition was aroused by the gathering laurels round his brother's brow; and he too would seek reputation in the stirring scenes of the Wyoming contest.

So vigorous had been the efforts on the part of the Proprietary Government, that in less than thirty days from the expulsion of the Pennsylvania party, although in the depth of winter, a force of more than one hundred men was displayed before Fort Durkee. But as a prudent officer, Ogden directed his first efforts to provide shelter and defence for his men. His old position at Mill Creek, was not only in ashes, but too far from his enemy. Such was his courage, he could not be brought too near them. Ground was broke and a fortification commenced on the bank of the river, sixty rods above Fort Durkee, at which his force wrought with such spirit, that in three or four days it was inhabitable. The baggage being secured, and a tolerable defence from a sudden attack prepared, Sheriff Hacklein, as civil officer, proceeded to Fort Durkee, declared his name and character, and demanded the surrender of the fortress, and all persons within it, in the name of the authorities of Pennsylvania. Capt. Stewart's men were all at their quarters, not intending to attack but ready to repel aggression; Stewart himself, with four or five trusty friends, stood on the battlements prepared to answer. To the summons he replied:—" That he had taken possession in the name and behalf of the Colony of Connecticut, in whose jurisdiction they were; and in that name, and by that authority he would defend it." Doubtless, the use of the name of Connecticut was unwarranted and improper; for so far, that colony was, officially, uncommitted in the civil war, although in fact almost all the members of the Government, in their individual capacity, were exerting their utmost influence to forward the interests of the Susquehanna Company, of which they were component parts, and shareholders. But the use of the name imparted consideration to the Yankee cause, and therefore it was boldly exercised.

Sheriff Hacklein withdrew, and every nerve was exerted to finish the defences of fort Wyoming,* (for so was the new fortress named,) and to prepare for a vigorous prosecution of the war.

On the 20th of January, 1771, Capt. Amos Ogden, drew out in armed array, and accompanied by his brother Nathan, marched

---

* The remains of this fort, directly opposite Mr. Butler's white house, were in tolerable preservation forty years ago, (1800,) but it has been swept away by the encroachment of the river on the bank.

forth to attempt the reduction of Fort Durkee. Stewart and his men were ready. Two more daring leaders never met. To part without a battle appeared improbable, and blood seemed destined again to flow in this unhappy contest. A peremptory demand was made for the surrender of the fort, and as peremptorily refused; when Ogden opened his fire, which was promptly returned. At the first volley, several of Ogden's men fell, and among the number, Nathan was mortally wounded by his side.* Of the deceased, we know nothing, except that he was brother to as gallant and noble a spirit as ever gained laurels or gathered cypress on the tented field. Amos, peradventure had persuaded him to leave his peaceful home, and engage in the expedition. In the bitterness of his grief, in the spirit, though not the words of David, we may conceive him exclaiming in pathetic strain:—"My brother,! oh, my brother! would to God I had died for thee." Little could our sympathies affect the survivor—less, could our regrets avail the dead; but every feeling breast will heave a sigh of pity for the living, and the eye shed a tear of unaffected sorrow for the fate of him who fell. It was the fortune of war. It was in fair open fight. He had chosen his lot. If his mother wept, so too wept many mothers for the loss of sons in this sharply contested conflict. Their bones rest together; they repose, side by side, on the lovely fields their valour sought to win.— Peace to their gallant shades!

Taking with them the lifeless body, and the three wounded men, the besieging party withdrew unmolested by the garrison, and slowly retraced their melancholy way to their own fortification.

Irritated as the Proprietary Government already was known to be against Capt. Stewart; exasperated as, from recent events, they would assuredly become, Capt. Stewart wisely thought, that a free foot on the mountains would be safer for him, and better for his friends, than confinement within the limits of a wooden fortress, however spiritedly defended. In the night following the battle, taking with him twenty or thirty trusty followers, he abandoned Fort Durkee, leaving about twenty persons, least obnoxious to the vengeance of the enemy. With the break of morning, his retreat was known to

---

* *From Hugh Gaines' New York Gazette, Nov. 11, 1771.*

"Philadelphia Nov. 4.—At the Supreme Court, held here on Tuesday last, William Speddy was arraigned and tried for the murder of Lieut. Nathan Ogden, who was shot from the block-house, at Wioming, while it was in the possession of Lazarus Stewart, and company; and after a long and impartial hearing, the jury soon gave in their verdict, 'NOT GUILTY.'"

Capt. Ogden, who, forthwith, took possession of the Fort, and, as was the invariable custom, sent the garrison to jail, at Easton; Sheriff Hacklein returning with them in charge. This, the reader will observe, was the fifth total expulsion of the Yankees.

An additional reward of three hundred pounds was now offered for the arrest of Stewart, and the Governor in his communication to the Assembly, represented the killing of Nathan Ogden, as a treacherous murder, demanding prompt and condign punishment.

Capt. Ogden now devoted himself assiduously to rendering Fort Wyoming impregnable, so far as his means would admit, to any force the Yankees could muster to assail it. February and March passed away without the slightest interruption, or even note of alarm. Too wary to be again so caught, Ogden this time, less assured that his conquest was safe, had remained with his men, to defend what they had purchased at, to him, a price so dear. It was well, though in vain, he did so, for early in April Capt. Zebulon Butler, with Capt. Stewart as an assistant, accompanied by an hundred and fifty armed men, entered the valley, and forthwith laid vigorous seige to Fort Wyoming. Three redoubts were thrown up, one on the opposite side of the river, chiefly with a view to cut off all access to water;—one on the river bank, between Forts Durkee and Wyoming; the other on the hill, known ever since as "The Redoubt," by the canal basin, at the upper part of the town of Wilkesbarre. The cannon, which had been carefully hid by the Yankees, too precious to be exposed to capture by a sortie, was placed on this elevation, and with skilful gunners, would have completely commanded Ogden's position. But distance and want of skill rendered it in a very slight degree effective.

Among the new body of emigrants, were two of the *Gore* family, from Norwich, (whose names will fill a bright and a bloody page in our subsequent annals.) Obadiah Gore, Esq., the father, and Daniel Gore his son, blacksmiths by trade, full of ardour, and replete with Yankee ingenuity. They conceived the design of adding to the ordnance, a new cannon. A large pepperage* log was fashioned, bored, and then hooped from breach to muzzle with stout bands of iron.— Painted black, with a red mouth, and mounted on a wagon;—its appearance at least was sufficiently formidable. The first discharge excited at once admiration and hope among its friends. Re-loaded,

---

* Presumed to be the *Nyssa-Sylvatica*, the Upland Tupelo-Tree—or Sour Gum of Marshall.

a heavier charge was driven home that a corresponding execution might be produced,—the cannon split, and so terrible was the explosion that one of the iron bands, thrown a thousand feet across the Susquehanna, was afterwards found in the willows on the river shore.

To courage no way inferior to that of Ogden, the Connecticut party, in Capt. Butler, had a commander, skilled in the arts of war by long service, and so thorough was the investment, and so closely pressed, that not a man could venture out for food, fuel, or water, without being met by a volley from one of the redoubts. The garrison, containing nearly an hundred souls, soon felt the pressure of actual want, (for all were placed on short allowance,) and the dread of approaching famine. Husbanding his resources however, in the most prudent manner, and in the darkness and stillness of night bringing up from the river sufficient water to last through the day, Ogden determined to hold out to the last extremity. But without aid, time must exhaust his provisions, and then to surrender would be inevitable. The descent of Capt. Butler had been made with such secrecy and celerity that not the slightest notice of his approach had been received, and instantly the fort had been so completely surrounded, no messenger could be despatched to the Proprietary Government, which was entirely ignorant of the recent events which had transpired at Wyoming, and the relief demanded by the critical state of the garrison. To convey intelligence to head quarters opened the only avenue of hope, and Ogden, as the achievement demanded the utmost boldness, promptitude and wisdom, determined to be himself the messenger. The deed alone was sufficient to immortalize any man, and stamp his name with the title of hero. A little past midnight on the 12th of July, when all was quiet, one of the Yankee sentinels saw something floating on the river having a very suspicious appearance. A shot awakened attention, and directed the eyes of every other sentinel to the spot. A volley was poured in, but producing no apparent effect; the thing still floating gently with the current the firing was suspended, while the "wonder grew" what the object could be. Capt. Ogden had tied his clothes in a bundle, and fastened his hat to the top; to this was connected a string of several yards in length which he fastened to his arm. Letting himself noiselessly into the water, swimming on his back so deeply as only to allow his lips to breathe—the whole movement demanding the most extraordinary skill and self possession, he floated down, drawing the bundle after him. As he had calculated, this being the only object apparent, drew the fire of his foes. He escaped unhurt, and when out of danger dressed himself in his drenched clothing and hat, perforated with bullets, and with the speed of the roebuck was in the city on the third day, having accomplished one hundred and twenty miles through a most rough and inhospitable wilderness. The services of that man, we are sure, have never been justly appreciated, and we fear have not been fairly rewarded.

Instantly the whole city was in commotion. Three hundred pounds were drawn from the public treasury to raise recruits. Captain Dick was hastened forward, Ogden in company, with a strong convoy of provisions. Captain Morris and his company was directed to follow with the least possible delay. Colonel Asher Clayton, a veteran of the French war, who was to have the chief command, (nominally, we presume, for it cannot be imagined Ogden would be superseded,) was ordered with a strong force to hasten his march. Captain Ledlie was put in requisition to follow with as much expedition as circumstances would admit.

In the meantime, while this apparently overpowering storm was gathering for his destruction, Captain Butler pushed on the siege, and with true Yankee providence, directed that at the same time the labors of the field should not be intermitted; and the flats, though with imperfect cultivation, from their extreme fertility, presented a waving sea of luxuriant Indian corn, and other summer fruits, a valuable possession or prize, as either party should be ultimately victorious.

Hurrying forward with about thirty men, and a number of pack-horses, loaded with ammunition and provisions, Captain Dick, on the last of July, descended into the valley. Nothing escaped the vigilance or sagacity of Captain Butler. Ogden's escape was soon known, and his speedy return with aid was not for a moment doubted. Sentinels were placed in proper positions to detect the approach of a hostile party. Every movement of Captain Dick was carefully watched. An ambush was laid in the most promising ground near the fort. Taking life so far from being desired, was sincerely deprecated, but to secure the provisions was an object of the first importance, and if the escort could be thrown into the fort, to help eat up the scanty remnant that was left, the garrison must so much the sooner capitulate; besides it was far better to have the enemy cooped up in the fortress, than free to make attacks on the rear. A volley from opposite coverts, a huzza, and a rush forward of the Yankees, had the desired effect. Captains Dick and

Ogden, with about twenty of their men, found refuge in the fort, while their pack-horses, and most of their loading, became a prize to Captain Butler, who had the satisfaction of seeing his well laid plan succeed to his utmost wishes.*

When the sad news of the discomfiture of Captain Dick reached Philadelphia, men were seen running in every direction in "hot haste." Another three hundred pounds were drawn from the treasury. New recruits were put in requisition. Ledlie was hurried on to overtake Clayton and Morris, and the greatest consternation reigned among the friends of the Proprietary Government. Not so the people. With few exceptions, those who had no direct interest in the lands, began to look on, at least with indifference, and many with favor to the Connecticut party. To this cause was to be ascribed the extreme difficulty of raising a sufficient force at once, to put an end to the contest.

The siege was now pushed with redoubled vigor; Colonel Clayton, with strong re-inforcements being expected, every hour's delay was pregnant with danger, that the chief objects of the campaign, on the point of being clutched, would be snatched from his grasp. To starve out the garrison without bloodshed, had been the humane purpose of Captain Butler, but more efficient action, in his estimate of duty, had become requisite. Blood began to flow. Several of the garrison were wounded. The gallant Ogden received a rifle ball in his left arm near the shoulder, and nearly fainting, reposed on the breast of Lieut. William Redyard, when a bullet struck the latter, and he fell lifeless upon the ground. A negotiation entered into on the 14th of August, was soon concluded by articles of capitulation,

*From Hugh Gaine's New York Gazette, August 12, 1771.

"Philadelphia, August 8.—The report of a party of men being cut off, who were despatched from Northampton county, with provisions for our people in the Block House at Wyoming, who are besieged by the Connecticut party, appears by the following extract of a letter, which came to town on the 6th, by express from the person who commanded the convoy, to be without foundation :—

"Wyoming, August 1, 1771.

Last Tuesday about break of day, I arrived at this place with 31 men and the provisions, and was attacked by the Connecticut party, who had information of our coming, by a letter falling into their hands with which an Indian was sent by Captain Ogden. We were surrounded by their fire, and lost two horse loads of our flour, and got in with the remainder and twenty-two men, two of whom are wounded. Nine of our men are missing; whether they retreated, or are killed, I cannot as yet give information. They have kept an almost continued fire on the Block House ever since from four entrenchments; but we are determined to hold out to the last extremity. I am Sir, your humble servant,

JOHN DICK."

by which the fort was surrendered. Colonel Clayton, Captains Dick and Morris, with Captain Ogden, and all the Pennsylvania troops, were forthwith to withdraw from Wyoming. Mr. Gordon states the terms of capitulation to have been, "That twenty-three men might leave the fort armed, and with the remainder unarmed, might proceed unmolested to their respective habitations; that the men having families might abide on the debateable land for two weeks, and might remove their effects without interruption, and that the sick and wounded might retain their nurses, and have leave to send for a physician." Signed on behalf of the Yankees by

ZEBULON BUTLER,
LAZARUS STEWART,
JOHN SMITH,

On the part of the Proprietary Government by

ASHER CLAYTON,
JOSEPH MORRIS,
JOHN DICK.

An anecdote is mentioned by Gordon so characteristic of the chivalry of Captain Butler, that we cannot doubt its correctness. That he offered to determine the rights of the respective claimants by a contest of thirty men to be selected by each party. Had not Amos Ogden been wounded, his spirit would have bounded with joy to the contest.* Captain Ledlie, who was on his march, met the retiring array of his discomfited friends, from whom he received an accession of eight or ten men, best acquainted with the valley, to act as guides, and as he was not included in the capitulation, continued his advance and took up a position on the mountain, intending to remain until he should receive orders to retreat, or a powerful reinforcement should be sent to his support. In the meantime he guarded the passes most frequented by the emigrating Yankees, who apprised of his position, evaded his sentinels, and every day added to the number of the Connecticut settlers. This great victory, achieved over a superior force with a sacrifice, comparatively so inconsiderable, established entire confidence in the ultimate success of the Yankee cause; and Captain Butler was hailed as the saviour of

---

* William Redyard was laid by the side of Nathan Ogden, who had been interred in what is now the street below the house of Colonel Welles, near the corner. Could their bones be found, or should they by accident be discovered, most certainly they should be removed to the burying place, and decently buried, with a stone and inscription to mark the spot.

Wyoming. His name was now a host, and multitudes flocked to the valley under protection of his standard.

Foiled in every attempt to establish a post on the disputed lands; becoming, daily, more and more unpopular as the difficulties with Great Britain and the colonies increased, the Proprietary Government ordered the return of Capt. Ledlie, and left the Susquehanna Company in undisturbed possession of the ground, who forthwith proceeded with all practicable celerity to increase their settlements, and consolidate their power.

Thus closes the first Pennymite and Yankee war. Commencing in January, 1769, it had continued, with what variety of incident, and alternation of success, the reader is apprised, to Sept. 1771—a period of nearly three years.

Judging, and probably not without truth, from the boldness and confidence of the proceedings of the intruding Yankees, that they were encouraged and sustained by the Government of Connecticut, Mr. Hamilton, President of Council, on abandoning all military demonstrations, opened a correspondence with Gov. Trumbull, upon the subject. In a letter, dated October 4, 1771, after detailing the events that had transpired at Susquehanna, he proceeds:—

"As the people concerned in these violent and hostile measures, profess to act under the authority of your Government, and have made a capitulation expressly on behalf of the Government, I have thought it proper and expedient to send a messenger to your Honour, on purpose to know, with certainty, whether they have proceeded in any sort under your countenance or authority, or that of your Assembly, and as this must be a matter within your knowledge, I make no doubt but you will despatch the express with a speedy answer."

In reply, Gov. Trumbull thus cautiously and ingeniously expresses himself.

"New Haven, Oct. 14, 1771.

"The persons concerned in those transactions have no order and direction from me, or from the General Assembly of the colony, for their proceeding upon this occasion, and I am very confident that the General Assembly, friends as they ever have been to peace and good order, will never countenance any violent, much less hostile measures, in vindicating the right which the Susquehanna Company suppose they have to the lands in that part of the country within the limits of the Charter of this colony."

The reader will, particularly, note the concluding line, in which the assumption is absolute, that the part of the "country is within the limits of the Charter of Connecticut." Such an official declaration at the time was well calculated to encourage new emigrations, and strengthen the hands of the settlers.

Governor Trumbull then proceeds to say, that each of the contending parties, it is understood, charge on the other the commencement of violence, of which he was not a proper judge. Here for the present, negotiations ended, to be renewed as will appear, a few years after, at a more propitious period.

LETTER XII.

1772-3.——List of Settlers—First white women in Wyoming—Stockade at Mill Creek, on the Ruins of Fort Ogden—Young Hollenback—Furniture—Mode of Living—Fifty miles to Mill—Indians—First Marriage in Wyoming—Doings of Committee—Famine—John Carey—Interesting Expedition—A Wedding, and the benevolent Scotchman—Sickness——First Mills—David Meade—Wilkesbarre—Ferries—Settlement of first Gospel Minister—Rev. Jacob Johnson—Toleration—Rev. Mr. Gray—Rev. Elkanah Holmes—Free Schools—Military organization—Prohibition of selling Liquor to Indians—Shares, and Half Share Rights—Constitution of Government, voluntarily established—Physicians—Vote of Connecticut Assembly—Renewed Negotiations.

In entering upon 1772, the fourth year of the permanent settlement by the Connecticut people upon the Susquehanna, we find the aspect of affairs essentially changed. The stern alarms of war were succeeded by the sweet songs of peace. Availing ourselves of the leisure afforded, we enter on a variety of civil and social details necessary to a perfect knowledge of the early history of Wyoming. So similar was the current of life, and so interwoven the events, that in this letter, we purpose to include a view of the two years, 1772 and '73, this period of time intervening between the close of the war with the Proprietaries, and the official recognition of the settlement by Connecticut, and the formal establishment of her jurisdiction west of the Delaware.

While some may turn away from a mere column of names; others, curious in such things may be pleased to see a list of the two hundred first enrolled as actual settlers to "man their rights" in the five allotted townships. The roll bears date June 2d, 1769. Especially will many of the grand children, or those of the fourth generation, look anxiously for the names of their progenitors. A few, after the first sharp collision, did not return, and their places were supplied by others. Several fell in the unhappy conflict, more in the revolutionary war; but we recognise in the list, a considerable number, whom time and war had spared, as the kindliest friends of our early manhood.

A more brave, hardy, and enterprising set of men never encountered danger in the field; or gave their stalwart arms to the settlement of a wilderness. Though perhaps an hundred others were concerned, from time to time, in the warlike scenes we have detailed, those, here recounted, it is believed, bore the chief brunt of the contest. At no time, until 1772, were there more than one hundred and thirty men on the ground at once, some being on the way out, and others returning home. As there was no mode of enforcing discipline, the association being voluntary, each man acted as prompted by his own sense of interest and propriety.

☞ Those names having a star [*] affixed to them, were of the Forty, or first settlers in Kingston.

David Whittlesey,
Job Green,
Philip Goss,
Joshua Whitney,
Abraham Savage,
Ebenezer Stearns,
Sylvester Chesebrough,
Zephaniah Thayer,
Eliphalet Jewel,
Daniel Gore,
Ozias Yale,
Henry Wall,*
Rowland Barton,
Gideon Lawrence,
Asa Lawrence,
Nathaniel Watson,
Philip Weeks,
Thomas Weeks,
Asher Harrot,
Ebenezer Hebbard,
Morgan Carvan,
Samuel Marvin,
Silas Gore,
Ebenezer Northrop,
Joshua Lampher,

Joseph Hillman,
Abel Pierce,
Jabez Roberts,
Jonathan Carrington,
John Dorrance,
Noah Allen,
Robert Jackson,
Zebulon Hawksey,
James Dunkin,
Caleb Tennant,
Zerobable Wightman,
Gurdon Hopson,
Asa Lee.
Thomas Wallworth,
Robert Hunter,
John Baker,
Jonathan Orms,
Daniel Angel,
Elias Roberts,
Nicholas Manvil,
Thomas Gray,
Joseph Gaylord,
Wm. Churchell,
Henry Strong,
Zebulon Frisbee,

Hezekiah Knap,
John Kenyon,
Preserved Taylor,
Isaac Bennett,
Uriah Marvin,
Abisha Bingham,
Moses Hebbard, Jr.
Jabez Fish,
Peris Briggs,
Aaron Walter,
James May,
Samuel Badger,
Jabez Cooke,
Samuel Dorrance,
John Comstock,*
Samuel Hotchkiss,
Wm. Leonard,
Jesse Leonard,
Elisha Avery,
Ezra Buel,
Gershom Hewit,
Nathaniel Goss,
Benjamin Hewit,
Benj. Hewit, Jr.,
Elias Thomas,
Abijah Mock,
Ephraim Fellows,
Joseph Arnold,
Ephraim Arnold,
Benjamin Ashley,
Wm. White,
Stephen Hull,
Diah Hull,
Joseph Lee,
Samuel Wybrant,
Reuben Hurlbut,
Jenks Corah,
Obadiah Gore, Jr.,
Caleb White,
Samuel Sweet,
Thomas Knight,

John Jollee,
Ebenezer Norton,
Enos Yale,
John Wiley,
Timothy Vorce,
Cyrus Kenne,
John Shaw,
James Forsythe,
Peter Harris,*
Abel Smith,
Elias Parks,
Joshua Maxfield,
John Murphy,
Thomas Bennet,*
Christopher Avery,
Elisha Babcock,
John Perkins,
Joseph Slocum,
Robert Hopkins,
Benjamin Shoemaker, Jr.,
Jabez Sill,
Parshall Terry,
John Delong,
Theophilus Westover,*
John Sterling,
Joseph Morse,
Stephen Fuller,
Andrew Durkee,
Andrew Medcalf,
Daniel Brown,
Jonathan Buck,
David Mead,
Thomas Ferlin,
Wm. Wallsworth,
Thomas Draper,
James Smith,
James Atherton, Jr.,*
Oliver Smith,*
James Evans,
Eleazer Carey,
Cyprian Lothrop,*

James Nesbitt,
Joseph Webster,
Samuel Millington,
Benjamin Budd,
John Lee,
Josiah Dean,
Zophur Teed,
Moses Hebbard,
Dan Murdock,
Noah Lee,
Stephen Lee,
Daniel Haynes,
Lemuel Smith,
Silas Park,
Stephen Hungerford,
Zerobable Jeorum,*
Comfort Goss,
Wm. Draper,
Thomas McClure,
Peter Ayers.
Solomon Johnson,
Phineas Stevens,
Abraham Colt,
Elijah Buck,*
Noah Read,
Nathan Beach,
Job Green, Jr.,
Fred. Wise,
Stephen Jenkins,
Daniel Marvin,
Zachariah Squier,
Henry Wall,

Simeon Draper,*
John Wallsworth,
Ebenezer Stone,
Thomas Olcott,
Stephen Hinsdale,
Benjamin Dorchester,
Elijah Witter,
Oliver Post,
Daniel Cass,
Isaac Tracy,
Samuel Story,
John Mitchel,
Samuel Orton,
Christopher Gardner,
Duty Gerold,
Peris Bradford,
Samuel Morgan.
John Clark,
Elijah Lewis,
Timothy Hopkins,
Edward Johnson,
Jacob Dingman,
Capt. Prince Alden,
Benedict Satterlee,*
Naniad Coleman,
Peter Comstock,
John Franklin,
Benjamin Matthews,
Jno. Durkee,
Wm. Gallop,
Stephen Hurlbut,
Stephen Miles.

Very few of the settlers had yet brought out their families; and in May, 1772, there were only five white women in Wilkesbarre:— Mrs. McClure, wife of James McClure; Mrs. Bennett, grandmother of Rufus Bennett, (who was in the Indian battle); Mrs. Sill, wife of Jabez Sill; another Mrs. Bennett, wife of Thomas Bennett, mother of Mrs. Myers, now living in Kingston, (to whose clear mind and retentive memory, we are indebted for most valuable information;) and Mrs. Hickman, with her husband; Mrs. Dr. Sprague, and her daughter, afterwards Mrs. Young. The second white child born in Wilkesbarre was a daughter of Mrs. McClure.

With increasing numbers, and prudent apprehensions of danger, more extensive stockades were thought necessary for protection, and the admirable position at Mill Creek, the ruins of Fort Ogden, was resumed, placed in the best condition, and made head-quarters of the chief men on the east side of the river.

Let us look in upon them. Huts were built all around the inside, against the wall, of upright timbers. They were one story high; several were divided into a number of small, but neat and comfortable rooms. The huts of Capt. Butler and Nathan Denison, adjoined each other. Next in the row was the store of Matthias Hollenback. He had brought up from Lancaster county a variety of indispensable articles. Denison and Hollenback, then young men, the latter twenty, the former twenty-three! Having seen, near forty years afterwards, their venerable forms wrapped in their cloaks, one on the right and the other on the left, as Associate Judges of Pennsylvania, his Hon. Judge Rush, presiding, we could not repress an allusion to the contrast.—The next in order, the largest building in the stockade, was a boarding house kept by Dr. Joseph Sprague. Neither a chair nor table, nor bedstead, except the rude construction of an auger and axe, was yet in the settlement. A samp mortar, that is a large stump, hollowed eight or ten inches by burning, the pestle worked by a spring pole, pounded corn, wheat, and rye, for bread; and this was their only mill. "Venison and shad," said the good Mrs. Young, "were plenty; but salt was a treasure."—Dr. Sprague would load his horse with wheat, and go out by the bridle path, for as yet there was no road, to the Delaware at Coshutunk, have his grist ground, get a few spices, and a runlet of Antigua rum. The cakes baked from the flour, and the liquor, were kept as dainties for some special occasion, or when emigrants of note came in from Connecticut.

The venerable and esteemed John Carey, who has given his name to Carey town is the only survivor of this interesting collection of early settlers. [He died, 1844.]

After the massacre of 1763, the Indians generally left the valley, but a number had returned, not as a tribe, but the scattered remnants of tribes, chiefly of those who had been partially christianized by the Moravians; though from subsequent events it is not doubted that spies of the Six Nations were kept among them, and reported from time to time the condition of the settlement, to the Council at

Onondago.—A small number, friendly, and good neighbors, lived on the flats half a mile above Mill creek, and frequently visited the stockade. Among them were Capt. Job Gillaway, Black Henry, and John Lystrum. The wife of Capt. Gillaway seemed pious and well disposed. From the Moravians she had derived the name of Comfort, and the knowledge to knit and to sew. The men were excellent hunters and supplied the fort with game.

The first marriage in Wyoming was that of Mr. Nathan, afterwards Col. Denison, and Miss Sill. The Rev. Jacob Johnson was the officiating minister, and the place where the knot was tied, and the nuptials celebrated, was a house on the spot now occupied by the mansion of the late Col. Welles, at the lower corner, on River street, of the Wilkesbarre town plot.

From the stockade the people, breakfasting early, taking with them a luncheon, went forth armed to their daily labour. The view here presented, with slight variations, was exhibited in four or five different places in the valley. Stockades, or block-houses were built in Hanover, and Plymouth. The celebrated Forty Fort in Kingston was occupied. Many returned to the east for their families, and new settlers came in. It was a season rather of activity than labour; moving and removing, surveying, drawing lots for land rights, preparing for building; hastily clearing up patches to sow with winter grain; the sad consequence of which was, the harvests of autumn were not sufficient for the considerably augmented number of inhabitants. Until the conclusion of 1772 very little of the forms of law, or the regulations of civil government had been introduced or required. Town Committees exercised the power of deciding on contested land rights.

Thus:—" Doings of the Committee May 22, 1772.

" That Rosewell Franklin have that right in Wilkesbarre, drawn by Thomas Stevens.

" That James Bidlack have that right in Plymouth, drawn by Nathaniel Drake.

" That Mr. McDowell be voted into the Forty town, (Kingston.)

" That for the special services done this Company by Col. Dyer, agreed that his son, Thomas Dyer, shall have a right in the Forty, if he has a man on it by the first day of August next.

" That the rights that are sold in the six mile township, or Capouse, shall be sold at sixty dollars each, and bonds taken;" etc.

It may be regarded as a transition year, full of undefined pleasure, flowing from the newness and freshness of the scene—a comparative sense of security—the exultation from having come off victorious—the influx of old neighbours from Connecticut, who must listen to the adventures and hair-breadth escapes of the narrator, an older settler by eighteen months than his hearer. Then the beautiful valley must be shown to the new come inquisitive wives and daughters, who had been told so much of its surpassing loveliness. The year passed without justice or lawyer—judge or sheriff—dun or constable—civil suit or crime; and from the representations of the old people, may be considered as a season of wild, joyous, almost unalloyed happiness.

The month of February, 1773, had so nearly exhausted the provisions of the Wilkesbarre settlement, that five persons were selected to go to the Delaware, near Stroudsburg, for supplies. Mr. John Carey, (an excellent soldier, a most worthy citizen, whom we shall again have pleasure to mention,) then a lad of sixteen, volunteered as one of the party. The distance was fifty miles through the wilderness; numerous streams, including the deep and rapid Lehigh were to be crossed. Had these been frozen over so as to be passable, their toils would have been sensibly mitigated, but the ice had formed on each side, many feet from the shore, leaving in the centre a deep rushing flood. Stripping naked, tying their clothes and sacks on their heads and shoulders, cutting a way through the ice from the shore to the stream, and from the stream to the opposite shore, they waded through, dressed themselves, and found warmth in marching rapidly. Arrived at the good old Scotchman's, and sending in to make known their errand, Mr. McDowell came out, rubbing his hands in great glee, bade them welcome, but in his Scotch dialect, broad as his benevolence, told them he had a house thronged with company, on the occasion of his daughter's wedding. Among the guests were magistrates and others, whose enmity was to be dreaded, if they knew a party of Yankees were within reach; but gave directions that they should warm themselves noiselessly at an out-house, then take shelter in the barn, where comfortable blankets were spread on the mow, a most royal supper sent them, with spirits and wine; their sacks were filled with flour, and their pockets with provisions. The four men took each an hundred pounds, young Carey seventy-five, and welcome was their return to their half-famished friends at Wilkesbarre. Never was an opening Spring, or the coming of the shad, looked for with more anxiety, or hailed with more cordial delight. The fishing season of course, dissipated all fears, and the dim eye was soon exchanged for the glance of joy and the sparkle of pleasure, and the dry, sunken cheek of want assumed the plump appearance of health and plenty.

The Spring too was attended with sickness. Several deaths took place. Captain Butler buried a son named Zebulon; and soon after, his wife followed her boy to the grave. Both were interred on the hill, near where the upper street of the borough is cut through the rocks, as it passes from the main street to the canal basin. This picture of the early settlement, simple in its details, we could not doubt would be agreeable to numbers now living, and not less so to readers in future years, when the valley shall become, as it is destined to be, rich and populous, not surpassed, if equalled in the Union.

Among the first objects of general interest was the erection of a grist-mill. This was undertaken by Nathan Chapman, to whom a grant was made of the site, where Hollenback's old mill now stands, near the stone bridge, on the road from Wilkesbarre to Pittston. Forty acres of land were part of the donation. Mr. Hollenback brought the mill-irons in his boat from Wright's ferry, and the voyage was rendered memorable by the loss of Lazarus Young, a valuable young man, who was drowned on the way up.

Immediately afterwards, the town voted: "To give unto Captain Stephen Fuller, Obadiah Gore, jr., and Mr. Seth Marvin, all the privileges of the stream called Mill Creek, below Mr. Chapman's mill, to be their own property, with full liberty of building mills, and flowing a pond, but so as not to obstruct or hinder Chapman's mills: Provided, they will have a saw-mill, ready to go by the 1st day of November, 1773, which gift shall be to them, their heirs and assigns, forever." And this was the first saw-mill erected on the upper waters of the Susquehanna.

The township of Wilkesbarre had been surveyed in 1770, by David Meade, and received its name from John Wilkes and Colonel Barre, members of Parliament, and distinguished advocates for liberty, and the rights of the Colonies. "Wilkes and Liberty— North Britain—45," was then heard from every tongue. A final division was now made of the back lots among the proprietors. The town plot, now the borough, was laid out by a liberal forecast, on a very handsome scale. On a high flat, on the east bank of the Susquehanna, above all fear of inundation, the position was chosen. Two hundred acres were divided into eight squares of twenty-five acres, and these into six lots each, containing, after the streets were taken off, about three and three quarters of an acre. A spacious central square was allotted for public buildings. The main avenue, perfectly straight for two miles, passing through the town plot from north-east to south-west, was cut at right angles by five streets. On the bank of the river a wide space was left, still beautiful, though much diminished by the ice and floods of the stream.

Two ferries were kept, one opposite Northampton street, the other at Mill Creek; and from these a revenue of some moment in those early times, was derived. From twenty-five dollars a year, the rent of the lower ferry soon rose to sixty dollars; that at Mill Creek yielding half that sum, until discontinued on the erection of mills in Kingston.

Mills and ferries having been provided, with true Pilgrim zeal, attention was immediately turned to the subject of a gospel ministry, and the establishment of schools.

"At a town meeting, December 11, 1772, Captain Stephen Fuller was appointed moderator. Voted, to give and grant, unto the Rev. Jacob Johnson, and his heirs and assigns forever, in case he settle in this town, as a gospel minister, fifty acres of land, &c."

In August following, feeling themselves more able, or more liberal (for the time it was munificent) provision was made.

"At a town meeting held at Wilkesbarre, August 23, 1773, Mr. Jacob Sill, chosen moderator, Joseph Sluman, clerk.

Voted, That a call or invitation, shall be given to the Rev. Jacob Johnson, late of Groton, in the colony of Connecticut, who for some time past has been preaching in this place, to continue a settler with us as our gospel minister.

2d. That Mr. Johnson shall be paid sixty pounds the year ensuing, on the present list, and his salary shall rise annually, as our list rises, till it amounts to one hundred pounds, etc." (Connecticut currency, six shillings to the dollar, or $333 1-3.)

In laying out the town originally, two lots containing about four hundred acres of back lands, had been set off for the first settled minister, and for schools. One of those lots, and the fifty acres above mentioned, together with a town lot of four acres, will show the liberal provision made for gospel purposes.

Mr. Johnson, a Presbyterian clergyman, was a graduate of Yale College, and was the grandfather of Ovid F. Johnson, Esq., the present (1842) Attorney General of Pennsylvania. Some highly interesting additional particulars of this eminent man, ("that wicked priest of Canojoharie") will be found in another page.

It is but just to observe, that amidst this zeal, there prevailed the most amiable spirit of toleration. Finding that a number of the inhabitants were Baptists, and attended the ministrations of Mr. Gray, at Kingston, the vote was rescinded which demanded a tax from them, and a different, but satisfactory arrangement made with their minister.

At a subsequent period, during the temporary absence of Mr. Johnson, the Rev. Elkanah Holmes officiated, preaching in Plymouth, Kingston and Wilkesbarre.

A vote was also passed, "To raise three pence on the pound, on the district list, to keep a free school in the several school districts in the said Wilkesbarre." A subsequent meeting specially warned, adopted measures for the keeping open free schools, one in the upper district, one in the lower, and a third on the town plot.

These votes, thus early in the settlement, passed in the midst of poverty and danger, may be referred to by the descendants of those pilgrim fathers, with honest pride. They will remain to all enduring time, monuments of religious zeal, and their earnest desire to advance the intellectual and moral condition of their children.

Military organization was not neglected. Following the order then existing in New England, discipline was enforced as indispensable to the existence of the settlement. In each township a company was enrolled, and led to the choice of officers; and in Wilkesbarre, from its being divided by natural boundaries into two sections, and its more rapid increase of inhabitants, at an early day two companies were formed. If the splendid uniform, the glittering bayonet, the evolution, rapid and precise, with the imposing band of many instruments of music, did not grace their trainings, there was yet upon the ground the strong-banded old French musket, the long duck shooting piece, and more efficient than either, the close-drawing rifle, little known in New England, but becoming familiar among the settlers on the Susquehanna. At a moment when it has become popular to deride the militia, I deem it proper to say, in defence of a thorough, and never relaxing organization and discipline, that in my opinion America owes her Independence to immediate and remote causes connected with the militia system, the enrollment and training existing in the colonies: and that Pennsylvania cannot too seduously encourage and preserve that right arm of her power, never forgetting, or encroaching upon, what should be deemed the sacred rights of persons conscientiously scrupulous of bearing arms.

Among the earliest resolutions adopted by the settlers, was one which has been, I think unjustly, censured as severe.

Any person selling liquor to an Indian was to forfeit his goods, and be expelled the colony. In justification of this seemingly harsh enactment, it may be observed:—That the massacre of 1763 had been ascribed to the Indians being intoxicated; and fears existed that under, to the Indians, the phrenzying influence of rum, another massacre might be attempted; or what was more immediately probable, that individual murders would be committed—retaliation follow, and the settlement be brought into hostile collision with the Six Nations, whose subjects the scattered Indians in the valley were. Penalties too severe, if effectual, could not be imposed, to avert so fatal a mischief.

Rights—shares—and half shares, being frequently mentioned in the ancient proceedings of the Susquehanna and Delaware purchases, or companies, it seems proper that they should be explained more fully. Those purchases of a degree of latitude, and two in longitude would give nearly five millions of acres.—The shares issued by the Susquehanna Company, increased from eight hundred and fifty, to twelve hundred and forty, several, perhaps an hundred, being granted for services rendered. A considerable number of half shares were given out, as many poor persons wished an interest in the purchase, whom, of course it was politic to oblige, and who did not feel able to buy a whole right. As dictated by prudence, only two thousand acres were allowed to be surveyed on a whole share, and one thousand on a half share, the balance being deferred until all the shares should have a chance of location.

Prices of whole shares varied from fifty to one hundred dollars. In a deed from Palmer Avery, dated March 7, 1767, the consideration is set down as thirty pounds. Another deed of subsequent date contains a consideration of twenty pounds. The last sales by the company, previous to the Trenton decree, were at fifteen pounds ten shillings. Like other stocks, the price varied with the varying prospects of the company.

Townships of six miles square, generally, were surveyed in the Delaware purchase, extending from the Delaware to within ten miles of the Susquehanna. The Susquehanna purchase was laid out, generally, in townships of five miles square.

To preserve order, and prevent interfering claims, a wise system was early adopted, and rigidly enforced. A land office was established—rights, full, or half shares, being produced to the amount of sixteen thousand acres, a survey by an appointed officer was made of the township, a patent, or grant issued and recorded, the shares being received and cancelled. For several years John Jenkins was surveyor general; and Joseph Biles his deputy ran more lines than any other surveyor in the purchase.

As the colony could not well subsist, with its greatly increasing population, and diversified interests, without a code of laws to govern them, and it did not yet accord with the cautious policy of Connecticut to avouch their proceedings, and extend her jurisdiction beyond the Delaware: a meeting of the Susquehanna Company, held at Hartford, June 2, 1773, adopted for the government of the settlement the following articles, in every aspect important: honourable to the pen that drew, and the people who accepted them.

"'1. *Whereas,* we the subscribers inhabitants of Connecticut in New England, in America, already settled, and about to settle on certain lands on the river Susquehanna in said Connecticut, by us and our associates sometime since purchased of the original natives, by, and with the consent of the said Colony of Connecticut.

And whereas, the same lands are claimed to be within the jurisdiction of the Province of Pennsylvania; and the Colony of Connecticut choosing to proceed with caution and deliberation, have applied to counsel learned in the law, in Great Britain, for their advice, which at present the colony have not received, by reason whereof we have as yet no established civil authority residing among us in said settlement, in consequence of which deficiency, disorders may arise tending to disturb the peace and happiness of the settlers, as well as the peace of our Sovereign Lord—the king, which to remedy, we have this day come into the following heads, or articles of agreement, with each other.

1st. We do solemnly profess and declare true and sincere allegiance to his Majesty, King George the Third, and that no foreign prince, person, prelate, state or potentate, hath, or ought to have any jurisdiction, power, or authority, ecclesiastical or spiritual, within the realm of England.

2d. We do solemnly promise and engage, that we will, so far as lieth in our power, behave ourselves peaceably, soberly and orderly towards each other, in particular, and the world in general, carefully observing and obeying the laws of this colony, as binding and of force with us equally in all respects, as though we actually resided within any of the counties of this colony.

3d. For the due enforcing such laws, as well as such other orders and regulations as shall, from time to time, be found necessary to be come into by said settlers and Company, we will immediately within each town, already settled, and immediately after the settlement of those that may be hereafter settled, choose three able and judicious men among such settlers, to take upon them, under the general direction of the Company, the direction of the settlement of each such town, and the well ordering and governing the same, to suppress vice of every kind, preserve the peace of God and the King therein, to whom each inhabitant shall pay such, and the same submission as is paid to the civil authority in the several towns in this colony; such inhabitants shall also choose, in each of their respective towns, one person of trust to be their officer, who shall be vested with the same power and authority, as a constable, by the laws of this colony is, for preserving the peace and apprehending offenders of a criminal or civil nature.

4th. The Directors in each town shall, on the first Monday of each month, and oftener, if need be, with such their peace officers, meet together, as well to consult for the good regulating thereof, as to hear and decide any differences that may arise, and to inflict proper fine or other punishment on offenders, according to the general laws and rules of this colony, so far as the peculiar situation and circumstances of such town and plantation will admit of; and as the reformation of offenders is the principal object in view, always preferring serious admonition and advice to them, and their making public satisfaction, by public acknowledgment of their fault, and doing such public service to the plantation, as the Directors shall judge meet, to fines in money, or corporal punishment, which, however, in extreme cases, such Directors shall inflict, as said laws direct.

5th. The Directors of each individual town or plantation, shall, once every quarter, or three months, meet together to confer with each other on the state of each particular town in said settlement, and to come into such resolutions concerning them as they shall find for their best good, as also to hear the complaints of any that shall judge themselves aggrieved by the decision of their Directors in their several towns, who shall have right to appeal to such quarterly meeting.

6th. No one convicted of sudden and violent breach of the peace, of swearing, drunkenness, stealing, gaming, fraud, idleness, and the like, before the Directors of the particular town in which he lives, shall have liberty of appeal to such quarterly meeting, from the sentence of such particular Directors, without first procuring good security, to the satisfaction of such Directors, for his orderly and sober behaviour until such meeting, and for his submitting to and complying with the sentence of such meeting.—No one, in matters of private property, shall have liberty of appeal from such particular Directors, to such quarterly general meeting of Directors, where the controversy is not more than twenty shillings.

7th. Such quarterly meeting of Directors, shall appoint an officer, statedly, to attend them as their clerk, who shall carefully register their proceedings, also an officer in the character of general peace officer, or Sheriff, who also shall attend them, and to whom the inhabitants of the whole settlement submit in the same manner as the inhabitants of any county within this colony, by law are obliged, to their respective High Sheriff.

8th. All persons within such settlement accused of the high handed crimes of adultery, burglary, and the like, shall be arraigned before such quarterly meeting, and if convicted, shall be sentenced to banishment from such settlement, and a confiscation of all their personal effects therein, to the use of the town, where such offence is committed, and should there still be the more heinous crimes of murder committed, which God forbid, the offender shall be instantly arrested, and delivered into the hands of the nearest civil authority in Connecticut, and should any person or persons be accused of counterfeiting the bills or coins of any province on this continent, and be thereof convicted before such quarterly meeting, the colony whose bills are thus counterfeited, shall have liberty to take such offender and punish him, he shall be instantly banished the settlement, and his personal effects confiscated as aforesaid, and all persons convicted of any heinous crime, in any province on this continent, and shall fly from justice, the inhabitants shall, as well directors and peace officers, as others, aid and assist their pursuers in apprehending them, that they may be duly punished in the Government where they have offended.

9th. No appeal shall be from the doings of such quarterly meeting, or their decrees, to the Susquehanna Company, in general, save where the property of land is disputed, in which case the appellant shall first secure the appellee for his costs, if he make not his appeal good before the Company.

10th. The inhabitants of each town, to wit:—All the males of twenty-one years and upwards, and a proprietor in one of the said towns shall annually meet, on the first Monday in December, and choose Directors for such town, with their peace officers, and other officers that shall be found necessary for the ensuing year, and the Directors, etc., that now may be chosen, shall have authority until new are chosen, and no longer.

11th. The Directors of each town shall make out and exhibit to their first quarterly meeting, a list in the rateable estate and polls of the inhabitants of each town, and such quarterly meeting shall have power to assess the inhabitants for defraying public expenses, as also to enforce the assessment made in each particular town, if need be.

12th. The law regulating the militia of this colony, shall be particularly attended to by the Directors of the respective towns, and the general regulation thereof, as the particular circumstances of the people require, shall be in the power of such general quarterly meeting.

Also, we do solemnly declare these and such other regulations as we shall hereafter come into, by and with the advice and consent of the Susquehanna Company, in full meeting assembled, to be of force and binding on us, and on each of us, our heirs and assigns, until the colony of Connecticut shall annex us to some one of the counties of this colony, or make us a distinct county, or we obtain from the said colony, or from his Gracious Majesty, King George the Third, whose true and loyal subjects we are, powers of Government in some more permanent method.

And lastly, it is further agreed and voted, that the Directors in each of the several towns now settled, and that shall be settled, shall forthwith procure a copy of the foregoing agreements, which shall be entered at large in a book for that purpose, and all the male inhabitants of the age of twenty-one years, shall, personally, subscribe the same with their own proper names, or mark, and strictly abide by and fulfil the same; and such inhabitants or settlers as are already come into, to settle, or shall hereafter appear to come in as settlers, as shall neglect, or refuse to subscribe to and abide by the foregoing agreements shall not continue there, nor be admitted as settlers on said lands.

Voted, that the following persons be, and they are hereby appointed Directors in the several towns hereafter mentioned, until the first Monday in December next, with the powers and authority according to the foregoing agreement.

To wit:—For the town of Wilkesbarre,—Maj. John Durkee, Capt. Zebulon Butler, and Obadiah Gore, Jr.

For the town of Plymouth,—Phineas Nash, Capt. David Marvin, and J. Gaylord.

In New Providence,—Isaac Tripp, Esq., Timothy Keys, and Gideon Baldwin.

For the town of Kingston,—Capt. Obadiah Gore, Nathan Denison, and Parshall Terry.

For the town of Pittston,—Caleb Bates, James Brown, and Lemuel Harding.

For the town of Hanover,—Capt. Lazarus Stewart, Wm. Stewart, and John Franklin.

Having given a brief picture of the Valley, and recorded the building of mills—settling a gospel minister—establishing schools—the first wedding—birth, and natural death: having given the early Constitution or Code of Laws, adopted, medical gentlemen may expect the result of our researches in respect to members of their profession. Dr. William Hooker Smith, justly eminent and highly successful, emigrated to the valley, in 1772; and his valuable services were continued through the revolutionary war; indeed, until very advanced age released him from active labour. But there came from New London, in 1773, a noted surgeon, whom many of the people desired to establish among them. A paper, drawn up by Henry Carey, (and it is a very neat piece of penmanship,) for subscription, proposes to "pay Dr. John Caulkins, in case he should settle among us in the quality of a physician," (the sums to be annexed,) "the money to be laid out in land for his benefit and use," etc. Among the names subscribed are, Anderson Dana, £2 8; James Stark, £1 4 etc., and other less sums. The issue of the negotiation, I have not been able to ascertain.

The most important exterior event that occurred, affecting the interests of Wyoming, during these two years, was an official movement on the part of the Government of Connecticut, asserting her Charter claim west of the Delaware. The progress of the new settlement had been watched with intense interest. As peace reigned and prosperity abounded: as the settlers had shown themselves competent to defend themselves, and their foot-hold seemed permanently established, it was deemed a fitting time for making a declaration of right, and opening a negotiation with the Proprietary Government, in respect to the disputed territory.

At the session of the General Assembly, in October, 1773, a Resolution was adopted, "That the Colony would make their claim to those lands; and in a legal manner support the same."

It was also Resolved, That Commissioners should be appointed to proceed to Philadelphia, to negotiate a mode of bringing the controversy to an amicable conclusion. Col. Eliphalet Dyer, Dr. Johnson, and J. Strong, Esq., were duly empowered, and about the middle of December, opened the matter, by presenting their credentials, and a letter from His Excellency, Gov. Trumbull to Gov. Penn. The notes, letters, replies and rejoinders, go so much into details in respect to title, repeating what, in substance, we have before fully stated, that a publication of them in extenso, in the body of this work, is regarded as unnecessary. A statement of the points made may, however, prove acceptable. On the part of Connecticut it was proposed, That Commissioners be mutually appointed to run the respective lines, and ascertain the extent of conflicting Charter claims.

The Governor and Council, on behalf of Pennsylvania, denying any right of Connecticut, west of New York, declined to accede to the proposition.

It was next proposed, in accordance with the Act of Assembly, " To *join* in an application to his Majesty to appoint Commissioners," to ascertain the rightful boundaries of the contesting colonies.

To this, Governor Penn and the Council replied, by decisively declining the proposition, but suggests that Connecticut should make *separate* application to his Majesty.

A third proposition was then made by the Connecticut Agents:— That Pennsylvania should continue to exercise jurisdiction over the West Branch, where her authority already extended, and Connecticut should extend her laws over Wyoming, and that part of the settlement which was not under the laws of Pennsylvania, so long as the dispute continued with the mother country, and until a decision by his Majesty, in Council, or some other amicable way might be obtained.

A negative, as decided, was given to the last, as to the two former propositions, and Messrs. Dyer, Johnson, and Strong, returned to Connecticut.

Throughout the proceedings, the greatest urbanity and mutual respect were manifested. Much ability was displayed on both sides; and the Connecticut Commissioners effected all that they could have expected when they opened the negotiation. An earnest appeal had been made to accommodate the unhappy differences by amicable means—a mutual commission—a reference to his Majesty—a division of jurisdiction, until a peaceable settlement could be made! What more fair could be offered? The moral influences at home and abroad, could not fail to prove of powerful aid to the offering, against the rejecting party.

Gov. Penn communicated the whole proceedings to the Assembly, whose answer on the occasion, though decided, is so mild, that it shows the favorable impression the Connecticut Delegates, personally, had made in Philadelphia.

"To prevent the mischievous effects of this unkind and unneighborly disposition in the Government of Connecticut, we beg leave earnestly to request that you will pursue every effectual measure to call the claimants before his Majesty, in Council, and to bring their claim to an immediate decision."

The important proceedings of the Connecticut Assembly, on receiving the report of their Agents, commencing a new year, will be noticed in the following letter.

LETTER XIII.

1774.—Connecticut assumes jurisdiction—town of Westmoreland—Town meeting—Districts—election of one hundred officers—Town sign-post established—Several town meetings—Civil and military organization—Representatives to Assembly—School committee—Insidious attacks—Alarm—meeting of Proprietors—Proceeding—Sales and price of lands—Census.

Two years of repose presented no event for the record of the historian's pen more exciting than the ordinary occurrences of peace and domestic prosperity. The succeeding year, 1774, though equally peaceful and prosperous, yet assumes in our annals an increased interest. It was *the* year, more than any other, in the memory of the ancient people, of unalloyed joy and gladness, even surpassing the two by which it was preceded. On the report of Messrs. Dyer, Johnson and Strong, the General Assembly of Connecticut adopted decisive measures to bring the settlement on the Susquehanna under her immediate jurisdiction. An act was passed early in January, erecting all the territory within her charter limits, from the river Delaware to a line fifteen miles west of the Susquehanna, into a town, with all the corporate powers of other towns in the colony, to be called WESTMORELAND, attaching it to the county of Litchfield. This most desirable event was hailed by the people with unbounded satisfaction. Venerating the law, they now felt that it pervaded the settlement with a holier sanction than their own mere agreement, or the resolutions of the Susquehanna Company, could impart. To all intents and purposes, in name as well as in fact, a portion of the ancient high standing Colony of Connecticut, eminent for order, learning and piety, the character of the parent was now felt to be officially imparted to this, her true, though distant offspring Moreover, the distinct legalization of what had before been done, and the pledge of protection for the future, implied in the extension of her laws to the settlement, were regarded as points attained of great importance. A sense of security existed, a feeling of confidence ensued, which gave force to contracts, encouraged industry, and stimulated enterprise.

In accordance with the Act of Assembly, Governor Turnbull issued his proclamation, forbidding any settlement within the limits of Westmoreland, except under the authority of Connecticut. Near the same time a proclamation from the Governor of Pennsylvania, prohibited any settlement on the contested claims, under pretended grants from Connecticut, or any other than the authority of the Proprietaries.

Proper measures had been adopted for the introduction of the laws and usages of the Civil Government of Connecticut. Zebulon Butler and Nathan Denison were commissioned Justices of the Peace, with directions to call a town meeting of the Freemen of Westmoreland, with a view to a perfect organization, and for the purpose of choosing town officers for the ensuing year. These gentlemen have been before noticed. Nature never formed two excellent men, in more distinct contrast. Butler, polished in manner, quick in perception, vehement and rapid in execution; Denison, plain, though courteous, slow to speak, as careful to consider, cool and firm, if not alert in action. Both universal favorites, we again advert to their characters because they were the two great and acknowledged leaders in Westmoreland.

The organization being now somewhat complicated, the reader will please to observe the difference between a *town* and a *township*. The *town* of Westmoreland legally incorporated for civil purposes, was about seventy miles square, and could only be established by supreme Legislative authority. Within this limit a number of townships of five or six miles square, were laid off by the Delaware and Susquehanna Companies, divided into lots, which were drawn for by Proprietors, or sold. These townships had power to make needful rules and bye-laws for their interior regulation, the establishment of roads, the care or disposal of vacant lots, and other matters entirely local. Of these there already existed Wilkesbarre, Hanover, Plymouth, Kingston, or the Forty, Exeter, Pittston, and Capouse, or Providence; more were from time to time added. A town meeting therefore, *now*, when "legally warned," called together all the Freemen, in all the townships or settlements, from the Delaware to fifteen miles beyond the Susquehanna, and from the Lehigh, north to Tioga Point.

The first town meeting:—But we are sure the curious reader will be pleased to hear the old records, page first, speak for themselves;

the more especially as they will exhibit the general organization of towns in Connecticut, the number and kind of officers chosen, and show the pure Democracy that prevailed in their system of Government. At that time the Assembly met twice a year. Delegates held their commissions only six months, so cautious were the people of intrusting power. Each town elected one or two members, according to their population.

Before we proceed to copy the votes, it may be proper to say—that every town in the colony kept, and we presume still keeps, a regular record of its elections, orders, votes, etc. While most of the valuable papers in the settlement were destroyed, by singular good fortune the volume of Westmoreland Records was saved, and is in a state of excellent preservation. The neat manner in which they were kept, the generally fine, liberal and patriotic spirit they breathe, reflect the highest honour on the ancient people. Bearing the "image and superscription" of the fathers of Wyoming, we shall quote them freely, both as curious from their antiquity, and interesting as reflecting the impress of those whose history our labours record.

"At a town meeting legally warned and held for Westmoreland, March ye 1st, 1774, for choosing town officers, etc., Zebulon Butler, Esq., was chosen moderator for the work of the day. Major Ezekiel Pierce was chosen town clerk.

"March ye 1st. Voted that this meeting is adjourned until tomorrow morning at this place, at eight of the clock, in ye forenoon.

"March ye 2d, 1774, this meeting is opened and held by adjournment. Voted, that ye town of Westmoreland be divided in the following manner into districts—that is to say, that ye town of Wilkesbarre, be one entire district, and known by the name of Wilkesbarre district: And that ye town of Hanover, and all the land south of Wilkesbarre, and west on Susquehanna river, and east on the Lehigh, be one district, by ye name of Hanover district. And that Plymouth, with all ye land west of Susquehanna river, south and west to the town line, be one district, by ye name of Plymouth district: and that Kingston, with ye land west to ye town line, be one district, by ye name of Kingston district: and that Pittston be one district, by ye name of Pittston district: and that Exeter, Providence, and all the lands west and north to ye town line, be one district, by ye name of ye North District: and that Lackaway settlement and Blooming Grove, and Sheolah, to be one district, and to be called by ye name of ye Lackaway district: and that Coshutunk, and all ye settlements on Delaware, be one district, and joined to ye other districts, and known by ye name of ye east district.

SELECT MEN.

"Christopher Avery, Nathaniel Landon, Samuel Ransom, Isaac Tripp, Esq., Caleb Bates, Lazarus Stewart, Silas Parke, were chosen Selectmen, for ye year ensuing. Isaac Tripp, Esq., refused to accept. John Jenkins was chosen Selectman in ye room of Esq. Tripp.

"Captain Stewart refused to accept. Rosewell Franklin was chosen Selectman in ye room of Captain Stewart.

TOWN TREASURER.

"Zebulon Butler, Esq., was chosen Town Treasurer.

CONSTABLES AND COLLECTORS OF RATES.

"Asa Stevens, Timothy Smith,* Jonathan Haskel, Asaph Whittlesy, Noah Adams, Phineas Clark, William Smith, were chosen Constables and Collectors of Rates.

SURVEYORS OF HIGHWAYS.

"Anderson Dana, Daniel Gore, Elisha Swift, Thomas Stoddart, Thomas Bennet, Perrin Ross, Rufus Lawrence, Samuel Ransom, Jonathan Parker, Isaac Baldwin, Zavan Tracy, Elijah Witter, John Ainsley, William Hibbard, James Lastley, John Dewit, John Jenkins, jr., Aaron Thomas, Anthony Chimer, Abraham Russ, Benjamin Vancampin, Benjamin Harvey, were chosen Surveyors of Highways.

FENCE VIEWERS.

"John Abbott, William Warner, Ezekiel Pierce, William Buck, Nathan Denison, Esq., Thomas Stoddart, Frederick Eveland, John Baker, Charles Gaylord, Samuel Slaughter, Abraham Harding, Captain Parrish, John Jamison, John Gardner, were chosen Fence Viewers, for ye year ensuing.

LISTERS.

"Anderson Dana, Daniel Gore, Elisha Swift, Eliphalet Follet, Perrin Ross, Nathan Wade, Jeremiah Blanchard, Zavan Tracy, Uriah Chapman, Gideon Baldwin, Silas Gore, Moses Thomas, Emanuel Consawler, John Jenkins and Phineas Clark, were chosen Listers, for ye year ensuing.

---

* This gentleman was sportively called "old-head," because of the ability displayed in inducing Connecticut to establish the town of Westmoreland.

LEATHER SEALERS.

"Elisha Swift, Ebenezer Hibbard, and Captain Silas Parke, were chosen Leather Sealers ye year ensuing.

GRAND JURORS.

"Jabez Sills, James Stark, William Buck, Elias Church, Phineas Nash, Thomas Heath, Barnabas Cary, Lemuel Harding, Hezekiah Bingham, John Franklin, Timothy Keys, were chosen Grand Jurors ye year ensuing.

TYTHING MEN.

"Philip Weeks, Elihu Williams, Luke Swetland, Justice Gaylord, James Brown, Isaac Parrish, Timothy Hopkins, were chosen Tything men.

SEALERS OF WEIGHTS AND MEASURES.

"Jabez Sills, Captain Obadiah Gore, Captain Silas Parke, Captain Lazarus Stewart, were chosen Sealers of Weights and Measures.

KEY-KEEPERS.

"Daniel Gore, Jabez Fish, Timothy Pierce, Uriah Stevens, Thomas Heath, Jeremiah Blanchard, Jonathan Haskel, Zipron Hibbard, were chosen Key Keepers." Thus was the town organized by the designation of one hundred officers.

April 11 and 12, the second town meeting in Westmoreland was held. Two hundred and six persons took the freeman's oath, as required by law. A tax was laid of one penny in the pound, "to purchase ammunition for the town's use, and other necessaries."

Application to the Assembly was directed for a Court of Probate, and the establishment of a Regiment. Pounds already built, were pronounced lawful pounds. Roads heretofore established, were declared lawful highways, on which taxes might be laid out.

"Voted—That for ye present, ye tree that now stands northerly from Captain Butler's house, shall be ye Town Sign Post."

This matter of the legal sign post, is of weightier import than, without explanation, might be imagined. Newspapers in those days were little known, save in the larger cities. It had therefore been enacted, that a sign post be established in each town, on which notices of public meetings, public sales, stray animals taken up, etc., should be nailed or placed, to render them legal. It is proper to add, that, as an accompaniment of the sign post, which was also the legal whipping post, a pair of stocks was provided for a punishment of the guilty, and a warning to deter from crime. These (now abjured) monuments of civilization and law, were derived from

England, and brought over, nay, almost venerated by our Puritan fathers. The ancient pillory and wooden horse, first disappeared, the whipping post and stocks soon followed.*

A third town meeting was holden April 28, 1774.

"Captain Butler was chosen Moderator, for ye work of ye day.

Voted that Captain Zebulon Butler, Captain Timothy Smith, Mr. Christopher Avery, and Mr. John Jenkins, be appointed agents in behalf of this company of settlers, to attend the meeting of the General Assembly, to be holden at Hartford in May next, etc."

The same gentlemen were also appointed as agents to the Susquehanna Company, which was to assemble at Hartford, on the 24th of May.

It is presumed that, at this time the number of the members of Assembly Westmoreland would be entitled to, had not been designated. Thereafter two were, or might be elected for each session, during the continuance of the jurisdiction of Connecticut.

The John Jenkins named, was the elder, and father of Colonel John Jenkins, both distinguished patriots, who will appear frequently and honorably on our pages.

The fourth town meeting was held June 27, Zebulon Butler Moderator. Votes were passed "to form themselves into companies in a military way." Each district in Westmoreland to be a company. And Zebulon Butler, Esq., Major Ezekiel Pierce, and Mr. John Jenkins were appointed as a committee to repair to the several districts, and lead each company to a choice of officers, etc.

On the 30th of September, a fifth town meeting was held, Captain S. Fuller, moderator.

Captain Butler, and Mr. Joseph Sluman, were chosen representatives to the next Assembly, and these were the first persons admitted to the full participation of the rights of members, not as delegates from territories, having a power to debate, but not a right

---

* The reader of Hudibras will recollect that he several times became intimately acquainted with those instruments of punishment, or persuasives to repentance, for his lady finds him sitting in a posture which occasions her thus to address the knight:—

"Quoth she, I grieve to see your leg
Stuck in a hole here like a peg,
And if I knew which way to do't
(Your honour safe) I'd let you out."

This mode of punishment is rendered classical by its extreme antiquity. Willis, in his charming "Pencillings by the Way," describing the ruins of Pompeii, says, "on the right were several small prisons, in one of which was found the skeleton of a man, with his feet in iron stocks."

to vote; but voting on all questions that arose, uniting in making laws for the rest of the colony, as the other members made laws for Westmoreland, and from henceforth, Wyoming, or Westmoreland, (we shall use the terms as synonimous) was in all respects a part of Connecticut, as much so as Stonington, or Saybrook, Hartford, or New Haven.

The name of Joseph Sluman, occurs frequently in the old records. From his being often named on committees, and several times chosen member of Assembly, it would appear that he was trusted and honoured; but we cannot learn whence he came, what was his fate, or whether he left any family in Wyoming. It is most probable that his generous spirit led him into the thickest of the terrible conflict, that afterwards overwhelmed the Valley, and that fortune, life, and all remembrance of him were extinguished together.

The sixth town meeting in that year was held on the 17th of October.

Voted—That Lieut. Elijah Shoemaker, Mr. Solomon Johnson, Mr. John Jenkins, Captain Timothy Smith, and Mr. Douglass Davidson, be a committee to meet such gentlemen, as shall be appointed at or near Delaware, " to mark out a road from that river to the Susquehanna." Up to this time therefore, we may assert that no road existed from any part of the inhabited country to Wyoming. Bridle paths were the only avenues to the Valley, except that by the Susquehanna river, on which boats brought from below, at great cost, heavy articles of indispensable necessity.

The seventh town meeting was held November 22, from which, in a page or two, we shall copy some interesting votes.

The eighth and last town meeting called during 1774, was held the 6th of December, at which, among a variety of other things, it was

"Voted—That Elisha Richards, Captain Ransom, Perrin Ross, Nathaniel Landon, Elisha Swift, Nathan Denison, Esq., Stephen Harding, John Jenkins, Anderson Dana, Obadiah Gore, jr., James Stark, Rosewell Franklin, Captain Stewart, Captain Parkes, and Uriah Chapman, were chosen School Committee, for the ensuing year.

It may be justly regarded equally honorable and extraordinary, that a people just commencing a settlement in a wilderness, wrestling with the yet rude and unbroken soil for bread, surrounded by so many extrinsic difficulties and causes of alarm, should be found so zealously adopting, and so steadily pursuing, measures to provide free schools throughout the settlement, and establish the preaching of the gospel.

The reader must have been amused by observing the great number of town meetings held this year. Human nature is illustrated by the review. After a long period of contest and suffering, now, for the first time, the lawful power existed to hold a " legally warned" meeting, and to give efficient votes. It was a new thing! What a pleasure! But where was the pleasure unless the right should be exercised. As the woodsman, when he has obtained the long wished-for rifle, is not satisfied till he has tried it again and again. Happy people! Every tint of brilliant morn or blushing eve, was to your delighted view a ray of hope and joy.*

Over the three years that had just passed, scarce a cloud had arisen to interrupt the cheering sunshine. But just towards the close of 1774, a policy began to develope itself, which occasioned no inconsiderable alarm and trouble. Persons came in as settlers, bought a Connecticut title to a lot, became regular inhabitants, and then avowed—That they did this from policy—that they considered the Connecticut claim, in fact, good for nothing, and held a better lying under that, which they had bought elsewhere. Pennsylvania surveyors were found, more or less openly, to be making surveys in various parts of Westmoreland, and some of the sagacious men began to speak doubtingly, for they saw breakers ahead.

To extirpate the evil before it should take deep root, the obvious policy led to prompt action.

" At a meeting of ye Proprietors and settlers, legally warned, and held in Wilkesbarre district, in Westmoreland, November 22nd, A. D. 1774—Zebulon Butler, Esq., was chosen moderator for ye work of ye day. Voted, that August Hunt, and Frederick Vanderlip, now residing on the Susquehanna purchase, being men that have, and now do so conduct themselves by spreading reports about ye town of Westmoreland, much to ye disturbance of ye good and wholesome

---

* The state of pleasurable excitement of this period, as represented by the old people, with whom I have conversed, tinges the whole with romance. Contrasted with the ills that awaited them, the lines of Gray often occur to my mind:—

"Fair laughs the morn, and soft the zephyr blows,
    While proudly riding o'er the azure realm
    In gallant trim the gilded vessel goes,
Youth on the prow, and pleasure at the helm;
    Regardless of the sweeping whirlwind's sway,
That, hushed in grim repose, expects his evening prey."

inhabitants of this town, and by their taking up and holding land under ye pretension of ye title of Pennsylvania, contrary to ye proclamation of ye Governor of this colony, and contrary to ye votes of ye Susquehanna Company, etc. It is now voted that ye said Hunt be expelled this purchase, and he be, as soon as may be, removed out of ye purchase and out of ye town of Westmoreland, by ye committee hereafter appointed, at ye cost of this Company, in such way as ye committee shall think proper.

"Voted,—That Capt. Stephen Fuller, Capt. Robert Durkee, Asahel Buck, Nathan Denison, Esq., Capt. Samuel Ransom, John Paine, Abraham Harding, Rosewell Franklin, John Jenkins, Jr., be a committee to make inquiry into, and search after all persons that are suspected to have been taking land under the title of Pennsylvania, etc., and that they have full power to expel any person or persons from this purchase and town, whom they or ye major part of them judge unwholesome inhabitants, on account of their taking land under ye title of Pennsylvania, and their conducting contrary to ye proclamation of ye Governor of ye Colony of Connecticut, and ye votes of ye Susquehanna Company, etc., and also remove them at such time and in such way as they shall think proper, out of this town and purchase, and that they be empowered by this company to call on the Treasurer for any of ye bonds in his hands that belong to this company, and put ye same in suit against any of ye persons who are indebted to this company, and are going out of town, or are spending their estate, etc., and that they collect ye same, or get good security of such other persons who are good able landholders in this town, and that they lodge ye same in ye hands of said Treasurer, as soon as they have obtained it, etc., and that they do ye same at ye cost of this company, if needful, and that they take ye most effectual method to prevent such great numbers of persons of evil name and fame, from going up and down this river under the pretence of laying out locations," etc.

The nine gentlemen named on the committee, embraced, as rightly it should in matters so delicate and important, one of the leading men from each township, or district. While the Pennsylvania party loudly censured this act of expulsion, as a high handed outrage, it was justified by the Yankees as a measure indispensable to self-preservation. But this game of settling real Pennsylvania claimants, on Connecticut rights, which could be purchased cheap, was too good to be abandoned. One or more gentlemen of character and intelligence, cautious and prudent, had been on the ground from an early day. The name of David Meade, is signed, in fair round hand, to a call of a meeting of Proprietors in Wilkesbarre, in 1770. When we say that the fine town of Meadville, the seat of justice in Crawford county, was established by him, soon after being expelled by the Yankees from Wyoming, the introduction of his name will be sufficient to awaken interest to his future course.

Having spoken of the facility with which lands could be obtained, from the lowness of price, at Wyoming, before closing this letter, I will state briefly the sums paid for certain lots in Wilkesbarre, in the year 1772-3, no later records of deeds, before the war, having rewarded my research.

"In the twelfth year of the reign of our sovereign lord, George ye Third, king, etc." July 6, 1772, Silas Gore sells to Jonathan Stowell of Ashford, Connecticut, for the consideration of twenty pounds, lawful money, one whole settling right in the township of Wilkesbarre, said right contains—the home or house lot, No. 28, the meadow lot, No. 50—and the third division, or back lot, No. 44, as by the drafts of the said town may appear, together with all the after divisions which may be made, etc."

"August 21, 1772. Asa Stephens sells to Enoch Judd, for the consideration of forty-three pounds, lawful money, ($143 34) one setling right in the township of Wilkesbarre, being meadow lot No. 20, house lot No. 27, and back, or great lot, No. 8, together with all the other divisions yet to be made.

"Elijah Loomis, of Harrington, in the county of Litchfield, sells to Elisha Swift, a whole right in Wilkesbarre, being town lot No. 2, meadow lot (about 33 acres) No. 28, back lot No. 36, for one hundred pounds, on the 22d of February, in the 13th year of the reign of our sovereign lord George the Third, king," etc. It was wise policy in the Susquehanna people to be particular in their deeds of conveyance to repeat "our sovereign lord George the King,"—for it was contemplated to refer the dispute to his majesty, and he could not fail to be conciliated by this evidence of devotion.

One more instance will close our present reference to prices. The burying ground lot, of near four acres, was bought, in 1772, for £9 10, or $31 67. At simple interest to 1842, seventy years, the amount would be, principal, $31 67, interest, $133; added, $164 67. Allow the sum to double every sixteen years, then in 1788, it would have cost $63 34—in 1804, it would have cost $126 68—in 1820, it would have cost $253 36—in 1836, it would have cost $506 72—add six years interest, up to 1842, $182 42, to the principal, gives $689 13. Allowing the rent of the land to have paid taxes, how would stand the investment? The corresponding town lot, on the opposite side of the street, would bring five times that sum. Several of the town lots would sell for ten times that amount; and many, independent of the buildings erected on them, would bring twenty times that sum. In a subsequent letter, the rise in prices of lands will be more particularly noted. We have indulged in this prospective speculation, to amuse the curious reader, who may trace our labours; and because the subject pressed strongly on the mind—that investments, judiciously made in lands, besides being safer than stocks, are far from being unprofitable. A census, taken this year, shows that Westmoreland contained 1922 inhabitants.

But the stirring events of 1775 demand our attention.

LETTER XIV.

1775.——Prosperity—Revolutionary War—Town Meeting—Patriotic Resolutions—Settlement on West Branch—Charleston and Judea destroyed by Col. Plunket—Vote of Congress; of Connecticut Council—of Pennsylvania Assembly—Plunket's invasion of Wyoming—Stirring Scenes—Interposition of Congress—Civil War—Col. Butler—Formidable Breastwork—Battle—Defeat of Plunket—Painful Incident—Connecticut prohibits further Emigration—Town Meeting—Rivalry between Kingston and Wilkesbarre—Amusements—Prices of Grain.

THREE years of tranquil enjoyment had increased the number of settlers at Wyoming, while unremitted industry upon a prolific soil, had diffused throughout the valley most of the necessaries, many of the conveniences, and some of the luxuries of life. Abundant food and clothing were enjoyed in every cottage. Numerous herds of cattle grazed upon the mountains. Hill and meadow were spotted with flocks of sheep. The flats, nearly cleared, yielded thirty and forty fold the seed that was sown. School-houses were erected in every district. The Sabbath was kept with Puritan strictness. Congregated in convenient places, the people listened to sermons from their gospel ministers. Prayer ascended to the Most High for grace in spiritual matters, and his protection in their secular concerns; while

> "They chant their artless notes in simple guise;
> They tune their hearts, by far the noblest aim:
> Perhaps *Dundee's* wild warbling measures rise,
> Or plaintive *Martyrs*, worthy of the name."

Such was the picture presented by Wyoming at the commencement of 1775. At the Spring election, John Jenkins, Esq., (the elder,) was elected member of Assembly, to be holden at Hartford, in May. The dispute between Great Britain and the colonies, now approaching to an open rupture, had already effected a sensible, and so far, not unfavorable influence on the settlement, as, by occupying the attention of the Proprietary Government with more important affairs, the Connecticut people had been left undisturbed to extend and establish their possessions. The battle at Lexington had taken place April 19th. On the 17th of June, the battle of Bunker's Hill was fought, so glorious to the American arms. The effect produced at Wyoming, by those soul-stirring events, will be best expressed by the simple record of a "town meeting legally warned."

"At a meeting of ye Proprietors and settlers of ye town of Westmoreland, legally warned and held in Westmoreland, August 1st, 1775, Mr. John Jenkins was chosen Moderator for ye work of ye day. Voted that this town does now vote that they will strictly observe and follow ye rules and regulations of ye Honorable Continental Congress, now sitting at Philadelphia.

"Resolved by this town, that they are willing to make any accommodations with ye Pennsylvania party that shall conduce to ye best good of ye whole, not infringing on the property of any person, and come in common cause of Liberty in ye defence of America, and that we will amicably give them ye offer of joining in ye proposals as soon as may be.

"Voted—This meeting is adjourned until Tuesday ye 8th day of this instant, August, at one of the clock in ye afternoon at this place."

"This meeting is opened and held by an adjournment August the 8th, 1775.

"Voted—as this town has but of late been incorporated and invested with the privileges of the law, both civil and military, and now in a capacity of acting in conjunction with our neighboring towns within this and the other colonies, in opposing ye late measures adopted by Parliament to enslave America.—Also this town having taken into consideration the late plan adopted by Parliament of enforcing their several oppressive and unconstitutional acts, of depriving us of our property, and of binding us in all cases without exception, whether we consent or not, is considered by us highly injurious to American or English freedom; therefore do consent to and acquiesce in the late proceedings and advice of the Continental Congress, and do rejoice that those measures are adopted, and so universally received throughout the Continent; and in conformity to the eleventh article of the association, we do now appoint a Committee to attentively observe the conduct of all persons within this town, touching the rules and regulations prescribed by the Honorable

Continental Congress, AND WILL UNANIMOUSLY JOIN OUR BRETHREN IN AMERICA IN THE COMMON CAUSE OF DEFENDING OUR LIBERTY.

"Voted—That Mr. John Jenkins, Joseph Sluman, Esq., Nathan Denison, Esq., Mr. Obadiah Gore, Jr., and Lieut. William Buck, be chosen a Committee of Correspondence for the town of Westmoreland," etc.

While all the votes of that meeting, breathe a spirit of patriotism, the notice of the reader cannot fail to be attracted to the second Resolve, offering the olive-branch to the Pennsylvania party, and proposing a truce of their private and local quarrels—that all hearts and all hands might be united in the general defence of liberty. Politic, as it was apparently patriotic and fair, both parties well knew, that time gained was greatly important to consolidate the strength of the settlement.

In no part of the thirteen colonies, neither in Massachusetts nor Connecticut, was there more lively zeal, or more perfect unanimity, in behalf of Independence, than among the settlers under the Connecticut Claim upon the Susquehanna and Delaware purchases. Among those who had taken the Freeman's Oath, previous to the above resolutions, there proved to be but one solitary tory. It was charged by the Connecticut people, that the interlopers, the transient persons, sent by the Pennsylvania landholders, to assume the mask of Connecticut settlers, were tories. To what extent this charge may have been true, we have now no means of forming an accurate opinion; but justice obliges us to say, in some instances *that* odious epithet was applied to such intruders, and assigned as a reason for expelling them from the settlement.

In a distribution of lots, two years previous, mention was made of the settlement at Muncy, on the west branch of the Susquehanna. Two townships had been surveyed including those inviting plains, so early as 1771. One was named Charleston, the other Judea. We are not able to designate the actual settlers, but the following is a list of the Proprietors of the former, embracing names of some of the most respectable families in Connecticut.

A List of the Proprietors of the Township of Charleston, in the Susquehanna Purchase, on the West Branch, June 1772.

Joseph Green,	Nathaniel Green,
Jonathan Root,	Daniel Foot,

David Bigelow,
David Carver,
Joseph Warters,
Capt. Thos. Loomis,
John Clemsted,
Amos Wells,
James Wells,
John Bigelow, Jr.,
Jonah Porter,
Capt. William Clark,
William Swetland,
Eunice White,
Benj. Kibben,
Thomas Heath,
William Buck,

Jonathan Harris' heirs,
Sam'l Fitch,
William Martin,
John Kellog,
Israel Kellog,
Charles Foot,
Samuel Carver,
Capt. Ebenezer Leech,
Dr. John Crocker,
Daniel Kellog,
David Barber, Esq.,
Nathaniel Clark,
Charles Dewey,
John Hastings,
Edward Lester.

We also subjoin a List of Proprietors in Judea.

"A List of the Proprietors of the Township of Judea, is as follows:—

Increase Mosely, Esq.,
John Leavensworth,
Ensign Caleb Wheeler,
Lieut. Peter Guernsey,
Samuel Jackson,
James Morris,
Samuel Slater,
Benjamin Hungerford,
James Hannah,
James Kasson,
Jonathan Smith,
James Frisbie,
Return Strong,
Capt. Nathan Hurd, Jr.,
Josiah Brownson,
John Gordon,

Asahel Hooker,
Joseph Easton,
Elijah Atwood,
Joseph Waugh,
Hezekiah Hooker,
Capt. Abner Mallory,
Titus Barnes,
Thomas Porter,
Josiah Averit,
Jesse Weeks,
Thomas Walsworth,
Deliverance Spalding,
William Choate,
Aholiab Buck,
Capt. Obadiah Gore.

It will be remembered that the General Assembly of Connecticut had not included this settlement in the limits of Westmoreland, the west line of that town extending only fifteen miles beyond the North Branch, not, therefore, reaching within twenty or thirty miles of

Muncy.* A comparatively small settlement, and unsupported, it offered at the same time an afflicting eye-sore to the well excited jealousy of the Proprietaries, and an inviting prize to the cupidity of those who, at some risk, should think proper to seize it. In September, 1775, Col. Plunket, under orders from the Government, detailed a strong force from the Northumberland militia, and marched to break up the settlements at Charlestown and Judea. The spirit or extent of resistance, is no where preserved, but is presumed to have been inconsiderable. One life was lost, and several persons of the Connecticut party were wounded. It has not been ascertained whether any loss was sustained by the Pennsylvania troops. After burning the buildings, and gathering together, for distribution among the victors, all the moveable property, the men taken were marched as prisoners, and confined in Sunbury jail; while the women and children were sent to Wyoming, where most of them had relations or friends.

This successful expedition extinguished forever all settlements, by the Yankees, west of Westmoreland. Leaving the prisoners closely incarcerated, our attention is attracted to the proceedings of Connecticut and of Congress.

Hartford, Nov. 3, 1775—"Letters were laid before Council by the Governor, which stated that the Pennites, on the West Branch of the Susquehanna river, were about to come 500 in number, armed, to drive off the Connecticut settlers from the Wyoming country.

---

* "I will here remark, that, in April 1769 the Susquehanna Company passed a vote to send on, in the whole, 540 settlers, 300 of which to have lands as a gratuity on the West Branch of the Susquehanna river—that several townships were soon after laid out on the West Branch for that purpose.

"By a subsequent act (May 1775) the western limits of the town [of Westmoreland] were extended "westward until it meets the line lately settled with the Indians at Fort Stanwix, called the Stanwix line." [The West Branch settlements, were therefore, included.]

"In May, 1775, one John Vincent, then residing on the West Branch, was appointed a Justice of the Peace for Litchfield county. The said Vincent, with several others, came to Wyoming in August, and requested a number of people to go on to the West Branch and make settlements, and extend the jurisdiction and authority of Connecticut to that country; whereupon, Maj. William Judd, and Joseph Sluman, Esq., and about 80 others, went on to the said West Branch in a peaceable manner in the month of September, and on the 20th of that month, immediately on their arrival there, were attacked and fired upon by about 500 Northumberland militia; one man killed, and several wounded—the party all taken prisoners," etc. "Messrs. Judd and Sluman sent to Philadelphia Goal—three remained in Sunbury, and the others dismissed."

FRANKLIN."

Col. Franklin subsequently states, that Messrs. Judd and Sluman (distinguished men among the Yankees, as will appear in the sequel) were detained several months in prison.

The Council viewed it as having a most dangerous tendency, to break the union of the colonies, and esteemed it a plan, probably concerted by enemies, with that view. The Governor was desired to address Congress on the subject, and endeavour to have the matter quieted."

On Saturday, the 4th of November, having been apprized of the destruction of Charleston and Judea, Congress came to the following resolution:

" The Congress, considering that the most perfect union between all the colonies, is essentially necessary for the just rights of North America, and being apprehensive that there is great danger of hostilities being commenced at, or near Wyoming, between the inhabitants of the Colony of Pennsylvania, and those of Connecticut,"

Resolved—" That the Assemblies of said colonies be requested to take the most speedy and effectual steps to prevent such hostilities."

"Ordered—That Mr. M'Kean, and Mr. Deane, wait upon the Honourable House of Assembly of Pennsylvania, now sitting, with a copy of the above resolutions."

"Ordered—That a copy of the said resolutions be transmitted by express, to the Magistrates and People of Pennsylvania and Connecticut, on the waters of the Susquehanna."

Unfortunately, the influence of the Continental Congress was not sufficiently powerful to quell the storm. On the 7th of the month, in reply to the resolutions quoted, an evasive verbal answer was made by the Pennsylvania Assembly, through Mr. Dickinson: "Desiring to know on what evidence the Congress grounded the apprehension therein expressed of hostilities commencing at, or near Wyoming, between the inhabitants of the Colony of Pennsylvania, and those of Connecticut."

The complete, perhaps easy conquest, and desolation of the Muncy settlement, instead of satisfying, only rendered more eager the Pennsylvania landholders, to strike a decisive blow against Wyoming. Col. Plunket had returned, his brow wreathed with victory, and a long line of Yankee prisoners graced his triumphal entry into Sunbury; while some of his followers, enriched by so much plunder, obtained with scarce a contest, were desirous of trying their fortunes in a new enterprise on a more extended scale, offering to their successful arms an hundred fold more valuable reward. More elated perhaps, than wisdom would have justified; proud and flattered for what he had already achieved, Col. Plunket was told by others, and seems not to have doubted himself, that he was the man for whom the honour had been reserved, of rescuing Wyoming (the desired,) from the unprincipled encroachments of the moss trooping Yankees. Had he known the gallant Ogden, and could he have appreciated half his worth, the Colonel would modestly have judged the task, without undervaluing his own prowess, much more difficult of accomplishment than seems to have been apprehended. But ample means were promised him, and those promises were fulfilled. An army, for it may be so termed, of seven hundred men, were placed at his disposal.*

During the continuance of the first Pennymite and Yankee war, from the commencement of 1769, to the close of 1771, it will be remembered that every expedition against Wyoming was of a civil character. Sheriffs Jennings and Hacklein being ostensibly the chief officers on duty, merely supported by Capt. Ogden, Capt. Francis, Col. Clayton, Capt. Dick, Captains Morris and Ledlie, with their several military companies; the burnished musket, the glittering bayonet, the four pounder—the whole martial array being simply an appurtenant to a peace officer while he should serve a civil process. The same policy was again assumed. Col. Plunket, with his seven hundred armed men, his train of boats, with store of ammunition, the leading and largest one armed with a field-piece ready for action, on board, or to be landed, were the mere accompaniments of William Cook, Esq., the High Sheriff of Northumberland, whose business at Wyoming was to arrest two or three individuals on civil writs.

A high degree of excitement prevailed on both sides. Several boats from Wyoming, trading with the settlements below, were seized on passing Fort Augusta, and their cargoes confiscated. Early in December, his preparations having been completed, Col. Plunket took up his line of march, the weather then being mild, the

---

" November 25, 1775.—Gov. Penn's Letter to Wm. Plunket and his associate Justices of the Peace, for the county of Northumberland.

"I have just now received a message from the Assembly, founded on a letter addressed to them from the county of Northumberland respecting the Connecticut settlers at Wyoming, etc., requesting me to give orders for a due execution of the laws of this Province in the counties of Northampton and Northumberland.

" In consequence thereof I do most cheerfully order you, to use your utmost diligence and activity in putting the laws of this Province in execution throughout the county of Northumberland; and you may depend on the faith of the House, and my concurrence with them, that every proper and necessary expense that may be incurred on the occasion will be defrayed," etc.

JOHN PENN."

river free from ice, a matter extremely unusual at that season of the year.

Justly alarmed at these formidable preparations, the Wyoming people despatched an agent to state the condition of affairs before Congress, and solicit their friendly interposition.

But while calling on Congress the inhabitants were far too wise to omit placing themselves in the best possible posture of defence. The military were reviewed. As there was no public magazine of provisions, every man able to bear arms was directed to hold himself in readiness to march at a moment's warning, his arms in order, with all the ammunition requisite for a weeks muster, and provisions for at least three days.

Scouts sent out for the purpose, returned, one every day with information of the advance of the enemy, who were coming up strong, and confident of success.

The cruelty of the contemplated attack was sensibly felt, intended, it was not doubted, like that on the Muncy settlement, to effectuate the entire expulsion of the whole people. It being in the midst of winter, those least given to despondence, looked to the probable issue with extreme inquietude, for defeat would assuredly devote the Valley to flames, and the inhabitants to famine. Seven hundred men! nearly double the force Westmoreland could bring into the field. Of those who had taken the Freeman's oath, the whole number amounted to two hundred and eighty-five, and of these several came from the Lackawaxen settlement, forty miles east of Wyoming, a few from Coshutunk, on the Delaware, and many aged men were on the list. There were probably in the valley twenty or thirty persons, like David Meade, (holding a Connecticut right, yet in heart and hand if need be, being secretly Pennsylvania landholders,) who, if they took no open part, wished success to the enterprise of Plunket, and at a proper moment would have lent their efficient aid in his behalf. These of course never took the Freeman's oath. The young men from fifteen to twenty-one, rallied with spirit on the occasion.

On the 20th December, the invading army was announced as having arrived at the mouth of the Nescopeck Creek, making their way now more slowly as the ice was gathering in the river, and checked the passage of their boats. Never did more earnest prayers ascend to Heaven for snows of Lapland to impede the march of the army, and ice of the Arctic circle to arrest their voyage.

Again Congress interposed, and on the 20th of December, adopted the following most important proceedings.

"The Congress taking into consideration, the dispute between the people of Pennsylvania and Connecticut, on the waters of the Susquehanna, came to the following resolution:

"Whereas, a dispute subsists between some of the inhabitants of the colony of Connecticut, settled under the claim of the said colony on land near Wyoming, on the Susquehanna river, and in the Delaware country, and the inhabitants settled under the claim of the Proprietors of Pennsylvania, which dispute it is apprehended will, if not suspended during the present troubles in the colonies, be productive of pernicious consequences, which may be very prejudicial to the common interest of the United Colonies, therefore

"Resolved, That it is the opinion of this Congress, and it is accordingly recommended, that the contending parties immediately cease all hostilities, and avoid every appearance of force until the dispute can be legally decided. That all property taken and detained, be immediately restored to the original owners; that no interruption be given to either party, to the free passing and repassing of persons behaving themselves peaceably, through the disputed territory, as well by land as by water, without molestation of either persons or property; that all persons seized and detained on account of said dispute on either side, be dismissed and permitted to go to their respective homes, and that things being put in the same situation they were before the late unhappy contest, they continue to behave themselves peaceably on their respective possessions and improvements, until a legal decision can be had on said dispute, or this Congress shall take further order thereon, and nothing herein done, shall be construed in prejudice of the claim of either party."*

But they came too late to arrest the attack of Colonel Plunket, whose force had arrived on the 23d, at the southwestern opening of the Valley. Colonel Zebulon Butler, who commanded the Yankees, by the most strenuous exertions had mustered about three hundred men and boys, but there were not guns enough to arm the whole, and several appeared on the ground with scythes fastened upon handles, projecting straight as possible; a formidable weapon in the hands of an active soldier, if they should be brought to close quarters, but otherwise useless. These weapons the men sportively called "the end of time." On the night of the 23d, he encamped on a flat near the union of Harvey's Creek with the river. From this point he

---

* This decisive interposition of Congress, and the acquiescence of Pennsylvania, it was thought by many, gave to the settlement a legal sanction, though it might not effect the ultimate question of title.

despatched Major John Garrett, his second in command, to visit Colonel Plunket with a flag, and desire to know the meaning of his extraordinary movements, and to demand his intentions in approaching Wyoming with so imposing a military array? The answer given was, that he came peaceably as an attendant on Sheriff Cook, who was authorized to arrest several persons at Wyoming, for violating the laws of Pennsylvania, and he trusted there would be no opposition to a measure so reasonable and pacific. Major Garrett reported that the enemy outnumbered the Yankees more than two to one. "The conflict will be a sharp one, boys," said he, "I for one am ready to die, if need be, for my country." Things wore a different aspect from what they had done formerly. Men then, were almost the only inhabitants. Now the Valley abounded with old men, women and children, brought out by the confidence inspired by three years of peace and prosperity. It was a season of gloomy apprehension.

Colonel Butler was humane as he was brave—politic as he was undaunted. Several positions existed below the Nanticoke falls where the river leaves the Valley, and takes its way for four or five miles between precipitous mountains, where a stand might have been made with almost certain success. It was thought better, however, justifiable as would have been such a course, to wait the attack within the Valley itself. Orders were also given to this effect—not to take life unless rendered unavoidable in self-defence. Leaving Ensign Mason Fitch Alden, with eighteen men on the ground where he had bivouacked, Colonel Butler retired on the morning of the 23d, and detached Captain Stewart with twenty men across to the east side of the river, above the Nanticoke Falls, with orders to lie in ambush, and prevent any boat's crew from landing on that shore.

On the morning of the 24th, about 11 o'clock, Ensign Alden was apprised of the approach of Plunket and his army, and, retiring slowly and in order, was followed by their van-guard, who came up with martial music playing. Keeping at a respectful distance, no shot was fired from either side, and Alden joining Col. Butler, reported the approach of the foe.

Displaying his columns on the flat just abandoned by the Yankees. Col. Plunket directed a spirited advance in pursuit of Alden, not doubting but the main forces of the Yankees were near, and the hour of battle had come. In less than thirty minutes the advancing line was arrested by the word, Halt! and Plunket, who was in the front, a little on the right, observing Col. Butler's position, was heard to exclaim, "My God! what a breastwork!"

Harvey's creek coming in from the north, cuts the high mountain which here approaches the river, deep to its base. A precipitous ledge of rocks, from near the summit, runs southerly to the river, presenting to the west by south a lofty natural barrier, for a mile along the ravine; and where the defence was not perfect, Col. Butler had made it so by ramparts of logs, so that it would require a powerful, as well as bold enemy, to dislodge him. Nothing could have been more perfectly military than the selection of the spot, and the whole preparations of defence. So it was regarded by his soldiers. Mr. John Carey says in respect to the conduct of Col. Butler, in all that affair " I loved the man—he was an honour to the human species." Such a declaration speaks the merits of Col. Butler in language more impressive than the most laboured eulogium. To take life was not the object, but orders were given for a general discharge all along the line of the defence by platoons, so as to impress Col. Plunket with a proper idea of the strength and spirit of its defenders. No one was hurt, but considerable confusion was seen to prevail in his ranks as Plunket's men recoiled from the formidable breastwork. A boat was forthwith dispatched by him, with a number of soldiers, to the opposite shore, it being the intention of the invaders to cross over and enter the settlement by a way apparently less obstructed, for sheriff Cook to serve his civil process. The passage of the boat and crew was watched by both parties with intense anxiety. A few minutes decided its fate. As it approached the shore, Capt. Stewart opened a fire, which wounded one man, and killed a dog that was on board, probably specially aimed at, when instantly pulling their oars with a will, the men gained the suction of the falls, through which they sped among the breakers with the rapid flight of an arrow, fortunately without further injury.

Thus closed the battle for the day. Col. Plunket retired, and encamped on the ground occupied by Col. Butler two nights previously. Early on the ensuing morning the contest was renewed, Col. Plunket returning to the attack, and determining to out-flank the Yankees, while at the same moment he should storm the breastwork. His troops displayed; they approached the line of Yankee defence, covering themselves by trees and loose rocks which lay below, and opened a spirited fire all along the line. While he thus assailed Col. Butler in front, a detatchment of his most determined and alert men was sent up the mountain on the left, by a rapid march, concealed as much as possible, to turn the right flank of the Connecticut people. But this danger having been forseen, and guarded against, the flanking party was repelled. During this contest several lives were lost, and a number on both sides wounded, how many, no record has been kept. A son of Surveyor-General Lukens fell in the engagement; a fine young man, deeply lamented on all sides; but it was the fortune of war.

A circumstance extremely affecting grew out of this battle. A great portion of the male population on the upper waters of the Susquehanna, it is known, in after times sawed lumber during the winter, and descended with it in rafts to market in the spring. The most cordial good understanding had for many years subsisted between the Yankee raftmen and the inhabitants below; the latter being remarkable for their hospitality and kindness. A person who was in the battle saw one of Plunket's men approach with great intrepidity very near the Yankee line, who, taking shelter behind a rock to load, would step out and fire wherever he could bring his rifle to bear. Already several men had fallen—the blood was up;— it had become a matter of life or death, and the aims became more close and deadly. The relator watched the opportunity, and as the head of Plunket's brave soldier rose above the rock, he fired, and the man fell. After the battle was decided, going to the place, the relator found a hat band cut by a bullet; the man and the hat were gone.

Being down the river on a raft, many years afterwards, and staying all night with a fine, hospitable old gentleman, they talked of Wyoming, and the ancient troubles there. "I lost a beloved son in the Plunket Invasion," said the aged father, as a tear fell. "See here," producing a hat perforated by a ball, "The bullet must have cut the band." The narrator said he never before experienced the depth of the calamities of war—the scene was most painful. Of course, he did not avow the deed, but most deeply deplored it, although never doubting he was doing right at the time, and under the circumstances, in defending his home from the invaders.

Finding Col. Butler's position too strong to be carried by storm, Col. Plunket concluded his rash enterprise by a retreat. On Christmas day he withdrew his troops, they marching as they had come up, on the west side of the river. In the mean time, a party of the Yankees followed on the east side, with a view to capture one of the boats, but Mr. Harvey, who was a prisoner on board, calling to them not to fire, for they might injure their friends, they returned, and left the retreating army to pass down without further pursuit.

The expedition of Col. Plunket* was, in every aspect in which it could be viewed, rash, and ill advised. After the resistance made in 1771, and the two previous years, when they were comparatively weak, the expulsion of the Wyoming people could not have been rationally calculated on, without a long and bloody contest. Just at the opening of the war with Great Britain, to commence a civil war, would seem to have been extremely unwise. In the depth of winter, when the Susquehanna is usually frozen up, to rely on transporting provisions, and the munitions of war in boats, appears to have been setting every precept of prudence at defiance. We see no reason to doubt the courage of Col. Plunket, and his men were unquestionably brave. But however zealous he and some of his troops may have been, the great body of them were extremely indisposed to adopt the harsh measures proposed against the Connecticut people. Though zealous for the rights of Pennsylvania, an impression prevailed that the Connecticut people, though in error, honestly believed their title good, and it was thought by most of them, that some peaceable mode of settling the controversy would be preferable to a resort to violence and arms. Had the Northumberland militia pursued the attack with the zeal of their Commander, they would have given the Yankees, brave and determined as they might have been, infinitely more trouble, and occasioned a much heavier mutual loss of life. It is probable too, that the Resolution of Congress had reached the camp, and rendered many unwilling to pursue the matter further. In recording the transaction, we cannot refrain from the expression of pleasure, that the consequences were to either, no further disastrous.

While these affairs were in progress, the colony of Connecticut had resolved to prohibit any addition being made to the settlement at Wyoming, unless under special license from the General Assembly.

Situated as the inhabitants of Westmoreland were, on the very borders of the Indian towns which spotted the upper branches of the Susquehanna, several of their villages at Tioga, Sheshequin, and Queen Esther's Flats, being in fact within the town of Westmoreland, and whose conduct already gave strong indications of hostility, this resolution prohibing any accessions of strength to the colony, they had sent out to assert and maintain their Charter rights west of New York, must appear to every candid reader, as of a very extraordinary character. Perhaps it may have been done in concert

---

* See Note at the close of this Letter

with, and to quiet the apprehensions of Pennsylvania. The times demanded union. Patriotism urged the most powerful persuasives that every proper sacrifice should be made to assuage jealousy, and lead to concert in council and action. Connecticut had previously forbidden any settlement on the disputed ground, except under her authority. Two years had not elapsed, and now she positively forbids any further settlement whatever, even under her claim, except upon special license of the Assembly, not likely to be easily obtained. The keeping at home all her able bodied men, and the wealth they might possess, to aid her in the war just commenced, it must be confessed, might have been a motive deriving some sanction from prudence and policy, but none from justice and good faith to the Wyoming settlement.*

A town meeting had been held December 6th, 1775, at which among other officers, Simon Spalding was chosen constable. The fact we quote in illustration of a previous remark, namely, that there was no office so high, or low, demanding the service of any freeman, which was not promptly accepted by the principal and leading men. Every station where the public was to be served, was a station of honour. Simon Spalding soon after held a captain's commission with distinguished honour, in the continental army, and was afterwards a general in the militia. The emoluments of office were a secondary consideration; to serve the country seemed to be, in those patriotic times, a hallowed duty.

But the meeting not having finished the business on which it had met, adjourned to Wednesday, the 20th of the month. Then, as the reader is aware, the whole valley was in commotion, preparing for the reception of Plunket. But a subsequent entry is made by Ezekiel Pierce, the usual Clerk. "This meeting was adjourned until Wednesday, the 20th of December, at 9 of ye o'clock in the forenoon, at ye house of Mr. Jabez Sill.

"But there was no meeting by reason of ye Pennimites," etc.

Though trifling in itself, yet as we mean to hold the mirror up to nature, and reflect a true picture of those ancient times, the fact must

---

* In addition to the Resolutions of the Connecticut Assembly, we find the following proceedings of Congress on the subject, passed Dec. 23, 1775.

Whereas, the colony of Connecticut has, by a certain Act of their Assembly, "Resolved, that no further settlements be made on the lands disputed between them and Pennsylvania, without license from the said Assembly."

Resolved, That it be recommended to the Colony of Connecticut not to introduce any settlers on the said lands, till the further order of this Congress, until the said dispute shall be settled.

be stated. A rivalry for power and precedence had sprung up between Kingston, or the Forty, and Wilkesbarre. The widely extended and rich bottom lands on the west side of the river, Abraham's Plains and Shawney, had attracted thither a large portion of the settlers. Why should they cross the river and pay ferriage to attend town meetings in Wilkesbarre? Aye, but Wilkesbarre, with its superb town plot, already seeing itself a county town in perspective, thought nothing could be more reasonable and pleasant than that public business should be transacted on her side. This jealousy had led to a town vote, and it had been decided by a small majority, that a certain tree in Kingston, " ten rods north of the house of Mr. Timothy Ross, shall be the Public sign-post;" repealing thereby, and repudiating the tree north of Mr. Butler's, in Wilkesbarre. Several town meetings were held in Kingston, and the prudence of Clerks would not, or failed to, state *where* they were holden. At length a compromise was made, as they had excellent precedent from Home, Hartford and New Haven possessing half-share rights in the honour of having the General Assembly meet in their respective cities. So, too, the County Courts were held alternately at the rival cities of Norwich and New London.

"Voted—That for the future the Annual town meetings, and Freeman's meetings shall be held, half the time on the east side of the river, and the other half on the west side of the river, for one year."

On the 29th of December, only four days after Col. Plunket had retired, we find the whole settlement together, in " TOWN MEETING." It was in importance equal to the Wittenagemote of our Saxon ancestors. The rigid Puritanism of the times allowing few amusements, the town meeting was a matter both of business and recreation. When met the most athletic threw the bar, rolled the bullet, wrestled, standing face to face, the right hand on each other's collar, the left hold of each other's elbow, the play with the feet, and the expert trip and twitch, affording a fine opportunity to display activity and skill. Or the parties took each other round the back, seizing by the waistband, the other hands interlocked, and then came the less neat and scientific, but more arduous struggle, the result depending greatly on strength. A third mode was for two to stand at a few rods distance, and rushing in, seize each other, and wrestle rough and tumble. Others again ran foot races, especially the lads, while some of the first in activity would run and jump the string. William Hibberd, it is told with a sort of bold pride by the old men, would cause a twine to be stretched so high that he could pass under it, just touching his hair—then stepping back a rod or two, he would leap like a deer, so light, so airy, as scarcely to touch the earth, and clear it with ease at a bound.

Several votes were passed in consequence of the Plunket invasion, too important to be omitted.

"That Mr. Christopher Avery be chosen Agent for this town, to proceed forthwith to his Hon. the Governor of this Colony, and lay our distressed case before him."

Obadiah Gore, jr., was also appointed to proceed to Philadelphia, "and lay before the Honorable Continental Congress, the late invasion made by the tory party of the Pennsylvania people."

"Voted—That Titus Hinman and Perrin Ross, be appointed to collect the charity of the people for the support of the widow Baker, the widow Franklin, and the widow Ensign."

How many single men were slain, or how many more married men whose circumstances were such that their widows would not need the aid of contributions we are not informed. It is probable six or eight were killed in all, and three times that number wounded.

It is not strange that money should have been scarce at Wyoming, as no market invited and rewarded the transportation of their surplus products, but grain, it is inferred, must have been plenty, from the prices at which it was valued. A vote was passed that in payment of taxes, corn should be received at two shillings a bushel, rye at three shillings, and wheat at four shillings, that is thirty-four, fifty, and sixty-seven cents.

So ended the memorable Plunket invasion, and thus closed the eventful year 1775.*

---

* On a recent visit to Northumberland, (May 1845) Mr. McC—— an intelligent gentleman, whose memory reaches back to Revolutionary times, related to me several characteristic anecdotes of Dr. Plunket. He was an Irishman (the name is distinguished in the history of the Emerald Isle,) whose loyalty to his king, neither the blandishments of ambition, the persuasions of interest, nor the terrors of proscription could shake for a moment. Up to the day of his death he would never take the oath of allegiance, which conceded the demise of royal authority in America. Not unfrequently assailed, for he was fearless and free spoken, he went armed with the loaded but of a riding whip, prepared to defend or chastise. A Justice of the Peace before the Revolution, if his decisions were just, his manner of inflicting punishment was frequently odd, if not arbitrary and severe. It would seem that the old English whipping-post and stocks, was unknown in Northumberland; but the Doctor had a stout worm-fence, and sometimes placed the neck of the prisoner between the rails, making them both pillory and stocks, at the same time. He died at an advanced age, a bachelor, and was buried at Sunbury. The father of Mr. McC—— was in the Plunket invasion, and some years afterwards received from the treasury (he thinks) $250 for his services on the expedition.

ADDITIONAL NOTE.

From Holt's New York Journal and General Advertiser, January 25, 1776.

" A letter from Westmoreland, dated the 27th of December, mentions that a body of six or seven hundred tories, under one PLUNKET, had assembled in arms, with two cannon, threatening destruction to all that opposed them. They were met on the 21st by Colonel ―――― with about two hundred of his regiment, who, after a short but brisk firing, which killed a number of them, drove one wing into the mountains, and obliged the main body to retreat. On the 23d, they, the Tories, attempted to cross the river, and destroy the settlements there; but a party was prepared to receive them, who, when they came near the shore, fired upon, and killed fifty or sixty of them, when all the rest retired precipitately, and will hardly return this winter. On the other side, there were but three killed and two wounded."

[Remark. The fifty or sixty stated to have been killed, was probably an error of the press. We have never previously seen the number estimated at half that amount.

Opprobious party names were applied to opponents at that day, with as little regard to fairness, as they had been for ages before, and have been for half a century since. Though the designation was applicable to Col. P., yet there is no reason to doubt but nine-tenths of his followers were as zealous whigs as their Yankee opponents.]

A THIRD NOTE.

For the following I am indebted to a literary friend. It is highly curious and will be read with interest.

From the Gentleman's Magazine, of September 1750.

"Several highway robberies having been committed on various persons on Hounslow Heath, among others on Lord Eglintoun; on the 27th July, James Maclean, who passed for an Irish gentleman of fortune, was apprehended, who afterwards confessed, he with one Plunket had committed the robberies.

In his defence on trial, he stated " that he had been in trade and had unhappily become acquainted with Plunket, an apothecary, who by his account of himself, induced me to believe he had travelled abroad, and was possessed of clothes and other things suitable thereto, and prevailed on me to employ him in attending on my family, and lend him money to the amount of 100 pounds and upwards. On giving up trade, I pressed Plunket for payment, and after receiving by degrees several sums, he proposed to pay me part in goods.

" These very clothes, with which I am charged, he brought there and made sale of towards paying my debt."

A MSS leaf states as follows :―" Plunket, the companion of Maclean, escaped, emigrated to America, reformed and became a very respectable character. He was for many years one of the Associate Judges of the Court of Common Pleas, of Northumberland county, Pa., and died."

" By his own acknowledgment he was concerned with Maclean in the attack upon Lord Eglintoun on Hounslow Heath. They engaged in this scheme to rob him, without the intention of committing murder, knowing that Eglintoun had left a gambling house with a large sum of money, and was going to his country seat. They found him armed, and in self protection, Maclean discharged his blunderbuss into the chariot.

" No injury was done, and they meeting with unexpected resistance, made off.

" Plunket was recognized in America by a person who had known him in England, and who kept his secret.

" He regretted this action, as one of his youthful crimes, and afterwards became a very useful member of society."

Extracted from the 21st volume of bound Magazines, in the Library of the Athenæum.

HISTORY OF WYOMING. 181

A FOURTH NOTE.

In the foregoing letter, page 168, will be found a note signed "*Franklin*." The following explanation is deemed proper.

Colonel Franklin's Book.—After the annunciation had been publicly made, that my history was ready for the press, a letter was received from my excellent friend, the Hon. John N. Conyngham, then on a circuit, holding courts in the upper part of his district, stating that Col. Kingsbury had placed in his hands a manuscript of Col. Franklin, in relation to the Wyoming claim and history. All the important papers of Col. Franklin had been, it was supposed, accidentally consumed by fire, occasioning universal regret. To his journal, obtained through Judge Conyngham's politeness from the kindness of Col. Kingsbury, is now added this manuscript volume, leaving nothing (except personal reminiscences and anecdotes illustrative of individual character) that Col. Franklin knew, or could have thought worthy of being related, to be wished for. The book is a quarto of 106 pages, in his own hand writing, and signed with the often seen, and well remembered autograph of

JOHN FRANKLIN.

It would seem that the first sixty pages were a syllabus of the Connecticut claim and settlement, made to be produced before Congress, or a new court (as petitioned for) if it had been raised, under the confederation, to try the private right of soil. For it begins with King James's Charter to the Plymouth Company, and runs regularly through all the documents, giving brief, but clear explanations or extracts, and to the marginal notes, or index, is added "a copy;" "*we* have a copy," "Charter produced, etc." Of the settlement of 1763, the massacre and expulsion, he says: "Proved by the deposition of Wm. Buck, Parshall Terry, and other witnesses may be had." Being intended for some important public purpose, it seems full, and prepared with great care.

The forty subsequent pages contain an epitome of the history of Wyoming, down to the establishment of Luzerne county, the marginal notes and index being continued, (as in our printed laws) but the remark "a copy," "we have a copy," or how proved, not continued. So that we infer it was intended as a memorandum for himself and friends, of the interesting events of the period he treats of. It has in no respect the form of a history written out for publication.

Having examined the venerable relic, with interest and care, the first remark we have to make is: An early possession of the manuscript would have saved us a year of patient labour. For here is gathered in a single sheaf, a vast variety of valuable facts, which we have been gleaning with solicitude and toil from a wide field, indeed, from almost innumerable sources. Our second remark is—that we are surprised—pleased, yea, proud—that our researches had been so successful. At present it is thought that not a single alteration or addition need be made in the text of our book; but that all proper emendations or additions may be introduced in notes, indicating their source by adding the name of——*Franklin*.

LETTER XV.

1776.——Alarm—Indians—Council at Wyoming—Indian Speech—Letter of Colonel Butler—Second deputation of Indians—Proceedings—Danger apparent—Numbers and strength of Wyoming—Precautionary measures—Strange and unwelcome settlers—Alarm increases—John Secord—Tories arrested—Sent to Connecticut—Members of Assembly—Forts built—County created—Enlistment of men—Important proceedings of Congress—Two Companies raised to defend the town—Immediately marched away.

The year 1776, was the most important to Wyoming both in immediate events, and ultimate consequences, that had yet been experienced.

Extreme anxiety had existed on the part of Congress and the country, in respect to the part the Six Nations and other Indians, would take in the contest between Great Britain and the Colonies. Every probable means suggested by prudence were adopted to conciliate their good will, and prevent them from taking up arms in favour of either party. Commissioners were sent among them with "talks" carefully prepared, stating the grievances which we suffered from Great Britain, and urging the Indians to leave the buried hatchet in repose, and maintain a position of peace and neutrality. Delegations of chiefs were invited to Philadelphia, where councils were held, and presents made to them; but amid general professions of friendship, it was apparent that a more powerful influence inclined them to side with the enemy, and anxiety all along the frontier, ripened into alarm. So very important were our Indian relations to the quiet, if not the existence of Wyoming, that a further exposition of the matter, appears to be required at our hand.

So early as the 1st of June 1775, a petition was laid before Congress from Augusta county, west of the Alleghany, Virginia, intimating "fears of a rupture with the Indians, on account of Lord Dunmore's conduct." In December of that year, Congress thought fit to publish an extract of a letter from General Schuyler, relative to measures taken by the ministerial agents to engage the Indians in a war with the colonies. In June, 1776, Congress were informed 'by a letter from the President of South Carolina, that the Cherokees had commenced hostilities, etc."

The ill temper of the savages is shown by the speech of Logan, a chief, to the commissioners at Pittsburg. "We still hear bad news. Connesdico and some of us are constantly threatened, and the Bear-skin, a trader from Pennsylvania, amongst others, says, a great reward is offered to any person who will take or entice either of us to Pittsburg, where we are to be hanged up like dogs by the Big-knife. This being true, how can we think of what is good. That it is true we have no doubt, and you may depend on it, that the Bear-skin told Metopsica every word of what I have mentioned."

August the 19th, Congress Resolved, "That the Commissioners be instructed to make diligent inquiry into the murder lately committed by Indians in the neighborhood of Pittsburg, on one Crawford; and that, as soon as they discover by whom the same was committed, they demand due punishment on the offender or offenders, which being granted, this Congress will not consider the same as a national act."

Still the Chief Head, the Council at Onondago, were making hollow professions of peace, and endeavoring to lull the frontiers into security. An outrage had been committed on a person named Wilson, who lived some distance up the North Branch, but within the limits of Westmoreland. Col. Butler, though not officially authorized to do so, thought proper on behalf of the people to send a messenger to the neighboring tribes, and ascertain their intentions. A chief returned with the messenger. His English name was John. We regret that his Indian name has not been preserved, for his speech is one of the most chaste, neat specimens of Indian oratory we have ever read. The Rev. Mr. Johnson acted as interpreter.

A Conference held at Wyoming, or Westmoreland, between Capt. John in behalf of the Six Nations, and Col. Butler of the Colony of Connecticut.

"Capt. John:—

"Brothers—We come to make you a visit and let you know we were at the Treaty at Oswego, with Col. Guy Johnson. We are all of one mind, we are friends, and bring good news.

"Brothers—We are also come to let you know, the Six Nations have been something afraid, but now are glad to see all things look like peace, and they think there will be no quarrel with each other, and you must not believe bad reports, or remember times that have been bad or unfriendly.

"Brothers—All our spirits are of one colour, why should we not be of one mind. Continue to be brothers as our fathers and grandfathers were.

"Brothers—We hope and desire you may hold what liberties and privileges you now enjoy.

"Brothers—We are sorry to hear two brothers are fighting with each other, and should be glad to hear the quarrel was peaceably settled. We choose not to interest ourselves on either side. The quarrel appears to be unnecessary. We do not well understand it. We are for peace.

"Brothers—When our young men come to hunt in your neighborhood, you must not imagine they come to do mischief—they come to procure themselves provisions—also skins to purchase them clothing.

"Brothers—We desire that Wyoming may be a place appointed where the great men may meet, and have a fire, which shall ever afterwards be called Wyomick, when you shall judge best, to prevent any jealousies or uneasy thoughts that may arise, and thereby preserve our friendship.

"Brothers—You see but one of our chiefs. You may be suspicious on that account, but we assure you, this Chief speaks in the name of the Six Nations. We are of one mind.

"Brothers—What we say is not from the lips, but from the heart. If any Indians of little note should speak otherwise, you must pay no regard to them, but observe what has been said and wrote by the chiefs, which may be depended on.

"Brothers—We live at the head of these waters, (Susquehanna.) Pay no regard to any reports that may come up the stream or any other way, but look to the head of the waters for truth, and we do now assure you, as long as the waters run, so long you may depend on our friendship. We are all of one mind, and we are all for peace."

A letter from Col. Butler to the Hon. Roger Sherman then a delegate in Congress, from Connecticut, will throw additional light on the subject.

"WESTMORELAND, Oct. 1st, 1776.

"Honored Sir:—In some of my last letters, you will recollect I informed you I had sent a messenger among the Indians upon the head waters of the Susquehannah, and thereby informed them of an assault made upon one of our people, whose testimony has some time since been sent to you. The Indians, you will see by the enclosed messages, are disposed for peace, and think it necessary that this place be appointed to hold their Council at, and, as they express it, to have a fire-place here. Their importunity was so pressing on that account, that I promised them to inform the Congress, and our Assembly of their request, and would beg the opinion of yourself, and our other delegates, whether it is best to lay it before the Congress, and that you would be pleased to inform his Honour, our Governor, immediately, what you apprehend will be best for the Colony to do, if any thing, in that matter. The Indians when they come here, expect presents, or at least to be supported while among us, and no one is appointed to treat with them. They come to me, and I have frequently given them, but find the burthen too great for one man to bear.

"They also insist upon a new flag, such as is used by the army of the United States. They say their old flag came over the great water, and they now want a new one, as a token of their friendship to the United States.

"By the last papers we find that the report of Col. Butler, etc., with Indians and Canadians being at Oswego, is disbelieved. By the accounts we had before received of that matter, some were much agitated here, but seem more easy at present.

"I expect to be at the Assembly, and shall gladly receive any information you shall think proper to send me.

"I am, sir, your humble servant,

"Z. BUTLER."

"N. B. The Indians deny having any hand in the attack made upon Wilson, and have engaged to let us know if they make any discovery of that matter.

HON. ROGER SHERMAN."

The earnest desire to have a *fire-place* erected at Wyoming, and that a great council should be held there, was probably a devised plan to introduce the savages into the settlement without creating alarm, and then treacherously to destroy the whole. Their importunity it seems, "*was pressing.*"

It would also appear that now, since war rumors were afloat, numerous chiefs, claiming consideration, visited Wyoming, expecting presents and entertainment. "I have frequently given" says Colonel Butler, "but find the burden too great for one man to bear."

But they wanted a new *flag*, such as the "United States Army used," probably as a decoy on a fitting occasion. In respect to the news of Colonel John Butler with his Canadians and Indians being at Oswego, Colonel Z. Butler says:—"SOME WERE VERY MUCH AGITATED HERE." The more sagacious men at Wyoming, could not fail to foresee and dread the danger. A tremendous avalanche hung over them, which the least jar might precipitate on their heads.

In September following, a deputation of three chiefs arrived at Wyoming, and brought a "Talk," the "Great Head" at Onondago having held a council. The talk was agreed upon at Chenango by certain authorized chiefs. While it professes peaceable intentions, the tone is one of complaint. The length is too great to render proper its publication entire. A paragraph or two will give its spirit.

"Brothers—There is a great deal between us. The Devil is always putting something between us, but this is to clear your hearts that you may speak clearly and pleasantly to us. A string of wampum.

"Well Brothers—There is a great deal of trouble around you. Your lids are all bloody, but we come to clear away all suspicion that your hearts may be pleasant." Three strings of wampum.

Still desirous that a great council fire should be kindled at Wyoming, they proceed:—

"Well Brothers—Our fire-place is almost lost, and our fire almost out. We think it hard, and desire it may be renewed, and the *fire-place fixed here*, that our mutual fire may give light from one end of this river to the other.

"Brothers—We are unwilling to have forts built up the river, but wish you would be content to build forts here among the lower settlers. A fort at Wyalusing will block up our new made, wide, and smooth road, and again make us strangers to one another."

Three other paragraphs urgently desire that a "Fire" may be kindled at Wyoming, "so that the flame and smoke may arise to the clouds," etc.

After complaining of some wrong by a white man, done an Indian in the exchange of cows, and demanding satisfaction, they ask a new flag, and beg for some flour to take home with them, and request that as they are for peace their guns and tomahawks may be put in order.

In conclusion, "Well Brother, Colonel Butler, you must have an Indian name; Koorenghloognana, (signifying a great tree,) we will henceforth call you."

The Chiefs present were

          WILLIAM NANTICOKE, Nanticoke Chief.
          INDIAN JOSEPH, Onondago Chief.
          NARONDIGWANOK, or ⎫ A Seneca Chief.
             CAPT. JOHNSON, ⎭

The "*Talk*" was regarded as evasive and unsatisfactory. It may be considered as creditable to the Wyoming people, that Indian jealousy could find nothing in their five years intercourse, for their friends scattered through the Valley to complain of, except the matter of the cow exchange.

In a letter from Colonel Butler to Roger Sherman, dated August 6, 1776, he says:—

"You will see by the representations from this town that we are under apprehensions of danger from the Indians, as our army has retreated to Crown-point, and every artifice using to set the Indians on us, by Johnson and Butler, at Niagara."

Colonel Butler also speaks of the settlement being in want of arms, "as those eighty guns taken from our people at Warrior's Run, have not been returned," etc.

A report reached the valley the same month, that Colonel John Butler, "with Indians and Canadians, was at Oswego." Notwithstanding the professions of the Six Nations, no one doubted before the close of 1776, but that they were pledged to the interest of Great Britain, and on the invasion by Burgoyne early in the following year, numbers of them were found arrayed under his standard, active, brave and cruel, as became their long established character.

Westmoreland extended north, five miles above the confluence of the Susquehanna and Chemung rivers. The upper part of the town was therefore not only within the range of the Indian paths, but as previously stated, actually included several of their settlements at Tioga Point, Sheshequin and the Great Bend. In the immediate neighborhood were the populous villages of Oquaga, (one of the head quarters of Brandt,) Chenango, Owego, Choconut and Newtown, the latter a place where many distinguished chiefs resided. The general, almost the universal, course of travel for the Indians going east or west, was through the upper part of Westmoreland. A moderate freshet in the river, would bring their boats and canoes, in twenty-four hours, from their place of rendezvous at Tioga, into the heart of the Wyoming settlement. Being therefore within easy striking distance, they were fully aware of their danger, and might well look with anxious solicitude to the public authorities for protection.

A colony projected out from her own bosom beyond New York, forty miles north of the Blue Mountains, and divided by an inhospitable wilderness, from any other settlement of sufficient strength to yield support in case of invasion, Connecticut seemed called upon by the strongest considerations of justice and mercy to take measures to afford effectual protection to this her exposed frontier.

An important inquiry presents itself; What were the numbers, and what the strength of Westmoreland? Trumbull states, and on his authority, Chapman copies the assertion, that there were five thousand inhabitants in the town. It will be observed that the number is stated roundly at five thousand, as if it were matter of guess, rather than of enumeration. From all the lights before me, I am confident the number is greatly exaggerated. In the first place, during the years of peace and prosperity from 1774 to 1776 only two hundred and eighty-five (285) persons had taken the Freeman's oath, and exercised the right of suffrage in town meetings, when there were many and obvious motives to do so, and none that we can conceive of, to deter.

Second. When, after the Declaration of Independence, a new oath was demanded, only two hundred and sixty-nine (269) had appeared and been sworn. Allowing an hundred freemen to have been absent with the army, and the whole number would be three hundred sixty-nine (369.) If we allow six persons to each voter, the number would be two thousand two hundred and fourteen (2214.) Third. A list of settlers at Wyoming for 1773, two years before, in Col. Butler's hand writing, numbers only two hundred and sixteen (216.) Fourth. An assessment for Wilkesbarre township in 1774, corrected January 1775, contains one hundred and twenty (120) names. The sum assessed was £3646. The whole assessment in Westmoreland that year was £13,083. Now if £3646 give 120 persons, how many would 13083 give? It is apprehended this would be one fair mode of approximating the truth. The answer is 430, which multiplied by 6, gives 2580.

In the Plunket battle, when full notice had been received of the impending and pressing danger, and every thing was at stake, only about three hundred men could be mustered, and not all those with fire arms. We see no reason to suppose the whole number of inhabitants exceeded about twenty-five hundred (2500.) Perhaps to impress the enemy with an idea of her formidable power, might have been regarded as a means to prevent invasion, and therefore warranting the exaggeration. The data on which our conclusion is founded, being submitted, every person who takes an interest in the matter will form an opinion for himself.

Having presented a brief view of the position of Wyoming, the dangers the people had reasonable ground to apprehend, and as accurate an estimate as possible of the number of inhabitants, we approach a matter of the utmost moment; but previous to entering thereon, duty and pleasure call on us to state some highly patriotic proceedings; while an equal sense of duty demands our notice of several painful events.

At a town meeting, held March 10th, "Voted, that the first man that shall make fifty weight of good salt-petre in this town shall be entitled to a bounty of ten pounds, lawful money, to be paid out of the town treasury."

"Voted, that the selectmen be directed to dispose of the grain now in the hands of the Treasurer, or Collector, in such way as to obtain powder and lead to the value of forty pounds, lawful money, if they can do the same."

The Continental Congress having recommended the appointment of committees of vigilance in every town, and the arrest of persons hostile to the cause of liberty, a committee of inspection was established, a measure that became the more pressingly necessary, as, with the breaking out of the war, and the prohibition on the part of Connecticut of any further emigration to Wyoming, there had come in strange families of interlopers from Minnisink, from West Chester, New York, from Kinderhook, and the Mohawk, neither connected with Pennsylvania nor Connecticut, between whom and the old settlers there was neither sympathy in feeling, nor community of interests—Wintermoots, Vangorders, and Von-Alstines. A path of communication was opened by the disaffected between New York and Niagara, to strike the Susquehanna twenty miles above Wilkesbarre. Some of those new and unwelcome settlers soon made their sentiments known, and disclosed their hostility to the American cause, while others for the time remained quiet, though subsequent events showed the purpose of their emigration to the Susquehanna.*

---

* This view is attested by the fact, that in January 1776, Mr. Hageman being examined before the committee of inspection, said, "that riding with Mr. S.—they *spoke of the people coming in up the river to join the enemy* ["as a familiar and well understood matter."] He, Hageman, observed that the Yankees would go up and take their arms from them. S. replied, he was the man, if it were done, who would see that they were returned to them."

John Secord, who had settled up the river near thirty miles above the Valley, was known to harbor suspicious persons, and was suspected of acting as a spy, and giving intelligence to the enemy. Several British prisoners, confined at Lebanon, Conn., had made their escape, viz: Captain Hume, Lieuts. Richardson, Hubbage and Burroughs, with their servants. Having a pilot, they struck the river twenty miles above the Valley, and were supposed to have been directed to, and entertained by Secord, furnished with provisions, and aided in their flight to Niagara.

The committee caused him to be arrested; but he petitioned Congress, complaining of the outrage on his rights, and by their order was liberated. A bold, bad man, he united himself to the enemy, the moment he could more effectually serve them in that manner, than by professing friendship for the Yankees, and acting as a spy upon Wyoming. Two of the Vangorders, Philip and Abraham, were taken by the committee, and sent to Litchfield for trial. Andrew Adams, Esq., was employed to conduct the prosecution, but the issue we have not been able to learn. About the same time eight or ten persons were arrested, and sent to Hartford for trial, but were dismissed.

Doubts have been expressed whether there was not more zeal than discretion in these proceedings. With the faint lights before us it is impossible to form an opinion entirely satisfactory upon the subject. Certain it is, such an influx of strangers was deemed, and not without reason, extraordinary. Some of them it is known immediately opened communications with the enemy. The issue showed that they were all enemies in disguise. We are not prepared to say therefore, that the people were to blame in taking the most energetic measures to remove, or over-awe the more avowedly disaffected, especially when the recommendations of Congress are considered.

John Jenkins, Esq., (the elder) and Captain Solomon Strong, were chosen members of the Legislature to attend at Hartford, in May, with express orders to request the Assembly to demand of the Pennsylvania Government £4,000 for losses sustained by their invasion, and if necessary to pursue the matter before Congress. As no further notice of the subject appears upon the records, and as it is certain no compensation was received, it is presumed that prudential considerations induced the General Assembly to decline interfering.

"At a town meeting legally warned and held, in Westmoreland, Wilkesbarre district, August 24, 1776,

"Colonel Butler was chosen moderator for the work of the day.

"Voted—As the opinion of this meeting, that it now becomes necessary for the inhabitants of this town to erect suitable forts, as a defence against our common enemy."

Recently there had been established by the General Assembly at Westmoreland, the 24th Regiment of Connecticut militia. The meeting voted that the three field officers should be a committee to fix on proper sites for the forts, lay them out, and give directions how they should be built. The Wintermoots, a numerous family, seeming to have extraordinary means at command, had purchased and settled near the head of the Valley upon a spot where a large and pure spring of water gushes out from the high bank, or upper flat. Here they had erected a fortification, known as Wintermoot's fort. This was looked upon with jealousy by the old settlers. A vote was therefore passed, that no forts be built except those which should be designated by the military committee. As it was too late to remedy the evil, the committee resolved to counteract it as far as possible, by causing a fort to be built a mile above Wintermoots, in the neighborhood, and under the supervision of the Jenkins and Harding families, leading men and ardent patriots. It was named Fort Jenkins, (but must not be confounded by the reader with the Fort Jenkins, half way between Wyoming and Sunbury, or Fort Augusta.) Forty Fort was to be strengthened and enlarged. Sites were fixed on in Pittston, Wilkesbarre, Hanover, and Plymouth. And then was adopted the following beautiful vote:—

"That the above said committee, do recommend it to the people to proceed forthwith in building said Forts without either fee or reward from ye town."

We leave it in its simplicity to speak its own eulogium.

The die was cast. Independence was declared. War assumed throughout the land his sternest aspect, and every day disclosed to Wyoming some new ground of apprehension. The savages, who yet dwelt in the Valley, theretofore peaceable and quiet, now began to assume an insolent carriage, demanding provisions and liquor, with an authoritative air, accompanied by expressions implying threats of vengeance if refused. Justly dreading the ill consequences of a quarrel, the town passed a solemn vote, similar in spirit to one previously adopted, forbidding, under penalty of forty shillings a gill, the sale to an Indian of any spirituous liquors, and also prohibiting the transportation of spirits upon the river above the Valley.

In November, Colonel Butler and Colonel Denison, representatives to the October session of the Assembly, held at New Haven, returned, bringing the good tidings that the town of Westmoreland was erected into a county, and henceforth its organization, civil and military, was complete. Jonathan Fitch, Esq., had received the commission of High Sheriff, and was of course the first person who ever held that responsible office on the North Branch of the Susquehanna.

During the summer Capt. Weisner, from New York, was sent to Wyoming, to enlist part of a rifle company for the continental service. Obadiah Gore, Jr., an active and enterprising man, offered Weisner his influence, received the commission of lieutenant, and raised about twenty men, with whom he marched to head-quarters. Soon after, however, it being deemed proper that, as they were enlisted in Connecticut, they should be credited to her, and not to the New York line of the army, they were transferred, it is believed, to the regiment of Col. Wyllis.

About the same time, Capt. Strong enlisted part of a company, at Wyoming, the number is supposed to have been inconsiderable, not exceeding eight or ten. These being the first enlisted men, took with them the best arms that could be obtained. That a man should have left the Valley, or that a musket or rifle should have been taken, is matter of surprise. But no where throughout the United Colonies, did the spirit of patriotism glow more intensely than in Westmoreland. We make the remark here, and shall repeat it again, that like the generous steed which exerts every sinew, till he falls lifeless under his rider, Wyoming never seemed to know when they had done and suffered enough, if further duty or suffering was demanded by the cause.

Col. Butler, in a letter to a member, complaining that no restitution had been made, as recommended by Congress, of property taken, partly in boats confiscated while trading down the river; and horses, arms, and other articles taken from Wyoming, says:—" Our other property, though valuable, we would not mention at this day, but OUR ARMS WE CANNOT FORBEAR SPEAKING OF, as there are none to be purchased, and we a frontier, and so unanimously willing to defend the United States of America, at the risk of our lives. But Congress must be best acquainted with the disposition of the Indians," etc. Congress being fully apprised of the situation of Westmoreland, determined to interpose and provide for the defence of the town. To this end—

"Friday, August 23, 1776.—Resolved, That two companies on the Continental establishment, be raised in the town of Westmoreland, *and stationed in proper places for the defence of the inhabitants of said town, and parts adjacent,* till further order of Congress; the commissioned officers of the said two companies, to be immediately appointed by Congress.

"That the pay of the men, to be raised as aforesaid, commence when they are armed and mustered, and that they be liable to serve in any part of the United States, when ordered by Congress.

"That the said troops be enlisted to serve during the war, unless sooner discharged by Congress."

August 26th.—Congress proceeded to the election of sundry officers, when Robert Durkee and Samuel Ransom were elected captains of the two companies ordered to be raised in the town of Westmoreland, James Wells, and Perrin Ross, first lieutenants; Asahel Buck, and Simon Spalding, second lieutenants; Herman Swift and Matthias Hollenback, ensigns of said companies."

Early in September, information was received of the Resolution of Congress, and rendezvous for the enlistment of men on the terms prescribed, were opened by Capt. Durkee on the east, and by Capt. Ransom on the west side of the river. As the troops raised were by the express pledge of Congress, "to be stationed in proper places for the defence of the inhabitants," while, of course, the existing danger should continue, the able bodied men flocked to the standard raised, and in less than sixty days, both companies were full, numbering about eighty-four each.

Washington's army, greatly impaired in numbers and spirit, by their expulsion from Long Island, were now sorely pressed by Gen. Howe. On the 15th of September, New York was taken possession of by the enemy. The battle at White Plains had been fought, and on the 16th of November, Fort Washington surrendered to the British arms, Gen. Howe claiming to have taken twenty-five hundred prisoners. Gloom—almost despondence—overspread the American camp. Howe pushed his advantage with energy. Washington was compelled to retreat, from post to post, through the Jerseys. "The Commander-in-Chief," says Marshall, "found himself at the head of this small force, less than three thousand soldiers, dispirited by their losses and fatigues, retreating, almost naked and bare footed, in the cold of November and December, before a numerous, well appointed and victorious army, through a desponding country, much more disposed to obtain safety by submission than to seek it by manly resistance."

On the 8th of December, Gen. Washington crossed the Delaware, and Congress immediately took measures to retire from Philadelphia to Baltimore. At this moment of peril, they " Resolved, Thursday December 12th, " That the two companies raised in the town of Westmoreland, be ordered to join Gen. Washington, *with all possible expedition*." And the very same day adjourned to meet on the 20th, at Baltimore.

Promptly obeying the order, the two companies hastened their march, and before the close of the month and year, were upon the lines, under the command of their beloved Washington.

LETTER XVI.

1777.—Wyoming Companies—Rivalry—Political jealousy—Town vote—The dreaded Small Pox—Pestilence spreads—First Student to Yale College—Adonijah Stansbury—Case curious and troublesome—Indian book debt—Citation for Toryism—Difficulty settled by marriage—Post established to Hartford—Yankee official titles—Tax—Preparations for defence—Lieut. Jenkins, first prisoner—Brave Old Fitzgerald—Companies of Durkee and Ransom—Battle of Millstone—Porter killed—Gen. Washington's letter—Mud Fort—Lieut. Spalding—Matthewson killed—Wealth and revenue of Westmoreland—Warrant—Excessive burdens on Wyoming—Beautiful resolve.

Lights and shadows alternately brightened and obscured the Wyoming sky during the year 1777. The gloomy aspect of affairs along the sea-board; Burgoyne with his powerful army descending from the north; the accession of the savage interest to the cause of Great Britain, carrying with it the certainty that the frontier settlements, as in the old French war, would be one long line of conflagration and murder, awakened in the breasts of the Wyoming people, great fears for the general cause, and extreme anxiety for their own safety.

The companies had marched with the utmost alacrity—not a murmur was heard, for every man felt that the case was one of imperious necessity, yet not one of them entertained a doubt, but that the moment affairs below the mountains were restored to a state of tolerable order, the pledge "to be stationed in proper places to defend their homes," would be regarded in good faith, and the soldiers ordered back to the Valley.

Treachery, a trick to entrap them into the service under so fair a pretence, and then to force them away, leaving their homes wholly exposed and unprotected, implied a degree of baseness and cruelty they could not even comprehend, and therefore did not fear. Cheerfully the soldiers marched to their duty, while hope of their speedy return sustained their families at home.

Town meetings were as heretofore, duly holden, and at the spring meeting, John Jenkins and Isaac Tripp, Esqs., were chosen members to the Assembly, which was to convene in Hartford, in May. Westmoreland being now a county as well as town, a place for the erection of public buildings must be fixed upon, and the old rivalry between Wilkesbarre and Kingston, or, more extensively, between the east and west sides of the river, was, by the magnitude of the subject excited to a pitch that absorbed for a time, almost exclusively, the public attention. An intelligent committee of impartial men was demanded of the Assembly to settle the dispute.

Another matter created no little excitement among the ambitious men. Rumours had reached Wyoming, that the Assembly intended to appoint to some of the more elevated judicial offices, certain persons not inhabitants of the Valley, but chosen from that part of the State east of New York.

Voted, as instructions to Messrs. Jenkins and Tripp. "If any person that is not an inhabitant of this town, should be nominated for an office in this county, that they immediately remonstrate against it in the most spirited manner, as unconstitutional, and an unprecedented thing in this colony in any former times."

The county town was established at Wilkesbarre, and the officers of the new county were selected from the town of Westmoreland.

Scarce had the summer opened when a new cause of terror and distress was developed in the Valley. The small-pox (how justly this then deadly plague was dreaded, the present generation can form but a faint idea,) made its appearance. One of the most respected citizens returned from Philadelphia, was taken sick with the disease, and died.* Want of the advice and protecting influence of the numerous heads of families, away with the army, was sorely felt. But a town meeting was held, where wise and energetic measures were adopted to obviate to the utmost of human power, the ill effects of the contagion. A pest house was established in each township or district, half a mile from any road, where persons were to resort for inoculation. No one in the settlement was to receive the infection except in one of these houses, nor unless by express warrant from an examining committee. A strict quarantine respecting persons connected with the pest houses was established, and regulations for the careful change of clothes. Physicians were prohibited from inoculating except in the places designated. How many deaths occurred from the contagion is not known, but the means adopted had the most salutary influence in quieting alarm, and preventing the spread of the fatal disorder.

* Jeremiah Ross, father of our late distinguished fellow-citizen, General Wm. Ross.

Throughout the proceedings of this year, schools appear to have engaged more than usual attention. State taxes, to go into the treasury at Hartford, were to be paid, county and town rates were levied, and yet the zeal for instruction was so unabated, that an additional tax of a penny in the pound was laid for free school purposes. Each township was also established as a legal school district, with power to rent the lands " sequestered by the Susquehanna Company therein, for the use of schools, and also receive of the school committee appointed by their town, their part of the county money, according to their respective rates."

It is also due to the pleasing fact, that it should be distinctly recorded, this year for the first time there was sent from Wyoming, a student to Yale College.

Were we the eulogist, instead of the impartial historian of Wyoming, we might inquire with emphasis, if there before was a people, surrounded by external dangers, pestilence in the midst, a large portion of their natural protectors away in the public service, who ever exhibited so praiseworthy a zeal to diffuse the blessings of education among the rising generation?

We have before adverted to the fact, that Pennsylvania landholders, masking their true character, came in, purchased a Connecticut right, and then denounced and undervalued the claim as of no validity. This was a mode of attack extremely annoying and difficult to repel. Chapman's mill was in full and successful operation. A person by the name of Adonijah Stansbury, from the State of Delaware, purchased Chapman's interest, and was placed therefore by his business in instant communication with multitudes of people. It became soon apparent that Stansbury was a disguised enemy. Intelligent, plausible, active, he laughed at the pretended Connecticut claim openly as a folly, and derided it more secretly to some as an imposition. The good people had no other mill to grind for them, and the nuisance became insupportable and dangerous. Stansbury had violated no law, but except through the law there was no way to reach him.

Voted at a town meeting, " that Col. Butler, Col. Denison and Maj. Judd, be a committee, (the high standing of the committee indicates the importance of the subject,) to write to the Connecticut Delegates, and give them a true character of Adonijah Stansbury, and the measures he has heretofore taken for the destruction of this settlement."

Stansbury disregarded the vote. More energetic measures became necessary, and as he owed no man in the town, an Indian, from the Oquago brought suit against him for a sum of money charged as being due on book, growing out of an ancient trade in horses. Active officers, and a willing court, found a heavy balance owing to the Indian. Suits accumulated.* A whole people had taken the law of him, and he found his position too warmly assailed to render it endurable. A young man, true to the Connecticut interest, happily at this moment formed a matrimonial connection with Stansbury's daughter, an amiable lady, and purchased the mill of his father-in-law, who retired from the settlement. Trifling as the incident in itself may be regarded, it is deemed worthy of preservation as showing that the dispute respecting title, although it slumbered, was still alive, and as indicating the means taken by both parties, to maintain their respective claims, or to annoy their opponents.

A more pleasing matter demands a passing notice. Surrounded by mountains, by a wide spreading wilderness, and by dreary wastes, shut out from all the usual sources of information, a people so inquisitive could not live in those exciting times without the news. Fortunately an old, torn, smoke-dried paper, has fallen into our possession, which shows that the people of Wyoming established a post to Hartford, to go once a fortnight and bring on the papers. A Mr. Prince Bryant was engaged as post-rider for nine months.

---

* Civil suits were not alone resorted to. The following paper has its interest as casting light upon the mode of proceeding with disaffected persons, as well as its direct reference to the case of Stansbury.

"CITATION."

To Adonijah Stansbury, (and two others) all of Westmoreland: You and each of you being suspected of toryism, and subverting the Constitution, and endeavouring to betray the inhabitants of this town into the hands of their enemies, etc.

You and each of you are hereby required without any manner of excuse to make your personal appearance before the committee of inspection for the town of Westmoreland, at the house of Solomon Johnson, Inn-holder in said town, on Wednesday the 3rd of instant, January, at 10 o'clock in the morning, then and there to answer unto divers complaints whereof you are suspected as above; hereof fail not, as you will answer the contrary at the peril of the displeasure of the public.

By order of the Chairman.
ANDERSON DANA, *Clerk.*

To any indifferent person to serve, and return."

On the trial, Garret Brinkerhoor saith, "that some time after Stansbury bought the mills of Chapman, he said he did not intend to pay any more for said mills, and he would go to Pennsylvania and make it appear that Chapman had no right to the lands."

More than fifty subscribers remain to the paper, which evidently must have been more numerous as it is torn in the centre. The sums given varied from one to two dollars each. In the list we find

Elijah Shoemaker,	Seth Marvin,
Elias Church,	Obadiah Gore,
George Dorrance.	James Stark,
Nathan Kingsley,	Anderson Dana,
Elisha Blackman,	Jeremiah Ross,
Nathan Denison,	Zebulon Butler.

Payment for the papers was of course a separate matter. It may well be questioned, whether there is another instance in the States, of a few settlers, especially as those at Wyoming were situated, establishing at their own expense, a post to bring them the newspapers, from a distance of two hundred and fifty miles!

It has been regarded as an amusing characteristic of the Yankees, that they never failed in ancient times, to give any man the title which he might claim, from the Governor of a colony, down to a Sergeant of a company. A quotation from the Westmoreland records will show that the practice was strictly adhered to by the emigrants from Connecticut.

"December, 1777, voted, that Capt. William Worden, Ensign Daniel Downing, Lieut. Daniel Gore, Capt. Nathaniel Landon, Capt. Jeremiah Blanchard, Lieut. Aaron Gaylord, Silas Parke, Esq., Isaac Tripp, Esq., Capt. Stephen Harding, Capt. John Franklin, be fence viewers for the ensuing year. The list contains two or three others without titles.

"December 30, voted by this town, to grant one penny on the pound as an addition to the two penny tax, granted August 6." Three pence on the pound, on an assessment of £20,000 would yield £350, $830. The town also vote to lend the county forty pounds.

During the summer active measures were in progress to place the settlement in the best posture of defence the circumstances of the people would admit. By detachments the people worked on the several forts; built upon a larger scale, and with greater strength, but in the same manner as those of Forts Ogden and Durkee. That at Wilkesbarre occupied the ground on which the Court House now stands. The venerable Maj. Eleazer Blackman says: "I was then a boy of about thirteen, but was called on to work in the fortifications. With spade and pick I could not do much, but I could drive oxen and haul logs." Every sinew from childhood to old age was thus put in requisition.

A system had been established by which scouts were sent up the river, to watch the Indian paths, and bring intelligence. Each party of five or seven, was generally absent a week, but their numbers, and the frequency of their tours of duty were increased as emergencies seemed to require.

Parties of Indians were occasionally heard of at no great distance, but they abstained from violence, except so far as to take off prisoners. Up to this time, they had committed no murder and burnt no dwelling. It is not doubted, that by profound policy, it was their wish the settlement should be lulled into security, that the companies of Durkee and Ransom might not be recalled, but the Valley left exposed, and reserved as a cherished victim for another campaign, when the main body of the Six Nations, now engaged in the northeast, in aid of Burgoyne, should be at liberty to detach a force competent to the certain destruction of the settlement.

An intercommunication it was known, or not doubted, was kept up between the disaffected settlers on the river, from near Tunkhannock to the Wyalusing, with the Indians at Tioga and Newtown, and the British at Niagara. Lieut. Asa Stevens was detached by the Committee of Inspection, with nine men, who returned bringing in five suspected persons, as prisoners. Lieut. John Jenkins having, as the commander of a scouting party, extended his march as far up as Wyalusing, (near the centre of Westmoreland,) was taken prisoner by a band of Indians and Tories. Three men were taken with him, a Mr. Yorke, Lemuel Fitch, and an old man, named Fitzgerald. The Indians and their allies, placed Fitzgerald on a flax-brake, and told him he must renounce his rebel principles, and declare for the King, or die. "Well," said the stouthearted, old fellow, "I am old and have little time to live, anyhow; and I had rather die now a friend to my country, than live ever so long and die a tory!" They had magnanimity enough to let him go; but took the other three to Canada.

As Lieut. Jenkins was, himself, an active officer, and the son of one of the most distinguished men in Wyoming, the father having several times been chosen member of Assembly, a proposal was made and accepted, to exchange him for an Indian chief, then a prisoner in Albany. Under an Indian escort he was sent to that city, and when they arrived, it was found the chief had recently died of the small-pox. The rage of the young Indians, who had escorted him, could scarcely be restrained. They would have tomahawked Lieut. Jenkins on the spot, had they not been forcibly prevented. They demanded that he should return with them. To have done so, would have been exposing him to certain death, probably lingering torture. But he was released, and instantly repaired to his post of duty. These were the first prisoners taken from Wyoming.

On an important occasion, a scouting party of thirty men under the command of Capt. Asaph Whittlesy, ventured up as far as Standing Stone, within twenty-five miles of the north line of Westmoreland. The Rev. Benjamin Bidlack, then a young man of twenty, who was out on this expedition, gives this picture of Wyoming, at that time. The young and active men were employed upon scouting parties, to guard the inhabitants from being surprised. Some portion of the militia was constantly on duty. It was necessary, as the able bodied men were away with the army, and the country so exposed. But the old men formed themselves into companies, and performed duty in the forts. Those companies of ancient men were called Reformados. Capt. Wm. H. Smith, (who acted also as physician and surgeon,) commanded one in Wilkesbarre, of which Elisha Blackman was lieutenant. The father of Mr. Bidlack commanded another in Plymouth.

In the mean time, Ransom and Durkee were stationed near the lines, between the two armies, in New Jersey; Washington, by his brilliant achievements at Trenton and Princeton, having wrested the western portion of that State from the hands of the enemy. They were termed "the two Independent Companies of Westmoreland," and kept from being incorporated with any corps or regiment, the intention being, it is not doubted, to order without unnecessary delay, their return to the duty for which they had been enlisted.

After joining the army, the first time they were under fire, was on the 20th of January, 1777, at the affair, or battle, at Millstone, one of the most gallant and successful actions, considering the numbers engaged, that was fought during the war.

"When Gen. Washington's army was hutted near Morristown," says Rogers, "and laboring under that fatal malady, the small-pox, a line of posts was formed along the Millstone river, in the direction of Princeton. One of these, established at Somerset Court House, was occupied by Gen. Dickinson, with a few hundred men," (consisting of Durkee and Ransom's Independent Companies, from Wyoming, mustering about one hundred and sixty, and three hundred militia.) Not very distant, and on the opposite bank of the stream, stood a mill, in which a considerable quantity of flour had been collected for the use of our troops. At this time, Lord Cornwallis lay at Brunswick, and having received information of this depot, immediately despatched a large foraging party, amounting to about four hundred men, and upwards of forty wagons, drawn by imported horses, of the English draft-breed, for the purpose of taking possession of it. The British troops arrived at the mill early in the morning, and having loaded the wagons with flour, were about to march on their return, when Gen. Dickinson, with an inferior force, which he led through the river, middle deep, attacked them with so much spirit and effect that they fled, abandoning the whole of their plunder."

The Mill Stone victory was, to their latest day, a darling theme with the old soldiers. By the unanimous declaration of those engaged, the attack was impetuous and well sustained. An order to charge was responded to with enthusiasm. Nor did the British yield the ground without a manly, though ineffectual resistance, The enemy retired in confusion, leaving to the victors a handsome booty, consisting of forty-seven wagons, and more than an hundred horses. Each man shared several dollars of prize money, and Capt. Ransom sent one of the wagons to his farm, at Wyoming, as a trophy. Nor was the victory achieved without loss. Several were killed, and a greater number wounded. Among the former, Porter, a gallant young fellow, the pride of Ransom's company, was cut down by a cannon ball.

His Excellency, Gen. Washington, in a letter to the President of Congress, dated Morristown, January 22d, 1777, gives this account of the occurrence.

"My last to you was on the 20th instant. Since that, I have the pleasure to inform you that Gen. Dickinson, with about four hundred militia, has defeated a foraging party of the enemy, of an equal number, and has taken forty wagons, and upwards of an hundred horses, most of them of the English draft-breed, and a number of sheep and cattle which they had collected. The enemy retreated with so much precipitation, that Gen. Dickinson had only an opportunity of making nine prisoners. They were observed to carry off a great many dead and wounded in light wagons. This action happened near Somerset Court House, on Millstone river. Gen. Dickinson's behaviour reflects the highest honour on him; for though his troops were all raw, he led them through the river middle deep, and gave the enemy so severe a charge, that although supported by three field pieces, they gave way, and left their convoy."

Gen. Lincoln's letter and Col. Butler's reply, will show the position of the companies, in May.

"BOUND BROOK, May 27th, 1777.

"Sir,—It is His Excellency, General Washington's orders, that you march immediately with the three detachments from Connecticut regiments, and the two companies of Wyoming men, to Chatham, there to take Gen. Stephens' orders, if there—if not, you will send to Head Quarters for directions.

"I am your humble servant,
"B. LINCOLN."

"CHATHAM, May 29th, 1777.

"Pursuant to orders received from your Excellency, by the hand of Major-General Lincoln, I have marched with the detachments from the Connecticut regiment, and a few of the Westmoreland Independent companies, and expect more of them will join me this day, and am now encamped upon the heights between Chatham and Springfield. I find Gen. Stephens has gone from this place, and no orders can be obtained from him, as I expected. My Quarter-Master waits on your Excellency, by my directions, to know your Excellency's pleasure concerning my detachment.

"Many soldiers in the Independent Companies have received no clothes since they entered the service, and are almost naked. Many of their arms are useless, and some of them lost. They are also destitute of tents, and every kind of camp equipage. I hope your Excellency will give special directions how they are to be supplied with those articles. I am, with the greatest esteem,
"Your Excellency's most obedient
"His Excellency   "Humble servant,
"GEN. WASHINGTON.   "Z. BUTLER."

The companies were at Bound brook, at Brandywine, at Germantown, and at Mud Fort. At that terrible bombardment, Lieut. Spalding commanded a detachment of Ransom's company. Almost every shot from the British tore through the fort, and the men fell on every side. A soldier of Spalding's threw himself flat on the ground. "No body" he said "can stand this!" "Get up, my good fellow," said Spalding, coolly, "I should hate to have to run you through—you can stand it, if I can;" and the man returned cheerfully to his duty. Constant Matthewson, who was with Spalding, a brave man and excellent soldier, a fine intelligent fellow, was blown to pieces by a cannon ball. Sickness carried off several. The two brothers,

Sawyers, died of camp distemper. Porter was killed—Spencer and Gaylord died; and three or four were reported as discharged or missing. The company of Ransom, in October, 1777, mustered still sixty-two.

The wealth and revenue of this infant colony, presents an interesting topic of inquiry. Before us is a warrant to Mr. John Dorrance, to collect the State tax for 1778; but as it is based on the assessment of 1777, this seems to be a fitting place to introduce it to the reader's notice.

STATE OF CONNECTICUT

[ARMS OF CONNECTICUT.]

CONNECTICUT IN AMERICA.

To Mr. *John Dorrance, Constable of Westmoreland, and Collector of the State Tax for said Town, for the Year* 1778, GREETING.

WHEREAS the General Assembly of this State, in October, 1778, granted a Rate or Tax of Two Shillings on the Pound, to be levied and collected on all the Polls and rateable Estates of this State, according to the List brought into the Assembly in October One Thousand Seven Hundred and Seventy-seven, and January 1778, to be collected and paid into the Treasury of this State, by the first Day of February One Thousand Seven Hundred and Seventy-nine.

THESE are therefore in the Name of the GOVERNOR and COMPANY of the State of CONNECTICUT, to require and command you, to collect of the Inhabitants of said Town, Two Shillings on the Pound, in Continental Bills, amounting to the sum of Two Thousand and thirty-two Pounds, five Shillings and eight Pence, Lawful Money, with all Additions made thereto. And if any Person or Persons shall neglect or refuse to make Payment of their just Proportion of said Rates, you are to make distraint of the Goods or Estate of such Person or Persons, and for want of Estate, their Person, as the Law directs. And you must make up and settle your Accounts with the Treasurer of this State, by the first Day of February next.

Dated at Hartford, the 10th Day of November, in the Year of our Lord, 1778.

JOHN LAWRENCE, *Treasurer.*

£20,322 17s. 0d., *a* 2s. £2,032 5s. 8d.

LIST, 1777.
ADDITIONS,
FOUR-FOLDS. . . . . Half is

It will be observed that the tax may be collected in Continental money, but at whatever depreciation, the sum must be made equal to "two thousand and thirty-two pounds, five shillings, lawful money (of Connecticut) that is, $6,667.

Without a remark from our pen, surprise, we are sure, will be excited, that a sum so considerable, or indeed any sum, should be demanded of Wyoming, for the general purposes of the State treasury at Hartford.

The whole assessment of the State amounted to £1,929,000, say, in round numbers, two millions. The assessment of Westmoreland to £20,332; say 20,000—so that the proportion of the town to the whole State was just about as 1 to 100. So too the population. Connecticut was estimated to contain two hundred and thirty thousand inhabitants. Westmoreland about two thousand three hundred, or again, as 1 to 100. The quota of troops demanded of Connecticut was three thousand two hundred and twenty-eight—the proportion then of Wyoming should have been the one hundredth part, (if indeed a frontier so exposed should have spared a man,) that would have been thirty-two. But the Wyoming companies still mustered one hundred and twenty-four—Gore and Strong's men thirty-six—making one hundred and sixty, five times the just proportion, admitting the State's quota to have been complete. But, from the urgent requisitions of Congress and the complaints of His Excellency, Gen. Washington, it appears none of the quotas of the States were kept much more than half full. Allow that of Connecticut to have been two thirds filled, then the number would have been two thousand one hundred and fifty-two. Wyoming, to have sent in proportion, should have had twenty-one men in service—but she had about one hundred and sixty, so that in fact the settlement sent eight times its just number. Admitting the thirteen colonies to have had a population of about three millions, then as Wyoming was nearly a thousandth part of the whole, the whole should have furnished to the army a thousand times as many men, that is 160,000.

While these calculations exhibit the great efforts made by Wyoming, they also show the powerful motives operating on the Government of Connecticut, to detain the two companies in the army. The relief to her was exceeding great and manifest. Accordingly they were numbered as a part of her quota, and their return, notwithstanding the solemn pledge at their enlistment, could not be complied with.

A brief recapitulation may give distinctness to the reader's view. As the three years of war, from 1769 to '71, should not be counted, the colony was now in the sixth year of its age. Nearly all their able bodied men were away in the service. The remaining population in dread of the Savages were building six forts, or stockades requiring great labour, and "without fee, or reward." All the aged men, out of the train bands, exempt by law from duty, were formed into companies to garrison the forts, one of the Captains being also Chief Physician to the people, and Surgeon to the military. Of the militia, the whole were in constant requisition to go on the scout, and guard against surprise. The small pox pestilence was in every district. A tax to go to Hartford was levied on the assessment of the year, of two thousand pounds!!

Such is the picture of Wyoming for 1777; but before we close the view, allow us to copy a heart touching resolve from the proceedings of a town meeting "legally warned," holden December 30.

John Jenkins, Esq., was chosen moderator for the work of the day.

"Voted by this town, that the committee of inspection be empowered to supply the Sogers' wives, and the Sogers' widows, and their families, with the necessaries of life."

Let it be engraved on plates of silver! Let it be printed in letters of gold! Challenge Rome in her Republican glory, or Greece in her Democratic pride, to produce, the circumstances considered, an act more generous and noble.

LETTER XVII.

1778.——Sketch—New oath of allegiance—Established prices, (curious)—Women of Wyoming—Scene darkens—Meditated invasion—Alarm—Congress orders a third company to be raised—Wm. Crooks murdered—Miner Robins shot—Indian spy—Inexplicable delay of Congress—Independent companies withheld—Wyoming defenceless—Vote of Congress—Reorganization of independent company—The four pounder—Bold and impudent treachery and deception of Congress by the Indians—Invasion—Murder of the Hardings, and Hadsells—Col. Z. Butler called to the command—Wintermoot's Fort surrendered——Fort Jenkins surrendered—Summons of Forty Fort—Array—Battle—Defeat—Dreadful massacre—Bloody ring—Soul stirring incidents—Cruel torture.

The first bright beams of a January sun, leading up the new year, lighted a scene at Wyoming of white and cold and placid beauty. Hill and valley were clad in virgin snow. Smoke rose, curling to the skies from hundreds of cottages. Barns surrounded by stacks of wheat showed that the staff of life was abundant. Cattle and sheep foddered from stacks in the meadow, or sheltered in rude sheds, sleek and thriving, gave evidence that they shared in the super-abounding plenty of these fertile plains. The deep mouthed watch-dog barked fiercely as the sled, drawn by a smart span of horses, with gingling bells and its merry load of girls and lads, going to some quilting, singing meeting, wedding, or other merry-making, passed swiftly by. The "sogers' wives, and the sogers' widows" were well provided for. Coffee was little known, but the fragrant and exhilarating cup of tea graced the table, on which smoked the buck-wheat cake, and the luscious honey-comb, the venison steak, and well preserved shad. If, perchance, a furlough had allowed some of Ransom and Durkee's men to visit their wives and little ones, the broiled chicken, the well fatted roasting pig, or the delicious turkey, bade them a thousand times welcome. Neighbours would flock in to hear—how they whipped the British at Millstone, and took an hundred horses! How Porter, poor fellow, and the gallant Matthewson, were cut in two by cannon balls. How Gen. Washington ("and did you see Gen. Washington? would, in the enthusiasm that beloved name inspired, burst from a dozen tongues.) How Gen. Washington, at Germantown, rode right into the mouths of the British cannon, as it were. The wearied scouts would come in, while others set off on tours of duty, creating little excitement, as no immediate danger impended, all seeming quiet above. Meanwhile the flail sounded merrily on the threshing floor—the flax-break and hatchell were in active requisition—the spinning wheel buzzed its round—while the shuttle sped its rapid flight. The arrival of the postman from Hartford created a sensation throughout the whole settlement. Such was the dawning of 1778 upon Wyoming, as pictured to the writer by a grey-headed survivor from that day.

Burgoyne had surrendered. It was a happy event, but many of the sagacious old men feared that the Indians, released from service in the northeast, would now turn their dreaded arms upon the southern and western frontiers; and who so hated, or exposed, as the people on the Susquehanna.

Under the recent law, requiring, since the Declaration of Independence, a new oath of allegiance to the State of Connecticut, instead of the King, one hundred and forty-nine freemen had been sworn in and recorded, beginning with the name of Nathan Denison, Esq., in the previous September, in open town meeting, and now, April 13, 1778, one hundred and twenty more appeared, and took the oath of fidelity; making in all two hundred and sixty-nine.

John Dorrance was chosen Collector of the State Tax.

Nathan Denison and Anderson Dana, were elected members to the Assembly, to be holden at Hartford, in May.

On the 21st of April, another town meeting was warned, and prices fixed on articles of sale and service of labour, in accordance with a recommendation of the Legislature. To gratify the curious, we will quote twenty items:—

Good yarn stockings, a pair,	10 s.
Laboring women, at spinning, a week,	6 s.
Winter-fed beef, a pound,	7 d.
Taverners, for dinner, of the best, per meal,	2 s.
Metheglin, per gallon,	7 s.
Beaver skins, per pound,	18 s.
Shad, a piece,	6 d.
Beaver hats, of the best,	4 l.
Ox work, for two oxen, per day, and tackling,	3 s.
Good hemp-seed, a bushel,	15 s.

Men's labour, at farming, the three summer months, pay day,	5 s. 3 d.
Good check flannel, yard wide,	8 s.
Good tow and linen, yard wide,	6 s.
Good white flannel, do.	5 s.
The above to be woven in a 36 reed, etc.	
Tobacco, in hank or leaf, per pound,	9 d.
Taverners, for mug of flip, with two gills of rum in it,	4 s.
Good barley, per bushel,	8 s.
Making, and setting, and shoeing horse all round,	8s.$1 33
Eggs, per doz.,	8 d.
Strong beer, by the barrel,	2 l.

From which we deduce several conclusions, namely:—That shad and eggs were plenty, as they were cheap—that tobacco, hemp and barley were extensively cultivated, and articles of considerable traffic—that the once popular, but now exploded, flip, had been introduced from New England, a most agreeable but pernicious beverage—that the luxury of beaver hats, costing more than thirteen dollars, had become fashionable, indicating considerable wealth—that metheglin was manufactured for sale, and therefore *honey* was abundant—that, in conclusion, the prices fixed to more than an hundred articles, are proof of extensive production, trade and prosperity.

An ancient document, of great interest, was found among the papers of Anderson Dana, Esq., being the Commission from the General Assembly and Governer of Connecticut, fixing the judicial establishment of Westmoreland for 1778, as was the annual custom. The names of judges and justices, with those of Governor Trumbull, and Secretary Wyllys, only are in manuscript, the remainder being printed. It is in perfect preservation, except that a few words of the printed matter are defaced by frequent folding. We insert it.

THE GOVERNOR AND COMPANY OF THE STATE OF CONNECTICUT, IN NEW-ENGLAND, IN AMERICA;

To *Nathan Denison, Christopher Avery, Obadiah Gore, Zera Beach, Zebulon Butler, William McKarrican, Asaph Whittlesey, Uriah Chapman, Anderson Dana, Ebenezer Marcy, Stephen Harding, John Franklin, 2d, Joseph Hambleton, and William Judd*, Esq's., GREETING.

KNOW YE, That We have assigned you, and every of you, jointly and severally, to keep the Peace within the County of Westmoreland, within the State aforesaid; and to keep, and cause to be kept, all the Laws and Ordinances that are or shall be made for the good, the Peace, and Conservation of the same, and for the quiet Rule and Government of the People within the County aforesaid: And to chastise and punish all Persons offending in the County aforesaid, against the said Laws or Ordinances, or any of them, as according to those Laws and Ordinances shall be fit to be done: And to cause to come before you, or any of you, all those Persons who shall threaten any one in his Person or Estate, to give sufficient Sureties for the Peace and good Behaviour, or in default of their finding Sureties, to commit them to Goal, or safe Custody, until they shall do so.

And we have assigned you, the said Nathan Denison, Christopher Avery, Obadiah Gore, and Zera Beach, Esq's., to assist the Judges of the County of Westmoreland [*a word or two torn*] enquire of, hear and determine by a Jury or otherwise, [*torn*] all matters and things, civil and criminal, cognizable [*half a line torn*]

And we do also assign you, the said Nathan Denison, Christopher Avery, Obadiah Gore, Zera Beach, Zebulon Butler, William McKarrican, Asaph Whittlesey, Uriah Chapman, Anderson Dana, Ebenezer Marcy, Stephen Harding, John Franklin, 2d, Joseph Hambleton, and William Judd, and each and every of you, to hear and determine all Causes, Matters and Things, civil and criminal, which any One Assistant in this Corporation, now hath, or hereafter shall have Power by Law to hear and determine. And I command you, and every of you, that you diligently intend the keeping of the Peace, Laws and Ordinances, and all and singular other the Premises, and perform and fulfil the same, doing therein what to Justice appertains, according to the Laws of this State. In Testimony whereof, We have caused the Seal of our said State to be hereunto affixed. *Witness* JONATHAN TRUMBULL, *Esq*; *Governor of our said State of Connecticut, and with the Consent of the General Assembly of the same, in Hartford, this first Day of June, Anno Domini,* 1778.

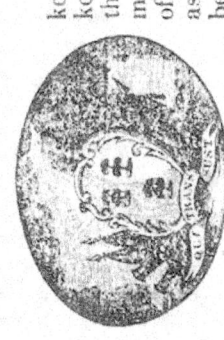

By His Excellency's Command.

GEORGE WYLLYS, *Sec'y.*

JONATHAN TRUMBULL.

Justice and gratitude demand a tribute to the praiseworthy spirit of the wives and daughters of Wyoming. While their husbands and fathers were on public duty, they cheerfully assumed a large portion of the labour, which females could do. They assisted to plant, made hay, husked and garnered the corn. As the settlement was mainly dependent on its own resourses for powder, Mr. Hollenback caused to be brought up the river, a pounder; and the women took up their floors, dug out the earth, put it in casks, and run water through it, (as ashes are leached). Then took ashes, in another cask, and made ley—mixed the water from the earth with weak ley, boiled it, set it to cool, and the saltpetre rose to the top. Charcoal and sulphur were then used, and powder produced for the public defence.*

Early in the Spring, Congress were apprised of a meditated attack on Wyoming. From Niagara, and the Indian country adjacent to, and within the town of Westmoreland, rumour followed rumour, that the British and Indians were preparing an expedition for the destruction of the settlement. Defenceless as the position was known to be, and exasperated as the enemy were, by the efforts of the people in the cause of Independence, nothing could be more probable than such a design. The only considerable post above the Blue Ridge, Wyoming was an important barrier between the Savages and the German settlements below those mountains; and could that place be desolated, bands of the enemy could easily penetrate the Great Swamp, and make incursions into Northampton and Berks, and immediately after striking a blow, hide themselves in those almost impenetrable forests, withdrawing thereby, those numerous and useful levies of men and provisions, which those populous and patriotic counties yielded to the army of his Excellency. Independent, therefore, of a just regard to the pledge noticed, and without considering the interests of the people, policy would seem to have dictated the taking early and ample measures to defend Wyoming. Gen. Schuyler wrote to the Board of War on the subject. The officers and men earnestly plead and remonstrated, that their families, left defenceless, were now menaced with invasion, and adverted to the terms of their enlistment. History affords no parallel of the pertinacious detention of men under such circumstances. Treachery

---

* Mrs. Bertha Jenkins. The statement of this lady, at the age of eighty-four, giving an account of the process of obtaining saltpetre, shows that it was a familiar and common transaction. We have been more particular in the quotation, as the fact is remarkable, showing that even powder was not furnished them.

is not for a moment to be lisped, and yet the malign influence of the policy pursued, and the disastrous consequences, could not have been aggravated, if they had been purposely withheld. Nothing could have been more frank and confiding, more brave and generous, than the whole conduct of the Wyoming people from the beginning of the contest; and it is saying little to aver that they deserved, both at the hands of Congress and Connecticut, a different requital. Connecticut could ill spare them. To her, they were inestimable. Mercy, justice, and policy, plead in vain.

All the Indians in the Valley had been recalled; and several white persons from Tunkhannock and Wyalusing, had joined the enemy.

In this state of things, Congress again interposed its authority for the protection of Wyoming. March 16th, 1778, " Resolved, That one full company of foot, be raised in the town of Westmoreland, on the east bank of the Susquehanna, for the defence of the said town, and the settlement on the frontiers, and in the neighborhood thereof, against the Indians and the enemies of these States; the said company to be enlisted to serve one year from the time of their enlisting, unless sooner discharged by Congress."

Several reflections arise out of this extraordinary resolution. In the first place, it establishes the fact that Congress was apprised of the danger from Indians, early in March, for it is predicated on a report of the Board of War, of a previous date, and had been some time under consideration. 2d. It is difficult to conceive how a company, then to be enlisted from among the inhabitants, could add any strength to the defence; for if at all, the enemy would probably come before they would have time to be disciplined, and a company, so enlisted, would not increase the force a single man. After so many had enlisted, and were away with the army, it sounds strange and almost unnatural to assume that more could be spared from the purposes of agriculture, the scout, and social protection!

But Wyoming seems to have been doomed by a selfishness, which cannot be designated except by terms which respect forbids us to employ.

The resolution proceeds—" That the company find their own arms, accoutrements, and blankets." But the difficulty was in obtaining them. Durkee and Ransom's men had armed themselves, and from the scant supply in the Valley, had taken away the best. Individual enterprise had been able, very imperfectly, to supply the deficiency.

In the month of May, scouting parties began to be met by those of the enemy, who hovered around the settlements at a distance of twenty miles, seeming intent to prevent all communication with the upper country, and it is presumed to cut off all chance of learning the preparations making for the descent, rather than to do mischief. No families were attacked—no houses burned. Shots were exchanged rarely, as the enemy rather kept aloof than courted battle; but one of the Wyoming men, William Crooks, coming out of a house near Tunkhannock, abandoned by John Secord, who had gone to the enemy, was shot dead at the door. This was the first life taken at Westmoreland by the Indians.

A few days afterwards a party of six, out on duty, were fired upon about four miles below Tunkhannock. Miner Robbins, and Joel Phelps were wounded; but regaining their canoes, escaped down the river. Robbins lingered until the next day, and died. Phelps recovered. These incidents increased the alarm already distractingly painful. But an event soon occurred of more exciting importance. Two Indians, formerly residents of Wyoming, and acquainted with the people, came down with their squaws on a visit, professing warm friendship; but suspicions existed that they were spies, and directions were given that they should be carefully watched. An old companion of one of them, with more than Indian cunning, professing his attachment to the natives, gave his visiter drink after drink of his favorite rum, when, in confidence, and the fulness of his maudlin heart, he avowed that his people were preparing to cut off the settlement, the attack to be made soon, and that they had come down to see and report how things were. The squaws were dismissed, but the two Indians arrested, and confined in Forty Fort.

Now the distress and alarm rose almost to phrenzy. To remain so entirely exposed, to have their throats cut, and their children's brains dashed out by the savages, without an effort for protection, was not to be endured.

Dethick Hewitt had been appointed captain to enlist the new continental company, but the order was looked upon as little better than a mockery. The people in the outer settlements fled to the forts; and the wives of the soldiers sent messages, calling upon them, by every tender tie, to come home and protect them. Still Congress and Connecticut, with more than Egyptian obstinacy, would not let the companies depart. Beyond all question they ought, as early as May, to have been ordered to Wyoming. Almost instantly, on hearing this last news, the companies became nearly disorganized. Every commissioned officer but two resigned, and more than twenty-five of the men, with or without leave, left the ranks, and hastened to the Valley. Imperious necessity, above all earthly law, consecrated the deed. That they did not all return shows the influence of discipline and their love of order.

Congress, by these measures, was compelled to interpose. On the 23d of June, only seven days before the arrival of the enemy, they resolved, "that the two Independent Companies lately commanded by the two captains, Durkee and Ransom, which were raised in the town of Westmoreland, be united, and form one company."

A preamble states that the number of men remaining was eighty-six, non-commissioned officers and privates. The two commissioned officers, made eighty-eight. Battle, sickness, and the vicissitudes of war, had reduced the companies to about sixty men each—of course nearly thirty must have returned on leave given, or assumed.

Simon Spaulding, a valuable officer, was appointed captain, Timothy Pierce and Phineas Pierce, lieutenants. The Board of War directed, (it is believed) the new company to march to Lancaster, and soon after, but too late, to Wyoming.

A vote was also passed that Hewitt's men should receive pay for their arms, accoutrements and blankets, but so tardy was the order, that few of them lived to hear of the benevolent design.

The concentration of the enemy at Newtown and Tioga, (the latter a part of Westmoreland town,) and the preparation of boats and canoes, being known, every man who could bear arms, was called into service, and trained. Two deserters from the British army were in the Valley, one by the name of Pike, who had fled from Boston several years before; the other named Boyd, a fine active young fellow, from Canada. The latter, a serjeant, was particularly useful in training the militia. Large bodies were sent up the river as scouts, and as the Yankee woodsmen, crossing the streams on fallen trees, would run over the roaring flood with the agility of a wild cat, the two foreigners, sitting astride on the log, hitching themselves awkwardly across, excited great merriment among their companions.* Both these names will appear conspicuously on another page. The forts were now filled with women and children. Every company of the militia was ordered to be ready at a moment's warning,—all was bustle and anxiety. Care sat on every brow, and fear on many

* "In sorrow's cup, still laughs the bubble joy."

a heart too firm to allow a breath of apprehension to escape from the lips. The one and only cannon, the four pounder, was in Wilkesbarre Fort. Having no ball, it was kept as an alarm gun. The indispensable labours of the field were performed by armed men. Soon and certainly the attack would be made, was known; but the precise time could not be calculated, for the enemy could descend the river slightly swollen, at the rate of five miles an hour, and could therefore be in the settlement in less than a day from leaving their rendezvous. So usually is there a rise of water in summer, that the "June fresh" is a familiar phrase, and had, it was supposed, been fixed upon for their embarkation.

Leaving the lovely and unprotected Valley in all its blooming beauty, the fields waving with the burden of an abundant harvest, but the people, like a covey of partridges, cowering beneath a flock of blood-scenting vultures, that soared above, ready to pounce on their prey; or like a flock of sheep huddled together in their pen, while the prowling wolves already sent their impatient howl across the fields, eager for their victims; we proceed to state one of the most impudent attempts at treachery and deception, ever recorded. It is known the Indian prides himself on his cunning. It is equally honorable by stratagem to take a scalp, as by force. So secure were they of Wyoming, that the whole expedition seems to have been a matter of sport, a holiday gambol with the savages. The Senecas were the nation principally concerned in the expedition, although detachments from the Mohawks, and other tribes, accompanied them. While the enemy were concentrating at their rendezvous, a delegation of Seneca chiefs, daringly presuming on the stolidity of Congress, repaired to Philadelphia, ostensibly to negotiate, really to amuse, put them off their guard, and prevent any troops being sent to the threatened frontier. Nor did the bold and dexterous chiefs leave the city, until the fatal blow was struck, as an extract from the journals will show. " July 8, 1778.—Resolved, That the Board of War be directed to send for the Seneca chiefs that have lately quitted Philadelphia, and inquire whether the Seneca Nation, as such, have committed hostilities against us."

The chiefs refused to return. Why should they? Their errand was accomplished! A motion was made July 17, that General Schuyler be directed, " to take effectual measures for detaining the Seneca chiefs at Albany," but it was decided in the negative.

The enemy numbering about four hundred British provincials, consisting of Col. John Butler's Rangers, a detachment of Sir John

Johnson's Royal Greens, the rest being Tories, from Pennsylvania, New Jersey and New York, together with six or seven hundred Indians, having descended the Susquehanna from Tioga Point, landed not far below the mouth of Bowman's Creek, on the west side of the river, in a north direction, about twenty miles above the Valley, (by the river, which here makes a large bend, the distance would have been nearly thirty miles.) Securing their boats they marched across the peninsula, and arrived on the western mountain, on the evening of the 29th, or morning of the 30th of June. At Fort Jenkins, the uppermost in the Valley, and only a mile above Wintermoot's, there were gathered the families of the old patriot, John Jenkins, Esq., the Hardings and Gardiners, distinguished for zeal, with others. Not apprised of the contiguity of the savages, on the morning of the 30th June, Benjamin Harding, Stukely Harding, John Harding, a boy, James Hadsell, James Hadsell, jr., Daniel Weller, John Gardiner and Daniel Carr, eight in all, took their arms and went up about three miles into Exeter, to their labour. Towards evening, at an hour when aid could not be expected, they were attacked. That they fought bravely was admitted by the enemy. Weller, Gardiner and Carr, were taken prisoners. James Hadsell, and his son James, Benjamin and Stukely Harding, were killed. John Harding, the boy, threw himself into the river, and lay under the willows, his mouth just above the surface. He heard with anguish the dying groans of his friends. Knowing he was near, the Indians searched carefully for him. At one time they were so close that he could have touched them.

This was the opening of the campaign.

Colonel Zebulon Butler, then at home, by common consent assumed the command of the Connecticut people. On the 1st of July he marched, Colonel Denison, and Lieut. Col. Dorrance, being also in command, with all his force, from Forty Fort to Exeter, where the murders of the preceding day had been perpetrated. The two Hardings, it appeared, must have contended to the last, for their arms and faces were much cut, and several spear holes were made through their bodies. Instead of shooting, it is probable the intention was to take them prisoners. All were scalped, and otherwise mutilated. Two Indians, who were watching the dead, expecting that friends might come to take away the bodies, and they might obtain other victims, were shot; one where he sat, the other in the river to which he had fled. Zebulon Marcy's rifle, it was supposed, killed one of them, and subsequently, he was waylaid and hunted for several years, a brother of the Indian killed, swearing he would have revenge. The bodies were removed and decently interred near Fort Jenkins, where many years after, Elisha Harding, Esq., caused a stone to be raised to their memory, with this inscription:—

"Sweet be the sleep of those who prefer death to slavery."

After Colonel Z. Butler returned, Colonel John Butler, passing through a notch in the mountain, near Wintermoots, took possession of the fort without opposition. Mr. Daniel Ingersoll, who was present, on learning the approach of the enemy, began to prepare for resistance, and his wife seized a pitchfork to aid, but the Wintermoots gave them to understand Colonel Butler would be at home there, and Ingersoll found himself a prisoner. This fort, beautifully situated on the upper river flat, from which gushed an abundant spring of pure water, was admirably calculated for the convenience of the enemy, for whose special purpose it was erected. The Wintermoots had built it amid the suspicions of their neighbours, and without their consent, but had, at the same time, in other respects conducted so discreetly as to give no ground for arresting them.*

The same evening, a detachment under the command of Capt. Caldwell was sent to reduce Fort Jenkins. Originally, the garrison consisted of seventeen, mostly old men; four of whom were slain, and three made prisoners, so that no means of resistance being left, the stockade capitulated.

Early the next morning, Mr. Ingersoll was sent under an escort of one white man and one Indian, to Col. Zebulon Butler, demanding the surrender of Forty Fort, and the Valley.

On the morning of Friday, the 3d, Mr. Ingersoll was again despatched from Wintermoot's to Forty Fort, accompanied as before,

* An anecdote connected with this celebrated fort may be introduced here. Colonel John Jenkins made the place his own after the Revolution, and it descended to his heirs. Eight or ten years ago, a shrewd son-in-law of Col. J's, in whose possession the property now is, was working on the flats below the spring, when a genteel stranger, mounted on a fine horse, rode up to the fence, alighted, looked eagerly round, and entered into conversation. He inquired for the spring—for the situation and extent of the fort, and other localities. "You seem to be a stranger in this place?" "Yes." "Yet you seem to know a good deal about it?" "Something." "Have you any interest here?" "My father formerly owned property here." Comprehending that the stranger was a Wintermoot, "I guess you don't own any now?" "No," answered the young man with a smile, seeing he was known and understood. His curiosity was gratified by every reasonable answer to his questions, when he mounted his horse and rode slowly away, turning every few moments, to take one more gaze at a spot, in regard to which, from infancy, he had heard his people speak with enthusiasm, and who had left it with the reluctance that Adam bade farewell to Paradise.

by two attendants, one Indian and one white man, both as guards and spies. The motive was perfectly comprehended, and the duty only undertaken because it would have been death to refuse. His guards did not allow Ingersoll a word with Col. Butler, or Denison, out of their hearing. Effectual care was taken that he should communicate nothing that he had discovered while a prisoner. But his guides had, by this means, an opportunity to see, partially, the condition of the fort, the number, and more than either, the spirit and bearing of the Connecticut people. A surrender of all the forts, the public property, Hewett's company and the Valley, was the least that was demanded, and of course refused. On his return, Col. Z. Butler called a council of war, and opinions were freely expressed. Many, and among the rest, Col. Butler, Col. Denison, and Lieutenant-Colonel Dorrance, were of opinion, that a little delay would be best—that the alarm of the sudden irruption would subside—that the absent militia companies would arrive, and that Capt. Spalding's company, supposed to be on its march, might be hoped for, and would be of great consequence—probably decisive of the issue. To these wise and weighty considerations, it was replied:—That the enemy had now been three days in the town—that they were fast carrying on their work of conquest and murder. Two forts had surrendered, and the cruel butchery of the Harding's, and their companions, was dwelt on. They would not be idle if we were disposed to be still. The Valley would be destroyed, piece-meal. All the craft in the upper part were in their possession. They could cross at Pittston, take that fort in spite of Capt. Blanchard, and murder the inhabitants. What then would prevent them from marching to any other point? Our little army could not be kept long together. Unless led to action, each man would fly to the protection of his own family. As to Spalding coming, no one doubted his hearty good will, but those who had detained him so long, would not be apt, now, to accelerate his coming. There was no certainty when he would arrive. We must depend on God and ourselves. To attack and defeat the enemy, was the only hope of salvation for the settlement. A large majority accorded with these sentiments; and the minority, though with reluctance, finally yielded their assent, and some time after noon, the column, consisting of about three hundred men, old men, and boys, marched from the fort. The little army consisted of six regular companies:—

1st. That of Capt. Dethic Hewitt, called regulars, but precisely like the rest of the militia, for they were just enlisted. He mustered about forty men.

2d. Capt. Asaph Whittlesey's company, from Plymouth, consisting of forty-four men.

3d. Capt. William McKarrican's company, from Hanover, numbering about forty men. Being also the schoolmaster, and little used to war, though a brave, active, and valuable man, he gave up the command to Capt. Lazarus Stewart; Rosewell Franklin was his lieutenant.

4th. The Lower Wilkesbarre company, commanded by Capt. James Bidlack, Jr., consisting of thirty-eight men.

5th. The Upper Wilkesbarre company, commanded by Capt. Rezin Geer, smaller, but the number not known.

6th. The Kingston company, commanded by Capt. Aholiab Buck, lieutenant Elijah Shoemaker, second in command.

In addition to those in the trainbands, the Judges of the Court, and all the civil officers who were near, went out. Many old men—some of them grandfathers—took their muskets and marched to the field. For instance, the aged Mr. Searle, of Kingston, was one. Having become bald, he wore a wig. Taking out his silver knee-buckles, he said to his family, "If I fall, I shall not need them. If I come back, they will be safe here."—Nothing could have been more incongruous, more pitiably unfit, than the mingling of such aged men in the rough onset of battle. Dire was the necessity that compelled it. The old gentleman had a number of grandchildren. Several boys, from fourteen to sixteen, are known to have been on the field. There was a company at Pittston, of thirty or forty men, under Capt. Blanchard, stationed at the fort, to guard the people gathered there. To leave them, and march to Forty Fort, would be to expose them to certain destruction, for the enemy were in sight, on the opposite bank of the river. Capt. Franklin's company, from Huntington and Salem, had not arrived. The other companies of the regiment were at Capouse, and at the "Lackaway" settlement, too far off to afford assistance. So that there were about two hundred and thirty enrolled men, and seventy old people, boys, civil magistrates, and other volunteers.

Every movement of Col. Z. Butler was watched by a vigilant and wary foe. No sooner had the march commenced than the news was communicated to Col. John Butler, at Wintermoot's, who immediately despatched a messenger up to Fort Jenkins, for the party there, who were destroying the defences, to hasten down, for the Yankees were coming out to battle. This was between two and three o'clock. A few sentinels alone were left at Forty Fort; and one of these by the name of Cooper, more brave than obedient to orders, said "Our people need all their strength on the field. If defeated or successful, my being here will do no good." And he hurried off to join his neighbours.

Miss Bennett, (since Mrs. Myers,) was one of the crowd of women and children who had resorted to the Forty Fort. After the troops had been gone about half an hour, three men were seen, spurring their jaded horses up the road. As they came to the gate and dismounted, the sweat flowed from the panting flanks of their generous steeds. Two of them were Capt. Durkee and Lieut. Pierce. In a moment they learned the state of things. "We are faint—give us bread; we have not broken our fasts to day." Such provisions as were at hand were placed before them. Pierce was a lieutenant in Capt. Spalding's company, then about forty miles off, through the Great Swamp. They had ridden nearly all night. Having snatched a morsel of food, they hastened to the field.

Among many patriotic volunteers, justice requires that Anderson Dana, Esq., should be particularly mentioned. He had just returned from duty as a member of Assembly at Hartford. It is impossible that any man could have conducted with a more cheerful spirit, or a more animating zeal. Christopher Avery, Esq., one of the Justices of the Court, who had filled many important stations, and possessed a large share of public confidence, though exempt by law, took post beside his neighbours. Many officers are mentioned, who strictly held no command. Captains Durkee and Ransom were in the battle, and no doubt were referred to, and obeyed by the militia officers, but they held no official station.

As the American troops approached Wintermoot's, they perceived that the fort was in flames. The motive for setting it on fire is not yet understood, probably to prevent its sudden assault and capture; probably to draw attention and conceal their number and movements.

At this point there are two plains, the upper and lower flats, divided by a steep bank of about fifteen or twenty feet in height; the lower a rich sandy loam; the upper a coarse gravel. The fort was on the bank dividing the two plains.

Col. Z. Butler, on approaching the enemy, sent forward Captains Ransom and Durkee, Lieutenants Ross and Wells, as officers whose skill he most relied on, to select the spot, and mark off the ground on which to form the order of battle. On coming up, the column displayed to the left, and under those officers every company took its station, and then advanced in line to the proper position, where it halted, the right resting on the steep bank noted—the left extending across the gravel flat to a morass, thick with timber and brush that separated the bottom land from the mountain. Yellow and pitch pine trees, with oak shrubs, were scattered all over the plain. On the American right was Capt. Bidlack's company. Next was Capt. Hewitt's, Daniel Gore being one of his Lieutenants. On the extreme left was Capt. Whittlesey's. Col. Butler, supported by Maj. John Garrett, commanded the right wing. Col. Denison, supported by Lieut. Col. George Dorrance, commanded the left. Such was the ground, and such the order of battle. Every thing was judiciously disposed, and conducted in a strictly military and prudent manner. Captains Durkee and Ransom, as experienced officers, in whom great confidence was placed, were stationed, Durkee with Bidlack on the right wing—Ransom with Whittlesey on the left. Col. Butler made a very brief address, just before he ordered the column to display. "Men, yonder is the enemy. The fate of the Hardings tells us what we have to expect if defeated. We come out to fight, not only for liberty, but for life itself, and what is dearer, to preserve our homes from conflagration; our women and children from the tomahawk. Stand firm the first shock, and the Indians will give way. Every man to his duty."

The column had marched up the road running near the bank on which our right rested. On its display, as Denison led off his men, he repeated the expression of Col. Butler—"Be firm, every thing depends on resisting the first shock."

The left of the enemy rested on Wintermoot's Fort, now on fire, and was commanded by Col. John Butler, who, divested of feathers and finery, appeared on the ground with a handkerchief tied on his head. A flanking party of Indian marksmen, were concealed among some logs and bushes under the bank. Johnson's Royal Greens, commanded by Capt. Caldwell, (if Johnson himself was not present,) formed on Butler's right. Indian marksmen filling the space between. The main body of the Indians, under Brandt, or Gi-en-gwah-toh,* formed the right wing, and extended to the morass or swamp.

From Wintermoot's Fort, to the river in a straight line, was about eighty rods—To Menockasy island, over the low flats in a south direction about a mile. The weather clear and warm.

---

* Gi-en-gwah-toh, a Seneca. "He who goes in the smoke."

COL. STONE.

About four in the afternoon the battle began; Colonel Z. Butler ordered his men to fire, and at each discharge to advance a step. Along the whole line the discharges were rapid and steady. It was evident, on the more open ground the Yankees were doing most execution. As our men advanced, pouring in their platoon fires with great vivacity, the British line gave way, in spite of all their officers efforts to prevent it. The Indian flanking party on our right kept up from their hiding places a galling fire. Lieut. Daniel Gore received a ball through the left arm. "Captain Durkee," said he, "look sharp for the Indians in those bushes." Captain D. stepped to the bank to look, preparatory to making a charge and dislodging them, when he fell. On the British Butler's right, his Indian warriors were sharply engaged. They seemed to be divided into six bands, for a yell would be raised at one end of their line, taken up, and carried through, six distinct bodies appearing at each time to repeat the cry. As the battle waxed warmer, that fearful yell was renewed again and again, with more and more spirit. It appeared to be at once their animating shout, and their signal of communication. As several fell near Col. Dorrance, one of his men gave way; "Stand up to your work, sir," said he, firmly, but coolly, and the soldier resumed his place.

For half an hour a hot fire had been given and sustained, when the vastly superior numbers of the enemy began to develope its power. The Indians had thrown into the swamp a large force, which now completely outflanked our left. It was impossible it should be otherwise: that wing was thrown into confusion. Col. Denison gave orders that the company of Whittlesey should wheel back, so as to form an angle with the main line, and thus present his front, instead of flank, to the enemy. The difficulty of performing evolutions, by the bravest militia on the field, under a hot fire, is well known. On the attempt the savages rushed in with horrid yells. Some had mistaken the order to fall back, as one to retreat, and that word, that fatal word, ran along the line. Utter confusion now prevailed on the left. Seeing the disorder, and his own men beginning to give way, Col. Z. Butler threw himself between the fires of the opposing ranks, and rode up and down the line in the most reckless exposure. "Don't leave me, my children, and the victory is ours." But it was too late.

Still on the fated left, men stood their ground. "See," said Westover to George Cooper, " our men are all retreating, shall we go?"

"I'll have one more shot first," was his reply. At that moment a ball struck a tree just by his head, and an Indian springing towards him with his spear, Cooper drew up his rifle and fired, the Indian sprung several feet from the ground, and fell prostrate on his face. "Come," said Westover. "I'll load first," replied Cooper—and it is probable this coolness saved them, for the great body of the savages had dashed forward after the flying, and were far in their rear.

On the right, one of his officers said to Captain Hewitt, "The day is lost—see the Indians are sixty rods in our rear, shall we retreat?" "I'll be d—d* if I do," was his answer. "Drummer strike up," cried he, and strove to rally his men. Every effort was vain. Thus he fought, and there he fell!

Every captain that led a company into action was slain, and in every instance fell on, or near the line. As was said of Bidlack, so of Hewitt, Whittlesey, and the others; "they died at the head of their men." They fought bravely—every man and officer did his duty, but they were overpowered by three fold their force. In point of numbers the enemy was overwhelmingly superior.

Darius Spafford was just married to Miss Blackman. Receiving a death wound, he fell into the arms of his brother Phineas, by whose side he fought. "Brother," said he, "I am mortally hurt; take care of Lavina." Stephen Whiton, a young schoolmaster from Connecticut, was also a bridegroom, having recently married the daughter of Anderson Dana, Esq. The father and son-in-law fell together.

The battle being ended, the massacre began.

A portion of the Indian flanking party pushed forward in the rear of the Connecticut line, to cut off retreat to Forty Fort, and then pressed the retreating army towards the river. Monockasy Island affording the only hope of crossing, the stream of flight flowed in that direction through fields of grain. Cooper, and those who remained near the line of battle, saw the main body of the Indians hastening after the fugitives.

At Forty Fort, the bank of the river was lined by anxious wives and mothers, awaiting the issue. Hearing the firing sharply continued, now, hope arose; but when the shots became irregular, and approached nearer and nearer, that hope sank in dismay. Lieut.

---

* "The accusing spirit flew up to Heaven's chancery with the oath, and as she wrote it down, dropped a tear on the word, and blotted it out forever."

Gore, whose arm was shattered early in the action, being intercepted in an attempt to retreat the way he had marched up, secreted himself in a thick covert of bushes and briars near the road, on the descending bank. Indians ran past him, their attention directed to those who were flying through the flats. One stood very near, gazed a moment, drew up his rifle and fired. Raising a yell, he rushed forward, probably to scalp his victim.

At the river near the Island, the scene was exceedingly distressing. A few swam over and escaped. Closely pressed, many were killed in the river. Sergeant Jeremiah Bigford, a very active man, was pursued by an Indian into the stream with a spear; Bigford faced him, struck the spear from his hand, and seizing him by the neck, dashed him under his feet, where he would have drowned, but another savage rushed forward to his aid, and ran his spear through Bigford's breast, who fell dead, and floated away. A month afterwards his body was found seven or eight miles below, much decayed, but was recognized by a silver broach he wore, which, with a piece of the shirt with the spear hole, was preserved by his family for many years. One of the fugitives by the name of Pensil sought security by hiding in a cluster of willows on the island. Seeing his tory brother come up, and recognize him, he threw himself at his feet, begged for protection, and proffered to serve him for life, if he would save him. "Mighty well!" was the taunting reply. "You d—d rebel," and instantly shot him dead. It was a dreadful hour; men seemed transformed into demons. The worst passions raged with wild and desolating fury. All the sweet charities of life seemed extinguished. Lieutenant Shoemaker, one of the most generous and benevolent-hearted men, whose wealth enabled him to dispense charity and do good, which was a delight to him, fled to the river, when Windecker, who had often fed at his board, and drank of his cup, came to the brink. "Come out, come out," said he, "You know I will protect you." How could he doubt it? Windecker reached out his left hand, as if to lead him, much exhausted, ashore, and dashed his tomahawk into the head of his benefactor, who fell back, and floated away.

Many prisoners were lured to shore by promise of quarter, and then butchered. The accurate Indian marksmen, sure of their prey, had coolly singled out officers, and broke the thigh bone, it is supposed, as so many are found perforated, so as effectually to disable, but leaving the victim alive for torture. Capt. Bidlack was thrown alive on the burning logs of the fort, held down with pitch forks, and there tortured till he expired. Prisoners taken under solemn promise of quarter, were gathered together, and placed in circles. Sixteen or eighteen were arranged round one large stone, since known as the bloody rock. Surrounded by a body of Indians, queen Esther, a fury in the form of a woman, assumed the office of executioner with death maul, or tomahawk, for she used the one with both hands, or took up the other with one, and passing round the circle with words, as if singing, or counting with a cadence, she would dash out the brains, or sink the tomahawk into the head of a prisoner. A number had fallen. Her rage increased with indulgence. Seeing there was no hope, Lebbeus, Hammond, and Joseph Elliott, with a sudden spring shook off the Indians who held them, and fled for the thicket: Rifles cracked! Indians yelled! Tomahawks flew! but they escaped, the pursuers soon returning to their death sports. The mangled bodies of fourteen or fifteen were afterwards found round the rock where they had fallen, scalped, and shockingly mangled. Nine more were found in a similar circle some distance above.

Young Searles, aged sixteen, fled, accompanied by William, the son of Asahel Buck, aged fourteen. Searles, almost exhausted, heard a person cry, "stop—you shall have quarter—we wont hurt you." Looking round, and almost inclined to surrender, he saw Buck stop, and yield himself: that moment a tomahawk struck him to the earth dead. Renewing his leap, from desperation, Searle escaped. "See," said one of the flying Yankees, who was pursued by a powerful Indian, and nearly exhausted. Richard Inman drew up his rifle, and the Indian dropped dead.* Samuel Carey, a young man of nineteen, had crossed the river at the island, where he was met by the Indians, who were already on the beach. At first they threatened him with death, placing a knife to his bowels, as if they meant to rip him open; but he was spared, and taken to the Indian country. With a single other exception, he was the only person made prisoner in the battle, whose life was not sacrificed.

While this scene of suffering and woe was in progress, night threw her kindly mantle over the field, and darkness arrested the pursuit. Lieut. Gore, who had lain still, now heard the tread of men, and their voices in conversation. "It has been a sore day for

* That shot was revenged on the family, as will be seen in the sequel.

the Yankees." "It has indeed—blood enough has been shed." So far he heard, and they passed on. He supposed it to be Col. J. Butler, and one of his officers.

Mr. Hollenback, who had swam the river, and so escaped, brought the anticipated tidings to Wilkesbarre, and having learned the position of Capt. Spalding, saddled his horse, and rode all night to apprise him of the state of affairs at Wyoming.

Col. Zebulon Butler repaired to the Wilkesbarre Fort, and cast himself exhausted on the ground. Col. Denison took up his quarters at Forty Fort, gathered the few soldiers who had come in—placed sentinels, and took all the precautions in his power, dictated by prudence, to guard against surprise, and save the women and children. The night throughout the Valley was one of inexpressible anguish and despair.

Although darkness had put an end to the pursuit, and most of the prisoners had been barbarously butchered, some who were supposed to be special objects of hate, were selected for slower torture, and the execution of more savage vengeance. It may be some unguarded word—perhaps the refusal, in gone-by years, of whiskey to an importunate Indian; some fancied, or real wrong; or, it is thought by some, to satiate the revenge of Indians who had lost relations in the fight: whatever may have been the motive, the vast depths of hell, boiling with demoniac passions, never could have devised or executed such horrid tortures, as many of the Connecticut prisoners were that night doomed to endure.

On the river bank, on the Pittston side, Capt. Blanchard, Esq., Whitaker, and Ishmael Bennet, attracted by fires among trees, on the opposite shore, took their station and witnessed the process of torture. Several naked men, in the midst of flames, were driven round a stake; their groans and screams were most piteous, while the shouts and yells of the Savages, who danced round, urging the victims on with their spears, were too horrible to be endured. They were powerless to help or avenge, and withdrew, heartsick from a view of their horrid orgies—glad that they did not know who were the sufferers. This was more than a mile above Wintermoot's. On the battle ground, the work of torture lasted till vengeance, satiated and weary, dropped the knife and torch, from exhaustion. Col. John Butler, much agitated, as the peculiar affluvium of burning human flesh came to his nostrils, said, in the hearing of Mr. Ingersoll, "It is not in my power to help it." In the morning, the battle field was strewed with limbs, and bodies torn apart, mangled and partially consumed.

About one hundred and sixty of the Connecticut people were killed that day, and one hundred and forty escaped. The loss of the enemy was never known. "Early the next morning," says Mr. Ingersoll, " all the shovels and pickaxes that could be mustered were taken out, and their dead buried in the swamp. Probably from forty to eighty fell."

The transactions of the next day must be reserved for another letter.

LETTER XVIII.

1778.——Morning of the Fourth—Consternation and Flight—Incidents of Suffering—Mr. Hollenback meets the starving Fugitives with bread—Pittston Forts surrender—Negotiations—Capitulation of Forty Fort—(*Note, Queen Esther)—(*Note, Brant)—Sergeant Boyd shot—Incidents—Col. John Butler withdraws from the Valley—His character—John Gardiner—The Indians that remain give up the Valley to fire, plunder and devastation—Murder of Hickman, wife and child—Murder of Leach and St. John—Murder of John Abbott and Isaac Williams—Murder of Keys and Hocksey—Swetland and Blanchard carried away prisoners—Col. Zebulon Butler returns with Capt. Spalding's Company to the Valley—Col. Hartley joins Col. Butler—Expedition to West Branch and Sheshequin—Remains of the slaughtered people buried—List of slain—Several interesting matters—Col. Hartley's Command withdrawn—Return of Savages—Indian murders—William Jameson—John Perkins—Wm. Jackson and Mr. Lester—Capt. Carr and Philip Goss—Robert Alexander and Amos Parker—The Utley family murdered—Isaac Inman murdered—Nathan Kingsley killed—Frances Slocum carried into captivity—Jonathan Slocum and Isaac Tripp murdered—The lost Sister—Thomas Neill, the generous Irishman—Terms of Capitulation, and official Papers, from British archives.

On the evening of the third of July, Capt. John Franklin arrived at Forty Fort, with the Huntington and Salem company, consisting of about thirty-five men; a most welcome reinforcement to Col. Denison, as they gave steadiness to the broken remnant of the army who had escaped. A consultation was held, at which it was concluded to send to Wilkesbarre for the cannon, to cause the whole settlement to concentrate at Forty Fort, the largest in the Valley, and defend themselves to the last extremity. A messenger, despatched on the morning of the fourth, hastily returned, and reported that the proposed measure was impracticable, for fugitives were flying in every direction to the wilderness, and all was confusion, consternation and horror. The only hope of safety seemed to be in flight. The several passages through the swamp were thronged. Few having been throughtful enough to take provisions, the greater part were destitute. On the old warrior's path, there were in one company, about one hundred women and children, with but a single man, Jonathan

Fitch, Esq., Sheriff of the county, to advise or aid them. The way towards the Wind Gap and Stroudsburg, was equally crowded. Sufferings from fatigue and hunger soon became extreme. The brave George Cooper, who would "have one shot more," with his companions, Westover and Stark, and their families, had made an effort to obtain provisions, but the Indians being discovered watching their dwellings, they were compelled to fly with scarce a morsel, though exhausted by the battle.

Of the little they had, neither of the men would partake, so that the children need not perish. Tears gushed from the eyes of the aged widow of Cooper, when she related that her husband had laid on his face to lap up a little meal which a companion, in their flight, had spilt on the earth. Children were born, and several perished in the "Dismal Swamp," or "Shades of Death," as it is called to this day. Mrs. Treusdale was taken in labour; daring to delay but a few minutes, she was soon seen with her infant, moving onward—a sheet having been fixed on a horse, so as to carry them. Jabez Fish, who was in the battle, escaped; but not being able to join his family, was supposed to have fallen; and Mrs. Fish hastened with her children through the wilderness. Overcome with fatigue and want, her infant died. Sitting down a moment, on a stone, to see it draw its last breath, she gazed in its face with unutterable anguish. There was no way to dig a grave—and to leave it to be devoured by wolves, seemed worse than death, so she took the dead babe in her arms, and carried it twenty miles, when she came to a German settlement. Though poor, they gave her food; made a box for the child, attended her to the graveyard, and decently buried it, kindly bidding her welcome, till she should be rested. The uniform hospitality of the Germans, is gratefully attested by the Wyoming people.

The wife of Ebenezer Marcy was taken in labour, in the wilderness. Having no mode of conveyance, her sufferings were inexpressibly severe. She was able to drag her fainting steps but about two miles that day. The next, being overtaken by a neighbour with a horse, she rode, and in a week's time, was more than a hundred miles, with her infant, from the place of its birth.

Mrs. Rogers, from Plymouth, an aged woman, flying with her family, overcome by fatigue and sorrow, fainted in the wilderness, twenty miles from human habitation. She could take no nourishment, and soon died. They made a grave in the best manner they could, and the next day, nearly exhausted, came to a settlement of Germans, who treated them with exceeding great kindness. Mrs.

Courtright relates that she, then a young girl, flying with her father's family, saw sitting by the road side, a widow, who had learned the death of her husband. Six children were on the ground near her. The group, the very image of despair, for they were without food. Just at that moment, a man was seen riding rapidly towards them, from the settlements. It was Mr. Hollenback. Foreseeing the probable destitution, he had providently loaded his horse with bread, and was hastening back, like an angel of mercy, to their relief. Cries and tears of gratitude and welcome went up to Heaven. He imparted a morsel to each, and hastened on to the relief of others.

The widow of Anderson Dana, Esq., and her widowed daughter, Mrs. Whiton, did not learn, certainly, the deaths of their husbands, until they were at Bullock's, on the mountain, ten miles on their way. Many then heard the fate of relations, and a messenger brought to Mr. Bullock, word, that both his sons were dead on the field. Then was there mourning and lamentation, and the wringing of hands. Mrs. Dana had been extraordinarily careful. Not only had she provided food, but taken a pillow-case of valuable papers, (the husband being much engaged in public business,) the preservation of which has thrown much light on our path of research. Depending chiefly on charity, the family sought their ancient home, at Ashford, Windham county, Connecticut. Those few instances selected from an hundred, will present some idea of the dreadful flight.

Early on the morning after the battle, Col. John Butler sent a detachment across the river to Pittston, when Capt. Blanchard surrendered Fort Brown, on terms of fair capitulation; and the Indians marked the prisoners with black paint on the face, telling them to keep it there, and if they went out, each should carry a white cloth on a stick, so that being known, they should not be hurt.* Colonel Butler also despatched a messenger to Forty Fort, requesting Col. Denison to come up, and agree on terms of capitulation. Taking with him Obadiah Gore, Esq., an aged man, and Dr. Gustin, Col. Denison immediately repaired to Head Quarters, near the ruins of Wintermoot's Fort. In discussing the terms, it was insisted that

---

* Tom Turkey, Anthony Turkey, David Singsing, and Anthony Cornelius, formerly residents in the Valley, and known to the inhabitants, were among the Indians. Squaws followed, hideously smeared with brains and blood, bringing strings of scalps; of which, with more than a demon's malice, they would smell, and exultingly exclaim, "Yankee blood!"

Col. Zebulon Butler, and the remains of Hewett's company, being continental soldiers, should be surrendered prisoners of war. Col. Denison desired time to consult with his officers, which was allowed. Returning, he hastened to Wilkesbarre, where, having an interview with Col. Z. Butler, it was judged expedient that he and the fourteen men remaining of Hewett's command, should immediately retire from the Valley. Ordering the men to Shamokin, Col. Butler threw a bed upon his horse, took Mrs. B. behind him, and that night tarried at the Nescopeck Valley, (now Conyngham,) twenty miles from Wilkesbarre. Having reported the fact to Col. John Butler, that all the continental men were beyond his command, negotiations were renewed—Zerah Beach, Esq. and the Rev. Jacob Johnson being present. Terms were agreed upon, verbally: but there remaining no conveniences for writing, at Wintermoot's, they were to be committed to paper at four o'clock, in the afternoon, at Forty Fort, when the surrender was to take place. It being known that among the stores there was a quantity of whiskey, Col. Butler desired it might be destroyed, for he feared, if the Indians became intoxicated, he could not restrain them. Before the hour, the barrels were rolled to the bank, the heads knocked in, and the liquor emptied into the river.

The two gates of the Fort were now thrown open, and what arms could be found, including those of Franklin's men, were piled up in the centre. So capacious was the fort, that notwithstanding the ranges of huts that lined the sides, there was ample room to drill a company of men. At the appointed time, the victors approached with colours flying and music playing; a column of white men, four abreast, on the left. On the right the Savages, also in four files; the whites, headed by Col. Butler—the Indians led by Queen Esther.*
"You told me to bring more Indians, Col. Den-i-son," said the old

* Col. Stone. For the opinions of my estimable friend, I entertain unaffected regard; but when compelled by proofs, his goodness will allow me to differ from him, without offence, He thinks it impossible Queen Esther should have conducted like a demon, especially as represented at the Bloody Rock. He may have misapprehended the person. It seems she and Col. Denison were acquainted. Col. Franklin, who also knew her, states the facts in respect to her conduct explicitly. That she was a person of consideration, is manifest, from her leading the Indian column, but more especially at the Fatal Ring, from which Hammond escaped. Remember the kindred atrocities perpetrated by women during the French Revolution. It required the purity of angels corrupted, to make perfect devils. One reason assigned for her intense malice, was, that one of the Indians slain, at Exeter, on the 2d, was her son.

From a narrative recently published in "Hill's Newhampshire Patriot," taken from a Journal of one of Sullivan's officers, we copy a paragraph.

Fury, drawling out his name, "See here, I have brought you all these." "Be silent," said Col. Butler, "women should be seen, but not heard." The column of Rangers, Royal Greens, and Tories, marched in at the north. Brant, or Gi-en-gwah-toh,* with his followers, at the south gate. The suspicious look of the wary chief, glancing his flashing eye, now to the right, now to the left, as if apprehensive of treachery, was well remembered, and graphically described by the late Col. Dorrance. Immediately on entering the fort, the Tories seized the arms. An order from Col. Butler to replace them, was followed by an address to the Indians. "See, a present the Yankees have made you!" Seeming much pleased, they took them into possession.

"August 10, [1779.] After advancing about a mile through a rich bottom covered with strong and stately timber, which shut out the sun, and shed a cool and agreeable twilight, we unexpectedly were introduced into a plain as large as that of Sheshukonah [Shesquequin,] called 'Queen Esther's Plantation.' It was in the plains, near the banks of the Susquehannah, that Esther, queen of the Seneca tribe, dwelt in retirement and sullen majesty. The ruins of her palace are still to be seen. In what we supposed to be the chapel, was found an idol, which might well be worshipped without violating the third commandment, on account of its likeness to 'any thing either in heaven or earth.' About sunrise, the General gave orders for the town to be illuminated, and accordingly we had a glorious bonfire, of upwards of thirty buildings at once."

* We had yielded rather to the confident opinion of Col. Stone, than to the proofs adduced, that Brant was not in command at the invasion. His own positive denial might well be received with hesitation and doubt; for in Europe, at least, he had no inconsiderable reputation; and so much infamy had attached to the Indian cruelties at Wyoming, that if guilty, he would gladly escape, even by the additional offence of falsehood. Little regard should be paid to his mere assertion. How much more to the denial of his Indian friends? Where was he? Col. Butler with his Rangers! Johnson, with his Royal Greens! Capt. Caldwell! Six hundred Indians to be commanded! Wyoming to be attacked! Assuredly, Brant, the great Iroquois leader, would not fail to be present! Such would be the reasoning. Add to this, the general, the universal belief, for forty years, during which time no other name was mentioned as the Chief-in-command. Gen. Ross, who lost two brothers in the battle, himself old enough to bear arms, having been in the array at Exeter, on the 2nd, highly intelligent, would not listen to a doubt on the subject; with such certainty, had half a century of unshaken belief, fixed the fact in his mind. Recently, Eleazer Carey, Esq., a gentleman of great candour and intelligence, tells me, in a note dated July 24, 1843,

"When a lad fourteen years old, I resided in the Genesee country, and in 1803, became acquainted with the family of Kanchilak, eldest son of Blue Throat, or Talaguadeak. He had sons and daughters, not differing much from my age; and he said the boys must teach me to talk Indian, and I, them, to speak Yankee. We thus became intimate. Blue Throat could speak our language, understandingly. He assured me, as did Little Beard, who held the rank of captain in the battle, that Brant was not present. This statement was confirmed by Stuttering John, and Roland Montour, the latter a half blood, who took my uncle, Samuel Carey, prisoner."

If the concurrent assertions of Brant, and his Indian friends, are to be credited, he was not present. Mr. Carey believes them. The public will form their own judgment.

The terms of capitulation were then reduced to writing, and signed (on a table still in possession of Mrs. Myers.) (Those, with other documents of interest—indeed, all that could be obtained at the London War Office, relating to Wyoming, will be found together at the close of this letter.)

As Col. Butler stood in the gateway, he recognized Serjeant Boyd, the deserter of whom we have before spoken. "Boyd," said he sternly, "go to that tree." "I hope," said Boyd imploringly, "your honour will consider me a prisoner of war." "Go to that tree, sir!" And at a signal the Indians poured in a volley, and he fell dead.

Soon after signing the articles, Col. Butler observed, "That as Wyoming was a frontier, it was wrong for any part of the inhabitants to leave their own settlements, and enter into the Continental army abroad; that such a number having done so, was the cause of the invasion, and that it never would have been attempted, if the men had remained at home. Col. Franklin, who heard the declaration, added, "I was of the same opinion."

In a few hours after the fort was surrendered, the Indians began to plunder, entering the huts, and breaking open trunks and boxes. The town papers were scattered around, the surveys, and other valuable writings destroyed, and the Westmoreland Records, with difficulty preserved. Col. Denison complained, saying he had capitulated relying on the honour of a British officer. "I will put a stop to it, I will put a stop to it," said Butler, and gave peremptory orders to the chief. "These are your Indians, you must restrain them." Soon after, open and flagrant robberies were renewed, and Col. Denison again, and with spirit, remonstrated. After another ineffectual effort, Col. Butler said: "I can do nothing with them, I can do nothing with them," and added, that Indians after a successful battle, never could be controlled. He professed to be, and probably was hurt, that such outrages should be committed, in violation of his plighted faith, and positive orders. "Make out a list," added he, "of the property lost, and I pledge my honour it shall be paid for."

Every hour growing bolder and more insolent, the savages soon threw off all restraint, seized on Col. Denison, and taking the hat from his head, demanded also the linen frock he wore. In the pocket were a few dollars, the whole military chest of the settlement, and he made some resistance, when they instantly lifting a tomahawk threatened his life. Obliged to comply, he, seeming to have some difficulty in slipping it over his head, stepped backward to where sat a young woman of his family, who comprehending the manœuvre, adroitly took out the purse, when he gave up the coveted garment to the spoiler.

So gross and widely circulated have been the errors, in respect to this capitulation, that it is time the truth of history should be vindicated. Gordon, Ramsey, Marshall and Botta, adopting the Poughkeepsie account, have all stated, that on Col. Denison asking what terms would be granted to him, was answered "the hatchet;" and that thereupon surrendering, fire was set to the fort, and the prisoners, men, women and children, pitched in on the burning pile, and given up to the flames. The facts, carefully collected by the labour of years, and now faithfully recorded, are sufficiently painful. "Give the devil his due," is an adage, just, as it is old. In another page, this matter being regarded as important, is set forth more at large. For the present it may be stated, that while in every other particular the terms were violated, no life was taken at Forty Fort, except that of Serjeant Boyd.

Col. Butler finding his commands disregarded, and his authority set at nought, by his own bands of enraged and licentious savages, flushed with victory and drunk with blood; apprehensive too, it is believed, of his own life being taken, if he attempted to enforce obedience, mustered all his force, whom discipline could control, and on Wednesday, the 8th, withdrew from the plains. He did not even indulge himself with a visit to Wilkesbarre, or the lower part of the Valley.*

---

* Mr. Finch, a prisoner liberated by the articles of capitulation, visiting the field with the writer in 1838, stated "that Col. Butler received a letter from a messenger on the 5th or 6th, that he immediately assembled round him his officers and the Indian chiefs, and read it to them. That he addressed the latter very earnestly in their own tongue, and was understood, among other things, to enjoin it on them, not to kill women and children. That when he ceased to speak, they raised a great shout, and he ordered preparations to be made for a retreat. It was supposed the letter hastened his march. Such a letter may have been received, or it might have been a scheme devised to hasten the departure of the Indians.

Col. Butler did not lack sense. All that duty, more than honour required, had been done. He must have been insensible to interest, as well as character, to countenance further atrocities. The Valley was in his absolute power. Had he meant to plunder and destroy the whole, certainly he would not have entered into written articles, voluntarily stipulating the reverse. Mr. Finch also states, that the knot by which Col. Butler's handkerchief was tied, was shot through, so that it fell.

An anecdote, too good to be lost, may as well be told here. Mr. Finch, and the writer, waited on Mrs. Jenkins, then more than eighty years of age, who lived near the field. She instantly recognized him, although it was near half a century since they had met. She, it will be recollected was a prisoner, having been taken on the 2d. "O yes, Finch," said the old lady with much archness and humour, in answer to his inquiry, "to be sure I remember you. An old squaw took you, and brought you in—she found you in the bushes—and as she drove

His retirement indeed, bore the marks of accelerated retreat. Fear of an attack from any probable force that could be brought to assail him, can hardly be imagined, and the anxiety to leave the ground can only be accounted for on the supposition that he was sickened by the tortures already committed, dreaded the further cruelties of the Indians, and desired by his absence, to escape the responsibility of their future conduct.

As we now part with this bold partisan leader forever, a page cannot be ill devoted in this history, which shall present a just sketch of his character. He was descended, we have great confidence in expressing the belief, from some of the younger branches of the family of the Duke of Ormond, whose name was Butler. Our own opinion is, that the two Colonel Butlers were from the same original stock, and perhaps three generations back, their fathers hailed at least as near as cousins. Col. John Butler was a fat man, below the middle stature, yet active; through the rough visage of the warrior, showing a rather agreeable, than forbidding aspect. Care sat on his brow. Speaking quickly, he repeated his words when excited. Decision, firmness and courage, were undoubted characteristics of the man. So detested is his name, associated with the atrocities perpetrated at Wyoming, that even now, it is not without some fear of offence, we draw of him, what we believe to be, a just outline. An old agricultural work says:—" In the town of Kilkenny, Ireland, and near the river side, stands on an eminence, a fine gothic building belonging to the Butler family, which was erected in the reign of Queen Anne, by the famous Duke of Ormond." Sir Walter Scott, in his Legend of Montrose, makes Dalgetty say: "I e'en gave up my commission, and took service with Wallenstein in Walter Butler's Irish Regiment. Col. John Butler, had a son *Walter*, who fell on the Mohawk. The ancestor of Col. Butler, as we have elsewhere hinted, probably came over as Indian agent, (in Queen Anne's reign, when Ormond was in great power,) with the delegation of Kings from the Five Nations, on their return.

It is certain Col. Butler could have commanded much more severe conditions. The settlement was wholly at his mercy. No one can deny but the capitulation, on its face, was, under the circumstances, in a high degree honourable, and favourable to Col. Denison. Col.

you along, patted you on the back, saying, my son, my son!" Though certainly no reflection on his courage or manhood, he did not relish the story half so much as the bystanders, especially as he had previously been playing the hero in his account of the battle. He very soon took leave of the Valley.

Franklin confirms the statement of Mrs. Myers, that Butler exerted himself to restrain the savages, seemed deeply hurt when he was unable to do so, and at once offered, if a list could be furnished of property lost, to make it good. Finally he withdrew his own men, proper, taking, so far as we learn, no plunder. His fault appears to us to have been in his position—his crime, in accepting command, lending his name, and associating with those blood-thirsty and unprincipled savages who were placed under his orders. Their stains, neither time nor charity can remove. But does it not attach with tenfold deeper crimson to the Government under whose administration such inhuman agents were directed to be employed? We have some reason to believe that many years after the war, the Government of Great Britain having withheld from Butler some token of honour, or expected emolument, otherwise his due, on account of his alleged treachery and cruelty, he sent a confidential agent to Wyoming to obtain certificates of the true state of the facts; in which he succeeded. That he was regarded as respectable, independent of his commission as a British officer, is shown from the fact, that the American commissioners appointed to treat with the Six Nations, under Washington's administration, (in 1795,) accepted an invitation from Col. Butler, crossed the line, and dined with him.*

With Butler, a large portion of the Indians withdrew, and their march presented a picture at once melancholy and ludicrous. Squaws to a considerable number, brought up the rear, a belt of scalps stretched on small hoops, around the waist for a girdle, having on, some four, some six, and even more, dresses of chintz or silk, one over the other; being mounted astride on horses, of course all stolen, and on their heads three, four, or five bonnets, one within another, worn wrong side before.

One prisoner taken at Exeter the 1st of July, when the Hardings and Hadsels were massacred, as we leave the battle ground, de-

* The deepest stain on the character of Butler, next to his taking the command of such a horde of merciless and ungovernable wretches, arises out of the fact that but two prisoners were taken, and saved at the time of the battle. With his own regiment of Rangers, and the detachment of Sir John Johnson's Greens, not including the tories who joined his army, he must have had several hundred white men under his command, no inconsiderable number disciplined soldiers. These, beyond all doubt, were the immediate servants of his will. That they took no part in the pursuit of the fugitives, is not for a moment to be imagined. It would seem, of course, that they must have participated in the cruelties which followed the flight; the refusal to give quarter to a yielding foe, or the subsequent murder of prisoners who had surrendered! Whatever may be said of the ungovernable character of the Indians, for the conduct of his own regularly enlisted and disciplined soldiers, he was unquestionably responsible.

mands our special notice. Mr. John Gardiner was a husband and father, a highly respectable man, against whom, some unappeasable spirit of enmity is supposed to have existed. On the morning of the 4th his wife and children were permitted to see, and take leave of him. Elisha Harding, Esq., then a boy, was present, and represents the scene as extremely affecting. When the last adieu was exchanged, an Indian placed a grievous load on his shoulders, which he could scarcely raise, then put a halter round his neck, and led him off as he would a beast. The farewell expressed the sentiment; "I go to return no more." Exhausted with fatigue before he arrived at his captor's home, he fell, crushed by the weight of his load, when he was handed over to the squaws, who tortured him to death by fire. Daniel Carr, a fellow prisoner, saw the remains the following day, and represented it as a sight to awaken the deepest pity.

The savages remaining, now freed from the slight restraint the presence of their white allies imposed, gave themselves to the wildest disorder. Separating in parties of from five to ten, they scattered through the Valley, marking their course as if in sheer wantonness, with fire. After stripping a house of every thing fancied, they would either leave, or set fire to it, as whim or caprice seemed to dictate. Such was their joyous exultation, they hardly knew how to give it expression. Constant Searle, Esq., the most aged man who went to the field, had fallen among the rest. An Indian was seen on horseback, wearing his wig hind side before, while his companions would frighten the animal, or prick him with a spear, laughing to see him fall.

From the farm of an aged man by the name of Weeks, in Wilkesbarre, originally from Fairfield county, seven persons had gone out to battle, (so imperious, so irresistible were demands for men, even to make up the three hundred.) Philip, Jonathan, and Bartholomew Weeks, his sons—Silas Benedict, who married a grand-daughter. Jabez Beers, and Josiah Carman, relatives, and Robert Bates, a boarder. Horrible slaughter! The whole seven lay dead on the field at night! A band of Indians came to the house of Mr. Weeks, and bade him remove. "How can I," said he, "my whole family you have slain." Getting provisions, they feasted heartily, when one of them wheeled a large rocking chair into the road, took the hat from the old gentleman, and putting it on his own head, sat down, and rocked himself. Allowing him to take a pair of oxen, they gave Mr. Weeks three days to prepare for his departure, when they set fire to the buildings, and destroyed all that was left.

The terms of capitulation being known, and regarded as favorable, the lives of the garrison having been spared, and the Savages thus far seeming satisfied with plunder and burning, hope of life dawned, for a moment, upon those that remained; but almost immediately the cheering ray was extinguished in blood.

News came down from the Lackawanna, that Mr. Hickman, his wife and child, were murdered at Capouse. The very next day two men, by the name of Leach and St. John, who were removing with their families, were shot six miles up the Lackawanna. One of them had a child in his arms, which, with strange inconsistency, the Indian took up, and handed to the mother, all covered with the father's blood. Leaving the women in the wagon unhurt, they took the scalps of their husbands, and departed. Again, alarm arose to phrenzy. Col. Denison, with all who had remained at Forty Fort, fled; some down the river and some through the swamp.*

Except a few who gathered about the fort at Wilkesbarre, the whole people abandoned the settlement. Every house and barn, not spared by caprice, was burnt. The Valley presented one wide scene of conflagration and ruin.

Col. Z. Butler, as soon as possible, wrote a hasty letter to General Washington, stating briefly the fate of the day, and soliciting succour, that if possible, a portion of the harvest might be preserved.

Joining Capt. Spalding, early in August, he returned to Wyoming.† A new stockade was erected in Wilkesbarre, and put in the best posture of defence. So sustained, a number of persons, whose families had fled, returned in the hope to save a portion of the wasting harvest, which had escaped destruction. John Abbott, who had been in the battle, and Isaac Williams, a young man, in attempting

---

* Through malice or misapprehension, blame was attempted to be cast on Col. Denison and the people, for taking up arms again. Surely they were released from every obligation of peace or neutrality, by the flagrant and wanton violation of all the provisions of the capitulation.

† Capt. Spalding was at Shupes', half way between the Pocono and Blue mountains, near fifty miles from Wyoming, on the day of the battle. Marching early on the 4th, he advanced thirteen miles to where the gate is now kept. Here he met Mr. Hollenback and Mr. Hageman, the first fugitives, and learned the fate of the day. Pushing forward, he came to the Bear Swamp, within twelve miles of Wilkesbarre, which he was anxious to reach. Resting his company, who had marched thirty miles through intolerable roads, he sent two men forward to reconnoiter. From the mountain, they saw the flames rising in all directions, confirming the statements of the retreating inhabitants, that the Valley was entirely in possession of the enemy. Victory, with a single company, being hopeless, Capt. Spalding returned, rendering all the aid in his power, to the distressed. Taking up a position at Stroudsburg, he waited the orders of Col. Butler.

to harvest their wheat on Jacob's plains, were waylaid and both shot and scalped. The widow of Mr. Abbott, who had fled to Cattawissa, with nine children, (their house and barn having been burnt, and all their property destroyed,) set out on foot, a journey of near three hundred miles, and begged their way home to Hampton, in Wyndham county.

About this time, three Indians took prisoners on the Lackawana, Isaac Tripp, Esq., the elder; Isaac Tripp, his grandson, and two young men, by the names of Keys and Hocksey. The old gentleman they painted and dismissed, but hurried the others into the forest, (now Abington,) above Leggett's Gap, on the warrior's path to Oquago. Resting one night, they rose next morning and traveled about two miles, when they stopped at a little stream of water. The two young Indians then took Keys and Hocksey some distance from the path, and were absent half an hour, the old Indian looking anxiously the way they had gone. Presently, the death-whoop was heard, and the Indians returned brandishing bloody tomahawks, and exhibiting the scalps of their victims. Tripp's hat was taken from his head, and his scalp examined twice, the Savages speaking earnestly, when at length they told him to fear nothing, he should not be hurt, and carried him off as a prisoner. Luke Swetland and Joseph Blanchard were taken prisoners, near Nanticoke, on the 24th of August, and carried away captives to the Indian country.

Surrounded by murderous parties, a very small portion of the grain could be preserved. Col. Hartley, of the Pennsylvania line, was now ordered to join Col. Butler, and thus strengthened, active offensive measures were instantly adopted, to hunt out and repel the Indians. Having pitched their lodges on the flats, at Sheshequin, within Westmoreland town, an expedition was set on foot, to break up their settlement. A detachment of one hundred and thirty men marched on the 8th of September, to the West Branch, and thence to Sheshequin. On the 29th a battle ensued. Several Indians were known to be killed, as their bodies were left on the field, and it was not doubted that a number more were slain. Two or three of Col. Hartley's men were killed and several wounded. The Indian settlement was broken up, and besides cattle and horses recovered, a considerable portion of plunder* was taken. Col. Hartley, in general orders, at camp Westmoreland, Oct. 3d, 1778, not only expresses

---

* So universally was the expression, *plunder*, used at that time, for property taken from an enemy, that we adopt it.

his satisfaction, generally, with the troops, "during a tiresome and dangerous march, amidst hunger—the wading of rivers at midnight, where not a complaint was heard," but adds, "In short, the whole detachment, with very few exceptions, have acquitted themselves with the highest reputation, and they have the satisfaction to know they have saved the lives of many, and served their country." The Colonel particularly compliments "Capt. Franklin, and the Wyoming volunteers." Serjeants Allison and Thornbury were raised to the rank of ensigns, in Col. Hartley's regiment, for their distinguished bravery in action. On the same day, Lord Butler was officially announced as "Quarter-Master at this post—to be obeyed as such;" a son, then a youth, of Col. Z. Butler. His name will frequently occur in these annals.

The middle of October had come and passed, and the dead yet lay on the field, unburied. Before the autumn frosts it had been impossible to perform the mournful duty.

"Camp Westmoreland, Oct. 21, 1778.—Ordered, That there be a party, consisting of a lieutenant, two serjeants, two corporals, and twenty-five men, to parade to-morrow morning, with arms, as a guard to those who will go to bury the remains of the men who were killed at the late battle, at and near the place called Wintermoot's Fort." On the 22d of October, therefore, the bodies were collected—a large hole dug, in which they were thrown, constant alarm from the enemy preventing a more ceremonious or respectful inhumation.

But few could be recognised. Two brothers of the Ross family had fallen—Lieut. Perrin, aged thirty-one, and Jeremiah, nineteen. The former was known by a ring he wore. Reserving for a chapter of personal narrative, a more particular account of many who fell, we may here observe, to give the reader an impression of the sacrifices families were obliged to make—that there were more than twenty who lost two in the battle; in several instances father and son. The slaughter in Mr. Weeks' family, of seven, we have recorded,—Anderson Dana and Mr. Whiton, his newly married son-in-law; old Mr. Searle, and Capt. Hewitt, his son-in-law, and two of Mr. Bullock's sons, have been mentioned. Of the Inman family, three lost their lives, (and one was subsequently murdered). Three of the Coreys fell. The Gores suffered most pitiably. Seven—five sons, and two sons-in-law, of Obadiah Gore, Esq., were in the battle, namely :—Daniel, Samuel, Asa, George, and Silas.—The sons-in-law were Timothy Pierce and John Murfee. At night, three of the sons, and the two sons-in-law lay on the field. Samuel escaped unhurt, Daniel with his left arm shattered. Another son, Lieut. Obadiah Gore, was then away with the main line of the army.

The following is a list of the killed, so far as the persons could be recollected. Probably there might have been twenty or thirty more whose names were not remembered.

FIELD OFFICERS.

Lieut. Col. George Dorrance,   Major John Garrett.

CAPTAINS.

Robert Durkee,
Dethick Hewitt,
Aholiab Buck,
Wm. McKarrican.
Samuel Ransom,

James Bidlack, Jr..
Asaph Whittlesey,
Rezin Geer,
Lazarus Stewart.

LIEUTENANTS.

James Welles,
Timothy Pierce,
Flavius Waterman,
Aaron Gaylord,
Lazarus Stewart, Jr.,

Perrin Ross,
Asa Stephens,
Elijah Shoemaker,
Stoddard Bowen,
A. Atherton.

ENSIGNS.

Asa Gore,
William White,
Silas Gore,

Jeremiah Bigford,
Titus Hinman.

PRIVATES.

Christopher Avery,
Jabez Atherton,
—— Acke,
A. Benedict,
Jabez Beers,
Elisha Bigsbee,
Thomas Brown,
Amos Bullock,
Asa Bullock,
John Brown,
David Bigsbee,
John Boyd,
Joseph Budd,
William Buck,

Samuel Bigford,
Henry Bush,
Samuel Carey,
Samuel Cole,
Joseph Crocker,
John Cortright,
John Caldwell,
Josiah Cameron,
Robert Comstock,
Kingsley Comstock,
Samuel Crooker,
William Coffrin,
Joel Church,
Joseph Corey.

HISTORY OF WYOMING.

Isaac Campbell,
James Coffrin,
Christopher Cortright,
Jenks Corey
Rufus Corey,
Anson Corey,
Anderson Dana,
—— Dutcher,
Jabez Darling,
William Dunn,
D. Denton,
Levi Dunn,
James Divine,
George Downing,
Conrad Davenport,
Thomas Fuller,
Stephen Fuller,
Elisha Fish,
Eliphalet Folet,
Benjamin Finch,
Daniel Finch,
John Finch,
Cornelius Fitchet,
Thomas Foxen,
John Franklin,
George Gore,
Silas Gore,
Samuel Hutchinson,
James Hopkins,
Silas Harvey,
William Hammer,
Levi Hicks,
John Hutchins,
Cyprean Hibbard,
Nathaniel Howard,
Benjamin Hatch,
Elijah Inman,
Israel Inman,
Robert McIntire,
Samuel Jackson,
Robert Jameson,
Joseph Jennings,
Henry Johnson,
Francis Lepard,
Daniel Lawrence,
Josh. Landon,
Conrad Lowe,
Jacob Lowe,
James Lock,
William Lawrence,
A. Meeleman,
C. McCartee,
Job Marshall,
Nicholas Manvil,
John Murphy,
Nero Matthewson,
Andrew Millard,
Thomas Neil,
Joseph Ogden,
J. Otis,
Abel Palmer,
William Parker,
Noah Pettibone, Jr.,
John Pierce,
Silas Parke,
Henry Pensil,
Elias Roberts,
Elisha Richards,
Timothy Rose,
Christopher Reynolds,
Enos Rockway,
Jeremiah Ross,
Joseph Staples,
Reuben Staples,
Aaron Stark,
Daniel Stark,
Darius Spafford,
Joseph Shaw,
Abram Shaw,
Rufus Stevens,
Constant Searles,
Nailer Swede.

James Stevenson,
James Spencer,
Levi Spencer,
Eleazer Sprague,
Josiah Spencer,
Able Seeley,
Ichabod Tuttle,
John Vanwee,
Abram Vangorder,
James Wigton,
Peter Wheeler,
Jonathan Weeks,
Philip Weeks,

Bartholomew Weeks,
Rufus Williams,
Elihu Williams, Jr.,
Parker Wilson,
Azibah Williams,
John Wilson,
John Ward,
Esen Wilcox,
Stephen Whiton,
Elihu Waters,
John Williams,
Wm. Woodward,
Ozias Yale.

From the records at Hartford, was obtained the following List of Officers in the Militia, whose commissions were "*established*" by the Assembly, in October 1775. At the time of the battle, most of them held different commissions. How dreadful the slaughter must have been, may be inferred from the heavy loss among the officers. The company that lost none, was not present in the battle.

October 1775.—24th Regiment of Connecticut Militia.

1st Company.
Capt. Stephen Fuller,
Lieut. John Garrett,*
Ensign Christopher Avery.*

2d Company.
Capt. Nathaniel Landon,
Lieut. George Dorrance,*
Ensign Asahel Buck,*

3d Company.
Capt. Samuel Ransom,*
Lieut. Perrin Ross,*
Ensign Asaph Whittlesey,*

4th Company.
Capt. Solomon Strong,
Lieut. Jonathan Parker,
Ensign Timothy Keys.

5th Company.
Capt. Wm. McKarrican,*
Lieut. Lazarus Stewart,*
Ensign Silas Gore.*

6th Company.
Capt. Rezin Geer,*
Lieut. Daniel Gore, (*wounded.*)
Ensign Matthias Hollenback.

Those marked with an asterisk [*] were killed; so that of fifteen, eleven were slain.

All the early historians, who have related the massacre, stated that the houses of tories left, looked like islands in a sea of fire, an error too important to remain uncontradicted. Below Wintermoot's, near the head of the Valley, it is not known that there was a single tory house or family. Individuals, labouring men, or hunters, there were a few, probably mingling with the inhabitants from policy. Above Wintermoot's, extending to Wyalusing, the tory families were scattered, their settlements being recent, holding but a partial intercourse, no sympathy existing between them and the Connecticut inhabitants. On a careful examination of a list found among the papers of Col. Butler, containing sixty-one names, three only are from New England. The names are of a different people. Wintermoots, Larraways, Van Alstines, Secords, etc., from the Mohawk, Kinderhook, Minnisink, and West Chester, New York. There is good reason to believe, on the breaking out of hostilities with Great Britain, that her comprehensive policy, which, while with gigantic grasp it embraced great interests, yet allowed nothing, however comparatively trivial or minute, to escape attention, foreseeing the necessity of cutting off all friendly communication between the zealous whig people of Wyoming and the Indians, and with views to ulterior measures, caused these tory families to remove, and take up the position they held. Gordon says: " An unusual number of strangers had come among them under various pretences." Certainly there was no disposition of the same number of most devoted partisans, that could have enabled them to render so much service. But this matter has been adverted to before.

Soon after Col. Hartley's return from the successful expedition just related, he was recalled from Wyoming, and a garrison left of about an hundred men, including Captain Spalding, and Captain Morrison's Companies, and Captain Franklin's Wyoming Volunteers, consisting of all the militia, who had returned to the Valley. Armed parties laboured in the fields, the necessity of sowing, though late, as much grain as possible, being apparent.*

---

* Fifteen years after the battle, a number of Indians, among whom were several chiefs of distinction, passed through Wyoming, on their way to Philadelphia, on business with the Government. Apprehending danger, they sent word to Wilkesbarre, and an escort of respectable citizens turned out to accompany them into the town. In the evening a council was held, in the Court Room, where mutually pacific assurances were given. It is not surprising, considering their cruel conduct during the war, that the Indians entertained fears for their safety. On their return, passing on the opposite side of the river from the battle ground, the old braves showed much excitement, talking and gesticulating, with great emphasis and spirit, as they seemed to be pointing out to the younger savages the position, and incidents of the conflict. I met Red Jacket at Washington in 1827 or 8, and strove to lead him to talk of Wyoming, but on that subject his lips were hermetically sealed.

Following almost immediately on the footsteps of Hartley's men, bands of marauding Indians again made their appearance. Surrounded as Wyoming is by mountains, whereon broken ledges of rocks afford innumerable places of shelter, parties would lie concealed, reconnoiter, and suddenly striking a blow, retire to their hiding places, where it was impossible to trace them.

On the 2d of October, four of Captain Morrison's men were attacked on the west side of the river, three of whom were killed, and one escaped. Monotonous and melancholy, as the record may appear, duty bids us to follow it out. Oct. 14th.—William Jameson, returning home from Wilkesbarre, was shot near where the canal crosses the road below Careytown. Being wounded he fell from the horse, and attempted to gain the woods, but was pursued, tomahawked and scalped. A valuable young man in the prime of life, being twenty-six years of age. He had been in the battle, and escaped, and his scalp was therefore a doubly valuable prize to the Indians.

November 7.—Mr. John Perkins was killed in Plymouth; a victim also, most gratifying to the revengeful savage, as Mr. Perkins had a son in Spalding's Independent Company. William Jackson, and Mr. Lester, taken from the mill at Nanticoke, were marched three miles up into Hanover, and then shot down. An aged man, spoken of as "old Mr. Hageman," a prisoner, escaped with six wounds, and survived, although the food he took oozed from a spear wound in his side. November 9th.—Captain Carr and Philip Goss, in attempting to fly in a canoe, were shot below Wapwallopen, and left; the latter dead, the other dying on the shore. Robert Alexander and Amos Parker, were about the same time found murdered in the lower part of the Valley.

Late in the fall, Isaac Inman was murdered in Hanover. We have stated the gallant array of determined men that family presented on the day of battle; and the shot of Israel, laying an Indian dead, thereby saving the life of a neighbour closely pursued, and nearly exhausted. The sweet hour of revenge had now come. Isaac said he was sure he heard wild-turkeys; he would take his rifle, and try to get one. This was in the afternoon. Not long after a gun was heard, but Isaac did not return. A heavy snow fell that night, and lay till Spring, when his body was found, shot, scalped, and a war club by his side, by its marks indicating the tribe that had done the deed.

Even a more distressing tragedy than we have recorded, was enacted near Nescopeck, on the 19th. A whole family were butchered—John Utley, Elisha Utley, and Diah Utley, were attacked. The two first were shot down, and soon despatched. Diah, the youngest, fled to the river, and swam over to the west side, (near Beach Grove,) but an Indian had crossed before him in a canoe, and struck him with a tomahawk as he reached the shore. He plead for his life, but there was no mercy shown. The savages then entered the house, and having murdered and scalped the aged mother, placed her as in sport, in a chair, and so left her. The Utley family were from the east side of the Connecticut river, in Hartford county. An eye witness of the scene that was presented the next morning, represents the remains of the slaughtered sons, and the ghastly appearance of the mother, as enough to awaken horror and pity in a breast of marble.

Jonathan Slocum, a man with a large family, a member of Friend's Society, had always been with characteristic benevolence, kind to the Indians. At first the savages left him unmolested, but probably learning that his son Giles was in the battle, the family were marked for vengeance. A respectable neighbour, Nathan Kingsley, had been made prisoner, and taken into the Indian country, leaving his wife and two sons to the charity of the neighbours. Taking them home, Mr. Slocum bade them welcome, until Mr. Kingsley should be liberated, or some other mode of subsistence present. On the 2d of November, the two boys being engaged grinding a knife, a rifle shot, and cry of distress, brought Mrs. Slocum to the door, where she beheld an Indian scalping Nathan, the eldest lad, fifteen years of age, with the knife he had been sharpening. Waving her back with his hand, he entered the house, and took up Ebenezer Slocum, a little boy. The mother stepped up to the savage, and reaching for the child, said: "He can do you no good, see, he is lame." With a grim smile, giving up the boy, he took Frances her daughter, aged about five years, gently in his arms, and seizing the younger Kingsley by the hand, hurried away to the mountains; two savages who were with him, taking a black girl, seventeen years old.* This was within an hundred rods of the Wilkesbarre fort. An alarm was instantly given, but the Indians eluded pursuit, and no traces of their retreat could be found.

The cup of vengeance was not yet full. December 16th, (or about forty days, allowing time for the war party to go to the Indian country with their prisoners, recruit themselves, and return,) Mr. Slocum, and

* The coloured girl was afterwards seen by prisoners, in the family of Col. John Butler, at Niagara, who had purchased her of the Indians.

Isaac Tripp, Esq., his father-in-law, an aged man, with William Slocum, a youth of nineteen, or twenty, were foddering cattle from a stack in the meadow, in sight of the fort, when they were fired upon by Indians. Mr. Slocum was shot dead; Mr. Tripp wounded, speared, and tomahawked; both were scalped. William, wounded by a spent ball in the heel, escaped, and gave the alarm, but the alert and wily foe had retreated to their hiding place in the mountain. This deed, bold as it was cruel, was perpetrated within the town plot, in the centre of which the fort was located. Thus in little more than a month, Mrs. Slocum had lost a beloved child, carried into captivity; the doorway had been drenched in blood by the murder of an inmate of the family; two others of the household had been taken away prisoners; and now, her husband and her father were both stricken down to the grave, murdered and mangled by merciless Indians! Verily the annals of Indian atrocities, written in blood, record few instances of desolation and woe to equal this.

I shall make no apology for anticipating more than half a century, in my narrative, to give a brief account of the lost sister, the little captive, Frances Slocum, so that the whole may be presented in one connected chain. The widowed mother heard nothing from her child. Peace came, and prisoners returned, but no one had seen, or could tell aught respecting her. As to those whom she knew were dead, they were at rest; the lamp of hope, as to them, had ceased to burn; and she bowed, as years passed away, in melancholy, but calm resignation, for those who could not return. But not so as to Frances; she might survive. She did live the cherished object of intensest love in the imagination of her fond mother, rendered ten-fold dearer by the blighting sorrows that crushed her house, when they were parted. Her first waking thought in the morning was for her lost one; her last, on retiring to rest, was for her child, her lost child. After the conclusion of peace, and intercourse with Canada was opened, two of her brothers, then amongst the most intelligent and enterprising young men in the Valley, led by their own sense of propriety and affection, and urged by a mother's tears, determined, if living, to find Frances, and restore her to home and friends. Connecting business with their search, they traversed the Indian settlements, and went as far as Niagara, making careful inquiries for Frances. The Indians, whom they saw, and inquired of in great numbers, did not know, or more probably would not reveal, the place of her location. High rewards, sufficient to tempt Indian cupidity, were offered in vain, and the brothers came to the conclusion that she must be dead, probably slain by her merciless captors; or, surely she would have been heard of; some one must have seen her!

Still, still, the fond mother saw in her dreams the cherished object of her love. Playful—smiling, as in infancy, she appeared before her. Frances was not in the grave; she knew she was not. Her afflicted soul clung to the idea of recovering her daughter, as the great and engrossing object of life. At length news came. A woman answering to the description was found, and claimed to be the child of Mrs. Slocum. About the proper age, she had been taken away captive when very young; knew not her parents, nor her own name, but had been carried off from the Susquehanna river. Mrs. Slocum took her home, and treated her with all possible tenderness and care. But soul did not answer to soul; the spirit did not respond to spirit; that secret and mysterious sympathy which exists between a mother and her offspring, did not draw them together. It might be her daughter, Mrs. Slocum said, but it did not seem so to her. "Yet the woman should be ever welcome." The unfortunate person, no impostor, an orphan indeed, simple and upright in intention, felt a persuasion in her own mind that these were not her relations, and taking presents, voluntarily returned to her Indian friends. At length time obliterated the last ray of hope, and Mrs. Slocum, at an advanced age, descended to the grave.

In August, 1837, fifty-nine years after the capture, a letter appeared in the Lancaster Intelligencer, written by G. W. Ewing, of Logansport, Indiana, dated January 20, 1835, a year and a half previous, stating:—"There is now living near this place, among the Miami tribe of Indians, an aged white woman, who, a few days ago told me that she was taken away from her father's house, on, or near the Susquehanna river, when she was very young. She says her father's name was Slocum; that he was a quaker, and wore a large brimmed hat; that he lived about half a mile from a town where there was a fort. She has two daughters living. Her husband is dead—she is old and feeble, and thinks she shall not live long. These considerations induced her to give the present history of herself—which she never would before, fearing her kindred would come and force her away. She has lived long, and happy as an Indian—is very respectable, and wealthy, sober, and honest—Her name is without reproach."

The sensation produced by this letter throughout Wyoming, can scarcely be imagined. "Is it Frances? Can she be alive? How wonderful!" Not an idle hour was lost. Her brother, Joseph Slocum, though near a thousand miles intervened, moved by affection, a sense of duty—and the known wishes of a beloved parent, made immediate preparations for a journey. Uniting with his younger brother, Isaac, who resides in Ohio, they hastened to Logansport, where they had the good fortune to meet Mr. Ewing. Frances, who resides about a dozen miles from that place, was soon apprised of their coming. While hope predominated, doubt and uncertainty, amounting almost to jealousy or suspicion, occupied her mind. She came into the village riding a high-spirited horse, her two daughters, tastefully dressed in Indian costume, accompanying her, with the husband of one of them, the elite among Indian beaux. Her manners were grave, her bearing reserved; she listened, through an interpreter, to what they had to say. But night approached. Cautious and prudent, she rode back to her home, promising to return the coming morning. At the appointed hour she alighted from her steed, and met them with something more of frankness, but still seemed desirous of further explanation. It was evident on all sides they were almost prepared for the recognition. Mr. Joseph Slocum at length said, what he had so far purposely kept back, that their sister, at play in their father's smith-shop with the children, had received a blow on the middle finger of the left hand, by a hammer on the anvil, which crushed the bone, and the mother had always said *that* would be a test which could not be mistaken. Her whole countenance was instantly lighted up with smiles, while tears ran down her cheeks, as she held out the wounded hand. Every lingering doubt was dispelled. Hope was merged into confidence. The tender embrace, the welcome recognition, the sacred, the exulting glow of brotherly and sisterly affection, filled every heart present to overflowing. Her father! Her dear, dear mother! Did she yet live? But they must long since, in the course of nature, have been gathered to their native dust. Her brothers and sisters? The slumbering affections awakened to life, broke forth in earnest inquiries for all whom she should love.

She then related the leading events of her life. Her memory, extremely tenacious, enabled her to tell, that, on being taken, her captors hastened to a rocky cave on the mountain, where blankets and a bed of dried leaves, showed that they had slept. On the journey to the Indian country she was kindly treated, the Indian carrying her, when she was weary, in his arms. She was immediately adopted into an Indian family, and brought up as their daughter, but with more than common tenderness. Young Kingsley, who was located near them, in a few years died. About the time she had grown up to womanhood, both her Indian parents, whom she loved and mourned, were taken away, and not long afterwards, she married a young Chief of the Nation, and removed to the waters of the Ohio. Treated with respect and confidence, few of the burdens women in the savage state are compelled to bear, were imposed upon her; and she was so happy in her family and connexions, that the idea of being found, and returned to live with the white people, was dreaded as the greatest evil that could befall her. On the death of her Chief, she married her last husband, but has been a widow for many years. After stating, though with much more minuteness, the principal events of her life, with great solemnity she raised her hand, and looking up, said:—" All this is true as that there is a God (or Great Spirit), in the Heavens."

It is evident from her wealth, the extreme attachment to her people, and mode of life, connected with the strength of mind and memory displayed, that Frances Slocum must have been a Queen among them. Doubtless her superior understanding gave great influence, and led to a flattering deference to her opinions every where, in savage or civilized society, so agreeable. All possible pains had therefore been taken to render life pleasant to her; and doubtless to imbue her mind with fear and dislike of the whites, so that she would not make known her name, and earnestly desired, when prisoners were inquired for, that she might not be betrayed, deeming a return, not a blessing to be desired, but a calamity to be deplored. Undoubtedly too, her strong sense told her, not by any process of reasoning, but by intuitive perception, that however much a mother's heart might yearn for the lost child, that child could only return so changed as to render living with the white people difficult, and embarrassing, if not impossible. Time and education had made her of another race, and the truest wisdom dictated acquiescence in her lot.

The next day the brothers, with the Interpreter, rode out to visit their sister. Every thing bore the appearance, not only of plenty, but of rude abundance. Numerous cattle grazed in the meadows—fifty horses pranced proudly over the fields. The house was half way between the Indian wigwam, and the more finished mansion of a farmer. An oven, well baked cakes of flour, venison nicely prepared, and honey, afforded an excellent repast. But the absence of milk and butter, so easily commanded in profusion, told of savage life. As a token of entire confidence being established, Frances placed a piece of venison under a snow white cloth, when one of the brothers lifted it up, and this was regarded as a formal covenant of recognition and affection. An agreeable visit of several days was passed, and has since been repeated by another branch of the family.

The Indian name of the lost sister was

Ma-con-a-quah—a young bear.

Eldest daughter.——Kich-ke-ne-che-quah—cut-finger; probably in allusion to the mother's wounded hand.

Youngest daughter.——O-saw-she-quah—yellow leaf.

Grand-children.——Kip-pe-no-quah—-corn tassel.

Wap-pa-no-se-a—blue corn.

Kim-on-sah-quah—young panther.

Congress recently passed a resolution exempting Frances (the lost sister) from the necessity of removing with her family from their present location. Several other Indian names, more remotely allied to her, are therein mentioned.

Mrs. Bennett, daughter of Joseph Slocum, and lady of the Hon. Ziba Bennett, with the most praiseworthy disregard of toil and danger, accompanied her father on his second visit to Indiana. Her account of the interview with her aunt, is of a most interesting and pleasing character. It is to be hoped she may be induced to give her journal and notes the form of letters, or a pamphlet for there are few so capable of sketching a lively and correct narrative, or of presenting a picture, of itself so full of interest, in a form more neat and attractive.

Their not comprehending each other's language, was of course a serious bar to social enjoyment, and that unreserved and affectionate intercourse, which, without the intervention of an interpreter, they would have indulged in. We regard this as one of the most remarkable series of events Providence, in its unsearchable wisdom, has ever permitted to be developed. It may gratify the distant reader to know, as it is a pleasure to record, that the encrimsoned night of bloodshed and woe, which seemed in 1778 to have settled forever on the family of Slocum, has long since broken away. Sunshine, and gladness, and prosperity have arisen, and shed their cheering rays over them in an especial manner, during the last forty years. A number of the sons, highly enterprising, have fulfilled their duties on the stage of action, with exemplary propriety. One was High

Sheriff of the county; another for many years a magistrate. Others might have shared the honours of office, if they would have given up their time to public concerns, to the neglect of their own. And now (1843) if the eye of the departed grandsire could look down on the Borough, he would see in the position of his descendants, sufficient to fill his heart to overflowing with pride and joy. Forgetting his own sufferings, his spirit would bless the day that he established his family—

"On Susquehanna's side, fair Wyoming."

Resuming our narrative, a paragraph of praise is specially due to Thomas Neill, an Irishman, of middle age, the most learned man in the Valley. A Catholic, a high-mason, fond of dress—remarkable for his fine flow of spirits and pleasing manners; a bachelor, and a schoolmaster, he was a favorite. With characteristic bravery, his Irish spirit broke out as the danger became pressing. "The Yankees are the weakest party—the odds are against them—though I have no special interest in the fight, so help me Heaven! I'll take a turn with them." Marching out in Capt. M'Karrican's company, he fell. Nor should the generous spirit of Wm. Jones of Virginia, be forgotten. A young man, quite accomplished, he taught school in the Valley, and, like Neill, volunteered his services on the day of battle. He went to return no more. The names of these two victims to those pure and chivalric sentiments that ennoble our nature, I owe to the memory of the late Mrs. Youngs.

---

*Copies and Extracts of Documents relative to the Expedition against Wyoming, in 1778, now in a volume in Her Majesty's State Paper Office, London, entitled "*MILITARY*, 1778.—No. 122."*

Extract of a Letter from Sir Henry Clinton, to Lord George Germain, dated New York, August 12, 1778.

* * * * "Reports, which seem to be credited, say that a body of Indians, assembled under the command of a Colonel Butler, have destroyed a number of settlements upon the frontiers of Pennsylvania, and repulsed what troops the rebels had collected to oppose them. When I receive certain intelligence of their proceedings, I shall take the earliest opportunity to acquaint your Lordship therewith." * * *

Extract of a Letter from Sir Henry Clinton to Lord George Germain, dated New York, September 15th, 1778.

* * * "I have at the same time, my Lord, the honour to transmit to you, a copy of a letter from Major Butler to Lieutenant Colonel Bolton, which I received from General Haldimand, a few days since, giving an account of the proceedings of the former upon the frontiers of Pennsylvania."

[Enclosures in the above.]

Copy of a Letter from Lieutenant-Colonel Bolton to Captain Le Maistre, dated Niagara, July 14th, 1778.

"Sir,—I have the pleasure of acquainting you with the signal success of the Rangers and Indians, with Col. Butler, over the rebels at Wioming, where they had no less than ten stockaded forts, and were defeated; enclosed, I send you the particulars, which I request you will lay before His Excellency. I received them this moment, by Lieut. Hare, of the Rangers. The Caldwell being ready to sail, I have only time to assure you that I am, with esteem, Sir, your most obedient humble servant.

"[Signed,]   MASON BOLTON.

"I request you'l inform Capt. Butler of the Colonel's success.
"Captain Le Maistre."

[Enclosed in the foregoing.—Copy of a Letter from Major John Butler to Lieut. Col. Bolton, dated Lacuwanack, 8th July, 1778.]

[Disallowed at the Foreign Office.].

Note by Mr. Brodhead.—This is the Report. It is about four foolscap pages long.   J. R. B.

[Third Enclosure.]

Copy of Articles of Capitulation, for Wintermoot's Fort, July 1, 1778.

ART. 1st. That Lieut. Elisha Scovell surrender the Fort, with all the stores, arms and ammunition, that are in said fort, as well public as private, to Major John Butler.

2d. That the garrison shall not bear arms during the present contest; and Major Butler promises that the men, women and children shall not be hurt, either by Indians or Rangers.

FORT JENKINS' FORT, July 1st, 1778.

Between Major John Butler, on behalf of His Majesty King George the Third, and John Jenkins.

ART. 1st. That the Fort, with all the stores, arms and ammunition, be delivered up immediately.

2d. That Major John Butler shall preserve to them, intire, the lives of the men, women and children.

Articles of Capitulation for three Forts at Lacuwanack, 4th July, 1778.

ART. 1st. That the different Commanders of the said Forts, do immediately deliver them up, with all the arms, ammunition and stores, in the said forts.

2d. Major Butler promises that the lives of the men, women and children be preserved intire.

WESTMORELAND, July 4th, 1778.

Capitulation made and completed between Major John Butler, on behalf of His Majesty King George the Third, and Col. Nathan Denniston, *of the United States of America.*

ART. 1. That the inhabitants of the settlement lay down their arms, and the garrisons be demolished.

2d. That the inhabitants are to occupy their farms peaceably, and the lives of the inhabitants preserved intire and unhurt.

3d. That the continental stores be delivered up.

4th. That Major Butler will use his utmost influence that the private property of the inhabitants shall be preserved intire to them.

5th. That the prisoners, in Forty Fort, be delivered up, and that Samuel Finch, now in Major Butler's possession, be delivered up also.

6th. That the property taken from the people called *Tories*, up the river, be made good; and they to remain in peaceable possession of their farms, unmolested in a free trade, in and throughout this State, as far as lies in my power.

7th. That the inhabitants, that Colonel Denniston now capitulates for, together with himself, do not take up arms during the present contest.

[Signed,]   NATHAN DENNISTON,
JOHN BUTLER.

Zarah Beech,   Samuel Gustin,
John Johnson,   Wm. Caldwell.

Extract of a Letter from Lord George Germain to Sir Henry Clinton, dated Whitehall, 4th of November, 1778.

* * * * "The success of Lieutenant-Colonel Butler, is distinguished for the few lives that have been lost among the Rangers and Indians he commanded; and for his humanity in making those only his object, who were in arms: And it is much to the credit of the officers and Rangers of his detachment, that they seem to partake of the spirit and perseverance which is common to all the British officers and soldiers." * * * *

[Copied from the originals in the State Paper Office, London, 11th April, 1843.]

J. R. BRODHEAD.

Some matters of interest will be found in this note. The letter of Judge Marshall, dated February 15, 1831, is curious in this respect. It acknowledges in simple style, the receipt of a letter written *twenty-five years before*, as if it had been a thing of day before yesterday. It may well be doubted, whether the records of correspondence, from remotest time, exhibit a similar instance.

WASHINGTON, Feb'y 15th, 1831.

SIR—I am much indebted to you for a letter received in April, 1806, correcting some errors into which our history has fallen, in its relation of the destruction of the Wyoming settlement, during the war of our revolution. The readiness you express in that letter, to give a true statement of that memorable tragedy, encourages me to make some further inquiries on the subject.

Your account of the battle is full, and I understand it perfectly; but you have entered into no detail of subsequent events, and I am not sure whether you contradict or agree with Gordon and Ramsay, respecting those events. They say that the two principal forts were Kingston and Wilkesbarre. That after the defeat, the men, women and children were collected in these forts, and after their surrender, were consumed by fire, in their houses. Is this representation correct? I should conjecture, from your letter, that the country was abandoned immediately after the defeat; but it seems impossible that all the circumstances relative to the surrender of the forts, and the horrors perpetrated afterwards, can be mere fable. You do not say from what place Colonels Dennison and Butler marched to the battle.

May I tax your goodness so far as to ask a statement of the occurrences which followed the battle, unless that made by Gordon and Ramsay, may be considered as perfectly correct?

I shall remain at this place until the middle of March, when I purpose to return to Richmond. With very great respect, I am your obliged and obedient servant,

J. MARSHALL.

RICHMOND, June 9th, 1831.

DEAR SIR,—I am greatly indebted to you for your letter of the 5th of May, and its enclosures, which reached this place, while I was in North Carolina. I have been closely occupied with the business of the court since my return; but should certainly have acknowledged its receipt immediately, had I not conjectured from the place of its date (Wilkesbarre,) that a letter written immediately, would not find you at home.

It is certainly desirable that historical narrative should be correct, and I shall avail myself of the information you have been so obliging as to furnish, so far at least as to omit the massacre and the charge of toryism on the inhabitants.

Mr. Ramsay, I presume, copied his statement from Mr. Gordon, and I relied upon both, as I knew Mr. Gordon made personal inquires into most of the events of the war, and that Mr. Ramsay was in Congress, and consequently had access to all the letters on the subject. It is surprising that they should have so readily given themselves up to the newspapers of the day.

It was certainly our policy during the war to excite the utmost possible irritation against our enemy, and it is not surprising that we should not always have been very mindful of the verity of our publications; but when we come to the insertion of facts in serious history, truth ought never to be disregarded. Mr. Gordon and Mr. Ramsay ought to have sought for it.

I must complain* of your paying the postage on your letter. It is my habit, when I write to a gentleman about my own affairs, not to charge him with my letter; but when a gentleman writes to me on my business, the case is entirely altered. I am pained at his incurring any expense on my account.

I repeat my thanks for your valuable communications, and my assurances that I am with respectful esteem, your obliged and obedient servant,

J. MARSHALL.

Gordon's (the Revolutionary historian) account of the massacre, we copy to show what has passed heretofore, for history; and what half the world seem still resolved to regard as such. A recent publication in a respectable city paper, retains the whole mass of early errors, and a letter to the author from a learned gentleman, whose wife's father was in Forty Fort, when it surrendered, written expressly to convey information for our annals, repeats the story of "the hatchet," and instant massacre of all who were in the fort, although his father-in-law and wife, both prisoners, escaped to relate to him the event. The pages of Botta, are yet more fanciful. But to Gordon's account :—

"At length, in the beginning of July, the enemy suddenly appeared in full force on the Susquehannah, headed by Col. John Butler, a Connecticut tory, and cousin to Col. Zebulon Butler, the second in command in the settlement. He was assisted by most of those leaders, who had rendered themselves terrible in the present frontier war. Their force was about 1600 men, near a fourth Indians, led by their own chiefs; the others were so disguised and painted as not to be distinguished from the Indians, excepting their officers, who being dressed in regimentals, carried the appearance of regulars. One of the smaller forts, garrisoned chiefly by tories, was given up, or rather betrayed. Another was taken by storm, and all but the women and children, massacred in the most inhuman manner.

July 3.—Col. Zebulon Butler, leaving a small number to guard Fort Wilkesborough, crossed the river with about 400 men, and marched into Kingston Fort, whither the women, children, and defenceless of all sorts, crowded for protection. He suffered himself to be enticed by his cousin to abandon the fortress. He agreed to march out, and hold a conference with the enemy in the open field, (at so great a distance from the fort, as to shut out all possibility of protection from it) upon their withdrawing according to their own proposal, in order to the holding of a parley for the conclusion of a treaty. He at about the same time marched out about 400 men well armed, being nearly the whole strength of the garrison, to guard his person to the place of parley, such was his distrust of the enemy's designs. On his arrival, he found nobody to treat with him, and yet advanced toward the foot of the mountain, where at a distance he saw a flag, the holders of which, seemingly afraid of treachery on his side, retired as he advanced; whilst he, endeavoring to remove this pretended ill impression, pursued the flag, till his party was thoroughly enclosed, when he was suddenly freed from his

---

* I had commenced the correspondence in 1806, as a Wyoming man, to vindicate our own people, and thought the payment proper.

delusion, by finding it attacked at once on every side. He and his men, notwithstanding the surprise and danger, fought with resolution and bravery, and kept up so continual and heavy a fire for three quarters of an hour, that they seemed to gain a marked superiority. In this critical moment, a soldier, through a sudden impulse of fear, or premeditated treachery, cried out aloud, "the Colonel has ordered a retreat." The fate of the party was now at once determined. In the state of confusion that ensued, an unresisted slaughter commenced, while the enemy broke in on all sides without obstruction. Col. Zebulon Butler, and about seventy of his men, escaped; the latter got across the river to Fort Wilkesborough, the Colonel made his way to Fort Kingston, which was invested the next day (July 4,) on the land side. The enemy, to sadden the drooping spirits of the weak remaining garrison, sent in for their contemplation the bloody scalps of one hundred and ninety-six of their late friends and comrades. They kept up a continual fire upon the fort the whole day. In the evening, the Colonel quitted the fort, and went down the river with his family. He is thought to be the only officer that escaped.

July 5.—Col. Nathan Denison, who succeeded to the command, seeing the impossibility of an effectual defence, went with a flag to Col. John Butler, to know what terms he would grant on a surrender, to which application Butler answered with more than savage phlegm, in two short words—*the hatchet*. Denison having defended the fort till most of the garrison were killed or disabled, was compelled to surrender at discretion. Some of the unhappy persons in the fort were carried away alive, but the barbarous conquerors, to save the trouble of murder in detail, shut up the rest promiscuously in the houses and barracks, which having set on fire, they enjoyed the savage pleasure of beholding the whole consumed in one general blaze.

They then crossed the river to the only remaining fort, Wilkesborough, which, in hopes of mercy, surrendered without demanding any conditions. They found about seventy continental soldiers, who had been engaged merely for the defence of the frontiers, whom they butchered with every circumstance of horrid cruelty. The remainder of the men, with the women and children, were shut up as before in the houses, which being set on fire, they perished altogether in the flames.

A general scene of devastation was now spread through all the townships. Fire, sword, and the other different instruments of destruction, alternately triumphed. The settlements of the tories alone generally escaped, and appeared as islands in the midst of the surrounding ruin. The merciless ravagers, having destroyed the main objects of their cruelty, directed their animosity to every part of living nature belonging to them: shot and destroyed some of their cattle, and cut out the tongues of others, leaving them still alive to prolong their agonies.

The following are a few of the more singular circumstances of the barbarity practised in the attack upon Wyoming. Capt. Bidlack, who had been taken prisoner, being stripped naked, had his body stuck full of splinters of pine knots, and then a heap of pine knots piled around him; the whole was then set on fire, and his two companions, Captains Ransom and Durkee, thrown alive into the flames, and held down with pitchforks. The returned tories, who had at different times abandoned the settlement, in order to join in those savage expeditions, were the most distinguished for their cruelty; in this they resembled the tories that joined the British forces. One of these Wyoming tories, whose mother had married a second husband, butchered with his own hands, both her, his father-in-law, his own sisters, and their infant children. Another, who during his absence had sent home several threats against the life of his father, now not only realized them in person, but was himself with his own hands, the exterminator of his whole family, mother, brothers and sisters, and mingled their blood in one common carnage, with that of the ancient husband and father."*

---

* Which particularly related facts, we believe, from careful inquiry, to be without the shadow of foundation.

LETTER XIX.

1779.——Projected expedition into Indian Country—(*Note*, Letter of Gen. Hand)—Lieut. John Jenkins—Gershom Hicks—Washington—Renewed invasion by Savages—Capt. Bidlack taken prisoner—Two hundred warriors' attack upon Wilkesbarre Fort, repelled—Serjeant Williams' gallant conduct—Lieut. Buck—Stephen Pettibone and Elihu Williams murdered—Follet, speared and scalped—Col. Butler reinforced—Maj Powell's advance——Capt. Davis, Lieut. Jones and four men killed on Laurel Run—Audacity of the Indians—Array for the Northern Campaign—Capt. John Paul Schotts—Sullivan's army arrive at Wilkesbarre—Military execution—Ascent of boats—Indian admirable war policy—McDonald and Hiockoto's attack near Sunbury on Sullivan's left—(*Note*, anecdote of McDonald)—Brandt's attack and massacre at Minisink—on Sullivan's right—Fixed purpose of Sullivan—Departure of the army for the North—Grand display—Incident of March—Union with Gen. Clinton at Tioga—Battle on Chemung—Indian country devastated—Melancholy fate of Lieut. Boyd and party—Army retires—Treat of welcome at Wyoming—Gen. Sullivan—Congress—Civil affairs—Town meeting—Answer to Mrs. Bidlack's Petition.

IMMEDIATELY after Col. Hartley's gallant excursion into the Indian territory, and victory at Sheshequin, his Excellency, General Washington, formed the design of sending a powerful force into the heart of the Six Nations, at once to chastise them for their cruelty, and by laying waste their settlements, to dislodge them from their position, so dangerously near to the American frontier. It was resolved to carry the war into their own country, and if possible to force the Savages back to Niagara. Having for centuries, not only inhabited the head waters of the Susquehanna, the Delaware and Mohawk; on the delightful borders of the lesser lakes; and westward to the beautiful Genesee, a perfect Indian Paradise; but time out of mind having established within those limits the council fire at Onondago, where the "Great Head" had exercised power and dominion over vassal nations; it could not be doubted but every impulse of a lofty ambition—the meaner, but not less active principle of revenge—the natural love of home and country, which warms with ardour even the savage breast, all sustained by the policy and power of England, would arouse the enemy to the most determined resistance. To send a force fully adequate to the object to be accomplished, was obviously the only effective, and consequently the most economical policy. An invasion during the winter had been proposed, but was wisely relinquished.*

Preparatory to a summer campaign, Gen. Hand, then at Minisink, by order from his Excellency, addressed a series of inquiries to Col. Zebulon Butler, in command at Wyoming, embracing every point on which information could be desirable. The distance and route to the nearest Indian settlements; their position and extent; facilities of obtaining subsistence; means of transportation in boats up the Susquehanna, &c. In his reply, Col. Butler takes pleasure in expressing his particular obligations to Lieut. John Jenkins, whose thorough knowledge, and judicious observations upon the subject, were of eminent service.

A letter from Col. Patterson, dated at Northumberland in March, 1779, to Col. Butler, throws light upon other measures adopted to obtain correct information. "Mr. Lemmon," says Col. P., "goes to your post, to wait the return, and take into his care Gershom Hicks, who is not to be examined or searched until he goes before his Excellency Gen. Washington. I inclose you his Excellency's letter. Be careful that your people, who are out on duty, or fatigue, receive Hicks, who may appear painted, and in a canoe. His regimentals I have sent by Mr. Lemmon." We cannot withhold the remark, that the duties of Washington, embracing generally all the civil, as well as military affairs of the country, and descending to the minutest details of every expedition, would seem to have been great and perplexing, beyond human power to perform. A frame of iron, and a mind of steel, would appear to have been requisite for the mere labour. But when to this is added his views, comprehensive, liberal, and accurate; his thorough knowledge of human nature; his profound wisdom and spotless patriotism, the whole warp and woof of his soul being composed of devotion to his country, without one single thread of selfishness or personal ambition, it is impossible to look

* A letter from Gen. Hand, dated Minisink, January 13th, 1779, to Col. Butler, says:— "Your favour of the 10th inst. now lies before me. I am much obliged to you for the diligence you have used, and the candour with which you give your information and advice on so important a subject. Your sentiments and those of Capt. Stoddart justify his Excellency General Washington's apprehensions of the impracticability, or at best the doubtful success of an expedition at this season, insomuch that I am persuaded the intelligence I now receive from the Susquehanna, which he has desired me to transmit to him, will determine him to give over all thought of it."

upon the great and good man, without reverently believing that he was specially raised up, and imbued with wisdom and strength from above, to rescue a nation from bondage, and establish freedom in America.

Savage hate, instead of being satiated by the sufferings of Wyoming, seemed, like the tiger that has tasted human blood, to be aroused to inappeasable fury.

The chief part of Col. Hartley's regiment having been withdrawn, Col. Butler was left in command of the fort at Wilkesbarre, with only about one hundred men. That vigilant officer, respectfully, but with spirit remonstrated with Gen. Hand, who returned for answer, that the power did not rest with him to remedy the evil.

In December of the preceding year several murders are recorded in our last letter as having been perpetrated. Scarcely sixty days of repose had been allowed to Wyoming even amid the cold and storms of winter. In March bands of savages began to make their appearance, as if, from the contiguity of their towns, an incursion into the Valley, instead of being a toil, was but a pleasure party. On the 21st of the month, unapprised of danger, Josiah Rogers and Capt. James Bidlack, both aged men, were crossing the flats, on their way to Plymouth. Springing from their covert, the savages failed in an attempt to seize the bridles of their horses. A race ensued of intense interest. The girth of Capt. Bidlack's saddle breaking, he was thrown and made prisoner. Several bullets perforated the clothes of Mr. Rogers, who happily escaped the painful captivity of his companion, whose misfortune was doubly distressing to his family, as his son James had fallen in the battle. A large number were seen advancing over the Kingston flats, towards a block-house erected on that side of the river, and in full view from the Wilkesbarre fort. The boldness of their advance showed confidence in their strength, and left no doubt but they were informed of the feeble state of the garrison. Plunder appeared to be their object, for while a small portion acted as a guard, the remainder, dividing into small parties, began to drive off all the horses and cattle they could find. Col. Butler immediately detached twenty-five men to the aid of those in the block-house. A charge was made on the enemy, who retreated, keeping at a respectful distance, evidently intending to draw the detachment into an ambuscade. On approaching the woods, a larger portion was discovered, which rendered a retreat prudent; whereupon the enemy advanced. A smart skirmish ensued, several men were wounded, but none mortally. Our people had to suffer the deep mortification of seeing sixty head of cattle, and twenty horses carried away by the marauding horde, without the power (from the most ill advised policy) of either protection or chastisement.

On the 23rd, the savages and tories, finding that their strength had been discovered, and an ambush was hopeless, boldly developed themselves, and showed by their numbers that this was in truth, a second invasion. Two hundred and fifty warriors, in a semicircle, approached the Wilkesbarre fort, as if with intent to carry it by storm. A brisk fire was opened upon them, the four pounder being brought to bear. After peace, it was ascertained the Indian chief who led the charge was killed by a cannon ball. What further loss they sustained is not known, but they were repulsed, not, however, until they had made themselves masters of fifty-one head of cattle, ten horses, and burnt three barns containing hay and grain, and two houses. A heavy snow fell on the 24th. Smoke from Indian fires, where they encamped at night, or burnt some house or barn, left by accident or caprice the preceding campaign, continued to mark their presence and route until the 28th. When these disgraceful and distressing particulars were communicated by Col. Butler to the Board of War, one of the members said hastily, in presence of the messenger:—" It is impossible—it can't be so!" So fatal was the folly or delusion, that Wyoming, on the very borders of the Six Nations of warriors, needed no defence. On learning the remarks of the gentleman, with the spirit of a soldier Col. Butler immediately wrote —" That no officer who properly regarded his own honour, would, without the slightest evidence, call in question the honour of a brother soldier."

The gallant defence of his father's house, by Serjeant Thomas Williams, deserves to be specially recorded. An officer in Capt. Spalding's company, he was now stationed in the Valley. Within eighty rods of the fort, and supposed to be within its protection, lived Mr. Thaddeus Williams, originally of Fairfield county, Connecticut. On the day the fort was attacked, a party of Indians made an assault on the house. The father, sick and confined to his bed, was unable to lend any assistance. Serjeant Williams, and a brother, quite young, were the only persons capable of offering the least resistance. Twice the Indians rushed up to the door, and attempted in vain, to force an entrance. Several balls were fired into the house through openings in the logs, one of which severely wounded the sick father. All this was accompanied by horrid yells, as if demons had visited the upper air. Having lost a brother the preceding fall, and belonging himself to the army, Mr. Williams knew his fate depended on his own coolness and courage. He could hope nothing from their mercy. He had two guns, one of which the lad loaded while he fired the other. Watching his time, and taking careful aim, one of the Indians fell, and was dragged away. Redoubling their shouts the Indians returned with brands of fire, but another discharge, which wounded their leader, finally repelled them, leaving Serjeant Williams victor, and his aged father and mother, rescued from death.

The Savages it was supposed had retired with their booty, but although the utmost caution was exercised, no vigilance could effectually guard every point from danger. A band of twenty Indians suddenly returned, and on the Kingston side of the river, in sight from the Wilkesbarre fort, in broad daylight, murdered three valuable citizens; Mr. Elihu Williams, Lieut. Buck, and Mr. Stephen Pettebone. Frederick Follet, who was with them, fell pierced by seven wounds from a spear, and with the others was scalped, and left for dead. Instantly a detachment of men was sent over; the Indians had fled. Follet, weltering in blood, gave signs of life, and was taken to the fort. Dr. William Hooker Smith, on examining his wounds, said, that while every thing should be done that kindness and skill could suggest, he regarded his recovery as hopeless. Yet he did recover. One spear thrust had penetrated his stomach, so that its contents came out at his side. Mr. Follet lived many years, and removed to Ohio, where he left a large family. Dr. Smith gained great credit for restoring Follet to health and usefulness.

Reinforced by a German regiment of about three hundred men, Col. Butler was enabled, not only to defend his position, but to clear the open portions of the Valley, of his cruel and insolent visiters; but small parties of Indians still hovered around Wyoming, like wolves around a sheep-fold. They waylaid the passes through the mountains, and occasionally exhibited extraordinary instances of courage and audacity.

Major Powell, commanding two hundred men of a regiment, which had been much reduced by losses in the battle of Germantown, having been ordered to Wyoming, arrived at Bear Creek, about ten miles from the fort, on the night of the 19th of April. Deeming themselves out of danger from a surprise by the Indians, orders were given that officers and men should dress in their best apparel, their arms be newly burnished, and every thing be put in order to appear respectably on entering the Valley. As was the fashion of the day, the officers wearing ruffles, were also powdered. The music, partaking in the excitement of the hour, played their liveliest strains as the party advanced. Deer were reported to have been seen by the vanguard, when Capt. Davis, and Lieut. Jones, armed with rifles, immediately hastened forward. Near the summit of the second mountain, by the Laurel Run, and about four miles from the fort, a fire was opened upon them by the Indians in ambush, by which Capt. Davis, Lieut. Jones, a Corporal by the name of Butler, and three men under his command, fell. Major Powell, not far in the rear, hastened forward at a moment when an Indian, with surprising audacity, had seized a woman, the wife of one of the soldiers who had fallen, and was dragging her from the path, into the thicket. A soldier in the act to fire, was stopped by Major Powell, but the woman escaped. The Major, it was thought, lost the self-possession so indispensable to a soldier, and his command thrown into confusion, retreated in disorder. Uncertain as to the power, though too fatally assured of the prowess of his enemy, Major Powell undoubtedly experienced a degree of fear, which the force of the enemy disclosed, or probably present, did not warrant; and seems scarcely to have remembered that he still commanded nearly two hundred veteran soldiers. Dispatching his Surgeon, who volunteered for the occasion, and John Halstead, a soldier of Capt. Spalding's company, who had met him, and acted as guide to Col. Butler, the German Battallion was immediately called to arms, and marched to the mountain, to escort Major P. and his men to the Valley.*

Major Powell, having leave to resign, soon left the army.

During the spring and early part of summer, vigorous preparations had been making for the contemplated invasion of the Indian country. A brigade from New York, under the command of General James Clinton, had wintered on the Mohawk. The brigades commanded by Maxwell, Hand and Poor, with Colonel Proctor's regiment of artillery, and a battalion of Morgan's riflemen, under the command of Major Parr, were ordered to rendezvous at Wyoming:—Major General John Sullivan, of New Hampshire, being appointed to the supreme command.

* The bodies of the two officers, hastily buried, were exhumed the July following, and on the 29th reinterred with military and masonic honours, by the brethren of General Sullivan's army, and the regiments of Col's. Proctor and Hubley. A band of music, the first whose soul arousing strains were ever heard in Wyoming, added interest to the solemn pomp, and gloomy splendour of the display. A rude stone, but the best and neatest the condition of the country allowed them to obtain, was erected by the masons, at the head of the grave, in Wilkesbarre burying ground, with a suitable inscription.

All the early part of the season, was a time of high excitement in the Valley. The German battalion, and Major Powell's command had arrived in April. In May, one regiment came in from York county, Pa. Another regiment from New Hampshire, and a company commanded by Captain John Paul Schotts.*

On the 26th of May, the 3d Jersey regiment reached Easton, where the 1st Jersey regiment, two regiments from New Hampshire, and Col. Proctor's artillery, were already assembled. A strong detachment was sent forward to open a passage for the artillery, who cut the way from Stroudsburg, crossing the Lehigh four miles above Stoddartsville, which has ever since been known as Sullivan's road, and is still occasionally traveled. While at Easton, two soldiers of Col. Hubley's regiment were executed for marauding; and two other men were arrested, and condemned to death for endeavoring to persuade soldiers to desert; one of them was pardoned, the other who had been a lieutenant in the militia, was placed in irons to be moved with the army.

On the 18th of June the troops left Easton, and encamped at Windgap, near Heller's—19th, at Larner's, on the Pocono—20th, at Chouder's camp—21st, at Fatigue camp—22d, at Sullivan's camp, at Great Meadows, seven miles from the Valley, and on the 23d, arrived at Wyoming. The whole army was encamped on the river flats, below Wilkesbarre, a portion of them occupying old Fort Durkee. Here on the 1st day of July, was executed the lieutenant of militia, condemned at Easton, the first, and only instance of capital punishment, ever witnessed within the limits of Luzerne county.

Boats having been provided on the lower waters of the Susquehanna for that purpose, a large fleet arrived on the 24th, loaded with provisions and military stores. The artillery thundered, and the music in sweeter strains sounded a joyous welcome.

Not a single movement of importance had escaped the observation of the vigilant and alert Indian Council, and their British allies. The numbers and aim of the American army were perfectly comprehended, and its strength known to be too powerful, successfully to be encountered by any force in their power to combine. A system of tactics, devised with skill, and executed with intrepid boldness, was entered upon, with the hope of distracting the attention of Gene-

---

* Captain Schotts was a Prussian officer of merit, who had served in the armies of Frederick the Great. Offering his services to Congress, that body on most respectable recommendations, immediately proffered him the commission of captain. Becoming a citizen of Wyoming, we shall have occasion to speak of him again.

ral Sullivan, dividing his army, and thwarting the great object of the campaign. During the month of July, attacks were made by strong bodies of Indians and British, on the right and left of the American army. The first attack was upon Freeland's Fort, fifteen miles from Northumberland, up the west branch of the Susquehanna. Two hundred and fifty men, of whom eighty were British troops, commanded by Captain M'Donald, the rest Indians, led by Hiokoto, a veteran brave of the Seneca tribe, appeared before the stockade, and demanded its surrender. The means of defence being wholly inadequate, and fair terms of capitulation being offered, the garrison capitulated. Gordon states, that contrary to Indian usage, the women and children, were suffered to retire into the settlements. Policy would obviously dictate some restraint on their savage ferocity, for their own women and children, it was quite probable, would soon be at the mercy of the Americans.

A party sent from Northumberland, to succor the garrison at Freeland's, were brought to action with a superior force, when two officers, Captains Hawkins and Boon, with fourteen of their men, were killed and scalped. The victorious enemy advanced towards Northumberland, with the addition of an hundred men, whom they had kept in reserve, creating in Fort Augusta, and all the neighboring settlements, the utmost alarm.*

The same week of the invasion by Hiokoto and M'Donald, Brandt, the dreaded Thayendenegea, with a party of warriors, fell upon the Minisink settlement, in Orange county, New York, killing several of the inhabitants, and making others prisoners. Ten houses, twelve barns and two mills, were consumed by fire. About a hundred and fifty militia from Goshen and the neighborhood, marched in pursuit. The wary Brandt, cunning as he was brave, saw in their hasty advance, victims to his superior prowess. The rarely failing expedient of exchanging a round or two, and then retreating as if driven back, and thus leading the too confident enemy into an ambuscade, was successfully resorted to, and it is melancholy to relate, that more than an hundred were left dead on the field. An attack followed on the Connecticut settlement on the Lackawaxen, within the town

---

* Some years after the war, Captain M'Donald, having business with the American government, on his way from Canada ventured, from pride or curiosity, to visit the ground of his victory, and tarried part of a night at Northumberland. Alarmed at certain movements, indicating hostility, he hired a servant to take him down the stream in a canoe, before daylight should expose him to his (as he had reason to suppose) excited enemies. His fine horse after remaining nearly a year with the inn-keeper unclaimed, was sold for his keeping.

of Westmoreland, which was broken up, several lives lost, and a number of persons taken prisoners. Brandt returned from this expedition, with trifling loss on his own part, having nearly double as many scalps and prisoners as he mustered warriors. Thus, messenger after messenger, express following express, came in to General Sullivan, from the east and southwest, from his right and his left, announcing invasion, massacre, and conflagration, all around him. Fixed in his purpose, pursuing his settled policy, he detached not a man from his main body, but gave immediate orders, that the artillery should be placed in the boats, and every preparation made for immediate departure.

Details are necessary to give the reader a just idea of the impudent boldness of these savage warriors. Three thousand men were encamped at Wyoming; yet on the 28th of July, a messenger came in haste from Shawnee, a mile or two from the tents, desiring the presence of Dr. Ellmore, the Indians having shot a man, both in his side and thigh.

From some cause, left unexplained, a large number of the German battalion had become disaffected and deserted. The deserters were arrested, and twenty-nine tried by a court-martial were condemned to die. After being held some time in confinement, being penitent, they united in a petition that their lives might be spared. A board of officers, over which Gen. Poor presided, on inquiry, recommended them to mercy; and the settlement and army were gratified with the pardon of the whole, who returned cheerfully to duty, and conducted themselves, thenceforward, with unexceptionable propriety.

On the evening of the 28th, Col. Reed arrived with ninety wagons loaded with stores, and on Saturday the 31st of July, the whole camp was in commotion, in obedience to marching orders.*

The artillery being destined to proceed by water, having been placed on board, the command was confided to Col. Proctor. An hundred and twenty boats following in line, with sufficient space between to avoid accidents, must have extended nearly two miles. The army that marched by land, consisting

1st. Of the brigade of Gen. Poor, composed, besides others, of the two regiments from New Hampshire, and one from Massachusetts—the latter under the orders of Col. Dearborn.

---

*₄ The drums beat and the fifes played, in sprightly unison, the *Reveillie*.

"Don't you hear your General say,
Strike your tents and march away."

2d. A brigade from New Jersey, of which the first, second and third regiments, from that state, composed a part; Gen. Maxwell.

3d. The Pennsylvania brigade, commanded by Gen. Hand, which among others included the regiments of Col. Richard Butler, Col. Hubley, and Col. Hartley, and the German battalion, (or regiment, as it is sometimes termed by the ancient people and old writers.)

4th. A strong detachment from Morgan's rifle corps, in command of Major Parr, in which were engrafted for the expedition a number of expert riflemen from Wyoming.

5th. Capt. Spalding's Westmoreland Independent Company.

6th. Capt. Schott's company of Riflemen.

7th. A company of Wyoming militia, chiefly riflemen, under the command of Capt. John Franklin; the whole under the orders of Major-General Sullivan. As chief guide, the General reposed on the skill of Lieutenant John Jenkins. The whole force consisted of about thirty-five hundred men; and in taking up the line from Wilkesbarre, the following was the prescribed order of march, to be adhered to as nearly as the extremely broken country, narrow defiles, and rugged roads would permit, until Gen. Clinton should be met at Tioga Point. "The light corps," says the journal of a brigade chaplain, "which, agreeable to general orders, were to march in three columns, were, by Gen. Hand, arranged as follows:—

Eleventh Pennsylvania regiment, and Capt. Spalding's Independent Company advanced by platoons from the centre of a line formed by them, and constituted a column to proceed on the main road. The German regiment, and Capt. Schott's Independent corps from the right of said regiment formed a column, and marched on the right of the eleventh, etc., having their right flank covered by one-third of the light infantry, of the eleventh, and Schott's riflemen in Indian file. Two thirds of the light infantry of the eleventh, and Capt. Spalding's riflemen marched in Indian file on the left of the column, to cover its left flank, and answer the purpose of a third column. Each column and flanking party had proportioned to their strength respectively, a small party advanced in front. The same order to be observed, if possible, until our arrival at Tioga Point." Two thousand pack horses attended the army. Col. Zebulon Butler was left with as many men as he deemed the circumstances to require, for the protection of Wyoming.

At nine of o'clock, every thing being in readiness, the fleet left their moorings, saluting the fort as they passed, with thirteen cannon. The honour was returned in the best style by the four pounder.

The army marching up on the east side, and extending more than a mile, now shut out, by hill or wood, from the sight of the boats, and now coming near the bank, and in full view, colours waved from each squadron of the advancing fleet: colours floated on the breeze from every column of the army; the rolling drums, the ear-piercing fifes, bands of music on board and on shore, pouring forth martial and patriotic airs, filled the Valley with the concord of sweet and inspiring strains. Hill answered to hill, mountain echoed to mountain. Here was all the pomp, and pride and circumstance of glorious war. The scene presented, was, in the highest degree, grand and sublime! But hark! How changed those notes! As the fleet approached Monockasy Island, a portion of the battle ground, the music struck a solemn dirge, in honour of the patriot dead. Then followed a moment of silence, when the whole proceeded in business order, to the accomplishment of the great object of the expedition.

The army encamped, the first night, on the large flat at the confluence of the Susquehanna and Lackawanna; on the 5th at Wyalusing; on the 9th, at Queen Esther's Plains, (Sheshequin,) and on the 11th, reached Tioga Point, having to wade the Susquehanna, deep to their armpits—their cartridge-boxes borne aloft on their bayonets. Here they encamped, being still in the town of Westmoreland. On the march, two soldiers died suddenly, and one of Col. Proctor's men was wounded. A number of cattle, and several pack-horses were precipitated from narrow defiles down the mountains, and dashed to pieces on the river bank.

General James Clinton, who had wintered on the Mohawk, had advanced to the head of the Susquehanna river, at Otsego lake, and had there built two hundred batteaux. Having dammed up the outlet, he prepared an artificial fresh, on which he was wafted down an hundred miles. On the 22d of August, escorted by Gen. Poor, who had advanced to meet him with a detachment from his brigade, the arrival of Gen. Clinton was welcomed by a salvo of artillery.

In the mean time the Indians had discovered themselves on several points; attacked some of our small parties, and taken the scalps of a serjeant and two or three men.* On the 25th of August, a captain of the New Hampshire troops was accidently killed.

At Tioga Point, a strong stockade was erected, into which all the stores, not absolutely needed, were placed. Two or three

---

* The journal of a New Hampshire officer, states " that Gen. Hand lost six men killed, three officers and seven men wounded in a skirmish on the 12th of August."

cannon were mounted. Convenient arrangements were made for the sick, and the fort left in charge of Capt. Shreive, of the second Jersey regiment, having two hundred and fifty men under his command.

On the 26th of August, having passed beyond the river mountains, and attained a comparatively open country, the army took up their line of march in this order.

Gen. Hand's brigade, in front, in eight columns.

Gen. Poor's brigade on the right, in eight columns, flanked by a strong body of light troops.

Gen. Maxwell's brigade on the left, in eight columns, flanked by light troops.

Gen. Clinton's brigade, in eight columns, in the rear.

Col. Proctor's artillery in the centre, flanked on the right and left by double files of pack-horses, which separated his command from Poor, and Maxwell's brigades.

The only important stand made by the enemy was below Newtown, eighteen miles above Tioga Point, on the Tioga, (or Chemung) river. Col. John Butler, Capt. Walter Butler, (his son,) the two Johnsons, Grey, and McDonald, commanded the British and Tories. Brandt, (Thayendenegea, the terrible,) was at the head of the combined Indian warriors of the Six Nations. Their numbers have been variously estimated, from fifteen hundred to two thousand fighting men.*

On the north side of the Tioga river, where there is a bend forming almost a right angle, on a steep gravelly bank, the enemy had thrown up a breast-work, extending nearly half a mile in length, north towards the hills, and here preparations were carefully made for a decisive battle. Their right and rear were guarded by the stream, their left only exposed; but on the neighboring heights on their left flank, strong bodies of their sharp-shooters were stationed. To mask their works, pine shrubs had been cut, and stuck up in front, as if still growing. The road ran to the foot of the gravel hill, on which they had fortified, then turning to the right, following a small brook in a line parallel with the breast-work, so that, had the army marched on without discovering their position, the whole left would have been exposed to a raking fire on the flank. Some skir-

---

* It has been stated, that there were but two hundred whites present This seems very improbable. Butler and Johnson had more than that number at Wyoming. So many Canadian and refugee officers could hardly have been in command of less than four or five hundred men.

mishing had previously taken place, and several men had fallen. Fortunately Major Parr, in advance with his riflemen, discovered the Indian line of defence, and gave immediate notice to the advancing columns. Gen. Hand forthwith formed the light infantry in the wood, about eighty rods from the enemy, and waited until the other columns should come up.

Gen. Sullivan promptly gave orders to Gen. Poor, to scale the hills on his right, rouse the Indians from their lurking places, who, he did not doubt, were there in force, at the bayonet's point, and pressing on with spirit, giving them no time to shelter themselves behind trees, and then to fall on the left flank and rear of the enemy. Proctor, with his artillery, took up a position to render his shot and shells most effective, and played with great vivacity. Parr, with the whole rifle corps, was actively engaged. Spalding and Franklin with the Wyoming troops were in the thickest of the fight. General Hand led his light infantry to the assault with the greatest gallantry. Clinton and Maxwell were held in impatient, though prudent, reserve. The enemy contested the ground with determined resolution, until the active and decisive movement of Poor cleared the hills, and unveiled their flank to his now descending and impetuous attack, when they fled with precipitation. The true Indian character was now exhibited. Cunning in expedient—patient under every privation in advancing on an enemy—impetuous and terrible in attack—overbearing, insolent and cruel in victory—so, when defeated, broken spirited, (like the tiger when he has missed his prey,) cowering almost into cowardice, for a time no power can rally them. The victory was decisive. No serious attempt was afterwards made to check the advance of the army. About thirty men fell in the battle. How many of the Indians, could not be known; as it is felt to be, among them, a most sacred duty to carry off their dead, and conceal the number of the slain. Capt. Franklin, of the Wyoming volunteers, received a ball in his shoulder, and several from his, Spalding's and Schott's companies, were wounded.

Not a moment of delay was allowed. Being now in the Indian country, hundreds of fields, teeming with corn, beans, and other vegetables, were laid waste with rigid severity. Every house, hut, and wigwam, was consumed. Cultivated in rude Indian fashion for centuries, orchards abounded, and near a town, between the Seneca and Cayuga lakes, there were fifteen hundred peach trees, bending under ripe, and ripening fruit; all were cut down. The besom of destruction swept, if with regret and pity, still with firm hand, through all their fair fields and fertile plains. Deeply were they made to drink of the bitter chalice they had so often forced remorselessly to the lips of the frontier settlers within their reach. Some idea of the extent of country inhabited by the Indians, the number of their towns, and the great quantity of produce to be destroyed, may be formed, when it is stated that an army of four thousand men were employed, without a day's (except indispensable) remission, from the 29th of August, until the 28th of September, in accomplishing the work of destruction. The furthest northwest extent of General Sullivan's advance, was to Genesee castle, at the large flats on the beautiful river of that name. Two or three incidents that occurred on the march have too much interest to be omitted. At Kanadia, on the 5th of September, Mr. Luke Swetland, one of the most respectable citizens of Wyoming, who had been taken prisoner the year previous, was relieved from captivity. At Canandaigua, on the 7th, a white child was found, indeed an orphan, without knowledge of its parents. We regret our inability to record its fate. A few days after, a woman who had been taken at Wyoming, came into the army, with a child in her arms of seven or eight months old. Her name we have not been able to learn. One old squaw, too old to be removed, was the only human being belonging to the enemy left by them, so totally was their country deserted. But a most melancholy occurrence demands a more particular narration.

On the 13th of September, Lieut. Boyd of the rifle corps, was directed to take five or six men, with a friendly Indian as a guide, and to advance towards the Genesee to reconnoiter. Numbers volunteering, he marched out at the head of twenty-four men; too few if battle was intended; too many if secresy and celerity were prime requisites of the enterprise. Striking Little castle, on the Genesee river, he surprised, killed and scalped two Indians. On his return, Boyd was surrounded by a strong detachment of the enemy, who killed fourteen of his men, and took him and a soldier prisoners; eight men only escaping. The next day the army accelerated their march, with the hope of releasing Lieut. Boyd. On arriving at the Genesee Castle, his remains and those of the other prisoner were found, surrounded by all the horrid evidences of savage barbarity. The torture fires were yet burning. Flaming pine knots had been thrust into their flesh, their finger nails pulled out, their tongues cut off, and their heads severed from their bodies. It is said that Boyd was brought before Col. Butler, who examined him, Boyd being on one knee, a warrior on each side firmly grasping his arms, a third at his back, with tomahawk raised. What a scene for a limner! "How many men has Sullivan? "I cannot tell you, sir." How is the army divided and disposed?" "I cannot give you any information, sir." "Boyd, life is sweet, you had better answer me." "Duty forbids, and I would not if life depended on the word—but Col. Butler, I know the issue, my doom is fixed." Another version of the affair omits the interview, and relates that Boyd was stabbed in the abdomen, an intestine drawn out and tied to a tree, around which the sufferer was driven. Both may be true. That a prisoner should be taken before Butler for examination is quite probable.

"While Sullivan" (we copy Marshall) "laid waste the county on the Susquehanna, another expedition under Col. Brodhead was carried on from Pittsburg up the Alleghany, against the Mingo, Munsey, and Seneca tribes. At the head of between six and seven hundred men, he advanced two hundred miles up the river, and destroyed the villages and cornfields on its head branches. Here too the Indians were unable to resist the invading army. After one unsuccessful skirmish, they abandoned their villages to a destruction that was inevitable, and sought for personal safety in the woods."

The army withdrew to Tioga point on the 29th September, and in the evening Capt. Shreeve gave an entertainment to the officers, in the best style in his power, the pleasure of which was heightened by learning the particulars of the surprise and capture of Stony Point by the gallant Wayne.

General Sullivan gave his troops three days of rest, and Oct. 4th marched to Standing Stone bottom. On the 5th the whole army, including the New York brigade, under General Clinton, except those who took charge of the pack-horses, embarked on board the boats, and were wafted, with hearts elate, down that chrystal stream, cheered alternately by songs and music; for rigid discipline was, on an occasion so joyous, temporarily relaxed.

Col. Zebulon Butler at Wyoming, having been apprised of their approach, welcomed them with a salute, and on the 8th, gave an entertainment, more sumptuous and profuse than the Valley had ever before witnessed. Venison and wild turkey smoked upon the board, and Gen. Sullivan, in fine spirits, imparted animation to the feast. Delaying only until the 10th, the army marched, and arrived at Easton on the 15th. On the 17th of October, a day of thanksgiving was held, and a sermon preached by the Rev. Dr. Evans, of Gen. Poor's brigade, when the several detachments of the victorious little army separated, taking up new positions assigned by his Excellency the Commander in Chief.

Throughout the whole campaign, the conduct of Gen. Sullivan was distinguished by courage, energy and skill. Unfortunately, soon after taking the command at Wyoming, in general orders, he animadverted with severity upon the Board of War, who had resisted what they deemed unreasonable demands for provisions, forage, stores, and means of transportation. Sept. 1st, 1779, in the Continental Congress, "a letter was read, dated August 31st, from the Board of War, enclosing a copy of general orders issued to the troops under his command, by Major Gen. John Sullivan, reflecting upon the Board, and representing that the characters of the Board are made free with in Gen. Sullivan's army, who, being under a deception, censure the Board with great bitterness; and, thereupon, request Congress to appoint a committee to examine into their conduct, &c."

October 14th.—On motion of Mr. Gerry: "Resolved, That the thanks of Congress be given to his Excellency General Washington, for directing, and to Major-General Sullivan, and the brave officers and soldiers under his command, for effectually conducting an important expedition, against such of the Indian nations, as encouraged by the counsels, and conducted by the officers of his Britannic Majesty, had perfidiously waged an unprovoked and cruel war against these United States; laid waste many of their defenceless towns, and with savage barbarity slaughtered the inhabitants thereof."

A second resolution proposes to set apart a day of general thanksgiving, which shows the importance attached to Sullivan's eminent success.

Still the voice of censure from the Board of War, and their partizans in Congress, was reiterated and loud.

On the 13th of November, a letter was read from General Sullivan, dated the 9th, "requesting leave, on account of ill health, to retire from the service." Whereupon a motion was made by Mr. Gerry, "that the resignation of Major-General Sullivan be not accepted, but that he have leave to retire from the service, as long as he shall judge it expedient for the recovery of his health." This motion, instead of being adopted, was referred to a committee, on whose report to Congress, on the 30th November, "Resolved, That Congress have a just sense of the services and abilities of Major-General Sullivan, and greatly regret the indisposition which deprives them of so gallant an officer; that as General Sullivan's health will not permit his continuance in the American army, his resignation be accepted."

On motion of Mr. Livingston, "Resolved, That the President be requested to return the thanks of Congress to Major-General Sullivan for his past services."

Thus was the gallant veteran politely bowed out. Imprudent in expression he may have been, but his meritorious services should have caused a few hasty words to be overlooked, and he should have been generously retained in his command.

It may well be regarded as one of the most extraordinary instances of healthfulness on record, that this army, exceeding three thousand men, (not including General Clinton's brigade) during the summer and autumn, in battle, by accident and sickness, should have suffered so inconsiderable loss. Marshall says: "The object of the expedition being accomplished, Sullivan returned to Easton, Pennsylvania, having lost only forty men, by sickness and the enemy.*

* Note 1.—In taking leave of General Sullivan, it may not be improper to add that he had displayed signal ability in various separate commands, previous to his being selected to direct the northern expedition. He had also been present at the battles of Long Island, Brandywine and Germantown. Immediately after the acceptance of his resignation, he was elected to Congress from New Hampshire; was afterwards President of that State, and a District Judge of the United States, appointed by Washington. Born in 1741, he died January 23, 1795, aged fifty-four years; so that when at Wyoming, he was about thirty-seven years old.

Note 2.—General Edward Hand, whose name has several times occurred in recounting the events of this campaign, as a distinguished Pennsylvanian, demands a further notice. He was from Lancaster county, and high in the confidence of Washington; so much so, that when in 1798-9, he consented to take command of the army being raised to resist the aggressions of France, that great and good man desired the appointment of General Hand as Adjutant General. He was extremely beloved by his men, and served with great usefulness and honour. When peace came he was called frequently by his fellow citizens, to perform high civil duties. His name is attached to the Pennsylvania Constitution of 1790. The old Wyoming soldiers, speak of his noble horsemanship, and attachment to his generous chargers. He rode a fine active grey; but a sorrel roan, remarkable for lofty carriage and spirited action, was his favourite parade horse. This he sent forward by his servant, the moment he arrived on the return of the army at Tioga-point, to Col. Butler at Wyoming, with a particular request, that he might be recruited against his arrival.

Note 3.—In 1790, Big-Tree, an Indian of the Seneca nation, being one of a delegation at Philadelphia, addressing Gen. Washington, thus feelingly refers to Sullivan's destruction of their settlements. "Father—When your army entered the country of the Six Nations, we called you the *Town destroyer* ; to this day when your name is heard, our women look behind and turn pale, and our children cling closer to the necks of their mothers." Big-Tree joined the American army under Wayne, in 1793, but committed suicide.

Barlow, in his Columbiad, referring to the Indian expedition against Wyoming, has these lines :—

"His savage hordes, the murderous *Johnson* leads,
Files through the woods, and treads the tangled weeds;
Shuns open combat, teaches where to run,
Skulk, couch the ambush, aim the hunter's gun ;
Whirl the sly tomahawk, the war whoop sing,
Divide the spoils, and pack the scalps they bring."

"After the return of General Sullivan," says Mr. Chapman, "several parties of Indians, stimulated by revenge for the losses they had sustained, continued to range among the mountains of Wyoming, in thirst of vengeance upon the white people, and occasionally caught and tortured, in the most cruel manner, any defenceless individuals that came in their way."

This paragraph, and a statement of the affair at Nescopeck, where the party under Lieut. Myers was cut off, is all that Mr. C. records of Indian depredations after 1779.

Even that excellent, and generally accurate work, the "AMERICAN ENCYCLOPEDIA," so late as 1840, speaking of Sullivan's expedition against the Indians, says, "By this one blow an end was put to their incursions and cruelties."

It will be seen from our annals of the three succeeding years, 1780, 1781, 1782, that, instead of "the danger of the Indian wars being in a great measure removed, the inhabitants returned in great numbers to their possessions at Wyoming, where their settlements again flourished," that, in fact, those three years were rife with Indian invasions, and that Wyoming was almost one continued scene of plunder and captivity—murder, conflagration and woe.

The civil transactions of the year afford few materials for history. The settlers who remained, or returned after the massacre, were generally gathered under the protection of the fort at Wilkesbarre. A mill on the borders of Hanover and Newport, was guarded by a few men, and three or four families ventured to reside in its vicinity. The civil organization was preserved by Col. Denison, and half a dozen citizens. At a town meeting held April ye 12, 1779, Giles Slocum, Christopher Hurlbut, Daniel Ingersoll, Asa Chapman and Joel Strong, were admitted freemen, and took the oath of fidelity to Connecticut; Colonel Nathan Denison, and Deacon John Hurlbut were chosen members of Assembly, to meet at Hartford the following May.

On the 6th of December, 1779, (the army having returned victorious, the enemy chastised, and it was hoped effectually broken and dispersed, hope and confidence being restored,) a town meeting was legally warned, and holden in the town of Westmoreland. Since April 1778, near two years, the entries had been brief, and imperfectly made in the old records, as if with trembling hand and broken heart. Now the record is full, bold, and beautifully written.

Colonel Nathan Denison was chosen moderator.

Obadiah Gore, town clerk, for the ensuing year. Selectmen, a Town Treasurer, Constables, Surveyors of Highways, Fence-viewers, Listers, (Assessors) a Tax Collector, Key-keeper, Brander of Horses, and School Committee, were appointed. The special confidence reposed in Col. Denison, may be inferred from his being not only chosen moderator, but treasurer, selectman, and one of the school committee. He was member of Assembly, Justice of the Peace, and Judge of the Court.

The names of James Nesbitt and John Phillips appear among the officers, and are now especially noticed, because April 14, 1843, as I now write, sixty-four years having elapsed since that town meeting, they still live, respected for their usefulness, and beloved for their virtues.

A single incident remains to be noted. Mrs. Bidlack, the mother of Capt. James Bidlack, who was slain in the massacre, applied for the release of her son Benjamin, (now the Rev. Benjamin Bidlack,) who was in the army, he being needed at home for her protection and support. The following neat letter, beautifully written, came to Col. Butler, in reply to her petition.

"WAR OFFICE, November 1st, 1779.

SIR,—The Board have received Mehitible Bidlack's representation of her case, and your certificate thereon, and much as they are inclined to alleviate the distresses of those who have suffered by the war, they cannot grant the petition for the discharge of her son. Her reasons, though very good, are such as thousands can plead, and to admit them as sufficien, would be to depopulate the army.

I am sir, with respect,
Your very obedient servant,
BENJAMIN STODERT, *Secretary.*

LETTER XX.

1780.——Renewed invasion—Bennet and Hammond taken—Noble exploit—Upson murdered—Van Campen, Pike and Rogers taken—Noble exploit and rescue—Town meeting—Civil affairs—Generous donation from Virginia—Good news from Assembly—Muster Roll—A prize—Capt. John Franklin—Justice's Court—Court martial—News from below—Death of Capt. Caldwell—Lieut. Lawrence Myers—Fifty miles to mill—Various Incidents—Massacre near Sugarloaf—Marriage of Capt. Schotts—J. Butler's Rangers—Seven prisoners taken from Shawney—sickly summer—welcome supply of provisions.

The sense of security and repose, so welcome to the wearied settlers after the distressing scenes of the two preceding years, they were not long permitted to cherish. Effectual as the punishment of the Savages seemed, instead of subduing, it only appeared to have exasperated their thirst for revenge, and 1780 was destined to be a year of extreme suffering.

Being confident that Sullivan had left in the whole Indian country nothing for them to subsist upon, it was not doubted but the Savages were necessarily within the British lines at Niagara, beyond striking distance; and the settlers resumed their farming at Kingston, Hanover, and Plymouth, the latter seven miles distant from the Wilkesbarre fort. A few adventured further. The main settlements had block-houses built, in case of attack, wherein to seek shelter and make defence.

In the latter part of March an alarm was given that Indians were in the Valley. On the 27th, Thomas Bennett and his son, a lad, in a field not far from their house, in Kingston, were seized and made prisoners by six Indians. Lebbeus Hammond, who had been captured a few hours before, they found tied as they entered a gorge of the mountain. Hammond had been in the battle, and was then taken prisoner, but had escaped from the fatal ring at bloody rock, where Queen Esther was pursuing her murderous rounds as previously related. He was a prize of more than ordinary value. No doubt could exist but that he was destined a victim to the cruelest barbarity. The night of the 27th they took up their quarters about twelve miles north from the Valley. The next day, having crossed the river near the three Islands, they pushed on towards Meshoppen with all the speed in their power. While on their march they met two parties of Indians and Tories, descending for murder and pillage upon the settlement. A man by the name of Moses Mount, whom they knew, was particular in his inquiries into the state of the garrison and the situation of the inhabitants. On the evening of the 28th they built a fire, with the aid of Mr. Bennett, who being an old man, was least feared, and permitted to go unbound. To a request from Mr. Bennett, of the Chief, to lend him an awl to put on a button, the Savage, with a significant look replied, "No want button for one night," and refused his request. The purpose of the Indians could not be mistaken. Whispering to Hammond, while the Indians went to a spring near by, to drink, it was resolved to make an effort to escape. To stay was certain death; they could but die. Tired with their heavy march, after a supper of venison, the Indians lay around the fire, Hammond and the boy tied between them, except an old Indian who was set to keep the first watch. His spear lay by his side, while he picked the meat from the head of a deer, as half sleeping and nodding, he sat over the fire. Bennett was allowed to sit near him, and seemingly in a careless manner, took the spear, and rolled it playfully on his thigh. Watching his opportunity when least on his guard, he thrust the spear through the Indian's side, who fell with a startling groan upon the burning logs. There was not a moment to be lost. Age forgot its decrepitude. In an instant Hammond and young Bennett were cut loose, the arms seized, three of the remaining Savages tomahawked, and slain as they slept, and another wounded. One only escaped unhurt. On the evening of the 30th the captive victors came in with five rifles, a silver mounted hanger, and several spears and blankets, as trophies of their brilliant exploit.

Another band of ten Indians, on the same day that Bennett and Hammond were taken, shot Asa Upson in Hanover, (near where the bridge crosses the canal below Carey-Town). On the 28th, two men were making sugar about eight miles below Wilkesbarre, one was killed, the other taken prisoner. On the 29th, Jonah Rogers, a lad of fourteen or fifteen, was taken prisoner from the lower part of the Valley. The Indians then pushed down the river to Fishing Creek, where, on the 30th they surprised the family of the Van Campens. Moses Van Campen was taken prisoner after they had murdered and scalped his father, his brother, and his uncle, and captured a boy named Pence. Directing their course northeast, the Savages passed through Huntington, where they were met by a scout of four men under the orders of Capt. Franklin. Shots were exchanged, and two of his men wounded. Too few to cope with the Indian party, Capt. Franklin took up a position in an old log house; but the enemy preferred to pursue their course, and the same evening came to a camp where Abraham Pike, with his wife, were making sugar. Pike, who was a British deserter, was a most desirable acquisition. The wife and her child they painted, and sent into the settlements. The party now bent their way to the lake country, crossed the Susquehanna at the little Tunkhannock, and pursued their course up the east branch of the river. Lieut. Van Campen, a man of true courage, brave and enterprising, formed a plan, with Pike, Rogers, and Pence, to rise on the ten Indians, and effect their liberation, or die in the attempt. It was a bold and hazardous enterprise. The party had ascended to within fifteen miles of Tioga Point, where they encamped on the night of the 3rd of April. The Indians, beyond the probability of pursuit, all lay down to sleep, five on each side of the prisoners, who were carefully bound. Van Campen had observed that a knife, used by one of the Indians, fell near him, and placing his foot on it, secured the inestimable prize. About midnight, finding the enemy buried in profound sleep, Van Campen cut himself loose, and with noiseless celerity liberated the hands of his companions. Springing to their feet, placing the guns in a secure place, tomahawks were used with the utmost vigour. The Indians made a desperate, but unavailing effort for the mastery, but were overpowered, and several of the ten killed, two others wounded, and two or three escaped unhurt. After scalping the dead, recovering the scalps of those of our people whom the Indians had slain, making a hasty raft, the party, taking the guns, tomahawks, spears, and blankets of the foe, descended the Susquehanna, and on the evening of the 5th of April arrived with their spoils in triumph at Wyoming. No nobler deed was performed during the Revolutionary war. In a narrative of his life and services, written 1837, and presented as a memorial to Congress, asking for a pension, Lieut. Van Campen represents his companions in this affair, except Pence, as terrified and inactive, thus impairing his own credit, and marring the beauty of a most chivalrous achievement. There was honour enough for all; there could be no motive but excessive self-glorification, for representing Pike and Rogers as cowards. But when that narrative was written Van Campen was an old man, Pike and Rogers were both dead, and he may have supposed no one remained to rescue their names from the odium. The writer of this knew Abraham Pike and Jonah Rogers well. Mr. Rogers was a highly respectable citizen, and was well understood, though quite a youth, to have performed his duty like a man. That he was collected and cool is evident from his observing that Pike struck his first blow with the head of his axe, then turned it and gave the edge. The former he has often heard recount the daring exploit, and until this recent statement of Van Campen, never heard a doubt of Pike's courage expressed. Familiarly he was called "Serjeant Pike, the Indian killer," and as such was every where welcome. An Irishman! A regularly disciplined soldier! The presumption would be strong against the charge of cowardice. But death was certain if taken to Niagara; even cowardice itself would have stimulated a man, so situated, to fight. That Van Campen's memory had become impaired, is apparent from the fact that he claims to have killed *nine* of the ten Indians. Col. Jenkins, in a memorandum made *at the time*, says: "Pike and two men from Fishing Creek, and two boys that were taken by the Indians, made their escape by rising on the guard, killed THREE, and the rest took to the woods, and left the prisoners with twelve guns," &c. No! without detracting from the bravery and good conduct of Van Campen, we cannot but conclude, that he had told the story of his own prowess, heightening the colouring in his own favour, as he found it gave him consideration with his wondering listeners, until, perhaps, he believed himself the sole hero of the victory.

On the 30th of March, three persons, named Avery, Lyons, and Jones, were taken off prisoners by the Indians, from Capouse.

The unfortunate, or fortunate Hammond, who, twice in such fearful jeopardy, had twice escaped, had now the pleasure of appearing at Head-Quarters, having been sent on the 3rd of April, by Col. Butler, express, with despatches for his Excellency.

In the course of these predatory excursions, the Savages set fire to the simple log buildings which the settlers had erected for their temporary residence.

In the midst of all this distress, the ever popular town meetings were not neglected.

"At a town meeting, legally warned and held, in the town of Westmoreland, on Monday the 10th day of April, 1780,

"John Franklin, Esq., was chosen Moderator for the work of the day.

"John Hurlbut, Esq., was chosen to negotiate the affairs of this town, before the General Assembly, to be holden in Hartford, in May next.

"Obadiah Gore, Esq., John Franklin, Esq., and Lieut. Rosewell Franklin are appointed a Committee to assist the Agent in drawing up a just representation of our circumstances, to lay before the Honorable the General Assembly, in May next."

"At a town meeting on the 20th of April, John Franklin, Esq., Lieut. Rosewell Franklin, and Ensign John Comstock, (titles as usual scrupulously given,) were appointed a Committee "to advise with the inhabitants of this town, about contracting their improvements to a smaller compass, and more defenceable situation, against the Savages, and to adopt measures for the security of their stock, and make their report to the commanding officer of the garrison, as soon as possible."

The next Resolve should be printed in letters of gold.

"Voted—That whereas the parish of Dresden, in the State of Virginia, have contributed and sent one hundred and eighty dollars for the support of the distressed inhabitants of this town, that the selectmen be directed to distribute said money to those they shall judge the most necessitated, and report to the town at some future meeting.

"Voted—That Col. Nathan Denison return the thanks of this town to the parish of Dresden, in the State of Virginia, for their charitable disposition in presenting the distressed inhabitants of this town with one hundred and eighty dollars."

Col. Butler's second Connecticut regiment consisted, at this time, of three hundred and fourteen men, fit for duty, and while he was stationed in Westmoreland, possessing, as he was known to do, more skill in Indian warfare, and enjoying in an eminent degree the confidence of the inhabitants, yet every man of his regiment was below the mountains, under the immediate orders of Lieutenant-Colonel Isaac Sherman. Visiting his command, to see that proper discipline and order were preserved, then hastening back to Wyoming, to a station of excessive care and responsibility, yet affording no chance to gather laurels, so dear to the high-souled military man, Col. Butler performed most arduous duties, in a manner to entitle him to the gratitude and praise of his country.

Early in July, Esquire Hurlbut returned from Hartford, bringing the cheering news, that the Assembly, in answer to the petition of her Wyoming people, had resolved to take an account of their losses, preparatory to making compensation therefor, when the public treasury should be in a condition to do so. The Resolve, itself, breathes a spirit, and shows an intention so just, that it should be carefully preserved.

"At a General Assembly of the Governor, and Company of the State of Connecticut, in America, holden at Hartford on the second Thursday of May, (being the 11th day of said month,) and continued by several adjournments until the 23d day of June following, Anno Domini, 1780.

——— " Upon the Memorial of the Civil Authority, and Selectmen of the Town of Westmoreland, representing that the inhabitants of said town have sustained great losses by the invasions and depredations of the enemy, and that the Rate Bills issued against the inhabitants of said town, for State Taxes, have been taken, burnt and destroyed ; the town depopulated, and the few remaining families greatly impoverished by the frequent incursions and depredations of the enemy. Praying this Assembly that an estimation of their losses may be made, and State Taxes abated in part compensation thereof, etc., as per Memorial.

"*Resolved by this Assembly*, That the whole of the State Taxes, for which warrants have already issued against the inhabitants of said town of Westmoreland, that are not paid into the hands of the State Treasurer, be, and the same are hereby abated, to be considered as in part compensation for their losses, whenever the United States shall order and direct the losses sustained by the citizens of said States, from the depredations of the enemy, to be compensated ; and John Hurlbut, Zebulon Butler, and Obadiah Gore, Esqs., be, and they are hereby appointed a Committee to repair to said Westmoreland ; first giving public notice in the several newspapers in this State, of the time and place of their meeting, and there examine into the damages, injuries, and losses sustained and suffered by the present or late inhabitants of said town of Westmoreland, holding under this State, who shall, by themselves or others on their behalf, being duly authorized, make application to said Committee, during their continuance in said town, and report make to some future session of this Assembly, of what they shall find in the matters aforesaid."

Capt. Simon Spalding's Independent Company, being the consolidated Wyoming companies of Ransom and Durkee, was stationed at Wilkesbarre fort, with Capt. John Paul Schott's rifle corps, and a detachment from the German regiment, under the command of Capt. Michael, making together, about one hundred and twenty men. The militia consisted of one company under the command of Capt. John Franklin. How entirely broken and reduced was the country, will be apparent from the returns of this company.

"July 29, 1780, there were twenty-nine on the roll. At Hanover, to guard the mill, one lieutenant, one serjeant, and ten privates. At Kingston, one serjeant and fourteen men; and two on the sick list. Small detachments were frequently made for scouting parties, the utmost vigilance being indispensable. On the 9th of June, Captain Franklin, with five men, being on a scout sixty miles up the river, at Wysox, took three prisoners, viz: Jacob Bowman, Adam Bowman, and Henry Hoover, with, according to the language of the day, a fine lot of plunder, valued at £46 18s. 11d. Capt. Franklin and Serjeant Baldwin each shared a silver watch, several pocket compasses, silver buttons, and sleeve buttons; a scarlet broadcloth coat, several gold pieces, and a beautiful spy-glass, attest the consequence of the prisoners. The canoes sold for £4 10s. They were probably confidential messengers on public service from the enemy in New York, to Col. John Butler at Niagara. Col. Z. Butler, purchased the spy-glass from the victors, estimated at three guineas, hard money."

In the midst of this scene of general distress, it is difficult to suppress a smile, when we contemplate the variety of character sustained, and duties performed by Captain Franklin. We have seen him taking an active part on several committees in town meeting. Indefatigable in the command of his little company; during all this time, he was farming with an industry, that showed his reliance for subsistence was on the labour of his hands. A hunter, scarce a week passed, that he did not in the proper season, bring in a buck. But he was a Justice of the Peace, and the civil laws were regularly administered. As it is our purpose to present an accurate picture of Wyoming as we can possibly sketch, one or two causes, tried before Justice Franklin, will be quoted.

August 19, 1780, —— ——, of Westmoreland, found guilty of playing cards, therefore ordered, that he pay a fine to the treasury of the town of Westmoreland of ten shillings, lawful money, with costs.

Test. JOHN FRANKLIN, J. P.

At a Justice's Court, holden at Westmoreland, August 31, 1780, present, John Franklin, Justice of the Peace, wherein Phineas Pierce, is plaintiff, and Lebeus Tubbs, defendant: Whereas, the said Pierce, as administrator on the estate of Col. George Dorrance, deceased, complains of the defendant as *disclosing*, (Q. secreting? withholding?) some of the estate aforesaid, the court proceeds to a trial by the consent of the parties, *and on the examination of the defendant on oath*, who testifies, etc. With these chancery powers of obliging the defendant on oath to reveal the whole truth, every thing was explained. Among many other articles, he had a rifle belonging to Col. Dorrance, a bed, a copper tea-kettle, and several other articles of valuable household furniture.

"The Court are of opinion, that the defendant deliver up the said articles to the administrator, and satisfy the costs of the court.

Test. JOHN FRANKLIN, Justice of the Peace."

Military courts were also held. Serjeant Leader was convicted of falsifying a provision return, breaking open the magazine; of conspiring to release the tory prisoners, and blow up the garrison. He was whipped one hundred lashes, and sent out with the prisoners to Head Quarters, as incorrigible. We make two or three brief extracts from Franklin's Journal. "July 12, 1780. A Court Martial.—Martin Breakall tried, Capt. John Paul Schotts, president; Capt. Spaulding, Capt. Franklin, Lieut. Gore, Lieut. Jenkins, Lieut. Kingsley, members. Breakall is found guilty of intending to desert to the Indians, take with him the tory prisoners, and threatening to scalp one Adam Sybert. It is the opinion of the court, that Breakall run the gauntlet four times through the troops of this garrison. The commanding officer approves the sentence, and the next afternoon, the 13th, was punished accordingly." A singing meeting this evening, says Capt. Franklin in his journal, at Mr. Forseman's.

"I went to Huntingdon, Saturday 15th, returned," says Capt. F. "Saturday the 22d, killed two deer, and took up Sherwood's flax."[*]

A boat arrived from down the river on the 20th of the month, with the welcome cargo of twenty-three barrels of flour. The boatmen state, "that on Friday the 14th, one man and three children were murdered by the Indians near Buffalo Creek, and on Saturday the 15th, one Capt. McMahon, was taken prisoner by an Indian and tory, six miles from Northumberland, on the West Branch, but he made his escape, killing the tory when the Indian had gone to his company, that lay near at hand. This tory was Capt. Caldwell, a noted villain." Probably the same Capt. Caldwell, who the day before the massacre in 1778, took possession of the fort at Jenkins'

---

[*] The development of Capt. Franklin's character and conduct in the sequel, will show the purpose of these minute details.

ferry. His conduct in that instance was neither marked by treachery nor cruelty. In a boat that arrived at this time, came Lieut. Laurence Myers, his first visit to Wyoming, a very worthy gentleman, of whom it will be our pleasure to speak more at large in our chapter of personal narratives.

"August 6. Last Thursday, Benjamin Clark with others, went down the river to mill. Same day, Lieut. Daniel Gore with others, set out to Col. Stroud's to mill." Col. Stroud's mill at Stroudsburgh, on the Delaware, was nearly fifty miles distant through the wilderness, from which may be inferred the privations and hardships the inhabitants had to encounter. No mill remained, but the small one near Nanticoke Falls, defended by a detachment of Captain Franklin's company.

On the death of Mason F. Alden's child on the 20th, Esquire Hurlbut preached two sermons. On the same day, Mr. Hollenback's boat loaded with goods arrived, having on board the three welcome "pounders," to enable the Wyoming people to make their own powder. Rumours were rife of murders by Indians below. The prowess and success of Bennett and Hammond, and of Pike, Rogers and Van Campen, had doubtless for a brief space, impressed on the enemy a lesson of extreme caution in regard to Wyoming.

Capt. Franklin and three men set out on a scout up the river early in September. At Tioga Point, they came to where large parties had encamped, and saw two Indians. At Tioga they found a canoe, and in two easy days sail arrived at the Wyoming Fort on the 10th. A week previous, Serjeants Baldwin and Searles exchanged shots with Indians at Tunkhannock, took a horse and some plunder from them, which it is supposed the Indians had taken in the neighborhood of Fort Allen, near the Lehi water gap.

After Wyoming was so reduced as to be unable to afford assistance in checking the excursions of the Savages, parties were in the habit of passing the settlement, and attacking the people both sides of the Blue Mountain, taking scalps, prisoners, and plunder. In May 1780, the settlement at Mahoning, not far from Mauch Chunk, was attacked, several were slain. Benjamin Gilbert, a quaker, and Abigail Dodson, a girl of twelve or thirteen, were among the prisoners taken to Niagara. In consequence of these repeated attacks, a chain of block-houses was built, at supporting distances, back of the Blue Mountain, from the Schuylkill in Berks county, to the Delaware in Northampton; and Nathan Beach was an orderly serjeant for two years under the command of Capt. Smeathers, on that line of defence. In September, a large party of Indians passing Wyoming, without giving the least alarm, crossed the Susquehanna, near the mouth of the Nescopeck Creek, leaving Wilkesbarre Fort eighteen miles on the left. On advancing into the Scotch Valley, now known as Conyngham and Sugar Loaf, moving with cat-like wariness, they discovered a party of Americans entirely off their guard, some eating, others at play, for it was noon, and entertaining not the slightest apprehension of an enemy being near, they were reposing or sporting, after a forenoon march. On counting their numbers, the Indians found the Americans had thirty-three men, their own being thirty. Some were for making a bold attack, others who had come for plunder, preferred to retire. It was however agreed upon, that they would all draw near, and take a shot; if the Americans were not broken, but should rally with spirit, they would retreat to a designated place. The fire was as deadly as unexpected. Our people who survived, ran in the utmost confusion. Lieut. Myers,[*] who commanded, did every thing an intrepid officer could do to rally his men, seized his rifle, and vowed he would die before he would retreat. One or two ran to his aid, but it was too late. He was seized by the gallant Indian chief, wounded slightly, and made prisoner. Satisfied with their thirteen scalps, their prisoners, and all the booty brought out by the party, the Indians hastened their retreat, doing what mischief they could, by burning the Shickshinny mills, and all the grain stacks on their route. The second night Lieut. Myers contrived to make his escape, and came into the Wyoming Fort with the melancholy tidings. After the war, the Miss Dodson, before named, was redeemed from captivity, and related the Indian account of the affair, as learned at Niagara.

As the preceding winter had been extremely cold, so the summer was marked by an unusual degree of heat. August especially was, to use an expression of the day, panting hot, severe thunder showers being frequent, followed by a close and oppressive atmosphere. The consequence was an autumn of greater sickness than had ever before been experienced. Remittent and intermittent fevers, prevailed to a distressing degree. The settlers in Kingston particularly suffered. Calomel, tartar emetic, and Jesuits bark, dispensed by Dr. William H. Smith, with skill, were efficacious, and the number of deaths, though considerable, bore a very small proportion to the great number afflicted. Every incident in a small community so excited,

[*] Not Laurence Myers.

awakened attention, and William Nelson, being badly bitten by a rattlesnake, was probably known in the course of a day, to every person in Wyoming. After much suffering he recovered.

On the 11th of October, the good Deacon Hurlbut, who preached in the absence of the Rev. Mr. Johnson, being chosen member of Assembly, set out for Hartford, accompanied by Asa Chapman, who went to visit his friends in Preston. Chapman had been sworn in a freeman of Westmoreland, a few months before. He returned, and his fate will be recorded in the annals of a subsequent year.

We have spoken several times of Capt. John Paul Schotts, who was stationed with his rifle corps at Wyoming, where he became attached to Miss Naomi Sill, sister to Col. Denison's lady. The banns were published on Sunday, October the 15th, and on Wednesday, the 18th, they were married; the occasion being one of great joy and festivity in the garrison, and among the whole people.

The 24th of the month, the settlement was thrown into commotion by the arrival of an express stating, that Col. Hunter, at Fort Augusta, (Sunbury,) had stopped the boats that were ascending the river with provisions for the garrison. Grain the people now had, but as we have seen, they were obliged to go to Stroudsburgh to mill. This was the first incident which had occurred for three years, exhibiting the smothered, but by no means extinguished jealousy, that existed on the part of Pennsylvania, towards the Connecticut garrison and settlement.

Nearly three months passed away, after the massacre at the Scotch Valley, in comparative peace. Alarms were frequent; scouts were on the alert; tidings of murder and robbery, weekly, came in from the West Branch, from near Sunbury, and more especially from the settlements along the Blue Mountains; but no direct attack was made on Wyoming. The harvest, though but little ground was cultivated, had come in satisfactorily. Hugh Forseman arrived from Philadelphia with a hundred head of cattle for the garrison, which fact, of itself, speaks of the general destitution of the country. Thus fear of absolute famine was removed. The comforts of life were not looked for, and all were satisfied with sufficient food to sustain existence.

In September, a town meeting voted—That a petition be prepared to the Assembly at Hartford, asking for an abatement of Taxes. It may be observed, that the ordinary assemblage, "legally warned," were called town meetings. Those more important, where all the town officers were chosen, holden the first Tuesday in December, each year, were sometimes, by way of eminence, denominated "*Freeman's Meeting.*" December 5th, 1780, the whole settlement was assembled in town meeting, legally warned, and held at the house of Abel Yarrington. John Hurlbut was chosen Moderator.

Voted—That John Hurlbut, Esq., Col. Nathan Denison, John Franklin, Esq., James Nesbitt, and Jabez Sill, be Selectmen for the year ensuing. A town clerk, treasurer, constable, surveyors of highways, fence-viewers, listers, collectors, leather-sealer, grand jurymen, etc. etc., were duly chosen. The fewness of inhabitants may be inferred from the fact, that James Nesbitt and Jabez Sill, were each chosen to three offices, and several others were voted in to the duties and honours of two. But the occasion was one of comparative cheerfulness. Winter had set in—snow had fallen—the enemy, kept at a respectful distance by the spirited conduct of Hammond, Bennett, Van Campen, Rogers and Pike, would not be likely, it was thought, soon to return. With frost, sickness had ceased; and Forseman's arrival with a supply of cattle, dissipated all fears of suffering from famine. These pleasing dreams of security were destined to be of brief duration. The very next day, December 6th, a party of the enemy, consisting of nineteen white men, and five Indians, under the command of Lieut. Turney, of John Butler's Rangers, broke into the settlement at Shawney, surprised and took off seven men prisoners, namely, Benjamin Harvey, Elisha Harvey, Nathan Bullock, James Frisbee, Jonathan Frisbee, Manassah Cady, and Samuel Palmer Ransom, highly respectable citizens. No lives were taken, and the party instantly retreated with their captives, and what plunder they could readily seize, marching with the greatest celerity. Capt. Franklin, with twenty-six men, pursued, the next morning, crossing the Susquehanna at Secord's, three miles above Tunkhannock; but the enemy were so far in advance, as to render further pursuit hopeless; and taking the canoes they had descended the river with and abandoned, Capt. Franklin returned to the fort. The facility of attacking Wyoming is here again illustrated. Scooping out a pine log into a canoe, the Indians could descend the river in twelve or fifteen hours, to within eighteen or twenty miles of the settlement. The easy mode of descent was in itself alluring, and tended greatly to the insecurity of the inhabitants.

One of Turney's men proved a traitor, if he did not come in as a spy, which is quite as probable. On the evening of the 11th, Col. Butler examined the deserter in the presence of Capt. Franklin.

The fellow said there were six hundred British troops at Niagara, and two thousand Indians. If he did not mean to exaggerate, to prevent Niagara being attacked, he must in both estimates have included women and children. He also stated that in October the Ontario, a new twenty gun ship, was lost in a gale of wind, and three hundred and fifty men, of the 34th British regiment, perished in her.

In several previous letters I have spoken of the vast numbers of the delicious shad that every Spring ascended the Susquehanna, attaining, from change of food and the salt sea for the fresh river water, their highest excellence. The picture of old times would be incomplete, were we to omit noting the immense quantity of eels taken in the Fall of the year, descending the river.

A wear was set in the stream, at Monockasy Island; the returns from which, for the last of September and the beginning of October, 1780, are before me. It would seem, a part of the time, the wear was visited but once in three days.

Friday, Sept.	15	they took	90	18 they took 178
	21		640	24 1888
	29		2800	30 1200
Oct.	1		1900	2 1400
	3		2100	4 1000
	5		500	6 250
	7		396	8 160
			8426	6076*

making upwards of fourteen thousand.

Thus the year 1780 passed in constant alarm, scouting and watchfulness. Several valuable lives had been lost. Many estimable citizens had been torn from their families and homes, and taken into captivity. Still hope, which "springs eternal in the human breast," was buoyant. Courage stimulated the settlers to action. Fortitude nerved their hearts to endure. Treacherous despair was allowed no lodgement in a single bosom. Matters must mend; it was impossible they could be worse. Congress would not be insensible to

---

* The greatness of the number will strike every reader with surprise. From Col. Franklin's Journal, the statement is carefully copied. No possible motive can be conceived for an erroneous entry.

their merits and sufferings. Connecticut, their parent State, who had planted them in the wilderness for noble objects, would not, could not be unmindful how much Westmoreland had done! How many men had been furnished to her line of the army! How much in taxes her treasury had, in time of pressing need, drawn from the exhausted people of Wyoming. Cheered and sustained by such reflections, especially after the noble resolve of the last Assembly, looking to indemnification, the year 1780 closed its sad and eventful term.

LETTER XXI.

1781-2.——The weather—Chorus—Indians attack Ransom's house—Marriage—Distant cannonading—Losses by the enemy—Assessments—Extreme poverty—Men killed below—Alarm—Capt. Spalding's company withdrawn, and Capt. Mitchell's substituted—Obvious policy—Indians renew their attacks—Rosewell Franklin—Priest Johnson—Bloody tragedy at Larned's—Capt. Bidlack's return—Representatives to Assembly—Courts of Law—Legal proceedings—Spirit of Blue Laws—Curious trial, Ayres, vs. Wolcott—Scene of deepest woe—Marriages—Hugh Forseman, Esq.—Murder of John Jameson and Asa Chapman—Touching incidents—Surrender of Cornwallis—Dawn of peace—Trial at Trenton—Jurisdiction of Connecticut ceases.

In this letter I propose to include the incidents of 1781-82. The winter of 1780-1, passed without any event worthy of particular record. The weather was exceedingly fluctuating and unsettled. January was so open, that Franklin, in his minute journal, speaks of the 1st being warm; the 2nd, 3rd, and 4th, as warm and muggy; the 5th, as warm and pleasant; and the fact is thought of sufficient note to be recorded, that in the night it froze. Early the preceding December the river was closed with ice for a day or two, but soon opened, and the 23rd, 24th, and 25th of that month, are spoken of as warm and pleasant. Singing meetings, called in the language of the day, " a Chorus," were the amusements of the evening—thus: " Monday, January 1st, a chorus at Mr. Ryan's."

On the 10th of March, the Savages made an attack on Samuel Ransom's house, in Plymouth, wounding him, though not severely. A spirited resistance was made, and one Indian left dead on the field.

At Plymouth, Shawney, (or more properly, and far more sweetly, *Chuanois*) the possession had been kept up. At the commencement of the war, the proprietors, forseeing danger, and the whole settlement being desirous that those beautiful, and productive alluvial lands, consisting of a thousand acres of the richest river bottoms, should not be entirely neglected, and run to waste

> "Wanting the scythe, all uncorrected, rank,
> ———— Where nothing teems
> But hateful dock, rough thistles,
> Losing both beauty and utility,"

they made an agreement with several persons to give them the use of all the land they could cultivate during the war, if they would build block-houses of sufficient strength to defend it and keep possession. Among those who associated for the purpose, were Major Prince Alden, Alexander Jameson, Joseph Jameson, Abraham Nesbitt, Jonah Rogers, Samuel Ayers, Mr. Ransom, and others. Except at the general expulsion after the massacre in 1778, the lessees, some of whom were proprietors, held their ground; attacked, defending themselves, fighting, suffering, they still maintained their position. Little, very little, were they able to farm, as less than two hundred acres were cultivated in 1781, in the whole Valley.

On Sunday the 18th January, Joseph Kinney and Sarah Spalding were called off, that is, the banns were published, and on Thursday the 22nd married. It was an occasion of unusual festivity and joy. The bride was the eldest daughter of Capt. Simon Spalding, the gallant commander of the Connecticut Independent Company. [Mr. Kinney* was a learned and accomplished gentleman, of a peculiarly philosophic turn of mind. He settled at Sheshequin, and had a large family. One of his sons represented Bradford county for several years in the Assembly. Recently, at the advanced age of eighty-four, he resigned his spirit to his Maker, and his body to its parent earth. I well remember the spirit, and ingenuity, with which he used to controvert the theory that the Sun was a ball of fire. He scouted the idea that it was perpetually wasting itself by combustion; or if it was fire, that its heat could be radiated to give effective warmth to the distant planets.]

It may, by the curious, be regarded as sufficiently remarkable to deserve preservation, that during the war, heavy cannonadings were heard at Wyoming, proceeding, as was supposed, from the forts on the sea board, or fleets near the coast. On the 28th of March,

---

* Brother of Newcome Kinney, known in 1785 as the popular writing and schoolmaster of Norwich, afterwards member of Assembly, and it is believed, now (1845) living in that city.

Chambers' Mills on the Delaware were attacked, and Joshua Farnham slain.

During the spring several meetings were holden by the Commissioners, under authority of the resolve of the General Assembly of the preceding year, to take an account of losses by the enemy, preparatory to making compensation. Whether a return was made to the Legislature is not known. It is presumed not, from the fact that the settlement was so broken, and the remnants of families so scattered, that it would have been impossible to obtain returns approaching to accuracy. Among Col. Butler's papers was found a memorandum of his loss, amounting to three hundred eighty-seven pounds. John Jenkins, Esq., by a memorandum made by his son, claimed £598 1s. 3d. Several other partial lists have been found among the papers of the old settlers. As the real extent of loss cannot be ascertained, the mode of approximating nearest to the truth seems to be to take the assessment, made under oath, of the year before the massacre, and comparing it with those taken after the battle.

In 1776, Westmoreland was assessed £16,996 13s.

In 1778, returned the January previous to the massacre, 20,322 pounds, 17 shillings.

November, 1780, the first assessment after the battle, 2,353 pounds; showing a diminution or loss, of 17,960 pounds, 17 shillings, or in dollars, 59,899.

The assessment of 1781, though larger than that of the preceding year, we here record, it having been found entire, as a document illustrating, with singular clearness, the utter destitution of the settlement, three years before flourishing in palmy prosperity and gladness.

"A true list of the Polls, and estate of the Town of Westmoreland, rateable by law, the 20th of August 1781.

114 male polls from 21 to 70, not especially exempted, at 18 pounds each, ... £18 00 00		£2,052 00 00
26 male polls, from 16 to 21, at . 9 00 00		234 00 00
45 oxen, four years old and upwards, 4 00 00		180 00 00
208 cows, three years old and upwards, 3 00 00		642 00 00
14 steers three years old, . . 3 00 00		42 00 00
18 steers and heifers two years old, 2 00 00		36 00 00
57 steers and heifers one years old, 1 00 00		57 00 00
Amount carried forward,		£3,243 00 00

Amount brought forward,		£3,243 00 00
173 horse kind, 3 years old and upwards	3 00 00	519 00 00
4 horse kind, two years old,	2 00 00	8 00 00
7 horse kind, one year old,	1 00 00	7 00 00
127 swine, one year old and upwards,	1 00 00	127 00 00
191½ acres of upland, mowing and clear pasture, at	08 08	76 12 00
95 acres bush pasture, at	02 00	9 10 00
2 silver watches, at	1 10 00	3 00 00

Assessment, traders and tradesmen.

Hollenback and Hageman, merchants,	£50 00 00	
Benjamin Bailey, blacksmith,	15 00 00	
Capt. John Franklin, one silver watch,	1 10 00	
Sarah Durkee, do. do.	1 10 00	
		68 00 00
Total,		£4,534 17 00
If from this we deduct the Polls		2,286 00 00
There will remain		£2,248 17 00

or in dollars, $7,496 17 !

Rumours of Indians on all sides of the settlement were rife. Lieut. Buck, from Sunbury, brought news that Capt. Campbell, Capt. Champlain and two other men, were killed or taken prisoners on the West Branch; that on the 8th of April, Mr. Dunn was killed, and Captain Solomon taken near Fort Augusta. A family was also taken near Fort Allen, and another near Brinkers. On the 28th of the month, orders were received that Capt. Spalding's company should march to camp. Earlier in the year, Capt. Michael had been directed to assume the command at Wyoming, in place of Colonel Butler, both movements being of deeper import than ordinary military regulations. The very natural, (perhaps very proper) certainly never sleeping jealousy of Pennsylvania, gloomy as was the hour, yet confident, since France had entered zealously into the contest, of ultimate independence, could not see Wyoming supported by a military force so hostile to her interests, and sought successfully to have the Connecticut troops withdrawn, and replaced by those in whose favour and fidelity the State could rely.

On Sunday, the 9th of June, a party of twelve Indians made an attack on a block-house at Buttonwood, in Hanover, three miles below the Wilkesbarre Fort. They met with a warm reception. The house was gallantly defended, the women aiding the men with alacrity and spirit. A party from the fort, on receiving the alarm, hastened down and found pools of blood, where Lieut. Rosewell Franklin had wounded, probably killed, an Indian. A terrible revenge followed. Scouts constantly on the alert, one going out as another returned, ascended the river from fifty to eighty miles, and sought the enemy in every direction. On Tuesday the 14th, Lieut. Crain shot at and wounded an Indian, within six hundred yards of the garrison. The Rev. Mr. Johnson, now returned with his family from their exile to Connecticut, having been compelled to fly after the massacre in 1778. Glowing with ardour for religion, liberty and the Connecticut claim, the return was welcomed by his flock, indeed by the whole settlement, with cordial congratulations. Sunday the 17th, he preached, and thenceforward "in season and out of season," he went from place to place, awakening sinners to repentance, arousing the people to new efforts, and sacrifices against the tyranny of England, and exhorting them by all means to adhere to, and support their righteous claim to their lands. But the cup of joy in coming to his devoted people, was almost immediately dashed from his lips by the death of Mrs. Butler, his daughter, consort of Col. Z. Butler. She died on the 26th of June, of typhus fever, and was buried the following day. The year, like the preceding, was extremely sickly, and more mortal; typhus fever being added to the remittent and intermittent, which had previously prevailed. A servant of Capt. Michael fell dead in the fort. A son of the late Capt. Durkee bled to death from the nose.

A party of Indians made their appearance at Shehola, and on the 17th of June killed an old man, and took three prisoners, on the Delaware. Pursuit being made, the prisoners were liberated, and one Indian mortally wounded, the American party having a man severely shot in the thigh. The Indian, before dying, said they had been long out, and were the party that had attacked the block-house at Hanover.

On the 3d of July, a bloody and most melancholy tragedy was enacted on the road leading from Wyoming to the Delaware, at Stroudsburg. Mr. Larned, an aged man, and his son George, were shot and scalped near their house. Another son, John, shot an Indian, who was left dead on the spot where he fell. The savages carried off George Larned's wife, and an infant four months old, but not choosing to be encumbered with the child, they dashed out its brains. Being pursued, they abandoned the horses and plunder taken, and left the old man's scalp behind them. Larned's was the scene of another tragedy several years afterwards, which, in due time, we shall record.

July 19th, Capt. Franklin says: "A cannonading has been heard for several days, and appears to be about New York." That the sound could travel so far over the ocean, would not seem strange, but considering the broken country, the deep forests, especially the high intervening Kittatiny mountain, may it not be regarded as extraordinary?

In the autumn, the settlement was surprised and gratified by the return of the aged Captain James Bidlack, and Mr. Harvey, also advanced in years, two of the prisoners taken from Shawney the preceding December. They had been liberated on parole by the British at Niagara.

As usual, the bustling and social town meetings, were "legally warned," and frequently holden. Capt. John Franklin and Obadiah Gore, were chosen representatives to the Assembly, that was to sit in October. A petition was agreed upon to be presented for an abatement of taxes, in consequence of the distressed state of the inhabitants; and it is honorable to the Assembly, that they remitted the taxes for the year.* But a town tax was agreed to be raised, and the County Court on proper representations made, issued their writ, (the town meeting having no authority to do so,) for its collection. Legal gentlemen who may honour these pages with a perusal, indeed other intelligent men may be pleased to look in upon the bench, see its organization, and note briefly their Honours proceedings.

---

* The severe and simple character of the times and people, is beautifully illustrated by two or three entries in John Franklin's Journal. He repaired to the Assembly at Hartford, debated with zeal, if not eloquently; returned November 10th, and immediately sat as one of the Justices of the Quorum as Judge of the County Court. "November 21st, Wednesday, thrashed wheat for Scott. Thursday thrashing wheat, and not long afterwards, dressed flax for Capt. Fuller." An example which, if generally followed, would ensure the perpetuation of liberty and prosperity.

"At a County Court, holden within and for the county of Westmoreland, etc.

Present,   NATHAN DENISON, ESQ., Judge.

JOHN FRANKLIN, ESQ.   } Justices
HUGH FORSEMAN, ESQ., } of
ABEL PIERCE, ESQ.,   } Quorum.

JONATHAN FITCH, ESQ., Sheriff.

"*Westmoreland County Court*, ss.,
Nov. Term, 1781.

Ordered—That there be a tax granted upon the List of 1781, on the inhabitants of Westmoreland, of two pence in the pound, to be paid by the first of January, 1782, either in hard money, or in specific articles, at the following prices: viz. wheat, at four shillings (Connecticut currency, sixty-seven cents.) Rye, at three shillings. Corn, at two shillings. Flax, at nine pence per pound.

The above specific articles to be delivered at the County Treasury."

"*Westmoreland County Court*, ss.,
Nov. Term, 1781.

Upon the memorial of Abigail Hadden, of said Westmoreland, praying for a Bill of Divorcement from Simeon Hadden, her husband, as per memorial, on file, which facts, in said petition, being sufficiently supported,

Therefore, Ordered, by the Court that the marriage of the said Simeon Hadden and Abigail, his wife, be declared null and void, and she is hereby declared single and unmarried."

In an action of Felony. In this case, the jury find that the Defendant is guilty, in manner and form, as the Plaintiff in his declaration hath alleged; therefore, find for the Plaintiff the sum of six shillings lawful money, damages, and his costs.

	£	s.	d.	
Damages,	0	6	0	
Costs Taxed,	5	18	6	Execution granted July 25, 1782.
	6	4	6	

As not a single lawyer remained, Dana and Bullock having been slain in the battle, where their courage and spirit of patriotism led them; although by law exempted from militia duty, and the Court having appointed Lieut. John Jenkins States-Attorney, and authorized either party to plead his own cause, or avail himself of the aid of any other person, in whose wisdom he could confide, it would seem probable that the technicalities of the law may have been not unfrequently violated; but it is believed that substantial justice was awarded by the Court. Disjointed as were the times; aroused as were the passions, and unloosed as moral ties generally are, during the prevalence of war, it is a just and a pleasing tribute to Wyoming, that neither tradition, the court records, nor any memorandum found, disclosed a single crime that deserves the character of heinous. There never was a record for the same number of years less stained with guilt, its pages more pure and free from the taint of malignity and corruption.

"*Jabez Sill* vs. *Susannah Reynolds.*

In action on Plea of Trespass, committed on a third division lot, in the District of Wilkesbarre, No. 33, demanding damages, etc. Upon which the Defendant set up title in the following manner:— That her late husband, Mr. Christopher Reynolds, (killed in the battle,) was the original proprietor of said lot. That he was lawfully seized and possessed of the same, at the time of his death. It appeared to the Court, that previous to administration being taken on said estate, Mr. Thomas Parke sold the lot aforesaid, and by sundry conveyances came into the hands of the Plaintiff. Whereupon the Court were of opinion, the Defendant is not guilty of the charge, therefore find for the Defendant her costs. It also appears at the investigation of the cause before the Court, that the property of the aforesaid thirty-third lot, in the third division of the District of Wilkesbarre, is in the Defendant (as being the relict of the said Christopher Reynolds, deceased,) and his children.

Costs taxed at six shillings."

It would seem that this was not a jury trial. In numerous instances, the jurors are named as part of the record. On one occasion, a special County Court was called at the instance of the Plaintiff, and a fellow promptly convicted of stealing an ox belonging to the public stores.

From the general character of fairness in the judicial proceedings, we find but two exceptions. The first; but let the Record speak for itself.

"*Westmoreland County*, Dec. 28th, 1782.

Mary Pritchard is found guilty of unnecessarily going from her place of abode, on the Lord's Day, on the 10th of November last:

Therefore, Ordered, that she pay a fine of five shillings, lawful money, to the Treasury of the Town of Westmoreland, and cost.

JOHN FRANKLIN, Justice of the Peace."

The other being also a trial not by the County Court and jury, but before a single Justice. We copy from the Justice's Docket.

"Samuel Ayres vs. John Wolcott.

At a Justice's Court, holden at Westmoreland, Dec. 26th, 1782, Present, John Franklin, Justice of the Peace, wherein John Wolcott, a transient person is brought before the said Court, by virtue of an advertisement put forth by Samuel Ayres, of said Westmoreland, wherein the said John Wolcott is accused of feloniously taking a buckskin from the said Samuel Ayres, about the 30th of November last, of the value of nineteen shillings, lawful money.

The delinquent pleads not guilty. The Court, on examining the delinquent, and hearing the evidence, and after taking the case into consideration, are of the opinion that the said John Wolcott is guilty of feloniously taking a buckskin from the said Samuel Ayres, of the value of nineteen shillings, lawful money.

Therefore Ordered, that the said Wolcott forfeit and pay to the said Samuel Ayres, the sum of nineteen shillings, lawful money, with the treble damages, as the law directs, together with costs. And also pay a fine to the Treasury of the Town of Westmoreland, of the sum of fifteen shillings, lawful money, or receive ten stripes upon the naked body.

	£	s.	d.
Bill of Costs, taxed at £10.			
Costs: viz. Reward of Advertisement,	0	18	00
Lieut. Ransom, pursuit to Juniata, and bringing back the delinquent,	2	04	10
Expenses, and a horse for the journey,	4	06	00
Hiring a man to assist,	1	10	00
Plaintiff look after delinquent,	0	06	00
Plaintiff, two days attendance,	0	03	00
Officers' Fees,	0	01	08
Two Evidences,	0	04	00
Subpœna,	0	00	06
Court Fees, Assignment and Indenture,	0	06	00
	£10	00	00

Whereas the above named John Wolcott, is unable to make restitution, or to pay the threefold damages and costs, it being the sum of £12 17s. in the whole: Therefore, Ordered, by said Court, that the said John Wolcott *be assigned in service to the said Samuel Ayres, for the sum of two full years* from this date, to be disposed of in service to any of the subjects of the United States. December 31, 1782. JOHN FRANKLIN, Justice of the Peace."

The whole proceedings bear the impress of extreme severity, at variance with the generally mild and equitable dispensation of the law. Sixty years, to be sure, have wrought a great alteration in our notions of justice, and public sentiment could now but ill endure what then was regarded as entirely proper. The pursuit of Wolcott to Juniata, an hundred miles, for so small an affair as a deerskin, worth perhaps a dollar, appears not a little singular. If nothing existed more than appears on the Record, we might be led to suppose that the spirit of the far-famed Connecticut Blue Laws was not yet entirely extinct. This was the last but two decisions before the jurisdiction of Wyoming was severed from Connecticut. At Trenton, the court had been in session two months. Their decision was anticipated, and indeed was rendered about the time of the trial of Wolcott. Whether he was regarded as an emissary of the Pennsylvania landholders, and the binding him out for two years was deemed the surest way to get rid of him, knowing, of course, he would run away, we cannot aver, but deem it probable, as the most charitable conclusion. We return back to our narrative, 1781.

On Friday the 7th of September, a band of Indians made an attack on the Hanover setttlement, and took off Arnold Franklin, and Rosewell Franklin, Jr., the sons of Lieut. Franklin, who had shot an Indian the preceding June. Several horses were stolen, and much grain, in stack, consumed by fire. Capt. Michael, with a detachment of men, went in pursuit; but the enemy eluded his vigilance. Perhaps the narrative of Lieut. Rosewell Franklin may be most properly concluded here, although events that subsequently occurred be anticipated.

A more distressing tragedy scarcely crimsons the page of history. In April following, Sunday the 7th, 1782, the Indians, still burning with rage, and intent on vengeance, rushed into Lieut. Franklin's house, and took off his wife and their four remaining children, one an infant, set fire to the building, which, with the furniture not plundered, was consumed to ashes. Parties went immediately in pursuit. Serjeant Thomas Baldwin, (Joseph Elliott second in command,) led seven determined men, with great celerity, taking an unfrequented course to head the Savages. Arrived at Wyalusing, near sixty miles, they were satisfied, by examining the fording place, that the Indians had not crossed the stream. Pushing on till they came to the mountain, nearly opposite Asylum, a slight breast-work was thrown up, and arrangements made to receive the enemy. Every precaution had been taken to conceal the defence by setting up bushes in front; but the wary chief, on approaching, discovered the snare, changed the route of his party, leaving the path, and attempted to ascend the hill, and pass our men, fifty or sixty rods more easterly. The attack was instantly commenced, a mutual fire was opened, and continued for some time with spirit, and yet with caution; the Indians being desirous to get off with their prisoners and plunder; the pursuing party being afraid of hurting Mrs. Franklin and the children. In the midst of the firing, the two little girls and the boy sprung from their captors, and found refuge with their friends! Instantly the Savages shot Mrs. Franklin and retreated; the chief, either to preserve the infant prisoner as a trophy, or to save himself from being a mark for the American rifles, raised the babe on his shoulder, and thus bearing her aloft, fled. Having recovered three of the children, and seeing the bleeding remains of the mother, the Yankees suspended pursuit. Mrs. Franklin was buried decently as circumstances permitted, and the children brought safely to Wyoming, where they arrived on the 16th. Two of the men, Serjeant Baldwin and Oliver Bennet, were wounded, the former severely, by the enemy's fire. The vigorous pursuit and spirited action were worthy of emphatic commendation.

 It would almost seem as if a fell spirit pursued the fortunes of Lieut. Franklin. He was a worthy man, of decided courage; in the battle, as ensign in Capt. McKarrican's company, having behaved with spirit. Enterprising and industrious, yet nothing prospered under his hand. When the troubles with Pennsylvania, after the war, were renewed at Wyoming, he sought repose from the long conflicts he had been engaged in, by removing with his family into the Genesee country, where he settled without title; the lands there being in controversy between Massachusetts and New York. After two years of arduous labour, winter approached and found his cellar stored and his granaries full, the product of a fruitful soil, and unremitted industry. A ray of gladness broke in on his dwelling, and " Hope and Pleasure smiled." Gov. Clinton had bided his time, and seizing the moment when his measures could not fail to be effective, veiling all the feelings of humanity, suppressing all the kindlier sympathies of our nature, under the pretence or plea of public policy, he sent a band of men, early in winter, into the Genesee country, to destroy the settlements making there. Every habitation was burnt, the improvements laid waste, and all the grain consumed by fire. Lieut. Franklin looked around him a moment on this new scene of desolation and woe, in utter despair; seized his rifle and put an end to his existence.

We must be allowed to relieve the gloom thrown around our pages, by the melancholy fate of the unfortunate Franklin,

> "And cause the sable cloud
> Turn forth her silver lining on the night."

The winter was cheered by several marriages of persons eminent in the Valley. Lieut. Lawrence Myers was married to Miss Sarah Gore, January 3rd, 1782. She, of the patriotic family that sent five brothers and two brothers-in-law into the battle. That she was very handsome cannot be doubted, for in 1837, then eighty years of age, the round face, regular features, and pleasing expression told of remarkable youthful beauty. [Lieut. Myers was of a German family from Frederick town, Maryland. Robust in early manhood, he became corpulent with advancing age, and presented a singular contrast with the spare forms of the Yankees, worn down by exertion and care.* But he was ever a favorite. His large round face seemed radiant with benevolence and cheerfulness. Besides several offices in the militia, he was for thirty years a magistrate, and in 1800, Commissioner of the county. The plan of the Court House, a cross, was introduced by him, taken from that at Fredericktown; which doubtless owed its origin to the Roman Catholic settlers of Maryland, under their liberal and tolerant founder, though that it was an emblem of Catholicism, or had any Christian allusion, was probably unknown to Mr. Myers, or those in Luzerne who approved thereof. The delight of his life was to talk of Frederick, and any thing that existed or came from there was an object of his special regard. Owning one of the noblest plantations on the Kingston flats, adjoining the Plymouth line, though he did not personally labour, he caused it to be highly cultivated, the produce of which

---

* I might almost say, if the Yankees would forgive me, he appeared a picture of plenty surrounded by famine.

yielded a liberal support. The ancient people are still pleased to tell of his almost daily crossing the river to Wilkesbarre, accompanied by the little shaggy water dog, spotted black and white, his unfailing attendant, running by his master's side, or sitting by his feet. If perchance the ferry-boat put off from shore without him, the dog would seem to measure the distance with mathematical precision, run up the river so far that the stream should not take him below the landing place, plunge in and swim over. In winter, the large and elegant cloth cloak, in those early days an article of dress too fine and costly not to be rare, gave to his noble person an imposing appearance. He died of dropsy, aged about fifty years, leaving, as he had no children, his fine estate to Mrs. Myers and his two brothers. In times of high excitement, from Washington's administration onward to the time of his decease, " Esquire Myers," which was the usual designation, was a zealous Federalist, but too liberal and kind to cherish a particle of ill will against his opponents. The fact is the rather noted, because it is believed he was the only one of the name who did not entertain different sentiments, and because his name and character for several years gave that party great influence, aiding to preserve it in the ascendancy. But this is a digression.]

Sunday, the 17th of February, 1782, Hugh Forseman, Esq., and Judith Slocum were called off; and on the succeeding Sunday, viz. the 24th, were married. Miss Slocum was the sister of the lost Frances, and daughter of Mr. Jonathan Slocum, who, with Mr. Tripp, was so audaciously murdered by the Indians in sight of the fort, three years previously. [Mr. Forseman we have seen as Justice of the Peace, and sitting as one of the Justices of Quorum in the County Court. A man of business and probity, few shared more highly the general confidence. As Clerk of the Town, his writing is singularly neat and accurate. To his care we are indebted that the old Westmoreland Records were preserved. Mr. Forseman was from Ireland, where a lease of considerable value depended on his life. The lessee being accustomed annually to send him a piece of fine linen, his receipt therefore being the proof that he was still alive.]

As shadows and sunshine chase each other over the plain, so do the events of our narrative alternate.

On Sunday, the 10th of March, the good deacon John Hurlbut departed this life; a life full of respect and usefulness. The confidence reposed in him, is attested by his having been, when, from the distressed state of the country, the sagest men for wisdom, and the brightest in virtue, were required for public trusts, three times chosen member of Assembly, besides fulfilling other offices of lesser note. If he did not live to enjoy the repose and prosperity that resulted from his labours, it is pleasing to be able to record that a son of his, Napthali Hurlbut, Esq., was in after days honoured by the citizens of Luzerne with the office of High Sheriff of the county.

A lad was murdered by the Indians near Bunkers, on Saturday, the 1st of June, 1782.

Hanover was the scene of another bloody deed on Monday, the 8th of July. John Jameson, and a lad, his brother, accompanied by Asa Chapman, were riding up from Nanticoke, their residence near (now) Lee's Mills, intending to go to Wilkesbarre. As they came opposite the Hanover meeting house, Jameson exclaimed, "there are Indians." Before he could turn his horse he received three rifle balls, and fell dead to the earth. Chapman being behind him, had time to draw the rein and turn, but was instantly wounded. Clinging to the saddle, the frighted horse bore him beyond their reach. The lad being in the rear, escaped. Chapman lingered several hours, sent for his wife, and took an affectionate leave of her. Capt. Franklin cut out the ball, but it had done its office, and he presently expired.

On the 26th of the month, a man, a woman, and two children, were killed near Catawissa, thirty miles below Wyoming.

Saturday the 27th.—The gloomy monotony of war was broken, and the settlement cheered by the return of George Palmer Ransom, one of the seven prisoners taken in December 1780. A young man full of courage and ardour, he could not brook confinement, made his escape encountering great hardships. The events of his captivity and return, will furnish an interesting page in our chapter of personal narratives. We have the satisfaction to say, that as I write, (April 20, 1845,) Col. Ransom still lives.

Saturday the 12th.—Daniel McDowal was taken prisoner at Shawney, and carried to Niagara. He was son of the benevolent Scotch gentleman at Stroudsburg, who, as we have previously seen, befriended with such disinterested and untiring perseverance, the Yankee settlers in their first efforts to establish themselves at Wyoming. He was the father of Mrs. McKean, wife of Gen. Samuel McKean, of Bradford county, recently United States Senator.

Imperfectly protected, constantly harrassed, wounded, bleeding at every pore, Capt. Spalding and the Wyoming Independent Company, consisting of nearly all the remaining able bodied men of the town, cruelly drawn away below the mountains, the handful of people remaining, in town meeting, with a fortitude and devotion never surpassed, still struggled for existence. In April voted,—" That the town treasurer be desired to grind up so much of the public wheat, (received for taxes,) as to make two hundred pounds of biscuit, and keep it made, and so deposited, as that the necessary scouts may instantly be supplied from time to time as occasion requires."

And subsequently, September the 10th,

" Voted—That Col. Nathan Denison be desired to send scouts up the river, as often and as far as he shall think it necessary, to discover the movements of the enemy; receiving his instructions from time to time, and to make immediate returns to him, as soon as they shall return back, and be subject to be examined under oath, touching their faithfulness; they to be found bread and ammunition, and be paid six shillings a day while in actual service, by this town. The selectmen to draw an order on the town treasurer for such sums, to be paid in produce at the market price.*

The ever memorable surrender of Lord Cornwallis had taken place on the 19th of October, 1781, which, in effect, decided the contest in favor of America and Independence. The Rev. Benjamin Bidlack and Nathan Beach, Esq., at that time young men in the prime of life, both from Wyoming, and both now living here, each having numbered more than four score years, were present at the capitulation.

General Conway, on the 27th of February, 1782, moved in the House of Commons: " That it is the opinion of this House, that a further prosecution of offensive war against America, would, under present circumstances, be the means of weakening the efforts of this country against her European enemies, and tend to increase the

---

* As has been previously explained, the town of Westmoreland, as laid off by Connecticut, and held under her jurisdiction, extended a degree of latitude on the Delaware, thence the present dividing line between New York and Pennsylvania, being the northern boundary, stretching west many miles beyond the Susquehanna. There were two distinct settlements proper—the main one in and about Wyoming Valley; the other, highly respectable, and for a time flourishing, on the Lackawaxen, which flows into the Delaware, called in the old records the Lackawa settlement. In respect to this second portion of Westmoreland, our narrative has but slightly adverted; and the writer is indebted for the extremely well written account, which will be found in a subsequent letter, to Warren J. Woodward, Esq., nephew of the Hon. George W. Woodward, President Judge of the 4th Judicial District, both of them natives of old "Lackawa." While I proffer my grateful acknowledgments for the aid thus afforded in throwing light on that part of the Wyoming history, I cannot withhold the expression of pride I feel in witnessing the deserved honours already won by descendants of one of the early settlers there.

mutual enmity so fatal to the interests both of Great Britain and America;" which was carried against the strenuous opposition of the ministry. On the 4th of March following, Parliament choosing to be more explicit, resolved, " That the house will consider as enemies to his Majesty and the country, all those who should advise, or attempt a further prosecution of offensive war on the continent of North America." An immediate change of ministry ensued, and negotiations for peace soon followed.

Although clouds still lowered, the thunder growled along the hills, and an occasional leven bolt burst in the Valley, yet the bow of promised peace, with its radiant hues, spanned the eastern sky, and awakened sweet hopes of security and rest.

The number of lives actually lost in Wyoming, during the war, it is impossible to estimate with certainty. Probably three hundred, being one in ten of every inhabitant, or exceeding one-third of the adult male population at the commencement of the war. Connecticut to have suffered in the same proportion, would have lost near twenty-three thousand, and the United Colonies three hundred thousand.

Almost immediately after Lord Cornwallis's surrender, the contest being regarded as virtually closed, that is, on the 3d of November, fifteen days after that event, a petition was presented to Congress, "from the Supreme Executive Council of Pennsylvania, stating a matter in dispute between the said State and the State of Connecticut, respecting sundry lands lying on the east branch of the river Susquehanna, and praying a hearing in the premises, agreeable to the ninth article of the Confederation."

Connecticut promptly met the overtures of Pennsylvania, and both parties during the winter made preparations for the trial. Preliminary proceedings were adopted early the following summer. On the 12th of August, 1782, the delegates from the two States announced, in a joint memorial to Congress, that they had mutually agreed on gentlemen to constitute the court:—the Hon. William Whipple, Esq., of New Hampshire; the Hon. Major-General Nathaniel Greene, of Rhode Island; the Hon. David Brearly, and William Churchill Houston, Esq., of New Jersey; the Hon. Cyrus Griffin, and Joseph Jones, Esq., of Virginia.

A subsequent communication August 23d, from the joint delegates, stated, it was ascertained that Gen. Greene and Hon. John Rutledge, (whose name does not previously appear on the journal,) could not attend, and substituting Hon. Welcome Arnold, of Rhode Island,

and Hon. Thomas Nelson, of Virginia; any five of whom to constitute a quorum.

Five commissioners, viz: Messrs. Whipple, Arnold, Houston, Griffin and Brearly, opened their court at Trenton, November 12, 1782. Messrs. William Bradford, Joseph Reed, James Wilson, and Jonathan D. Sergeant, appearing as counsel on behalf of Pennsylvania. Messrs. Eliphlet Dyer, William S. Johnson and Jesse Root, being the agents from Connecticut.

The court having declined to order notice to be given to the settlers at Wyoming, claiming the land—as the right of soil did not come before them; the question they were empowered to decide, being solely that of jurisdiction, the parties proceeded with their several allegations and pleas, and after a sitting of forty-one judicial days, viz: on Monday, December 30, 1782, gave their decision in these words:—

"We are unanimously of opinion that Connecticut has no right to the lands in controversy.

"We are also unanimously of opinion, that the jurisdiction and pre-emption of all the territory lying within the charter of Pennsylvania, and now claimed by the State of Connecticut, do of right belong to the State of Pennsylvania."

Clear, comprehensive, and explicit, Pennsylvania was satisfied, and Connecticut submitted without breathing a sigh for the loss of so noble a domain, the right to which she had so strenuously maintained, or a murmur at a decision which seemed to the surrounding world so extraordinary.

But as this trial, spoken of before in our examination of the titles of the two States, to Wyoming, will be found more fully treated of hereafter, we take leave of it, with this brief notice for the present.

With the close of the year 1782, and the Trenton decree, the jurisdiction of Connecticut, which had continued nine years, ceased; the cheerful and salutary town meetings were no longer holden, and we close the old parchment bound book with the most profound sentiments of respect, and with feelings of sincere regret, as if parting from a long cherished friend. A box of finely polished oak should be made for it; as the descendants of the old settlers may look back upon that humble volume, from seats of affluence or high places of power, centuries hence, with honest pride at the recorded transactions of their fathers.

LETTER XXII.

Being a chapter of great moment.

1782.——A paragraph of Retrospect—Opening of a very interesting matter—Eloquent Petition—Important Letter—Proceedings of Pennsylvania Assembly—A military force sent to Wyoming—Fort Dickinson—Negotiations—Joseph Montgomery—John Jenkins—Extraordinary proposition of compromise—Alexander Patterson—Rupture of negotiations—Consequent proceedings—Report of Commissioners to Assembly—Peace with Great Britain—Incidents—Settlers, broken-hearted, look out for a new home—"Act to stay suits"—Military preparations—Col. Butler returns from the army with his bride—Is arrested by Patterson, and sent to Sunbury jail—Major Prince Alden, Capt. James Bidlack, and Benjamin Harvey, arrested—Further arrests—Violent proceedings.

In the preceding Letters I have endeavored to give you a brief sketch of the Natives who formerly held dominion over Wyoming. Secondly, the origin and grounds of the controversy respecting jurisdiction and soil, that existed between Pennsylvania and Connecticut. Thirdly, the efforts to settle the country, and the accruing conflicts, known at the "old Pennymite and Yankee war." Fourthly, the events of the Revolutionary war, to its close, including the trial and decision at Trenton; the whole intermingled with civil and personal details, necessary to give you a perfect view of Wyoming as it then existed.

I now proceed to trace the further history of Wyoming, from 1782 to 1790, some portions of it of singular vicissitude and interest.

Immediately on the promulgation of the Trenton decree, we have seen that Connecticut withdrew her jurisdiction, and the county and town of Westmoreland ceased to exist, except as its memory was preserved in the records of the past.

An intimation has been suggested that the Trenton trial was not, in fact, what on its fair pages it purports to be, a bona fide examination, and impartial judgment upon a matter of right, in respect to territory and jurisdiction between the two states; but in fact, by a secret understanding and collusion, a legal form of transfer (something in the form of a common recovery) of the claim of Connecticut to Pennsylvania, within the limits of the Pennsylvania Charter, with the confidential understanding that Connecticut was to receive an equivalent, or indemnity, in the Western Reserve. As we proceed, facts that arise, bearing on that point, will be particularly noticed.

From the commencement of the war for Independence the Susquehanna Company had pretermitted their meetings, no one being found recorded from May 1774 to Nov. 13th, 1782, when, preparatory to the trial at Trenton, the Company were convened at Hartford, and appointed Messrs. Dyer, Root, and Johnson (who had been selected by the state to appear as counsel before the court), to act also as their agents, and those of the settlers. Surprised at the unlooked for decision, the Company seem darkly to have surmised that there was something behind the curtain not avowed, nor perfectly understood, and at a meeting holden at Hartford, May 21st, 1783, they appointed "Col. Talcott, Gen. Parsons, and Samuel Gray, a committee to lay a memorial before the General Assembly, in behalf of the Susquehanna Company, that the Assembly would desire Dr. Johnson and Col. Root, agents of this state, to give said Assembly an account of the trial of the cause between this state and the state of Pennsylvania, at the court holden at Trenton." It will be observed that of Col. Dyer, the other agent, no explanation is requested, as probably of him no suspicion existed. It is not known that the Assembly took any order on the petition.

The condition of the settlers was embarrassing and gloomy in the extreme. By a Resolution of Congress the Commander in Chief had been authorized, previous to the trial, to withdraw the garrison from Wyoming, Connecticut concurring. Their place was supplied, of course, by troops from Pennsylvania. A comparative handful remained, the broken remnants of the war; a great portion of those who had been expelled after the massacre, remaining in exile, especially the young men growing up to manhood, the natural hope and stay of the settlement, who being left orphans, had been bound out to mechanics and farmers, and whose time of apprenticeship had not yet expired. Thus situated they were advised to cast themselves at the feet of the Pennsylvania Government, and solicit protection, pardon and mercy. A petition was drawn up, in many points eloquent and touchingly pathetic, and signed by John Paul Schotts, Esq., with a number of the inhabitants, and presented to the Assembly, January 18th, 1783. Being but eighteen days after the

Trenton decree, the process of its drawing up, circulation, signature, transmission to the city, and presentation, exhibit a celerity that bears any impress rather than that of cool deliberation. The style is markedly peculiar. We pronounce with great confidence, from internal evidence, that it could not have been written in Wyoming. It exhibits in no particular the peculiar characteristics of the style, either of Franklin or Jenkins, the ready writers of the settlers. From all which we infer, that the petition was prepared below the mountains, probably by the Connecticut agents at Trenton, with the concurrence of those of Pennsylvania; its signature and presentation being hurried on without giving time to the inhabitants to recover from the shock produced by that highly politic, but nevertheless extraordinary decision.

In such a variety of aspects does the petition appear to warrant especial attention, that we publish it here entire, in preference to throwing it into the Appendix.

"*To the Honorable the Representatives of the freemen of the Commonwealth of Pennsylvania, in General Assembly met.*

" The memorial and address of Nathan Denison, Hugh Forseman, Obadiah Gore, Samuel Shephard and John Paul Schott, inhabitants, settlers, and proprietors of a territory of country situated on the waters of the Susquehanna river, under the claim of the State of Connecticut, on behalf of themselves and others of the inhabitants, settlers, etc., of the said country,"

" Most respectfully sheweth, That in the year 1754, a number of the inhabitants of Connecticut, finding all the lands eastward of the line of the State of New York settled and appropriated, proceeded to purchase of the Six Nations a large territory of country, extending from Delaware, westward, about one hundred and sixty miles, and in breadth, the whole forty-[second] degree of north latitude, and gave a valuable consideration, supposing, that without dispute, the aforesaid territory was included in the charter granted them by King Charles the Second, April 3d, 1662, and formed themselves into a company of proprietors, by the consent of the Legislature, and regulated by the laws of said State, and proceeded to locate the valuable lands situated on the eastern branch of the Susquehanna river, the full breadth of the forty-[second] degree, extending six miles east, and twenty miles west of said river. Having no apprehension that any royal grant covered the same, either previous or subsequent to the aforesaid Charter of Connecticut, they proceeded to plant themselves through said territory, and [cultivate] the same, among which number of settlers are your petitioners, and those whom they represent, in full confidence of the justice of our title, under Connecticut, with the most honest intentions, we uniformly maintained our supposed right, by opposing persons claiming under the Pennsylvania Proprietary, who frequently interrupted us in what we esteemed our lawful business. Constantly wishing for an absolute decision between the two States, concerning jurisdiction, we used every effort to expedite such decision, resolutely determined to maintain the title which we had acquired, until a more equitable one could be established. In the year 1763, and a number of successive years, appeals were made to the Crown, by one and the other State, for a final decision, which were yet depending when the commencement of the present war put a period to all appeals to the Crown. In the course of which appeals, the opinion of the Counsel, most eminent and learned in the law, was taken, who advised (as we apprehended,) fully in the favour of the claim of Connecticut. This greatly encouraged your Memorialists that they were right in supporting their claim.

"In 1774, the Legislature of the State of Connecticut asserted their claim, erected civil jurisdiction, and complete civil and military establishments according to the laws and usages of said State, which led your Memorialists into a greater confidence of their security under said State, and induced them to build houses and mills for their convenience, and to cultivate a country which we esteemed our own. Since that time, attempts have been made to dispossess us in a hostile manner, which the law of self preservation obliged us to oppose, in the course of which there were faults on both sides, which we hope may be cancelled and buried in oblivion.

"The right of jurisdiction was always esteemed important to the claiming State, and more especially to the settlers and tenants, who have ventured their all there, and who were combatting difficulties and dangers in every shape.

"After recourse to Great Britain was cut off, it was provided, that in all disputes concerning boundaries, jurisdiction, etc., the United States, in Congress, shall be the last resort and appeal. That judges be appointed to hear and determine the matter in question; and that the sentence of the Court be decisive between the parties. And also all controversies, the private right of soil being claimed under different grants of two or more States, etc.; said grants, etc., shall, on the petition of either party to the Congress of the United

States, be finally determined, as near as may be, pursuant to this provision. The Honorable Congress established a Court; both States were cited, and appeared; the cause was heard for more than forty days; the grounds stated on which each State asserted their right of jurisdiction. On which, the Court finally adjudged in favour of the State of Pennsylvania, by which the jurisdiction of the disputed territory, on which your Memorialists live, is adjudged yours. By this adjudication, we are under your jurisdiction and protection. We are subjects and free citizens of the State of Pennsylvania, and have to look up to your Honours as our fathers, guardians and protectors, entitled to every tender regard and respect, as to justice, equity, liberty and protection, on which we depend, and which we are warranted to do by the impartial treatment that all, even strangers have received, when once they became inhabitants and citizens of this great and flourishing State.

"Thus have we stated the grounds on which our title was established; which, though determined to be ill grounded by the honorable Court, appeared to be founded in the highest reason, we verily thought it our duty to do as we did. If we have committed faults, we pray for mercy and forgiveness. If we have deserved any thing, we hope something from the gratitude of our country. We have settled a country (in its original state,) but of little value, but now cultivated by your Memorialists, is to them of the greatest importance, being their all. We are yet alive, but the richest blood of our neighbours and friends, children, husbands and fathers, has been spilt in the general cause of their country, and we have suffered every danger this side death. We supplied the continental army with many valuable officers and soldiers, and left ourselves weak and unguarded against the attack of the Savages, and others of a more savage nature. Our houses are desolate—many mothers childless—widows and orphans multiplied—our habitations destroyed, and many families reduced to beggary, which exhibits a scene most pitiful and deserving of mercy. If the greatest misfortunes can demand pity and mercy, we greatly deserve them. That the country twenty-six miles in breadth, the length aforesaid, when compared with the extended territory of the State of Pennsylvania, is trifling indeed. That the present population is of far more consequence to this State than it could have been in an uncultivated state. We are yet entitled to another trial for our particular possessions, according to the ninth article of the Confederation, but reduced in every respect, we are unable to maintain a trial against an opulent State. We therefore present a request, which the laws of justice and policy suggest, and which the dictates of humanity demand.

"That your Honours of your abundant goodness and clemency, would be pleased to grant and confirm to your Memorialists, and those whom they represent, the inconsiderable part of the claim contested, extended as above, to be appurted [held?] as they were before the decision. Thus will you increase the inhabitants of this flourishing State, will add to its wealth and strength, will give joy to the widow and fatherless. Sure these must be irresistible motives to a just, generous and merciful Assembly. Our only resource is in your decision:—If that is unfavorable, we are reduced to desperation; unable to purchase the soil, we must leave our cultivations and possessions, and be thrown into the wide world, our children crying for bread, which we shall be unable to give them.

"It is impossible that the magnanimity of a powerful and opulent State will ever condescend to distress an innocent and brave people, that have unsuccessfully struggled against the ills of fortune. We care not under what State we live, if we can be protected and happy. We will serve you—we will promote your interests—will fight your battles; but in mercy, goodness, wisdom, justice, and every great and generous principle, do leave us our possessions, the dearest pledge of our brothers, children, and fathers, which their hands have cultivated, and their blood, spilt in the cause of their country, has enriched.

"We further pray, that a general act of *oblivion and indemnity* may be passed, and that Courts of Judicature be established according to the usages and customs of this State; that we be, not only a happy but a well organized and regulated people, and that all judicial proceedings of the prerogative courts, and the common law courts, held by, and under the authority of the State of Connecticut, be ratified and fully confirmed.

"And they, as in duty bound, will ever pray.

"JOHN PAUL SCHOTT.

"*Philadelphia, Jan'y* 18*th*, 1783."

Observation will be attracted, in the outset, by the full and accurate knowledge of the Connecticut title exhibited, dates as of King Charles the Second's Charter, granted "3d April, 1662," being so minutely correct. Moreover, the boundaries set forth being specifically accurate. Whether this does not indicate the pen of a lawyer, whose mind was imbued with the recent examination of the whole subject, or whether it reads like the setting forth of an unlettered, though strong-minded farmer, the reader will determine.

Furthermore, the petition says: " Thus have we stated the grounds on which *our* title was established, which though determined to be *ill grounded*, etc. Assuredly the *settlers* would not, could not, deliberately and understandingly declare, that the decision of jurisdiction pronounced *their* title " ill grounded." " If we have committed faults, we pray for mercy and forgiveness." Was this the style and tone proper for the brave and suffering Wyoming settlers to assume, who had defended the country through a seven years war, or that of conscious criminals?

Again: " If the greatest misfortunes can demand pity and mercy, we greatly deserve them."

Speaking of a trial, as provided under the ninth article of Confederation, they are made to say, " Reduced in every respect, we are unable to maintain a trial against an opulent State." " Our only resource is your decision; if that is unfavorable we are reduced to desperation. Unable to purchase the soil, *we must leave our possessions* and be thrown into the wide world, our children crying for bread." And again: They pray for an act " of oblivion and indemnity," as if they had been robbers, instead of being upright, hardy settlers, on property they honestly believed to be their own. Certainly if an understanding existed between the Agents of Pennsylvania and Connecticut, that, not only jurisdiction should be given up, but the Wyoming people abandoned to the mercy of the landholders; a course of proceeding could not have been adopted, and especially a petition framed to be signed by the settlers, more completely calculated to effect the dishonorable sacrifice. Bearing in mind, that in every other controversy, in this and in every other State, where lands were settled under claims from different States, the actual settlers were quieted in their possessions, it would seem that this benevolent principle, if not measure of justice, should have been unhesitatingly extended to the Wyoming people.

A paper, before adverted to, bearing on this point, is too important not to be noticed in this connexion: namely, the Letter of the Court, at Trenton, to the President and Executive Council of Pennsylvania. It will doubtless be regarded as extraordinary, that, for twelve years, this paper remained in the Secretary's Office, unnoticed and unknown beyond its walls. How much weight it was imagined the settlers would have derived from the letter, is attested by the scrupulous care with which its contents were concealed. In

1795, thirteen years afterwards, in the trial of Vanhorne vs. Dorrance, it was discovered and made public.

"Trenton, 31st Dec. 1782.

"Sir—We take the liberty to address your Excellency, as private citizens, lately honored with a commission to hear and determine the controversy between the States of Pennsylvania and Connecticut, relative to a dispute of territory. In the course of executing this commission, we have found that many persons are, or lately have been, settled on the land in question. Their individual claims could in no instance come before us, not being in the line of our appointment. We beg leave to declare to your Excellency, that we think the situation of these people well deserves the notice of government. The dispute has long subsisted. It may have produced heats and animosities among those living in or near the country in contest, and some imprudencies may take place, and draw after them the most unfavorable consequences. With all deference therefore, we would suggest to your Excellency and Council, whether it would not be best to adopt some reasonable measures to prevent any, the least disorder or misunderstanding among them, and to continue things in the present peaceable posture, until proper steps can be taken to decide the controversy respecting the private right of soil, in the mode prescribed by the Confederation. We doubt not an early proclamation from the Executive of Pennsylvania, would have all necessary good effect; and we feel ourselves happy in the fullest confidence that every means will be adopted, or acquiesed in by the State, to render the settlement of this dispute complete and satisfactory, as far as may be, to all concerned.

" We have the honour to be with great respect,
" Your Excellency's most obedient and humble servants,
Wm. Whipple,
Welcome Arnold,
W. C. Houston,
David Brearly,
Cyrus Griffin.

His Excellency
President Dickinson."

The explicit declaration that " their individual claims could in no instance come before us, not being in the line of our appointment ;" The suggestion that the settlers be permitted to remain in undisturbed possession, " until proper steps can be taken to decide the controversy respecting the private right of soil, in the mode prescribed by the confederation," evinces a lively sense of justice and humanity, and shows that the court, who, in the investigation, must have as thoroughly understood the parties' claims to the soil, as that of the States to jurisdiction, did not doubt the perfect right of the settlers at least to a trial.

Acting on the petition of the settlers, the Assembly declared that the persons now settled at Wyoming, yielding obedience to the laws, are undoubtedly entitled, in common with other citizens of this State, to protection, and the benefits of civil government.

"Therefore Resolved, That commissioners be appointed to make full inquiries into the cases respectively, and report to the House.

"That in order to make the inquiry effectual, the committee have authority to send for persons, papers and records.

"That they be instructed to confer with all or any of the claimants under Pennsylvania, of any land now in the possession of, or claimed under the State of Connecticut, by persons now being actual settlers, as well as with the said settlers, or any of them, and to endeavour as much as possible, by reasonable and friendly compromises between the parties claiming; and where this cannot be done, to consider of and report such plans of accommodation as may be most advisable for accomplishing an equitable and final adjustment of all difficulties.

"That as soon as may be, after the commissioners shall report, an act be passed providing fully for the cases of the inhabitants of the said country; more especially for the extending to them of the advantages of civil government, for authorizing and directing the choice of Justices of the Peace; for appointing places for holding their annual elections; for giving time for entering their slaves, if any, according to the spirit of the act for the gradual abolition of slavery; for consigning to oblivion all tumults and breaches of the peace, by whatsoever name they may be called, which have arisen out of the controversy between the colony, or State of Connecticut, and the said settlers on the one part, and the Province or State of Pennsylvania, and the inhabitants thereof, or any of them, on the other part; and for such other purposes as circumstances shall appear to require.

"That an act be immediately passed for staying proceedings at law, during said inquiry, against the settlers, for dispossessing them by writ of ejectment or otherwise, until this House shall decide upon the report, so to be made by the said commissioners.

"And as the guard of continental troops which has been stationed at Wyoming, is about to be withdrawn, it is necessary for the protection of the said settlement against the savages, to replace the guard immediately with the two companies of Rangers commanded by Captains Robinson and Shrawder."

In accordance with these resolves, an act was forthwith passed to stay the prosecution of suits against the settlers; and on the 25th of February, commissioners were appointed, consisting of Joseph Montgomery, William Montgomery, and Moses M'Clean.

Notwithstanding the recall of the continental guard, and the doubtful measure of sending Robinson and Shrawder's companies to Wilkesbarre, the proceedings were received at Wyoming by many with no little satisfaction; by the sanguine with joy; by a few with misgivings and distrust: for the two military companies, as the war with Great Britain was regarded at an end, and the danger of Indian incursions no longer existed, awakened the jealousy of the more sagacious old men, who remembered the invasion of Plunket, and who saw, or thought they saw, in this array, not protectors, but agents of a hostile interest experience had shown them they had great reason to dread. But the highly respectable names of the Montgomery's were pledges of honour and fairness, that on the whole inspired confidence, and hope of an honorable adjustment.

Prompt to obey orders, Robinson and Shrawder, with their respective companies, marched immediately to Wyoming, and took possession of the fort, which they named "Fort Dickinson," in honour of the President of the Supreme Executive Council.

On the 15th of April, the commisioners arrived at Wilkesbarre, where they were met, and welcomed by a committee of the settlers. It was a moment of intense, of painful anxiety. Negotiations were immediately opened by a letter from the committee. It is deemed proper to publish the whole correspondence, as necessary to a perfect understanding of the matter, and more especially as it was the prelude to re-opening the civil, or "Pennymite and Yankee war," which the revolutionary conflict had suspended.

"To the commissioners appointed by the Honorable Legislature of the Commonwealth of Pennsylvania, to inquire into the circumstances of the Wyoming inhabitants of said State.

"GENTLEMEN,—We are happy to find that the Legislative body of the State, have condescended to treat our late petition lying before them, with that coolness and candour, as to appoint commissioners to come and make full inquiry into our cases, and make report to the House. And as we shall think it our duty, straitly, strictly and truly, to adhere to our petition, and shall think ourselves happy to give every true information to any inquiries that shall be thought necessary further to be made respecting our settlements, etc.

  April 19th, 1783.   JOHN JENKINS,
            NATHAN DENISON,
 The Hon. Commissioners. OBADIAH GORE, } *Committee.*"
            SAMUEL SHEPHERD,

Letter from the Pennsylvania Commissioners to the Committee of Settlers:—

"GENTLEMEN,—As it is our duty, so we will with pleasure pay attention to every piece of necessary information with respect to your settlements at this place.

Although it cannot be supposed that Pennsylvania *will, nor can she consistent with her constitution by any ex-post facto law, deprive her citizens of any part of their property legally obtained;* yet, willing to do every thing in her power to promote the peace and happiness of her citizens, wishes to be informed fully of your case, that if your peaceable demeanour and ready submission to Government render you the proper objects of clemency and generosity, she may be prepared to extend it to you.

Therefore we wish you to communicate to us as speedily as possible, the names and numbers of those who first settled at Wyoming, who are now alive, and by whom those that are dead are represented.

The names and number of those now actual settlers here, the quantity of land they respectively occupy, and time they last came and settled at this place.

    Signed in behalf of the Commissioners,
     By your humble servant,
       JOSEPH MONTGOMERY, *Chairman.*"

JOHN JENKINS,
NATHAN DENISON,
OBADIAH GORE, } *Committee.*"
SAMUEL SHEPHERD,

Wyoming, April 19th, 1783.

The distinct declaration, "*It cannot be supposed that Pennsylvania will, nor can she consistent with her constitution, by any ex-post facto law, deprive her citizens of any portion of their property legally obtained, etc.,*" was perfectly comprehended. Expulsion, the entire abandonment of their possessions was understood as preliminary, and indispensable to any adjustment. The cold sarcasm of Jenkins in reply, as well as in a subsequent letter, will not fail to arrest attention.

Reply to the Commissioners, from the Committee of Settlers:—

"GENTLEMEN,—It is with pleasure we observe in yours of the 19th, your readiness to attend to every piece of necessary information we shall be able to give in respect to our settlement in this place. How far the State can or will, by virtue of any ex-post facto law, undertake to deprive any of the citizens of this State of any part of their property legally obtained by any of the claimants under their different claims, we shall not undertake to say or determine, as we suppose, that in general, Common law is to determine in such cases. Yet we are happy to hear that this State is willing to do every thing in their power to promote the peace and happiness of her citizens.

"We take notice that if our peaceable demeanor and ready submission to Government, render us proper objects of clemency and generosity, we may probably expect to be made the happy partakers of such generous gratuities, as they in their abundant goodness shall be pleased to bestow; whilst our necessitous circumstances oblige us to wait the happy period, and if received will no doubt deserve our sincere and hearty thanks. As to our peaceable demeanor, and ready submission to Government, our petition now before the Honorable the Legislature of this State, suggests to them, that we are under their jurisdiction and protection, from which we have no disposition to recede. However, would request to have a tender regard paid to the new and extraordinary circumstances in which we stand with regard to law matters. We have made continuance of our actions commenced, with a view to have them taken up under the jurisdiction of Pennsylvania, agreeable to our aforesaid petition, and have neglected to pay any attention to the appointment of representatives or government officers, under the Connecticut jurisdiction, which facts evidence our intentions better than protestations.

"With regard to the next requisition, the calamities of war have so put it out of our power to give you that concise account we could wish at present, as most of our papers and records were thereby destroyed. But the Susquehanna purchase was made in the year 1754, at the treaty at Albany, as set forth in their petition, by upwards of fourteen hundred adventurers, who were joint tenants in common, one with another; and in 1755, said proprietors proceeded to locate and survey the Susquehanna river, taking the latitude, etc. That in the year 1762, one hundred and nineteen of the aforesaid proprietors were here to possess themselves of the said lands in behalf of themselves and fellows, of which number John Jenkins, William Buck, etc., are contained in a list herewith exhibited, marked No. 1. In October, 1763, we were dispossessed by the savages with the loss of many lives, and much property. In the beginning of the year 1769, we again resumed our possessions and improvements, which we had made before with great labour and expense, with the number of about four hundred, being partly of the aforesaid one hundred and nineteen, or their representatives, whose names, according to our best recollection, are herewith annexed, and marked No. 2. A line being in the meantime settled with the natives, we proceeded to lay out our lands agreeable to our former surveys, into a large number of towns, up and down the river Susquehanna, nearly across the whole latitude of forty-two, of five miles square, and proceeded to part them out to the inhabitants, according to the number of inhabitants each town or district was to contain; in lots of between three and four hundred acres to a man, since which, said lands have been divided and subdivided, according to the agreement of the settlers of each town or district, a particular detail of which we are not able to give, without having recourse to our records and papers, which we are at present deprived of, and from that until the year 1776, our numbers were increasing, at which time we were required by the State to number the inhabitants of this place, which, according to our best recollection, amounted to upwards of six thousand souls, so that at the time Independence was declared, we had got to be very numerous, and were still increasing until the fatal third day of July, 1778, when great numbers of our friends and most valuable inhabitants were slain by the savages and those of a more savage nature, and their whole country laid waste, our houses and buildings consumed by fire, our household goods and large stock of cattle, horses, sheep and hogs, with our farming and other utensils, destroyed and carried off by the enemy, and we in a most savage and inhuman manner drove out into the country, in a state of desperation and distress. A scene which must astonish all human nature to describe, and we are not able to paint it. Our old men, women, widows and children, were dispersed into all parts of the country, destitute of bread, clothing, or any thing to subsist on. But a large number of the yet remaining and living inhabitants being fired with a fervent zeal for the cause of their country, were determined, instead of throwing themselves on the clemency of their friends and fellow-citizens of the world, to surmount all danger, collected themselves together, and on or about the fourth day of August then next, resolved with the assistance of the company of brave continental troops raised here, and then commanded by Captain Simon Spalding, came into this place, retook the country, drove off the savages, regained some trifling part of our effects and the possession of our lands, being our all; since which we have, by many hard and hazardous skirmishes, attended with the loss of many lives, and a considerable of the effects acquired by our industry, held the same to this time, which has afforded great comfort to the widow and fatherless children, the destitute and naked, not only to those at present improving here, but by the people who improve here paying rent for the lands that belong to the widow and fatherless, that are dispersed into the wide world, they are greatly relieved and comforted. The most, or all of this has been done at our expense and charge, and been a safeguard to the frontiers of our good neighbours and friends, with whom we wish to live in peace.

April 20, 1783.   Signed in behalf of the Committee,

JOHN JENKINS, *Chairman.*

JOSEPH MONTGOMERY, *Chairman.*

N. B. We herewith transmit a list of the names of part of the first settlers in 1762 and 63, as far as we can at present recollect. Also a list of the widows and orphans."

Letter from the State Commissioners to the Committee of Settlers.

"GENTLEMEN,—We herewith transmit you a copy of an address of the committee representing the landholders under this State, handed to us this morning, containing terms on which they declare themselves willing to compromise the dispute now unhappily subsisting between you and them, and which it is our duty to endeavour to have adjusted, and settled in an amicable manner.

"Therefore, we wish you, with all calmness and despatch, to consider of, and duly weigh the said proposals, and to furnish us with a clear and explicit answer to the same, which will enable us to transact the business committed to us by the General Assembly, with more precision, and to take such measures as may effectually answer the ends of our mission. We have only further to add, that should we be so happy as to find that these terms are agreed to, and ratified by the contending parties, we shall think it our duty to recommend your distressed situation to the notice of the Legislature of this State.

"We have the honour to be, Gentlemen,
 Your most obedient and humble servants.
  JOSEPH MONTGOMERY, *Chairman*.

The Committee representing the Settlers.

Wyoming, April 22nd, 1783."

There would seem to be no question but the terms proposed met the entire approbation of the Commissioners.

"Address from the Committee of Pennsylvania Landholders, to the State Commissioners with their proposals of compromise.

"GENTLEMEN,—The committee are honored with your answer to their address. The assurance you are pleased to give them of attention to the rights of the citizens of this State calls for their grateful acknowledgments, and so perfectly harmonizes with the sentiments of the committee, that we are instructed to commit ourselves wholly to your direction in future, and in doing this we are confident that our rights are in the hands of those who will have a watchful eye over them.

We are sorry to observe so much of the old leaven remaining in the sentiments of the people of Connecticut, and expressed in their last conference before your honours. Their humanity would, it seems, permit us and our associates to go any where over the wide world, no matter where, provided they may enjoy our lands; they cannot conveniently spare us one foot for the support of our families. We think this an ungrateful return to the good people of the State, and far short of the expectations of the Legislature, whose humanity and pity alone proposed to consign to oblivion all past offences, by a law for that purpose, and where wisdom pointed out the only way of information to the House of Assembly, of the real disposition of the contending parties.

"We beg leave only to suggest to your honours that we have reason to think the obedience to laws of this State by many of those people, will not be durable, unless such pledges are taken by your honours, as cannot admit of any evasion or denial hereafter. If that assurance be once given, and the pretended claims under Connecticut relinquished in writing, publicly, plainly, and unequivocally, we wish afterwards to give them every indulgence that your honours may judge generous in us, and worthy the approbation of the Assembly of Pennsylvania, and all the world.

"We propose to give leases with covenants of warranty for holding their possessions one year from the first day of April inst.: at the end of which they shall deliver up full possession of the whole, they shall have liberty to occupy half the lands, one half the meadows: dwell in the houses they now possess, and cultivate their present gardens, and if they have any opportunities of disposing of their *hutts*, barns, or other buildings, they shall have liberty to do it, and to remove them off at any time between the present day and the first day of April next, 1784, and the other moiety or half of the cleared lands and meadows to be possessed by us and our associates and no impediment to have in our way to enjoy them. The Rev. Mr. Johnson to have the full use of all the grounds he formerly held, for two years, ending the first of April, 1785. The widows of all those whose husbands were killed by the savages, to have a further indulgence of a year after the first of April, 1784, for half their possessions, and a square in the town to be set apart for their use, to which they may remove their houses, and at the end of the term, sell them to the best advantage for their own use.

"We think a refusal of these terms *hardly possible*; But if stubbornness and disaffection to the laws of this State, are yet to continue, we trust your honours will be convinced that on our parts we have not in view merely our own private interests, but that our offers will appear just and equitable before God and men.

With every sentiment of respect,
Sir, your most obedient and humble servant,
ALEXANDER PATTERSON, *Chairman.*

Wyoming, April 22nd, 1783.
Signed in behalf of the Committee.
To the honourable Joseph Montgomery, Chairman of the Board of Commissioners."

A true Copy. Attested,—MOSES MCCLAIN, *Clerk.*"

The conditions of compromise then, offered the Wyoming people, were these:—

1st. Pledges to be given, such as could not admit of denial or evasion, for their obedience.

2d. A disclaimer in writing, publicly, plainly, and unequivocally given, of all claims to their lands held under title from Connecticut. Then follow the merciful terms.

3d. The settler to take a lease of half his farm for about eleven months, giving up possession at once of the other half. On the first of April following to abandon claims, home, possession, to his adversary.

4th. The widows of those who had fallen by the Savages, to be indulged in half their possessions a year longer.

And 5th. The Rev. Mr. Johnson to be allowed to occupy his grounds (under disclaimer and lease, of course,) for two years.

It will be obvious to every reader that instead of being terms of conciliation and compromise, they bear the impress of an imperious master, conscious of his power, dictating to revolted slaves, broken, hated and despised. That the Montgomerys should ever have lent their respected names to proposals, so fraught with injustice and contumely, appears at this day incredible. Those gentlemen were superior to the least suspicion of corruption; but their minds were probably too deeply imbued with prejudice against the Connecticut claim and claimants, to leave room for the exercise of their naturally just judgments, and more generous and elevated sentiments.

"If the terms should be agreed to and satisfied," say the Commissioners most graciously, "we shall think it our duty to recommend your distressed situation to the notice of the Legislature!"

The address from the Committee of Landholders brought a new personage into the discussion, but an old acquaintance of the settlers, ALEXANDER PATTERSON, ESQ. As this gentleman acted a very prominent part in the events which ensued, it seems fitting that he should be more particularly introduced to the reader. In a petition presented by him to the Legislature, in 1802, asking remuneration for his faithful services he set forth,

"In the year 1769, he was solicited by the late proprietary, John Penn and Chief Justice Allen, to take an active part against the Connecticut intruders, who were pursuing an unbounded claim," etc. "In the month of February, same year, he proceeded with John Jennings, Sheriff of Northampton, and others, and brought to Easton gaol, the first forty of the intruders, who had attempted to seat themselves at Wyoming." "The ensuing Fall, there came upwards of two hundred intruders: they attempted to dispossess the Pennsylvania settlers with axes, scythes and clubs. Your Petitioner was in the front of the opposition, and was severely wounded in the head with an axe. Notwithstanding the loss of much blood, he that evening set off for Fort Augusta (Sunbury,) in a batteau, and brought up a cannon,* etc. The next year the intruders "drove the Pennsylvania settlers into the garrison, wherein was your Petitioner, with many women and children, where they were besieged nearly seven

---

* "The terrible four-pounder."

weeks, and were obliged to capitulate through famine, to Butler," etc. "The September following, your petitioner was among the most active who again took their garrison, with much enterprise." Prisoners who escaped, " with others, accompanied those bravos to Wyoming, where by palpable perjury they instantly joined their associate ruffians"—" He has gone with his associates through the wilderness at night; taken particular captive offenders; abated the marauders' settlement; and expelled the despicable herd."

If such was the strain in which Mr. Patterson spoke of the settlers, a quarter of a century after the conflict, well may be imagined the spirit of hatred and revenge that rankled in his breast while the events were recent. Yet this gentleman was chosen as the fitting dove to bear the olive of peace, and be the messenger of conciliation.

Supported by the two companies of Robinson and Shrawder's Rangers, confident of his strength, and exulting in his power; determined to " feed fat the ancient grudge he bore them," Patterson had gathered around him Capt. Dick and a number of his former companions in arms, to witness his triumph, and share in the utter humiliation of his Yankee foes. But "there is a Divinity that shapes our ends," and the conclusion was not so near as anticipated. We publish:—6th. Letter from the Committee of Settlers, in reply to the offered proposals of Compromise.

"GENTLEMEN,—We duly received yours of the 22nd instant, enclosing the address, and proposals of the landholders of this State by their committee; and although we must confess that their elegant manner of address is far beyond us, yet we hope our plain country way of communicating our ideas will be forgiven. But we cannot help taking notice that in their address they complain of a proposal that was made by us before your honours, being very ungrateful, which to the best of our remembrance was that it had been intimated by some that it was probable this State would out of courtesy bestow something in the land way on the settlers, and claimants of the lands here under Connecticut; they were only asked, that if that was granted out of courtesy, whether they would not exchange and suffer us to enjoy our peaceable possessions here, by way of compromise? Their answer was, that they were as able to apply for lands as we. We are extremely sorry to entertain the idea that in a compromise, we, or they, instead of looking at the designed, and desired object, be forming mountains out of mole hills. We do not think the lawful defence of what we esteem to be our own, can with any justice be termed a disaffection to Government. We would add, the petition we laid before the Legislative body of this State, we were in hopes would be considered of as we find it is, and if that is granted, or any other satisfactory measures can be come into by way of compromise, as we would first take all lenitive measures, and if nothing is effected by this method of treating, we must have recourse to the ninth article of Confederation, as that is the only mode pointed out for the trial of these lands claimed under grants of different States. As we conceive that the proposals of the committee, in which they offer as a compromise, will not tend to peace, as they are so far from what we deem reasonable, we cannot comply with them without doing the greatest injustice to ourselves and our associates, to widows, and fatherless children. And although we mean to pay due obedience to the constitutional laws of Pennsylvania, we do not mean to become abject slaves, as the Committee of Landholders suggest in their address to your honors.

Signed in behalf of the Committee of Settlers.

JOHN JENKINS, *Chairman*.

Wyoming, April 22, 1783.

To the honorable Joseph Montgomery, Chairman of the Board of Commissioners.

The last letter was an address from the State Commissioners, to the Committee of Settlers.

GENTLEMEN,—We are now possessed of your answer to the proposals of the Committee of Landholders under Pennsylvania.

We are sorry that there does not appear any prospect of accommodation between you. Therefore we must beg the favour of you, to notify your people to meet with us to-morrow morning at 8 o'clock, when we shall take the liberty to lay the whole proceedings before them, and take our leave of them, and you.

We shall be glad to have a friendly interview with you this afternoon at 4 o'clock, and that you will bring with you the returns.

We have the honour to be, Gentlemen,
Your most obedient and humble servants.
Signed in behalf of the Commissioners, by

JOSEPH MONTGOMERY.

Wyoming, April 23, 1783.

The Committee representing the Settlers from Connecticut."

And here terminated the correspondence; but not the action of the commissioners. Forthwith they divided Wyoming into three townships, naming the two new ones Stoke and Shawanese. Justices of the Peace for the county of Northumberland were immediately chosen by Mr. Patterson, and his New Jersey and Northampton friends, who had accompanied him to Wyoming; David Mead, Robert Martin, John Chambers, and Nathan Denison, for the northwestern district: Alexander Patterson, John Seely, Luke Brodhead, and Henry Shoemaker, for the southeastern. The inhabitants were equally unconscious of the division of the townships, and of the election of Magistrates, Col. Denison's name being used without his knowledge. None of the others were, or had been for years, inhabitants of Westmoreland. David Mead, formerly an active Connecticut partizan, and the surveyor of Wilkesbarre township, had resided during the war at Northumberland. This gentleman is again especially noticed, as he will appear a conspicuous actor on a subsequent page. No proceeding could possibly have been more illegal, arbitrary, and unjust.

Having been nine days at Wyoming, the commissioners withdrew on the 24th of April, to make their report to the Assembly, which was to convene early in August. Their report recommended that a reasonable compensation in land [in the western part of the State] should be made to the families of those who had fallen in arms against the common enemy, and to such other settlers as had a proper Connecticut title, and "did actually reside on the lands at the time of the decree at Trenton, provided they immediately relinquish all claim to the soil where they now inhabit, and enter into contracts to deliver up full and quiet possession of their present tenures, to the rightful owners under Pennsylvania, by the first of April next."

Waiting the reception of the commissioners, uncertain whether the course pursued would be disallowed or confirmed, Justice Patterson and his troops, although indulging in every species of petty insult and contumely, seemingly intended to drive the settlers to violations of law and order, yet restrained themselves from overt acts of cruelty, and flagrant instances of oppression.

Eventual and preliminary articles of peace having been signed with Great Britain the 30th of the preceding November, on the 11th of May all Wyoming, echoing with shouts, and congratulations, indulged in feasting and merry-making, it being a day set apart for rejoicings at that happy event. Sorrow forgot her woes; care assumed the gay laugh of mirth; and even the melancholy mother, beholding in her blooming boy, growing into manhood, a freeman, whose liberty had been sealed by his father's blood, shook off the tear of fond remembrance, and smiled.

Benjamin Bidlack returned from the army on the 12th of June; on the 22nd, Lieut. Rosewell Franklin, whose wife was so barbarously butchered by the Indians the preceding summer, was married to Mrs. Lester, whose husband had also fallen by the hands of the Savages; thus assuaging mutual sorrow in the arms of mutual, and honourable endearment.

With prudent forecast, the settlers, aware of the overwhelming power of the State, if vigorously put forth, and sensible of the spirit with which, under Patterson's vice-royalty it would be exercised, began in earnest to look out for a place of retreat. An association was formed to establish a settlement in New York, north of the Pennsylvania line. Capt. J. Franklin, sent out on an exploring party, was absent from the 15th of May to the 7th of June, examining, chiefly, the country near Oquago on the east branch of the Susquehanna, and thence north to the Butternuts. Mr. Jenkins actually began surveying a tract in the Genesee country, but several Indians came to his camp, ostensibly to beg provisions, promising to return the value in venison; their real purpose was evinced by a visit in a different character, two nights afterwards. While the party was sleeping in perfect unconsciousness of danger, a fire was opened into his cabin; one man killed outright, and three wounded. Lieut. Jenkins sprang to his feet, seized his Jacob staff, struck down an Indian upon the fire, and killed him. To remain would have been certain death, and he withdrew with his wounded men. Whether the attack was made for plunder, or what is more probable, revenge still boiling in the savage breast against Wyoming, or as is not unlikely, jealousy of the whites encroaching on their hunting grounds, could not be certainly determined.*

Capt. Spalding and several of his military associates, with Obadiah Gore, Esq., and some others, immediately withdrew from the Valley, and made a settlement at Sheshequin, a few miles below Tioga point, on the east side of the Susquehanna, and by the river seventy miles above Wyoming; yet in the old town of Westmoreland. Two or three Indian families remained there, demeaning themselves peaceably for awhile, and then removed to the west.

* The date of this transaction in Col. Jenkins' journal is set down as 1783. The imprudence, not to say rashness, of venturing to survey on the Indian lands so soon after the war, and some other circumstances, would lead us to give to it a posterior date.

In May, 1783, when Capt. Spalding arrived on the ground, the Indian grass on the flats was so tall as to reach to a man's shoulders when on horseback. To this his people set fire: the raging flames ascending to the heavens—sweeping—coursing—whirling along the plain for several miles, was long dwelt on by the inhabitants as a scene, exceeding any thing they had ever witnessed, or imagined of sublimity and grandeur.

With more than even hoped for promptitude of approbation, the Assembly, at their August session, received the report of the commissioners, and confirmed all that had been done, or was recommended.

The division of Wyoming into three towns was approved, and made legal, as was the election of magistrates. A law was forthwith passed to repeal " An act to prevent and stay suits from being brought against the inhabitants of Wyoming," which had not yet been six months on the statute book. The terms proposed to the inhabitants were recognized as " generous offers," and the commissioners were complimented by a flattering eulogium for the " laudable zeal and industry" displayed by them* in the execution of their mission.

After the conclusion of peace, the company of Capt. Robinson had been withdrawn from the Valley, leaving that of Capt. Shrawder, the intimate friend of Alexander Patterson, to afford such protection as was intended to be granted to the inhabitants. In view of ulterior measures, shadowed forth by the proceedings of Assembly, a resolution was adopted, September 22, 1783, " That the Supreme Executive Council are hereby empowered, and required to take into the service of this State, one major, two captains, four subalterns of the officers of the Pennsylvania line, who are forthwith to be instructed to enlist two full companies of the soldiers who have served in the Pennsylvania line, to serve such time as to the Supreme Executive Council, or the succeeding Assembly shall seem meet, etc." This resolution was passed with closed doors, in secret session, and recorded on the secret journals of the House; and was regarded when known, as a direct infraction of the articles of confederation. Major James Moore was appointed to the supreme command. Capt. Shrawder re-enlisted his company, while Capt. Christie enlisted a company near Philadelphia, and repaired immediately to Wyoming.

---

* It may excite a smile when known, that the committee who thus laud, and the commissioners praised, consisted in part of the same persons. Messrs. Joseph Montgomery, William Montgomery, and Mr. McClean, being members of both.

Capt. Patterson having received his commission as magistrate, returned from the city, where he, the sole and prime agent, had been to superintend, to advise and direct all these movements, preparatory to the decisive measures so manifestly contemplated. Brave undoubtedly he was, full of enterprise, overflowing with zeal, he took up his quarters at Wilkesbarre, near the fort, changing the name of the place to Londonderry, from which, in his communications, he dated.* And fully armed with legal and illegal power, forthwith commenced its exercise.

Col. Zebulon Butler, (by whom Patterson had in 1770 been starved out and made a prisoner,) returned from the army with his lady, (having married Miss Phœbe Haight at West Point, the previous winter,) arriving at Wilkesbarre on the 20th of August. How welcome was his presence to friend or foe, may be easily imagined. The licentious soldiery, freed from the restraints of discipline, which the presence of an enemy tends to enforce, and encouraged by the civil authority, became extremely rude and oppressive. They took without leave, whatever they fancied. Several persons had been arrested and brought before Captain Shrawder. Col. Butler, indignant at the treatment the inhabitants suffered, expressed his opinions freely, and for himself, said he was going to camp, was still a continental officer, and swore his soldier's oath, "*set fire to 'em*," they shall not stop me. It was enough. A writ was issued, and Col. Butler arrested on the 24th of September, as it was said, for high treason. Surrounded by a guard of soldiers, he was conveyed to the fort, and treated with great indignity. The next day under a military guard, the gallant veteran was sent by Esquire Patterson to Sunbury, a distance of sixty miles. When delivered at the jail, lo! there was no mittimus, and Sheriff Antis said he could not legally detain him. But that day two of the new Wyoming justices having taken the oath of office at Northumberland, made out a mittimus, directing Sheriff Antis to hold the prisoner in custody, until more accurate documents could be procured from Justice Patterson. Very soon after, satisfactory bail being offered, Sheriff Antis set Col. Butler at liberty, and he returned to his family.†

---

* We cannot help adverting to the gallant Ogden. Where was he? What was his fate? His name does not appear that we have been able to learn, during the war. Death alone could have subdued so noble a spirit.

† Thus the patriot soldier, who had served with reputation through the war, had periled his life again and again for Wyoming, in one short month from his arrival at his home, was seized, and without law cast into prison as a felon! Indignation must have been lost in

On the 1st of October, Capt. Franklin was arrested on a charge of trespass, for proceeding to farm his land, and brought before Justice Patterson. Mr. F. plead title, and desired that a fair trial by court and jury might decide the matter. Such course not according with his policy, he was dismissed by the justice.

Capt. Christie arrived with his company on the 29th of October, and forthwith the two companies of soldiers were quartered upon the inhabitants, in some instances where special oppression was meditated, eight and ten were placed with one family. Col. Butler was particularly distinguished by having twenty billeted upon him, the more distressingly unwelcome, as Mrs. Butler was then recently confined. We cannot refrain from adding that the daughter then born, has been for thirty years, and is now moving in the first circles of New York, respected and beloved, the lady of one of the most eminent legal gentlemen of that city, (1845.) The house being small, hastily erected after the conflagration of the Savages, the people poor, and the soldiers insolent, their sufferings were exceedingly severe, too great for human nature patiently to endure. But seeing it was the purpose to drive them to some act of desperation, the injury and insults were borne with forbearance and fortitude.

His strength being now equal to any probable emergency, Justice Patterson proceeded to adopt measures of greater energy. October 31, the settlement of Shawney was invaded by the military, headed by the Justice in person, and eleven respectable citizens arrested, and sent under guard to the fort. Among the prisoners was Major Prince Alden, sixty-five years old, feeble from age, and suffering from disease. Compassion yielded nothing to alleviate his sufferings. Capt. James Bidlack was also arrested. He was between sixty and seventy. His son of the same name had fallen, as previously recorded, at the head of his company in the Indian battle; another son, Benjamin, had served in the army through the revolutionary war. Mr. B. himself had been taken by the Savages, and suffered a tedious captivity in Canada. All this availed him nothing. Benjamin Harvey, who had been a prisoner to the Indians was also arrested. Samuel Ransom, son of Capt. Ransom, who fell in the massacre, was most rudely treated on being taken. "Ah ha!" cried Patterson, "you are the jocky we wanted; away with him to the guard-house, with old Harvey, another damned rascal." Eleven in all were

---

amazement at the audacious deed. Added to the iniquity of the illegal arrest, was an attempt, amply proved to compel Harding, a witness, to give a false deposition against Col. Butler.

taken, and driven to the fort, where they were confined in a room with a mud floor, wet and comfortless, with no food and little fire, which, as they were sitting round, Capt. Christie came in, ordered them to lie down on the ground, and bade the guard to blow out the brains of any one who should attempt to rise. Even the staff of the aged Mr. Alden was taken from him. On demanding what was their offence, and if it was intended to starve them, Patterson tauntingly replied: "Perhaps in two or three months we shall be at leisure, and you may be set at liberty." At the intercession of D. Meade, Esq., three of the elder prisoners the next day were liberated, the remaining eight being kept in their loathsome prison, some a week, others ten days, and then dismissed without arraignment or trial. But the object had been accomplished; their several families had been turned out of their houses, and creatures of Patterson put in possession. Oppression will drive a wise man mad; but the people still endured their sufferings, being alleviated by the charity of those who had been less unfortunate.

It is scarcely possible to conceive the insolence of manner assumed by Justice Patterson. Meeting by accident with Capt. Caleb Bates, and learning his name, "Why have you not been to see me, sir?" Capt. Bates answered, he did not know him. "I will recommend myself to you, sir—I am Esquire Patterson of Pennsylvania," and almost instantly ordered a serjeant to take him to the guard-house.

The following documents seem necessary to a more perfect understanding of the situation of the people, subsequent to the transfer of jurisdiction by the decree of Trenton; and after the recommendation of the Assembly to the landholders and settlers, to make "reasonable compromises" under the prefecture of Alexender Patterson.

RESOLUTION passed 22d September 1783.

"*Resolved*, That the Supreme Executive Council, are hereby empowered and required to take into the service of this State, one major, two captains, four subalterns of the officers of the Pennsylvania line, who are forthwith to be instructed to enlist two full companies of the soldiers who have served in the Pennsylvania line, to serve such time as the Supreme Executive Council, or the succeeding Assembly shall seem meet; and that one month's pay shall be advanced to the said officers and soldiers, who shall be armed and accoutred at the expense of the State, the money for which purpose, shall be drawn by order of the Supreme Executive Council, out of the money collected by virtue of the impost law of this State, and now in the hands of the Naval Officer, or which may hereafter come into his hands by virtue of the aforesaid law."

ADDRESS.

The Honorable the Representatives of the Commonwealth of the State of Pennsylvania, in General Assembly met:—

The petition, address and remonstrance, of us the subscribers, in behalf of the rest of the inhabitants of Wyoming, humbly sheweth: That after the judgment at Trenton, changing the jurisdiction from that of Connecticut to that of Pennsylvania, since which we have considered ourselves as citizens of Pennsylvania, and have at all times by our peaceable demeanor, and ready submission to government, duly submitted ourselves to the laws of the State of Pennsylvania, and not only so, but as we were not made duly acquainted with the laws of the State, have tamely submitted to every requisition of the executive and military authority, although the same appeared in many instances to us to be unconstitutional and unlawful. We beg leave to observe, that nothing special happened until the resolve of the Assembly, appointing commissioners, in which we observed that after the report of those commissioners so appointed, we were to have a time and place appointed for choosing of authority, holding elections, etc. But to our great surprise and grief, it seems that there was a choice made, as we understand, by those that called themselves landholders, some from one part of the State, and some from other parts. Some from New Jersey and elsewhere, and principally not inhabitants of this county, of a number of persons to be commissioned in authority, all without our knowledge, and before the report of the commissioners or the appointment of a time or place for that purpose, and a return of those persons was, by some way or means to us unknown, made to the Honorable the General Assembly of the State, and have since been commissioned, which has produced the following facts, viz: Some time in September 1783, Col. Zebulon Butler was met at the ferry boat, by a man that is called a constable; but how he came by his authority, we know not; however this man, Brink by name, seized his horse by the bridle, told him he was his prisoner, took him into the fort, delivered him up to the martial department. He, the said Butler, was kept there twenty-four hours under guard, then sent off under a strong guard of soldiers to Northumberland, without either civil officer or writ, and was not made acquainted with any crime for which he was taken, he has been taken three times since by different officers under pretences of the same crime, and yet knows not what it is, although he got bail for his appearance at court. Since this the property of sundry persons has been taken by force under a pretence, and the persons that take it, say by the advice of the authority, and upon application to the authority, no redress can be had. That persons taken for pretended crimes have been told by the Justices that if they would take a lease, they should be set at liberty, and have in fact been obliged to comply, or suffer in prison in a guard house. Widows and fatherless children, in a sickly condition, turned out of their houses and sick beds, and drove off in a tedious storm, and said to be done by advice of the authority, and no redress could be obtained from the authority, though application was made. Some taken under pretence of some crime, and when confined, their wives were told if they would submit to their carnal desires, their husbands should be set at liberty. Some taken by a guard of armed soldiers in presence of the Justices, and their wives and families turned out of doors. The possession of a grist mill taken away by force, and given to another man, and although frequent application has been made to the Justices for redress, none can be had. That eleven persons were taken at Shawney by a guard of twenty-five armed men, in company with Esquire Patterson and Seely, under pretence of some crime, although not any was alleged, neither any writ ever produced, nor yet sheriff or constable, and were drove at the point of the bayonet for six miles in a tedious storm to the fort. Confined in an open guard-house without any floor, and the mud shoe deep, ordered to lie down in the mud, and the sentinel ordered, that if one raised his head from the ground to shoot him through. A staff taken from an old gentleman and ordered to be burnt. This old gentleman and sundry others, were at the same time sick with a fever, yet closely confined for six days in that situation, and then dismissed without ceremony. That persons when taken and brought before the Justices, not suffered to speak a word in their own defence, or to hear a witness, although requested, and judgment given without ever being made acquainted with the cause. That writs are given out for sixpence against children fifteen years of age, and that said to be lawful, although it was for one gill of whiskey, and parents, guardians, nor masters, never notified. Locks and doors broke, when the families were from home, under pretence of quartering soldiers in the house, and public buildings at the same time that might have received them. That one of the inhabitants having business with Capt. Schott, Esquire Patterson being present, asked his name. He informed him, and, said " Patterson, I do not know you." " I am Alexander Patterson, Esq., of Pennsylvania, one of the magistrates of this place, G—d d—n you, I will make you know me;" then called a guard of soldiers, took him to the guard-house, confined him twenty-four hours, then dismissed him without ceremony, all which facts we conceive to be done without law or right, and merely to distress the poor distressed inhabitants of this place, and is an infringement on the rights, liberties and privileges, of free citizens of this State.

Therefore, we as sincere friends to the rights, liberties and privileges of the United States and citizens of this State, under our distressed circumstances, gratefully request your Honorable body to take our distressed case under your wise and serious consideration, and in some way grant relief, as may appear most just and reasonable to your Honours; hoping that every unconstitutional and unlawful act may be redressed, and removed into oblivion, and we your petitioners as in duty bound will ever pray.

Wyoming, November 18th, 1783.

Signed by John Jenkins and a number of others, in behalf of themselves and the rest of the inhabitants of Wyoming.

STATE OF PENNSYLVANIA. In General Assembly, Tuesday, December 9th, 1783, A. M.

The petition from divers inhabitants of Wyoming, in the county of Northumberland, was read the second time, whereupon

Resolved, That the members from Northampton county, or a majority of them, be a committee to inquire into the charges contained in a petition from a number of the inhabitants of Wyoming, in the county of Northumberland, and report to the House at their next meeting, and that the said petition, and other papers accompanying it, be put into their hands.

Extract from the minutes.

       Signed,   PETER Z. LLOYD,
               Clerk of General Assembly.

             Philadelphia, December 9th, 1783.

In compliance of the above resolution, we, or a majority of us, the committee therein mentioned, will attend on the 29th of December instant, at the house of Capt. Shott, in the township of Stoke, (Wilkesbarre) in order to inquire into the charges by you set forth in the above petition, of which time and place you are hereby notified, that you be and appear before us, when and where we shall be ready to hear your evidence to support the charges by you set forth in said petition.

             JACOB ARNDT,
             JACOB STROUD,
             JONAS HARTZEL,
             ROBERT BROWN.

To Mr. John Jenkins and others, the petitioners, etc.

A similar note was sent to Alexander Patterson, and to the officers of the garrison; and Robert Martin was also desired to be in attendance, to aid in taking the testimony in the case.

       A. PATTERSON to President DICKINSON.

         LONDONDERRY, (Wilkesbarre,) December 20th, 1783.

SIR,—Since Mr. Meade and I wrote you last, the purport of which was informing the measures taken to have in confinement that flagrant offender Col. Zebulon Butler, who has threatened the dissolution of the citizens of this State and its laws. Notwithstanding he was committed from under the hands and seals of three Justices of the Peace for treason, he has found security, and is sent back to this place to the terror of the good citizens in this neighborhood. The Sheriff has not done his duty, nor do I believe he intends it, being a party man, among which I am sorry to see so little principles of humanity and honour, men who wish for popularity at the expense of the property, and perhaps blood of their fellow citizens. Strange as it may appear it is absolutely true, that the banditti at Wyoming have been solicited for their votes at the election, caressed and patronized in their villainy, encouraged in their claims to land, which they now hold in violation of all law, from men who have distinguished themselves and taken a very decided part in the late revolution. Sure I am that it would be an act of justice not to commissionate Antis—the other person on the return I do not know, but worse he cannot be. Pardon this freedom. Nothing but a wish for the peace of the citizens would have induced me to have said so much upon this head. I have wrote the Chief Justice, concerning Butler, and have prevailed upon the bearer, Capt. John Dick, to carry those despatches, he will return to this place, and may be depended upon. I am very uneasy having heard nothing of Major Moore. I wish he was here. I hope your Excellency will think it right to order the troops forward as soon as possible.

I have the honour to be with sentiments of the highest esteem,
Your most obedient humble servant,
ALEXANDER PATTERSON.

His Excellency John Dickinson.

REPORT.

The committee appointed on the petition of divers inhabitants of Wyoming, exhibiting complaints against Alexander Patterson, Esq., and stating also other grievances, beg leave to report; That your committee repaired to Wyoming, agreeable to the orders of this House, and having given due notice to all parties concerned, proceeded to the investigation of the different charges contained in the petition before the House, in the presence as well of the persons accused as the persons accusing. And the evidence taken on the inquiry has been reduced to writing by a person employed for that purpose by your committee, which depositions your committee beg leave to lay before the House.

This report was endorsed as follows, viz: Read first time, February 3d, 1784, and on motion read second time, and referred to Mr. Work, Mr. Miller, Mr. Johnson, Mr. Lutz and Mr. C———.* [Name uncertain.]

PETITION.

To the Honorable the Representatives of the Freemen of the Commonwealth of Pennsylvania, in General Assembly met:—

The petition and address of John Jenkins, Nathan Denison, Obadiah Gore, Hugh Forsman and John Franklin, inhabitants of Wyoming, in behalf of themselves and others, inhabitants of said place.

Most respectfully sheweth, That whereas upon a petition and remonstrance from divers inhabitants of Wyoming, bearing date November 18th, 1783, complaining of certain illegal proceedings had against them by Alexander Patterson, Esq., and others, your Honours of your abundant goodness, by a resolution appointed a committee from your Honorable House to inquire into the charges contained in said petition.

That timely notice being given to the said Alexander Patterson, Esq., and others concerned, as well as to the petitioners, an inquiry was held at Wyoming by your committee near ten days. Witnesses called for and fairly heard, and depositions taken, as well on the part of those complained of, as on the part of the petitioners. Liberty of questioning the witnesses when under examination in support of the petition was granted to the defending

---

Col. Franklin again attended the Legislature, on the part of the inhabitants. He stated to me (says Mr. Ward,) that Patterson and those who were concerned with him, had full access to the committee, laying before them private letters and ex-parte depositions taken after the first committee had left Wyoming—while he was never allowed to go before them during the whole forty-six days the subject was before the committee.

Finding this unfair course was likely to prejudice the interests of his constituents, he prepared and had presented the above petition.

party, and a fair and legal hearing of all such witnesses as they see fit to make use of. That since the return of your committee from Wyoming, we understand that sundry private letters and a number of ex-parte depositions, taken since the inquiry aforesaid, have been presented to your House, reporting or presenting to your Honours, that the inhabitants of Wyoming who settled that territory under the Connecticut claim, do not manifest submission to the laws and authority of this State, but appear designing against the same, and that there is danger of ill consequences proceeding from the opposition of said inhabitants.

Conscious that no opposition from us has been made to the laws and authority aforesaid, and that no such designs are existing, we humbly conceive that such reports must have originated through misinformation or mistake.

We have the highest esteem for the constitution of the Commonwealth of Pennsylvania, and are well satisfied with the laws of this State.

We are under your jurisdiction and protection, are subjects and free citizens of the State of Pennsylvania. We have voluntarily taken and subscribed the oaths and affirmations of allegiance and fidelity, as directed by a supplement to an act of General Assembly of this State. And it is our will and pleasure to serve you in doing our duty as good and faithful subjects of this State, in supporting the rights, liberties and privileges of the same. We have to look up to your Honours for protection, for justice, equity and liberty, on which we depend. We have the greatest confidence that upon the examination of the depositions taken by your committee in their inquiry at Wyoming, your House will be satisfied that the charges contained in the aforesaid petition are fully supported, and that no opposition has been made on our part. That by our peaceable demeanor and ready submission to Government, we have duly submitted to every requisition, whether civil or military, and that the proceedings had against us, and which we complained of, were unconstitutional and unlawful, and that we had the greatest reason to appeal to your Honours for redress.

Relying on the justice and impartiality of your Honorable House, we are assured that reports by private letters and ex-parte evidence, will not avail against legal and well grounded testimony, either to condemn an innocent people, or screen the guilty from justice.

We humbly request to be protected, and continued quiet and unmolested in our possessions, (which is our all) until a legal decision shall be had thereon, with which we are ready to comply, and shall quietly resign to any claimant or claimants whose title shall be adjudged preferable to ours. We press your Honours to grant us protection and redress, and that the liberties and privileges, which subjects and free citizens of this State are entitled to, may not be denied to us. And your petitioners, as in duty bound, will ever pray.

JOHN FRANKLIN,

Philadelphia, February 23, 1784.   Agent for the inhabitants of Wyoming.

Read in the House the first time on Monday, the 23d of February, and by motion and special order, taken for a second reading, ordered that it be referred to Mr. Work, Mr. Miller, Mr. Johnson, Mr. Lutz and Mr. C———, (the same committee to whom the former petitions were referred.)

REPORT—19th March, 1784.

The committee to whom was referred the report of the committee on the charges contained in the petition from divers inhabitants of Wyoming, the letter from Alexander Patterson, Esq., the petitions from the inhabitants of Wyoming, beg leave to report :—

That after examining the different depositions accompanying the report of the committee on the charges contained in the petition from the inhabitants of Wyoming, they do not find that the same contain any matter of complaint, but such as if true, the laws of this State are fully sufficient to redress, and that therefore an application to this House was unnecessary and improper. A greater part of the irregularities alleged against Alexander Patterson, Esq., appear to have been done by people in his name, but no orders or warrant appears to have been given by him for any such acts. Your committee therefore submit the following resolution to the House:

Resolved, That the petition from divers inhabitants of Wyoming to this House, presented the eighth day of December last, be dismissed, and that the parties be referred to common law for redress, if any injuries they may have sustained.

LETTER XXIII.

1784.——Rife in stirring incident—Proceedings of Settlers—Petition to Connecticut—To Congress—Committee from Northampton—Pennsylvania Assembly—Deceptive movement of Patterson—Other influences dawn on the path of the Settlers—Action of Congress—Ice flood—Generous proposition of President Dickinson—Patterson's inhuman conduct—Expulsion of inhabitants—Generous feeling aroused throughout Pennsylvania—Negotiations—Settlers surrender their arms—Resume them—Proclamation—Base treachery of Armstrong—Settlers made prisoners, and sent to Sunbury and Easton jails—Prisoners released—War Renewed—Swift wounded—Henderson and Reed shot—Smith and Stevens killed—Cool courage of Ogden—Satterlee drowned—Council of Censors—Highly important proceedings—Armstrong returns with armed men—Capt. Bolin killed—Franklin's oath on the bloody rifle—Pleasing information—Withdrawal of troops enlisted by Patterson—Third Pennymite and Yankee war—Battle—Garrett and Pierce killed—Capt. John Franklin—Fort Dickinson invested—Part of Wilkesbarre burnt—Negotiation—Fort assaulted—Yankees defeated—Patterson indicted—Civil authority arrives at Wyoming—Affair at Locust Hill—Jacob Everett killed—Hon. John Armstrong.

MEANWHILE the inhabitants were not idle. Knowing the influence of public opinion, they sent petitions to the Pennsylvania Assembly, to the Assembly of Connecticut and to Congress, setting forth their wrongs, and praying for redress. With commendable promptitude, the Pennsylvania Assembly appointed the members from Northampton county, viz: Jacob Arndt, Jacob Stroud, Jonas Hartzel and Robert Brown, Esqrs., a committee to repair to Wyoming, and examine into the charges made. Having arrived on the 29th of December, and given notice to accusers and accused, they proceeded to take depositions, remaining in the Valley about ten days.*

Hearing that new and ex-parte depositions had been sent down by Justice Patterson, a second petition was sent forward by the settlers, declaring their entire submission to the constitution and laws of Pennsylvania, as became good citizens, and beseeching protection. The whole matter was referred to a committee, which reported

* "To the honour of this committee of Assembly, their inquiries were conducted with the strictest justice and impartiality."—*Franklin.*

January 23, 1784, briefly, that there was nothing proved which might not be remedied by process of law, and that there was no evidence that the irregularities were authorized or sanctioned by Justice Patterson. Daniel Clymer, Esq., of Berks county rose, and reading one of the depositions declared, " there was evidence enough in that to show that Alexander Patterson ought to be removed." General Robert Brown said, " he was certain no member of the House could imagine him in the interest of the people of Wyoming beyond the bounds of truth, and a desire to do justice. He had visited Wyoming as one of the committee upon the subject, and had heard all the evidence on both sides. The wrongs and sufferings of the people of Wyoming, he was constrained to declare, were intolerable. If there ever on earth was a people deserving redress, it was those people. Let the depositions lying on the table be read, and afford the House an opportunity to judge." An evident desire was manifested summarily to get rid of the subject, the landholders' interest predominating. Speaker Gray, somewhat irregularly remarked from the chair, that Justice Patterson had returned to Wyoming, that he could not be prosecuted without being present, that the session was drawing to a close, and important business pressing, which must be laid over if this matter was pressed." In accordance with these suggestions the subject was allowed to rest.

While these measures were in agitation, the policy of Justice Patterson was displayed, in causing a petition to be presented, signed by names distinguished among the settlers, complying with his demands, relinquishing the pretended claim under Connecticut, and soliciting the bounty of the Assembly, which was somewhat ostentatiously extended to them, grants being made to Shephard, Spalding, and a dozen others, of lands in the western part of the State. The gentlemen answering to those names among the settlers disavowed the proceedings, and whatever became of those land warrants we have been unable to learn.

Other influences, in free States ever potent, began now to affect the interests of the settlers. At the preceding fall election, Capt. Simon Spalding, and twenty-three others, repaired to Northumberland, some of them traveling an hundred miles, and none of them less than sixty, to reach the nearest place for balloting. After taking the oath of allegiance, their ballots were deposited in separate boxes, lest they should be deemed irregular; but this caused it to be known for whom they had voted. So nearly were parties divided, that these twenty-four votes decided the election of a member of the Supreme Executive Council, two Representatives to the Assembly, and the Sheriff. Justice Patterson remonstrated vehemently, but unsuccessfully, against the commission being given to Henry Antis, Esq., thus chosen Sheriff of Northumberland. The Assembly rejected the votes for members, which produced a protest from the minority, brief, but so well drawn, and being the first political Pennsylvania party movement, bearing on the affairs at Wyoming, we insert it entire.

"We whose names are hereto subscribed, considering the security of elections the only safeguard of public liberty and the peace of the State, do protest against the determination of the House on the Northumberland election, for the following reasons.

"We conceive the twenty-four votes set aside as illegal, were given by legal voters, inasmuch as the persons giving them were in fact in the government (though not in the territory) of Connecticut, which exercised a full jurisdiction over them, until the decree at Trenton.

"We observe, that allowing it to be Connecticut, as was contended until the decree at Trenton, then they may be deemed persons coming from another State, who producing certificates of their having taken the oath to this State, become by law entitled to vote: this, it was fully proved they had done. Of this construction we apprehend there is clear and express precedent in the case of the inhabitants of Westmoreland and Washington, on the settlement of the Virginia line, who were admitted to vote immediately, as persons coming from another State.

"We cannot but lament the fatal policy, which, instead of conciliating these people, and adopting them as our subjects and citizens, and endearing them to us in political bands, we are straining the laws against them, and making such difference between them and the adopted inhabitants of Virginia; and hold ourselves clear of the consequences which must flow from such unadvised proceedings, which in our judgment has a strong tendency to revive the dispute, which they may yet do under the articles of confederation, and drive them back to the jurisdiction of Connecticut, which will be more ready to receive them, and renew the old claim, when they find the actual settlers excluded from the common privileges of the citizens of this State. Therefore we wish it to be known to our constituents, and to the world at large, that we have borne our testimony against the determination on said election."

Subscribed by twenty members of the minority.

Congress, on the petition of Zebulon Butler and others, on motion of Mr. Jefferson, Chairman of the committee,—Resolved, January 23, 1784, "That a court, under the 9th article of the confederation, should be raised, to try and determine the private right of soil, as derived from Pennsylvania and Connecticut, and notice was ordered to be given to the respective parties to attend by their agents, on the fourth Monday of June following." A spirited remonstrance from the Pennsylvania Assembly, adopted the succeeding February, arrested further proceedings. Preferring to present this interesting matter in one connected view, the details are delayed to a future letter.

It seemed as if the very elements had conspired to augment the woes, or to try the fortitude of the Wyoming people. After a winter of unusual severity, about the middle of March the weather became suddenly warm, and on the 13th and 14th rain fell in torrents, melting the deep snows throughout all the hills and valleys in the upper regions watered by the Susquehanna. "The following day," says Chapman, "the ice in the river began to break up, and the streams rose with great rapidity. The ice first gave way at the different rapids, and floating down in great masses, lodged against the frozen surface of the more gentle parts of the river, where it remained firm. In this manner several large dams were formed, which caused such an accumulation of water that the river overflowed all its banks, and one general inundation overspread the extensive plains of Wyoming. The inhabitants took refuge on the surrounding heights, and saw their property exposed to the fury of the waters. At length the upper dam gave way, and huge masses of ice were scattered in every direction. The deluge bore down upon the dams below—which successively yielded to the insupportable burden, and the whole went off with the noise of contending storms. Houses, barns, fences, stacks of hay and grain, were swept off in the general destruction, to be seen no more. The plain on which the village of Wilkesbarre is built, was covered with heaps of ice which continued a great portion of the following summer."

To this admirable and graphic description, it may not be uninteresting to add several instances of special adventure and loss. Abel Pierce, Esq., (whom we have before seen on the bench, as one of the justices of quorum, and whom we shall again be obliged to present in weeds of deepest woe,) had his residence on Kingston flats, opposite Wilkesbarre. Suddenly in the night, the family was aroused by a rushing sound and mighty convulsions, which shook the house, when the waters, a dam having broken above, flowed in upon the floor, giving them scarcely time to ascend for safety to the chamber, rescuing a few things from destruction. Huge masses of ice, one following another, struck against the side of the house, seeming to be rending it from its foundations, and the water had already risen nearly to the upper floor. A craft, which they had secured the day before, tied to a tree close by the window, now afforded them the only ray of hope and shelter, as they were almost certain the building must be swept away. Passing from the chamber window into the boat, the family waited in intense anxiety the subsiding of the deluge, and the break of morning. A daughter was thus exposed to the winds, the waves, and the storm, (who afterwards, as the honoured wife of Gen. Lord Butler, and the beloved mother of a numerous family, who still adorn every walk of life which they have chosen;) and a son, whose melancholy fate, before the close of this letter, must be recorded. The waters suddenly fell, so that when light appeared aid arrived, and the family were saved; but their stock of horses and cattle were all lost in the deluge. In Fish's Eddy, at the lower point of the town, forty head of cattle were seen floating at one time. But one life, so far as we learn, was lost, namely, that of Asa Jackson, in the upper part of Wilkesbarre, (Jacob's Plains.) He was the son of Mr. William Jackson, killed by the savages in 1779. His fate was peculiar—Daniel Gore and Mr. Jackson were standing on the river bank observing the ice break up, when suddenly there came a rush of waters deluging the flats, and pouring in huge masses between them and the hill. Jackson sprang on a horse he had beside him, and rode for life to reach the high lands, but becoming entangled in the ice he was borne away by the flood, man and steed, and were no more seen. Mr. Gore stood still: flight for him seemed impossible, when providentially a canoe of his own, broken from its moorings, floated near him, and he contrived by skill and care, to reach the shore in safety.

Reduced by successive visitations of ill fortune to poverty, this providential infliction, sweeping off many dwellings with their furniture, rude though they were hasty substitutes for those the savages had destroyed; the loss of provisions, clothing, cattle and hay, left numbers a prey to extreme sufferings, which their neighbours were in no condition effectually to relieve. Learning the distressing event, President Dickinson (with gratitude and honour be it recorded,) sent the following message to the Assembly on the 31st of March:

"GENTLEMEN,—The late inundation having reduced many of the inhabitants of Wyoming to great distress, we should be glad your honourable House would make some immediate provision for their relief."

Pennsylvania, in every other instance just to a scruple, and generous to profusion, yet under the influence of land-speculators the Assembly labored under too deep a prejudice to regard the settlers as objects of commiseration or charity, and no aid was afforded. The welcome and abundant shad fishing that ensued, alone prevented actual starvation.

With the opening of spring the soldiery began to remove fences, disregarding the Connecticut boundaries, and establishing those of the Pennsylvania surveys.* Resistance was made, and a determination avowed not to submit peaceably to the measure, the people insisting on a legal trial, declaring that to a regular and fair judicial decision they would yield implicit, if not cheerful obedience. Forthwith more vigorous and decisive measures were resolved upon, and justice Patterson, to prepare the mind of Council, wrote to the President, the last of April, the following pregnant intimation: "I therefore humbly hope, that if any dangerous, or seditious commotion should arise in this county, so remote from the seat of Government, that it may not be construed into a want of zeal or love for the Commonwealth, *if we should, through dire necessity, be obliged to do some things not strictly consonant to the letter of the law.*"

On the 13th and 14th of May the soldiery were sent forth, and at the point of the bayonet, with the most highhanded arrogance, dispossessed an hundred and fifty families; in many instances, set fire to their dwellings, avowing the intention utterly to expel them from the country. Unable to make any effectual resistance, the people

---

* "The soldiers were set to work removing the fences from the inclosures of the inhabitants —laying fields of grain open to be devoured—fencing up the highways, and between the houses of the settlers, and their wells of water—that they were not suffered to procure water from their wells, or to travel on their usual highways. The greatest part of the settlers were in the most distressed situation—numbers having had their horses swept off by the uncommon overflowing of the river Susquehanna in the month of March preceding; numbers were without a shelter, and in a starving condition; but they were not suffered to cut a stick of timber, or make any shelter for their families. They were forbid to draw their nets for fish—their nets were taken from them by the officers of the garrison. The settlers were often dragged out of their beds in the night season by ruffians, and beat in a cruel manner. Complaints were made to the justices, as well as to the commanding officers of the garrison; but to no purpose—they were equally callous to every feeling of humanity."

FRANKLIN.

implored for leave to remove either up or down the river, in boats, as with their wives and children, in the state of the roads, it would be impossible to travel. A stern refusal met this seemingly reasonable request, and they were directed to take the Lackawaxen road, as leading most directly to Connecticut. But this way consisted of sixty miles of wilderness, with scarce a house; the roads wholly neglected during the war, and they then begged leave to take the Easton, or Stroudsburg road, where bridges spanned the larger streams, still swollen with recent rains. All importunities were vain, and the people fled towards the Delaware, objects of destitution and pity, that should have moved a heart of marble. About five hundred men, women and children, with scarce provisions to sustain life, plodded their weary way, mostly on foot, the road being impassable for wagons; mothers carrying their infants, and pregnant women literally waded streams, the water reaching to their armpits, and at night slept on the naked earth, the Heavens their canopy, with scarce clothes to cover them. A Mr. Gardiner and John Jenkins, Esq., (who had been a Representative in the Connecticut Assembly, and was Chairman of the Town Meeting, which, in 1775, had adopted those noble resolutions in favour of liberty,) both aged men and lame, sought their way on crutches. Little children, tired with traveling, crying to their mothers for bread, which they had not to give them, sunk from exhaustion into stillness and slumber; while the mothers could only shed tears of sorrow and compassion, till in sleep they forgot their grief and cares. Several of the unhappy sufferers died in the wilderness, others were taken sick from excessive fatigue, and expired soon after reaching the settlement. A widow with a numerous family of children, whose husband had been slain in the war, endured inexpressible hardships. One child died, and she buried it as she could beneath a hemlock log, probably to be disinterred from its shallow covering, and be devoured by wolves.*

Wherever the news extended of this outrage, not on the Wyoming settlers alone, but on the common rights of humanity and justice,

---

* It is probable that the ostensible reason for compelling the exiles to this route, the fear lest their old and kind friends at Stroudsburg should afford them aid, was not without weight. Esquire Elisha Harding was one of the exiles. He says, "It was a solemn scene: parents, their children crying for hunger—aged men on crutches—all urged forward by an armed force at our heels. The first night we encamped at Capouse; the second, at Cobb's; the third, at Little Meadow, so called. Cold, hungry and drenched with rain, the poor women and children suffering much. The fourth night, at Lackawack; fifth, at Blooming-

feelings of indignation were awakened and expressed, too emphatic to be disregarded. In no part of the Union were the sympathies of the people more generously aroused than among the just and good people of Pennsylvania. The influence brought to bear on the Government, produced the instant dismissal of the troops; and Captains Shrawder and Christie were ordered, on the 13th of June, to discharge their respective companies. Justice Patterson forthwith, by his own authority, re-enlisted for the land-claimants, about one-half of the most desperate, already in their interest, in whom he could rely, and set at once the settlers and the Commonwealth at defiance. Henry Antis, Sheriff of Northumberland, on learning the disorders that prevailed, hastened to Wyoming to restore, if possible, the reign of law. Messengers were despatched after the exiles, with invitations to return, and promises of protection. Gladdened by these cheering tidings the settlers returned, assisted by the never-failing benevolence of the people of New Jersey and Pennsylvania, along the Delaware; but on their arrival, they found that Sheriff Antis was powerless against the illegal and desperate forces of Patterson. No homes opened their doors to receive them, for their farms were in the possession of others. Thus situated they encamped among the clefts of the rocks on the eastern mountains, where a cave was strengthened for their head-quarters, and received the name of "Fort Lillo-pe." Justice Patterson, unbroken in spirit and inflamed to the most vengeful resentment by the return of the fugitives, sent a flag of truce, and offered to those who had resided in Wilkesbarre, leave to return to their habitations in town, promising them protection. Several men, who placed confidence enough in his honour to visit the place, were seized, tied up and cruelly beaten with iron ramrods. Capt. Jabez Fish, of Wilkesbarre, and Mr. John Gore, of Kingston, were two who thus suffered. Sheriff Antis being set at defiance by the now lawless garrison, returned to Northumberland, inculcating patience, and promising early assistance to the people. Tired of their comfortless residence, Fort Lillope, which had been

grove; sixth, at Shehola; on the seventh, arrived at the Delaware, where the people dispersed, some going up and some down the river. I kept on east, and when I got to the top of Shongum mountain, I looked back with this thought: shall I abandon Wyoming forever? The reply was, No! oh no! There lie your murdered brothers and friends. Dear to me art thou, though a land of affliction. Every way looked gloomy, except towards Wyoming. Poor, ragged and distressed as I was, I had youth, health, and felt that my heart was whole. So I turned back to defend or die.'

occupied since the 30th of May, was abandoned on the 3d of July, and the Yankees removed to Kingston, taking up their quarters at Abraham's (now Tuttle's) Creek.

In the mean time a company of thirty young men had associated to defend the settlers, and secure the ripening harvests. Armed, and prepared for labour or war, on the 20th of July they were marching from Kingston to Shawney, when on Ross's Hill they met a larger party of Patterson's new levies, who opened a fire upon the Yankees, by which Elisha Garrett and Chester Pierce were slain. The former fell dead on the spot; the latter lingered until the next morning, when he expired. The Yankees promptly returned the fire, by which several of Patterson's men were wounded; Henry Brink and Wilhelmus Van Gordon being left on the field, and another returned to the fort, his broken arm swinging in his sleeve. Both Pierce and Garrett were highly esteemed for their virtues, and beloved for their open, frank and manly spirit. In the bloom of youth, manhood opening upon them with its fairest promise of usefulness and honour, their untimely death shrouded the whole settlement in gloom. Chester Pierce was the son of the good Justice, Abel Pierce, Esq., of whom we have before spoken. They were buried amid deep execrations at the cruelty of Patterson, which had led to this civil war, mingling with the cries of woe.

A general rally of the settlers, able to bear arms, was the consequence. Forty-two effective and twenty old men, mustered under Capt. John Franklin at Kingston, marched down on the west side of the river to Shawney, dispossessing every Pennsylvania family, (except from humanity those of Brink and Van Gordon, who lay wounded.) Franklin then crossed over to Nanticoke, and marched up, turning out every settler that did not hold under the Connecticut claim, driving them to the fort, which was immediately surrounded. Civil war to blood now openly prevailed. With equal spirit and policy the garrison, to dispossess the Yankees of several houses from which they were annoyed, made a sortie and set fire to twenty-three buildings, which were consumed. The fort mounted four pieces of cannon, the ancient four-pounder and three others, left by Sullivan's army, but destitute of suitable ammunition. The small arms, with cartridges provided for the companies of Shrawder and Christie, amounting to an hundred and thirty, were in good condition, and afforded the besieged party, consisting of more than a hundred men, ample means of resistance. From time to time, messengers arrived from Northumberland, dissuading from hostilities, and promising protection from the civil authorities. Well inclined as the magistrates doubtless were, they had no authority to embody an armed force, without which their presence, in the existing state of excited passions, would, they well imagined, prove wholly inefficacious.

Having taken possession of the grist-mill at Mill-Creek, the only one in the settlement, the settlers kept it running night and day, to provide flour for themselves and friends, for future emergencies, as well as their present wants.

Capt. John Franklin was entrusted with the command of the besieging forces; and before storming the fort, sent in the following summons.

"WYOMING, July 27, 1784.

"Gentlemen:—In the name and behalf of the inhabitants of this place, who hold their lands under the Connecticut claim, and were lately, without law, or even the colour of law, driven from their possessions in a hostile and unconstitutional manner, we, in the name of those injured and incensed inhabitants, demand an immediate surrender of your garrison unto our hands, together with our possessions and property; which, if complied with, you shall be treated with humanity and commiseration, otherwise the consequences shall prove fatal and bloody to every person found in the garrison.

We give you two hours for a decisive answer, and will receive the same at Mr. Bailey's.

Signed, JOHN FRANKLIN,
In behalf of the injured."

Whatever might be the faults committed, the garrison, as Pennsylvania soldiers, never wanted courage to dare, or fortitude to endure. The summons was received with scorn. A vigorous, but unsuccessful attack was made on the fort, several lives were lost, both parties being sufferers, but the Yankees were compelled to retire, and took up their former position above Forty Fort.

Forty of the Pennsylvania party, concerned in the expulsion of the inhabitants, among whom were Justice Patterson and Major James Moore, were indicted by the Grand Jury at Sunbury, and Sheriff Antis was sent to Wyoming to arrest them; but his efforts were unavailing, as Patterson and Moore, secure behind their ramparts, set him and his authority at defiance.*

* At a trial subsequently held, Chief Justice M'Kean presiding, the majesty of the laws was nobly vindicated; the rioters, (who, mortifying enough, had been arrested by Franklin and Swift, Yankee leaders, deputed by the Sheriff) severely fined. The charge of the Judge was long remembered for its just sentiments, its deep feeling, and the impressive manner in which it was delivered; but the fines were never collected.

In obedience to orders from the Supreme Executive Council, Thomas Hewit, Esq., a Justice of the Peace, accompanied by John Scott, Esq., Coroner of Northumberland County, repaired to Wyoming, where they arrived on the 29th of July. A few days afterwards they were joined by Sheriff Antis, and Justices Mead and Martin, with directions, by the interposition of the authority of the Commonwealth with both parties, to put a stop to hostilities. But the Yankees, having learned that an armed force, partly collected in New Jersey, were assembling at Larner's, under the command of Major Moore, to reinforce Patterson, had previously detached Capt. John Swift, a determined officer, with thirty picked men, to meet, dislodge and defeat them before they could reach the Valley. It was certainly unfortunate, for on the 2nd of August, the day Sheriff Antis and the Magistrates arrived, Swift met an advanced party at Locust Hill:* a battle ensued, Jacob Everett, one of Moore's men, was killed, and several others wounded on each side, when both parties retired, Moore to Easton, and Swift to his post in Kingston. In this instance the Yankees were charged with an unprovoked murder, as the men attacked were in Northampton County, and had not participated in the disturbances at Wyoming. It was defended as a measure of absolute necessity and justifiable self defence, the destination and object of the troops being perfectly understood, and their commander being Major Moore, the active oppressor of the settlers, and confidential coadjutor of Patterson. It afterwards appeared that Moore's company was the advanced guard of a larger force, raised by order of the Supreme Executive Council, and placed under the command of Col. John Armstrong, Secretary, and the Hon. John Boyd, a member of the Council, who were appointed Commissioners to restore the reign of law and order in the disturbed district. Three hundred Infantry, and fifteen light dragoons, were ordered to be raised from the militia of Northampton, and placed at their disposal.†

* Locust ridge was on the old Sullivan road, near the south bank of the Lehi, three or four miles east of Stodartsville.

† The Yankees affirm that Logan, a mulatto, was under Patterson, with a company of thirty men, raised on the Delaware. A rude old song spoke of Logan:—

>> The 20th of September,
>> We marched the rebel route;
>> From Easton to Wyoming,
>> To drive the Yankees out.
>>> The weary dogs and savage beasts
>>> Would rather steal than show their face.

In introducing a gentleman of so much eminence as Col. Armstrong upon the scene of action, a few words illustrative of his character may not be deemed inappropriate.—Col. Armstrong was then most distinctly known as the author of the Newberg Letters to the army, written with a power and eloquence rarely equalled, if ever surpassed, and which it required the whole force of Washington's influence to disarm of its envenomed poison. Though passed by with marked neglect by Washington, succeeding Presidents, deeming that his talents might be rendered serviceable to the country, called him into public life, and he was successively appointed to the stations of Minister to Madrid, then to France, and afterwards, during the last contest with Great Britain, to that of Secretary of War. In whatever station placed, his style, formed on the model of Junius, equally terse, vigorous, and epigramatic, attracted universal attention, and wrung even from his enemies unwilling applause. " To appeal to the Laws of Nations," said he to Napoleon, " is literally to appeal to the dead." In his incendiary letter to the army, he thus speaks—" Can you consent to be the only sufferers by this revolution, and retiring from the field, grow old in poverty, wretchedness and contempt? Can you consent to wade through the vile mire of despondency, and owe the miserable remnant of that life to charity, which has hitherto been spent in honour? If you can, GO, and carry with you the jest of tories, and the scorn of whigs—the ridicule, and what is worse, the pity of the world.—Go, STARVE, and be FORGOTTEN!"

But in style alone was his vigour displayed. As Secretary at War, the duty of providing for the defence of Washington devolved especially on him; and with its capture he lost, with his friends, all that was desirable of popularity, and all that was estimable in confidence; while his enemies, and he had many, in the bitterness of their execration, quoting the line of Homer, " Thou dog in forehead, but a deer in heart," insisted it was only that the lion skin was removed, and the man exposed in his true character. From 1812

> We halted all at Romig's,
> Our forces to review;
> Our chief commander LOGAN
> Encouraged thus his crew—
> " Brave lads he cried, who steals the most,
> He shall obtain the highest post."

Prejudice probably dignified a servant of Patterson, or Van Campen, with the title of an officer.

he lived at his seat on the Hudson, in affluent neglect, until 1843, when at past the age of eighty years his career was closed in death. If some slight bitterness may seem to be infused into this sketch, his conduct at Wyoming will be found to have richly deserved it.

Previous to the arrival of Col. Armstrong, negotiations had been opened by the magistrates, with both the contending parties. The letters which passed; their communication to the President of Council, and their report to Messrs. Boyd and Armstrong, are regarded of great importance, as they show, officially and incontestibly, that the Wyoming people were the suffering party; willing to pay obedience to the laws; but driven to arms by unendurable oppression.

"Wyoming, 5th of August, 1784.

"Gentlemen:—In obedience to our instruction from the Supreme Executive Council of the State of Pennsylvania, we have repaired to this place, and find two distinct parties in actual hostilities. Therefore, in the name of the Commonwealth we command you, and that without delay, to deliver to us the arms of your party, and such a number of your men as we shall think proper, to put in charge of the High Sheriff until the pleasure of the Chief Justice is known, and those that remain to be bound to the peace and good behaviour in sufficient security.

"We are, etc.   Thomas Hewit,
                 David Mead,
                 Robert Martin."

"Messrs. Phinehas Pierce,
    Giles Slocum,
    John Swift.

"N. B.—The Connecticut party dispersed in our presence."

"Wyoming, August 5th, 1784.

"Gentlemen:—We received yours of the present date as magistrates, and as such we revere you in your exalted sphere; and as you have, in the name of the Commonwealth of Pennsylvania made a demand of our arms, declare our promptitude to comply with your requisition, and we shall rely, gentlemen, upon your honours, that we shall have the benefit of the laws of this State, in all respects, for the future; at the same time lamenting the neglect of the law in times past, which has been the occasion of all the hostilities we are charged with.

"Gentlemen, we are, with respect, etc.

John Franklin,
John Swift,
Giles Slocum,
Phinehas Pierce.

"Thomas Hewit,
David Mead,
Robert Martin. } Esquires."

"Wyoming, 5th August, 1784.

"Gentlemen:—In consequence of our instructions from the Supreme Executive Council of the State of Pennsylvania, we have demanded of the Connecticut party their arms, and such a number of their men as we think proper to put in charge of the High Sheriff of the county, until the pleasure of the Chief Justice is known, and those that remain to be bound to the peace and good behaviour, in sufficient security, which they have complied with. Therefore, in the name of the Commonwealth, we demand the same of you and your party; also the delivery to us of all the State property, and your flag to be taken down.

"We are, etc.

Thomas Hewit,
Robert Martin,
David Mead.

"Messrs. Alexander Patterson,
Blackall W. Ball, Samuel
Reed, Andrew Henderson."

"Wyoming, August 6th, 1784.

"Gentlemen:—In obedience to the instructions of Council, of the 24th of July, we repaired to this place, and found the Pennsylvania and Connecticut parties in actual hostilities, and yesterday made a demand of the Connecticut party, of a surrender of their arms, and submission to the laws of this State, *which they complied with;* reference being had to the enclosed papers. We also made a demand of the same nature, of the party in the garrison, but have received no direct, but an evasive answer, at the same time expressing fear of their lives; in reply to which, they were promised protection, agreeably to law, in every respect; but still hold the garrison, and have not dispersed. We believe that a due execution of the laws will be the most effectual means to quiet the country; as to the pretended titles of the Connecticut party we have nothing to fear, *and are convinced that had it not been through the cruel and irregular conduct of our people, the peace might have been established long since, and the dignity of this Government supported.*

"We are, etc.
THOMAS HEWIT,
ROBERT MARTIN,
DAVID MEAD.

"His Excellency the President and Members of the Supreme Executive Council of Pennsylvania. Pr. Express."

"WYOMING, August 7th, 1784.

"Gentlemen:—We are sorry to have occasion to write to you on so disagreeable a subject as the hostilities of this place. We have dispersed the Connecticut party; *but our own people we cannot.* Yesterday, when we despatched a message to Council, we had some expectation of introducing the laws of Government here; but this day, when a civil officer attempted the service of legal process on persons in the garrison, admission and service was denied; the proper depositions of which we have taken, in order to transmit to the Chief Justice: Therefore, we think it our indispensable duty to request you to come forward with the militia, with as much despatch as possible.

"We are, gentlemen, etc.
DAVID MEAD,
ROBERT MARTIN.

"JOHN BOYD,
JOHN ARMSTRONG.} Esquires."

"We are convinced," say the commissioners, "that had it not been through the CRUEL and IRREGULAR conduct of *our people, the peace might have been established long since*, and the dignity of this Government supported." And this representation derives weight from the fact that David Mead, Esq., was one of the illegally elected Justices, and for a year the coadjutor of Justice Patterson. His better judgment, and moral sensibility, shocked at the wrongs perpetrated on the settlers, led him to this official declaration.

Again, "we have dispersed the Connecticut party, *our people we cannot.*" Being set at defiance; their messenger to the fort told, that "Capt. Patterson desired him to go home about his business, if any he had,"—and bid him begone, begone immediately:" the commissioners wrote to urge the march of Boyd and Armstrong, to reduce the refractory Pennsylvanians.

Upon the refusal of Patterson to yield obedience, the commissioners permitted the Connecticut people to resume their arms for self defence, and they immediately concentrated their forces at their former post, on Abraham's Creek, where they waited, as far as brave men may ever be said to do so, with fear and trembling, the arrival of Cols. Armstrong and Boyd. Having assembled a force of four hundred men, those gentlemen marched from Larner's on the 6th, and on the 8th of August* arrived at Wyoming. A proclamation was immediately issued, declaring that they came in the name of the commonwealth, as commissioners of peace, to repress violence from whatever quarter, to establish order, and restore the reign of law; demanding an immediate cessation of hostilities, and the surrender of their arms by both parties, promising impartial justice and protection. A conference having been opened with the Connecticut party, serious doubts and misgivings existed in the breasts of several of the Yankee leaders, who had so far experienced, as they said, "nothing but oppression and treachery;" but Col. Armstrong pledged his faith as a soldier, and his honour as a gentleman, that Patterson's party should also be disarmed, and equal protection should be extended to all. They paraded, were ordered to "ground arms"†—they were then commanded —"right about—march ten steps—halt—right about!" which they obeyed; when Col. Armstrong ordered his men to advance and take up the grounded arms. Thus far was according to their expectations; but their surprise was merged in bitterest mortification, when Col. Armstrong gave rapid orders, as rapidly obeyed, to surround the disarmed settlers, and make them all prisoners—resistance was vain,

---

* Chapman says the 16th. Col. Franklin's journal is precise as to this and twenty succeeding dates, mentioning also the day of the week. He has it—"Sunday 8, Col. Armstrong, and Esq. Boyd with four hundred Northampton militia arrived here.

Tues. 10. Lay down our arms to Col. Armstrong, and Esq. Boyd, after having given us every engagement that no advantage should be taken," &c.

† Elisha Harding in his letter to the author says, "Col. Armstrong came with his regiment, and with great parade entered the fort, and then wrote to Col. Franklin stating that he had orders from the Governor to march to Wyoming, to stop the effusion of blood; that he had heard the Yankees had laid down their arms to the Sheriff, in submission to the law; but in order that he could assure the Governor he had seen it, desired Col. Franklin would parade his men, and again lay down their arms, pledging his honour and the honour of the state, that they should not be detained more than an hour, and that no advantage should be taken of their submission." The rest is known. I suppress the terms of indignation used at the treachery. The name of Brandt was scarcely more execrated by all the ancient people.

and escape hopeless. Not a musket was taken from Patterson's forces, but they beheld the successful treachery of Col. Armstrong with unrestrained delight, and taunting exultation. A soldier's faith should be unsullied as the judicial ermine—the pledged honour of a gentleman, more sacred than life. Both were basely violated, and language is too poor to paint in proper colours the detestable deed.*

Bound with cords, the thirty who had been with Swift at Locust Hill were thrown into the guard house, charged with murder, and orders given to put to death instantly, any man who should attempt to escape.† Had not civil war, open war, prevailed? Had not blood been shed and lives been lost? If self defence justified hostilities, and did it not? is there any maxim in military affairs better established, than that you are warrantable in attacking an enemy concentrating on your frontiers, to invade you, before his reinforcements come up? The expedition, then, of Swift, to Locust Hill, however deeply to be deplored, was justified on the plea of necessity and self defence. The thirty men, as soon as irons could be provided, were marched to Easton, under a strong guard and committed to prison.‡ Forty-six others were bound and confined, part in an

---

* Remote and obscure as Armstrong may have regarded the scene of treachery, and however inconsiderable the sufferers, the transaction was soon bruited abroad, and adding infamy to the ignominy of his Newberg Letters, tended long to exile him, fine as was his address, and considerable as were his talents, from public confidence and employments.

"I will remark that the Northampton militia, in general, appeared to be humane."

FRANKLIN.

† The account given of this affair by Elisha Harding, Esq., is minute and interesting. "When the Yankees were marched to the fort from the place where they laid down their arms (a mile below the bridge, on the Carey Town road, near the new white house of M'Cleans, [1813,]) Armstrong sat on horseback in imposing state, and ordered the roll of the prisoners to be called. As a name was spoken that was at Locust Ridge—he nodded towards Giles Slocum's house, whither the man was sent. When one was called, not at the Ridge, he nodded, like another Jove, towards Col. Butler's, whither the man was sent, and so on until all were called off and separated. Those destined for Easton were treated with great severity, being deprived of any food for twenty-four hours. When the irons were ready, they were hand cuffed in pairs, right and left, a long rope tied to the irons, and that fastened to two soldiers, who marched next; then came two more prisoners, and a pair of soldiers; thus a very long column was formed, all fastened together, flanked by a strong guard, with bayonets fixed. Going up the mountain, some hung back, and impeded the march; some contrived to loosen their hands, and cut the cords. Threats of instant death did but increase the mischief. Maj. Abbot and Waterman Baldwin escaped at Larner's. Wm. Ross, by superior activity, took leave from Heller's. The rest were lodged in prison; our allowance being a pound of bread with water a day. But there was an old gentleman of Easton, who every Friday sent us a dinner good enough for men who were well fed. He has been long dead, but his memory will live with me while I have life. His name was MICHAEL HART, an Israelite. This meal did but give us an appetite for more; so we concluded to break up house keeping, and seek better quarters,"—&c.

‡ "Aug. 14. The Locust Hill party being coupled two and two in irons, and all bound

out-house of Col. Butler; part in the red house (still standing,) on Bank Street. Among the latter were Jehoiada Pitt Johnson, (father of the present Attorney-General of Pennsylvania,) and Lieut. John Jenkins.—Their hands were tied behind them. Turning back to back, some of the prisoners were fortunate enough to loose the bands of their fellows, who proceeded to untie the rest. Lieut. Jenkins, with characteristic spirit, swore by the God who made him his hands should never be untied if they rotted off, unless by the very man who had bound him. The day following his wrists being so swollen, as nearly to bury the cord, the man was sent, and he was released. Justices Martin and Mead, having full confidence in Messrs. Franklin, Pierce, and Slocum, with whom they had previously negotiated, admitted them and Mr. Johnson to bail, binding them to attend the next court to be holden at Sunbury.

On Thursday, the 19th, the remaining forty-two prisoners were again bound, and sent under a strong detachment of men to Northumberland jail, two of whom made their escape by the way, and four after arriving at Sunbury. Thus sixty-six men of the Connecticut party were in prison, it being apparent that Col. Armstrong was acting under the influence of the landholders, in the same line of policy with Justice Patterson, namely, to dispossess by fraud and force the settlers from the beautiful, and, from the long and bloody contests for them, the inappreciably rich and lovely Wyoming alluvial lands, her fertile meadows, and extensive plains. The conquest seemed to be complete;* the work effectually done; the pacification of the Valley

---

together with ropes, were sent to Easton under guard. As they were marching off Mr. Secretary Armstrong gave orders to the guard, that if any one prisoner attempted to make his escape, *to put the whole immediately to death*, and that Government would indemnify them for so doing."

"August 19. Forty-two others were bound together with ropes, in a team, and sent under a military guard to Sunbury goal. The Sheriff of the County proposed to take charge of the whole that were to be sent to Sunbury, before they left Wyoming, *and to be accountable for them all, but could not be permitted*. In a word, during the confinement of the prisoners at Wyoming, they were treated in a most cruel and barbarous manner,—suffered with hunger—and suffocated in a nauseous prison, for the want of fresh air; and insulted by a banditti of ruffians—the prisoners were not even suffered to go out of their house to perform their most necessary occasions for the ease of nature, for the term of nine days."

FRANKLIN.

[Oh! this was but one degree less horrible than the Black Hole at Calcutta.]

* A letter to the author, dated Hartford, Con., June 3d, 1845, says—" A few days since, a gentleman of this city (Joseph Morgan Esq.,) furnished me with an original letter which relates to Wyoming, and which he thought might be of service to you, if your work had not gone to press. It was presented to him by John Potter, Esq. of Centre County, the grandson of one of the persons to whom it was addressed. The superscription of the letter

accomplished; and tenants of the Pennsylvania claimants took possession of the empty dwellings; the only difficulty that remained, was how to get rid of the wives and children of those in jail, and of the widows and orphans whose husbands and fathers slept beneath the sod.

is as follows. "The Honourable Gen. James Potter, and Col. William Montgomery, Esqrs. Members of Council of Censors, Philadelphia,—hand by Mr. Johnson."—

This paper is from the pen of Robert Martin, Esq., one of the Pennsylvania Justices, sent by the government to restore order at Wyoming. A person so eminent as Col. Armstrong, being deeply implicated by our narrative, the letter is deemed of great importance, fully sustaining as it does the facts we had derived from other sources.

Wyoming, 14th August, 1784.

Gentlemen :—

I beg leave to give you a detail of matters at this place. I must confess I am much disappointed as to the conduct of the Commissioners, to wit, Captain Boyd and Col. Armstrong. Esquire Mead and myself repaired to this place, in obedience to our instructions from Council, a copy of which hope you will call on Council for, and peruse, whereby you'll find we are required by every legal means in our power to investigate matters and to proceed impartially, in order that offenders of every description may be brought to justice. At our arrival we found that both the Pennsylvania and Connecticut parties had actually proceeded to hostilities, which we are well assured began five miles from the Garrison on Shawney Plains, about the 20th July last. Which party first began the fire at that time we cannot with certainty say; but we view both parties guilty of hostilities: previous to this, it can be proved, that numbers of the Connecticut party have been fired upon by the other party when they were about their lawful business. But to return to the subject of our mission or duty; soon after we came to this place, we called on the Connecticut party in the name of the commonwealth, to lay down their arms, and submit themselves to the laws; which they accordingly did, which will appear by papers inclosed in our letter to Council of the 6th inst., August; and at the same time declaring their willingness at all times to be law abiding; we accordingly made a demand of the like nature of Patterson and his party, or in other words, the Pennsylvania party; their answer was that they would comply, but said they would every one be murdered by the Connecticut party; we in answer to them said, we did not apprehend the least danger from their opponents, as they had solemnly engaged to us they would not molest or hurt one of them on any pretence whatever; we further assured them that we would not ask them to deliver their arms to us, before we put the arms of the Connecticut party on board the boat within sight of the Garrison; but all our arguments and proposals was to no purpose. Then we returned to the Connecticut party, and informed them that they were at liberty to take up their arms and disperse, and go to their habitations about their lawful business, which we believe they did, as we were of opinion that it would not be prudent to disarm one party and not the other. Our proposals to both parties were, that if they would submit to the laws, and deliver up their arms to us, we would put as many of the leading men of both parties, as we should see proper, in custody of the sheriff, to be taken to Sunbury. Had these proposals been complied with by Patterson and his party, we should have had no use for the Commissioners, or Militia, which plan we thought most likely to answer the objects of Government, and quiet the minds of the people, and at the same time be acting up to our instructions from Council. We had solemnly engaged to the Connecticut party on their submission, they should have equal justice with the other party, and the benefit of the law, which engagement we made known to the Commissioners on their arrival, who approved of our conduct, and assured us that they were sent here to do complete justice without distinction of parties; which gave us the highest expectations that matters would soon be settled in such a manner as would do honour to Government; but to our astonishment, no sooner had the Connecticut

Crowned with victory if not with laurel, Col. Armstrong returned to Philadelphia, to report formally to Council, and confidentially to his real, though less ostensible employers, the success of his mission. Scarcely had he time to receive the congratulations of friends on the promptitude and vigour with which he had brought to a close an enterprise that had baffled the efforts of his predecessors for more than a year, when the mortifying tidings reached the city, that the Sunbury prisoners were all released on bail, and the Locust Hill banditti had risen on their keepers, and only eleven were retaken and remanded to prison, while fourteen made their escape, and had returned to the contested district.* With signal celerity, Col. Armstrong raised a force of fifty men, and by rapid marches reached Wilkesbarre, on Monday the 20th of September.

party yielded themselves prisoners, and laid down their arms to the Commissioners, they were immediately marched under a strong guard, and crowded into two small houses, unfit for the reception of any human being, at the same time, to the great mortification of those prisoners, and contrary as they say, to the promise of the Commissioners, were insulted by the other party, with their arms in their hands, which we think by no means accords with the declaration of the Commissioners, which was, that they were sent here to do complete justice. It appears very clear to us, that the proceedings now at this place, are carried on in so unfair, partial, and unlawful manner, that we despair of establishing peace and good order in this part of the County; therefore, as for my own part, think it not prudent to act for the future in my office, unless properly supported, as we are very sure, nothing short of law, impartially distributed without distinction, will ever restore peace, and quiet the minds of the people in this place; sorry we are, and with reluctance we mention the partial proceedings here by the officers of Government, but at the same time think it our indispensable duty to bear testimony against them; *we are much alarmed at the horrid abuse of power* lodged in the hands of designing and biased men; we fear eventually it may bring on an intestine war between the states, to prevent which, we hope the authority of Pennsylvania will execute justice to every citizen thereof. The Connecticut party have generally declared themselves as such, by taking the oath of allegiance to this state as directed by law. God forbid that I should have any desire or inclination to favour the Connecticut party or their claims. I can honestly declare, that I should be as well pleased to see them legally removed from this place as any man in the State; as my interest here is under the Pennsylvania right. It must appear to every one acquainted with this circumstance, much to my interest to have them dispossest. I again say that I have nothing in view respecting the unhappy disputes here, but to do equal justice to every person, as I hope my conduct will at all times stand the test, and I be esteemed a faithful servant to Government."

I am with due respect, Gentlemen,
Your Humble Servant,
Rob. Martin.

Honourable James Potter, and Wm. Montgomery, Esquires.

N.B.—Gentlemen, you may make what use you please of this letter either public or private.

* Edward Inman, one of the Easton party, a man of great strength and personal courage, seized the keys from the jailor, knocked him down and gave the whole company liberty. A hot pursuit was immediately commenced. By scattering in all directions fourteen got free, while eleven were taken. After lying in jail three months, a court was held at Easton

In addition to Mr. Boyd, there came with Col. Armstrong Mr. James Read and Mr. John Oakley, as commissioners to bring about a compromise, but the latter speedily returned, without as is known, making any endeavour to effect the purpose of his mission.

While at Sunbury, Mr. Franklin was arrested on two warrants arising out of affairs at Wyoming, and on the 21st of September, the day after Armstrong's arrival, Mr. Johnson, Phineas Pierce, and Mr. Franklin were arrested for treason, on warrants from Justice Seeley. The object of those constantly recurring, expensive and harrassing arrests, is easily comprehended.

The sufferings of the Connecticut people had excited indignation and pity throughout the whole country, and several Green Mountain boys, who had gone through a similar struggle with the authorities of New York, had come to Wyoming, and volunteered their assistance to the settlers. An attempt by Patterson's men to secure a portion of the Yankee harvest was met and repelled. An occurrence which happened on Sunday night, the 26th of September, is differently represented. Col. Armstrong reported that the Yankees, wholly unprovoked, made an attack on his quarters in Wilkesbarre, but were vigorously met and speedily repulsed, giving this as a proof of the evil disposition of the people. Mr. Franklin and others, in a memorial protest, "We declare to God that the report is false, and the Connecticut party had no hand in it;" charging Armstrong and Patterson with making the attack, or pretended attack. themselves, for the purpose of criminating the settlers. Exhausted patience could endure no longer. Forbearance had ceased to be a virtue, while fear and cowardice began to be so distinctly imputed against the Yankee leaders, that they resolved to bring the matter to a crisis by attacking the garrison. A frame work of plank was formed and placed on wheels, so that pushed forward, it would shield the assailants from the small arms of the enemy. A number of men all armed, and some of them carrying brands of fire, under

Chief Justice M'Kean presiding, and bills sent up to the Grand Jury, charging the prisoners with the murder of Jacob Everett. The Jury promptly returned the bills "*ignoramus*," when Judge M'Kean said, "he did not see how they could render such a return," but in conclusion remarked, "that killing by either side was no way to settle the title to the land." The Jury considered the settlers as fighting in self-defence; and such was the popular opinion throughout the State. This and the subsequent refusal of the Jury of Northumberland to find bills against the prisoners sent to Sunbury, and the fact that Major Moore, and a large number of Patterson's party were indicted and convicted, will show the prevailing feeling throughout Pennsylvania, in respect to the parties.

the command of Capt. Swift, on the evening of the 29th September, supported by a strong corps in reserve, pushed up their frame towards a house occupied by Patterson. A battle ensued; the house was abandoned and set on fire, and Messrs. Henderson and Reed, in attempting to escape to the fort were shot down. Capt. Swift received a wound in the throat, which was supposed to be mortal.*

The garrison was now closely invested, the Yankees occupying two houses from which the opposing party had been driven. Two of the same name belonged to the investing company, designated as little William and big William Smith. The latter, in attempting to obtain water from the river, was shot through the body. He reached the house and said, "they have killed me," and almost instantly expired. Capt. Franklin was wounded in the wrist. Keen as were the Yankee sharp shooters, the Pennymites showed themselves in no respect their inferiors. A small opening, or eye-hole had been made in the house to watch the garrison, the distance being about fifty rods. Nathan Stevens in taking an observation from this aperture, received a rifle ball directly in his eye, and fell dead on the floor. The loss of Franklin and Swift wounded, with two or three others, whose names we have not been able to ascertain; Stevens and Smith, having been killed, the Yankees were compelled to abandon the siege. Col. Armstrong returned a day or two preceding, or immediately subsequent, to Philadelphia.

An incident happened about this time well deserving to be recorded, as it exhibited a high degree of promptitude, courage and self-possession, marking the hero. A Pennymite named Ogden, out reconnoitering, had been taken prisoner by William Slocum and John Satterlee, pinioned tightly and placed in a canoe, to be conveyed to the west side of the river. "Be careful," said Satterlee, "our canoe is very unsteady, and I can't swim." "Nor I neither," replied Slocum, "so you need n't fear." "Ah ha!" cried Ogden, "but I can—good bye gentlemen," and instantly upset the boat, throwing himself coolly upon his back, his arms tied behind helping to buoy him up; thus he floated, and swam with the ease of a duck till he reached the shore, and escaped to tell the tale to his companions in the

* The following day, two companions, to remove Swift to a place where he could be safely and carefully nursed, took him in a canoe, and began to ascend the river, when one of them observed, 'There is a deer on yonder shore.' The ruling passion "strong in death" was exhibited by Swift, who suffering, and as all believed dying, begged they would turn him over and place the rifle in his hands. The old hunter still true to the mark, dropped the deer in his tracks and fainted. Though slowly, and long first, Swift recovered.

fort. Slocum seized the rope of the canoe, and escaped. Satterlee sunk to the dark shades of death. He was a fine young fellow, of noble port, a generous spirit, and unquestionable bravery. Whether this gallant young Pennymite, who so daringly escaped, was a relative of Capt. Amos Ogden, we cannot ascertain.*

On arriving in the city, Col. Armstrong learned to his surprise, if not dismay, that his proceedings at Wyoming, and those previously of justice Patterson, had aroused a spirit of opposition and resentment, which now began to display itself in official acts, which could not fail to produce an important influence on the course of policy pursued.

By the first constitution of Pennsylvania, which was established immediately after the declaration of independence, the Government of the Commonwealth was vested in a House of Representatives, and a President, and Council. Another Council was also established, called the "Council of Censors," who were chosen by the people, and directed to meet every seventh year; "and whose duty it shall be," says the constitution, "to inquire whether the constitution has been preserved inviolate in every part, and whether the Legislative and Executive branches of the Government have performed their duty as guardians of the people, or assumed to themselves, or exercised, other, or greater powers than they are entitled to by the constitution. They are also to inquire whether the public taxes have been justly laid, and collected in all parts of the Commonwealth; in what manner the public moneys have been disposed of, and whether the laws have been duly executed. For these purposes they shall have power to send for persons, papers, and records. They shall have authority to pass public censures, to order impeachments, and to recommend to the the Legislature the repealing such laws as appear to them to have been enacted contrary to the principles of the constitution."

This Council of Censors met at Philadelphia in the summer of 1784, and having received information of the transactions at Wyoming, on the 7th of September, ordered that the President and Supreme Executive Council should furnish certain documents in relation to their proceedings in the case of the Connecticut settlers, at and near that place; and that William Bradford, Jr., and James Wilson, Esqrs.,

---

* Our admiration for their valour, leads us earnestly to wish we could trace those gallant Ogdens up into seats of honour and prosperity. They deserved it. There is still existing in New Jersey, a noble family of that name, if every manly virtue can constitute nobility.

Counsel for Pennsylvania in this case, should furnish all the documents in their hands on the subject. On the 8th, Mr. Bradford surrendered the documents in his possession, in obedience to the order, and the Secretary of the Supreme Executive Council informed the Council of Censors by letter, that the documents required of them had been transmitted to the General Assembly. On the following day, the Council of Censors passed a resolution requiring the General Assembly to furnish the said documents. The Assembly proceeded immediately into the consideration of the order, and passed a resolution refusing to comply with it. In consequence of this refusal on the part of the Assembly, the Council of Censors, on the 10th of the same month, issued process against the General Assembly in the following words:

" The Council of Censors in the name, and by the authority of the people of Pennsylvania, to the General Assembly of the State of Pennsylvania, *Send greeting*:—We demand of you that you without delay, or excuse, forthwith send into this Council of Censors, the documents and papers hereunder mentioned, now, as it is said, in your keeping; that is to say, the report of the committee appointed the 9th of December last, to inquire into the charges contained in a petition from a number of the inhabitants of Wyoming, and the papers and affidavits accompanying the same, and the letter from Zebulon Butler, and others of Wyoming, read in the Supreme Executive Council on the 28th of May 1784, and which was by them transmitted to the House.

Signed by order of the Council of Censors, now sitting in the State House, in the city of Philadelphia, on this 10th day of September, Anno Domini, one thousand seven hundred and eighty-four.*

Frederick A. Muhlenberg,
President of the Council of Censors.

Attest—Samuel Bryan, *Secretary*."

* The list of the Council of Censors who met in the summer of 1784 will be found to contain numerous names distinguished for talents and patriotism, viz:—

    Philadelphia city—George Bryan, Thomas Fitzsimons.
    Philadelphia county—Frederick A. Muhlenberg, Arthur St. Clair.
    Bucks county—Joseph Hart, Samuel Smith.
    Bedford county—Daniel Espy, Samuel Davidson.
    Chester county—Anthony Wayne, James Moore.
    Lancaster county—John Whitehill, Stephen Chambers.
    York county—Thomas Hartley, Richard McAllister.
    Westmoreland county—John Smiley, William Finley.
    Cumberland county—James McLene, William Irvine.

The mandamus of the Censors was disregarded by the General Assembly, and the House declined even to answer the demand; whereupon the Council proceeded to make the following important declaration, or as it may well be characterized, most solemn denunciation of the measures pursued against the Wyoming settlers:

"It is the opinion of this Council, that the decision made at Trenton, early in 1783, between the State of Connecticut and this Commonwealth, concerning the territorial rights of both, was favorable to Pennsylvania. It likewise promised the happiest consequences to the Confederacy, as an example was thereby set, of two contending sovereignties adjusting their differences in a court of justice, instead of involving themselves, and perhaps their confederates, in war and bloodshed. It is much to be regretted, that this happy event was not improved on the part of this State, as it might have been. That the persons claiming lands at, and near Wyoming, occupied by the emigrants from Connecticut, now become subjects of Pennsylvania, were not left to prosecute their claims in the proper course without the intervention of the Legislature. That a body of troops was enlisted after the Indian war had ceased, and the civil government had been established, and stationed at Wyoming, for no other apparent purpose than that of promoting the interests of the claimants under the former grants of Pennsylvania.—That these troops were kept up, and continued there, without the license of Congress, in violation of the Confederation. That they were suffered, without restraint, to injure and oppress the neighboring inhabitants, during the course of the last winter. That the injuries done to these people excited the compassion and interposition of the State of Connecticut, who thereupon demanded of Congress another hearing, in order to investigate the private claims of the settlers at Wyoming, formerly inhabitants of New England, who from this instance of partiality in our own rulers, have been led to distrust the justice of the State, when in the mean time, numbers of these soldiers and other disorderly persons, in a most riotous and inhuman manner, expelled the New England settlers, before mentioned, from their habitations, and drove them towards the Delaware, through unsettled and almost impassable ways, leaving those unhappy outcasts to suffer every species of misery and distress. That this armed force, stationed as

Berks county—James Renie, Baltzer Gehr.
Northampton county—John Arndt, Simon Dreisbach.
Washington county—James Edgar, John McDowell.
Northumberland county—William Montgomery, James Potter.

aforesaid at Wyoming, as far as we can see, without any public advantage in view, has cost the Commonwealth the sum of £4,460, and upwards, for the bare levying, providing, and paying of them, besides other expenditures of public moneys. That the authority for embodying these troops was given privately, and unknown to the good people of Pennsylvania, the same being directed by a mere resolve of the House of Assembly, brought in and read the first time on Monday the 22d of September, 1783, when on motion and by special order, the same was read a second time and adopted. That the putting this resolve on the Secret Journal of the House, and concealing it from the people, after the war with the Savages had ceased, and the inhabitants of Wyoming had submitted to the Government of the State, sufficiently marks and fixes the clandestine and partial interests of the armament, no such condition having been thought necessary in the defence of the northern and western frontiers during the late war. And lastly, we regret the fatal example which this transaction has set of private persons, at least equally able with their opponents to maintain their own cause, procuring the interest of the Commonwealth in their behalf, and the aid of the public treasury. The opprobrium which, from hence, has resulted to this State, and the dissatisfaction and prospect of dissension now existing with one of our sister States, the violation of the Confederation, and the injury hereby done to such of the Pennsylvania claimants of lands at Wyoming, occupied as aforesaid, as have given no countenance to, but on the contrary, have disavowed these extravagant proceedings. In short, we lament that our Government has in this business manifested little wisdom or foresight; nor have acted as guardians of the rights of the people, committed to their care. Impressed with the multiplied evils which have sprung from the imprudent management of this business, *we hold it up to public censure*, to prevent, if possible, further instances of bad government, which might convulse and distract our new formed nation."

Contemptuously, and totally disregarding the proceedings of the Council of Censors, the Supreme Executive Council, and the Assembly, still, it is supposed, acting under the influence of the land-claimants, and stimulated by Col. Armstrong, whose pride was now combined with those motives and passions which had at first engaged him in the enterprise, proceeded to advance that officer, as a token of approbation for extraordinary merit and honorable services, to the rank of adjutant-general of the State, and authorized him to raise a competent force, from the militia of Bucks, Berks and Northampton, with which to proceed to Wyoming, and complete the work of expulsion, which, there is every reason to believe he had pledged himself thoroughly to accomplish. But new obstacles presented themselves. President Dickinson, whose humanity had been shown in desiring supplies to be sent to the inhabitants suffering from the ice flood, and whose sense of justice, as well as ideas of policy, was shocked by the violences committed on the people, now encouraged by the proceedings of the Council of Censors, interposed in this feeling and impressive strain.

"October 5th, 1784.
" To the Supreme Executive Council.

" Gentlemen :—Being still indisposed and unable to attend in Council to-day, I think it my duty, notwithstanding what has been already offered, to request that you will be pleased further to consider the propriety of calling a body of militia into actual service, on the intelligence yet received, and in the manner proposed. If the intention is, that the militia should assist the Pennsylvania claimants in securing the corn planted on the lands from which the settlers were expelled last Spring, such a procedure will drive those settlers into absolute despair. They will have no alternative but to fight for the corn, or suffer, perhaps to perish, for want of it in the coming winter. The Commissioners have informed the Council that their determination on that alternative will most probably be " [Here is a space left in the entries of this letter, in the book containing the minutes of the Council, over which is a long black mark drawn, as if some cause prevented the insertion of this part of the President's letter, which thus proceeds :]*. " They will regard this step as the commencement of a war against them, and perhaps others, whose sentiments are of vastly more importance, may be of the same opinion. I am perfectly convinced of the uncommon merit of Col. Armstrong, but the appointment of an adjutant-general upon this occasion, and bestowing that appointment on the Secretary of the Council, when it is well known that the settlers view him in the light of an enemy, are circumstances that may promote unfavorable constructions of the conduct of Government.

" The public bodies which have lately assembled in this city, have fully testified their disapprobation of hostilities on account of the disputes at Wyoming; and upon the whole, there is too much reason to

* Chapman.

be persuaded that the plan now meditated will, if carried into execution, produce very unhappy consequences.

"Knowing the uprightness of your intentions, gentlemen, I feel great pain in dissenting from your judgment; and if the measure is pursued, from esteem for you, and affection for the Commonwealth, I have only to wish, as I most heartily do, that I may be proved by the event to have been mistaken."

Signed,   JOHN DICKINSON.

The Council, on consideration of the letter from the President, "Resolved, That the measures adopted on the second instant, be pursued;" and on the same day issued a proclamation, offering a reward of twenty-five pounds for the apprehension of eighteen of the principal inhabitants, whose names were mentioned.

No time was to be lost. An adverse storm to the Pennsylvania land claimants' interests was already bursting upon them, and Gen. Armstrong, without a moment's delay, entered on the duties of his renewed appointment, with his accustomed zeal. But the influences which had operated with such effect on the Council of Censors and upon President Dickinson, also pervaded the people, and the militia generally declined obedience to orders. The emergency was too pressing for delay, for if the Pennsylvania party could secure the fall harvest, the Yankees must abandon their possessions or perish, and General Armstrong hastened back to Wyoming with less than an hundred men, where he arrived on Sunday, the 17th of October, and on the very next day put his forces in motion, and made an attack on Brockway's, above Abraham's Creek, where Wm. Jackson of the Yankees, was severely wounded, Capt. Bolin of Armstrong's men, killed and left on the field of battle, three or four of his men being wounded, who were borne off in the retreat.

This action was sharply contested on both sides for an hour. The Yankees occupied four log houses placed in form of a diamond. General Armstrong in a letter to Council deprecating his repulse, said; "I need scarcely observe to your Excellency, that four log houses, so constructed as to flank each other, became a very formidable post."

After the attacking party had retired, Capt. Franklin seized the rifle of his friend William Jackson, bloody from his wound, and calling his companions in suffering around him, swore thereon a solemn oath "That he would never lay down his arms until death should arrest his hand, or Patterson and Armstrong be expelled from Wyoming, and the people be restored to their rights of possession, and a legal trial guaranteed to every citizen by the constitution, by justice, and by law!"

In pursuance of his settled policy, or in revenge for his defeat, General Armstrong the next day dispossessed thirty families, who had been restored or returned to their farms. In a skirmish which ensued, Jonathan Terry was severely wounded. The flats of Kingston opposite the fort, had been extensively sowed with buckwheat, and General Armstrong's men were now engaged in threshing out the abundant produce. A body of Yankees under Major Abbott, approached the laborers undiscovered, and rushing forward, surrounded them before they could seize their arms, and took all the grain, wagons having been prepared to transport it to head quarters. Meanwhile the alarmed garrison paraded the cannon, but the Yankees placed their prisoners as a shield, and thus prevented the firing. More than an hundred bushels rewarded the enterprise, the supply of bread being very seasonable to the settlers, who had been prevented from sowing or reaping enough for food. The fact is mentioned by Elisha Harding, to the praise of Mr. John Hollenback, whose mill was in possession of Armstrong's men, and who was compelled to appear friendly to his cause, that a confidential understanding was kept up with the settlers, their grain ground, or flour supplied, to the utmost extent of his power without detection.

The pleasing information now came that the Assembly had ordered the settlers to be restored to their possessions. This bears date, September 15, 1784, and is explained by the preamble.

"Whereas, several persons at or near Wyoming, in the county of Northumberland, were in the month of May last, violently dispossessed of the messuages, lands and tenements, which they then occupied, and which are still detained from them by force; and the peculiar circumstances of these cases require that the possession of the premises so forcibly entered and detained, should be without delay restored to the persons who occupied them as aforesaid,"

"Be it enacted, etc." Then follows the just and benevolent enactment.

It must appear obvious to the reader, from the proceedings of the Council of Censors; from the letter of President Dickinson to the Supreme Executive Council; from the refusal of the Bucks and Berks militia to march; from the spirit of pity and indignation awakened in the public mind, and from the obstinate and successful resistance of the settlers; and especially from the recent act of Assembly, that hostile measures against them must soon be abandoned. Armstrong and Patterson were recalled.

In tracing the negotiations which took place during the year, the reader must have observed, that both Jenkins and Franklin, the chief scribes of the people, without making any pretensions to literary elegance, yet conveyed just and manly thoughts in a clear and nervous style.

Franklin's Journal says: "November, Thursday 25. Sent two guineas to the prisoners, (Easton,) by Robert McDowell.

"Saturday 27. The Pennymites evacuated the fort at 11 P. M.

"Tuesday 30. The Yankees destroyed the fort."

Thus have we narrated the events that transpired, to the close of 1784; two years having elapsed since the transfer of jurisdiction by the Trenton Decree. Peace, which waved its cheering olive over every other part of the Union, healing the wounds inflicted by ruthless war—soothing the sorrows of innumerable children of affliction, and kindling the lamp of hope in the dark chambers of despair, came not to the broken-hearted people of Wyoming. The veteran soldier returned, but found no resting place. Instead of a joyous welcome to his hearth and home, he found his cottage in ruins or in possession of a stranger, and his wife and little ones shelterless in the open fields, or in the caves of the mountains; like the ocean-tossed mariner approaching the wished for harbour—driven by adverse winds far, far from shore, to buffet again the billows and the storm. It is true and honorable to those who effected it, that the New England people were repossessed of their farms; but a summer of exile and war had left them no harvest to reap, and they returned to their empty granaries and desolate homes, crushed by the miseries of the Indian invasion; mourners over fields of more recent slaughter—destitute of food, with scarce clothing to cover them, through the rigours of a northern winter, while clouds and darkness shrouded all the future. Assuredly the people of Wyoming were objects of deepest commiseration, and the heart must be harder and colder than marble, that could look upon their sufferings and not drop a tear of tenderest pity.

LETTER XXIV.

Sketch of John Franklin—Civil Government.

1785.——Petition to Congress for a Federal Court to try the right of soil—Proceedings of Congress—Spirited resolves of Pennsylvania Assembly—Interesting details—Remarkable conclusion—Gathering storm—David Mead, Esq.,—Oliver Harmless—Revival of old Susquehanna Company—Danger threatening—Proceedings Pennsylvania Assembly.

GENERALLY, the two years intervening between the close of the Pennymite and Yankee war, in 1784, and the erection of the contested lands into a new county towards the close of 1786, have been regarded as affording little to record, and less to repay the labour of perusal.

To those who can only find pleasure in the ambush, and the fight; in the clash of arms, houses in flames; the shout of victory and the wail of woe, that period may appear dull, and uninteresting. So far otherwise, we confidently aver, will it be found by the philosophical reader, who searches for the springs of action, and delights to trace important consequences to their remote, or originating causes, that he will regard it as among the most interesting in the course of our annals.

In the preceding letter, the oath, not less solemn than that of Hannibal, taken by Franklin on the bloody rifle of his wounded friend, has been recorded. It was no unmeaning ceremony, nor sudden impulse, but the deliberate pregnant appeal to heaven, of a man of powerful mind, deeply impressed with the wrongs of his people, and resolved to protect and avenge them. This extraordinary man, for thirty years the prime and popular leader of the Yankee interest in northeastern Pennsylvania, already distinguished, and destined to become eminently conspicuous, deserves a more formal introduction.

John Franklin was a native of Canaan, Litchfield county, Connecticut. An instance of his remarkable memory, when a lad of seventeen, will show that he was no ordinary boy. Having accompanied the family to the place of worship, the meeting house being only enclosed, but neither ceiled nor plastered, the beams and rafters were all exposed to view. John saw that his austere father sat through the sermon with great uneasiness, but could not divine the cause. On returning home, "John," said his father, "it is my duty to give you a severe thrashing, (common in old times,) and you shall have it presently, so prepare yourself." "But you won't whip me, father, without telling me what for?" "No, certainly—your conduct at meeting, sir, is the cause. Instead of attending to the sermon, you were all the while gaping about as if you were counting the beams and rafters of the meeting house." "Well, father, can you repeat the sermon?" "Sermon! no. I had as much as I could do to watch your inattention." If I'll tell you all the minister said, you won't whip me? "No, John, no; but that is impossible."—Young Franklin immediately named the text, and taking up the discourse, went through every head of it with surprising accuracy. "Upon my word," said the delighted parent, "I should not have thought it." "And now, father," said John, "I can tell you exactly how many beams and rafters there are in the meeting house." His ever springing affection for this parent is beautifully evinced by his journal. Almost every other page has the entry, "*wrote a letter to father.*"

Not long after removing to Wyoming, his wife died, leaving three small children, one an infant of a week old. Having no person to take care of them he determined to place them in charge of his kind friends in Canaan. Harnessing a horse to a little cart, he put in the three children, tied a cow by the horns, to follow, and drove on, having a cup in which, as occasion required, he milked, and fed the babe. Thus he traveled the rough way, more than two hundred miles, in safety, exhibiting all the patience and tenderness that might be expected from a mother.

Some may be curious to learn the appearance of this extraordinary man. Of excellent proportions, nearly six feet in height, thick set, and well knit, he seemed built for strength and endurance, without being too heavy to be active. His courage was unquestionable. Elisha Harding, Esq., who was an associate with him through those times of trial, says:—"He was as brave a man as ever carried a gun." The small pox had treated him roughly, his face being much pitted, yet his countenance was not unpleasing. One peculiar feature was the upper lip, which was long, and the indentation in the centre, from the nose to the mouth, remarkably deep. The chin and lower part of the face were full of manly expression. His complexion was florid, the hair light, if not inclining to red, showing the high Saxon blood. Open, frank, fond of talking, full of anecdote, the Connecticut claim, and the sufferings of the settlers, his hobby, Col. Franklin would visit from house to house, from neighborhood to neighborhood, taking a circuit of miles, never in a hurry, yet always busy, tarrying a night with one, spending a day with another; the neighbours, hearing Col. Franklin had come, men, women and chilren gathering in to hear him; he would inform, argue, arouse, and cheer, in aid of the cause to which he had devoted his life; and every where was thrice and cordially welcome. Ambitious he certainly was. The love of popularity became his ruling passion, nor did he woo the pleasing and delusive gale in vain. For thirty years he was the idol of the people whose interests he especially espoused, and they would mutually and cheerfully have died for each other. As a public speaker, fond to display his knowledge, and not averse to behold a crowd listening to his voice, he could make no pretensions to eloquence; yet he rarely failed to command attention, even from the learned and accomplished, for he exhibited a thorough knowledge of his subject, a surprising memory, day, date, names, the purport of every document being stated by him, without referring to paper or note, with an accuracy rarely equaled. Earnest, often vehement, his whole soul seemed to be in the matter. He quoted no poetry, attempted no flight of the imagination, but illustrated his subject by an occasional quotation from scripture, and the introduction of popular aphorisms. After remaining many years a widower, he married Mrs. Bidlack, daughter of Capt. Fuller, whose husband, Capt. James Bidlack, had fallen in the battle.

Immediately after the garrison was withdrawn and the people restored to their possessions, committees were appointed in the interregnum of law, to regulate affairs in the settlement, adjust controversies, punish offenders and preserve order. Town meetings, not "legally warned," but informally called together, were holden, and taxes collected; while the militia were organized with a good deal of care, and led to a choice of officers. At a general parade in Shawney, Capt. Franklin was elected to the command of the regiment, and thenceforward was called through life by the well-known appellation of COL. FRANKLIN.

The first object of the settlers, both ostensible and real, was to obtain a trial for the right of soil. What ulterior scheme Colonel Franklin had then devised, will appear in the sequel. Petitions prepared to the Assembly of Connecticut, praying their interposition, had been sent forward. Ardent, indefatigable, the rifle resting on his knee, he knew well the power, and kept the pen in motion. "Wrote to William S. Johnson, Jesse Root and Eliphalet Dyer." "Sent a letter to Esquire Antis." "Wrote a letter to the Justices of the Supreme Court." "Sent by Zerah Beach, Esq., copies of letters to the Governor of Connecticut and the committee." Wrote to Esquire Grey." "Wrote to Major Smith." "Wrote to Major Smith." And these entries are made in his journal, intermixed with constant skirmishing, fighting and dying, and show the earnestness with which he devoted himself to the cause.

After the proceedings of the Council of Censors, the Connecticut Assembly, saying they had no jurisdiction, yet powerfully solicited by the settlers, and their petitions being sustained by the Susquehanna Company and friends at home, too numerous and influential to be wholly disregarded, passed a resolution that the settlers ought to have the advantage of a fair trial, and also requesting Governor Griswold to write to the Government of Pennsylvania in their behalf. The letter was just and appropriate, and doubtless not without salutary influence.

Petitions to Congress having before been presented, were now renewed, and as this seems the most fitting place to trace the extraordinary action of that honorable body, we shall do so without interruption to the close.

Col. Franklin set out on the 6th of March, 1785, for New York, as agent of the settlers. Preceding this time, the following action had taken place:—

Friday, January 23, 1784.

"Congress assembled: Present—Massachusetts, Rhode Island, Connecticut, Pennsylvania, Maryland, Virginia, North Carolina and South Carolina; and from the State of New Jersey, Mr. Beatty, and from Delaware, Mr. Tilton.

"On the report of the committee, consisting of Mr. Jefferson, Mr. Lee and Mr. Williamson, to whom was referred a petition of Zebulon Butler and others, claiming under the State of Connecticut, private right of soil within the territory westward of the Delaware, formerly in controversy between the said State and that of Pennsylvania, and lately determined by a court, constituted and appointed agreeably to the ninth of the articles of confederation and perpetual union, to be within the jurisdiction of the State of Pennsylvania, complaining that they are disturbed in their right by others, claiming under the said State of Pennsylvania, and praying that a court may be instituted under the ninth article of the confederation, for determining the said right,

"*Resolved*, That a court be instituted according to the said ninth article of the confederation, for determining the private right of soil within the said territory, so far as the same is by the said article submitted to the determination of such a court.

"That the fourth Monday in June next, be assigned for the appearance of the parties, by their lawful agents before Congress, or the Committee of the States, wheresoever they shall be then sitting.

"That notice of the assignment of the said day, be given to the parties in the following form:—

"To the claimants of the private right of soil within the territory westward of the Delaware, heretofore in controversy between the States of Connecticut and Pennsylvania, and adjudged by the sentence of a court constituted and appointed agreeably to the ninth of the articles of confederation and perpetual union, to be within the jurisdiction of the State of Pennsylvania, it is hereby made known: That sundry individuals claiming private right of soil under the State of Connecticut, within the said territory, have made application to Congress, stating that they have been disturbed in their said right of soil by others, claiming under the State of Pennsylvania; and praying for the institution of a court for determining the said private right of soil, in pursuance of the ninth article of confederation: And that the fourth Monday in June next is assigned for the appearance of the parties by their lawful agents before Congress, or a Committee of the States, wheresoever they shall be then sitting, to proceed in the premises as by the confederation is directed.

By order of Congress.

CHARLES THOMSON, *Secretary.*

"*Resolved*, That the said notice be transmitted by the secretary, to the Executives of the States of Connecticut and Pennsylvania, with a request that they will take proper measures for having the same served on the parties interested under their States respectively."

"Saturday, April 24, 1784.

Congress assembled: Present as yesterday.

A motion was made by Mr. Hand, seconded by Mr. Montgomery, in the words following:

"Whereas, Congress have by their resolution of the 23d day of January last, on the petition of Zebulon Butler, and others, directed the institution of a court to determine the private right of soil within the territory westward of the Delaware, formerly in dispute between the states of Connecticut and Pennsylvania, agreeably to the ninth of the articles of confederation, and have assigned the fourth Monday in June next, for the appearance of the parties by their lawful agents, before Congress or a committee of the states, to proceed in the premises, as by the confederation is directed. And whereas, the General Assembly of the State of Pennsylvania have, by their resolutions of the 14th day of February last, instructed their delegates in Congress, as follows:

[" In General Assembly, Saturday, February 14, 1784, A. M.

Resolved, 1st. That the delegates of this State be instructed to apply immediately to Congress for an explanation of their act of the 23d day of last month, it appearing to be uncertain whether the fourth Monday in June next is fixed for the purpose of appointing commissioners or judges to constitute a court for hearing, and determining the matter in question, or for the purpose of deciding how far the same is, by the ninth article of confederation, submitted to the determination of such a court.

"2d. That if Congress by their said act meant the appointment of commissioners or judges next June, then the said delegates move for a reconsideration of the said act, and represent to Congress, that the agents for the state of Connecticut did, upon the late trial at Trenton, suggest to the court there, that the tenants in possession of the lands in controversy, and particularly the companies of Delaware and Susquehanna, were improving and holding large tracts of land under title from the State of Connecticut; and that by the same article of confederation, a court is to be established for the trial of the private right of soil, only where it is claimed, under different grants of two or more states, so that Zebulon Butler and the other claimants cannot be entitled to such a court, unless they come within the description aforesaid, which it is apprehended they do not. That if Congress should consent to establish courts at the instance of persons, not first proving themselves to be included in the description aforesaid, the citizens of this State may be harrassed by a multitude of pretended claims at the suit of adventurers or invaders of the state, and in the present instance at the suit of persons who have settled in defiance of the resolution of Congress of the 23d day of December, 1775.

3d. That if Congress shall resolve that the matter in question is, by the said article of the confederation, submitted to the determination of such a court, then the said delegates insist that Zebulon Butler, and the other claimants, be required, immediately, to exhibit to Congress schedules particularizing their claims."]

Then proceeds the resolution of Mr. Hand.

"*Resolved*, That it was the intention of Congress, by their act of the 23d day of January last, that commissioners or judges should be appointed on the fourth Monday in June next, agreeably to the ninth of the articles of confederation, to determine the private right of soil within the territory westward of the Delaware, formerly in controversy between the States of Connecticut and Pennsylvania, and lately determined to be within the jurisdiction of the State of Pennsylvania. Nevertheless, as the petitioners aforesaid have not shown to Congress that their claims to the private right of soil, within the territory aforesaid, originate from grants obtained from the state of Connecticut,* which alone can entitle them to a court, agreeably to the ninth of the articles of confederation. Resolved, that the resolution of the 23d day of January last, directing the institution of a court for determining the private right of soil within the territory westward of the Delaware, formerly in controversy between the States of Connecticut and Pennsylvania, and appointing the fourth Monday in June next for the appearance of the parties, by their lawful agents, before Congress, or a Committee of the States, be, and it is hereby suspended, until Zebulon Butler, and the other petitioners claimants as aforesaid, exhibit to Congress, or a Committee of the States, schedules, particularizing their claims. Resolved, that the parties, claimants as aforesaid, be informed, that their appearance by their agents before Congress, or a Committee of the States, as specified by the resolution of Congress of the 23d day of January last, will not be necessary, until the further determinations of Congress, or a Committee of the States, in the premises, be made known to them."

A motion was made by Mr. Howell, seconded by Mr. Montgomery, that the foregoing motion be committed; and on the question for commitment, the yeas and nays being required by Mr. Hand.

N. HAMPSHIRE.			MASSACHUSETTS.		
Mr. Foster,	ay	ay	Mr. Gerry,	ay	ay
Blanchard,	ay		Patridge,	ay	

---

* This, notwithstanding the authorized agents of Connecticut had twice officially stated at the Trenton trial, that the Wyoming settlers derived their claim from Connecticut, and that solemn declaration was recorded on the Journals of Congress.

RHODE ISLAND.		MARYLAND.	
Mr. Ellery,	no ⎫ div.	Mr. Stone,	ay ⎫ ay
Howell,	ay ⎭	Chase,	ay ⎭
CONNECTICUT.		VIRGINIA.	
Mr. Sherman,	no ⎫ no	Mr. Jefferson,	ay ⎫
Wadsworth,	no ⎭	Hardy,	ay ⎬ ay
NEW YORK.		Mercer,	ay ⎪
Mr. De Witt,	ay ⎫ ay	Monroe,	ay ⎭
Paine,	ay ⎭	N. CAROLINA.	
NEW JERSEY.		Mr. Williamson,	ay ⎫ ay
Mr. Beatty,	no ⎫ div.	Spaight,	ay ⎭
Dick,	ay ⎭	S. CAROLINA.	
PENNSYLVANIA.		Mr. Read,	ay ⎫ ay
Mr. Mifflin,	ay ⎫	Beresford,	ay ⎭
Montgomery,	ay ⎬ ay		
Hand,	ay ⎭		

" So it was resolved to commit it."

Certainly the resolutions of the Pennsylvania Assembly are drawn with consummate ability. Whether the cogency of reasoning, or other causes then in operation, produced the decision, the impartial reader must determine. At a subsequent session,

" Wednesday, September 21, 1785.

Congress resumed the consideration of the letter of the 24th of December, 1784, from the Governor of Connecticut, stating claims of settlers of Wyoming, with a copy of a memorial of sundry inhabitants at Wyoming, and a copy of the proceedings of the Legislature of Connecticut relative thereto, which was the subject of debate on Monday and Tuesday.

And a motion having been made by the State of Pennsylvania, in the words following :—

" Are the proceedings on the first application of the persons alleged to be settlers at Wyoming, continued and in force, notwithstanding the non-appearance of the applicants on the 28th of June, 1784, and the recess of Congress and the Committee of the States, at that time.

A motion was made by Mr. King, seconded by Mr. Johnson, to postpone that motion in order to take up the following :—

" Whereas, on the fourth Monday of June, 1784, being the day assigned for the appearance of the parties under the act of Congress of the 23d of January, 1784, upon the petition of Zebulon Butler and others, claiming under the State of Connecticut, private right of soil within the jurisdiction of the State of Pennsylvania, Congress were then in recess, and a quorum of the committee of the States, did not assemble,

"*Resolved,* That further day be given to the parties, and that the   Monday of   be assigned for the appearance of the parties by their lawful agents before Congress, wheresoever they shall be then sitting; or if Congress shall not on that day be in session, then on the day of their session next following the said Monday of   that notice of the assignment of the said day, be given to the parties in the following form:" etc.—

"On the question to postpone for the purpose aforesaid, the yeas and nays being required by Mr. Wilson,

"It was resolved in the affirmative.

"After debate, the motion before the House was withdrawn by the mover, and a motion was made by Mr. Smith, seconded by Mr. Pettit, as follows:—

"Whereas, the petition of Zebulon Butler and others, claiming private right of soil under the State of Connecticut, and within the jurisdiction of the Commonwealth of Pennsylvania, doth not describe with sufficient certainty the tract of land claimed by the said Zebulon Butler and others, nor particularly name the private adverse claim, under grants from the Commonwealth of Pennsylvania,

Resolved, That the resolutions of Congress of the 23d day of January, 1784, relative to the claim of Zebulon Butler and others, be, and hereby are repealed.

"A motion was made by Mr. Read, seconded by Mr. Grayson, to postpone that motion, in order to take up the following:—

Whereas, the United States in Congress assembled, on the 23d day of January, 1784, on the petition of Zebulon Butler and others, claiming under the State of Connecticut, private right of soil within the territory westward of the Delaware, formerly in controversy between the said State and that of Pennsylvania, and lately determined by a court constituted and appointed agreeably to the 9th of the articles of confederation and perpetual union, to be within the jurisdiction of the State of Pennsylvania, complaining that they are disturbed in their right, by others claiming under the said State of Pennsylvania, and praying that a court may be instituted under the 9th article of the confederation for determining the said right,

"*Resolved,* That a court be instituted according to the said 9th article of the confederation for determining the private right of soil within the said territory, so far as the same is by the said articles submitted to the determination of such a court. That the fourth

Monday in June next be assigned for the appearance of the parties by their lawful agents before Congress or the Committee of the States, wheresoever they shall then be sitting." And whereas, on the said fourth Monday in June, Congress was not in session, and a sufficient number of the Committee of the States, appointed by Congress on the 29th day of May, 1784, did not assemble on the said 4th Monday in June; and whereas, it does not appear to the United States in Congress assembled, that on the said 4th Monday in June, 1784, either the parties petitioning, or the claimants of the private right of soil under the State of Pennsylvania, did appear at the city of Annapolis, to prosecute or defend their respective rights; therefore

"*Resolved*, That the force of the said recited resolution of the 23d of January, 1784, is determined, and that the same resolution ought not to be considered at the present day as having any validity or effect."

" And on the question to postpone for the purpose above mentioned, the yeas and nays being required by Mr. Wilson, it passed in the negative.

"A motion was then made by Mr. Pinckney, seconded by Mr. Johnson, to postpone the consideration of the motion before the House, in order to take into consideration the motion moved by Mr. King, as before recited, and which was withdrawn.

"And on the question to postpone for the purpose mentioned, the yeas and nays being required by Mr. Wilson, it passed in the negative.

"On the question to agree to the motion before the House, the yeas and nays being required by Mr. Wilson, it was resolved in the affirmative, as follows:—

" Whereas, the petition of Zebulon Butler and others, claiming private right of soil under the State of Connecticut, and within the jurisdiction of the Commonwealth of Pennsylvania, doth not describe with sufficient certainty the tract of land claimed by the said Zebulon Butler and others, nor particularly name the private adverse claims under grants from the Commonwealth of Pennsylvania,

"*Resolved*, That the resolutions of Congress, of the 23d day of January, 1784, relative to the claim of Zebulon Butler and others, be, and hereby are repealed."

The unanimity was remarkable, every State but two voting affirmatively. New Hampshire, interested in the Vermont grants, and Connecticut being obliged to do so, to save appearances, a powerful interest at home being concerned. It might have been supposed that the Wyoming people should have notice and time to amend their plea. It might have been supposed that the questions whether

"Z. Butler and others," had with sufficient accuracy set forth their boundaries, was one, not for Congress, but the court to decide. If no Wyoming settler could have a trial until he could say with certainty who was the adverse claimant, a matter it was almost impossible he could know or ascertain, his chance was hopeless.

If, on the other hand, a secret understanding prevailed throughout Congress, that Pennsylvania, by a previous arrangement with Connecticut, was to possess all within her charter, the settlers being at her mercy, and Connecticut to receive an equivalent west; and now, after the renewed troubles at Wyoming, if secret pledges were given that a more liberal course should be pursued towards the unfortunate inhabitants, then the resolution, otherwise so extraordinary, is easy, plain, and perfectly comprehensible. Certain it is that immediately thereafter, the course of policy pursued by Pennsylvania assumed an aspect of conciliation and justice, interrupted, it is true, by violent efforts of her land claimants to stimulate the government to renew coercive measures against the settlers; but those efforts were in vain, and the State, in sincerity it is believed, resolved, by equitable terms of compromise, to quiet those claimants in their possessions who inhabited Wyoming before the Decree of Trenton. But the seeds of violent commotion, if not of revolution, were already sown. The fruit will be seen in the sequel.*

---

* A very curious matter demands notice. In Col. Franklin's accurate and invaluable Journal, proceedings of Congress are recorded, which the journals of that body do not notice. New York, Thursday, September 22, 1785, Messrs. John Franklin, Ebenezer Johnson, Phineas Pierce and Lord Butler, (presented a petition) "to know the grounds and reasons of the resolve of Congress of the 21st; and to be quiet in our possessions at Wyoming, until a petition could be brought in, and a decision had thereon." Mr. Butler set off for Wyoming; send letters.

"Friday 23d, our petitions referred to Col. Johnson of Connecticut, Mr. Smith of New York, and Mr. Bedford of Delaware."

"26th and 27th, waiting on Congress."

"28th. This day the committee report in favour of our petition. That the repeal of the resolution of Congress was founded in the insufficiency of the allegations, and defective description of the lands in controversy, and was not intended to foreclose the proprietors, settlers and claimants of lands at and near Wyoming, for the appointment of a Federal court to try their rights of soil, to the land included in the purchase made of the natives by the Susquehanna and Delaware Companies, by the leave and approbation of the then colony of Connecticut, when a petition shall be brought describing the land, and naming the adverse claimant with due degree of certainty." "The report was disapproved."

"Friday, Sept. 30th. Report reconsidered, but nothing done."

"Monday, October 3d. The report reconsidered, but was lost for the want of one vote to carry the resolve. Thus the Connecticut settlers were "shuffled off," denied a trial by the interposition of unreasonable obstacles. Pierce and Johnson set off for Wilkesbarre. Friday 7th. I set off for White Plains. 8th. To Danbury, &c.," making a fourth journey to Connecticut within the year. Truly Col. Franklin may be termed the "INDEFATIGABLE."

Col. Franklin, comprehending the hopelessness of any favorable action on the part of Congress, pursued his way to Connecticut, and mingling with his old friends and the active members of the Susquehanna Company, visited—talked—proposed—suggested—opened to the ambitious new scenes of honour—to the young, an exciting if not a noble field for enterprise,—to all a source of wealth, in the rich and widely extended limits of the Connecticut claim on the Susquehanna. Pennsylvania, all branches of her government united, and with a military force upon the ground, had not been able to dispossess a handful of settlers from the Wyoming Valley. The wrongs suffered by those people had awakened universal sympathy. Public sentiment, a host in itself, was in favour of the Connecticut claim. What could Pennsylvania do, if the Susquehanna and Delaware Companies resumed the making of grants, and New England poured on a stream of hardy adventurers, and took possession of the land? By the Hampshire grants, Vermont had been successfully settled and defended in spite of all the power of New York, close neighbours, whereas the settlements of Pennsylvania were separated from those of Wyoming, by mountains and forests extremely difficult to penetrate. A chord was struck that vibrated through all New England. Franklin, in the spirit of his oath, infused his own soul, glowing with resentment and ambition, into the people with whom he conversed, from which most important consequences resulted; and had not his schemes been counteracted by a timely and prudent change of policy on the part of her authorities, Pennsylvania had lost her fair northern possessions, or by new civil war, extinguished the Connecticut claim in blood.

On Col. Franklin's return, April 24th, having been absent nearly two months, a town meeting [not "legally warned"] was held, and the people given to understand that movements in their behalf might be expected from abroad. On the 30th, in company with Messrs. Pierce and Johnson, he warned Van Gorder, one of the few Pennsylvania settlers remaining, to quit the land. Monday, May 2d, a meeting of the Wilkesbarre proprietors was holden; and on the 14th, Col. Franklin again set off for Connecticut, to attend an expected meeting of the Susquehanna Company at Hartford. The inert mass was not yet sufficiently warmed, to be moved to his wishes. Doubts and fears seem to have hung around and retarded the action of the prudent Yankees. No meeting had been called; the committee, still slumbering, had neglected to give the proper notice. Supported especially by Maj. Wm. Judd, of Farmington, Col. Franklin went from town to town, to Windham, to Hartford, to Watertown, to Colchester; and again to Hartford, where, from the public records he took copies of papers to aid him in sustaining the Connecticut claim, which he every where preached with apostolic zeal.

Having now made arrangements for a meeting of the company in July, he hastened back to Wyoming, where he arrived on the 29th of June. Immediately a town meeting was called, the people addressed, and encouraged to be firm in defence of their rights.

Among the few who still held the lands they occupied, under title derived from Pennsylvania, was David Meade, Esq., who was seated on the farm a mile below the Court House, on the Carey Town road, a charming situation, to be sought for with eagerness, and to be abandoned with reluctance. Justice Meade was one of the earliest Connecticut settlers, the accurate surveyor of Wilkesbarre. During the war he had removed to near Fort Augusta, as a place of greater security, where, undergoing a change of principles or opinions, he made up his mind to take part with the Pennsylvania land claimants, against his old Wyoming neighbours. At Patterson's election, as has been related, he was appointed one of the Justices of Peace, and being commissioned, removed to Wilkesbarre. His conduct as a magistrate seemed to have been marked by forbearance, and as a man, often by kindness. The Yankees frequently appealed to him, when in distress, and he yielded his good offices in their favour. Tall, slender, bent a little forward, with a countenance mild, and of a grave deportment, Justice Meade was calculated, under other circumstances, and in less boisterous times, to have been a favorite. But it could illy be brooked, that one of Patterson's Justices should hold possessions under the " Pennymite claim," as it was termed, on the rich bottom lands of Wilkesbarre too, and he a renegade and traitor from the Yankee ranks; moreover, and probably with justice he was regarded as still the agent of the land claimants, and a spy on the conduct of the Connecticut people. His expulsion was, therefore, under the new spirit awakened by Col. Franklin on his return, determined on. Rising one morning Mr. Meade beheld a dozen men mowing his meadow, and all orders to desist, or requests for explanation, were equally disregarded; they went on openly and carted off the hay. A warrant was forthwith issued, and several arrested on a charge of riot, and brought before Justice Meade. Evasive answers to his questions were given by those whom he knew, and first interrogated. "And who are you, Sir?" said he, to one whom he was not acquainted with, "and what have you to say for yourself?" "My name," said the fellow, with affected simplicity, " is Oliver Harmless,* and if I ever did you any good in the world, I am sorry for it." A burst of laughter followed this sally, when Mason F. Alden spoke up and said, " Squire Meade, it is you or us; Pennymites and Yankees can't live together in Wyoming. Our lines don't agree. We give you fair notice to quit, and that shortly." Meade immediately called to his aid thirty or forty men, and having garrisoned his house, resolved to defend himself. Writs were obtained against the rioters, and Maj. Crawford, as Sheriff's Deputy, was sent up from Sunbury; but finding it difficult to serve them, left the writs with Col. Butler, that he might request the persons to go voluntarily to Sunbury, and give themselves up, or enter bail. Displeased with this lenient course, complaint was made by Meade against Sheriff Antis, and the parties were cited before the authorities in Philadelphia, Capt. Shott being called to attend as a witness. On the return of Justice Meade, the cannon, that terrible four pounder, was paraded before his house, and on Monday, the 8th of August, he retired with his men from the Valley, leaving, it is believed, no Pennsylvania claimant on the Wyoming lands. We have been more particular in tracing these events, from the character and consequence of the gentleman concerned, both on the Susquehanna, and as the founder of the fine town of Meadville, in Crawford County, the scite of which, then a wilderness, was allotted to him as an indemnity for his losses at Wyoming. The Assembly also, by an Act of Sept. 22, 1785, in consideration that " he was requested to continue there (at Wyoming,) as long as possible, by which means he has been subjected to heavy expenses in giving information to the Government, and other matters," &c., provided, " That the Supreme Executive Council be, and they are hereby authorized to draw an order on the Treasurer of the State, for the sum of sixty-seven pounds, and three pence, the balance due him." What seemed an evil, thus proved to him a singular advantage; wealth beyond his fondest imaginings, having resulted from his expulsion.

A month having been occupied in dispossessing Meade, Colonel Franklin had, in the mean time, made his third visit within five months, to Connecticut, and must have traveled nearly two thousand miles. The meeting of the Susquehanna Company was holden at Hartford on the 13th of July, 1785. No moderator is named—no clerk appointed. Instead of the usual title, it is styled, " A meeting

---

* Ephraim M'Coy was his real name.

of the Proprietors, Purchasers and Settlers of the land on the Susquehanna river, under the countenance and title of the State of Connecticut, legally warned," etc. It is a State paper of altogether too much consequence to be omitted, or passed lightly over; nor can it be regarded as much less than a manifesto of war. Malign and portentous to the State, as were its apparent indications, it proved most benign and salutary in its ultimate effects, for from thence sprung those measures, and that course of policy, that has peopled northeastern Pennsylvania, Luzerne, Wyoming, Susquehanna and Bradford counties, with so great a portion of hardy, moral, industrious New Englanders, faithful to the laws, ready, with cheerfulness, if necessary, to fight and die for the good old Commonwealth; who have by unremitting toil, caused a rugged wilderness to blossom like the rose, thus showing, that

> "Though man proposes,
> God disposes."

The chief part of proceedings we copy.

"At a meeting of the Proprietors, Purchasers and Settlers of the land on the Susquehanna river, under the countenance and title of the State of Connecticut, legally warned and held at Hartford, July 13, A. D., 1785.

This meeting taking into consideration the situation of their claim, the large sums of money expended in the purchase, settlement and defence of the same, and the justice of their claim to the said land, do resolve:—

1. That the purchase they made of the Indian natives, proprietors of said lands, was fair, *bona fide*, and for a valuable consideration paid previous to any other purchase of said lands from said Indians.

2. That at the time of making said purchase, there was not, nor ought there ever to have been, a doubt respecting the right of Connecticut to the jurisdiction and right of pre-emption of that territory, the charter and letters patent to Connecticut being in fact eighteen years prior to the patent to Sir William Penn, which in terms the most explicit did cover said lands.

3. That in confidence in the Charter of Connecticut, which they judged to be as sure and secured as the solemn acts of any public body can be, and with the countenance and approbation of the colony of Connecticut, they made the purchase and settlement afore-

said, and have at vast expense of blood and treasure, purchased and defended their possessions against the common enemy to the great emolument and security of the United States.

4. That although the Court constituted to determine the right of jurisdiction between the States of Connecticut and Pennsylvania, have astonished the world with the decision in favour of Pennsylvania, yet our right to those lands in possession, as founded in law and justice, is clear and unquestionable; and we cannot and will not give it up.

5. That the conduct of the State and people of Pennsylvania, towards the proprietors of the lands on the river Susquehanna, in consequence of the decree of Trenton, in A. D. 1782, was impolitic, unjust, and tyrannical, and has a tendency to interrupt the harmony of the States.

Voted—That this Company will support their claim and right of soil, to all lands laying on the waters of the river Susquehanna, included in the Deed of Purchase from the Six Nations of Indians, native owners, and proprietors thereof, and confirmed to said Company by the Legislature of the State of Connecticut, agreeble to the laws of said State, and that the Committee of said Company be, and they are hereby authorized to dispose of all non-resident delinquent proprietors' rights, who have or shall neglect to pay their taxes, agreeable to the vote of said Company, taking the previous steps pointed out in the act of Assembly regulating the same.

Voted—That this Company will support the proprietors, owners, settlers, and claimers of the country aforesaid, in their new application to Congress for a trial of the right of soil, agreeable to the second paragraph of the ninth article of the Confederation of the United States of America, and that we will protect our settlers in said country from all lawless outrage, unjustifiable and wanton depredations of property or personal abuse, whether under countenance of law, or otherwise, until such their right is judicially determined.

Voted—That every able-bodied and effective man, approved by any one of the Company's Committee, not being a proprietor, and that will repair to Wyoming, submit himself to the orders of this Company, and their Committee at that place, shall become a half share proprietor in said Company, entitled to all the benefits of any proprietor thereof, that has paid his full taxes to this time, provided he remains in said country for the space of three years, and do not depart therefrom without the permission of such Committee; and also provided that such half share proprietors do not exceed four hundred, and provided they arrive there by the first day of October next.

Voted, that Col. Ebenezer Gray, Col. Thomas Dyer, Ralph Pomeroy, Esq., Timothy Edwards, Esq., John Franklin, Esq., Ludwick Updike, Esq., Mr. Moses Sherrard, Joseph Hamilton, Esq., Zerah Beach, Esq., Col. Zebulon Butler, Obadiah Gore, Esq., and Captain Samuel Street, be, and they are hereby appointed committee men, in addition to the standing committee of this company.

Voted, that the standing committee be, and they are fully authorized to dispose of six hundred rights in said general tract of country, for the use of said company, using their discretion therein, and to account when required; and the clerk of said company is hereby directed to furnish said committee with such number of certificates, as they or any of them shall require, not to exceed the number of 600 in the whole, each committee man to be accountable for the number he receives.

Voted, this company will circumspectly conform themselves to all decisions of their claim constitutionally had, but, at the same time, cannot omit despising the treatment this State met with upon a former trial, the secretion of material papers by our opponents, until after the trial was over; and being fully assured the New England ancient royal charters were the only ground of the northern and western extensions of the United States, in the settlements of the late peace with Great Britain, viz., as far south as the completion of the 40th degree of northern latitude, cannot content themselves with idle speculations only, and tamely yield a tract of country, the grant of their ancestors, that purchased, of themselves, established by the only Legislature on earth that had right to confirm the same, and defended through a long and cruel war, at an amazing expense of property, and the lives of more than one thousand settlers."

A tax of one dollar on every whole share, and half a dollar on every half share right was then imposed, and the meeting dissolved, with no other attestation of its proceedings than their being transcribed into the book of records.

"Half share rights," much spoken of in early times, were now extensively used as a bounty for enlistment. "Every able bodied and effective man," who would move on to the land, "submit himself to the orders of the company," was to be entitled to a half share, the quantity of land exceeding two thousand acres: three hundred acres only to be located in a township.

Immediately on Col. Franklin's return, he called a meeting of the inhabitants at Kingston, and addressed them, explaining what had been done at Hartford. Proceeding to Plymouth, the settlers were called together; from thence he crossed over to Nanticoke, or Hanover; and thus journeying from town to town, public meetings were holden, contemplated measures, as far as politic, explained, and the people prepared for action. Adventurers were invited to enlist, or accept half share rights, on the terms proposed, and numbers received the bounty, Col. Franklin being engaged several days in issuing certificates.

It would be an imputation on the vigilance and sagacity of Pennsylvania, to suppose that these proceedings were not known to, and watched by her with jealous solicitude. What could she do to avert the threatened evil? Another invasion and civil war, so injudiciously had the last been managed, were too unpopular to afford hope of success. But December 24, a law was enacted, "For quieting disturbances at Wyoming, for pardoning certain offenders, and for other purposes therein mentioned." After reciting in preamble, according to the excellent fashion of the day, that "a spirit of licentiousness, and disobedience to the laws" prevailed, and "to strengthen the hands of Government and quiet the disturbances," "It is fit that lenient means be tried, before the most coercive ones are used," it proceeds to provide,

Sec. 2. That all offences committed before "the 1st of Nov. be pardoned, and put in oblivion."

Sec. 3. Provided all offenders surrender themselves before the 15th of April next, and enter into recognizances.

Sec. 4. Authorizes the militia to be called out.

Sec. 5. Repeals the act dividing Wyoming Township into three districts, and annuls Patterson's commission, and that of the other justices then elected.

To suppose the whole people, for all were concerned, would go forward, acknowledge their guilt, and sue for pardon by entering into bonds for their good behaviour, was a presumption founded elsewhere than in reason. No notice was taken of the law, and it remained a dead letter on the statute book. Thus close the annals of 1785.

LETTER XXV.

786.——Susquehanna Company's Resolves, at Hartford—Ethan Allen—Civil Government—Trials at Law—Ludicrous Defence—Susquehanna Whole and Half Share Rights in market—Conciliatory Policy—Luzerne county established—Name of Luzerne—('curious Note)—Pumpkin Fresh—New and important Personages appear on the stage—Joel Barlow—Hosmore—The Wolcotts, etc.—Grand Scheme to dismember Pennsylvania—New State contemplated.

THE most interesting event occurring in the early part of 1786, was the holding a second meeting of the Susquehanna Company, at Hartford, in May, the Assembly being then in session, following up the policy developed in their proceedings of the preceding year. Important in their bearing upon the interests of Wyoming, we copy whatever is of general concern.

At a meeting of the Susquehanna Company held at Hartford, May 17, 1786 :—

"Col. Elizur Talcott, Moderator; Samuel Gray, Clerk; Then Voted—That all persons settled under the authority of the State of Pennsylvania, now actually inhabiting upon that tract of country, situate upon the westerly waters of the Susquehanna river, and purchased of the natives, by the company called the Susquehanna Company, be, and the same are hereby fully established and confirmed in their full and absolute possession of the lands by them actually possessed, under the said State of Pennsylvania.

" Voted—That this Company, conscious of the equity of their title to the lands *bona fide* purchased of the natives, and situate upon the waters of the river Susquehanna, *will support and maintain their claims to the lands aforesaid, and effectually justify and support their settlers therein.*"

"Voted—That Col. John Franklin, Gen. Ethan Allen, Major John Jenkins, Col. Zebulon Butler, be, and they are hereby appointed a Committee, with full power and authority to locate townships within the territory aforesaid, agreeable to the votes of said Company, in the room and stead of the former Committee appointed for that purpose; and the said Committee are also hereby fully authorized and empowered to inquire into the claim of all persons now settled at Wyoming, and such as shall make out their claim in pursuance of the votes of said Company; said Committee are hereby authorized to quiet them in such lands as they shall find them justly entitled to, agreeable to the votes of said Company; and that Col. John Franklin, be, and he is hereby appointed clerk of the said Committee, and directed to keep fair records of the proceedings of said Committee, and the tranfer of all property in said settlement; and that said Clerk transmit, from time to time, fair copies to the clerk of this Company, of all such locations of townships, and the names of such as shall be admitted proprietors by such Committee, in virtue of the authority aforesaid. Col. John Franklin was duly sworn faithfully to execute the office of clerk of said Committee, according to the above vote, before Samuel Gray, Justice of the Peace."

It was doubtless politic, as well as liberal, to quiet the Pennsylvania settlers in their possessions, although the formal resolve to do so, may now excite a smile.

A declaration that the Company would "*effectually* justify and *support* the settlers," shows the boldness and earnestness of their proceedings.

Gen. Ethan Allen, of Vermont, too well known to require any introduction from my pen, it will be observed is appointed with Col. Franklin and Major Jenkins, as a Committee to "locate townships," and as a court to try contested titles.*

In the intermediate time, between those meetings, Wyoming was in a state of comparative repose. Hundreds of scattered settlers, who had been expelled by the war, many of them boys, now grown up to manhood, returned to claim their own or their fallen fathers' possessions. New adventurers, attracted by the wonderful tales of its richness and beauty, came in to purchase; and a productive year, diffusing plenty—such is the elastic spirit of man—restored cheerfulness and invigorated industry. Frame buildings began to take place of the log hut; and in Wilkesbarre Townplot one or two

---

* "General Allen arrived at Wyoming, April 8th, 1786. "In April 1786, General Ethan Allen paid us a visit at Wyoming, and proposed to settle amongst us *and to bring on with him* a number of his Green Mountain Boys, and assist us in supporting and defending our rights against the Pennsylvania Claimants. A large number of Proprietors' Rights were given to General Allen, to induce him to espouse our cause. FRANKLIN."

houses were painted, besides that on the river street, of which we have before spoken.*

While, nominally, the laws of Pennsylvania, administered by the magistrates of Northumberland, extended to Wyoming, in point of fact the settlers governed themselves, avoiding the service of writs, rather than opposing the officer. Indeed, from the well known friendship of Sheriff Antis, it is supposed that for the present, he did not deem it politic to pursue the eluding Yankees with much earnestness; relying, and relying wisely, on the measures of conciliation, or more determined and effectual coercion, which the Assembly must very soon adopt. For the year, the people had chosen Col. John Franklin, Major John Jenkins, Capt. John Paul Schott, Ebenezer Johnson, Esq., and Dr. William Hooker Smith, " A Committee to regulate the police of the Settlement." General and voluntary obedience was paid to their authority.† No record, that we have been able to discover, contains their proceedings, but by the aged inhabitants, several trials are remembered, two of which we preserve as a sample.

---

* A common exaggeration, in the olden time, to convey an idea of the fatness of the soil, was to say, " That it only needed melting, and you might dip candles." For some miles on the old " Lackaway" road, from the Delaware to the Susquehanna, there is a super-superabundance of stone. It was a standing joke, that Satan coming from New England with a load for Wyoming, his apron string broke on those hills, covering them with stones, and so the Valley was left free.

† In this way the settlements of Wyoming were governed under the directions of the Committee of Directors according to the form of government established by the people, regulating the affairs respecting new settlers, etc., agreeably to the rules adopted by the Susquehanna Company. We in a short time increased our numbers to upwards of six hundred effective men; and were determined to support our claims and interest, until decided by a legal course of law. We were also determined to oppose any authority from Pennsylvania, residing among us, until we could have a regular establishment on Constitutional principles, and our lands in some way secured to us. We continued firm and united in our resolutions, until the county of Luzerne was established, and the Confirming Law took place, which put a stop to our settlements being made under the Susquehanna Company. I will remark, that a large number on the west branch of the Susquehanna river had proposed to join us, and extend the claims of the Susquehanna Company into that part of the country. A Committee was appointed in 1786, and sent to Wyoming for that purpose. JOHN FRANKLIN."

This is the closing paragraph of Col. Franklin's book. It will be admitted that in the actual posture of public affairs, the promised Green Mountain Boys, with Ethan Allen to head them—the Wolcotts, and Barlow, and Hosmer and Judd, to back them by aid from Connecticut—the proposed auxiliaries from the West Branch, and six hundred enrolled effective men on the ground, with a civil government in operation, and a military organization complete, it was time for Pennsylvania to throw aside such agents as Patterson and Armstrong, and to exercise her utmost wisdom and vigilance.

A fellow, who had found his way to the Susquehanna, was charged with stealing honey. Having confessed the fact to the prosecutor and offered a very inadequate compensation for the pilfered sweets, the matter was brought before the Court, where the defendant plead not guilty, asseverated his innocence, and demanded proof. A witness was sworn who testified that he saw honey and honeycomb at the house of the defendant, the day after the alleged theft. "And what have you to answer to this testimony?" inquired one of the Committee. "May it please your worship, it is all a mistake; that man isn't capable of being a witness. He can't tell the difference between honey and molasses, and don't know honeycomb from a johnnycake." The merriment excited saved the prisoner from a severer punishment than a fine sufficient to pay for the honey and costs of suit. The other was a case of theft; the property having been taken from William Stark. The Court met near the house of the prisoner, heard the evidence, and decided—That the goods be forthwith restored; and as it was an aggravated case, the family being wandering interlopers, they were warned to leave the Valley in two weeks, or," etc. Some indefinite, but severe punishment was, probably, menaced by that "*or*."

These incidents, while they may excite a smile, are recorded chiefly to show, that so late as 1786, four years after the transfer of jurisdiction, the settlers still preserved some form of Government, trying offences and enforcing obedience. But it must be apparent, the high moral sanction of legitimate and acknowledged authority being wanting, that *habit* rather than *law*, was the chief defence of the inhabitants.

During the summer, an active business was going on in the disposal of whole and half share rights in the Susquehanna Company's purchase. Townships were "located" and surveyed; settlers began rapidly to people the lands on both sides of the Susquehanna from Wilkesbarre to the line of New York.

Deeming them curious to the antiquarian, and worthy of preservation, in this, and on two succeeding pages, will be found

First. A Certificate of a Susquehanna Whole Share Right, to a no less personage than SAMUEL HUNTINGTON, some time President of the Continental Congress ; and for many years Governor of the State of Connecticut.

Second. A Grant, by the Susquehanna Company, of a Township of Land, called LORANA, issued so late as 1796, situated on the State line, in McKean county, it is one hundred and ten miles west of Athens. It is neatly written upon parchment, and the reader will observe the Certificate of Approval, by the Deputy Surveyor-General ; and the Certificate of Record, in page 112 of Book F. (or 6th) giving evidence that the Records must have embraced many pages.

Third. A Grant, dated 1797, of a "GORE" of Land, by the "CONNECTICUT DELAWARE FIRST COMPANY ;" this is also carefully written on parchment ; and certificates are annexed, as in the Susquehanna Grant.

WINDHAM, 7th July, A. D. 1773.

THESE PRESENTS WITNESS.—That we the Subscribers, Committee of the Susquehannah Company : In consideration of Sundry beneficial Services, done by SAMUEL HUNTINGTON, of Norwich, for said Company—Do hereby Institute him, to one whole Share in the Lands, in sd Susquehannah Purchase in equal proportion, with the other Proprietors.

ELIPHALET DYER,
JED'A ELDERKIN,
SAM'L GRAY,
NATH'A WALES, JR.
} Committee.

Recorded on the Records of the Susquehannah Company. Liber E Page 364. Sept. 6th, 1796.
Attest,
DAVID PAINE, Ass't Clerk.

WHEREAS, THE CONNECTICUT SUSQUEHANNA COMPANY, voted and entered on their Records, that the Subscribers with others, (three of whom were to be a quorum) should be Commissioners under said Company, duly authorized to make out and sign GRANTS for Lands within the limits of the Purchase of said Company, to such applicants as made it manifest they were proprietors in said Purchase. *And whereas,* Mr. JOSHUA DOWNER, of Preston, and EZEKIEL HYDE, of Norwich, in Connecticut, and Mr. SAMUEL ENSIGN, of Whitstown, Harkemer county, State of New York, have, on the day of the date hereof, exhibited in our Office, to us, the Subscribers, (three of said Commissioners,) sufficient vouchers; and have, in other respects, complied with the rules and regulations of said Company; so as to entitle them to a Grant of a Township of Land; which said township is bounded and described as follows: to wit.—BEGINNING at the northwest corner of Conde, then west on the north line of the purchase, two hundred and forty chains, to the most northwesterly bounds of the purchase; thence south eight hundred chains, to a post standing in the west line of the purchase marked for a corner; thence east two hundred and forty chains, to a black cherry tree, being the northwest corner of Trumbull and southwest corner of Minerva; thence north, on the west line of Minerva, and west line of Conde, eight hundred chains, to the place of beginning; containing nineteen thousand two hundred acres of land—and known by the name of LORANA.

NOW, KNOW ALL MEN to whom these presents shall or may come, greeting, That we the undersigned Commissioners as aforesaid, in consequence, or by virtue of the power and authority vested and reposed in us as aforesaid, have granted and confirmed, and by these presents do grant and confirm unto the said Downer, Hyde and Ensign, their heirs or assigns, forever, the aforesaid Township of Land, with all and singular, the privileges and advantages thereunto belonging or in any wise appertaining; subject, however, to the rules and regulations of the aforesaid Company. IN TESTIMONY WHEREOF, we, the undersigned Commissioners, have hereunto set our hands and affixed our seals, at our office in Athens, April 1st, seventeen hundred and ninety-six.

JOHN FRANKLIN,
SIMON SPALDING,
ELISHA SATTERLEE,
} *Commissioners.*

The Survey of the above Township of Land } *is Approved of pr me,*
Jos. BILES, D. S. for JNO. JENKINS, Super't of Surveys.

Recorded in Liber F. page 112, of the Records of the Susquehanna Company.
Test,
BILLA FRANKLIN, *Assist. Clerk.*
Sept. 29th, 1796.

WHEREAS, THE CONNECTICUT DELAWARE FIRST COMPANY, voted and entered on their Records, That the Subscribers with others, (three of whom were to be a quorum,) should be a Committee under said Company, duly authorized to make out and sign Grants or Locations of Land, within the limits of said Purchase, to such Applicants as made it manifest they were Proprietors therein. AND WHEREAS Charles Hill, of Cazenevia, county of Herkemer, and State of New York, ... and . . . . Ezekiel Hyde, of Norwich, in Connecticut, have this day exhibited to us, the Subscribers, rights sufficient to entitle them to a Grant of a tract or parcel of Land which is bounded as follows:—Beginning at the southeast corner of Usher, on the west line of Manor; thence south four hundred and eight chains, to the line between the Delaware and Susquehanna Purchases; thence north forty-eight degrees west, on said Purchase line, six hundred and seventy-two chains to the south line of Usher; thence east four hundred and sixty-two chains to the place of beginning.—Containing ten thousand eight hundred acres of land.

NOW, KNOW ALL MEN BY THESE PRESENTS, That we, the undersigned Committee, have apportioned and set off to the aforesaid Charles —— and Ezekiel, the aforesaid tract or parcel of land, in severally, from said general tract or purchase, with all the privileges and appurtenances thereunto belonging, to themselves, their heirs and assigns, forever. IN TESTIMONY whereof, we the undersigned Committee, have hereunto set our hands and seals, in the City of Norwich, Jan'y 20th, seventeen hundred and ninety-seven.

The aforesaid tract or parcel of Land adjoining the town of Usher, and the Connecticut Susquehanna Purchase, does not interfere with any Grant of a previous date.

EZEKIEL HYDE, *Super't Surveys.*

ANDREW TRACY,
OLIVER CRARY, } *Committee.*
ROBERT GERE,

Recorded in Liber A, page 399.—Records of the Connecticut Delaware First Company.
January 21st, A. D. 1797.
Attest, ANDREW TRACY, *Proprietor's Clerk.*

That the speculation in those rights was general, is shown by the fact, that gentlemen of the first distinction and property engaged in the purchase. Matthias Hollenback, Esq., took a whole share, numbered 264. Capt. Dudley, Capt. Spalding, Hugh Forseman, Esq., Col. Denison, William Slocum, and other principal men of the settlement are set down as purchasers. Capt. Schott paid 28 1-3 dollars for share No. 160. John Hollenback paid 40 dollars for No. 83. Capt. Peter Loop paid 40 dollars for No. 82. Samuel Church gave 20 dollars for half share No. 272. Aaron Cleaveland gave 40 dollars for a share, and Samuel Decker received a half share, numbered 283, "for services rendered prisoners at Easton." From whence it may be seen that several hundred shares of the new emission had been already disposed of at Wyoming, the prices paid, and the respectability of the persons engaged. In different parts of New England the numbers, probably were seven fold greater. Many of the half shares it may be observed, were disposed of as a condition of actual settlement, to " man the rights."

It may reasonably be supposed that these measures on the part of the Yankees accelerated the action of Pennsylvania. A new and more liberal policy was resolved upon, coercion giving place to conciliation, and compromise being beneficially substituted for civil war.

To extend to the remote settlement at Wyoming the advantages of civil government, in which they might participate; affording them an opportunity to administer their own local affairs, by persons having the confidence of the inhabitants chosen by themselves; to give the people an efficient representation in the Council and Assembly, so that their voice might be heard, their interests explained, and their influence fairly appreciated, was the first grand healing measure adopted on the part of the State. That it was full of wisdom in its conception, subsequent events proved beyond question. On the 25th of September, 1786, an act was passed for erecting the northern part of the county of Northumberland into a separate county. The limits of the new county were these: beginning at the mouth of Nescopeck creek, and running along the south bank thereof, eastward to the head of said creek; from thence a due east course to the head branch of Lehigh Creek; then along the east bank of said Lehigh Creek to the head thereof; from thence a due north course to the northern boundary of the State; thence westward along said boundary till it crosses the east branch of Susquehanna, and then along said northern boundary fifteen miles west of said river Susquehanna; thence by a straight line to the head of

Towanda Creek; thence along the ridge which divides the waters of the east branch of the Susquehanna, from those of the west branch, to a point due west from the mouth of the Nescopeck creek; thence east to the place of beginning, which shall henceforth be known and called by the name of Luzerne county.

In respect to the boundaries, it may be remarked that they include about the western half of the old town and county of Westmoreland. When the act was drawn, the northern line was evidently imperfectly known, for it crosses the Susquehanna three times instead of once, as seems to have been supposed. But the limits were fair and liberal, and included all the New England emigrants, excepting those in the ancient "Lackawa" settlement, and a few on the Delaware.

The five succeeding sections were in the usual form, and invite no comment. Sect. 8, provides that "on the second Tuesday of October next, there shall be chosen (in the town of Wilkesbarre) one representative to serve in the Assembly, one counsellor, two fit persons for sheriff, two fit persons for coroner, and three commissioners. Section 9 provides, "that Zebulon Butler, Nathaniel Landon, Jonah Rogers, Simon Spalding and John Phillips,"* shall be commissioners to purchase land whereon to erect the necessary public buildings.

But no provision had been made for the "little election" to choose judges and inspectors, and the day passed over, no counsellor, assemblymen, or county officers having been chosen.

The least curious reader will be led to inquire, whence the name of "*Luzerne?*" And especially the young and intelligent citizen of the county, may be presumed earnestly to desire full information on the subject. In the fall of 1778, the alliance with France was formed, and in the following year the Sieur Gerard had leave to return, and a new minister was accredited to the United States. In Congress, "Wednesday, November 17th, 1779, according to order, the Honorable Chevalier de la Luzerne, Minister Plenipotentiary of his most Christian Majesty, was introduced to an audience by Mr. Matthews and Mr. Morris, the two members for that purpose appointed, and being seated in his chair, the Secretary of the Embassy delivered to the President a letter from his most Christian Majesty, of which the following is a translation:—

* While his companions in the commission are all long, long since gathered to their fathers, we have the pleasure to say that John Phillips, Esq., was last winter married, and is still a highly respectable, hale old gentleman, (May 1843.)

To our very dear, great friends and allies, the President and Members of the General Congress of the United States in North America.

"Very dear, great friends and allies:

The bad state of health of the Sieur Gerard, our Minister Plenipotentiary to you, having laid him under the necessity of applying for a recall, we have made choice of the Chevalier de la Luzerne, a colonel in our service, to supply his place. We have no doubt but he will be agreeable to you, and that you will repose entire confidence in him. We pray you to give full credit to all he shall say to you on our behalf, especially when he shall assure you of the sincerity of our wishes for your prosperity, as well as of the constancy of our affection, and of our friendship for the United States in general, and for each one of them in particular. We pray God to keep you, our very dear, great friends and allies, in his holy protection.

Your good friend and ally,
LOUIS.

(Underneath)   GRAVIER DE VERGENNES."

Done at Versailles, the 31st of May, 1779.

"The Minister was then announced to the House: Whereupon he arose, and addressed Congress in a speech, which, when he had finished, the Secretary delivered in writing to the President, and of which the following is a translation:

"Gentlemen, the wisdom and courage which have founded your republic; the prudence which presides over your deliberations; your firmness in executing, the skill and valour displayed by your generals and soldiers, during the course of the war, have attracted the admiration and regard of the whole world. The king, my master, was the first to acknowledge a liberty acquired amidst so many perils, and with so much glory. Since treaties, dictated by moderation, have fixed upon a permanent base the union of France, with the American Republic, his Majesty's whole conduct must have demonstrated how dearly he tenders your prosperity, and his firm resolution to maintain your independence, by every means in his power. The events which have successively unfolded themselves, show the wisdom of those measures. A powerful ally hath acknowledged the justice of those motives which had compelled the king to take arms, and we may reasonably hope for the most solid success, from the operations of the united fleets. The naval force of the enemy hath been diverted from your Continent.—Compelled to flee to the defence of their own possessions, all their efforts have been too feeble to prevent our troops from conquering a considerable part."

Such was the letter of introduction from the Count de Vergennes of the Chevalier de la Luzerne; such was a part of his address to Congress; and from this gentleman is derived the euphonious, the sweetly flowing name of the newly erected county. Still surprise might exist that the name of a foreigner, however worthy, should have been selected for the honour, in preference to many equally worthy, who were citizens of Pennsylvania, who had distinguished themselves in council, or in the field; or if a foreigner was to be so honoured, why Rochambeau, the commander of the French forces, who aided Washington to capture Cornwallis, was not preferred? So early as May, 1784, the Chevalier had taken leave, and returned to France. What Minister is now remembered two years and a half after his departure for a distant home? The difficulty is solved by relating, that, in 1782, on the birth of the Dauphin of France, the Chevalier de la Luzerne gave an entertainment in Philadelphia, then, except by the Maschienza, never equalled; and the account of it, written in an extremely popular style to a lady in the country, was first published, or republished about the time Luzerne was erected, and probably, nay, almost certainly, led to the selection of the name. Not doubting such to be the fact, both for the instruction and amusement imparted, I have copied the letter in a note.*

PHILADELPHIA, July 16, 1782.

MADAM,—For some weeks past our city has been amused with the expectation of a most splendid entertainment to be given by the minister, to celebrate the birth of the Dauphin of France. Great preparations, it was said, were made for that purpose. Hundreds crowded daily to see a large frame building, which he had erected for a dancing room, on one side of his house. This building which was sixty feet in front, and forty feet in depth, was supported by large painted pillars, and was open all round. The ceiling was decorated with several pieces of neat paintings emblematical of the design of the entertainment. The garden contiguous to this shed was cut into walks, and divided with cedar and pine branches into artificial groves. The whole, both of the building and walks, were accommodated with seats. Besides these preparations, we are told that the minister had borrowed thirty cooks from the French army, to assist in providing an entertainment suited to the size and dignity of his company. Eleven hundred tickets were distributed, most of them two and three weeks before the evening of the entertainment. Forty were sent to the Governors of each State, to be distributed by them to the principal officers and gentlemen of their respective governments; and I believe the same number to General Washington, to be distributed among the principal officers of the army.

For ten days before the entertainment, nothing else was talked of in our city. The shops were crowded with customers. Hair dressers were retained, and tailors, milliners and mantuamakers, were to be seen covered with sweat and out of breath, in every street.

Monday, July 15, was the long expected evening. The morning of this day was ushered in by a corps of hair dressers, occupying the place of the city watchmen. Many ladies

If history be philosophy teaching by example, the deduction might be that the road to immortality was not that of war, sacrifice, or privation, but the primrose path of hospitality, of courtesy, of display.

were obliged to have their heads dressed between four and six o'clock in the morning, so great was the demand, and so numerous were the engagements this day of the gentlemen of the comb. At half an hour after seven o'clock in the afternoon, was the time fixed in the tickets for the meeting of the company. The approach of the hour was proclaimed by the rattling of all the carriages in the city. The doors and windows of the street, which leads to the minister's, were lined with people, and near the minister's house, there was a collection of all the curious, and idle men, women and children of the city, who were not invited to the entertainment, amounting probably to ten thousand people. The minister was not unmindful of this crowd of spectators. He had previously pulled down a board fence, and put up a low fence before the dancing room and walks, on purpose to gratify them with a sight of the company and entertainment. He intended further to have distributed two pipes of Madeira wine, and six hundred dollars in small change among them; but he was dissuaded from this act of generosity by some gentlemen of the city, who were afraid that it might prove the occasion of a riot, or some tumultuous proceedings. The money devoted to this purpose was charitably distributed among the prisoners in the jails, and the patients in the hospitals in the city. About eight o'clock, our family, together with Miss —— and Miss ——, and our good neighbours Mr. and Mrs. ——, entered the apartments provided for this splendid entertainment. We were received through a side gate by the minister, and conducted by one of his family forward towards the dancing room. The scene now almost exceeds description. The numerous lights distributed through the garden—the splendour of the room that we were approaching—the size of the company, which was now collected, and which amounted to about 700 persons—the brilliancy and variety of their dresses, and the band of music which had just began to play, formed a scene that resembled enchantment. Our companion, Miss —— said "her mind was carried beyond and out of itself." We entered the room together—and here we saw the world in miniature. All the ranks and parties, and professions in the city, and officers of our government were fully represented in this assembly. Here were ladies and gentlemen of the most ancient, and of the most modern families. Here were lawyers, doctors, and ministers of the gospel. Here were the learned faculty of the college, and with them many who knew not whether Cicero plead in Latin or Greek, or whether Horace was a Roman or a Scotchman. Here were painters and musicians, poets and philosophers, and men who were never moved by beauty, nor harmony, nor by rhyme nor reason. Here were merchants and gentlemen of independent fortunes, as well as many respectable and opulent tradesmen. Here were whigs, and men who formerly bore the character of tories. Here were the president and members of Congress, governors of States—generals of armies—ministers of finance, and war, and foreign affairs, judges of superior and inferior courts, with all their respective suits of assistants—secretaries and clerks. In a word the assembly was truly republican. The company was mixed, it is true, but the mixture formed the harmony of the evening. Every body seemed pleased. Pride and ill nature for awhile forgot their pretensions and offices, and the whole assembly behaved to each other as if they had been members of the same family.

It was impossible to partake of the joy of the evening, without being struck with the occasion of it. It was to celebrate the birth of a Dauphin of France. How great the revolution in the mind of an American! to rejoice in the birth of an heir to the crown of France! a country against which he had imbibed prejudices, as ancient as the wars between France and England. How strange! for a protestant to rejoice in the birth of a prince, whose religion he has been taught to consider as unfriendly to humanity—and above all, how new the phenomenon, for republicans and freemen to rejoice in the birth of a prince, who must one day be the support of monarchy. Human nature in this instance seems to be

An event occurred in the autumn of this year, regarded by all the ancient people as too important to be omitted. In October the waters of the Susquehanna rose to a height never known except at the ice

turned inside outwards. The picture is still agreeable, inasmuch as it shows us in the clearest point of view, that there are no prejudices so strong, no opinions so sacred, and no contradictions so palpable, that will not yield to the love of liberty.

The appearance and characters, as well as the employments of the company, naturally suggested the ideas of Elysium, given us by the ancient poets. Here were to be seen heroes and patriots in close conversation with each other. Washington and Dickinson held several dialogues together. Here were to be seen men conversing with each other, who appeared in all the different stages of the American war. Dickinson and Morris, frequently reclined together against the same pillar. Here were to be seen statesmen and warriors from the opposite ends of the continent, talking of the history of the war, in their respective States. Rutledge and Walton from the south, here conversed with Lincoln and Duane, from the east and the north. Here and there too, appeared a solitary character, walking among the artificial bowers in the garden. The celebrated author of " Common Sense," retired frequently from company to enjoy the repast of his own original ideas. Here were to be seen men who had opposed each other in the councils and parties of their country, forgetting all former resentments, and exchanging civilities with each other. Even M——n and R——d, accosted each other with all the kindness of ancient friends. Here were to be seen men of various countries and languages, such as Americans and Frenchmen, Englishmen and Scotchmen, Germans and Irishmen, conversing with each other like children of one father. And lastly, here were to be seen the extremes of the civilized, and of the savage life. An Indian chief in his savage habits, and the Count Rochambeau in his expensive and splendid uniform, talked with each other, as if they had been the subjects of the same government, generals in the same army, and the partakers of the same blessings of civilized life.

About half an hour after eight o'clock, the signal was given for the dances to begin. Each lady was provided with a partner before she came. The heat of the evening deterred above one half of the company from dancing. Two sets however, appeared on the floor during the remaining part of the evening.

On one side of the room were provided two private apartments, where a number of servants attended to help the company to all kinds of cool and agreeable drinks, with sweet cake, fruit and the like. Between these apartments, and under the orchestra, there was a private room where several ladies, whose dress would not permit them to join the assembly, were indulged with a sight of the company through a gauze curtain. This little attention to the curiosity of these ladies, marks in the strongest manner the minister's desire to please every body.

At 9 o'clock, were exhibited a number of rockets from a stage erected in a large open lot before the minister's house; they were uncommonly beautiful, and gave universal satisfaction.

At 12 o'clock, the company was called to supper. It was laid behind the dancing room under three large markees, so connected together as to make one large canopy. Under this canopy were placed seven tables, each of which was large enough to accommodate fifty people. The ladies, who composed near one-half of the whole assembly, took their seats first, with a small number of gentlemen to assist in helping them. The supper was a cold collation, simple, frugal and elegant, and handsomely set off with a desert consisting of cakes, and all the fruits of the season. The Chevalier de la Luzerne, now appeared with all the splendour of the minister, and all the politeness of a gentleman. He walked along the tables, and addressed himself in particular to every lady. A decent and respectful silence pervaded the whole company. Intemperance did not show its head—levity composed its flood two years previously. Wilkesbarre was partially inundated, and many were preparing canoes to take off the inhabitants to the hills. This was termed the "Pumpkin fresh," from the immense number that floated down the stream to the astonishment of the people below. Great and irreparable losses were sustained in hay, grain and cattle, occasioning much suffering during the ensuing winter. Several houses and barns were swept away, and one or two lives were lost.

Other important personages crowd on the scene of action. The last grand movement of the Susquehanna Company, having in view the establishment of an independent government and State, in defiance of Pennsylvania, her power and her laws, was now in bold and energetic progress. Col. Franklin, "the hero of Wyoming," in the spirit of his oath on the bloody rifle, had aroused into action some of the boldest and most influential spirits in the land. In the proceedings which follow, fraught as Pennsylvania might well regard them, with war and treason; and justified as Franklin, and those gentlemen who connected themselves with his scheme, conscientiously believed, by the unendurable wrongs and oppressions inflicted with unsparing hand and remorseless rigour, on the poor settlers at Wyoming, will be found names conspicuous in the annals of the nation; official functionaries of the highest grade, and men of genius, whom literature as well as politics, was proud to crown with the chaplet of enviable distinction.

Joel Barlow, already known to fame, eminent for learning and distinguished by genius, which subsequently ensured his elevation to the honourable office of minister plenipotentiary to the court of France, acted, it will be seen, as secretary.

The Wolcotts, of Connecticut, were themselves a host. No less than three of the name will be found on the list of the grand commit-

countenance, and even humour itself, forgot for a few minutes its usual haunt; and the simple jest, no less than the loud laugh, were unheard at any of the tables. So great and universal was the decorum, and so totally suspended was every species of convivial noise, that several gentlemen remarked that the "company looked and behaved more as if they were *worshipping* than *eating*." In a word, good breeding was acknowledged by universal consent, to be mistress of the evening, and the conduct of her votaries at supper formed the conclusion of her triumphs.

At two o'clock in the morning the company broke up, and we returned home. Our ladies speak with great pleasure of the entertainment, and, as far as I have heard, no offence was given or taken the whole evening.

If this long letter gives you half as much pleasure in reading it, as I have had in writing it, it will add greatly to my proportion of pleasure derived from the entertainment. With great respect, I am madam, your sincere friend, and most humble servant.

* * * * * * *

tee of twenty-two. The name of Hosmer was also there. Oliver Wolcott, jr., was afterwards Secretary of the Treasury, and subsequently Governor of Connecticut. Such men did not move without high purpose and elevated aim. A prize to gratify ambition could alone have secured the co-operation of gentlemen holding station, enjoying consequence, and with prospects so flattering in society as theirs. But to the proceedings.

"At a meeting of the proprietors of the Susquehanna purchase, duly warned, and held at the State House of the city of Hartford, December 26, A. D. 1786,

"Col. Gad Stanley, moderator, Joel Barlow, clerk pro tem., several public papers and private letters relative to the present situation of the settlers at Wyoming were read. It was then moved that a committee be appointed to prepare the business for to-morrow, and that the meeting adjourn to that time; accordingly Major Judd, Mr. Pomeroy, Mr. Hamilton, Mr. Beach, Mr. Barlow, Mr. Barton, Mr. O. Wolcott, Mr. A. Wolcott, Mr. Hosmore, were appointed, the meeting adjourned till ten o'clock to-morrow morning.

"December 27. The meeting opened according to adjournment, and the committee reported: whereupon the following resolves were passed.

"Whereas, it is an object of great importance that the rights of the proprietors under the Susquehanna purchase be ascertained, and the claims of the settlers be reduced to a certainty, and their titles confirmed, therefore

"*Resolved*, That Maj. Judd, Saml. Gray, Esq., Joel Barlow, Esq., Oliver Wolcott, jr. Esq., Al. Wolcott, jr. Esq., Col. Gad Stanley, Joseph Hamilton, Esq., Dr. Timothy Hosmore, Col. Zebulon Butler, Col. Nathan Denison, Obadiah Gore, Esq., Col. John Franklin, Zerah Beach, Esq., Capt. Simon Spalding, Major John Jenkins, Major Paul Schott, Abel Pierce, Esq., Capt. John Bartle, Capt. Peter Loop, jr., John Bay, Esq., and Col. Ebenezer Gray, be, and they are hereby authorized and appointed commissioners, with full powers to ascertain, by reference to the records of the clerk of the Susquehanna Company, and the records of the settlers at Wyoming, the names of the proprietors claiming under said purchase; that as soon as may be they make out a fair and complete list of the names of all the proprietors, and annex thereto the proportions of land to which they are severally entitled. That as soon as said list may be completed, it shall be entered at large on the records of the said Company, and shall be considered as full and complete evidence of the title of said proprietors.

" That said Commissioners shall thereupon make a scrutiny of every person settled upon said lands, and that such settlers as shall appear to have been proprietors, heirs or assigns of proprietors, shall immediately procure their locations to be surveyed and ascertained, which after being approved by said Commissioners shall be accorded as parcel of their proprietary right.

" That whenever it shall appear that any settler or proprietor has made a location by permission, and under authority from any proprietor, or the Company, the quantity of land located shall be surveyed as aforesaid, and if approved by said Commissioners, shall be recorded, and considered as parcel of the right of said original proprietor, unless otherwise provided by the vote of this Company; that said Commissioners be, and they are hereby directed to ascertain, locate and survey, to each and every person, who has in consequence of any person, vote, or agreement of said Susquehanna Company, gone and settled on said lands, the amount of his grant, which being recorded, shall vest a full and complete title thereto, in favour of such person. That said Commissioners be also directed and empowered to locate and survey, in favour of such persons as they shall judge proper, who shall actually settle and occupy said lands, by themselves, their heirs or assigns, not exceeding 200 acres on any proprietor's right, who has either by himself, or by some person under him, settled and remained on said lands; which survey and location being recorded shall vest a complete title in such settlers, and shall be considered as parcel of such proprietor's right.

" That said Commissioners shall locate and survey all such grants as they may make in favour of any new settler on said lands, in such towns as have been already granted, as far as vacant lands can be found for that purpose, or on such gores of land as remain ungranted between said towns: Provided that nothing herein shall be construed to affect the title of any actual settler in such town. Said Commissioners are to take especial care that the property of widows and orphans be in no instance infringed.

" That said Commissioners shall, as soon as may be, convene together and appoint some particular place for holding their court, and they shall in no instance hold their court in any other place than that first agreed upon, unless it shall not be convenient to meet at such place, in which [case] it shall be in their power to adjourn to any other place, and they shall appoint some proper person for their secretary, who shall keep fair and accurate records of all their proceedings and determinations.

"That said Commissioners be, and they are hereby authorized to make locations and surveys in favour of any settlers or proprietors, on any of the broken or mountainous lands lying within five miles of the river, not convenient to lay out townships five miles square, and annex the same to such townships as they judge proper, provided that such locations shall in no instance exceed six hundred acres to the proprietor of a full right, or in proportion to the proprietor of a less quantity than a full right, including any location heretofore made by such proprietor, or any person under him, and also including such locations as may by the said Commissioners be made in favour of any settler on his proprietary right.

"And said Commissioners are hereby authorized to grant new townships, agreeable to the former votes of this company, and the powers heretofore granted to any Committee for that purpose are hereby declared to cease and determine.

"And said Commissioners are hereby authorized to inquire into the particular circumstances of any locations and settlements that have been made contrary to the former regulations of this Company, and confirm or disallow the same, as they shall judge most conducive to the interests of this Company:—And it is hereby ordered that no location which may hereafter be made contrary to the regulations contained in this act, shall in any instance be admitted or confirmed.

"That any three of the said Commissioners, together with their Secretary, shall be a quorum to transact any of the business aforesaid.

"That the expense of locating, and surveying and determining all matters aforesaid, shall be paid by persons in whose favour such locations, &c., shall be made or done: and that said Court of Commissioners shall in no instance exact or receive unreasonable or exorbitant fees.

"That any five of said Commissioners, with their Secretary, shall be a COURT, with power to hear and finally determine all controversies between actual occupants respecting the title of lands, and to award equitable costs in the usual forms of trials at law; this power to determine *whenever a form of internal government shall be established in that country.*

"Resolved likewise, That the Commissioners aforesaid, or a majority of them, be, and they are hereby *fully authorized and empowered to do and transact any other matters and things which they may judge necessary for the security and protection of the settlers on said lands, and for the benefit of the Company of Proprietors, hereby ratifying and confirming whatever said Commissioners may do in the premises.* Test, Joel Barlow, *Clerk, pro tem."*

Long as this document is, we have chosen to place in our pages the full record of all that it contained of material import. Except the copy before us, there is not, probably, another in existence. It will be seen that, in truth, the Committee is an Executive Directory, with full powers, or rather a Government; and doubtless meant, in its appointment, to be a provisional government, in and over the new State, contemplated to be erected by the dismemberment of Pennsylvania.

These proceedings were a prelude to the highly important and stirring scenes which it will be our duty to record in the annals of the coming year.

On the 27th of December a Supplement was passed to the Act establishing Luzerne county, within four days of the close of the year, its whole operation being thrown into 1787; and moreover, as it introduces a person of far too high distinction to bring forward at the close of a letter, we shall postpone its consideration till our next.

LETTER XXVI.

1787.——Col. Timothy Pickering—Col. Butler—Wyoming People divided—Elections—Grand Measure of Conciliation—The Confirming Act—Organization of Luzerne county—Policy of Pickering—Adverse Policy of Franklin—Great Meeting—Stormy Discussion—Broken up in confusion and riot—A stream of Settlers flowing in from the East, on Share and Half Share Rights—Ethan Allen on the ground—A Crisis impending—Constitution for the new State—Arrest of Col. Franklin for Treason—Spirit of Mrs. Slocum—Bloody Scene—A City Paper—Commotion—Pickering withdrawn—Is elected member of the Convention—Another year closes in storms and tempest.

THE Act of December 27th, 1786, provided, that Timothy Pickering, Zebulon Butler, and John Franklin, notify the Electors that an election would be holden to choose a Counsellor, Member of Assembly, Sheriff, Coroner, and Commissioners, on the first day of February. A mode was pointed out by which Inspectors and Judges were to be appointed. Oaths of allegiance were to be taken by the voters; and provision for the election of Justices of the Peace was made.

Col. Pickering was one of the most eminent men in the Union. Having the confidence of Washington and Congress, he had executed with fidelity and approbation the office of Quartermaster-General of the army. A native of Massachusetts, after the peace he settled in Philadelphia, becoming a citizen of Pennsylvania, and was selected, in addition to his great abilities and weight of character, for the reason that he was a New England man, to organize the new county, and introduce the laws of the State among the Wyoming people. Too politic, as well as too just not to desire that the controversy should be settled on terms reciprocally satisfactory, there is reason to suppose, that, before accepting this delicate and arduous appointment, assurances had been given him that the settlers, before the Decree of Trenton, should, by some fair terms of compromise, be quieted in their possessions. To believe otherwise would be an imputation at once upon his sagacity and his honour.

Col. Butler, with great prudence, had kept himself aloof from all active measures of opposition. A captain in the old French war; a colonel in the revolutionary contest, having served with reputation, and retired with honours; ambition having been satisfied, and age cooled the fever of his ardent temperament, he desired peace; he longed, ardently, for repose, if it could be attained with safety to his neighbours and credit to himself. But if expulsion or war were the only alternatives, "Set fire to 'em," he was prepared for the course pointed out by the duty of a patriot and the spirit of a soldier.

Franklin, except in education and polish, was in no respect the inferior of Pickering; and it was a wise, though as it proved, an unavailing stroke of policy, to endeavour to conciliate the great Yankee leader, by naming him as one of the Deputies to regulate the elections.

But Col. Franklin was too deeply committed in interest and pledged faith to the grand scheme of establishing a new State, to take a new oath of fidelity to Pennsylvania; and either directly, by himself, or through the agency of his attached partizans, every obstacle, short of absolute force, was interposed to prevent the election being held.

And now, for the first time was presented the spectacle, equally gratifying to foes and painful to friends, of open and decided hostility among the Wyoming people. Whatever difference of opinion may exist in respect to the justice of their claim, no liberal mind could have traced their arduous course, through toil and privation, through suffering and oppression, through civil and foreign war, and observed the fortitude, fellowship and harmony among themselves, that had prevailed, without a feeling of admiration for rare and generous virtues so signally displayed. In an equal degree was the mortification at the spectacle now presented. It was now no longer, "Pennymite and Yankee;" but the "Old settlers against the wild Yankees, or Half Share Men."

Col. Pickering came with assurances, that on the introduction of the laws, and the organization of the county by the election of proper officers, which of course implied the oath of allegiance, measures of compromise would be forthwith adopted. Probably three-fourths of the ancient people sided with him, and were in favour of submission to the law. Among these were Col. Butler, Col. Denison, the Hollenbacks, the Rosses, the families of Gore, Carey, Nesbit, etc. while Franklin, the Jenkins, the Slocums, Satterlee, Dudley, and others, especially the residents up the river, wished to defeat the election, insisting that confirmation of title to the settlers should precede, and not be left to follow, complete submission to the power of the State. It was a day of high excitement, even for Wyoming; indeed of riotous commotion. Many a stalwart Yankee was engaged in combat fierce, and sometimes bloody, though not mortal, with a former friend, by whose side he had fought. In the midst of the wild uproar, when overwhelming force was apprehended, Col. Butler mounted his war steed, and rode up and down amid the crowd, exclaiming; " I draw my sword in defence of the law; let every lover of peace and good order support me !" The romance of life was all over. That secret charm which has led us so long to cherish the behalf of a united band struggling for the right, was, by their disunion dissipated at least for a season. In despite of opposition, the election was consummated. Col. Nathan Denison was elected to the Supreme Executive Council; John Franklin was chosen member of Assembly, and Lord Butler, Esq., High Sheriff.

Immediately upon the favorable issue of the election being made known, the Assembly, then in session, proceeded to perfect the work of conciliation so happily begun. At the suggestion of Col. Pickering, a large number of the people united in a petition, setting forth that seventeen townships, of five miles square, had been located by the Connecticut settlers before the Trenton Decree; and the lots, averaging three hundred acres, been set off, specifically, to settlers and proprietors, and praying that these might be confirmed: Whereupon the Assembly, on the 28th of March, passed the Confirming Law, which after the recitation of the subject matter of the petition, enacted "That all the said rights or lots now laying within the county of Luzerne, which were occupied or acquired by Connecticut claimants who were actual settlers there at or before the termination of the claim of the State of Connecticut, by the Decree aforesaid, and which rights or lots were particularly assigned to the said settlers prior to the said Decree, agreeably to the regulations then in force among them, be and they are hereby confirmed to them and their heirs and assigns." Such was the essence of the law. The Act, consisting of nine sections, provided for the appointment of Commissioners, the exhibition of claims, compensation in land to Pennsylvania Claimants, and whatever appeared necessary to carry its beneficent provisions into complete effect. Peter Muhlenburg, Timothy Pickering, and Joseph Montgomery, Esqs., were the Commissioners named, (Chapman says Stephen Balliott. Did Montgomery decline?) who repaired early in May to Wyoming, to enter upon the duties of their appointment.

In the mean time the general organization of the several departments demanded for the due administration of the Laws in Luzerne had taken place, a brief official view of which cannot fail to be read with interest.

COUNTY OF LUZERNE, to wit. May, 1787.

Be it Remembered, That on Tuesday, the twenty-seventh day of May, in the year one thousand seven hundred and eighty-seven, William Hooker Smith, Benjamin Carpenter, and James Nesbit, Esq'rs., Justices of the County Court of Common Pleas for said County, convened at the dwelling house of Zebulon Butler in Wilkesbarre, in the said County, when and where the following proceedings were had.

Proclamation having been made by the Sheriff of said County, commanding all persons to keep silence, there were read:

I. The Commissions issued by the Supreme Executive Council of Pennsylvania to the said William Hooker Smith, Benjamin Carpenter, and James Nesbit, and also to Timothy Pickering, Obadiah Gore, Nathan Kingsley, and Matthias Hollenback, constituting them Justices of the County Court of Common Pleas for the said County.

II. The Dedimus Potestatum to Timothy Pickering and Nathan Denison, Esquires, issued by the Supreme Executive Council, impowering them to administer the oaths to persons who were, or should be commissioned in said County.

III. Then William Hooker Smith, Benjamin Carpenter, and James Nesbit, Esquires, took the oaths of allegiance and of office, and Justices of the Peace, and of the County Court of Common Pleas for said County, (as required by the Constitution of Pennsylvania,) before Timothy Pickering, Esq., impowered as aforesaid to administer them.

IV. The Court of Common Pleas was then opened, and Joseph Sprague appointed Crier.

V. Then were read the other Commissions granted to Timothy Pickering, Esq., by the Supreme Executive Council, constituting him,

1. Prothonotary of said Court of Common Pleas,
2. Clerk of the Peace,
3. Clerk of the Orphans' Court,
4. Register for the Probate of Wills, and granting letters of Administration,
5. Recorder of Deeds,

for said County.

VI. The Court, upon application to them made, admitted and appointed Ebenezer Bowman, Putnam Catlin, Roswell Wells, and William Nichols, to be attorneys of the same Court, who were accordingly sworn.

VII. Then appeared Lord Butler, Esq., Sheriff of the same County, and petitioned the Court to take some order relative to the erecting of a jail within the said County, Whereupon

It is ordered, that he immediately apply to the trustees for that purpose appointed, and request them to execute the powers granted them by the law of the State, so far as respects the erecting of a County Jail.

Thus Luzerne, being politically organized, Courts established, and the laws introduced under the auspices of Col. Pickering, sustained by the confirming law, he proceeded with wisdom and promptitude to conciliate the good will of the people—to assuage passion, to overcome prejudice, to inspire confidence. If Franklin was busy, Pickering was no less active. Without, in the slightest degree, lessening his dignity by unworthy condescension, he yet rendered himself familiar,—talked with the farmer about corn and potatoes, and with their wives about the dairy, maintaining his own opinions with zeal, yet listening to others with respect. " He was no way a proud man," was the general expression of the ancient people. But they thought he farmed rather too much by books, and smiled to see him cart into his barn damp clover, to cure by its power of generating heat in the mow. To show his entire confidence in the faith of the State, and the beneficial effects to be expected from the confirming law, Col. Pickering immediately purchased several tracts of land of Connecticut Claimants; (the prices paid, and those for which they have since been sold, may furnish an interesting paragraph in a subsequent letter.) How entirely he sought to conform to the simple habits of the people, is shown by the record in his own hand writing, that Timothy Pickering, and some other citizens, " were elected fence viewers and overseers of the poor."

Franklin, meanwhile, with characteristic industry visited from town to town, from settlement to settlement, and from house to house, kindling by his burning zeal the passions of his adherents to resist the laws, not by open violence, but by avoiding to commit themselves by taking the oath of allegiance, or participating in any measure that should seem to acknowledge the jurisdiction of the State, unless some law more comprehensive, liberal and specific, should first be enacted to quiet the settlers in their lands.

At length a proposition was made and acceded to by both parties, that the whole people should be called together, and a general meeting be held to talk over the matter in common council, a sort of ancient "Town Meeting," though not "legally warned," to hear speakers on either side, and if possible, to preserve union among those who had so long fought and suffered together, now separating into the most exciting and acrimonious divisions. Old Forty Fort was chosen as the ground. The day fixed, the north and the south, the east and the west poured forth their anxious hundreds, plainly, nay, rudely dressed, for they were yet very poor; but with firm tread, compressed lip, and independent bearing, for though rough and sunburnt, (on this great occasion who would stay at home,) they were at once a shrewd and a proud, as they were a hardy and brave people. A platform had been erected for the Moderator and Clerks of the meeting, and a stand for the speakers, convenient to address the Assembly.

Samuel Sutton was called on to preside.

The meeting had come together to take into consideration the important matter, whether the *terms offered by the Confirming Law should be accepted;* which involved the point whether the laws of Pennsylvania should be received and obeyed. On these questions, as we have previously intimated, there was a wide diversity of opinion. Throughout the Valley of Wyoming proper, wherein the earliest settlements were made, and the principal sufferings had been experienced, including the townships of Kingston, Pittston, Wilkesbarre, Hanover, Plymouth or Shawney; and all the country below, a great majority were in favour of coming in kindly under the jurisdiction of the State, and accepting the terms held out by the Confirming Law. The older men, wearied with contests, and desirous of repose, more especially took the part of obedience, compromise and peace. A few, perhaps a third, some smarting under the treachery of Armstrong and the insolence of Patterson, distrusted all promises made on behalf of Pennsylvania, however plausible and fairly made. Others, young men, brave and ardent, still "loved the rocking of the battlements," and wooed the storm that brought action and imparted distinction. Up the river, above and beyond the limits mentioned, the settlers, new and old, with greater unanimity, though some division of opinion existed, preferred to rely on their Connecticut titles, cherishing hopes of aid, not official but effective, from Connecticut, Massachusetts, and Vermont. So great a gathering had not been known in the Valley for years. Matters of the highest moment were to be discussed and decided. Indeed the future fate of Wyoming seemed to rest on their deliberations, and the decision of that day. Little less than war or peace appeared to be involved in the issue. All felt the magnitude of the question to be resolved. But Wyoming was no longer united. Discord had reared its snaky crest; malign passions were awakened. Brother met brother, and friend confronted friend, not with the all hail of hearty good will, but with beating heart, knit brow, and the frown of anger and defiance.

Col. Pickering, sustained by the Butlers, the Hollenbacks, the Nesbits, and the Denisons, appeared as the advocate of law and compromise. Col. Franklin, supported by the Jenkinses, the Spaldings, the Satterlees, came forth the champion of the Connecticut title. Col. Pickering first ascended the rostrum, and opened the meeting by an able address, urging every motive in his plain common sense, strong and emphatic manner, that could operate, leading to a fixed government of law—freedom from harrassing contests for their homes; the terms of compromise including all the seventeen townships established before the Trenton Decree, embracing nearly all the old settlers, and containing two hundred and seventy thousand acres of land. He pledged his honour, dearer than life, that Pennsylvania was honest in her purpose, sincere in her offer of compromise, and that full faith might be reposed in her promise. Half convinced, yet distrustful, Stephen Gardiner spoke up : " Your lips speak fair, but O that there was a window in that breast, that we might read your heart !"

Col. Jenkins, in his brief, and sententious way, demanded: "What security have we, that if we comply and put ourselves into your power, the State won't repeal the law, and deal as treacherously as in the case of Armstrong ?"

Col. Franklin now rose, and replied with all the bitterness he was master of. Dwelt on the justice of the Connecticut title; the land was their own, purchased by their money, their labour, and their blood; the sufferings of the settlers, the wrongs and insults they had received from Pennsylvania, he set forth; and declared the terms of compromise hollow and deceptive, and in no measured strains, (as if the spirit or his oath on the bloody rifle reanimated him,) denounced all those who took part with Pickering. At this moment, passions, long with difficulty suppressed, overpowered all prudential considerations, and Col. Hollenback, one of the earliest and bravest of the settlers, drew the butt of his riding whip and aimed a blow at Franklin's head. Caught by some friendly arm, it missed its aim; but the whole meeting was instantly thrown into wild confusion. The parties ran to the neighboring wood, and each cutting a stick, returned, and blows, furious and severe were exchanged, until, in the wild melee, the meeting separated, after a vote, not very orderly taken, was adopted to support the laws, and accept the proposed terms of compromise.

Franklin and his party excited to still greater activity, continued to throw every obstruction in the way of the confirming law, and made the most spirited opposition to the laws being received and obeyed. Surveyors were now out in various directions, locating townships under the Connecticut claim. Whole share rights and half share rights had become a stock of lively speculation, and no inconsiderable value. The dormant titles throughout Connecticut, and the neighboring States, were drawn forth from their long neglected repose, and purchased by speculators, or entered and surveyed for the owners; while a stream of population was literally pouring in from the east, and settling along the Susquehanna, and the chief branches that empty into the river, more especially in the more northern limits of the county.

Soon after the dispersion of the great meeting, no little sensation was produced in the Valley, by the appearance of the far famed General Ethan Allen, from Vermont, arrayed in cocked hat and regimentals. The purpose of his visit was as well understood by Pickering as by Franklin and his associates. A grant of several thousand acres of land was made to him by the Susquehanna Company. How many men he was pledged to lead from the Green Mountains we have no means of ascertaining; but it was not doubted that his object was to reconnoiter, and concert measures for early and decisive action.

A crisis was depending of highest moment, pregnant with civil war and revolution. Barlow and the Wolcotts, as has been previously intimated, had not embarked even their names, without purposes of import and ambition. A constitution for a new State was actually drawn up,* the purpose being to wrest Wyoming and the old county

---

* Gen. William Ross told the writer, that being at New Haven in 1803 or 4, a gentleman assured him such was the fact, and that it was understood William Judd, Esq., of Farmington, was to be the first Governor, and John Franklin Lieutenant Governor. The late

of Westmoreland from the jurisdiction of Pennsylvania, and establish a new and independent government. as Vermont was established in despite of New York. Nor will the design be regarded as impracticable, when the success of the settlers on the New Hampshire grants is considered, and when the extreme weakness of the Federal government under the confederation is regarded. Indian hostilities raging in the west; the Shays' disturbances still prevailing in Massachusetts, and the arm of government every where unnerved and powerless, to say nothing of the wrongs and contumely heaped upon the Wyoming people, and the general sympathy that existed throughout the whole country in their favour.

How far the details of the plan were known to Col. Pickering, cannot now be ascertained; but that his intelligent and sagacious mind fully comprehended the danger is not to be doubted. He saw that Franklin was the prime mover, the head and grand leader of the conspiracy, and determined that a stop should be put to his machinations. A writ was obtained from Chief Justice M'Kean, to arrest John Franklin on a charge of high treason. Not choosing to entrust even the secret to any officer in Luzerne, four gentlemen, of known resolution, activity and strength, were deputed on the perilous duty. Captain Lawrence Erbe, Capt. Brady, and Lieut. McCormick, who had held commissions in the army, were the principal personages entrusted with the confidential service. Col. Franklin, at the close of September, had been on a political tour down the west side of the river to Huntington and Salem, and returned by Hanover to Wilkesbarre, when, as he stood by Mr. Yarrington's, near the ferry, it being about two o'clock in the afternoon, a person whom he knew came up and said, "a friend at the red house wished to speak to him." Unconscious of danger he walked down, when suddenly he was seized behind, and an attempt made to pinion his arms. By powerful efforts he shook himself loose; was again seized, but by the most vigorous exertions kept his opponents from their purpose, till a noose was thrown over his head, and his arms confined; the power of all four being requisite to tie him. To get him on horseback was

---

Capt. Richards, a highly intelligent and worthy man, being from Farmington, it occurred to me to inquire of him. His reply was prompt and distinct, leaving no doubt in respect to the matter. "Yes, perfectly familiar to me. Capt. Judd showed me the draft of the constitution. It was drawn up by Oliver Wolcott. I well remember it commenced like the Declaration of Independence, by setting forth a series of wrongs, or the declaration of rights, justifying the deed, and then came the organization, &c."

the next object. Col. Franklin now cried out: "help, help! William Slocum! Where is William Slocum?" and drawing his pistols, for he went armed, discharged one of them without effect, when a heavy blow struck him for a moment almost senseless, and covered his face with blood. The hour had been judiciously selected,—in the midst of seeding time. William Slocum, with nearly all the male population, were at work in distant fields sowing grain. But the spirit of the good Quaker mother was aroused. Her Yankee blood was up. A lovely and amiable woman she was, but for the moment she thought of nothing but the release of Franklin. Mrs. Slocum seized the gun, and running to her door, "William," she cried, "Who will call William? Is there no *man* here? Will nobody rescue him?"

From the river bank Capt. Erbe had got his prisoner into the main street near Col. Pickering's, but with tremendous power, in despite of his four captors, Franklin threw himself from the horse, as often as placed on him, when Col. Pickering was obliged to come from behind the curtain, and decisively to interpose. Accompanied by his servant, William A. George, he ran to the door armed with a loaded pistol, which he held to Franklin's breast, while George tied his legs under the horse, and bound him to one of his captors.

Col. Pickering says: "The four gentlemen seized him, two of their horses were in my stable, which were sent to them; but soon my servant returned on one of them, with a message from the gentlemen that the people were assembling in numbers, and requested me to come with what men were near me, to prevent a rescue. I took loaded pistols in my hands, and went with another servant to their aid. Just as I met them, Franklin threw himself off his horse, and renewed his struggle with them. His hair was disheveled and face bloody with preceding efforts. I told the gentlemen they would never carry him off unless his feet were tied under his horse's belly. I sent for a cord. The gentlemen remounted him, and my servant tied his feet. Then one taking his bridle, another following behind, and the others riding one on each side, they whipped up his horse, and were soon beyond the reach of his friends." Thus subdued by six, he was hurried with painful speed to the jail of Philadelphia.

A paper of that city announces the event, showing its estimated consequence by the following exciting paragraph:—

"October 6, 1787. We are informed that John Franklin, the hero of Wyoming, has been seized by several of the friends of government, and brought to this city. It is hoped that some legal steps will be taken to subdue the turbulent spirit of this modern Shays, who has been the chief cause of the discontents in the county of Luzerne, and has uniformly labored to involve the county in a civil war. Every overture that has been made on the part of government has been rendered ineffectual by his machinations, and even his election as a representative in the General Assembly was not sufficient to gratify his ambition.* "Better to reign in hell, than serve in heaven," has ever been a favourite sentiment with the demons of sedition."

All Wyoming was in commotion from Nescopeck to the State line, on hearing of the abduction of Franklin, and the part Col. Pickering had acted in the scene.

Immediate measures were adopted by the partizans of the Yankee leaders to seize Col. Pickering, and carry him off as a hostage for the safety of Franklin. A guard had been detailed for the protection of his family by Dr. W. H. Smith, of which Col. Butler volunteered to take the command. Under the lead of Swift and Satterlee, the Tioga boys, or wild Yankees, surrounded the house in the evening, and demanded admittance, threatening in case of refusal or resistance, to set the buildings on fire. No satisfactory reply being given, a fire was absolutely kindled, when Col. Butler went out to the besiegers. "I pledge you my word," said he, "that Col. Pickering is not within; but to satisfy your party, Capt. Swift, as I have confidence in your honour, and that of Mr. Satterlee, we will allow you to come in and search—more would only give unnecessary disturbance to the family." A stipulation was made, that all the arms of both sides should be placed in the custody of a committee mutually chosen. While the search was making, old friends and comrades chatted socially together. Col. Pickering apprised of their approach had escaped to the fields. But his own account of the matter possesses too much interest not to be quoted.

"The rising of Franklin's men was expected from the opposite side of the river. I desired my friends to place sentinels along the bank, where they might discover the first movements for crossing the

---

* The fact we have not been able officially to verify, but presume Col. Pickering in his profound policy had procured the choice of Franklin to the Assembly, at the February election; knowing if he took the oath of allegiance his honour would not suffer him to pursue measures hostile to the integrity of the State; but he would neither accept the office, nor take the oath. His previous oath on the "bloody rifle" yet forbade.

river, and then sat down to sup with my family. Before I had finished that meal, a sentinel came in haste from the river, and informed me that Franklin's adherents were crossing in boats. My house was within a furlong of the river. I took up a loaded pistol, and three or four small biscuits, and retired to a neighboring field. Soon the yell of the insurgents apprised me of their arrival at my house. I listened to their noises a full half hour, when the clamour ceasing, I judged that the few armed neighbors, who had previously entered and fastened the doors, had surrendered. This was the fact. The rioters, (as I afterwards learned from your mother,) searched the house for me, and for concealed arms, if any there were.

"While I was listening, Griffith Evans, secretary to the board of commissioners, and a lodger at my house, retiring from it, fortunately taking the same course, joined me. Believing that when they should have searched the house in vain, they would proceed to the near fields to find me, I told Mr. Evans it would be well to retire still farther. When we had gained the side of Wilkesbarre mountain, we laid ourselves down and got some sleep. In the morning I descried at the distance of a mile or more, a log house, which was on a lot of land I had purchased, and near a mile from the village, and occupied by an honest German, whose daughter lived with your mother as a maid. I proposed to Mr. Evans, as he had no personal injury to apprehend from the rioters, to go to the log house, and ask the German, in my behalf, to go down to my house, (which, as his daughter was there, would be perfectly natural,) and if he could see your mother, inquire what was the state of things, and whether I could return with safety. Mr. Evans waited his return; and then brought me word from your mother, that I must remain concealed, for they were still searching for me. It was now about eleven o'clock. I told Mr. Evans that as I could not return to Wilkesbarre, we had better proceed for Philadelphia, and inform the Executive of the state of things at Wyoming. He readily assented, and we immediately commenced our march. It was through pathless woods, and we had no provisions except the three or four biscuits I had put into my pocket the preceding evening. That we might not get lost, I proposed turning short to our left, to strike the road leading from Wyoming, and thence take our departure with more safety. We did so; and then again darting into the woods, proceeded as nearly as we could judge, in a line parallel to the road, but not in sight of it. A little before sun-setting we came to a small run of water, which I supposed to be the "*nine mile run,*" being at that distance from Wilkesbarre. I therefore desired Mr. Evans to go cautiously down the run till he should strike the road which crossed it. He did so, it was not far off. On his return we concluded to lie down to get some sleep, intending to rise when the moon should be up, at about two the next morning and prosecute our journey. About two miles from the nine mile run was Bear Creek, a stream perhaps forty or fifty feet wide, and without a bridge. Having several times traveled that road, I knew when we approached it. There I thought it probable the insurgents had posted a small guard to intercept me, leaving their main guard at a deserted cabin four miles back. Mr. Evans proposed to advance alone, to reconnoiter, and if he discovered there any armed men to halloo, that I might escape into the woods. I told him that was impracticable; fatigued and destitute of provisions, I could not fly; that each of us had a loaded pistol; that I presumed the guard at the creek would not exceed three men; that if they attempted to take us, we must each kill his man, when the third would be glad to escape. With this determination we proceeded. The creek was not guarded, we forded it, and then marched at our ease. In the morning, we reached the first inhabited house about twenty-five miles from Wilkesbarre.* Here we were refreshed

---

* A letter, obligingly furnished me by J. Jordan, jr., Esq., one of the Secretaries of the Pennsylvania Historical Society, throws light upon this part of our narrative.

October 6, 1787. Dr.s   † Smithfield, writes to the Council, viz: "Yesterday morning being on the Wyoming road, at a small distance from Larner's house, I met Timothy Pickering and Mr. Evans, secretary, entering our settlements in a distressed situation. Being informed of the coup de main executed on Franklin, and apprehensive of the natural consequences attending such conduct, I asked for information, when to my great surprise, I understood from Mr. Pickering, that although he narrowly escaped the vengeance of the Connecticut banditti, and had left behind his lady and children, likely to be taken as hostages for Franklin; he was going to Philadelphia, to compromise matters with John Franklin. His expressions I believe started from a repenting and disappointed heart, in the expansion of which I understood he had wrote a letter to J. Swift, present leader of the faction, promising an act of amnesty for him, Franklin and party, provided they would submit to his fugitive plan of submission to our laws. He further added that his first exertion in the city would be to pay a visit to the prisoner Franklin, and should propose to him once more to make him and Swift, men of great importance on the above condition. It hurted my feelings to conceive, that one individual as Mr. Pickering, in a free and constitutional government, should confer or pretend to dispose of the three branches of our political existence, at the same time that he confesses of the necessity of coercive measures and sees the dignity of government exposed. The tumult continues in Wyoming—the apprehension of Franklin, I believe has only hastened the period of their clandestine opposition to Government. I hope it will convince our legislators of the impropriety of purchasing peace at the expense and ruin of individuals, from a set of men devoted to disturb public tranquillity.

FRANCIS SMITH.

with a comfortable breakfast, and then went on our way. Having traveled some miles farther, we came to some farmers' houses, where we hired horses, and then continued our journey to Philadelphia.

"On my return to Wilkesbarre, I was informed that the arrangement of the guards to intercept me, was precisely as I had conjectured. A subaltern's command marched to the deserted cabin, whence three men were detached to Bear Creek, where they waited till night, when they returned to the cabin; concluding that I had reached the creek before them.

"The insurgents, soon brought to reflection, and deprived of the counsel and direction of their leader, Franklin, began to relent, and sent a petition to the Executive Council, acknowledging their offence, and praying for a pardon. This was readily granted; and Colonel Denison, the Luzerne counsellor, went up with the pardon. It was natural to infer from this, that I might return in safety to my family. I proceeded accordingly; but when within twenty-five miles, I sent by a servant who was with me, a letter to your mother, desiring her to consult some of the discreet neighbours, who were my friends, relative to my return. She did so. They were of opinion that I could not return with safety at present. So I went back to Philadelphia.

"In September, 1787, the Convention of Delegates from the several States, to form a Constitution for the United States, which had been sitting several months in Philadelphia, concluded their labours. They recommended that the Constitution should be submitted to a Convention of Delegates, to be chosen in each State, by the people thereof, under the recommendation of its Legislature, for their assent and ratification. Such a Convention being called by the Legislature of Pennsylvania, *the people of Luzerne county chose* ME *their delegate to represent them in it.* This Convention assembled in Philadelphia, (where I still remained,) I think, early in December. After a great deal of discussion, the Convention assented to and ratified the Constitution. It was engrossed on parchment, and received the signatures of nearly all the Delegates, including the opposers while under discussion, with the exception of some three or four obstinate men, and, to the best of my recollection of their characters, as ignorant as obstinate. The opposers of its adoption were the extra-republicans or democrats—the same sort of men who afterwards were called anti-federalists, and who uniformly opposed all the leading measures of the federal administration of the General Government.

"I could now no longer doubt that I might return to Wyoming. I arrived there the beginning of January, 1788."

At the Fall election Col. Denison was again returned to the Executive Council, and Capt. John Paul Schott was chosen member of Assembly.

Thus closed the year 1787, and no bow of promise gave hope that the succeeding year would be less distinguished by violence and disorder.

LETTER XXVII.

1788—Col. Pickering's return—Violent Abduction—His Account, with Notes—Yankee War—A saucy Boy—Capt Ross wounded, Joseph Dudley killed—Col. Franklin in Philadelphia Jail—The Lion Tamed—Released on Bail—Chief Justice M'Kean and Judge Rush—Trials—Dawn of Peace.

COL. PICKERING from his honourable exile to Philadelphia, where he had performed the acceptable service of a delegate to ratify the Federal Constitution,* returned to Luzerne early in January, 1788.

No incident of importance marked the first part of the year; but the violent abduction of that gentleman in June, was a measure of the most exciting character, leading up civil war in its train, and again staining the fair fields of Wyoming with blood.

Col. Pickering's own narrative of that event I have chosen to copy, from the deep interest which the recital, by himself, cannot fail to excite and gratify; but, at the same time, as much matter presents itself in his letter for observation, I shall throw into notes, a free commentary as we proceed.

"On the 26th of June, at about 11 at night, when your mother and I were asleep, and your brother Edward, nine months old, was lying on my arm, I was awakened by a violent opening of the door of the room. "Who's there?" I asked: "Get up," was the answer. "Don't strike," said I, "I have an infant on my arm."—I had no doubt that the intruders were ruffians come to execute the long menaced attack.

---

* Col. Stone seems to think it an extraordinary instance of inconsistency, that the people of Luzerne should "select Col. Pickering of all others, to sit in judgment, upon an instrument, which if adopted was to become the grand regulating machinery of their political and religious principles, the charter of their liberty, and that of their posterity in all time to come, while they would not trust the same individual to decide for them in a matter of a contested title of a few hundred dollars worth of land!" It may be remarked that the people of Luzerne were now divided in twain. Those who elected Col. Pickering had no hand in his exile. Those who would have laid the hand of violence on him, would not take the oath of allegiance, and were, therefore, not voters.

"I rolled Edward from my arm, rose, and put on my clothes. Your mother slipped out of the other side of the bed; and putting on some clothes went to the kitchen, and soon returned with a lighted candle. Then we saw the room filled with men armed with guns and hatchets, having their faces blacked, and handkerchiefs tied round their heads. Their first act was to pinion me; tying my arms together with a cord, above my elbows, and crossed over my back. To the middle of this cord they tied another, long enough for one of them to take hold of, to prevent my escaping from them. They told me it would be well to take a blanket or outer garment, for I should be a long time in a situation where I should want it.* I desired your mother to get me an old surtout, which was in the chamber.† She quickly returned, and I received it on one of my arms. They then led me off, and hastened through the village of Wilkesbarre, in perfect silence. Having traveled a couple of miles, they halted a few minutes. Then resuming their march, proceeded to Pittstown, ten or eleven miles up the river from Wilkesbarre. Here they stopped at a tavern and called for whiskey—offering some to me, which I did not accept; I drank some water.

"In twenty minutes, they left this house, and pursued their march. —There were about fifteen of them—arranged in my front, my rear, and on both flanks. We were in the darkness and stillness of night. As we proceeded, one of the ruffians at my side thus accosted me— "Now if you will only write two or three lines to the Executive Council, they will discharge Col. Franklin, and then we will release you." Instantly I answered—"The Executive Council better understand their duty, than to discharge a traitor to procure the release of an innocent man."—" Damn him, (exclaimed a voice before me) why don't you tomahawk him?" this wrath of the ruffian (1) was

[* Two Notes by Col. P.—When I stepped out of bed, the first garment I took up was a coat, in a pocket of which was a packet of letters which I had written to one or more of my acquaintances, Members of Congress, (then sitting at New York) detailing the conduct and characters of some of the leaders in the nefarious measures of the Susquehanna Company; which letters Mr. Andrew Elicot, then at Wilkesbarre, and who was to set off for Philadelphia the next morning, was to take with him. I dropped the coat, and felt for a pair of fustian trowsers, and fustian jacket with sleeves. These I put on—and my shoes.

† Your mother afterwards informed me that one of the ruffians followed her to the chamber, and threatened to tomahawk her, if she made any noise.]

Note 1. (To Pickering's letter.) "This wrath of the ruffian." This is the third time within the limits of a page, that the word ruffian is applied to his captors. Granting to Col. Pickering, which we cheerfully do, the possession of unspotted integrity, we still think his narrative should be read with a knowledge that strong prejudice was a marked characteristic of his otherwise manly mind. It does not appear that more severity was used, than was excited by the word "traitor," applied to their old leader, Franklin. No more words were uttered on this subject.

We soon reached the river Lachawannack, about two miles from the tavern. After searching a little while, they found a canoe, in which some of them passed over. On its return I stepped in, with the others of the gang. The water was low, and the canoe touched the bottom before we reached the shore. I was going to step out and wade to the shore. "Stop"—said one of them, who had a pack on his back. He waded to the shore—laid down his pack—returned to the side of the canoe, *and carried me on his back to the shore.* (2)

"Proceeding upwards, we in a little while came to a ferry. The day had dawned. They crossed over in a scow (a large flat-bottomed boat) to the western side of the Susquehanna; and we continued our march, on the shore of the river, for an hour or two; then struck into the woods, and pursued the course upwards, out of sight of the river. About four in the afternoon, they arrived at a log house near the bank of the river about thirty miles above Wilkesbarre. Here they had victuals cooked, and I ate with a good appetite; having fasted since I was taken the preceding night.

"Seeing a bed in the room, I laid myself down upon it. I do not recollect when they unpinioned me. I had lain but a little while, when a man arrived in a boat from Jacob's Plains, a small settlement about two miles and a half above Wilkesbarre. I knew the man. The ruffians (supposing that I was asleep) inquired with eagerness, what was the news below; and whether the militia had turned out to pursue them. He answered in the affirmative. I immediately saw that I should not be suffered to keep my place on the bed. In a few minutes, one of them came to the bed side and said "get up." I

---

indispensable to his safe keeping. Such refreshments as they obtained for themselves at Lackawanna, were freely placed at his service. With considerate thoughtfulness they advised him to take a blanket, showing that they desired he should be comfortable. "Now only write two or three lines to the Executive Council—they will release Franklin, and we will release you." This key unlocks the whole affair. No ruffian malevolence mingled in the abduction. The sole object was the release of their friend and leader in a thousand troubles. To almost any other mind it would have occurred, that those men, though in error, might be actuated by noble and generous sentiments. After the violence, the wrongs, the perfidy exhibited towards the settlers, by Armstrong and Patterson, acting in the name of Pennsylvania, no great stretch of charity was requisite, to allow that a very honest man might doubt the sincerity of the new overtures for compromise.

Note 2. Col. Pickering crossed over in the canoe with others of the "*gang.*" But it seems they would not allow him even to wet his feet. One of this *gang of ruffians* absolutely took him on his shoulders to the shore. Courtesy and kindness appear to have marked their conduct.

rose, and they took me directly back from the river, a quarter of a mile; and behind a rising ground they rested for the night. It thundered; and a heavy rain soon wet us to the skin. At day-light one of the crew went to the house: and finding all quiet, he returned, and we all went thither. The drying of our clothes, and eating breakfast, employed us till about ten o'clock. Standing with them on the bank of the river, I observed a man on the other side, leading a horse. It was on the shore of the river. Being near sighted, I did not know him. But one of them exclaimed—" There goes Major Jenkins, now,—a damned stinking son of a bitch." By this *courteous* observation on the second man of the party, and the first in Franklin's absence, it was apparent, that after encouraging and engaging them in the diabolical outrage upon me he had deserted them.(3) He, in fact kept on his route, went into the State of New York, and there, being a land surveyor, found employment, during the residue of the season, and until tranquillity was finally restored to the county.

"By this time the blacking had disappeared from the faces of the ruffians; when I found two of them to be sons of one Dudley, a carpenter and a near neighbour at Wilkesbarre. The others were all before unknown to me.

"They now prepared to cross over to the eastern side of the Susquehanna. Gideon Dudley came up to me with a pair of handcuffs, with which to manacle me. To this I objected, as they were going to cross the river in a small canoe, and I desired to have a chance of saving my life by swimming, if it should overset. At this moment Mr. Earl (whom I had not known, but who was father to two of the party) interposed—telling Dudley that there was no danger of an escape, and advising him not to put the irons upon me. He accordingly forbore.—We crossed the river; and they pursued their march. In an hour they halted; the leader of the band selected four,

---

Note 3. "*Ruffians,*" "*Crew,*" "*Diabolical Outrage,*"—garnish the next page, showing the bitterness of his feelings that existed after thirty years had passed away. The harsh remarks on Col. Jenkins do not warrant the inference, we think, which has been drawn from it. Col. Jenkins never put his hand to an enterprize, however hazardous, and then shrunk from it, leaving his companions. Col. Jenkins had warned Col. Pickering of the danger. "Fore-warned, fore-armed," he might have taken it as a friendly caution, but chose to regard it as a threat. It was no new enterprise on the part of Col. Jenkins to go into the Genesee country surveying. For two or three years he had been engaged with Dewit, in laying out the fine western lands in New York, and the reader must have observed that his name does not appear, or if at all, seldom in the contests of 1785-6. With a large and growing family, no one more sincerely desired repose, that industry might reap its just reward.

and bid the rest go on.—With these four and me, he darted directly into the woods. This excited some apprehension in me, of personal mischief; especially as one of them, by the name of Cady, sustained, as I understood, a very bad character. The leader of this band was a hunter, and had his rifle gun with him. As we proceeded a fawn was started, and as he bounded along, the hunter shot him, and in five minutes had his skin off, and the carcass slung on his back. At the distance of three or four miles from the river, they halted, close by a very small run of water. A fire being quickly kindled, they began to cook some of the venison. The hunter took his first cut. They sharpened small sticks at both ends, running one into a slice of the fawn and setting the other end into the ground, the top of the stick bearing so near the fire as to broil the flesh. Being hungry, I borrowed one of their knives, and followed their example.—I observed the hunter tending his steak with great nicety; and sprinkling it with a little salt, as soon as it was done, he with a very good grace, presented it to *me!* (4)

"Before night, they cut down some limbs of trees, and formed a slight booth, to shelter us from the dew. One of them taking post as a sentinel, we lay down on the ground: my pillow was a stone.—In this situation we remained about a week. (5) At first, they had some good salt pork, and wheaten bread that lasted two or three days; after which they got Indian meal, which they made into cakes, or fried, as pancakes, in the fat of the pork. Of the pork they were very sparing; frying only two or three small slices at a time, and cutting them up in the pan. Such was our breakfast, dinner and supper: my share did not exceed five mouthfuls of pork at each meal.* (6) They fared better—sopping up, with their bread or cakes,

Note 4. Considering that Cady was the worst of the *ruffian gang*, this was very civil.

Note 5. Perhaps the first night; but with attendants so obliging, we can hardly suppose Col. P. kept his stone pillow the whole week. A bass-wood log we have often used in the woods, a stone seldom—never. Attention is called to this point to show that prejudice tinges the account, and it must therefore be received with some slight grains of allowance; nothing to detract from the outline, but something to be softened in the colouring.

[* " Yet I never felt more alert and vigorous in my life; which I ascribed to my *necessary extreme temperance.*"]

Note 6. The Colonel was a soldier, and took proper note of his rations. At Tunkhannock "they cooked victuals, and I ate with a good appetite." At another time, Cady "with a good grace, presented him a nice venison steak." Now they have pork and johnny cake; but he repines that for his share he got only " five mouthfuls of pork at each meal." That is fifteen mouthfuls, or about half a pound a day. And venison could not have been scarce. But Col. Pickering was remarkable for his fine appetite and powerful digestion. Afterwards all the fat in the pan, of which I felt no inclination to participate.—It was here I told them they would repent of their doings; and instead of being supported by four hundred men in the county, as they had professed to believe, that they would be abandoned to their fate.

"From this station they marched a few miles, and took another, in a narrow valley, a sequestered place, and about two or three miles from the Susquehanna. We had no sooner halted than they came to me with a chain five or six feet long, having at one end a band like the bands of horse-fetters. Col. Franklin, they said, had been put in irons, in the Philadelphia jail, and they must put irons on me, although it was not agreeable to them to do it; "but their great men required it." Satisfied that it would be in vain to remonstrate, I was silent. They fixed the band of the chain round my ankle, securing it with a flat key, which they twisted, to prevent its being cut off without a tool to untwist the key. The other end of the chain they fastened by a staple to a tree. In this situation I remained an hour or more; and they employed themselves in forming a booth with the boughs of trees. This chain, besides its conformity with the orders of their "great men," saved my gentlemen from the burden of mounting guard every night. When we lay down, they placed me in the middle, and one of them wrapped the chain round one of his legs; so that I could not rise to attempt an escape, without waking him up. But I determined not to make the attempt—for I soon considered that my life was not in danger; and I expected them to grow weary of their enterprise: so I patiently endured present affliction. Besides, if I escaped they could take me again, unless I quitted the county; which was the precise object of the outrage—to get rid of me.

We had been in this valley but two or three days, when, one morning, whilst all my guard were fast asleep, I heard a brisk firing of musquetry. It was a skirmish, I had no doubt, between the "Boys" (as these fellows called their party) and the militia who had come from below to discover *them*, and rescue *me*. But I let them sleep on; nor did I tell them of the firing after they awoke. After breakfast, one of them went down to a house by the river, in their interest, and returned in haste, to tell his comrades that the "Boys"

---

during Washington's administration, when negotiating a treaty with the Indians, a vast table was surrounded by commissioners, contractors, attendants, and braves. The conversation turned upon the characteristic designation of the chiefs; one was that of the eagle, another of the tortoise. An old warrior seeing Col. P. swallowing his eleventh cup of coffee, with viands in proportion, exclaimed—"*He; Wolf Tribe.*"

and militia had met, and that in the battle, captain Ross, who commanded the militia, was mortally wounded.* At the close of this, or the next day, they marched down to the river, and sought for a canoe to cross to the western side; but could find none. We were now at Black-Walnut Bottom, about forty-four miles above Wilkesbarre. Thus disappointed they marched back into the woods, and we lay down for the night. The next day, towards evening, they went again to the river and crossed it. It was so dark that at the distance of thirty or forty yards we might pass unseen. They passed through a thick wood to the house of one Kilborn, father to two of the party. There we lodged. The next morning they pushed back into the woods, about four miles from the river. This was the third and last station. This changing from place to place, was to prevent their being discovered by the militia, who came from below, at different times to find them.

"On the 15th of July, Gideon Dudley (who now appeared to have the command) with two others came out to our station. It was late in the afternoon. After lounging about for some time, as if they did not know what to do with themselves, they approached me; and Dudley asked—" Don't you wish to be set at liberty?"—" To be sure I do "—was my answer. After a little pause, Dudley accosted me—" What will you do for us if we will set you at liberty?—" What do you wish me to do for you?" was my reply. " Will you intercede for Col. Franklin's pardon?" (7) " No, I will not." This answer was evidently unexpected; they were confounded; and retiring, they for some time laid their heads together. Then again coming near, one of them asked—" Will you intercede for *our* pardon?—After a momentary pause, I aswered—" While I have been in your hands, you have told me of your ' Great Men,' and that you have been acting in obedience to their orders. By them you have been misled and deceived. Give me their names, and I have no doubt of obtaining *your* pardon."—This they could not do, they said, without going down to their Head Quarters, and consulting the main body; and turned on

[* " He was badly wounded, but recovered. Gideon Dudley received from the militia a ball through his hand."]

Note 7. " Will you intercede for Col. Franklin's pardon?" Neither retaliation, revenge, nor malicious mischief, actuated them. Only " intercede for Franklin," was the generous purpose. But for their own pardon he would solicit, if they would disclose the names of their " great men," their leaders and advisers. This they with true honour refused to do. While these incidents were transpiring in the sequestered glen, where the distinguished prisoner was held in durance, all the rest part of the country was in a state of extreme agitation.

their heels to depart—"Stop," said I, "and knock off this chain." They instantly took off the chain, that I had carried about for ten days.

"I lay down with my guard that night, not doubting of my speedy release. As soon as it was light, I rose, put the fire-brands together (in the woods, a fire is generally kept up at night even in the warmest weather;) mixed up some of their miserable coarse Indian meal for cakes, spread the dough on pieces of hemlock bark (the usual trenchers) and set them to the fire. As soon as it was light enough to see *our green tea*, I went to gather it. This was the *winter green*, bearing red berries, which went by the name of partridge berries. Infused in boiling water, the winter green makes a tolerable warm beverage.*

By this time my guard were awake, the tea was boiled and the cakes were baked. I told them that expecting to be released, I had risen and got the breakfast ready, in order to gain time; for if released, I had a particular desire to reach home the next day.† I then proposed that we should go to their head-quarters, without delay; where, if released, it would be well; if not, I would come back with them again into the woods. They readily assented—took up their kettle and frying-pan—(our kitchen furniture) and down we marched. When arrived near to their head-quarters, they halted. One went to announce our arrival. Two or three came out, Gideon Dudley at their head—when he put to me the original question, "Will you intercede for Col. Franklin's pardon?" "I will answer no question till I am set at liberty," was my return. They conducted me into Kilborn's house.

"It was now the 16th of July. Nineteen days had passed away, while I had been their prisoner. Having no razor, nor a second shirt, I had neither shaved nor changed my linen during that whole time.— They had told me, if I desired clothing or any thing else from home, and I would write for them, they should be brought to me. (8) I

[* "They once asked me if I should like a dish of coffee. 'A dish of coffee by all means,' I answered. They went to work. Boiling water in their iron pot, to make it clean, then emptying it, they set it over to heat. They next strewed into it some Indian meal; and when it was roasted, they poured in water; and as soon as it was boiled, the coffee was made. It was an agreeable change for our green tea."]

[† "It would be the 17th of July—my birth day."]

Note 8. "Clothing or any thing else" that you want, Col. Pickering, shall be brought you from home. This does not look like wanton oppression. "Only intercede for our beloved Franklin." Noble fellows—they scarcely deserved from him the harsh epithet of a "gang of ruffians."

accordingly wrote to your mother for clothing—and for a book. She sent them up as directed, and they arrived at Zebulon Marcy's at Tunkhannock; and there I found them, after I was released. The shirt I wore from home, I repeatedly took off, and washed as well as I could, in cold water and without soap.

"As soon as I entered Kilborn's house, they brought me a razor and soap to shave, and a clean shirt, and pair of stockings; and told me I was at liberty. They roasted some chickens, and gave me as good a dinner as the poor wretches could furnish. (9)

"While dinner was preparing, they renewed their request, that I would intercede for Franklin's pardon. This I again peremptorily refused to do. Then they made the same request for themselves; and I again told them that I could venture to assure them of pardons, if they would give me the names of their "Great Men" who had instigated them to commit the outrage I had endured at their hands. They consulted together for some time; and finally told me they could not give up their names. "This (I said to them) is a very unwise determination. Here are two-and-twenty of you (I had counted them) who may all obtain pardon, if you will give me the names of your employers; and among so many, some one at least, to save himself, will turn state's evidence; you had better therefore give me the names of the men who have engaged you in this wicked business." "Whoever does it, said Gideon Dudley, ought to go to hell, and be damned everlastingly." (10)

"They then made a last request, that I would write a petition for them to the Executive Council praying for pardons, and carrying it with me to Wilkesbarre, take an opportunity to send it to Philadelphia. With this, undeserving as they were, I complied.

"It was now late in the afternoon; and unless I went to Tunkhannock (distant twelve miles) that night, I could not reach home the next day. They had a good boat in which they carried me down. It was dark when they landed. I had only set my foot on shore, when the two Earls came to me, aside, and offered to become evidences for the state upon an assurance of pardon. This I ventured to give them: but the rogues, when brought before the court, divulged none of the

---

Note 9. The "poor wretches,"—not so harsh. The savory odour of the "roasted chickens," in some measure softened his ire.

Note 10. The expression of Dudley is rough enough; but the rugged coat cannot conceal from view the noble sentiment of integrity, fidelity and honour, that lies beneath it.

names of their "Great men;" and reluctantly furnished any evidence against their companions. (11)

"Walking from the landing place about a mile, across the Tunkhannock bottom land, we arrived at the house of Zebulon Marcy, to get supper and lodging. There I found the bundle of clothing which your mother had sent up for me; and there, also, I found an inhabitant of Pittstown, going down the river as far as Lachawannock Creek. And Tuttle, one of the 'Boys,' said he would go down with us, and take his chance. The next morning, we three set off in a canoe. Landing the man destined for Lachawannock, the other went on with me to Wilkesbarre. On the way, he told me that he had joined the 'boys' but two or three days before, in order to discover where I was, and get me rescued out of their hands. (12)

"Stepping ashore at Wilkesbarre, I walked directly to our house. You were standing at the front door. As I drew near, you looked a moment—appeared frightened—and retired. Before I reached the door, your mother came with Edward in her arms. Consternation marked her countenance—as if I had been an apparition. My return so soon was wholly unexpected; and she looked at me as if to satisfy herself of the reality.

"Without waiting the result of their petition to the Executive Council, most of the actual perpetrators of the outrage upon me, fled

Note 11. Though a man of unusual intelligence, as well as fortitude, Col. P., it is evident, did not perfectly comprehend the Yankee tactics. The Earls were not traitors—there was not a drop of traitor blood in their veins. Doubtless the measure was adopted with the assent of their companions. Having two witnesses secured, of course little pains would be taken to search for, or summon others, and with them their companions were safe.

Note 12. Nor was Tuttle a recreant to his faith. "Deceive your enemy," is a maxim of war. It was important to their safety that Pickering should be conciliated and watched. The Earls and Tuttle, shrewd men, were best able to throw him off his guard; draw out his opinions, and fathom his purposes. There was not one of that "gang of ruffians," we firmly believe, who would not sooner have sacrificed his life, than betrayed his fellows. An anecdote of Benjamin Earl is too good to be lost, and yet so nearly approaches the indelicate, that pardon must be solicited for its recital. A writ issued for his apprehension growing out of the Yankee disturbances, was put into the hands of our old friend Westover, (who stood by Cooper in the Indian battle,) now a constable, to serve. Mr. Earl, a very small man, though he had a large spirit, had just married a buxom girl of four times his size. In the dead of night Westover and his assistants demanded admittance. Pressing her little spouse deep in the feathers, for the object of the visit was known, and placing herself on her back over him, so that there appeared but one person in bed, she answered, "Come in, who is there?" "Westover!" "Come, Earl, you are my prisoner," and entered the room with a light. "For shame, Mr. Westover," said Mrs Earl. "I here a lone woman to be so encroached upon." "But where is Ben?" "You know he was expecting the writ, and needn't think he was such a fool as to be at home—he has more wit than that, I hope." Satisfied the lady was alone, Westover retired.

to the northward, to escape into the state of New York. On their way, as they reached Wysock's Creek, they encountered a party of militia, under the command of Capt. Rosewell Franklin, and exchanged some shots. Joseph Dudley was very badly wounded. The others escaped. Dudley was put into a canoe. and brought down to Wilkesbarre, a distance of perhaps sixty or seventy miles. The doctor who was sent for, had no medicine. I had a small box of medicines which had been put up under the care of my friend Dr. Rush. Of these, upon application of the physician, I furnished all he desired. But Dudley survived only two or three days. On his death, his friends sent to your mother, to beg a winding sheet—which she gave them.

"In the autumn, a court of Oyer and Terminer was held at Wilkesbarre, by M'Kean, Chief Justice, and Judge Rush. A number of the villains had been arrested—were tried and convicted—fined and imprisoned in different sums, and for different lengths of time, according to the aggravation of their offence. The poor creatures had no money to pay their fines, and the new jail at Wilkesbarre was so insufficient, that all of them made their escape excepting Stephen Jenkins, brother to Major John Jenkins. Stephen was not in arms with the party; but was concerned in the plot. He might have escaped from the jail with the others, but chose to stay; and in consequence received a pardon, after about two months confinement.

"John Franklin, so often mentioned, having been indicted on the charge of treason, for which he had been arrested, remained a good while in jail. At length he was liberated on giving bond with a large penalty; and finally all opposition to the government in Luzerne county, ceasing, he was fully discharged. The people of the county afterwards chose him to represent them in the State legislature, where, in the House of Representatives he sat, I believe for several years. During this period, chance, once or twice, threw him in my way. He was very civil, and I returned his civilities."

Immediately on the abduction of Col. Pickering being known, vigorous measures were adopted for his rescue. Four companies of militia were ordered out. That of Wilkesbarre, under the command of Capt. William Ross. A troop of horse, commanded by Capt. John Paul Schott. The Hanover boys, Capt. Rosewell Franklin, and a company from Kingston, under Maj. Lawrence Myers, the whole military moving by direction of the civil authority, as part of the posse comitatus, directed by Lord Butler, Esq., the high sheriff of the county. What a change! "Circumstances alter cases." Capt.

Ross and Sheriff Butler, as violators of the law at Laurel Hill, sent in irons to Easton, were now the effectual vindicators of the violated laws. At Osterhout's, a few miles above Keeler's ferry, they made a halt to take refreshments; when a guard of two or three men, placed by the river side, observed a boat with three persons on board, to push out suddenly as in haste from beneath a bunch of willows. Refusing to answer, a shot was fired, and they changed their course. Another bullet struck near, when two men threw themselves into the river, and swam to the opposite shore, while a boy hove the canoe about and surrendered. "Who are you, and who were those in the canoe?" inquired Sheriff Butler, who had come down to the spot. "None of your—business," said the boy, with great apparent indignation. "Tell us who you are, and where you are going?" "I won't—you are all a pack of rascals not to let honest men go to mill in their own boat, but they must be shot at as if they were wolves." Finding they could get no information from the fellow, amused with the spirit displayed, and respecting his faithfulness to his friends, Mr. Butler took him to the house, gave him a good dinner, and then told him to go tell "the boys," the whole country was in arms against them, and they had better give up Col. Pickering. The story of young Hillman, for that was his name, may as well be concluded here. He was arraigned with others, and it was in proof that he was for some time one of Pickering's guard. When Chief Justice M'Kean was about to pass sentence, Col. P. with great magnanimity rose and said: "The boy had evidently been misled by older persons. That though in error, the spirit and faithfulness exhibited, in what he probably thought was right, showed that he was no ordinary character. He might yet under better advisement become a useful member of the community, and it was his desire that the lad should receive as mild a punishment as the law would admit." Of course Hillman was permitted to escape under a very mitigated sentence. We have sought to learn his subsequent fate, but he is lost to us.

The company of Capt. Ross, in ascending the east bank of the Susquehanna, encountered near Meshoppen, a party of the wild Yankees, under the lead of Gideon Dudley. An action ensued, in which Capt. Ross received a severe wound in the body, the ball passing through him, lodged in the skin of the opposite side, from which it was some time after extracted. He was removed with all possible care to Wilkesbarre, where he slowly recovered. A ball struck Dudley in the wrist, when his party retreated.

Finding, from the inflexible fortitude of their prisoner, that he could not be induced to write to obtain the release of Franklin, that being their sole object, and cherishing no feelings of malice or revenge against him, Col. Pickering was liberated as detailed in his narrative.

Joseph Dudley, of whom he speaks, was subsequently wounded in an encounter with Rosewell Franklin's men near Wysox. From the first it was supposed the wound must prove mortal, as the gall issued therefrom; but in hope of relief, he was placed in a canoe, and brought to Wilkesbarre, where he in a few days died. A fine formed, generous natured, brave young man of twenty-four, his death was regretted by friend and foe.

Col. Pickering being at liberty, immediate measures were taken to vindicate the authority of the laws, by the arrest, trial and punishment of the rioters.

Col. Franklin was still detained a prisoner in the Philadelphia jail. After remaining in prison six months, being closely confined in a rear apartment, and excluded from society, maintaining himself, for he was not apprised that any provision had been made by Government for his subsistence, although he might have claimed the usual jail allowance; suffering from a protracted fever, as well as by confinement so uncongenial to health, and so irksome to an active mind, the iron will and the iron frame of this "hero of Wyoming" began to give way, and in April he petitioned the Justices of the Supreme Court that he might be liberated on finding bail that should be deemed sufficient. Assurances were given him that if he would obtain securities in the sum of two thousand pounds, he should have his liberty. Josiah Rogers, Jonah Rogers, Christopher Hurlbut, John Hurlbut, Nathan Carey, John Jenkins, Hezekiah Roberts, Benjamin Harvey, Daniel Gore, Samuel Ayres, and Jonathan Corey, were named by Col. Franklin, any or all of whom would become pledged for his good behaviour, and appearance at the time of trial. But delays were interposed. Perhaps the spirit that prevailed in respect to himself and his adherents, may best be exemplified by an interview held between him, and a member of the Supreme Executive Council, who visited him in prison. Col. F. in June, had been allowed the indulgence of coming to the front of the jail, and receiving such company as the keeper deemed it prudent to admit. On the 8th of that month, a member of Council called. Col. Franklin urged the injustice and cruelty of longer confinement, and earnestly desired that he might be admitted to bail. The Hon. Counsellor replied, "that the bail offered was insufficient. That no ten of the Wyoming settlers were worth two hundred pounds, much less two thousand—that the whole of them were a pack of thieves from Connecticut, who had robbed others of their property, and now presumed to call it their own."

Strong must be the frame and stout the spirit, that more than a year's close confinement would not subdue. Accustomed to the morning breeze upon the mountain; to strike down the noble buck with his trusty rifle, or arrest in full spring the flying doe: drinking from pure springs at their fountains, joining in the labours and the carols of the joyous harvest, the loss of these exhilerating pleasures must have rendered his prison walls dreary as desolation itself. As the letter of Col. Franklin, declaring "*I was fully determined to return to Wyoming, and to use my influence in quelling the disturbances,*" &c., was regarded as an honorable surrender and pledge, we publish it entire, except the omission of a few lines contained in a preceding page.

"Prison, *Philadelphia, Sept.* 17, 1788.

Gentlemen :—

You will please to pardon me, while I address you upon a subject that most nearly concerns me—the subject to which I relate in my petition, lately presented to your Honourable House, and which is referred to you, to inquire into, and report thereon.

The notice taken of me in this my unhappy situation, and the opportunity I had yesterday with Doctor Logan, who was pleased to honour me with a visit on the subject of my petition, demand my grateful acknowledgments. But, as some matters have since occurred more fully to my memory, you will permit me to lay before you a state of facts, which I would wish to do only for information.

The Honourable Justices of the Supreme Court, on the 16th of April, agreed to admit me to bail, upon my entering into a recognizance with two good securities, in a sum therein required, as stated more fully in my petition. I obtained a certificate accordingly from the Clerk of the said Court, after which I addressed his Honour the Chief Justice in a letter, stating the difficulty which would probably take place in procuring any two persons at Luzerne to be my bail, who would be adjudged equal to the sum required, and requested that four or more persons might be taken as security, and that some such person, within the said County, as his honour thought proper, might be directed to take the recognizance;—he was pleased to grant my request: however, not any thing was done to effect until the 9th of May, when a friend of mine was permitted to see me, he being accompanied with an Honourable Member of Council, by whom I was informed that the Chief Justice had agreed to direct the Prothonotary of Luzerne to take four persons as security for my appearance at court, &c." * * * "However, before the business was complete, the Chief Justice had set off on the western circuit. My friend went on as far as Chester, and returned on the 10th, when I was informed that he had a letter from the Chief Justice, to send forward to the Prothonotary at Luzerne, to take the security at that place, and that whenever the recognizance was sent, that Justice Bryan would take my own recognizance. This letter, together with a letter which I was permitted to write to my friends at Luzerne, on that subject, was immediately sent forward. May, 31, I had information that security was taken, and the recognizance came to hand by a young man sent for that purpose. I expected to be liberated the same day; but heard nothing further until the 4th of June, when the young man was permitted to see me, he being in company with a Member of Council. I was then informed that nothing could be done until the Chief Justice returned, who accordingly returned soon after.

Application was made to him by my friends in my behalf, to obtain my discharge on the bail. I did all in my power to obtain my discharge from prison, or to know what prevented me from being liberated. I was informed that the Chief Justice gave for answer, that he had nothing to do with it, that it lay entirely in the breast of Council. Application was made to that Board, in my behalf. It rested until about the 8th of June, when an Honourable Member of Council came to see me." * * * * * * *

"After hearing the remarks of the visiting member, the young man who was present at that time, returned to Wyoming, after waiting nine days in this city at my expense. I was still kept in close confinement, deprived of the advantages of social society as I before had been, and could not be informed of any reason why I was not liberated, except as before represented, neither did I ever, by any authority, know what other reasons were assigned, until Doctor Logan informed me, yesterday, that the security was deemed insufficient—that some of those who were taken as security, had, at the same time, used threatening language, &c., which probably prevented me from being liberated. I have not heard the names of *all* those who are my security, but have been informed, that some of those nominated were absent, and others accepted by the Prothonotary in lieu thereof,—ten persons being required to enter bail. If any person who has been accepted as security for me, has been so imprudent as to use threatening language on that subject, I hope that their misconduct will not prejudice those equitable rights to which I may be judged entitled to. I wish, if the Honourable Commissioners think proper, that the matter may be fairly investigated whether the persons who entered bail for me are the identical persons who made use of threatening language, (I do not pretend to know to the contrary,) but I have enemies, who would, perhaps, wish to injure me, and be fond to have me wear out the last remains of life in prison. I therefore only wish that such inquiries may be made, as to prevent any undue measures operating to my hurt, that equal justice in that as well as in every other case, may be done me: I must confess, that I earnestly expected to be liberated on bail, conformably to the encouragement given me, and really thought that I had right so to expect, and I most solemnly declare, that, in case I had been liberated, I was fully determined to return to Wyoming and to use my influence in quelling the disturbances at that place, if any there should be, and to prepare myself to take my trial when called, therefor before a jury of my country, as the constitution directs: but as I was not liberated, I made my appeal to the legislative body, the guardians of the people, from whose justice and humanity, I am induced to believe, I shall in some way obtain relief. As to the circumstances of my confinement, that is fully set forth in my petition.

* A letter to the author from Joseph Jameson, an intimate friend of Franklin, written in 1831, gives this account of his imprisonment, derived from himself.

"When war with the Indians ceased, he found a more formidable foe in Pennsylvania, and a far more cruel one as respected himself, by their inhumanly imprisoning him better than seventeen months in the City of Philadelphia, with only twenty-seven pounds of iron upon him. The State gave a reward of six hundred dollars for his apprehension, for he had previously twice refused to be bought by the land-jobbers, and they were determined to punish him for slighting their generosity. The last time the offer of a bribe was made, he cautioned them never to propose the thing to him again. The proposals were to pay him a sum of money sufficient to make him and family independent if he would quit the country and not return."

[As our limits do not admit of the publication of this letter entire; as it was recovered too late to be interwoven in the text, and as every thing relating to Col. F. is of interest, I transcribe here a paragraph shewing his early labours and sufferings.

"He told me many years ago that he was the first white man that ever made a settlement in Huntington. He spent one whole summer there entirely alone—not a soul to speak to. He carried his provisions on his back from Plymouth, and when they were expended he would go up and fetch down another back load, through a pathless wilderness. He sometimes traveled this in the night, not leaving his work until about sun-down, the distance he had to go being about eighteen miles. At one time he was under the necessity of going up in the night, and entirely barefooted, among snakes, rocks and stones—not the appearance of a thing like a shoe to his feet." This was about the year '75.]

I have lately been very sick with a fever, but am now recovered from the disorder, though my sickness, together with a long confinement, has reduced me to a feeble state, which is hard to be recovered in a place of confinement. I was destitute of money at the time of my commitment, but agreed with a friend to support me with provisions, and never knew that any provision was made for me by Government, until I was liberated to the front of the gaol, the 24th of June, since which I learn that the person who supported me has had his bill allowed by Council, for my weekly subsistence, though paid in depreciated currency, which I shall be under obligation to make good, unless the sum he has received is made equal to my weekly subsistence, which I am not able to determine; my retired situation has prevented me from doing any thing for myself to any advantage which I might otherwise have done.

If after a full investigation it should be thought proper to admit me to bail on the security already taken, it would prevent a pecuniary expense which would take place in procuring other security if required; but in case I am liberated in any other way I shall make myself satisfied, and if continued in prison, I am resolved to be submissive to whatever Providence has assigned me. I have only wrote to give you information. I earnestly hope that whatever may be alleged against me, will not prejudice any equitable right to which your committee and the Honourable Assembly may adjudge me entitled, as equal justice is all that I demand. I am, gentlemen, with every sentiment of respect,

Your Obedient Servant.
JOHN FRANKLIN."

GEORGE LOGAN,
PETER MUHLENBURGH, } Esquires.
and JOHN. P. SCHOTT.

Having perfect reliance on the honour of Col. Franklin this explicit declaration was regarded, rightfully, as an abandonment of his plan to establish a new state. Intercourse secret and confidential, had without doubt been kept up between Col. Franklin, and the Wolcott's, Barlow, Judd, Hosmore, and other chief men engaged in the enterprise, in Connecticut, alluded to by Col. Pickering, when he speaks of their " great men," and " Such a project, to be accomplished by such desperate, flagitious means, it might be expected would meet no countenance from, *much less be the very offspring* of men, of whom some were of respectable standing in Connecticut," &c.

It seems probable that the energetic measures adopted by Pickering, the arrest, and close confinement of Franklin; the failure to obtain Franklin's release by the abduction of Col. P., had convinced them that their plan could not succeed, and under their advice he had resolved to submit to the laws. Moreover, the establishment of the Federal Constitution opened to those ambitious Connecticut spirits, a larger and more inviting field for the exercise of their talents.

The Lion being tamed; the purpose of a new and independent government being abandoned, and the pledge contained in his letter to the committee, being received with confidence, Col. Franklin was visited by the magnates of the city, and treated with all the respect and courtesy of a prisoner of state—detained on political considerations, not affecting his moral integrity or personal character. Knowing his great influence, particular pains were taken to conciliate him, and to bring him into the scheme of compromise, devised by Col. Pickering. Without committing himself to that point, he satisfied those who were interested, that he would offer no further obstruction to the free introduction of the laws.

Means to bring Franklin, and the rioters to trial, were adopted (merely, we presume, for form sake,) and a Supreme Court was ordered to be holden at Wilkesbarre in November. Chief Justice M'Kean was met on the mountains, several miles from the Valley, by Sheriff Butler, the Coroner, and a large number of the principal inhabitants. When they arrived at the point which commanded a full view of the beautiful Valley, Judge M'Kean stopped and surveyed it for a quarter of an hour with deep apparent interest. At length he broke silence: "It is indeed a lovely spot—I cease to wonder that it has been so zealously contended for."

The court was opened by the Chief Justice, supported by his honour Jacob Rush.* Col. Franklin had been brought up from the city, and was indicted on a charge of High Treason, "*in endeavouring to subvert the government, and to erect a new and independent state in the room and stead thereof.*" Messrs. Biddle and Clymer appeared as his Counsel, and on the ground that important witnesses, needed on his defence, were absent, the trial was postponed, and he remanded to prison, not to Philadelphia, but at Easton. Bail, however, was taken,

---

* A letter writer, to a friend in Philadelphia, who dates "Wilkesborough, Nov. 8, 1788," says:—"A Supreme Court was opened last Tuesday in this place before their honours the Chief Justice and Judge Rush, the first ever held for the County of Luzerne."

"It gave me pleasure to see the order and decorum that prevailed; *nothing could exceed the respectful silence and attention of all ranks of people, while the Court was sitting.*

and Franklin set at liberty, and the prosecution, after remaining unacted upon for some time, finally abandoned.

Twenty-five concerned in the "diabolical outrage" on Col. Pickering, were indicted. Of sixteen arraigned, nine submitted to the mercy of the Court, seven pleaded not guilty, of whom three were acquitted, and five convicted. A fine of twenty shillings, and six months imprisonment was imposed on four of them; fifty dollars without imprisonment, on the fifth. Those who submitted to the Court, were fined each one hundred dollars. Of the "poor creatures" imprisoned, all escaped, that is, went home without let or hindrance, immediately after the Court adjourned. Stephen Jenkins alone remained, who would not go. It cannot have escaped the sagacity of the reader, that, with all the harshness of epithet used by Col. Pickering, he was at once too politic, too placable, far too noble minded, to desire that the rioters should suffer, and doubtless connived at their escape. We believe that none of the fines imposed were ever collected.* It is worthy of note that the Rev. Jacob Johnson, already well known to the reader, could not, or would not suppress the ebulition of his Yankee and patriotic ire, at the course of proceedings. He made the pulpit echo with his soul stirring appeals. So open were the denunciations of the pious old man, that he was arrested, called before M'Kean, and obliged to find security for his peaceable behaviour.

Christmas of 1788, found Luzerne abounding in the necessaries of life; the laws of Pennsylvania in perfect operation, receiving every where cheerful obedience. Franklin at liberty. Col. Pickering in his office, issuing writs, or recording deeds, with the same devoted industry that characterized the performance of every other duty, high or low, allotted to him in life—a most extraordinary man, in whom were combined those rare attributes of wisdom to devise measures, decision to resolve on their execution—energy to carry them through, the whole tempered by consummate prudence, and perfect integrity, tinged nevertheless by a degree of prejudice, that occasionally misled him; yet ever commanding the respect of friend and enemy. Indeed, perhaps he was the only man who could have introduced the laws, and averted the calamity of a new and more disastrous civil war in Wyoming.

* Among those concerned, we find Noah Phelps, two or three Kilbourns, and some others, distinguished names now in Connecticut; and that of Garret Smith, a christian name so unusual as to lead us to wonder whether he might have been the father, or relative of the distinguished New Yorker?

LETTER XXVIII.

Legal matters—Particularly dedicated to gentlemen of the Bench and Bar.

THE Confirming Law has been briefly adverted to in a preceding page. In every aspect, historical and legal, the very great importance of this act demands a more extended consideration, as it is the ground-work of compromise, and the root from which springs no inconsiderable portion of the existing titles of the Wyoming settlers to their lands, notwithstanding the law was repealed by the Assembly, and pronounced unconstitutional by the court. In this letter it is our purpose to trace through to their issue, historically and argumentatively, in a connected chain, the measures of the Commonwealth resulting in the issuing of patents to Connecticut claimants.

To suppose that a Pennsylvania land claimant shall appear in court with a warrant, survey, and patent of 1794; and a Connecticut settler with a certificate of 1804, and a patent for the same piece of land—that here the prosecution and defence close; and the court gives its charge to the jury, that, from the face of the papers, the warrant and survey of 1794, being oldest, must of course recover;—would be gross error.

Our thesis presupposes such case to be depending. In fact such an issue was on the list when this paper was written.

The CERTIFICATE, a paper so peculiar, and wholly unknown in any other part of the Commonwealth, would on presentation instantly strike a court as something extraordinary, and lead to the inquiry "What is this? whence comes a paper so very unusual?"

A copy will be found on the next page.

WILKESBARRE.

DRAUGHT of a Tract of Land, situate in Wilkesbarre, one of the seventeen Townships in Luzerne County, being Numbers Fourteen and Fifteen in the Third Division of that Township and containing 432 Ac's, 157 Ps. and the usual allowance of Six per Cent for Roads, resurveyed for Thomas Wright, the Eighteenth day of August, 1802, by order of the Commissioners appointed to put in execution an act of the General Assembly of the State of Pennsylvania, entitled "An Act for offering compensation to the Pennsylvania Claimants of certain Lands within the seventeen Townships in the County of Luzerne, and for other purposes therein mentioned."

December 1st, 1802.

THOS. SAMBOURNE,
Surveyor to the said Commissioners.

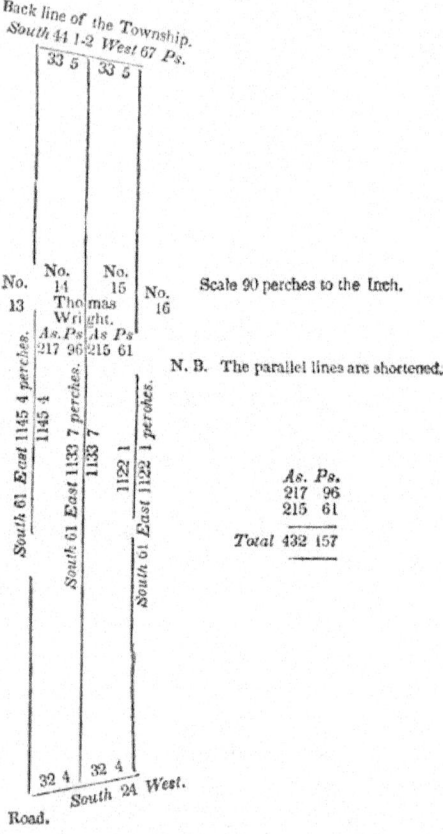

WE the undersigned Commissioners, duly appointed for putting in execution an Act of the General Assembly of the State of Pennsylvania, entitled "An Act for offering compensation to the Pennsylvania Claimants of certain Lands within the seventeen Townships in the County of Luzerne, and for other purposes therein mentioned," passed the 4th day of April 1799, and the Supplement thereto passed the 15th day of March, 1800, and the further Supplement thereto passed the 6th day of April, 1802, DO CERTIFY, That Thomas Wright is the Owner as a Connecticut Claimant of Four hundred and Thirty-two Acres and One hundred and fifty-seven perches of Land in the Township of WILKESBARRE, one of the before mentioned seventeen Townships; being Lots, Number Fourteen and Fifteen, in the Third Division in the said Township; WHICH Lots Number Fourteen and Fifteen were severally occupied and acquired by a Connecticut Claimant, an actual Settler there before the time of the Decree of Trenton, and was particularly assigned to such actual Settler, prior to the said Decree, agreeably to the regulations then in force among such Settlers. The said Land (a Draught of Survey whereof is hereto annexed) is included in the application of Thomas Weeks, under the provisions of the acts aforesaid: of which application an official transcript has been transmitted to us from the Land Office of the Commonwealth of Pennsylvania. No. 215, Of the said Tract, one hundred and sixty-five Acres, part thereof are of the third Class, and the residue thereof is of the fourth Class.

November 10th, 1803.

THOMAS COOPER,
JNO. M. TAYLOR.

It will be apparent that the question has its origin in a controversy between sovereign States: That the certificate has its foundation in the benign and politic principle of compromise—to arrest bloodshed and put an end to civil war. It involves high matter of State policy, and should be decided, after a full view of the case in all its aspects, (not by the complex fettered rules of special pleading,) but on the broad ground of its own peculiar merits. He therefore, who examines it through the microscope of mere legal technicalities, must necessarily grope in darkness; the broad expanse can only be embraced by the telescope which sweeps from the zenith to the horizon. It is a vast State question of mingled equity and law.

We mean to be studiously brief, both because I feel myself to be a trespasser, and because generally, an intimation of the point or principle being given, legal gentlemen can follow it out with a force and clearness I could make no pretensions to.

The historical part of the origin of the Connecticut claim has already been set forth, and is presumed to be too well known and familiar to be here repeated at length, all important as it is regarded in considering the equity of title under the compromise.

The First point I propose to establish is this:

That the decree of Trenton, adjudging the jurisdiction to Pennsylvania, was a decision of *policy* and not of *right*. That it could not and did not affect the right of soil.

But a page of recapitulation is deemed proper. In the exhibit of claims by the Connecticut commissioners before the court at Trenton, it is set forth that the Susquehanna Company in its purchase and settlement of these lands acted " under countenance of the authority of said colony." And that "the Legislature of the colony of Connecticut have approved of the purchases and settlements of the adventurers aforesaid, and have *actually exerted and exercised jurisdiction* in and over said territory, as part and parcel of said colony." In fact in 1773, resolutions were passed declaring the intention to support their claim west of New York, and in January 1774, the jurisdiction and laws of Connecticut were, by formal enactment, extended to Wyoming, a town called Westmoreland was erected, and attached to the county of Litchfield, civil officers were appointed, taxes were levied and paid into the treasury of Connecticut, and representatives chosen to her Assembly. The power of State authority was as perfect here as at Hartford or New Haven; and thus it continued through the Revolutionary war, until the decree of Trenton in December 1782.

After the surrender of Lord Cornwallis it was obvious that the British power in America was broken, independence secure, and peace near at hand. Immediately all the States began to look with increased anxiety to the settlement of disputed points among themselves of boundaries, jurisdiction and soil.

By the second and third sections of the ninth article of confederation, provision was made for raising two separate courts; one to try questions of jurisdiction between contending States; the other to try the right of soil between persons claiming lands under grants from different States. Thus clearly and distinctly admitting—that jurisdiction might be awarded to one State, and the soil to claimants under grants from another State. That is, that the right of jurisdiction and the right of soil did not necessarily go together. My impressions are clear that these sections were introduced having particular reference to the dispute existing between Pennsylvania and Connecticut, Massachusetts and New York. It must have been manifest to the sagacious heads then on the stage of action, from the relative position of the parties, and the land claimed, that however just the title of Connecticut and Massachusetts, to the soil west of the Hudson, policy should award the jurisdiction relatively to Pennsylvania and New York. The application of nice technical and legal rules to the settlement of these controversies would have led to endless litigation, heart burnings, and most probably to civil war. Charter claims lapped on to each other—these were met by Indian deeds, rights of possession, and various equitable and political considerations, which ought not, and which could not be disregarded. Wisdom uttered her voice with emphatic solemnity, urging an adjustment upon broad and liberal grounds of State policy and equitable compromise. Chesterfield, in a letter to his son, says: "Where a variety of concurring incidents, and a chain of circumstantial evidence, all combine to support a proposition, he would believe it sooner than the most direct human testimony."

The reason of the thing, and concurring circumstances, lead strongly to the conclusion, that *policy* and not *law* governed the decision of this great cause at Trenton.

To give my impressions in familiar language, and make them more easily comprehended, I will suppose the great men in Congress in social chat, talking over the subject of these perplexing controversies.

South Carolina.—" Well, gentlemen, the power of Britain is broken—we shall now have a release from foreign war—shall we be able to preserve domestic peace? What do you say, Mr. Wolcott, for Connecticut, will you maintain jurisdiction to your Wyoming lands, in defiance of my friend Clymer here, and the good State of Pennsylvania? Come, come, you are both ready to speak up very short—both for war! So, too, with my friends Floyd, from New York, and Osgood, from Massachusetts. They are ready for a battle for the rich lake and Genesee lands! But this is all nonsense, gentlemen. Wisdom, prudence, policy, these must come in and adjust the matter. There are twenty millions acres of unseated land in New York, claimed by that State and Massachusetts; you must divide these. There is enough for both. The jurisdiction should of course remain in New York—what does Massachusetts want to do with jurisdiction beyond the North River. She has plenty to attend to at home, and besides has the province of Maine to take care of."

Pennsylvania.—" Very well, you have settled the dispute of those States: give us a plan for Pennsylvania and Connecticut."

South Carolina.—" O, easy—leave Pennsylvania to herself—she is just large enough, as bounded by her charter—nothing to want and nothing to spare. Take off the degree of latitude claimed by Connecticut, all along her longitudinal limits, and you leave her razeed down to a fourth rate State. You deprive her of nearly all unseated lands, and she has no pretence of claim elsewhere. It will never, never answer."

Connecticut.—" But what is Connecticut to do?"

South Carolina.—" All easy and practicable. Connecticut must take a good slice out of her chartered limits west of Pennsylvania—the beautiful Ohio lands, at present neither adversely settled nor claimed; enough, an hundred miles or more, if she please. Jurisdiction west of the Hudson cannot be an object of desire to her. And then all the States whose charters extend far west, must release the remainder of their claims to the United States, according to the resolves of Congress. And thus the whole matter may be satisfactorily adjusted."

Connecticut.—" Upon my word, you reason well. But what shall be done with the Wyoming settlers?"

South Carolina.—" O there can be no question about them. Their rights cannot be affected by any relinquishment the State may now make. Besides it will be the manifest policy of all parties to quiet the actual settlers. Land is plenty. All the States want good, contented, industrious citizens, to subdue the wilderness. And moreover, the Wyoming people have fairly bought these lands of Pennsylvania by their blood and sufferings, standing as a frontier against the cruel savage, as they have done."

Pennsylvania.—"Certainly, certainly. If Connecticut will be satisfied with that arrangement, we pledge ourselves, give us all the rest within our charter peaceably, there shall be no difficulty in respect to the Wyoming settlers."

Connecticut.—"It seems rational; but the thing must be done in a legal way. The grant to Pennsylvania must pass by decision of court; for it would cut out so many of our people at home, who have claims in the Susquehanna country, there would be great dissatisfaction—the Wyoming settlers too, would be extremely offended if we give it up without a trial."

Pennsylvania.—"We understand you. You shall have a trial. An application shall be made forthwith to raise a court to decide the matter."

Fifteen days after Cornwallis surrendered, to wit:—November 3d, "A petition from the Supreme Executive Council was read" in Congress, stating the matter of dispute between Pennsylvania and Connecticut, praying a hearing in the premises, agreeable to the 9th article of confederation.

[See Journal of that date.]

A court was accordingly raised, composed of the Hon. William Whipple, of New Hampshire; Welcome Arnold, Rhode Island; David Brearly and William Churchill Houston, of New Jersey; Cyrus Griffin, Joseph Jones and Thomas Nelson, of Virginia. The two latter did not attend. The five first named convened at Trenton Nov. 12, 1782.

William Bradford, jr., Joseph Reed, James Wilson and Jonathan D. Sergeant, attended as counsel and agents, on the part of Pennsylvania.

Eliphalet Dyer, William S. Johnson and Jesse Root, appeared as counsel and agents, on behalf of Connecticut.

Early in the proceedings, to wit: November 19, a motion was made as follows: "The agents of the State of Connecticut, saving to themselves all advantages of other and further defence in said cause, beg leave to suggest, inform, and give the court to understand, that there are many persons who are tenants, in possession of the lands in controversy, holding, improving and claiming large quantities of said lands, under titles from the States of Pennsylvania and Connecticut, respectively, particularly the two large companies of

Delaware and Susquehanna, consisting of more than 2000 persons, many of whose people are in, possessing, improving and holding large tracts of said land in controversy, *under title* from the State of Connecticut, whose titles under said States respectively, will be materially affected by the decision in this case, yet have not been cited, or any way legally notified to be present at said trial, to defend their titles respectively, which, by the rules of proceeding in a court of justice, ought to be done, before any further proceedings are had in said case: and thereupon the said agents move this honourable court, to cause said companies of Delaware and Susquehanna, and other tenants in possession, holding under title from either of said States, to be duly cited in some proper and reasonable manner, to appear and defend at said trial, if they see cause, before any farther proceedings are had in said cause. And of this they pray the opinion of this honourable court.

    E. Dyer,
    Wm. S. Johnson, } Agents for Connecticut.
    J. Root,

After argument, the court adjourned till to-morrow, ten of the clock.

                        Wednesday, November 20, 1782.

The court met. The court gave their opinion on the motion of yesterday, made in writing by the agents of Connecticut.

"That the same cannot be admitted according to the construction of the 9th article of the confederation, and the tenor and designs of the commission under which they act."

I have quoted this at length for the purpose of more clearly establishing two points. 1st. That the right of soil was not decided at Trenton—that it could not be under the authority by which the court was constituted—that notice was therefore refused to be given to the settlers to appear; and the principle distinctly recognized—that jurisdiction might be awarded to one State; and the right of soil be awarded to claimants under grants from another State. This matter will be adverted to hereafter: The other point is this—that the agents of Connecticut do therein, officially declare, not only once but twice, that the Susquehanna Company and the settlers, under their grants, derive title *under Connecticut;* a matter of some moment.

The court continued its sittings until December 30th, when they rendered this very brief and very explicit judgment.

"We are unanimously of opinion, that the State of Connecticut has no right to the lands in controversy.

"We are also unanimously of opinion, that the jurisdiction and pre-emption of all the territory lying within the charter boundary of Pennsylvania, and now claimed by the State of Connecticut, do of right belong to the State of Pennsylvania.

        Wm. Whipple,
        Welcome Arnold,
        Wm. C. Houston,
        Cyrus Griffin,
        David Brearly."

In all which the Connecticut agents and counsel acquiesced without protest or murmur. After, to say the least, the plausible exhibit on the part of Connecticut, the perfect unanimity of the Court would strike an impartial observer as in no slight degree remarkable. The very brief judgment, not a solitary reason being given, would excite surprise. There is nothing extraordinary, or in the least degree surprising, admitting the position which I maintain to be correct—that the whole trial was a political movement, a mere "*common recovery*," intended to convey, and carry into effect a previously understood arrangement between Pennsylvania and Connecticut.

It seems probable that Connecticut, before coming to the understanding with Pennsylvania, had made an offer to Congress to cede her western lands beyond the limits of that State; most likely without any reservation. The reserve I take it was an after thought. On a careful examination I find no such proposition on the journal. If a new and different proposal was to be made, it might have been politic to withdraw the old one, and leave no trace of it. The fact comes out by a side wind. On the 31st of January, 1783, just a month after the Trenton decree, in a report of Mr. Carroll and others, on the finances, it is said " Virginia and *Connecticut have also made cessions*, the acceptance of which, for *particular reasons* have been delayed." The matter was wisely permitted to sleep awhile. In May 22, 1786, on motion proceeding from a committee, to wit:

"*Resolved*, That Congress, in behalf of the United States, are ready to accept all the right, title, interest and claim of the State of Connecticut, to certain western lands, &c."

Debate and several motions arose thereon. The question was not decided until the 26th, five days being devoted to its consideration. Seven times the yeas and nays were recorded. It is worthy of emphatic remark, that Pennsylvania and Connecticut voted together five times! Once all the other States voting against them. Connecticut was once excused from voting; and only in one solitary instance out of the seven times, did they vote against each other, and that on a motion of no great moment made by another State. What new-born love! What brotherly affection! Can any one doubt its origin?

As adopted, the resolution was in these words—"That Congress accept the said deed of cession, and that the same be recorded and enrolled among the acts of the United States, in Congress assembled."

By the deed Connecticut grants "all right, title, interest, jurisdiction and claim to certain western lands, beginning at the completion of the 41st degree of north latitude, one hundred and twenty miles west of the western boundary line of the Commonwealth of Pennsylvania, as now claimed by the said Commonwealth, and from thence by a line drawn north parallel to, and one hundred and twenty miles west of the said west line of Pennsylvania, and to continue north, until it comes to forty-two degrees and two minutes of north latitude." All west of this line is ceded, and of course, all east is reserved. The reservation is of 120 miles east and west, (bounding it easterly by the west line of Pennsylvania,) by a degree and two minutes north and south latitude, containing several millions of acres. It is well known by the name of New Connecticut, or the Western Reserve. It may be here proper as a historical fact to say, that about the year 1800, Connecticut made a formal release of all claim to jurisdiction or soil, west of the eastern limits of New York, excepting to the western reserve; and received from the United States letters patent for that tract.

By the proceedings detailed it will be seen that the right of Connecticut west of New York was recognized by Congress, accepting her cession, and admitting the reservation. Pennsylvania, by voting for the acceptance, did also distinctly recognize that right. How could she have a right west of Pennsylvania, and not through Pennsylvania, when her charter was nineteen years the oldest? From which, the whole circumstances taken together, a rational doubt we think cannot be entertained, but that the decision at Trenton was made on grounds of *policy* and not of *right*.

There remains a most important matter bearing on this point, yet to be noticed, which pours in a flood of light, dispelling every shade of darkness or doubt, if any should still rest upon it.

The Hon. Cyrus Griffin, one of the Judges of the court at Trenton, in answer to inquiries from Barnabas Bidwell, wrote a letter in 1796, of which the following is a copy. Before transcribing this important paper, it seems proper to observe that Cyrus Griffin was a distinguished member of Congress from Virginia. I find he was a delegate early in 1778; in 1780, he was elected a Judge of the Court of Appeals; in 1788, he was chosen President of Congress. Such is the character of the witness we produce. To the letter:—

"SIR,—Being upon a tour of duty in the line of my office, I had not the pleasure of reading your letter until yesterday.

"Before the Commissioners determined that important contest between Pennsylvania and Connecticut, it was agreed:—

"1st. That the reasons for the determination should never be given.

"2d. That the minority should concede the determination as the unanimous opinion of the court.

"No doubt sufficient reasons appeared to us to adopt these preliminary points. Whether strictly justifiable, or at present would be adopted, I will not undertake to say; perhaps a different course might be pursued; but this I will undertake to say, that no court ever met and decided a great question, less subject to partiality or corruption, or in which more candour and freedom of debate were exercised.

"As you seem to suppose, I do not know in what manner the jurisdiction might be considered if tried again; and especially since a number of important discoveries have been made, and a mass of evidence can now be produced which was not known at that time.

"But I can assure you, sir, that the commissioners were *unanimously of opinion*, that the *private right of soil should not be affected by the decision*.

"The decision was *not to reach the question of property in the soil*.

"We recommended *very strongly*, derived from *legal* and *political grounds, that the settlers should be quieted in all their claims by an act of the Pennsylvania Assembly;* and that the right of soil, if I recollect truly, as derived from Connecticut, *should be held sacred.*

"Such, however, I AM CERTAIN, was the opinion of the individuals who composed that court."

No comment could make the matter clearer; and I assume again, with the utmost confidence, that my proposition is well established, viz: "That the decree of Trenton, adjudging the jurisdiction to Pennsylvania, was a decision of *policy* and not of *right*—that it could not, and did not affect the right of soil."

Yet there is an additional fact of great weight, bearing on and supporting this conclusion. The claim of Massachusetts west of the Hudson, rested on precisely the same ground as that of Connecticut. Preliminary measures were adopted to raise a court, to try the question. Wisely preferring compromise to law, New York adjusted the matter by liberal and just concession; the States divided the land between them. In 1787, New York recognized the right of Massachusetts, conceded and confirmed her claim to the land, in all that part of western New York, beginning at a point on the Pennsylvania line, eighty-two miles west of the north-east corner of Pennsylvania, [the point of beginning is in Tioga county] thence north to the British boundary, and including with a trifling exception the whole of the Genesee and Lake country, west of that line. The exception was more than made up by 230,000 acres confirmed to Massachusetts east of that line, between the Oswego and Chenango rivers. The quantity of land retained by Massachusetts cannot be much less than 10,000 square miles, and probably exceeded seven millions of acres.

It would be an insult to the understanding, a mockery of common sense, to suppose that New York conceded this princely domain to Massachusetts, after the decree of Trenton, if that decree was regarded by any one living being, lawyer or politician, statesman or philosopher, as a decision of law and right—as any thing else, but a legal process of consummating a wise political arrangement.

Passing from these historical facts and speculations we proceed more directly to those which are strictly legal. An act was passed September 15, 1784, directing that the dispossessed settlers should be restored to their farms. Col. Antis, Sheriff of Northumberland, was ordered to perform the duty. A most important law and proceeding; as now, beyond controversy, the settlers had a clear legal Pennsylvania possession.

On the 30th of Dec., 1786, an act was passed for giving, during a limited time, a right of pre-emption.

I rather suggest than argue, the effect this act would have upon the rights of those persons in actual possession, claiming against warrant holders, whose surveys were made, and warrants obtained, subsequently thereto.

The great plan of conciliation; the grand healing measure of compromise, which should quiet the Wyoming people in their possessions, and staunch the wounds which so many years of disorder had inflicted, was the CONFIRMING LAW, passed March 28, 1787, (to which we adverted in a preceding letter.) It provided, "That all the said rights or lots now lying within the County of Luzerne, which were occupied or acquired by Connecticut claimants who were actual settlers thereat or before the termination of the claim of the State of Connecticut, by the [Trenton] decree aforesaid, and which rights or lots were particularly assigned to the said settlers prior to the said decree, agreeable to the regulations then in force among them, be and they are hereby confirmed to them, and their heirs and assigns." [*See the Act.*]

Certain conditions were to be complied with by the settlers. The most important one is, that within eight months they should make application for the benefits of the act. The disturbances of the country already detailed, occasioned the withdrawal of the commissioners appointed to carry it into effect.

In a year and a day the act was suspended. April 1, 1790, it was repealed. It must be admitted the day was fitly chosen for the deed.

Two Dissents, arguing with consummate ability the impolicy and unconstitutionality of the repeal, were entered on the Journal. The first from the able pen of William Rawle; the other emanating from the luminous mind of William Lewis. Both are appended to this letter, and are deemed of great importance.

Now, the only pretence, the only spider thread on which it could be pretended that titles under the Confirming Law were not valid *to those lands owned by the State*, when the act passed was, that within the eight months assigned the settlers did not make application under it, &c. There is not the slightest evidence that they did not. There is every reasonable presumption that they did, as far as possible, for the law granted all they asked. They were required to pay nothing to the State for the land—the sums for surveying and patenting, were not a consideration as purchase money, but merely to pay expenses and office fees. The consideration stated in the preamble was fully acknowledged to be received. The time was manifestly too short for all to come in. From the whole spirit of the law, it being an Act of Grace and Equity, it could not have been the intention of the Legislature, to exclude from its benefits the widow—the orphans —the ignorant or even the dilatory, who might not come in by the very short day named. It would take the Commissioners several months to get to Luzerne, and some time to explain the law and mode of proceeding. The people interested were scattered over a territory, along the river an hundred miles, their papers dispersed, and a number, whose fathers had fallen by the Savages, were minors, serving their apprenticeship with masters to whom they had been bound in Connecticut while very young, whither they had fled or been carried on the general expulsion. That these were intended to be embraced is evident from the fact, that the commissioners were required to give notice in one or more newspapers printed in Pennsylvania and Connecticut." In this view of the matter, if a mere simple application or assent was all that was required to exclude every one who did not assent or apply in time, would be a most forced and hard construction, inequitable, no mercy in it, no justice in it, and therefore not a true construction.

But this point is too important, not to be pursued further. The words of the proviso are, "Provided that *all* the claimants whose lots are hereby confirmed, shall by themselves, guardians, or other lawful agents, within eight months next after passing this act, prefer to the Commissioners hereinafter mentioned, their respective claims to the lots aforesaid, therein stating the grounds of their claim, and sufficiently describing the lots claimed, so that the same may be made known or ascertained, and support the same by reasonable proofs."

If strictly and rigidly construed, here was a great deal of work to be done in a short time. Several thousand persons, so widely dispersed, their papers and titles necessarily in confusion, from their Indian expulsion and more recent troubles—*all* these, every one, for if *all* do not come in, in strictness, the whole failed—they must not only prefer their claims, generally, but describe their lots—every river and back lot is to be particularly described, and in addition to all this their titles must be supported before the Commissioners by reasonable proofs. Impossible—utterly impossible—every man of common sense must see that the literal rigid demands of the law could not be complied with in eight months. To demand it or say that on failure the whole law might be repealed—the solemn confirmations of titles be abrogated, would be worse than Turkish despotism. Such injustice never stained the deliberate legislation of Pennsylvania. Such construction never soiled the pure ermine of her Jurisprudence.

Courts justly hold that an impossible condition is void. Suppose a law had said, "whereas, a certain five hundred persons having paid £10,000 into the treasury, the receipt whereof is acknowledged; now, in consideration thereof, the said persons, their heirs and assigns, shall each be quieted and confirmed in one hundred acres of land, belonging to the State, on which they are seated; provided that within one month all of them bring to the Secretary of the Land Office a survey of their respective lots;"—and in two months after the law should be repealed. If any speculator should afterwards lay a warrant on one of their farms, is there a Court on earth that would oust the settler, or adjudge the land to the warrant holder? In principle the cases are precisely parallel.

On these legal points I have been purposely brief, suggesting merely the outline. because legal gentlemen can with so much more ease and correctness give them their appropriate illustration.

But the confirming law was pronounced unconstitutional and void by Judge Patterson of the United States Circuit Court, in the case of Vanhorn, vs. Dorrance—Vanhorn, a lesse under a Pennsylvania claimant, under a warrant before the confirming law; Dorrance being an early Connecticut settler. The trial took place in 1795.

Judge Patterson made short work of the Connecticut title. The decree of Trenton had settled that matter. Connecticut had no right, and therefore no person claiming under her, could have any right.

Far more justly, as the counsel for Dorrance admitted, he decided that Vanhorn, claiming under title derived from the State before the confirming law was passed, did not, and could not have his claim taken from him by the proffer of a land compensation. The State could only resume the title for public purposes, and the payment of a just price therefor in money.*

The confirming law might be unconstitutional, and a dead letter, in respect to *one* set of claimants—yet perfectly constitutional and valid as regarded *another class*. To make this plain, it should be noted—and this distinction is vitally important—that the State had disposed of *part* of the lands confirmed to the settlers, to Pennsylvania claimants, *before the confirming law* passed. In respect to *these* it *was* unconstitutional for the reason stated. But at the time that law passed, the State was proprietor of a large portion of the lands so confirmed to the settler. In respect to these, it cannot doubted she had a right

---

* The proceedings never were followed up. No attempt was made to put Dorrance out of possession. A movement was made to take the case up to the Supreme Court, but the Yankees ailedged that Vanhorn (an irresponsible person—a man of straw) could not be found to serve a writ upon. Col. Pickering, writing March 2, 1798, says "By this repeal [the confirming act] the Courts of Law were opened to the Pennsylvania claimants, who *were soon to get* possession of the disputed lands, and rid the State of the burden of compensation! They brought many actions, and in *eight* years they have *partly* tried *one cause*."

to do as she pleased. She did please, for valid reasons and satisfactory considerations, to confirm them to certain Connecticut claimants.

Judge Cooper, in his observations to the legislature of Pennsylvania, March 1802, says, "however unconstitutional that law might be, as it respects the Pennsylvania claimants, whose property was taken on a land compensation, it certainly was binding on the legislature in favour of the actual settler before the decree of Trenton, who had applied for the benefit of it; for the State had the power, *and the right to give away her vacant lands*; and also to take the lands of her citizens, on paying a just compensation in money."

Judge Patterson says, "the *intention* of the legislature was to vest in Connecticut claimants of a particular description a *perfect estate* to certain lands in the County of Luzerne." Mark this distinct and solemn adjudication of the *intention* of the legislature.

Again the Judge says, "*if the property to the lands in question had been vested in the State of Pennsylvania, then the legislature would have had the liberty and right of disposing or granting them to whom they pleased, at any time, and in any manner.*"

In the case we are now considering, "the property of the land was vested in the State."

I contend then, that by the confirming law, for the great and valid considerations of the equity and policy of the case, the legislature did convey the right that was, at the passing the law, still vested in her, to the settlers. By that act virtue went out of the State, and attached to the settler. From that moment, those settlers who were on lands yet belonging to the Commonwealth, were clothed with the State title, or unquestionable legal *right* to the State title. Forms were yet to be gone through; the land was yet to be surveyed and patented, but the right of title was in them; the inception of title was perfect.

But the confirming law was repealed. The law was not a simple gift, it was a grant for a good consideration, the value received was expressly acknowledged; it was a sufficient consideration in the sight of an impartial world. The grant took effect the moment it was passed. It shook the pollen from the tassel upon the silk, and the impregnation was complete, though time was requisite to bring the ear to perfection. The legislature had no more power to repeal it than to annul any other patent or land title granted by its authority. I need not say a grantor cannot annul and make void his deed. Even kings, in the plenitude of their prerogative or sovereign power, cannot revoke a charter, or abrogate a conveyance of land.

The view which I take of the effect of that law has been recognized and maintained by the government of Pennsylvania, from that day to this, with the utmost uniformity and steadiness.

1. They have constantly acted under the clear and solemn conviction that the settlers in the seventeen towns had a valid right to their lands, which the State was bound to make perfect in form.

2. They have purchased back all Pennsylvania titles that originated *before* the confirming law, by a money compensation, and perfected titles to settlers on them.

3. They have refused in every possible shape and manner to recognize any right in warrant holders, whose titles originated in the seventeen towns *after the confirming law*, one hasty and ill considered decision excepted; showing that they regarded such warrants void, like any other second set of warrants laid on previously appropriated lands, with which in the wild rage of speculation in 1793 and 4, the State was shingled over frequently four or five deep.

Advancing to another topic. Luzerne County having been established, her voice was heard in the Assembly. Public opinion in and out of the State, with accumulated strength, demanded the formal redemption of the pledged faith of the Commonwealth to the old settlers. Comparative peace and prosperity prevailed at Wyoming, for the influence of the confirming law was felt, though nominally struck from the statue book. In 1799, April 4, an act was passed, entitled "An Act for offering compensation to certain Pennsylvania claimants therein named, and for other purposes."

This compromising law and its supplements provided that all Pennsylvania claims to lands in the seventeen towns which originated *before* March 28, 1787, (the date of the confirming law) should be paid for, at a price proffered, or the claimants might, at their option, sue the State, and have the value fixed by a jury.

Commissioners were to re-survey lots claimed by Connecticut settlers, whose titles (precisely as in the confirming law) originated *before* the decree of Trenton. A certificate was to be issued to the settler, on presenting which to the land office, and paying the compensation fixed, he should receive a patent.*

---

* Terms of the compromising law of April 4, 1799.

Commissioners were to divide the lands into four classes. Pennsylvania claimants, who preferred to release their lands to the state, rather than have them appraised by a Jury, were to receive,

for the first class, $ 5.00 *an acre.*
second class, 3.00

Is it not preposterous to say that the title of the settler is to be dated as beginning with the date of the certificate? The thousand warrants of '93–4, were perfectly known to have been laid on these lands. Was it expected that after some years the two claims would come into Court, to be decided which was the *oldest*, and *therefore*, which was best? Did the State so understand it? Did the settlers so understand it? Did those warrant holders, who have suffered the matter to sleep forty years, so understand it? No, the legal Pennsylvania title must be dated as beginning at the passage of the confirming law, or the right of pre-emption, Dec. 30, 1786; the equitable claim having existed from or before the decree of Trenton.

It is here proper to say, that to Thomas Cooper, Esq., one of the commissioners under the compromising law, in 1803 and 1804, the settlers within the seventeen townships, and the Commonwealth at large, are deeply indebted. He gave to the subject the most devoted attention of a mind remarkably sagacious, vigorous, and clear. He unraveled with unexceeded patience and perspicuity, the mazes of this most intricate subject; aided by the practical good sense and dignity of character of Gen. Steele of Lancaster County, and Mr. Wilson of Lycoming; afterwards assisted by John M. Taylor, Esq., of Philadelphia.

On obtaining certificates the settlers were required to give up all deeds or evidence of Connecticut title, so that, very properly, thereafter, they should rest *solely on the pledged faith of the Commonwealth*. In point of fact, however, the certificate is of itself the best possible evidence of Connecticut title, adjudicated and decided to be perfect by a Pennsylvania Court.

I submit the remark here, that *all the laws* tending to confirm titles to the settlers ought to be taken and construed, not as *separate, independent* acts, but as parts and parcel of *a system*, as bricks of one edifice, constituting together one whole and perfect structure of compromise.

It is a striking fact, that the certificate issued under the compromising law of '99, makes use of almost the literal words to designate Connecticut claimants, employed by the confirming act; thereby referring to and recognizing that act, to which in truth the compro-

	third class, 1.50	*an acre.*
	fourth class, 25	"
Connecticut claimants were to pay for lands of the first class,	2.00	"
	second, 1.20	"
	third, 50	"
	fourth, 08½	"

mising law is a mere supplement. The certificate reads: "Which number was severally occupied and acquired by a Connecticut claimant, an actual settler there before the time of the decree of Trenton, and was particularly assigned to such actual settler prior to the said decree, agreeably to the regulations then in force among such settlers."

The words of the confirming law are—"which were occupied or acquired by Connecticut claimants, who were actual settlers there before the decree aforesaid, and which rights or lots, were particularly assigned to the said settlers prior to the said decree, agreeably to the regulations then in force among them."

If the confirming law did not convey the State title to the settler, it recognized in him and legalized a peculiar settlement made, or claim acquired "before the decree of Trenton." And to such and such only, could certificates issue. The fact of such settlement or acquisition was to be proved, and the commissioners under the compromising law were constituted a competent tribunal to decide upon it. Their certificate is complete proof of the fact. The holder may go into court, and produce his certificate: 1st. As evidence of title under the compromising law, or 2d. as proof positive *of settlement or acquired claim, before December* 30, 1782, recognized and legalized by the confirming act.

The compromising law went fully into operation. Peace and harmony have since prevailed. Those claims under Connecticut, within townships on which settlement had been made after the Trenton decree, already numerous and rapidly increasing, threatening wide extended and serious mischief, forthwith fell before this act of mingled policy and justice. Separated from the old settlers, who had borne the hardships of early emigration, and the crimsoned severities of savage war, the new grants plausibly urged for awhile, now found little favour, and soon sunk to oblivion.

DISSENTIENT from the vote adopting the report of the committee in favour of repealing the act entitled "An act for ascertaining and confirming to certain persons called *Connecticut claimants*, the lands by them claimed within the county of Luzerne, and for other purposes therein mentioned.

1st. Because we consider the act which the resolution adopted by the House, proposes to repeal, to be either in the nature of an absolute, or a conditional grant to the *Connecticut settlers*. If the latter, it has not yet been proved to our satisfaction, that the insurrection at Wyoming, which occasioned the commissioners to fly, proceeded from a general determination to resist the authority, and reject the bounties of this State, or from the turbulent dispositions of some of the adherents of *John Franklin*, who were incensed at his sudden and secret arrest; few of whom could derive any benefit from the law which the commissioners were then carrying into execution, and consequently, it has not appeared with that clearness which the importance of the subject requires, that there has been any breach of the implied condition of the law, viz: that the Connecticut settlers would submit to the authority of the State.

2d. Because if the grant is absolute, it is obligatory upon the State, and can only be revoked upon the terms mentioned hereafter.

We conceive that a law vesting an interest conveys the most (authentic) and (solemn) title that can be annexed to property, after which the State has not the same power over the law which it most unquestionably possesses over its own acts of another nature. But in no instance can the power of repealing laws affect their obligations while in force, and consequently, if the effect of the law while in force is permanent and perpetual upon the subject to which it relates, a repeal, although it may destroy the law, cannot diminish the effect it has already produced.

3d. Because, although it is universally conceded that private property may at any time be taken for public uses, yet it can only be so taken on condition of making full and adequate compensation to the private proprietor; and hence it *may* follow that the State, from whatever motives, having conveyed the title to the lands in dispute, under certain terms and modifications to the *Connecticut settlers*, will at a future day be liable to make a more expensive compensation to those settlers. than the whole amount of the demands of the *Pennsylvania claimants.*

4th. Because it is introducing a most dangerous principle to repeal a law of any kind from an impression, however strong, that the Legislature was deceived at the time of passing the law. A law contrary to the constitution, may and ought to be repealed; for in that instance there is a certain guide, which although it may be disobeyed, cannot be misunderstood. But to pass our own judgment in a legislative manner, upon the sufficiency of the motives which induced a former Assembly to enact a law of the nature of that which it is now proposed to repeal, and to collect those motives from other sources than the law itself, appears to us to endanger the authority even of our own proceedings, by rendering them liable at a future day, to be subverted in the same manner, with perhaps still less evidence, than we have to proceed upon. And it will directly tend to destroy the order, safety and happiness, derived from civil society; for as the obligation of the laws is rendered less solemn and conclusive, the Legislature will naturally become less impressed with their importance, and the people will gradually learn to disregard their authority.

Signed,   WILLIAM RAWLE,   JACOB HILTSHEIMER,
          RICHARD THOMAS,   HENRY DENNEY,
          RICHARD DOWNING, jr.,   SAMUEL ASHMEAD,
          LAWRENCE SICKLE,   OBADIAH GORE,
          JONATHAN ROBERTS,   HERMAN HERSHARD"

[Would it be too presuming to doubt whether the Philadelphia Bar, at all times distinguished for ability, but sixty years ago pre-eminent for the talents which adorned it, has often exhibited a paper of superior merit? The historical exposition in the third point taken, is remarkable for clearness, force and eloquence.]

DISSENTIENT from the vote for enacting the law entitled, an act to repeal an act, entitled an " Act for ascertaining and confirming to certain persons, called *Connecticut claimants,* the lands by them claimed within the county of *Luzerne,* and for other purposes therein mentioned."

1st. Because the passing of the bill into a law in the same session in which it originated, and within eight days after it was first read to the House, is beyond all example heretofore furnished by the rage or folly of party, a flagrant violation of the constitution, which declares, that " to the end that laws before they are enacted may be more maturely considered, and the inconvenience of hasty determination as much as possible prevented, all bills of a public nature shall be printed for the consideration of the people, before they are read in General Assembly, the last time for debate, and except on occasions of sudden necessity, shall not be passed into laws until the next session of Assembly."

That this bill was of "a public nature," all who have understanding to comprehend, and candour to acknowledge the obvious meaning of words, must confess; inasmuch as the compensation to be made to the *Pennsylvania claimants* related to the whole State, and affected all its members; and no one will have the effrontery to say, that any "occasion of sudden necessity" had occurred for dispensing with the express provision of the constitution.

This wanton precipitation in passing the bill, is inconsistent with its preamble, in which one motive assigned for the repeal of the confirming law is, that it was passed hastily, and without due consideration had, and another contradiction equally glaring is, that after stating that the said act divested many citizens of this State of their lands, without their consent, *and without making them any just compensation*, it assigns as a reason for the repeal, that the carrying said act into effect would impose a grievous burthen on the good citizens of this State, to *make compensation* to those who would thereby be divested of their property.

The constitution further declares that "for the more perfect satisfaction of the public the reasons and motives for making laws shall be fully and clearly expressed in the preambles." Whatever might be the reasons and motives for passing the bill, the facts assumed in the preamble, but which were neither proved nor admitted, seem to have been intended to give colour to a proceeding which stood in need of it, if not to bring reproach on a former House, equally respectable at least with the present one for wisdom and virtue.

2d. Because the House had no proper evidence in support of the allegations contained in the preamble, and refused to inquire either in the House or in committee of the whole House, whether they were true or not. In a measure highly interesting to the honour dignity and justice of the State, in a measure consigning to misery and ruin many hundred families, who had trusted to its good faith; and calculated to bring severe and merited reproach on a former Assembly, a decent regard for the opinions of men should have induced the House to have heard the evidence which was called for, so as to give some semblance of justice to their proceedings. This was nevertheless refused, and an example set for preferring rumour to facts, assertions to proof, and conjecture to full and complete information. A solemn vote precluded probing inquiry, and then the House assuming facts, assigned them as grounds for repealing a law founded in wisdom, justice and sound policy. If this proceeding is not a mockery of justice, and satire on the House, it must be admitted to be of the most dangerous example.

3d. Because the confirming act was founded in *wisdom and sound policy*, and the allegations in the preamble to the bill repealing it, that "it was unconstitutional, and of the most dangerous consequences;" and that "the reasons set forth in the preamble of the said act, do not appear sufficient to warrant any legislative interference," are without foundation.

The *salus populi* or safety of the people, is the supreme law of the land, to which all inferior rights and regulations must yield. They originate from and are auxiliary to society, and may, on reasonable compensation made, be lawfully resumed, whenever the great ends thereof require it, *for the accomplishment of some great good, or to arrest an impending evil*. These important truths result from the very nature of society, and the first principles of government. They are sanctioned by the principles of individuals, and the practice of nations. They are confirmed in abundant instances by our municipal laws, and recognized by our bill of rights. The Legislature who enacted that law were neither so weak nor so wicked, as men less informed and not more virtuous, have supposed them to have been. The state of the Commonwealth called for the system which they adopted, and had a policy equally just and wise been since pursued, the faith of *Pennsylvania* would not have been broken, or her honour tainted by her own sons.

If the House had designed to inquire for themselves of witnesses at the bar, or in committee of the whole, instead of trusting to others, the truth might have appeared on our journals, and a curious spectacle would have been exhibited by contrasting it with the preamble of the bill. But the hurry with which they charged a former House with proceeding "hastily and without due consideration had," not admitting of the necessary inquiries, has exposed them to that censure which has been wrongfully imputed to others. The conduct of the Legislature in November 1787, when the same business came before them, was very different. Instead of listening to idle rumours, they called witnesses to their bar, and examined for themselves. They had written documents laid before them, and became well acquainted with all the facts which led to the quieting act, as well as with its effects. The charter boundaries of Pennsylvania and Connecticut were supposed to clash, and had long been contested before and since the revolution. Each asserted her claim to the country at and about Wyoming, and manifested a resolution to maintain them at every hazard. The *Connecticut claimants* settled themselves on the lands, under grants from the *Susquehanna Company*, and the patronage of *Connecticut*. They maintained and cultivated their lands, until the decree of Trenton in 1782 That decree settled the rights of soil and territory, as between the contending States, in favour of *Pennsylvania*, but it neither did nor possibly could affect the private rights of individuals. The judges who pronounced that decree, nevertheless became well acquainted with the nature of the settlements, and the equity resulting from them. Under the impressions made thereby, they wrote a letter to the Executive authority of *Pennsylvania*, which is perhaps lost, but the following account of it has been given by one of the same judges in a subsequent letter.

"We had many strong reasons for writing the letter to the President of *Pennsylvania* We were fully acquainted with the circumstances of the New England settlers. We knew that many of them had honestly paid for their possessions; that they verily believed the title under which they claimed to be perfectly good; that they had cleared, built upon, and improved the land; that in doing this they had encountered many dangers, and suffered innumerable hardships; and beyond all these things, and what cannot be estimated, many of their nearest connexions had spilt their blood in defence of their possessions.

"Thus circumstanced it was manifest that they had become enthusiastic for the land; that the reasoning of legislators and statesmen would have but little weight with them; that if the State should attempt to dispossess them, they would become desperate, and a civil war would be the consequence. On the contrary, if the State should quiet them in their possessions, they would become peaceable good citizens, and that the State could compensate those who held the *Pennsylvania* title, by giving them an equivalent in lands or money, at a less expense than that of dispossessing the New England settlers. That therefore the interest, the humanity, and the policy of the State, would lead them to adopt the measures that we recommended. The letter bore no official authority. We subscribed it as private citizens. Nevertheless we did conceive that it would have some weight, as it must be apparent that our means of information have been better than those of any other persons who were disinterested."

A different policy from that which had been so warmly recommended was adopted by Pennsylvania. She levied troops, and marched them into the hapless country, dispossessed the settlers without any trial of their rights. The horrors of war were renewed, and from the supposed inclemency of our measures, or some other cause, a dangerous confederacy was forming against us. The *Connecticut claimants* were a bold and hardy race of men, inured to toils and trained to arms. Their enrolled militia, between the ages of eighteen and fifty-eight, amounted to 685, exclusive of those of some townships, whose returns had not come to hand. Besides these, it appears that there were many able bodied men among them, not between those ages, but who were capable of being brought into action to great advantage, as occasion might call for it. Many fruitless efforts had been made by *Pennsylvania*, at the expense of some blood and much treasure, to subdue the country, and establish her authority within it; but experience had evinced that the inhabitants, when assailed by a superior force, only retreated to the fastnesses of a rugged country, till that force was removed. Thus situated, they had for many years there kept *Pennsylvania* at bay, or made momentary retreats as circumstances dictated. At the time of passing the act, the affairs of that country had assumed a very different and still more menacing aspect.

The number of settlers was increasing. The *Susquehanna Company*, under whom they held, was composed of influential characters in the States of *Connecticut and New York*. The efforts of *Pennsylvania* after the decree of *Trenton*, to dispossess the settlers by an armed force, united that company in a resolution to support them. They offered a bounty of two hundred acres of land, to every able bodied man who would settle among them. Many had already accepted of these terms of enlistment, and marched to the land of conflict. The settlers were emigrants from *Connecticut*, where their friends, connexions and adherents, remained. The Legislature of *Connecticut*, their parent State, which had by her public acts countenanced the forming of that settlement, were, to use the words of some of the witnesses. in 'a flame the moment they heard of the conduct of *Pennsylvania*, which they branded with the epithets of "cruel and unjust;" and with much difficulty the cooler members abated their resentment.

But danger did not threaten from these quarters only, and *Pennsylvania* had perhaps still more to apprehend from another. It was made appear at the bar of the House, and if inquiry had not been precluded, it might have appeared again, that shortly before the passing of the act, *Col. Ethan Allen*, one of the principal founders of Vermont, had been at Wyoming, and joined in the plan of erecting a new State, and that he and his followers were to be rewarded by a share of the lands for their services; that he had returned home, as was probable from circumstances, with the view of collecting his strength to carry this plan into execution. It would not have become *Pennsylvania* at any time, much less in her then feeble and distracted state, to behold such a dangerous combination with indifference, or to be inattentive to the breaking of it.

Nor was this all; for it appeared from very respectable evidence given at the bar, that a gentleman of high rank in the late army, had at the same time resolved on marching with a large train of his followers to *Wyoming*, and after settling there, to share one common fate with those who had alone baffled *Pennsylvania* in all her attempts to expel them. And it is equally certain, that as the insurrection in *Massachusetts* had just been quelled, there was too much reason to fear, that the ringleaders and their followers might take the same course. What was it but this that induced *Pennsylvania* to offer additional rewards for apprehending them? Whether a mistaken policy on the part of *Pennsylvania*, prejudice against her, or the feelings of humanity in favour of devoted victims, led to these confederacies, is not now material, since they did exist, and her faith was plighted by solemn contract in order to break them.

Thus situated, did sound policy call for girding on the sword against numerous bands of gathering foes, or for the adoption of those lenient but honourable measures, which had been so warmly recommended by disinterested and well informed judges. *Pennsylvania* remembered that the *Connecticut* claimants, had alone and unsupported for many years baffled all her exertions to establish her authority among them. She had seen them increasing in numbers and prowess, amid all their difficulties. She saw dangerous combinations formed and forming against her. She saw herself but just emerged from a long, a burthensome and a bloody war. She saw her treasures exhausted, and her citizens overburthened with taxes. She saw general reluctance, and sometimes a refusal in her militia, to risk their lives in what was considered by some as the quarrel of individuals about their speculations in lands. By party broils she was enervated at home, and from the prejudice which had been excited by her preferring arms to the lenient, but dignified measures which had been recommended after the decree at *Trenton*, she had little to hope and much to fear from abroad. Political exigencies determined her choice, and called for immediate action. A small delay might have plunged her into a long and expensive war, or obliged her to retreat with the loss of reputation. For these reasons, the act appears to have been founded in wisdom, justice and sound policy, and if the epithets now bestowed upon it apply at all, it must be to the bill for its repeal.

4th. Because the act hath, so far as depended on the *Connecticut claimants* had the effects proposed, and the allegations to the contrary, in the preamble to the bill for its repeal, are unfounded. *It was incontestibly proved on a former occasion, at the bar of the House*, that the Connecticut claimants whose rights had been acquired previous to the decree at Trenton, and who were the only persons included in the act, were perfectly satisfied therewith, and that all of them, except six or eight, had submitted to the government and laws of Pennsylvania ; that all those who had been disposed to join them, had abandoned their design, except the half-share men, who had come among them since the decree at Trenton, and who were not included in the act. These being too insignificant to make any formidable opposition, have either abandoned the settlement, or, encouraged by the wavering conduct of *Pennsylvania*, remain ready to renew their mischiefs, if by her breach of faith, others should be induced to join them.

Hence the most salutary effects have been derived from the law ; and war, perhaps more expensive than the compensation to have been made, was avoided ; peace and tranquillity were restored, or rather took place for the first time. The government and laws of *Pennsylvania* have been established and had their free operation, and allies, formidable from their numbers and situation, abandoned their hostile views.

Thus the great objects which the Legislature had in view, in passing the Confirming Law, have really been accomplished. They were principally these.—1st. To conciliate the mind of those *Claimants* ; to induce them to relinquish their designs of absolutely rejecting the jurisdiction of this State, and in conjunction with others who had associated, and were preparing to associate with them, of erecting a new and independent State in that and the adjacent country. 2d. To put an end to the distresses, expense and bloodshed, which, during a series of years had attended this dispute ; and to prevent the still more serious evils of a civil war, which not only a contrary policy, but a delay of that salutary confirmation were likely to produce ; the measures which those people were then pursuing having a direct tendency to that fatal issue. 3d. A further object of that law was, that by having their lands confirmed to them, those people might be induced not only to relinquish the designs already mentioned, but to submit to the government, and become useful as well as peaceable citizens of this State. 4th. Another object and it was an object of high importance, was to render practicable the settlement of an extensive adjacent country, to which the contention about the Wyoming lands had for many years proved a fatal bar. These were the great objects of the Confirming Law ; these were the effects proposed and expected to result from it ; and the event has justified the expectation. The adjacent country is in a train of settlement, and if the county of *Luzerne* itself has not greatly increased in population and improvement, it is to be attributed to the long suspension of the Confirming Law.

5th. Because the preamble contains most indecent and unwarrantable reflections on the Assembly, by which the Confirming Law was enacted. That Assembly was impressed with the weighty considerations above stated ; considerations which received additional force from many collateral circumstances, which a retrospect to the numerous mischiefs which had flowed from the dispute about the Wyoming lands could not fail to bring to remembrance. That Assembly must have recollected the many fruitless attempts of government to extend its jurisdiction over that country, and have seen that the obstacles to it were daily increasing. They saw that there was but this alternative, either to confirm the lands to the old *Connecticut* settlers, or immediately to raise a military force, with the hope of subduing them. They chose the former, and disinterested men of sound judgment, approved the choice. It is well known that at the time when that law passed the union of these States was but a rope of sand ; that the people of Wyoming, amidst many sufferings and oppressions, received countenance from their parent State, *Connecticut* ; that they had numerous and interested connexions in that State ; and that under such circumstances, a war commenced against the Wyoming settlers might have drawn after it very serious consequences. A Legislature passing the Confirming Law, for such reasons and under such impressions, ought not to be charged with doing it hastily and without due consideration. It was a measure which we have seen had been recommended to the State by men to whose judgment, in this case, the highest deference was due, and whose discernment and impartiality ought not to be impeached by this House. And various transactions of the Legislature, at different periods, before the Confirming Law was made, clearly manifest their opinion that some equitable provision ought to be made for the *Connecticut Claimants*, who had settled in that country before the decree at Trenton, and for the widows and children of such as had fallen, (and a multitude of them *had fallen*,) fighting against the savages. A law passed under such circumstances cannot justly be called unconstitutional. At the time when the Confirming Law was passed, the General Assembly had the exclusive right to judge of its expediency, propriety and necessity; and even admitting, (which we do not admit) that the Assembly had on those points formed an erroneous judgment; yet so far as its grants or engagements extended, they are irrevocably binding on the State, and cannot be canceled without the consent of those to or with whom they were made.

6th. Because all the acts of the Legislature which appear on their journals since the Confirming Law was passed, manifest an intention, ultimately, to establish the claim of the *Connecticut Claimants*. When accidental causes had rendered it impossible for all of them to exhibit their claims within the time prescribed by the Confirming Law, the power of the Commissioners was suspended by a law made for that purpose; lest by a partial establishment of claims, (which could apply only to such as they had an opportunity to receive and examine,) much mischief and confusion should arise. But the suspension of a law is in its nature only a temporary measure; and in this case it was expressly declared to be only until the Legislature should make further provisions and regulations in the premises. At the same time a bill was introduced, adopted, and published for consideration, for the purpose of granting the seventeen towns entire to the *Connecticut Claimants*; a grant that there is sufficient evidence to show would greatly have exceeded the claims which could have been admitted under the Confirming Law. The next day a resolve was passed, to authorize the Supreme Executive Council to take proper measures for ascertaining the quantity and value of the land claimed by *Pennsylvania* owners, to be reported at the next Session, "that the House might the better be enabled to decide upon the compensation to be made them." All these transactions took place long after the Confirming Law had been enacted, and they will admit of but one or two meanings:—Either that the Legislature still judged it proper and necessary substantially to carry the Confirming Law into execution, and meant eventually to do it; or, that the cogent reasons which induced the passing of it, still continued in such force, that a repeal of it would have been dangerous, and therefore, that the Suspending Law, the bill for granting the seventeen towns entire, and the resolution preparatory to the making compensation to the *Pennsylvania Claimants* were necessary to excite in the *Connecticut Settlers* an expectation of a final establishment of their claims, to soothe and keep them quiet, to prevent any accession of force, and to detach from them their new associates; but that when these views should be accomplished, and when it should be found that the jurisdiction of the Commonwealth was completely established in Luzerne county, the Confirming Law should be repealed. But if some, by their conduct in this business are disposed to impute such base and dishonorable motives to a former Legislature, we are not. The obvious construction of those public acts forbids the suspicion.

7th. Because the grants of land solemnly made by the Confirming Law to the *Connecticut Claimants*, assure to them effective titles, and the property thereby vested in them cannot be taken from them, without providing for them a complete compensation. But such compensation would far exceed that which has been engaged to the *Pennsylvania Claimants:* Therefore, if the mere *interest* of the State be regarded, the Confirming Law ought not to be repealed. The journals and files of the Legislature clearly show that the Assembly which enacted the law for confirming to the *Connecticut Claimants* the lands by them claimed in the county of *Luzerne*, were not ignorant of the magnitude of her grant.

The petition of those claimants explicitly states, that their claims extended through seventeen towns generally of five miles square, and to some detached lots, and the Committee on that petition reported to the Assembly that the petition was for entire and extensive tracts.

In addition to this, the law by relative terms refers to the petition; is founded upon and confined to it; and as the claims are there stated, it is but a trifling with words to say, that "The Legislature had not proper information of the magnitude of the grant."

8th. Because, if we should say that at the time the Confirming Law was enacted, there did not exist sufficient reasons for passing it; if we should declare in the words of the preamble of the repealing law, "that it was hastily passed without due consideration;" it would be to accuse that Legislature of criminal improvidence, and inattention to their duty. But no subsequent Legislature can be justified in doing this, unless (which is impossible) they can see and feel all those reasons and impressions under which the law originated.

9th. Because, if the repealing law could possibly produce the effect intended by its supporters, it will nevertheless bring an indelible disgrace on the State. It will show that not honour and justice, but mere mercenary views, governed its conduct; that it held itself bound by its contracts, only when a fulfilment of them coincided with its interests; and that though by its laws, it will compel the honest performance of disadvantageous contracts, entered into by individual citizens, yet in its own case, setting itself above the law, it will pay no regard to them.

10th. Because the formal repeal of the Confirming Law, while it prostrates the faith, honour and dignity of the State, will not procure any equivalent, if, in the nature of things, there can be any possible equivalent for the sacrifice of those great principles of society and government; because the repeal, itself, will be nugatory, for it is an infraction of the laws of nations, a violation of the Constitution of the United States, an *ex post facto* law, a law violating the obligation of a solemn public contract, and the courts of the United States must pronounce it to be of no effect. Hence the folly of the repeal will equal its injustice; for there will not remain even the paltry consideration of *interest* to console the State for the loss of its honour, dignity and faith. It is too probable that the mischiefs resulting from the measure may be serious in their nature and of long continuance. Those who were appeased by a good policy, will not be appeased by a faithless one; and those who formerly joined them, from motives of humanity, may do it again, from the additional one of our having added treachery to violence. Whatever may be the event, we dissent from the vote passing the bill into a law, and desire that our reasons may be recorded in justification of our conduct, and for the information of our constituents.

WILLIAM LEWIS,
JOHN NEVIL,
OBADIAH GORE,
SAMUEL ASHMEAD,
HENRY DENNY.

OPINION.

"Judge Brackenridge, in Carkhuff versus Anderson, (Binney's Reports, Vol. iii, page 10.) "The appearance of *right* which the Susquehanna Company, a people of Connecticut, had to advance a claim to this district of country, is in my mind in considering the case before me. I do not view them in the light of trespassers, with a full knowledge of their want of title. At all events, the bulk of them do not appear to have been apprised of their want of title, and I make a great distinction between trespassers, knowing, or having good reason to know, their defect of title, and such as may reasonably be supposed to be ignorant of what they are about.

"Before the decree of Trenton, the most intelligent and the best informed, might have been led to believe that the part of the country in question *was settled under* a GOOD TITLE from the State of Connecticut."

"But" In favour of those who had settled under the idea of a good title, and with an expectation of enjoying the land which they were *improving* and *defending*, at a great risk and with much loss, from the *common enemy during the Revolutionary war*, THERE IS A CLAIM which ought not wholly to be disregarded. I do not call it a right, but a claim, on the ground of moral obligation."

LETTER XXIX.

Our readers have been apprized that a part of the people of Westmoreland were located on the Lackawaxen, [now Wayne county,] and that it was designated in the ancient records as the "Lackawa" settlement. To Warren J. Woodward, Esq., I am indebted for the interesting details which follow.

Separated by many miles of wilderness and mountain, although under the same government, and the people coming to Wilkesbarre to Courts and Elections, the intercourse could not be frequent, and distance divided their interests and their fortunes. The memoir will be found full of interest, rescues from oblivion fast fading facts, and adds valuable matter to the history of Wyoming, and the early settlements in north-eastern Pennsylvania.

THE WALLENPAUPACK.

A tract of country lying upon the Wallenpaupack creek, and contained in what is now Palmyra township, Pike county, was settled at the time of the emigration of the Wyoming pioneers from Connecticut. The details that are subjoined, contain the entire history of its settlement, which tradition has preserved.

In 1752, the county of Northampton was erected. Of this county, the country along the Wallenpaupack was a part. Whether Connecticut, at the time of the emigration, claimed the ownership of, and civil jurisdiction over this colony, I have had no means of ascertaining.

A warrant was issued out of the Proprietary Office, 25th November, 1748, under which a tract of land upon the Wallenpaupack creek, containing 12,150 acres, was surveyed 14th October, 1751, "for the use of the Proprietaries of Pennsylvania," called "The Wallenpaupack Manor." 21st February, 1793, this manor was conveyed to the Hon. James Wilson, who gave mortgage to John Penn, elder, and John Penn, younger, the vendors. In 1804, when this part of Northampton had become Wayne county,* the mortgage of Judge Wilson was foreclosed, and the land purchased by Samuel Sitgreaves, of Easton, in trust for the Penn heirs. The settlers at that time residing on the manor, bought the land of Sitgreaves, who made to them the first title that was ever in the hands of the actual occupants of the land.

Some time between the years 1750 and 1760, a family, named Carter, settled upon the Wallenpaupack creek. This is supposed to have been the first white family that ever visited the neighborhood. The spot upon which the house was built is in view of the road leading from Sterling, (☞ this is the road running parallel with the Wallenpaupack, the whole extent of the settlement) in Wayne county, to the Milford and Owego turnpike, seven miles southwest from Wilsonville. The old Indian path, from Cochecton to Wyoming, crossed the Wallenpaupack about thirty rods below the house of the Carters. During the French and Indian war, which commenced in 1756, the members of the family were all murdered, and the house was burnt by a tribe of Indians in the service of the French. When the emigrants from Connecticut arrived on the banks of the Wallenpaupack, the chimney of the house and a stone oven alone were standing.

When the first Wyoming emigrants from Connecticut reached the Wallenpaupack, the main body halted, and some pioneers were sent forward in a westerly direction to procure intelligence of the position of the country on the Susquehanna. The pioneers followed the Indian path before alluded to, leading from Cochecton in New York, across the Lechawaxen, to the point on the Wallenpaupack below the Carter house, where there was an "Indian clearing," and thence to the "Indian clearings" on the Susquehanna. This path crossed "Cobb's mountain." The pioneers attained the summit, from which the Susquehanna was in view, in the evening, and built up a large fire to indicate to the settlers the point to which they should direct their course. The next morning the emigrants commenced their journey, building their road as they proceeded. That road, leaving the Sterling road before mentioned about a mile down the creek below the site of the Carter house, is the one which is now constantly traveled between Wilkesbarre and Milford. It is said to have been most judiciously located. The point on which the fire

---

* Wayne county was erected in 1798. 3 *Smith's laws*, 316.

Pike county, in which all that was the Wallenpaupack Manor is now contained, was erected in 1814. 6 *Smith's Laws*, 190.

was built on Cobb's mountain, was near the present residence of John Cobb, Esq., and is pointed out by the people residing on the Wallenpaupack to the present time.

At some period, shortly before the revolutionary war, a settlement was commenced at Milford, on the Delaware, now the capital of Pike county. The settlers were all Pennsylvanians. This was the only inhabited part of what are now Wayne and Pike counties, except the Connecticut colony planted on the Wallenpaupack. The emigrants to the latter left Connecticut in 1774. Within a year after their arrival, two townships were erected under the names of Lackaway and Bozrah. The former was all in the "Wallenpaupack Manor;" the latter lay further up the creek, and but a small, if any, part of it was included in the Pennsylvania Proprietary warrant. The original settlers all located themselves in the township of Lackaway. This township was surveyed into farms, and each emigrant had one of them alloted to him. Each lot extended, in uniform width, back from the creek to the mountain, the distance of a mile. The width of the several lots was graduated by the quality of the bottom land lying along the creek. The settlement extended four miles and a half along the creek. The farms still remain of the same size as originally fixed, and with two exceptions, they still remain in the possession of the descendants of the settlers in 1774.

The names of the first emigrants, so far as they are remembered by the present residents upon the Wallenpaupack, were Uriah Chapman, Esq.,* Capt. Zebulon Parrish, Capt. Eliab Varnum, Nathaniel Gates, Zadock Killam, Ephraim Killam, Jacob Kimble,* Enos Woodward,* Isaac Parrish,* John Killam, Hezekiah Bingham,* John Ansley,* Elijah Winters, John Pellet, Sr., John Pellet, Jr., Abel Kimble, and Walter Kimble, all of whom returned to the settlement after the revolution: Joshua Varnum, who was killed by the Indians during the war; Doctor Amos Parks, who moved to Goshen, in Orange county, New York, between 1774 and 1778; Silas Parks,*

---

* It appears from the Westmoreland Records, March 1, 1774, "That Isaac Parrish was chosen tithing man; Silas Parks, sealer of weights and measures; Hezekiah Bingham, grand juror; Uriah Chapman, lister, [assessor]; John Ansley, surveyor of highways; Silas Parks, selectman.

Jacob Kimball was chosen tithing man, December, 1775.

Capt. Zebulon Parrish was elected tithing man, December 13th, 1776; at which election Enos Woodward was chosen one of the grand jurors, [the ancestor of the Hon. G. W. Woodward, and of my excellent young friend to whom I am indebted for this memoir.]

It therefore appears that the "Lackawa" settlement was not merely within the territorial limits of Westmoreland, but united in jurisdiction; taking part in the Government, and attending the elections at Wilkesbarre.

who had two sons, one, Moses, afterwards a clergyman in New Jersey, and Silas, who was a fifer in Capt. Dethic Hewit's company, and was killed in the battle of Wyoming, never returned after the revolution; David Gates, Jonathan Haskell, William Pellet, Charles Forsyth, Roger Clark, —— Strong, James Dye, Nathaniel Washburne, Joseph Washburne, —— Fry, who was the schoolmaster of the settlement, and James Hallet, none of whom returned to the Wallenpaupack after the flight in 1778; Jesper Edwards and Reuben Jones, who were taken prisoners by the Indians in the course of the war of the revolution.

One of the first labours of the settlers after their emigration was the erection of a fort. This fort, which was probably somewhat primitive in its construction, was a field containing about an acre, surrounded by a trench, into which upright pieces of hewed timber were firmly fixed. The spot was selected from the circumstance of its containing a living spring. The fort was erected on the eastern side of the Sterling road, almost immediately opposite the point where the road leading through Salem, over Cobb's mountain, and along the Lackawanna to the Wyoming settlements, called the "Old Wyoming road," branches off from the Sterling road. It is six miles southwest from the hamlet now marked on the maps as Wilsonville. Within the enclosed space was a block-house, also built of squared pieces of hewed timber, upon the top of which was a sentry-box, made bullet-proof. There was, beside, a guard-house standing just east of the block-house. The defences were so constructed that a rifle ball fired from the high ground on the east into the fort, would strike the palisades on the opposite side above a man's head. After the rumours of the Indian troubles on the Susquehanna reached the Wallenpaupack, the settlers constantly spent the night in the fort. The spring, whose existence and situation governed the colonists in their selection of a stronghold, still bubbles by the way side, and nothing but a pile of loose stones indicates to the traveler the formidable neighborhood to which it has been exposed.

Once fixed in their new abode, and prepared to defend themselves from the incursions of the savages, the emigrants agreed upon the form of their civil, military and ecclesiastical form of government. Silas Parks was the first Justice of Peace, in the settlement. He brought a commission, it is supposed, with him from Connecticut. His views of magisterial dignity and decorum were, however, somewhat more liberal than those which the people among whom he administered justice, entertained. It was discovered that he played cards. The intelligence was immediately forwarded to Connecticut, and he was superseded; Uriah Chapman* being appointed in his place.* The settlers elected a constable, and this office was administered by Mr. John Killam, during, probably, the whole of the time between the emigration and 1778. Capt. Zebulon Parrish, was the tithing man of the settlement. [From the etymology of this word, and from its meaning in the English law, I should think there must have been three tithing men, as there were near thirty families; but I was able to learn the name of no other than Capt. Parrish.]

Capt. Eliab Varnum, had the command of the troops of the colony. Jonathan Haskell was lieutenant, and Elijah Winters, ensign.

The population was generally composed of Presbyterians. On the Sabbath the whole settlement was collected together, when a sermon was read. The observance of the Lord's Day was rigidly enforced, and the morality and decorum of the settlers carefully insisted upon.

The most perfect equality existed thoughout the settlement as to rights, privileges and property. The lands were disposed of, it is believed, by lot. The title of each man to his land was the consent, and the proof of his title was the memory, of his neighbours. Until 1804, when the land was purchased at sheriff's sale, by Mr. Sitgreaves, no deed had been held by an occupant for a single acre.

A saw-mill was built upon a creek flowing into the Wallenpaupack, about a mile from the latter. The mouth of this creek is a mile and a quarter above the site of the fort. The mill was burnt by the Indians in 1779.

During the years 1777 and 1778, the settlers upon the Wallenpaupack were harassed and disturbed by some Indians who had their head-quarters at Cochecton, on the eastern side of the Delaware river, now in Sullivan county, New York, and a gang of tories who infested that neighborhood. Brant† had given orders to the Indians under his control, not to molest the Wallenpaupack. Those, therefore, by whom the settlement was plundered, were a band of vaga-

---

* " I tell the tale as 'twas told to me." During the whole of my conversations with Esquire Killam, and my other informants, one of whom was a daughter of Esquire Chapman, now eighty-five years old, (Mrs. Sybil Kimble) I endeavored to procure some intelligence as to the character and extent of the jurisdiction of Connecticut. I think she had no jurisdiction whatever, *at first.*

† He gave a passport to one Jenkins, a collector of taxes in Wyoming, who was taken prisoner on the Wyalusing, in which he stated that the Wallenpaupack people "had always been kind to the Indians."

bond scamps, outcasts from all the recognised tribes, with no associates except the skinners and cow-boys of New York.

In 1777, a body of men, eighteen in number, were seen lurking in the "Great Swamp," as the bottom land along the Wallenpaupack was called. They were discovered by a young girl, a daughter of Nathaniel Gates,* (a serjeant in Dethic Hewet's company, and a survivor of the Wyoming massacre,) as she was looking for some cows. She gave notice to the officer in command of the troops, Lieut. Jonathan Haskell, and he collected the force of the settlement, and succeeded in capturing the whole body. They proved to be tories, who had deserted from the American army. Lieut. Haskell conducted them to Hartford, where they were confined.† It is supposed that the Lieutenant's journey was a profitable one, for whereas he had but one cow when he went to Hartford, he had five cows when he returned. (So says Mrs. Bennett.)

On the night of the 3d of July, 1778, the officers in command, to try the temper of the troops, caused a false alarm of danger to be made. The moveables of the settlement were hurried into the fort. The whole force of the colony was collected, and the arms and ammunition prepared for service. While the noise and clamour, which were the consequence of the alarm, were going on, a body of sixty Indians and tories, from the neighborhood of Cochecton, approached from the direction of Wilsonville to within half a mile of the fort. They told some prisoners, afterwards captured, that their object was to carry off the cattle belonging to the settlement. The preparations at the fort, however, induced them to believe that the New York Indians, under Brant, had attacked the settlement. And as the orders were distinct from Brant, that they should not interfere with the Wallenpaupack; and feeling that their presence would be unwelcome to the Susquehanna Indians, they retreated to the Lechawaxen, four or five miles above the mouth of the Wallenpaupack, burning a gristmill built by Joseph Washburne, at what is now Wilsonville.

Among these tories were two, named Bryant McKean and Hugh Jones. From the traditions that have come down to us, McKean appears to have been one of the very worst of the very bad class of men to which he belonged. Both he and Jones were at one time

---

* This girl afterward married Stephen Bennett. I saw her on the 5th of May, 1842. She was seventy-eight years of age. She retains a singularly distinct recollection of minute details and is in perfect health.

† About this time, probably, the government of Connecticut began to exert a control over the Wallenpaupack settlement.

arrested by Ensign Elijah Winters upon a suspicion of their connexion with the Cochecton Indians, and brought before the authorities of the Wallenpaupack settlement. No satisfactory proof of their guilt, however, appearing, they were discharged. Some time during the last years of the war of the revolution, McKean, who had quarrelled with one of his neighbours, one night procured the Indians with whom he was connected, to burn his house and murder his family. He described the situation and appearance of the house, informing the Indians that his neighbour lived upon the opposite side of a small stream from himself. The Indians proceeded to do his bidding, but in doing it, they made a mistake, and murdered the family and burnt the house of McKean himself. For years after the war, the old tory was traversing the towns in the neighborhood, seeking sympathy for his misfortunes and soliciting charity from the humane, carrying with him a statement of his calamities, only omitting the single fact that they were calamities of his own procuring.

On the 3rd of July, 1778, the Wyoming tragedy was enacted. A young man by the name of Hammond, who escaped from the Indians, brought the news the next afternoon to the Wallenpaupack. The inhabitants, alarmed by the probably exaggerated account they received of the number and ferocity of the enemy, prepared for immediate flight. Preparations were hastily made, and before sunset on the fourth of July the settlers were on their way to the Delaware river. A number of the women and children were so sick that they had to be carried in carts. They were put on beds placed in the bottom of the carts, and in that situation traveled the whole night and all the next day. The next night, 5th July, the settlers arrived at a point three miles above Milford, upon the "old Wyoming road." Here they intended to pass the night. Shortly after they halted, they heard, however, that the Indians, (probably the Cochecton gang) were in pursuit of them, and they were compelled again to commence their march, and did not stop until they had reached the eastern bank of the Delaware. The cattle belonging to the settlement and such moveable articles as were portable, were carried away. All that was left fell into the hands of the Cochecton Indians and cow-boys.

When the news of the Wyoming massacre was received in the settlement, Captain Zebulon Parrish, his son Jasper, and Stephen Kimble, a son of one of the settlers, went down on horseback, each with a led horse, to the Lechawaxen, a short distance above the mouth of the Wallenpaupack, for the purpose of giving notice of the danger to some families who resided on the Lechawaxen. The names of the settlers were Benjamin Haynes, David Ford, and James Hough. They were Pennsylvanians, who had located themselves upon the river, with a view to support themselves by the game in the neighborhood. When the three men from the upper settlement were near the mouth of the Wallenpaupack, they were called to by the same body of tories and Indians who had long been prowling about the country, who told them that the Susquehanna Indians had attacked and captured the inhabitants of the settlement, and invited them to cross the creek and surrender themselves prisoners, threatening to fire upon them if they did not do so, and assuring them of kind treatment if the invitation should be accepted. The men crossed the creek and surrendered themselves. Five of the horses fell into the hands of the Indians. One horse escaped and was recovered by the settlers in their retreat to the Delaware.

The three men were carried into the State of New York, and retained prisoners until the close of the revolutionary war. After peace was made Capt. Parrish returned to his family. Jesper, his son, was soon after appointed Indian interpreter by the authorities of the United States, being employed in the intercourse of the Government with the Six Nations. He remained in that capacity until the time of his death. He lived near Canandaigua. Stephen Kimble died a prisoner among the Indians.

Stephen Parrish, or " Doctor Parrish," as he was called, another son of the Captain, and one of the settlers named Ruben Jones, were also taken prisoners about the time of the flight from the Wallenpaupack. Stephen was a weak, feeble man, and while a prisoner was taught the mysteries of the Indian materia medica. He returned after the war and resided with his family until 1818, when he removed to the State of New York, and died near Canandaigua. He was learned in the herbs and charms that constituted the scientific knowledge of the aboriginal Doctor. Ruben Jones returned also, and died in Wayne county thirty years ago.

In their retreat from the Wallenpaupack, most of the settlers fled to Orange county, in the State of New York, where they remained until the close of the war. Some few families went back to Connecticut, and one or two settled down on the Delaware a few miles above Milford. Many of the young men had previously enlisted in the American army. Ephraim Killam, son of Zadock Killam, and Abel Kimble, son of Jacob Kimble, were in the battle that led to the retreat of General Washington from Long Island.

In August, 1778, four young men—John Pellet, Junior, Walter Kimble, Charles Forsythe, and Uriah Chapman, Junior, returned to the Wallenpaupack for the purpose of cutting hay. They commenced working at the upper end of the settlement, and had cut all the hay except that on the land of Uriah Chapman, who occupied the farm lowest down the creek. It was in the afternoon. Young Chapman left his work to go to a neighboring spring for water. In going to the spring, he stopped for a moment, and sat, whistling, upon a fence. Thus occupied, an Indian rose from a covert and fired at him. He sprang from the fence towards a sled near him, on which the young men had deposited their guns. As he attempted to raise a gun, he first discovered that he was wounded. The gun dropped from his hand, and he ran for the fort, which at that time was still standing. The other young men had heard the report of the Indian's rifle, but they were at a much greater distance from their arms than the Indians were, and they also fled to the fort for safety. The Indians seized the guns as soon as Chapman sprang from the fence. Young Chapman, although weak from the loss of blood, was able to reach the fort the same night, though some time after the other young men arrived there. The ball fired by the Indian passed through his right arm into his shoulder, and at the time of his death, fifty-one years afterwards, it was found lodged against his back-bone. The Indians did not molest the settlers that night, though they lurked around the fort. The next day the young men left the settlement.

In the spring of 1779, five young men went back to the settlement to make maple sugar. Their names were Ephraim Killam, Jeptha Killam, Silas Killam, Ephraim Kimble and Walter Kimble. They chose for their residence a log house standing upon a point now on the road from Sterling, in Wayne county, to the Milford and Owego Turnpike, seven miles and a half from Wilsonville, and about half a mile southwest from the site of the fort. The fort at this time had been destroyed. A stable was standing seven or eight rods from the house, between it and the river. A day or two after their arrival, when they had tapped some maple trees, and while they were fitting up their house for temporary use, they were again disturbed by the Indians. One evening, two of the young men—Silas Killam and Walter Kimble, were out of the house, the former collecting sap for coffee for breakfast, and the latter shooting ducks, when the Indians suddenly surprised them. Silas Killam, who was nearest the house, immediately ran towards it, some of the Indians pursuing him. He succeeded in reaching the house, when the door was opened for him by his brother Ephraim. As he entered, one of the Indians fired. The ball struck a nail in the door-post, and met such resistance that the ball was shivered to pieces. Some slivers struck Ephraim in the arm. The scars left by the wound were perceptible to the day of his death. Walter Kimble, finding his retreat to the house intercepted by the Indians, ran towards the hills, and commenced a very sudden and expeditious journey to the Delaware. The Indians followed him some distance, but he is said to have been remarkable for capacity to endure fatigue and for speed of foot,* and his pursuers soon abandoned the chase. He had on a pair of loose shoes, so large that he could not retain them on his feet. It snowed during the night, the snow melting nearly as fast as it fell. He was compelled to throw away his shoes, and took a pair of Indian leggins he had on, and bound them around his feet. Thus provided he traveled the whole night. The next morning, about breakfast time, he arrived at the house of his brother Abel, at a place called "Vantyne Kill," a mile above Milford. Mrs. Sybil Kimble, the wife of his brother, who is still living, says she never looked upon a human being presenting an appearance so pitiable and wretched. He had not eaten a morsel in more than twenty-four hours, and he exclaimed, as he entered the house, with tears in his eyes, "the boys are all dead." The boys were not dead, however. Immediately after the Indians had driven Killam into the house, they built up a fire upon the side of the stable opposite the house, and settled themselves down with the evident intention of besieging the whites and starving them out. As the Indians were building their fire, one of them exposed himself in gathering wood and was fired at and wounded in the hip by Ephraim Kimble. Of this wound the Indian afterwards died. In the evening after the savages became still, the young men in the house built up a large fire in the house and left it, getting out of the window. They took their course towards the Delaware. The next morning they crossed the river seven miles below Milford. The house was burned that night. After the peace, all the young men returned to the Wallenpaupack, and all of them resided in Pike county until their

---

* This Walter Kimble is still spoken of as having presented a singularly interesting specimen of the manners of his age. His appearance must have been striking and imposing. He is described as having been a tall, strongly-formed, athletic man, of a dark complexion, grave, even saturine in his disposition, of great vigour of mind and force of character. He had all the virtues of his generation, with probably most of their attendant faults. Resolute, determined, brave, he was uncompromising, obstinate and rash. He died in Ohio.

death, except Walter Kimble and Jeptha Killam. They left large families, and their descendants are among the wealthiest and most respectable citizens of Wayne and Pike counties. No further attempt was made to occupy the Wallenpaupack until the close of the war of the revolution.

In the summer of 1779, Brant at the head of three or four hundred Indians descended the Delaware to the mouth of the Neversink, seven miles above Milford. The depredations committed in the neighborhood aroused the fears of the inhabitants of the lower counties of New York. A force was raised in Orange county and the vicinity, and placed under the command of Colonel Benjamin Tustin. There were four or five hundred men collected, who were armed in the best way the necessity of immediate action permitted. The savages retreated as soon as they learned they were about to be molested, and the whites pursued them. The Indians crossed the Delaware at some point between the mouth of the Neversink and "Butler's Falls," it is supposed about five miles above the former. The New York troops also crossed the river. About three or four miles below the mouth of the Lechawaxen, both parties passed to the eastern side of the Delaware, Brant shortly afterwards turning to the right and ascending a hill on the east, a mile or a mile and a half from the river. The Indians passed over the brow of the hill, and the whites incautiously followed in pursuit. When the militia reached the top, a few Indians were seen in front, but the great body of them had circled round the hill, as their pursuers had ascended, and the first intimation the latter received of the error they had committed, was conveyed by the reports of the rifles of the former upon every side of them. The militia for a time attempted to withstand the assaults of their concealed enemies, and some of the soldiers shielded themselves with breast-works thrown up from the loose stones scattered around them. The top of the hill, however, was completely bare of timber, and the Indians were defended by the trees growing upon its sides. The New York troops were suffering dreadfully, whole companies falling at every fire, while their enemies scarcely lost a man. Finding all efforts to make resistance unavailing, the whites, after the massacre of nearly one-half of their number, commenced their flight. It is supposed that more than two hundred men were killed—among them Colonel Tustin, the Commander. Moses Killam, a settler upon the Wallenpaupack, who died there in 1831, and from whose intelligent and hospitable son, Moses Killam, Esq., the foregoing details have been derived, was in the battle. He collected the stones around him into a sort of temporary breast-work, and he believed that if the same means of defence had been generally and concertedly resorted to, the troops might have been preserved from the catastrophe in which the contest terminated. It is said that the heaps of stones collected by the soldiers still remain undisturbed, to mark the spot were these ill-fated men were sacrificed to the craft of their enemies, and the thoughtlessness and inexperience of their officers. The Delaware and Hudson Canal now passes within little more than a mile of the scene of the battle, which was fought a short distance below a point opposite the point of the Lechawaxen. In 1828 or 1829, the bones of the slaughtered troops were collected by the citizens of Orange County, and conveyed to Goshen, where they were interred.

Major Wood, one of the officers of the Orange county troops, was taken prisoner by the Indians, and carried with them in their retreat to their fastnesses. He was detained even after the close of the revolutionary war, and every effort to escape was rendered fruitless by the vigilance of his captors. He left a wife. His family and his friends received no intelligence of his fate after the battle, and it was supposed he had shared the death of his fellow soldiers. Seven years after his capture he procured his release by some means from the Indians, and returned to his home. The lady's situation was a somewhat delicate one, and the other parties interested seemed to appreciate its delicacy. The matter was compromised in a manner characteristic of the age and country. The old husband and the new bridegroom agreed to submit the arbitrament of their respective claims to the possession of the double wife, to the lady herself. They did so, and the lady chose the Major.

After the close of the revolution the original settlers returned to the Wallenpaupack, and located themselves on the farms first allotted to them. Some of them settled in 1783. With less of danger to encounter than attended their first residence, they suffered much more of hardship. The year of their return the corn crop failed, generally, and the little that was raised had to be pounded into a shape fit for use in mortars constructed of pieces of wood. The flour used in the settlement was carried on the backs of the inhabitants from Milford. The winter of 1783-4, was a very severe one and the snow was very deep, during most of the winter the only mode of getting to and from Milford was upon snow shoes.

From the close of that winter the affairs of the settlement have been prosperous and promising. The population have always been industrious, energetic, hospitable, and honest. They became successful and wealthy. Their descendants have always retained the peculiar features of person and character which distinguished the first settlers. This is partly owing to the isolated situation of the settlement, and to the great age to which most of the inhabitants lived. Mrs. Sybil Kimble, already spoken of, and one of my authorities for the facts I have collected, is now living, at the age of 85 years. Mrs. Bennet, from whom also many of the facts related have been procured, is 78 years of age. Mrs. Mary Woodward, wife of Enos Woodward, died in 1818, aged 87. Jacob Kimble died in 1826, aged 91. His son, Jacob, died in 1834, aged 67. Abel, another of his sons, died in 1832, aged 77. Hezekiah Bingham died in 1811, aged 74. Moses Killam died 1831, aged 72. John Pellet died in 1801, aged 85. John Pellet, Jr. died in 1838, aged 90. Ephriam Killam died in 1836, aged 87. Mrs. Lucretia Woodward, a daughter of Jacob Kimble, died in April last, 1842, aged 67.

LETTER XXX,

AND LAST.

My Dear William:—

The Annals of Wyoming are written. It is confidently hoped the general reader, in pursuit of novelty, may find in the story something of interest to amuse a leisure hour. If the intelligent searcher for truth shall be satisfied that our labours throw some useful rays of light upon the heretofore dark and confused history of Northeastern Pennsylvania, we shall be well pleased.

The severity of labour being over, the last proof but one read, I breathe more freely; and fettered by no rules but my own taste and fancy, I mean to expatiate in this letter with unrestrained freedom. I had some reputation as a paragraph writer and essayist, and stood well generally with the Press; hence, when my work was announced, many praised because they thought "Poor Robert, the Scribe," or "John Harwood," must, of course, write a valuable book. More spoke favorably with the generous purpose of aiding the sale and helping a brother printer to dispose of the productions of his pen to pecuniary advantage. Flattered I was, and grateful I am, for so much kindness; but my morbid sensibility awakens a thousand painful fears, that public expectation, so excited, will demand something that the incidents of Wyoming could not yield; that even the polished pen of Prescott, or the exuberantly gifted Bancroft could not have satisfied. A Puritan settlement, quite limited in numbers and very poor, projected into one of the valleys beyond the mountains, "that look so distant here," and there, for twenty years, enduring an unremitting succession of sufferings. What could be made of it? What could I do, but in a simple manner as possible tell their story—draw a faithful picture?

Then again, and with reason, have I dreaded censure, lest I should be regarded as prejudiced and partial—I plead guilty. My fault, which I did not perceive in my manuscript, is apparent in my printed narrative. My honest purpose was to have been strictly impartial in coloring as well as in fact. But a Yankee, and an Intruder—having resided seventeen years in Wyoming—courted and wedded there—sent early to the Assembly—petted by her rude and hardy woodsmen, like a spoiled child—how *could* I help it, if affection led me, or misled me, to view their cause with partial favour? In truth, no one who did not make it a labour of love, ever could or would have taken the pains I have done, to gather the materials of which my history is composed; and the facts, according to the best of my knowledge, are accurately stated.

But would I do injustice to Pennsylvania? Heaven forbid. A New England man—I avow it—love for the rocky hills and stone-clad valleys of my native Connecticut, the residence of my ancestors for more than two hundred years, can never cease to glow with ardour, while there remains a pulsation in my heart. I am bound to old Norwich by all the ties that hallow the remembrance of childhood—gay with the recollection of a delightful circle of lads and maidens—the sports of the green—the mischiefs of the school—the solemn pleasures of the ever welcome Sabbath—the kindly blessing of our beloved Pastor—a father's affection—a fond mother's tenderness—the sweet regards of sisters and a brother, without the remembrance of a day that was not gilded by sunshine. New England! I love thy stern and manly virtues, that have filled a country—so cold and rugged, that nature seemed to have marked it for desolation—with flourishing towns and populous cities; the abode of industry and intelligence, wealth and refinement; an elevated standard of morals; and where a reverential regard for the worship of HIM, who planted and sustained them, is every where a familiar and cherished sentiment. But do I love Pennsylvania less? Does the bride who leaves the paternal roof to abide with her husband, therefore forget the sweet attachments of home? A Pennsylvanian of choice, ever since in 1799, a lad of nineteen, I came within her borders, every year has added to my regard, founded in reason, for her people, in all the generous virtues that ennoble our nature, are inferior to none on earth. It is impossible to regard the great Founder of our noble Commonwealth without awe, at his sublime virtues—reverence for his profound wisdom—love for his abounding goodness. WASHINGTON, first amidst those who established the Republic! PENN, foremost on the file among the founders of the individual States; in his household came the progenitors of my children. So far from intentionally doing wrong to Pennsylvania, I must be the most ungrateful of beings, treated with so much confidence as I have been, if I would not cheerfully die for her, if necessary. So that if the Wyoming sufferers find in me a somewhat favourer of their side, set it not down for malice.

This I solemnly charge. Let no one who comes after me alter a a single word of the text. If alterations or additions shall be deemed proper, let them be made in notes. I choose that the book should go down to posterity precisely as I leave it.

Our work in no slight degree bears the impression of a Drama of five acts—The introduction and brief preliminary chapter being the Prologue—The Indian story—the first act.

The exhibition of Title—the second act.

The civil war and incidents, including the Plunket invasion, to 1776—the third act.

The tragic events of the revolutionary war to the Trenton decree—the fourth act.

From that period, the second civil war, and mighty scheme to dismember Pennsylvania, up to the establishment of Luzerne, and onward to the cheering and happy compromise—the union—the marriage of the parties—the gloom breaking away—the clouds of sorrow dispersing, and peace and joy taking place of war and woe—the fifth and concluding act.

Prospectively large as is the mass of interesting matter which patient research has accumulated on my hands, I regard it as having more appropriate reference to the history of Luzerne. Neither to interrupt the current of our narrative by too precise a detail, nor to incumber our pages by voluminous documents, I have reserved for the Appendix a variety of what I cannot but consider amusing and instructive anecdotes, facts and incidents, which could not well be omitted, and which will, I doubt not, prove acceptable to the reader.

Though Col. Pickering was pledged to the liberal adjustment of the controversy, and was deeply chagrined at the repeal of the confirming law, he did not remain in Luzerne to see his desired purpose effected; but although elsewhere engaged in affairs of engrossing moment, he never lost sight of the subject, and was efficaciously instrumental in procuring the enactments of the compromising law of 1799.

That he was chosen to represent Luzerne in the Convention which ratified the United States' constitution, has already been stated. Subsequently he was elected to the convention for forming a new State constitution, and his name will be found appended to the beautiful frame of Government adopted in 1790.

When the new Federal Government went into operation, under the auspices of Washington, Col. Pickering was invited to take charge of the Post Office department. Selecting as his Assistant Post Master General, Abraham Bradley, Esq., then, though a very young man, an Associate Judge of the court in the county, he removed to Philadelphia, having sold the Connecticut claim to lands he had bought for £500, to William Ross for £2600, notwithstanding the repeal of the confirming law. Although it would be equally unnecessary and foreign to the rightful purpose of our narrative to trace the life of Col. Pickering with minuteness to its close, I may add, that after serving his country in the various capacities of Post Master General, Secretary of War, and Secretary of State, he removed to Massachusetts his native State, a number of liberal friends having purchased his wild lands and relieved him from pressing pecuniary embarrassments.* From Massachusetts Col. Pickering was sent to the Senate of the United States. During the whole of his life he devoted much attention to agriculture, and the papers of the day were frequently enriched by essays on that most interesting subject, from his pen. Col. Pickering closed his active and honourable life at his farm in Wenham, Massachusetts, January 29, 1829, in the eighty-fourth year of his age.

Col. Franklin, after his return from captivity, submitting to the laws, and giving rein to his strong but honourable ambition, sought and obtained for many years a large share of public favour. In 1792, little more than four years after his incarceration in a Philadelphia prison, and indictment for high treason, there came a commission from his excellency Gov. Mifflin, running thus: "*Reposing special trust* and *confidence* in *your patriotism, integrity* and *ability, etc*," constituting John Franklin High Sheriff of Luzerne.

He was succeeded in that office by his friend William Slocum, for whom he called so earnestly in the extremity of his distress, when arrested by Capt. Erbe. Immediately and frequently afterwards Franklin was chosen member of Assembly, sometimes by a vote of

---

* Considering the exact method and carefulness of Col. Pickering, it is matter of surprise that he was not rich. When at Wilkesbarre, if he lent a neighbour a bag, he was particular to make a minute of it in his day book, and to note its return.

three to one over any opponent. Having removed to his farm, situate on the east bank of the Susquehanna, opposite Tioga Point, keeping himself as he supposed within the limits of the law, he led off strongly as the advocate of the Connecticut claim generally, discountenancing all compromise that did not embrace the "half share men," or recent settlers; as well as those before the Trenton decree. A zealous federalist, wielding a large influence in Luzerne; in the then nearly balanced state of parties in Pennsylvania, he was courted or countenanced by eminent men, and even the heart of his old enemy, Col. Pickering, so far relented, that they "exchanged civilities," that is, it is understood, dined together at the Secretary's table. Whether at Philadelphia, Lancaster or at home, his ever busy pen was in requisition, and he filled the papers with essays upon the Connecticut title. At length, under the intrusion laws he was indicted, but the court dividing in opinion, Judge Yates affirming, Judge Breckenridge denying the constitutionality of the act, the matter slept, and the prosecution was lost sight of from the favorable progress of the compromising law, and the rapid decline of the new claims under the Susquehanna and Delaware Companies. A few months before an election, with great tact Franklin would commence his essays, awaken new and old prejudices and hopes, kindling the spirit of the people to that degree of warmth, that "Col. Franklin *must* go to the Assembly," and he went. Determined to rid themselves of a man so obnoxious, the Legislature enacted a law dividing the county of Luzerne, and setting off a very small part, including the district in which Col. Franklin lived, to Lycoming county. After several efforts one proved successful, and behold the great Yankee leader was chosen a representative from Lycoming county, appeared in triumph at Lancaster, and took his seat, December 1805. As it was his crowning, so it was his closing victory. Age had come with its whitening frost and chilling influence. The warm Saxon blood began to flow languidly, and that eye of fire to gleam with faded lustre; the stalwart frame gave way, and the once powerful arm fell nerveless; but the old gentleman, still revered and beloved, used to give and receive delight, by gathering round him a circle of eager listeners in the village of Athens, where he would recount the eventful stories connected with the early settlement of Wyoming.

John Franklin was born in Canaan, Connecticut in 1749, and in 1828, then more than 78 years old, his iron memory was so retentive, that he would relate with minute accuracy, stating numbers and dates, series of events that had happened half a century before. A vein of sly humour often mingled in his conversation. Giving in testimony before the Court, referring to some transaction that took place about the time of his forcible abduction, he said with much gravity, though a smile lighted up every other countenance, " Having at that time a call on important business to Philadelphia, I had just gone in company with several gentlemen to that city."

He died on the 1st of March, 1831, having attained the great age of 82 years.

Lord Butler succeeded Col. Pickering, as Prothonotary, Clerk of the Quarter Sessions and Orphans' Court, Register and Recorder.

HON. JACOB RUSH, *President.*

OBADIAH GORE,
MATTHIAS HOLLENBACK,
NATHAN DENISON,
JESSE FELL,
} *Associates.*

Such was the constitution of the court in 1798, and the reader will recognize in its members three of the Wyoming settlers, introduced to them twenty-seven years before.

Of the Sheriffs of Luzerne, of whom there have been twenty, Lord Butler, John Franklin, William Slocum, were themselves actively engaged in the scenes we have described; Benjamin Dorrance lost his father in the battle, Jabez Hyde was connected with the Jenkins' family, having married the oldest daughter of John and Bertha Jenkins; Elijah Shoemaker was son to Lieut. Shoemaker who fell, and he had married the daughter of Col. Denison. Naptha Hurlbut was son to Deacon Hurlbut, preacher in the absence of Priest Johnson, and representative to the Assembly at Hartford. James Nesbit, son of one of the early settlers in Plymouth. Thomas Myers, grandson of Mr. Bennet, who with Hammond, rose on the Indians. Caleb Atherton, son of Mr. Atherton of Plymouth, still one of the clearest chroniclers of Dr. Plunkett's defeat, which he witnessed and aided; George P. Steel, grandson of Col. George P. Ransom.

In the minutes of the sessions in 1794, it is stated that the only attorneys in Luzerne are Ebenezer Bowman and Putnam Catlin, (Rosewell Welles had been appointed judge.) That E. Bowman has declined practice, and P. Catlin was about to decline—that Nathan

Palmer* and Noah Wadhams, jr., having been admitted in the Supreme Court of Connecticut, be " under the circumstances" admitted, &c., (the two years residence and study within the State, being dispensed with.) So great is the contrast between the fewness of attorneys in 1794, and the number of gentlemen at the bar in 1844, that we have preserved the fact.

Among the lawyers from other counties admitted to practice from time to time, we find the names of Wm. R. Hanna, Evan Rice Evans, Archibald T. Dick, Charles Houston, Thomas Cooper, John Carson, William Nichols, Daniel Clymer, John Kidd, John Ross, Daniel Smith, Daniel Levy, Samuel Sitgreaves.

An allusion has been made to the rise of property. Col. Pickering, January 1787, bought of Col. Z. Butler, town lots numbered 27 and 39, for 100 dollars, containing nearly seven and three-quarter acres, or about fifteen dollars an acre. In 1842 a piece of ground for building, cut out of one of these lots, 30 feet front by 225 deep, sold for $990, or at the rate of $6,000 an acre.†

So striking does the contrast of assessed property between 1781 and 1845, exhibit to those who take an interest in Wyoming, that it is a pleasure to present them with the gratifying picture; exclusive of polls, the assessment of the former year was £2,248—$7,493 33. 1844, in Luzerne county the real and personal property was assessed, $4,291,058
    Bradford,   3,793,957
    Susquehanna,   2,658,813
    Wayne,   1,238,425
    Pike,   847,515

                                        $12,829,768

Those six counties constituting the old town of Westmoreland. Of this value the township and borough of Wilkesbarre are assessed $910,580.

---

* Afterwards, 1809, distinguished as a Senator from the District in the Pennsylvania Assembly.

† Among the various items of expense paid by the county, in suppressing the riot, at the abduction of Pickering, we note the following:— *L. s. d.*
Major Lawrence Myers, and his command on duty, seven days, fifty-two men, 66 5 7
Capt. John Paul Schott's expense, his troop, eight days, - - - - 23 10 0
And our old friend Abraham Westover, for extraordinary services in taking rioters, with approbation of Court, - - - - - - - 9 17 6

Referring to the census, the view is equally pleasing. Westmoreland in 1781, contained 114 males from 21 to 70, and 26 from 16 to 21, making 140, quadruple this and we shall have 560 inhabitants. At the first census under the constitution, viz: 1790, there were in

Luzerne,	4,904
In 1800,	12,839

[An increase of nearly 300 per cent., of which about 6000, or one-half, were located in townships up the river from the Valley, a large proportion of them being new settlers under the Connecticut claim.]

In 1810, an increase of 50 per cent.,		18,109
Luzerne, in 1820,	20,027	
Bradford county, taken from Luzerne,	11,554	
Susquehanna, taken from Luzerne,	9,990	
		41,571

An almost unprecedented increase of 120 per cent.

During this period of ten years, the full influence of the compromising law, and the settlement of titles generally, was felt.

	Passing to 1830	1840.
Luzerne,	27,365	44,006
Susquehanna,	16,777	21,195
Bradford,	19,699	29,335
Wayne,	7,663	11,849
Pike,	4,843	3,832
An increase of 40 per cent.	76,347	110,216

Hence it will manifestly appear that the part of Pennsylvania, settled under the Connecticut Claim, so far from having been retarded in population and wealth, has advanced in both in a ratio not exceeded by any portion of the Commonwealth. Compared with the counties within the Connecticut Charter, west of Westmoreland, where the controversy, in effect did not extend, the increase is obvious. Without meaning the slightest invidiousness of distinction, it may yet be said, that no part of the State presents a more intelligent, moral, or industrious people. Since conciliated by her kindness, and won by the steady exhibition of her justice, the once outlawed Yankees have become attached, with all the enduring ardour of

New England affection, to Pennsylvania, her mild laws and her equitable and liberal administration of public affairs.

We not unfrequently hear from the pulpit an aphorism which we quote again, "That man proposes, and God disposes;" or, in the language of the Bard:—

> "There is a Divinity that shapes our ends,
> Rough hew them as we will."

What many regarded as an evil to be ever deplored, has proved, in the wise and beneficent dispensations of Providence, like charity, a double blessing; the settlers deriving widely extended comfort from well cultivated farms, and many of them ease and affluence; while the Commonwealth beholds a district of country, most of it in a state of nature, repulsively rugged from its stony hills, rocky mountains and dense forests, now smiling with cultivation, and teeming with a loyal and happy people, the true wealth of a State. The hardy sons of New England, trained to labour and economy on the rocky fields of their native homes, could alone have been led to see in the forests of the Susquehanna, a country which industry could render "a land flowing with milk and honey:" But such they have made it. Those, then, were the proper pioneers to settle such a wilderness. The rich alluvial lands along the streams served to attract sufficient leading spirits to the enterprise, and all the concurring circumstances, even the blood-stirring romance of the conflicts and woes of the early settlers, tended to awaken and keep alive, throughout the eastern States, thoughts of Wyoming, and increased instead of checking emigration.

A great and noble duty on the part of the New England inhabitants on the Susquehanna and their descendants, of ever abiding obligation, remains to be performed: namely, by their industry, economy, attention to the cause of religion, and the education of their children, to elevate the Yankee character in public estimation, and by their obedience to the wise and salutary laws of Pennsylvania; by their earnest devotion; by every liberal and honorable means to promote the welfare of the State; to conciliate the regard of the good old Commonwealth, flowing in so generous a stream towards them, that both may regard the day as blessed which made them one.

NOTE.—It should be borne in mind, that the landholders, frequently spoken of with asperity, as the stimulators of the Assembly, of Patterson and Armstrong, to unjust measures against the Wyoming people, were generally claimants under leases from the Proprietors, or warrants of 1784. The landholders under warrants of 1793 and '94—the Tilghmans, Drinkers, Francises, etc., having no special interest at Wyoming, in that early time, are in no respect implicated in the censure.

RECAPITULATION.

List of Persons murdered by Savages at Westmoreland, other than those who fell the day of the battle.

1778.	May.	Wm. Crooks, near Tunkhannock.
	Early in June.	Miner Robbins, four miles below Tunkhannock.
	June 30.	Benj. Harding, Stukely Harding, James Hadsell, James Hadsell, Jr., Wm. Martin, of Exter; John Gardiner, killed on his way up the river; Mr. Finch, Kingston, near Shoemaker's Mills.

These before the battle.

	July 8.	Leach and St. John, near Atherton's, Providence; Mr, Hickman, his wife and child, near Tripp's, Providence.
		Timothy Keys and Mr. Hocksey, Abington, six or seven miles north of Liggett's Gap.
		A crazy man below Wilkesbarre.
	July 18.	John Abbott, Isaac Williams, of Wilkesbarre.
	Sept.	John Utley, Elisha Utley, Diah Utley and their mother, Mrs. Utley, opposite Beach Grove, Nescopeck Township.
	Oct. 2.	Philip Goss and Capt. Carr, below Beach's.
	Nov. 2.	Nathan Kingsley, Wilkesbarre.
	" 5.	Jackson and Lester, taken at Nanticoke, brought up near Christman's Tavern, there shot down and scalped.
	" 7.	John Perkins, Shawney.
		Isaac Inman, Hanover; William Jameson, Hanover.
	Dec.	Isaac Tripp, Esq., and Jonathan Slocum, Wilkesbarre.
		[Old Mr. Hagaman, wounded same time, and escaped.]
1779.	March.	Abel Dewey, Robert Alexander, Amos Parker, below Salem, on the opposite side of the river.
		Elihu Williams, Lieut. Asahel Buck, Stephen Pettebone, Kingston.
		[Frederick Follett, speared, scalped and left for dead.]

	April 24.	Capt. Davis, Lieut. Jones, and three men, on Wilkesbarre mountain.
1780.	March 27.	Upson, Hanover.
	April.	Mrs. Rosewell Franklin.
1782.	July 8.	John Jameson, Asa Chapman.
		Thirteen men in Nescopeck Valley, now Conyngham, when the attack was made on Capt. Myers.

Making sixty-one. It is probable there were ten or twelve more; but we have not been able to ascertain the facts, sufficiently, to fix the dates or name them. The last thirteen being armed and in military array, may rather be regarded as slain in battle, than murdered.

RECAPITULATION.

List of Persons taken Prisoners during the War, from Westmoreland.

1777.	June.	John Jenkins, near Tunkhannock.
		Mr. York, Do.
		Elemuel Fitzgerald, Do.
1778.	June.	Daniel Weller, Exeter.
		Daniel Carr, Do.
	Aug. 24.	Luke Swetland and Joseph Blanchard.
	July.	Samuel Carey, from the battle ground.
		Isaac Tripp, Jr., in Providence.
		Wilcox and Pierce, near Tunkhannock.
		Mr. Kingsley.
	Nov. 2.	Frances Slocum, Young Kingsley, and a colored girl, servant of J. Slocum, of Wilkesbarre.
1779.		Michael Kelley, and daughter; the girl, it was said, married a British officer in Canada.
	March 21.	James Bidlack, and two others, of Shawney.
	April 24.	Two of Maj. Powell's men, Wilkesbarre mountain.
	March.	Bennett, Son and Hammond.
	"	Abm. Pike, Jonah Rogers, Huntington, Van Campen, from below.

488 HISTORY OF WYOMING.

1780. Dec. 6.   Benjamin Harvey, Elisha Harvey, Nathan Bullock, Jonathan Frisby, James Frisby, Manassah Cady, George Palmer, George Palmer Ransom, of Shawney.
Jonathan Smith.
1781. Sept.   Rosewell Franklin, Jr., Arnold Franklin and Mrs. Franklin; and the Spring following, four others, children of Rosewell Franklin, of Hanover.
1782. Sept. 12. Daniel McDowal, Shawney.

Our list embraces only forty-two. The number, I am persuaded, did not amount to less than sixty—probably more.

RETROSPECT.

Members from Westmoreland to the Connecticut Assembly.

It would seem that in April, 1774, four Representatives to the Assembly, were chosen or appointed. Among the votes recorded is this:—"That Zebulon Butler, Esq., Capt. Timothy Smith, Christopher Avery, and John Jenkins, be appointed Agents from the town of Westmoreland, to lay our circumstances before the General Assembly, in May next. Sept. 30, 1774."

Capt. Butler and Mr. Joseph Sluman, Agents to New Haven, April 1775.
Sept. 19. 1775. Capt. Zebulon Butler, and Major Ezekiel Pierce,
We find no appointment to the May Sesssion, 1776.

Oct.	1776.	Col. Zebulon Butler, Col. Nathan Denison.
May	1777.	Mr. John Jenkins, Mr. Isaac Tripp.
May	1778.	Nathan Denison, Anderson Dana.
Oct.	1778.	Col. Nathan Denison, Lieutenant Asahel Buck.
May	1779.	Col. Nathan Denison, Deacon John Hurlbut.
May	1780.	Mr. John Hurlbut, Mr. Jonathan Fitch.
Oct.	1780.	Capt. Nathan Denison, Mr. John Hurlbut.
May	1781.	John Hurlbut, Jonathan Fitch, Esq.
Oct.	1781.	Mr. Obadiah Gore, Capt. John Franklin.
May	1782.	Mr. Obadiah Gore, Jonathan Fitch.
Oct.	1782.	Mr. Obadiah Gore, Jonathan Fitch.

EXPLANATION OF MAP No. I.

1. Massachusetts and Connecticut, with a general view of their Charter Claims, west.

2. The Connecticut County and Town of Westmoreland, from the Delaware west to the Fort Stanwix line; which sent Representatives to the Assembly at Hartford and New Haven from 1774 to 1783.

3. The north and south line, one hundred and twenty miles west of the line ten miles east of the Susquehanna, indicates the western limits of the Connecticut Susquehanna Company's Indian purchase at Albany, in 1754. Nearly to this line ranges of Towns five miles square were granted and surveyed; the five most western in M'Kean county, named Lorana, Conde, Turrenne, Newtown and Addison, are designated.

4. The Western Reserve, or New Connecticut, in Ohio, being one hundred and twenty miles in length, the width of the Connecticut Charter claim, confirmed to that State on the final adjustment of Western Land Claims; the United States having accepted the cession from Connecticut of the territory west to the Mississippi. Five hundred thousand acres of this reservation, called "Fire Lands," were granted to New London, Fairfield, Norwalk, and other towns burnt by the enemy. The remainder being sold, is the source of the noble School Fund of that State.

5. About seven millions of acres of the beautiful Genesee country, being, with slight reservations, all the territory in New York west from a line beginning at the eighty-second mile stone from the Delaware, on the northern boundary of Pennsylvania, running north to the British possessions—confirmed by compromise between New York and Massachusetts in 1786, to the latter State—together with 230,400 acres east of that line.

EXPLANATION OF MAP No. II.

CONNECTICUT SURVEYS.

The towns marked with a star thus, * within the Susquehanna Company's Purchase, namely, Huntington, Salem, Plymouth, Kingston, Newport, Hanover, Wilkesbarre, Pittston, Providence, Exeter, Bedford, Northmoreland, Putnam or Tunkhannock, Braintrim, Springfield, Claverack, Ulster, are designated in ancient Pennsylvania proceedings as "The seventeen towns occupied or acquired by Connecticut claimants before the Decree of Trenton," and were, with the addition of Athens, confirmed to Connecticut claimants by the Compromising Law of April 4, 1799, and its several supplements.

The Delaware Company's Indian purchases comprised the land west from the Delaware river to the line within ten miles of the Susquehanna.

The Susquehanna Company's Indian purchase at Albany, (1754) extended from the line ten miles east of the river, one hundred and twenty miles west, and included the chief parts of M'Kean and Elk counties.

Ranges of towns, west of our map, were granted and surveyed (some as late as 1805) embracing more than a million of acres; the most western on the State line being in M'Kean county, (as will be found indicated in Map No. 1.) But we have deemed it useful to give place only to those wherein, or in the neighbourhood of which, the New England people commenced settlements.

Allensburg, on the Wyalusing, was a grant to Gen. Ethan Allen of Vermont, of several thousand acres, for his expected aid in the grand scheme of treason and rebellion, as it was designated by one party, and of just resistance to unendurable oppression, as it was regarded by the other, in 1787. It is supposed he derived no value from the grant.

The square townships in the Delaware purchases contain 23,000 acres. Those in the Susquehanna purchase, being five miles square, contain 16,000 acres.

Bozrah, on the Lackawaxen, shews the compact part of the "Lackawa" settlement, and was the birthplace of the Hon. Geo. W. Woodward.

The mark in Usher (lot No. 39,) three miles west from Mont-Rose, designates the place of the Author's bark cabin, where, in the spring of 1799, then a lad of nineteen, assisted by Mr. John Chase (the pleasant bar-keeper at Wilson's Hotel, Harrisburg,) he commenced a clearing.

The mark further west in Usher shews the boyhood residence, in 1800, of the Hon. Andrew Beaumont.

The designation of "Barnum," at Lawsville, in the town of Cunningham, shews the log-cabin tavern (1800) of that prince of Hotel keepers, afterwards of Baltimore.

The triangle marked "Hyde," west of Usher, indicates the head-quarters of Col. Ezekiel Hyde, Yankee leader in the Delaware purchase in 1800. Also the store of Enoch Reynolds, Esq., (in 1799,) afterwards at the head of one of the Bureaus in the Treasury Department, at Washington, for many years; and since, till his decease, the residence of Judge Jabez Hyde.

To avoid embarrassing the map by the insertion of too many names, letters are placed in Wilkesbarre, Exeter, and Pittston, as points of reference, and their explanation is made here. A, Fort Durkee; B, Fort Wyoming; C, Fort Ogden; D, Wintermoot's Fort; E, Jenkins's Fort; F, three Pittston Forts: G, Monockacy Island.

After years of search, two maps only of those Connecticut Surveys could be found. Our efforts probably have rescued them from hopeless oblivion.

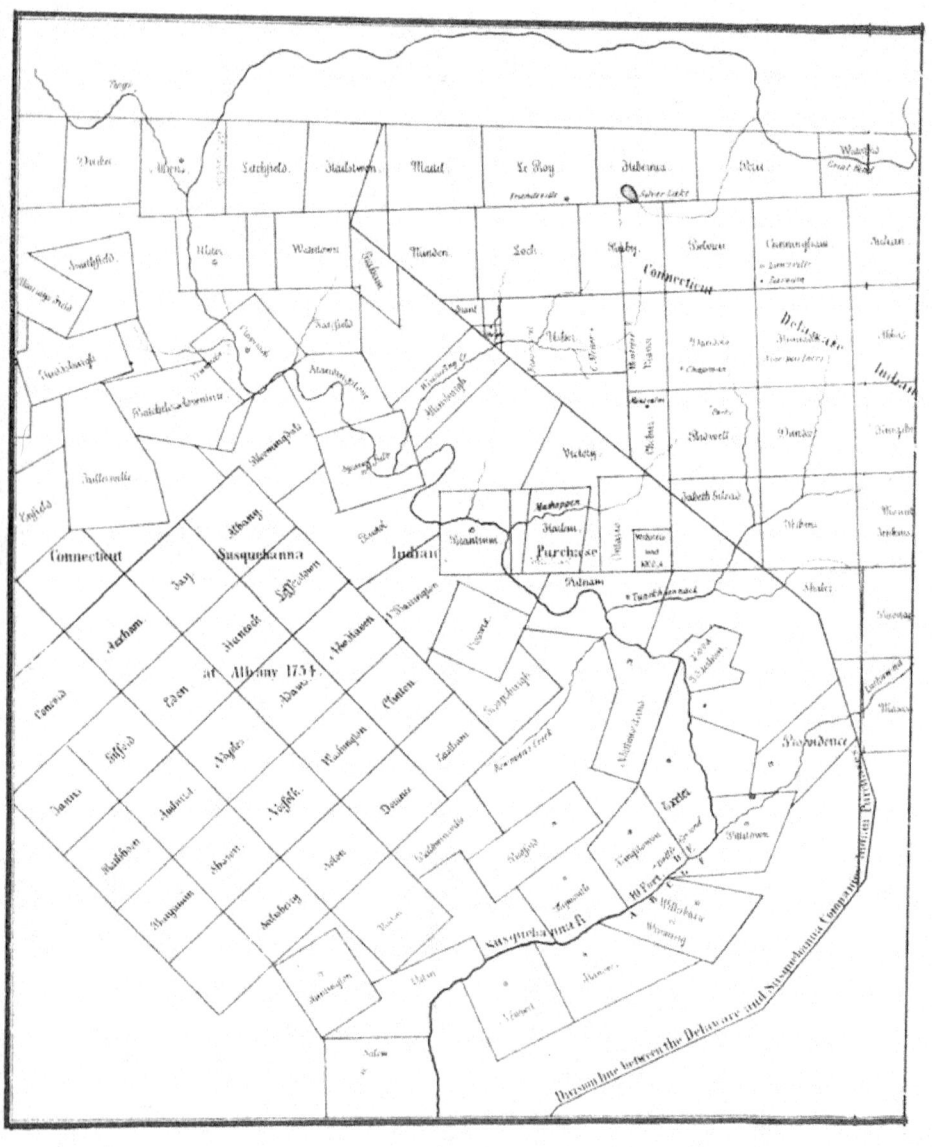

APPENDIX

TO THE

HISTORY OF WYOMING:

CONTAINING

THE HAZLETON TRAVELLERS;

OR,

NUMEROUS PERSONAL AND FAMILY SKETCHES OF THE ANCIENT SUFFERERS.

TOGETHER WITH

VARIOUS INCIDENTAL AND ILLUSTRATIVE MATTER, INCLUDING
A DESCRIPTION OF THE MONUMENT, AND A

BALLAD

ON THE TERRIBLE MASSACRE OF 1778, WRITTEN IMMEDIATELY
AFTER THE EVENT.

As introductory to the HAZLETON TRAVELLERS and the accompanying Family and Personal Sketches, it may not be improper to say, that several numbers, originally published, are omitted, because the principal events detailed are interwoven in our annals: that, for instance, of Colonel Franklin, Sergeant Thomas Williams, the Slocum Family, Rosewell Franklin, and some others. More than half the Sketches are new, and those before published are revised and corrected with all possible care. In some instances facts are repeated, which it was impossible to omit in the main body of the work; but these are comparatively few, and are more than compensated by an extra number of pages.

APPENDIX.

THE HAZLETON TRAVELLERS.

NO. I.

GEN. ROSS.

Good morning, Mr. Printer.—We left Hazleton on the 22d at about 8 A. M., and came in on the State Road. My companion had often visited Wyoming, and was acquainted personally, or by character, with most of the inhabitants, especially the early settlers.

"Ah! my friend," said I, "then we are at length here. I have heard much of this beautiful valley; and beautiful, indeed, it is. But come, tell me as we pass through, something of its inhabitants. Let us loiter a little. It is but ten miles you say to Carpenters', and we may easily get there by dark. So, Wilkesbarre is a fine town, larger than I expected. Whose white house is this on the right?"

"That is the residence of Gen. William Ross. The property was formerly owned, and the house occupied, by Col. Pickering."

"O, I recollect having read that he, being an eminent New England man, was selected to introduce the Pennsylvania laws here."

"He was. After the arrest of Franklin and consequent abduction of Pickering by the wild Yankees, Capt. Ross marched his company to release Col. P., and arrest the rioters. An engagement ensued and Capt. Ross received a severe wound in the body, which for some time was regarded mortal. Recovering, his gallant services were so highly estimated that the Executive Council of the state presented him an elegant sword with an appropriate inscription.* When Col. Pickering left the valley he sold to Mr. Ross his plantation, on easy terms of payment, which, by improvements and the rise of property, has advanced in value to 80,000 dollars."

[That his two and only brothers, Perrin and Jeremiah, were slain in the battle, has been previously related; as also the decease of his father, the preceding year.]

"The day previous to the massacre, Mr. Ross was with our little army in its march to Exeter, where the Hardings had been murdered, and would have been in the battle, but that his older brothers needed his arms. At the flight, the family were scattered, passing through the wilderness by different paths, in a state of extreme privation and suffering, young Ross and his mother, taking the lower or Nescopeck way. Soon after the coming in of Spalding's Company they returned. Having a taste for military affairs, he rose by regular gradations from Major to

---

* Inscription on the sword:
"Capt. Wm. Ross,
"The Supreme Executive Council present this mark of their approbation, acquired by your firmness in support of the Laws of the Commonwealth on the 4th of July, 1788.
"Charles Biddle, Secr'y."

Brigade Inspector, and General in the militia. For twenty years he held the Commission of a Magistrate, and during the last war was chosen to represent the District composed of Northumberland and Luzerne in the senate of the state. A strong minded man, he had studied human nature in the school of active life, to great advantage, and performed the duties of all the various stations to which he was called with intelligence and integrity. He was tall, straight, extremely active; he started early and he moved fast who ever got ahead of him. A zealous Democrat, of ardent temperament, he was among the most influential leaders of his party, and most feared by his opponents, [as the writer, for many years somewhat active on the other side, had occasion to know.] In 1803 or '4, having so far made his payment as to feel the full force of independence, Col. Ross resolved with natural pride, and not an incommendable spirit, to visit his birth-place in Connecticut. Mounted on a high-spirited and elegant steed, black as jet, with holsters and pistols, his dress elegant though unostentatious, he visited New London county, his native home." "Ay, ay, that was right. Who, among the emigrants in search of fortune, girls or lads, have not again and again sighed to make a favourable settlement, to acquire honour, to accumulate property, or to do some noble deed to be talked of in their far away native town? Who has not

'Borne in each season the heat and the cold,'

cheerfully, in special reference to, and with the hope of some day returning and exhibiting to his old neighbours the evidences of his success?" "Another anecdote, illustrative of character, permit me to mention. It so happened in Wilkesbarre, that in seven cases out of ten the Federal lads married girls of Democratic parents." "Ay, ay! that was right again. If the young people can agree I wish it were everywhere the fashion. Democratic lads, girls of Federal parents!" "Much absorbed in politics, always on the alert, we said one day to an intimate friend: 'There's mischief afoot I strongly suspect; young Covell has been here two or three evenings lately. He has some political scheme, you may depend, and desires to find out from me what will be our plan of operation. Don't you think so?' 'You had better,' said Gen. B., 'ask Sarah.' 'Hut tut!' cried he, with a merry laugh, as the right view flashed in upon him. And the young people were married before the lilies bloomed."

[William Sterling Ross, an only son, now (1845) occupies the seat of his father in the senate of the state. Gen. Ross had established a family burying-ground, in which he had erected a tablet of marble to the memory of his brothers. Having lived to the good old age of 82 years, on the 9th of August, 1842, he closed his active and honourable life. Every fitting demonstration of respect was paid to his remains: the court adjourning to attend the funeral. One incident was too remarkable not to be noted. A thunder cloud arose above the North East mountain, a most unusual place, as the procession moved, and cast its dark shadow over the plains. For some time the repeated peals of thunder were regarded as minute guns from the cannon placed in some proper position. The cloud passed away without rain, and as the train arrived at the mansion house the sun came out again in all its brightness.]

NO. II.

COL. HOLLENBACK.

"AND this long, ancient white building on the left?" "Ah yes, this brings up very interesting recollections. This for many years was the residence of Judge HOLLENBACK. You perceive, although under one roof, the building was divided into a house and store. Hundreds of thousands, perhaps I might say a million of dollars worth of goods have been from time to time upon those shelves, or in the adjoining store-rooms; and many a quarter cask of fine Madeira has been rolled into that cellar."

"Come, come; methinks the Madeira exhilarates you. Are you not in advance of your story?"

"I believe I am. Let us turn back to the beginning. Matthias Hollenback was a native of Virginia. Attracted by the wonderful tales of the beauty and richness of Wyoming valley, like many other young men of ardour and enterprize, he came to see, was pleased, determined to make it his home, and commenced those arrangements, which, steadily pursued, raised him to a point of wealth far exceeding that of his most successful competitors.

"So early as 1771, when the whole white population on the east side of the river, occupied a stoccade at the point where Mill-creek unites with the Susquehanna, Mr. H., then aged eighteen, was one of its inhabitants. Huts were erected around the inside against the upright timbers. One was possessed by Capt. Zebulon Butler; next in the row was the store, containing the humble beginnings of the object of this notice. A boarding hut, having two rooms, was the third in order, kept by Dr. Sprague; Mr. Nathan Denison, a young bachelor from Stonington, making one of the family. [Our annals show the conspicuous part three of these gentlemen acted in the eventful scenes that followed.]

"On the enlistment of two independent companies being directed at Westmoreland, Congress appointed Matthias Hollenback an ensign. Serjeant Williams used to take pleasure in relating the battle at Millstone, and the daring spirit exhibited by ensign H., when he led and cheered his men, wading the river waist deep to attack the British regulars, ensuring victory.

"When danger to Wyoming became imminent, and Congress turned a deaf ear to pressing calls for protection, throwing up his commission he returned, not to avoid, but to meet danger. The skill acquired by eighteen months' service in camp, was imparted to the militia, and his undaunted and elastic spirit infused into all around him. When the invasion came, when that terrible descent was made by Butler and his savage allies, when the war tocsin rung, and the alarm trumpet sounded from hill to hill, calling to battle, young Hollenback was among the foremost who sprang to their arms, and prepared to meet the foe.

"Our little army was composed chiefly of aged, or very young men, hastily called together. An enemy, fearful for his numbers, and terrible for his ferocity, was descending upon them. A vast distance, and howling wilderness intervened between the settlement and any hope of assistance." "It was indeed the moment to try the firmness of a soldier."

"Nearly all who were able to bear arms assembled; and Mr. Hollenback took his station in the midst of them. Fear was a stranger to his bosom. I have heard several say, who saw him there, and afterwards recognized him in the battle, that a braver soldier never marched out to meet an enemy. But two, or nearer three to one, was hopeless odds; while the right under our gallant Butler, where Hollenback was stationed, was advancing, the left, outflanked by hordes of savages, was compelled to give way. Thrown into confusion, the retreat became a route, which no human courage or conduct could arrest. Mr. H. was among those who escaped to the river. Expert in all manly exercises, he swam to Monocacy Island, and then to the eastern shore.

"Foreseeing the necessity of instant aid from abroad, mounting his horse he rode all night, gave information to Capt. Spalding's company, which so tardily had been permitted to advance, and with praiseworthy thoughtfulness, rapidly returned, laden with bread, for the relief of the flying widows and their suffering children. Imparting a saving morsel to one, and then hastening on to another starving group, he came, said the ancient people, 'like an Angel of mercy.'

"Ever prompt at the call of duty, Mr. Hollenback was actively engaged in collecting the remains of the slain, and giving them the most decent burial circumstances at that time permitted.

"On the passage by the Connecticut Assembly of a resolve, allowing Wyoming to make their own powder, Mr. H. was looked to, to provide the requisite machinery. His arrival with the 'Pounders,' was spoken of by Mrs. Jenkins, with exultation, as an important event; for previously powder for the settlement was (chiefly) brought from Connecticut on horseback.

"After the enemy retired, Mr. Hollenback was among the first to return and resume his wonted business. Fortune smiled on his enterprise; wealth and independence soon dawned upon his active career. Of middling height, compact and well made, remarkably active; his spirits always buoyant, and his frame seeming incapable of fatigue; he was an extraordinary instance of bold enterprise and untiring industry. He established stores at various points betweeen Wilkesbarre and the Genesee county, along the Susquehanna. If business called, neither heat nor cold, hail, rain nor snow, high water, bad roads nor darkness, arrested his progress while the way was practicable. In almost every instance where a store was erected, a farm was bought, and the cultivation of the soil went hand in hand with the disposal of merchandize. Such enterprize, spirit and industry were undoubtedly of great advantage to the settlement and improvement of the country.

"After the jurisdiction of Connecticut ceased, and the laws of Pennsylvania were introduced, Mr. Hollenback received repeated marks of public favour. He was chosen to command a regiment of militia, at an early day. Having a strong mind; being intelligent in all matters which concerned the people here; and moreover, the government reposing confidence in his integrity, Col. Hollenback was appointed, on the organization of Luzerne county, to fill the responsible station of one of the associate judges; Col. Denison receiving a similar commission: so that the two youthful adventurers under the Connecticut claim, who dwelt in the stoccade in 1771, now twenty eventful years having intervened, were seen sitting beside the president judge of the court, 'their honours,' clothed with official dignity, dispensing justice as magistrates of Pennsylvania.

"The duties of his judicial office he performed to very general satisfaction, for nearly forty years, retaining the commission to the time of his decease. Judge Hollenback, like Stephen Girard, having accumulated wealth by his own industry, was perfect master of his own. Attention to business was his chief pleasure; but he could unbend with his friends; and no one knew how to be merrier in the social circle. For the times when Judge Rush and Judge Cooper presided, he was in the habit of giving an annual dinner to the bench and the bar, when the Madeira flowed like water, and the cares of business were laid aside for the pleasures of hospitality and social enjoyment.

"Judge Hollenback, an ardent friend to internal improvement, watched the progress of the ascending canal to Wyoming with intense interest. The bridge and meeting-house were aided by his zealous exertions. Wonderful were the changes that had taken place since he, a lad of eighteen, first visited the valley, to the time of the commencement of the canal system, surpassing even the anticipation of his own clear and sagacious mind.

"But he did not live to see the work completed. More than seventy years had thinned his locks, and made inroads on his constitution. He had performed the arduous duties of life faithfully in his day and generation. Where he had seen fields flowing with blood and strewed over with the slain, he had lived to witness smiling harvests garnered in the lap of peace; where he had heard the war whoop and the death shrieks he had lived to listen to songs of joy and chants of praise. But his time had come. Born on the 15th of February, 1752, he departed on the 18th of February, 1829, aged therefore 77 years, leaving to his children and grandchildren a splendid property for this northern county, variously estimated at from three to four hundred thousand dollars.

NO. III.

GEN. LORD BUTLER.

"To the left—to the left—let us turn to the left and go down to the river."
"Why not keep up the main street? Is not the bridge in that direction?"
"We come to the bridge in the same distance going either way; but I wish

APPENDIX.

you to reach the bank of the noble Susquehanna at the termination of this street, for two or three reasons. The view is remarkably beautiful; and the way takes us past the house, formerly the residence of one of the magnates of the land."

"Lead on: and give me a traveller's sketch in passing."

"This large white house to the left, standing in a little from the street, was the home of GEN. LORD BUTLER."

"A fine situation, upon my word—the Susquehanna flowing in front, commanding a prospect of two miles above and one below—the bridge sufficiently near to render the scene picturesque—the house having a handsome yard in front; it is, indeed, a charming situation. My good wife would sit at those chamber windows, with Gertrude in her hand, and watch the thousands of rafts and arks descending, which at times make the river a scene of busy animation, and count it the very romance of life. But who was this Gen. Butler? not the American colonel, who commanded in the battle?"

"No—his eldest son. Col. Butler's given name was Zebulon—the son, of whom we speak was called LORD, that being the family name of his mother."

"LORD BUTLER was but a youth in the time of the Revolution; yet he was some time in camp with his father. I mention this, because associating then with officers of rank had doubtless an influence on his manners in after life. He was tall—more than six feet, straight as an arrow, his countenance manly, with bold Roman features; his manners grave and dignified. Courteous he was, but it was the courtesy of a gentleman who felt the dignity of his own character. Lofty and reserved to those who loved him not, no one approached him with a joke or a slap on the shoulder. A man of active business habits, he wrote a bold, free, and excellent hand, and his accounts and affairs were always in the strictest order. He rode admirably, and appeared extremely well on horseback—no one loved a noble steed better than he. An iron gray was his favourite. I have seen him an hundred times on horseback, and never indifferently mounted—never without a handsome riding whip—never without gloves. These trifles will give you a better idea of the man—his appearance and habits—than perhaps a more studied description. He was always and everywhere the gentleman. Decided in his political opinions, and free in expressing them, his opponents said he was proud. If an unworthy pride was meant, the charge was unjust. But if an election was depending, and he a candidate, he would neither shake hands with nor smile on a man with whom he would not have done the same as cordially if he had not been on the lists. His delicacy, in this particular, was probably carried rather to excess: for no truer republican ever lived—no one had a more sincere regard for his fellow-men—no man was more devoted to the independence and liberty of his country. But his reserve, which enemies construed into hauteur, was the result of early associations. His father, the gallant Colonel Butler, who had been much with British officers in the old French War, and with the accomplished French officers in the war of the Revolution, had a good deal of dignity and gravity about him. A lady told me, when she first came to Wyoming, she saw a gentleman step from a door into the street, and meet a friend. With a slight bow, the gentleman, stopping, placed his silver headed cane under his left arm, took out his snuff box, rapped the lid as he took it off, and offered it to his friend; took a pinch himself, and brushing his face slightly with his doubled bandanna, bowed and passed on—the whole in such manner as to induce her instantly and eagerly to inquire, 'What gentleman is that?' The answer was, 'La! don't you know!—that's Col. Butler. I thought everybody knew him.'"

"Mr. Butler was for many years one of the most active public men in Luzerne County. Besides the militia offices which he filled, until he rose to the rank of general, he held the commission of sheriff. For several years he was a member of the executive council of the state. By Governor Mifflin's appointment, he held the offices of register, and recorder, and prothonotary. He was many years later chosen to the assembly, and county commissioner; and for some time held the station of county treasurer. In all these various offices Gen. Butler sustained the highest character for faithfulness and ability. No public servant ever deserved better of the public. If he would not condescend to flatter their prejudices, he yet delighted all with his intelligence and zeal to promote their best interests. He was a man of stern integrity, and lived and died highly respected and esteemed; while in the family and social circle he was justly and tenderly loved."

"And did he accumulate wealth?"

"A very handsome independence. After we cross the bridge I will show you one of his noble farms, now in the enjoyment of a son of his, one of the worthiest among a number of highly worthy descendants."

"You avoid saying anything of party politics in your sketches. Pray, whisper it in my private ear, what were the party designations of the three distinguished gentlemen you have told us of?"

"I will, frankly, if you choose it. Gen. Ross and Judge Hollenback were both zealous democratic republicans. The Aurora and Democratic Press were their favourite sources of political information; and Mr. Jefferson, in an especial degree, the object of their confidence and regard, in respect to national affairs, while Gov. M'Kean and Simon Snyder commanded their support in the administration of state matters. On the other hand, Gen. Butler was one of the chiefs among the leaders in Federal politics. The United States Gazette, glowing with zeal under the management of Chauncey, Wayne, Bronson, &c., came for more than thirty years to his address; and he preferred James Ross, of Pittsburgh, the Federal rallying point, to his more successful competitors. Mr. Butler was deprived of the county offices which he held, on the memorable political revolution which brought in Gov. McKean. I speak of this without reserve and without passion. The storm has subsided—the winds are hushed—the mild beams of truth, calm as a summer evening, are shed abroad over the whole subject. They saw the matter from different points of view, and saw it differently. All were equally patriotic, equally sincere. They were all ardent lovers of liberty and of their country; and however momentarily divided in times of high party excitement, in latter life mingled socially together. But here is the bridge."

"Stay—who inhabit these beautiful mansions on our right?"

"Another generation! Fine fellows, they! The active—the eloquent—the bustling men of business; among the *elite* of those on the stage of action. My sketches are meant merely to bring to your view the more active spirits of the last generation. You shall have several portraits before we get to Carpenter's, and a dozen more on our return."

NO. IV.

COL. BENJAMIN DORRANCE.

——"This bridge is a noble structure. I am proud that I am a Pennsylvanian, a state that has done so much to improve her condition and promote the common welfare. Her canals; her railroads; her bridges: The number of her literary, scientific, and benevolent institutions! Ah, my friend, Pennsylvania is indeed a state to be proud of. Her policy and success are once at honourable monuments, and persuasive arguments, to a republican form of government, where the people are their own masters, and under God, the conservators of their own happiness."

"I am glad to find you in this vein. It is apropos of the next subject for my pencil."——

"Stop—give me a moment to wonder and admire at the extent and richness of these bottom lands. I had heard of the extraordinary river meadows of Wyoming, but they far exceed my utmost expectations; who owns the fine farm we are passing through?"

"It happens quite in order. This belongs to the heirs of Judge Hollenback. The next above—(you observe the farm house beyond the orchard)—is the one I spoke of as belonging to a son of Gen. Butler. But see, we come to the pleasant and thriving village of Kingston. Yonder is the Academy. This large wheat field at the right is still a part of the Butler property; and that neat white house, standing in from the road, and those three barns—that below the house, that beyond, and the one across the way, with a noble plantation of four or five hundred acres, extending a mile to the river and a mile to the mountains—this is the home of Col. Benjamin Dorrance."

"A name familiar to me. I have heard my father speak of him. I think they were members of Assembly together."

"Very likely. He was many years in the legislature; but that is anticipating our story. O, there he is, going down to the village. Observe him—not tall, but of good height; fleshy, but not corpulent; his head large—face round—Grecian in contour—good sense and good humour mingling in the expression of his countenance."

"Yes, I see—but I thought he had been an older man—his step is that of a man of fifty."

"He is older than that; for, though not in the Indian battle, he was in the fort that was afterwards surrendered; but he has good stamina; an excellent constitution; while cheerfulness, independence, and benevolence give him health and happiness superior to many a younger man. Col. Dorrance, sir, is prominent among the distinguished men that the county of Luzerne has produced. All his life he has been the favourite of the people. Few men in any state or county ever, for so long a period, to use a common expression, carried all before him. He has been certainly the most popular man of his day. Was Dorrance on the ticket, no matter who else was there, it was agreed on all hands HE would go in. Even in the highest days of party, implacable party spirit relented before his popular name, and gathering friends, breaking through all the restraints of party discipline, flocked to the polls to support him. He has been all his life, sir, the favourite of the people."

"And did he deserve it?"

"None more so: He was every way worthy; but it seemed as if he was peculiarly formed to be popular. Easy of access, of bland and pleasing manners, extremely hospitable, always ready, when proper, to oblige; withal, sensible and discerning, the popular heart leaped towards him, confided, and loved. It is but rigidly just to say—he never deceived the people. He disdained to sustain himself by rash and plausible promises, to be violated when his present purpose was accomplished. With principles decided, and with opinions avowed, such was the popular confidence and regard, that many political opponents would always support him. In old times, when Bradford and Susquehanna were parts of Luzerne, and numbers going to court had more than sixty miles to travel, I have heard it said, his friends would ride to the door, turn their horses into his rich pastures and walk in, certain of welcome as at their own houses. Undoubtedly it is true that his hospitality was almost unbounded. Yet there were no unworthy—no improper compliances. But there were severe trials to both his patience and his prudence, when the bank was first established in Wilkesbarre. The people were eager to get patents for their lands, deeming their titles not secure until patented. Hence, to raise money, innumerable applications came to Mr. Dorrance to endorse—to endorse. His name, they said, would insure the discount of the notes. Mr. D. saw that embarrassment certainly, if not ruin, would follow a general compliance. You wonder how he got along? I'll tell you. His answer was simple and frank. 'Situated as I am here and being a director of the board, applications are daily coming to me to endorse. If I do for one friend, how can I deny another? You will see it is impossible for me to do so for all, and I am obliged to prescribe to myself a course which I am sure you, yourself, will on reflection, approve.' The propriety of his course was seen and he did not make an enemy. Indeed the remark has often been made, that Col. Dorrance could decline a request in such a manner that the man would go away better pleased than with half the rest of this world who should have granted it.

"When a very young man, Mr. Dorrance was chosen sheriff of Luzerne county. Soon after his term expired, he was elected county commissioner. In 1808 he was chosen member of Assembly; and, at intervals, he has sustained the duties of that responsible station, seven or eight or nine years. I do not remember the number, but as often as he would consent to serve, and always to the satisfaction of his constituents. His enemies—no, I do wrong—he has no enemies—but who that is eminently fortunate, is without the jealousy of rivalship?—jealousy would sometimes intimate that he owed much of his extraordinary popularity to the circumstance that his father, Lieut. Col. George Dorrance, was slain in the Indian battle; and that the universal sympathy and kindness, so honourable to human nature, felt for the memory of those noble patriots who fought and died in that dreadful conflict for liberty, were transferred to their children. This, doubtless, had its influence in bringing young Dorrance forward into the sheriff's office so unusually early in life; but his own good sense, intelligence, aptness for business, and pleasing manners, would, wherever known, have made him popular without such extrinsic aid. Such a circumstance might introduce a man with favour into public life, but rely on it, before the rigid and scrutinizing ordeal of public opinion, a man must depend on his own intrinsic merits.

"Among the characteristics of Col. Dorrance, conspicuously shone the virtues of firmness and moderation. As our excellent friend, Ebenezer Bowman, used to say, he united in an extraordinary degree the SUAVITOR IN MODO with the FORTITER IN RE. Concession and conciliation, when no principle was involved, restoring harmony and inspiring confidence by healing councils, were his weapons and policy. Grave at the council board, merry at the banquet—his life has been highly useful, respectable and happy."

"We must call and see him when we come back—I should like an introduction. But did you not say he was in the fort when it surrendered?"

"O! yes, and that recalls an incident which must not be omitted. After the capitulation, the British marched into the fort by the northern or upper gateway The Indians, under Brandt, as is supposed, their commander, marched in at the southern portal. Col. Dorrance, though quite a lad, remembers the look and conduct of the Indian leader: all eye, glancing quickly to the right—then glancing to the left, with all an Indian's jealousy and caution, lest some treachery or ambush should lurk in the fort. Alas! the brave and powerful had fallen; no strength remained to resist—no power to defend."

"Many years and countless blessings be the lot of the excellent man whose interesting sketch you have given me! But we approach the monument—Push on! I long to see it before the shades of evening shall darken the view."

[The Dorrance family came from Windham county, Connecticut. There were two brothers, George and John, who settled in Kingston; both men of intelligence and energy. Lieut. Col. George Dorrance, in 1777, led a large scouting party up the river consisting of 80 men, to disperse or capture a settlement of Indians and Tories on the Wyalusing. Having accomplished the object, an unseasonable snow storm detained them beyond their expected time, and they suffered extremely from cold and hunger. By Col. Dorrance's order rafts were made of the huts from which the enemy had been driven, and the whole of the company were safely wafted down to Forty Fort. In the battle Lieut. Col. Dorrance commanded on the left wing under Col. Denison. His coolness in the midst of the fight, when one of his men gave way, is shown by the firm command, instantly obeyed—"Stand up to your work, sir."—That he fell, in the prime of life, being about 45, and that he was cruelly mangled by the savages, is else where recorded. In the Independent company of Capt. Ransom, was Robert, the oldest of his two sons. He served to the close of the war; afterwards in the western army; and was in the battle resulting in St. Clair's defeat. A good soldier, he was said to have been one of the few who did not abandon his gun in the flight. True to his colours to the last, he died in the army, supposed to have fallen in a subsequent engagement. Col. Benjamin Dorrance, of whom we commenced to speak, departed this life in August, 1837, aged 70 years, and was interred in the Kingston burying-ground with every possible mark of respect and affection. He left two sons. Col. Charles Dorrance, resembling much his father, resides at the homestead. The Rev. John Dorrance is the beloved pastor of the Presbyterian Church in Wilkesbarre.

Our legal readers are, of course, familiar with the celebrated land trial before Judge Patterson—Van Horn, (Lessee), vs. Dorrance.

APPENDIX. 11

The defendant in that suit was John Dorrance, the elder brother of George. John was born in 1733, lived a bachelor, and died in July, 1804, aged 71 years, commanding general confidence and respect through his whole life.]

NO. V.

REV. BENJAMIN BIDLACK.

"The Pilgrim's spirit has not fled—
It walks in noon's broad light,
And it watches the bed of the glorious dead
With the holy stars by night."—*Pierpont*.

"——Leaf after leaf as I turn over the pages that record the early history of Wyoming, the virtues of courage, fortitude, and patriotism of her inhabitants, stand out in bold relief. Wherever danger was to be met, or glory was to be won, there were they found alert and cheerful at the post of duty. The battle was disastrous in the extreme, but without a shade of dishonour! What else could have been expected? The bone and sinew of Wyoming, raised for our special defence, had been called away to defend the country below. Washington needed them: Our country required their services elsewhere, and Wyoming was left exposed to attack. The enemy came! How could our people fly? What chance for life if they attempted a retreat through the wilderness? It is apparent that to fight or be unresistingly slaughtered was their only alternative. I do not mean to discuss the question, here, what they ought to have done: though, I declare, I do not see among the thousand difficulties that surrounded them, that they could have done otherwise than meet the enemy, and decide their fate by arms. I purpose, by and by, to give a picture of the battle—Not now.

"I will now, my friend, present you with a sketch of another patriotic family, who fought, and suffered, and bled in the righteous cause of liberty.

"There lives in the village of Kingston, (the house stands at the left as we came up, not far below the residence of Col. Dorrance,) an aged and venerable man, a minister of the Gospel in the Methodist Episcopal persuasion Though four score years and more have passed over him, he still moves erect, with dignity and grace. Tall, of fine form, in early life he was a powerful man, all nerve and muscle. Full of energy—full of ardour—glowing with patriotism, he entered into the service of his country at the very commencement of the Revolutionary war. He was at Boston when Washington assembled the first American army, to oppose Gage and his bloody myrmidons, and to resist British aggression. He was afterwards at the lines before New York; he had a brother taken prisoner in the battle at Long Island, and, as was the fate of many a fine fellow at the commencement of the war, while we were regarded as rebels, to be despised and slaughtered, instead of an enemy to be respected—he was starved to death!

"But who is it you are speaking of?"

"The Rev. Benjamin Bidlack. Attend, and you shall judge if his family do not stand out most honourably and conspicuously among the patriots of that day. Mr. Bidlack's term of enlistment being out, he joined his father's family at Wyoming in 1777. Here he entered immediately into active duty. A large party under the command of Capt. Asaph Whittlesey, of the Plymouth company, was ordered up the river from whence rumours of the enemy had come. Mr. Bidlack was one of the volunteers. They marched about 50 miles. Mr. Bidlack then entered again into the regular service, and continued in the army till the close of the war. Besides other events in which he participated, he was present at the glorious and crowning struggle at Yorktown, where Cornwallis, the pride of the British army, was hemmed in. The lion was brought to bay. It is exhilarating to hear Mr. B. speak of that event, and recount the incidents of the contest. Our batteries played away night and day. It was one incessant blaze and thunder—roar and flash! Midnight was lighted up so that you might pick up a glove almost anywhere on the field. The result you know."——

"Truly that family did their part worthily——"

"Stay, my friend; I have more to tell, and of events that occurred in this valley. James Bidlack, Jr., another brother, commanded the Wilkes-barre Company, which he led into battle on the fatal 3d.—He died where he stood, at the head of his men. Only eight of all his company escaped. They were of the true blood, the whole family of Bidlacks—mild in private life, remarkably clever and obliging; the social virtues, in the peaceful circle, seemed to find in them their happiest illustrations: but called to arms! and roused to action! they were all and each every inch the soldier.

"The circumstance is certainly extraordinary—it is nevertheless true: The day that Capt. James Bidlack led his men into action, his father, James Bidlack, Sen., commanded a company of aged men and kept garrison in the fort at Plymouth. Father and sons—all of them were in the service, and two of them sealed with their lives their attachment to freedom. Nor yet is the eventful story ended. When the savages returned the following year in force to Wyoming, old Mr. Bidlack, the father, was surprised and taken prisoner, and carried into a deeply suffering captivity, from which he was only relieved by the return of peace. But he did return to the beloved valley, and lived to see his country rise into almost unhoped-for prosperity, the fruit of the services of the patriots of the Revolution. It is nearly thirty years since the father was called, we trust, to a better world. The circumstances that occurred in many years of active life after the close of the war, to Mr. Benjamin Bidlack, it does not belong to the purpose of these sketches to portray. Many years ago he became a preacher of the Methodist persuasion, and spoke, as he had fought, with impressive earnestness, and ardent sincerity. Indeed, the Bidlack family seem in their conduct to have kept the true end of life in view:

'Still to employ
The mind's brave ardour in heroic aims;
Such as may raise us o'er the groveling herd,
And make us shine forever—THAT IS LIFE.'"*

* May, 1845. The worthy old Patriot still lives, blessed with abundance, and the evening of life is cheered by the well-merited fortune of his son, the Hon. Benjamin Alden Bidlack, who has been the past four years member of Congress from this District; and recently has been appointed minister to Grenada, carrying with him not only the approbation of his political friends, but the hearty good will of all his neighbours.

NO. VI.

NOAH PETTEBONE.

The fine farm, after passing that of Col. Dorrance, has belonged, from very early times, to the Pettebone family. Observe that white house on the right,—the barn, an hundred feet long, on the left—those beautiful flats, extending more than a mile from the river towards the mountain! Attractive to the eye, prolific of every good thing kind earth can yield. Nature must have been in excellent humour when she formed those lovely plains.

Noah Pettebone emigrated from Hartford county. He had three sons and four daughters; the names of the sons were Noah, Stephen, and Oliver. When the Independent companies of Durkee and Ransom were raised, Stephen, the second son, enlisted and marched, near the close of 1776, to join the army of Gen. Washington, leaving Noah, the oldest brother, and Oliver, then a lad of 14, at home with their father.

When the alarm gun gave notice that the enemy was in the valley, Noah repaired promptly to the post of danger; was in the dreadful conflict that ensued,

APPENDIX.

and was slain, leaving a young wife to mingle her tears with those of his aged father, for his loss.*

Stephen, having come in with Capt. Spalding's company, was murdered the following spring by a band of savages, on the flats, a little beyond where the western abutment of the bridge terminates. Mr. Williams and Mr. Buck, fell at the same time, and Mr. Follet was shot, pierced through several times with a spear, scalped and left for dead—but recovered. His own account of the matter was, that knowing they would strike while signs of life remained, summoning his utmost power he lay perfectly still, notwithstanding repeated wounds, pretending to be dead. The bold and daring deed being perpetrated in plain sight of Wilkesbarre, the Indians, having brief space to effect their purpose, did not strike him with the tomahawk. The unflinching firmness displayed was almost more than human; we know of but one parallel instance.†

Thus two of the old man's sons poured out their life blood, victims to Indian barbarity, martyrs in the holy cause of Liberty and Independence.

The younger brother Oliver was in Forty Fort at the time of its surrender. On the decease of his father the care of the family and estate devolved on him. The writer remembers him well as he appeared thirty years ago. He was tall, slender, but well made, of frank and agreeable manners. We knew him in public life as commissioner of the county, a vigilant and faithful officer; and as a private gentleman liberal and kind, ever assiduous to please. He was a man of perfect integrity and honour. Having lived to the good old age of 70, he died in March 1832.

Such is the mingled painful and pleasing record of one of the most patriotic families of Wyoming, and among the deepest sufferers.

The plantation is now owned by Noah (it is right to preserve the old family name), and his brother, the Hon. Henry Pettebone, in the possession of whose descendants we hope it may remain a thousand years. Judge H. Pettebone, of whom we speak, has recently received that appointment in place of Judge Bennett, resigned.‡

* The widow intermarried with Amariah Watson, a respectable farmer of Huntington.
† Related by Capt. Basil Hall.
‡ Col. Erastus Hill, who owns that very handsome seat, next above William Sweetlands, married a daughter of Oliver Pettebone, and residing near the spot, has taken great interest in the erection of the monument. In his possession are a number of sculls and thigh bones taken from the pit, where they were first deposited. For several years, not only the deep stroke of the tomahawk was visible, but marks of the accursed scalping knife were plain to be seen; while the rifle bullet hole in the thigh bone, smoothly cut, without the least splint or fracture, as with a sharp bit or gouge, excited much interest. But they are fast crumbling by exposure to the air.

[P. S. It would appear that patriot blood ran warmly through the hearts of the whole Pettebone family, for our researches show us that those who remained in Connecticut, if less deeply sufferers, were not less active in the service of the country. In 1775, Col. Jonathan Pettebone assembled his regiment and addressed them. "The spirit was so generous," says the Record, "that a number sufficient to form three companies of 68 men each, exclusive of officers, immediately enlisted, and were ready for any expedition on the shortest notice."

When the militia, two or three years afterwards, were re-organized, Col. Pettebone received the command of the 18th Regiment.

A gallant enterprise was effected in 1777, in which Capt. Abel Pettebone of Enos' Regiment, and Capt. Levenworth and Ely of Meigs' Regiment took the lead. Having by great celerity surprised the enemy at Horse Neck, they took six light-horse prisoners, a number of horses, cattle, and arms, burnt three vessels loaded with provisions for New York, and broke up a pestilent nest of cow-boys; returning after travelling more than sixty miles, having been absent only 10 hours.

NO. VII.

MRS. MYERS.

——"You say we have passed Forty Fort?" "Yes—its position was sixty rods to our right when we were at the meeting-house." "I am sorry we did not tarry long enough to take a view, ruined and dilapidated as I know it is, of that so much talked of fortification. But are there not some of the ancient people living near, who were here in those times of peril and suffering, whose recollections could furnish us with incidents worth remembering, and characteristic anecdotes of some of the distinguished men of that day?" "There are several in the neighbourhood, and among them a highly intelligent and respectable lady, who was 16 years old at the time of the battle. I refer to Mrs. Myers. I think she is mother of the present sheriff of Luzerne; her maiden name was Bennett, daughter of ——Bennett. Some years ago, when Professor Silliman was in the valley, led by the same liberal curiosity which seems to animate your breast, he visited Mrs. Myers, and I had the good fortune to be present at the interview. Mr. S. was almost an enthusiast in whatever related to Revolutionary story. An ardent friend of liberty himself, his gallant father was an officer in the war for independence; so he entered with that hearty zeal upon his inquiries, which, from sympathy, awakened in Mrs. Myers a lively recollection of the time.

"Our men, Mrs. M. said, marched out two or three abreast, with drums beating and colours flying. They were all conscious that there was great danger; they knew not the strength of the enemy, for they had concealed it with great skill. She mentioned this fact: One of the people, a Mr. Finch, had been shot and scalped two days before the engagement, near the gorge of the mountain, not far from where Shoemaker's tavern now is. A Mr. Hewitt at the same time was shot through the hand. A considerable party went out on the 2d of July to bring away the remains of Finch, and did so without interruption. Afterwards it was known that several hundred Indians were concealed within striking distance, and could easily have destroyed our whole party, but did not choose to unveil their strength, lest our people should become too cautious.

"After our men had marched forth from the fort, several horsemen were seen galloping up from towards the Ferry. All eyes were upon them: their horses jaded, were yet in a foam—the sweat dropping from their panting sides. They proved to be Capt. Durkee, Lieut. Phineas Pearce, and another officer from Capt Spalding's company, which had advanced as far as Shupp's, about fifty miles distance; and these gallant men had ridden all night. They learned that our people had gone out to meet the enemy. 'A morsel of anything, Mrs. Bennett,' said they to her mother—'a morsel of food, and we will follow.' The table was hastily spread, and they partook of their last meal. Of course they had not slept, and were very unfit for the field action. Country!—liberty!—home!—wives!—children!—and friends!—all were in danger; and they allowed no selfish consideration to weigh a feather against the behests of duty. Forward they went—rushed into the thickest of the fight, and when the sun cast his last bright glance on the valley, they slept in the arms of honourable death, or wounded, were prisoners to demons incarnate, reserved (the thought is distressing—horrible!) reserved for agonizing torture.

"During the battle, those left at Forty Fort could step on the river bank and hear the firing distinctly. For a while it was kept up with spirit, and hope prevailed; by and by it became broken and irregular, approaching nearer and nearer. 'Ah!' exclaimed one, 'all is lost—our people are defeated—they are retreating!' It was a dreadful moment. The battle began about four in the afternoon. Just at evening a few of the fugitives rushed in and fell down exhausted—some wounded and bloody. Through the night, every hour, one or more came into the fort. On the 4th, the day after the massacre, terms of capitulation were agreed upon between Col. John Butler and Col. Denison. The enemy marched in six abreast, part at one gate, part at the other, their banners flying and music playing. On paper the terms are fair, and security promised by the victor to life and property.

"But the Indians immediately began to rob and burn, plunder and destroy. Col. Denison sent for Col. Butler; they sat down together by a table on which the capitulation had been signed, (which is yet carefully preserved by Mrs. Myers.) She and a girl a little older sat on a seat within the fort, close by, and heard every word they said. Col. D. complained of the injuries doing to the inhabitants by the savages. 'I will put a stop to it, sir, I will put a stop to it,' said Butler. The plundering continued; Col. D. sent again for Butler, and remonstrated with energy:—'Col. Butler,' said he, 'we have surrendered our fort and arms to you on the pledge of your faith that life and property should be protected. Articles of capitulation are considered as sacred by all civilized people;' this was, perhaps, the third time. 'I'll tell you what, sir,' replied Col. Butler, waving his hand impatiently, 'I can do nothing with them—I can do nothing with them.'

"The Indians, to show their entire independence and power, came into the fort, and one took the hat from Col. Denison's head. Another demanded his rifle, frock, a dress much worn by officers as well as soldiers. It did not suit Col. D. to be thus stripped—whereupon the Indian raised his tomahawk menacingly, and Col. Denison was obliged to yield; but seeming to find difficulty in taking off the garment, he stepped back to where the young women were sitting; the girl who sat by Miss Bennett was one of Col. D.'s own family—she understood the movement, and took from a pocket in the frock a purse, and hid it under her apron; the frock was delivered to the Indian, and the town money (for the purse, containing a few dollars, was the whole military chest of Wyoming) was saved.

"Mrs. Myers represents Col. Butler as a portly, good-looking man, perhaps 45, dressed in green, the uniform of Butler's rangers, with a cap and feather. Col. Butler led the chief part of his army away in a few days; but parties of Indians continued in the valley burning and plundering. Her father's house was left for a week; she used to go out often to see if it was safe. One morning as she looked out from the fort, fire after fire rose, east, west, north and south—and casting her eyes towards home, the flames were bursting from the roof, and in an hour it was all a heap of ruins.

> 'Why flames yon fair valley—why shoot to the blast,
> Those emblems like stars, to the firmament cast?
> 'Tis THE FIRE SHOWER OF RUIN, all dreadfully driven!'

In a week or ten days it was seen that the articles of capitulation afforded no security—and those that remained followed their friends who had fled immediately after the massacre into exile.

"Having returned, peace returned not with them. Early the following spring Mr. Bennett, the father of Mrs. Myers, a lad, her brother, and Lebeus Hammond, who were out at work, were captured by a party of six savages, and hurried away to the north. One evening the 2d or 3d day, Mr. Bennett asked one of the Indians for his moccason awl, to help put on a button. 'No want button for one night,' replied the savage—from which the prisoners inferred that after another day they were to be murdered. While the Indians went to a spring to drink, they concerted a plan to escape. Mr. Bennett being in years, was permitted to travel unbound. Hammond and the boy had their arms tied. At night they all lay down to sleep except an Indian and Mr. Bennett; the latter brought in dry wood, kept up the fire, busied himself as if to make everything as comfortable as he could, and then seating himself by the fire, took the Indian's spear, laid it on his lap, and rolled it playfully on his thigh. Every now and then the savage would cast a look at him, half of suspicion, and then go to picking the deer's head again which he had roasted and held in his hand, nodding the while, half asleep. Tired, the other Indians who had laid down wrapped in their blankets, snored loudly, and Bennett was soon assured of their being in a deep sleep. Watching his opportunity, he thrust the savage through with the spear, who fell across the burning logs with a groan. In an instant Hammond and young Bennett were cut loose, and the other Indians attacked. Five were killed, and the other got away wounded, a spear sticking in his back. The victors came in, bringing with them the Indians' scalps and their arms as trophies."

"Upon my word! there was trial, suffering and courage. But none of Mrs. Myers' family, it seems, were in the battle?"

"O yes—not her father, but her brother Solomon was in the thickest of the engagement, and had the good fortune to escape. The BENNETT family stands forth conspicuously among the patriots of that day, who fought and suffered for the glorious cause of liberty."

"Blissful rest to those who have departed! Prosperity and happiness to the living!"*

---

* Mrs. Bennett has been, and yet is one of the clearest chroniclers of early scenes. Though the light
"Revisits not those orbs, that roll in vain
To find its piercing ray,"
the mental eye retains all its early power and lustre. Though now (1845) 83 years of age, it is a pleasure to sit by her side and hear
"Of most disastrous chances—hair breadth 'scapes,"
witnessed in her eventful youth. A beautiful situation on the left, half a mile above Col. Dorrance's, is the property and residence of that brother's son who was taken with her father. All around the house there is a display of neatness and taste, delightful to behold. John Bennett, Esq., besides being one of the very best farmers in the valley, during the location of our canal, proved himself an able engineer, combining with accurate mathematical knowledge, that soundness of judgment which no teaching could impart. It has been stated that one of the sons of Mrs. Myers was high sheriff of the county; another was for a number of years an approved magistrate; and a daughter is married to the Rev. Dr. Peck, the able editor of the Methodist Episcopal Review, published in New York, and a polished gentleman, as well as a most eloquent preacher. It is pleasant to trace up the fortunes of deeply suffering families from the gloom of the olden time to the brightness which now gilds their path.

NO. VIII.

THE SHOEMAKER FAMILY.

"STOP! Draw the reins, boy. Stay your horses! Let us tarry a moment before this beautiful mansion. A double house, set in from the avenue far enough to allow a spacious yard, lofty shade trees, fruits, flowers and shrubbery in exuberant profusion, yet nothing crowded! See that Peacock spreading his golden honours as he moves upon the velvet lawn. Upon my word, this would be thought handsome in New Haven itself!"—"Yes, and possibly the pattern may have been taken from that fine city, for the owner was educated at Yale!" "And is he a descendant from an old Wyoming patriot?" "Ay, by both sides of the house. The Hon. Charles Denison Shoemaker is the son of the late Elijah Shoemaker, formerly sheriff of Luzerne, who, it will be recollected, was the son of Lieut. Benjamin Shoemaker, so treacherously slain by *Windecker*, on the day of the massacre. Benjamin had married the daughter of the good old Cameronian Scotchman, frequently spoken of in our preceding pages. That the alliance is cherished as it should be is shown by "M'Dowal" being given as a middle name by Sheriff Shoemaker to one of his sons. Elijah Shoemaker had married a daughter of Col. Nathan Denison, whose name is itself an eulogy, and synonymous with every manly virtue."

"In respect to the two grandfathers our annals are so full as to leave no details necessary here, further than to say, that their plantation was the original allotment of Mr. Shoemaker when, as one of the Forty, he came in on the first settlement of Wyoming. Elijah, the father, added to it several lots.—Between the avenue and the mountain, he held a mile square, bounded on the four sides by roads, and subject, when the crops became inviting, to the depredations of cattle. During those summer months, just at dawning of day you might see him mounted, two strong and favourite dogs his companions, starting for a four mile ride round that favourite portion of his place. The early and stirring activity of the master kept alive a similar spirit in all around him, and it required the abundant product of his large plantation to support his numerous family and meet the demands which his hospitality and too greatly obliging disposition made upon him. Every one who wanted a favour was sure of an obliging answer, and almost certain of aid from his purse, his granary, or his name.

"After finishing his studies and graduating at New-Haven, C. D. Shoemaker returned, and was soon after appointed prothonotary of Luzerne, subsequently judge of the county, which he held for several years. Among the active business men of the county, he has several brothers, all in prosperous circumstances.

"Pleasing as are the speculations and beautiful the review, we must not linger too long, but hasten on to other inviting scenes."

NO. IX.

JUDGE DENISON.

"More gently here: we approach the hallowed spot where the aged and the young men of Wyoming, gathering around their wives, their mothers, and their little ones, to shield them from the fury of the ruthless savages—to protect their hearths and their altars from violation—presented, in array of arms, their own breasts to the foe. Many were old and feeble; many were young and tender; few had been accustomed to war, and all were undisciplined."

"Why then did they go out?"

"What could they do? The effective men of Wyoming were away with Washington's army. Already had the enemy made a lodgment in the upper part of the valley; and unless defeated and driven back, the whole settlement would become a scene of murder and conflagration from their scattered bands. To bring all together into forts was impracticable, and, dispersed as they were, where were they to obtain provisions?"

"I see how it was—they must fight and conquer, or be slaughtered, without the honour of a manly resistance."

"As brave men were wont to do, they took counsel of their courage, and marched out to meet danger in the very teeth. It is not my purpose now to describe the battle; but look to the left. Do you observe that ancient looking red house, standing in a dozen rods from the road, surrounded by those venerable trees? That was the residence of Col. NATHAN DENISON, who commanded the left wing of the American troops. Though unfortunate, his conduct on that day was that of a faithful and brave officer. Outflanked and overpowered by a vast superiority of numbers, the change of position, wisely ordered, became a retreat—the retreat a rout—the battle—a massacre."

"I tremble—my heart sinks within me, and a cold shivering comes over my frame, when I hear of that bloody affair. But pray tell me, is it true that Col. Denison took command of the fort? Is it true that when called on to surrender and he asked, 'What terms?' they answered—'THE HATCHET,' and nevertheless, without further attempt at defence, he gave up the fort to certain destruction, and almost every soul was murdered before his eyes?"

"No—it is not true."

"Such is the statement of Ramsay, Gordon, Botta, Marshall, and I think the London Gentleman's Magazine for 1778." "All false—all different versions of the same story, but agreeing in the grossest errors."

"He did not then surrender his command to the cruelty of the enemy, who threatened them with the hatchet, and that without effort to protect them?"

"No—no. All these statements do great injustice to Col. Denison; and it is strange, in his lifetime, he did not take means to remove this impression from his fair fame. No. His conduct in the very trying hour, when the fort was surrounded by an exulting and victorious enemy, was that of a wise, firm, and pa-

APPENDIX.

triotic officer. I love to take every occasion to rescue his name from those aspersions. Knowing his worth and venerating his memory, I take pleasure to vindicate his character and to speak his just praise. Col. Denison surrendered on terms of capitulation, considering the circumstances in which he was placed, honourable to his character as an officer; above all, shielding and protecting the women and children—all who were in the fort, from violence.* Perhaps higher powers—a more consummate prudence—equal boldness and self-possession, are necessary to save the remnants of a people so situated, than to lead successfully in battle. Marshall, in his late edition, has corrected the error, and given a more correct account of the transaction. The universal respect and confidence that attended Col. Denison, from the battle to the time of his death, attest the high estimation in which his character was held among the inhabitants of Wyoming, who were witnesses of, and affected by, his conduct.

"When the jurisdiction of Connecticut ceased, and the laws of Pennsylvania became supreme in Wyoming, Col. Denison was appointed from policy, as being a favourite of the people, in whom they had entire confidence, one of the associate judges of the court. Four were commissioned: Denison and Gore—selected as being partial to the Yankee interest; Fell and Hollenback—one a Pennsylvania Quaker, the other a Virginian—were preferred as having the confidence, in a peculiar degree, of the other party. A man of good sense and stern integrity—the selection was made with great wisdom and propriety."

"Do you remember Wyoming so long ago as to be able to recall the court to recollection, when all four of the judges were on the bench?"

"O, yes—perfectly: I see them now. Courts were held in the chamber of what was the old academy, the jail being below. Behold Sheriff Colt with his white staff in advance—see that short, fat, somewhat aged, but active man, with a smart cocked hat, coming up.—Look again: they are arranged on the bench. The President of the Court, Judge Rush, in the centre; on his right Judges Denison and Gore—on his left, Judges Hollenback and Fell. Dignity and decorum mark their appearance and proceedings, so far as it was possible to restrain the impetuosity, the wit, or mischief of a numerous bar of highly talented, but somewhat ungovernable lawyers. Judge Denison, though cheerful in the social circle, never laughed and seldom smiled. His looks were grave, but pleasing—not sad, but extremely sedate. Such was the character of all his deportment. His judgment was sound, as his heart was pure; but there was nothing showy about him—no attempt at effect—but all reposed in him, because his integrity was undoubted, while his good sense and intelligence inspired unlimited confidence.

"The president judge with a slight cast in his eye, that gave a peculiar but not unpleasant expression to his countenance, had a look full of intelligence, quickness and sagacity:—'Are you ready, gentlemen, on the part of the defendant?' How clear his voice, how distinct his enunciation! To the grand jury his charges were models of purity of style, soundness of sentiment, and impressiveness of delivery. But look at the bar—there is Lawyer Dick, a thick, stout set gentleman of five and thirty. Wit, humour, sarcasm, playing about his round face. He comes out in thunder—he sets the court in a roar of laughter, and having thrown them off their guard, by a few powerful but pertinent remarks, drives his cause home, and wins it, if possible to be won.—That tall, delicate looking gentleman, so neatly, I might say, elegantly dressed, is Dan Smith, of Northumberland. See! he turns pale and actually trembles as he rises to speak: you are interested by such exceeding modesty, and half fear he will not be able to go on. Fear nothing. What grace—how sweetly his voice breaks on the ear—what words of persuasive wisdom begin to flow—and now, pour along in a rapid torrent. Ah! that is eloquence. Just such a man, were I a girl of twenty, methinks, I should fall in love with—were he ten or fifteen years younger.—Observe that heavy stout gentleman, with large head and florid complexion: Stop—he is about to speak. How rapid

---

* After the surrender, there was but one life lost in the fort. It is important that this matter be rightly comprehended. Teh execution of Boyd was the only instance of life being taken, after the capitulation, *until Col. John Butler left Wyoming with his army.* THEN began scenes of murder and conflagration, by hands of marauding Indians, whom he averred he could not control.

his delivery—the words crowd so, one upon the other, they sometimes choke utterance: then the stream flows again. He talks good sense. Why shouldn't he? His head has more law in it than half a modern library."

"Who is he?"

"It is EVAN RICE EVANS, a powerful advocate with a good fee and an intricate cause. This very handsome man on the left is CHARLES HALL, of Sunbury. His dress is rich—how neatly his ruffle is plaited! Slow, distinct, and very pleasant in speaking, he prepares with care, and argues his cause with excellent skill. But here is the distinguished THOMAS COOPER going to speak in a criminal cause. Short, round, stooping forward—his head nodding as if too full of matter to hold still—a florid and right English countenance and complexion."

"Will he speak long?"

"Not he. His forte is to seize two or three strong points and present them forcibly to the court and jury. He never wearies by long speeches: never uses a word, an illustration, or an argument that is not to the purpose. A man of extraordinary endowments—of most distinguished genius: But there rises an answerer to Mr. Cooper. Observe that tall—raw, I had almost said—and awkward man; how he scratches his head—depend on it there is something in it. How high he pitches his voice: how loud he speaks: how plain, unselected, almost coarse in his language. Yet is there matter in him."

"But who is he?"

"That is JOHN ROSS, of Easton. He has not a particle of grace, but he is indefatigable: his dress, though good, is awkwardly put on; what does he care? the law is his study—the practice his delight. He mingles freely with all classes, high and low, and has a thorough knowledge of human nature. Hence he is a most successful jury lawyer: and not only remarkable, but renowned, in all the courts he practices in, for his technical accuracy in drawing indictments, and his almost irresistible ingenuity in pulling them to pieces, when drawn by another."

"You amuse me with these sketches of the old bar. Can't you give us a portrait of Sitgreaves, Dan Levy, Duncan, Charles Houston, Bowman, Wells, Griffin, Dyer, Catlin and Palmer?"

"Stop—stop—you are cutting out too much work for one afternoon." "Yes, I could give you a characteristic trait or two of each; but not now. Besides, it was not my purpose to speak, at present, of any of the Luzerne lawyers. Of all these, as time, opportunity, and humour shall prompt. Soon after the establishment of peace, Judge Denison returned to Stonington, Connecticut, and with filial piety brought out his aged father to reside with him. The old gentleman survived until 1803, and then was gathered to his native earth, aged 88 years.

"Col. Denison departed this life January 25th, 1809, aged 68 years.

"His piety was ardent. The sweet influences of religious faith and hope chastened and elevated to saint-like purity his naturally amiable disposition. One of his sons, now no more, was several years a representative from Luzerne in the Assembly, and afterwards in Congress, in both of which stations he served with distinguished ability. It is conceded that to Mr. George Denison, with Judge Scott and Judge Mallery, we owe, in a great degree, all that is beneficial in our system of internal improvement, especially as regards northern Pennsylvania:—But yonder is the monument."

NO. X.

LUKE SWEETLAND.

STRANGERS who visit Wyoming, besides having in view a visit to the monument, the battle ground and bloody rock, should cross the bridge and pass up through Kingston for the pleasure of the ride. The road, or rather noble avenue, for five miles, is an hundred feet wide, showing that the minds of the early settlers were graduated on no narrow scale. The Kingston gentlemen (thanks probably to their ladies), have displayed a much greater degree of taste in their buildings, the improvement of their grounds, and in ornamental shrubbery around their dwellings, than their neighbours. A companion, quick to hear, intelligent to relate, and with sufficient tact not to annoy by talking too much, would add to the pleasure of the jaunt. From among fifty elegant country seats, one on the left, half a mile after passing Col. Denison's, would immediately attract admiration and elicit praise. It is the residence of William Sweetland, Esq. For many years an enterprising merchant, wealth has flowed into his coffers as if they were its natural deposit. Besides the embellishment around his mansion, his having brought in pipes from the mountain more than a mile, water from a spring, that he might have a cool and gushing stream at his door, shows that he has the right spirit to render home an agreeable place. His mills within the ravine of the mountain, and several farms with white cottages further up upon the hills, tell at once of taste, enterprise, and true economy.

Mr. Sweetland was one of the delegates to form the present constitution; and, if inclination had led him, might have entered into public life in any station he should have chosen.

This is another pleasant instance of prosperity, among descendants from early Wyoming settlers who were doomed to dreadful suffering.

Luke Sweetland, the grandfather, bore arms in defence of Wyoming, although it is not certainly known whether he was in the battle. Immediately after the expulsion, he, with twenty-five or thirty others of the inhabitants, united together and joined (not enlisted) the company of Capt. Spalding. The fact is shown by the receipt they gave to Col. Butler for continental arms, issued to them at Port Penn. Their aid thus strengthening Spalding's company enabled him earlier to march to Wilkesbarre and arrest the depredations of the Indians. Mr. Sweetland was taken prisoner with Joseph Blanchard, near Nanticoke, where they had gone to mill, (this was August 24, 1778,) and were carried by the savages to their country, near Geneva Lake. Besides the constant dread of torture, his sufferings from cold and want of food during the winter were intense. A man of ardent piety, the confidence and hope imparted by religion sustained him. To trace his weary days of captivity would be but a repetition of ever-recurring sorrows. After having failed in several attempts to escape, he was at length rescued by our army under Gen. Sullivan. Returning to his native Connecticut, he had a narrative of his captivity and sufferings printed at Hartford, which is in the possession of the writer. In later days I knew, and knowing, could not but esteem the good old man. His taste and pride took a right direction, and were of much value to the settlement: I refer to his establishment of a nursery for fruit, and his introduction from New England of various kinds of apples, selected with care. It is long since he was withdrawn from life. The contrast between the sufferings of the grandsire and the prosperity of his descendant, leads to agreeable reflections. I cannot close this very brief notice, without a passing tribute to the memory of William Sweetland and Belding Sweetland, sons of the old gentleman, who in early life were the attached, the respected friends of the writer. Though in a position remarkable for general health they were both taken away in the midday of activity and usefulness. Peace to those who have departed; prosperity and honour to the living!

NO. XI.

CAPT. M'KERACHAN.

CAPT. WILLIAM M'KERACHAN was the first officer of the Hanover company. Evincing at once a spirit of singular modesty and patriotism, he said to Capt. Stewart, on the morning of the battle: " My pursuits in life have thus far been those of peace; you have been used to war and accustomed to command. On parade I can manœuvre my men; but in the field no unnecessary hazard should be run;

a mistake might prove fatal. Take you the lead, I will fight under you, with my men, as an aid, or a private in the ranks. Your presence at the head of the Hanover boys will impart confidence." So it was arranged, and they fell together.

Mr. M'Kerachan was a native of Ireland. Not classically, but well educated, he left Belfast, county Antrim, in the summer of 1764, then a young man, to seek his fortune in America. Landing in Philadelphia, he passed into Chester county, and taught school in Nantmel, for a season; from thence he went to Bucks county. There, and in New Jersey, he spent a year or two, occupied in the honourable profession of a schoolmaster. As early as 1774, the romance of the Wyoming contest attracted and pleased his ardent imagination, and he became a settler at Nanticoke, Hanover township. After instructing children a brief period, scenes of wider scope and more commanding interest engaged his attention. Having accumulated by industry and economy sufficent funds, he set up a store, and purchased lands. Among his papers recently found, are a number of deeds for valuable tracts, showing that he had become a very respectable landed proprietor. In his memorandum book are several passages, indicative of his studies, knowledge and character. Mathematical problems, some of them belonging to navigation, show that that branch of science was familiar to him. An entry, made June 24, 1768, would indicate that serious subjects occupied his thoughts, and that he was of the Presbyterian persuasion. "The Saturday before the sacrament, Mr. Foster had his text in Matthew the 12th chapter 42d verse. The sacrament morning Mr. Carmichael had his text in the 12th chapter and 3d verse of Isaiah.

"The evening sermon by Mr. Foster.—Text, 6th chapter and 11th verse of the Ephesians."

That he was not only esteemed in his immediate neighbourhood, but by the community at large, is shown by his commission from the authorities in Connecticut, as a magistrate in Westmoreland, and one of the judges of the court.

Several stanzas of poetry are in his hand-writing. Whether original or copied, it is impossible for us to determine. If his own, they show talent; if selected, they certainly display taste, though they may sound old fashioned:

To ——
" Now let my cares all buried lie,
My griefs be ever dumb;
Your sorrows swell my heart so high
They leave my *own* no room."

Were we sure the poetry was his own, we would copy the preceding four verses, which have some pretty lines of thought. But though desiring to give as perfect a picture as possible of Wyoming and its distinguished men, we must not swell our volume too much by extraneous matter, however interesting. He was tall, had a fine person—an alert step—a cheerful disposition, and a countenance pleasingly expressive.

He fell, as the reader is apprized, on the 3d of July, 1778, in the Indian battle. Farewell to the brave, the generous, the true-hearted Irishman. Gentle sleep and a happy resurrection to his manly spirit, who, in the midst of gathering honours and accumulating prosperity, in the very prime of manhood, laid down his life for Wyoming!

NO. XII.

MR. SAMUEL CAREY.

WHILE our minds are on the opposite side of the river, at *Jacob's Plains*, as the upper part of Wilkesbarre is termed, sketching a brief outline of the Abbott's—the Searle's—and the Williams', who reside there, methinks I may as well fulfil a promise previously made, and give you some account of the family of CAREY, their neighbours; a name which stands conspicuous on the list of those patriots who served and suffered at Wyoming, in the cause of liberty and their country.

APPENDIX

Mr. Samuel Carey is now 79 years old; of course he was 19 in 1778, the year of the battle. Active, ardent and patriotic, he was enrolled in Captain Bidlack's company—was out on several scouting parties before the invasion—was up at Wyalusing, and with our men at Exeter, aiding to bring away the remains of the Hardings and others, murdered by the Indians a day or two before the battle. On the fatal third he was at his post, and marched with the brave Bidlack to the contest. Their position was near the right. The left wing was earliest pressed and retreated, being thrown into entire confusion before the centre or right gave way; but retreat had become inevitable. Mr. C. left the road and passed down on the low flats near where the monument is now being erected; Zipperah Hibberd was nearest to him. Hibberd was in the prime of early manhood, six feet high, built at once for strength and activity; he was straight as an arrow, and moved with a light elastic step. Of him it is told by several of the old settlers, that in their athletic sports Hibberd would take off his hat and shoes—let two companions hold a string extended so that, in walking under it, he could just touch it with his head: he would then step off a few paces till he got his proper distance, return on the spring, and leap over the string with the alertness of the bounding deer. His activity, and manly and social qualities, rendered him a general favourite. Mr. Hibberd was but recently married. Preparations for the engagement had been made the day previous. Fear was a stranger to his breast; but he was sensible and sagacious, and he saw from the unprepared state of our people, enfeebled by the two companies, raised for our special defence, being marched and kept away, and from the evidence of great force on the part of the enemy, that the chances were all against us. Perhaps, and it is thought there was a particular presentiment, that go the battle as it would, he should not survive. But listening to nothing but the dictates of patriotism and duty, he fitted himself for the field—went to the door—looked abroad to the bright heavens and the beautiful earth, then clothed in the rich robe of approaching harvest—gazed a moment—rested his gun against the door-post—hastened into the house and impressed one parting kiss on the pale lips of his trembling bride—spoke not a word, but tore himself away; and the next hour there was not a soldier that marched to the field with more cheerful alacrity. He went to return no more.

Hibberd and Carey ran together towards the river, Hibberd in advance, breaking a path through a heavy piece of rye. The obstruction, perhaps, proved fatal to him; for by the time they got through he was nearly exhausted, and showed signs of great fatigue. On coming near the river bank and leaving the rye field, Mr. Hibberd sprang to the sandbar, but was closely pursued by an Indian, who overtook him before he could gain the stream. As Hibberd turned to defend himself he received the accursed spear in his breast, and fell lifeless on the sand.

Mr. Carey got to the river lower down, and succeeded in swimming across, but the savages had crossed over before him, and he was instantly surrounded by several. One who seemed to have authority took charge of him, but a small Indian, pitted with the small-pox, and having lost an eye, (as he stood naked, for Mr. C. had stripped off all his clothes that he might swim,) with a malicious smile, drew a knife up and down his breast and abdomen, about an inch from the skin, saying the while, "Te-te—te-te." They then made him swim back, bound his hands, and he was conducted to Wintermoot's. The fort had been set on fire by the enemy at the commencement of the engagement, and Mr. C. saw the remains of one or two of our people, who had been thrown on the burning pile, but they were then lifeless. That night he lay on the ground, bound, and without food. The next morning an officer struck him on the mouth with his open hand. "You are the fellow," said he, "that threatened yesterday morning you would comb my hair, are you?" He then learned that the Indian who had taken him was Capt. Roland Montour, who now gave him food, unbound, and led him to a young savage who was mortally wounded. What passed he could not then perfectly comprehend, but afterwards learned the purpose was to show him to the dying Indian, and ask if his life should be preserved and he be taken to the Indian's parents to be adopted instead of their lost son. He assented, and young Carey's life was saved. They then painted him, and gave him the name of the dying Indian—Coconeunquo—of the tribe of Onondagoes.

APPENDIX.

When the enemy marched from the valley, Mr. Carey, carefully guarded, was taken with them, and when they reached the Indian country, was handed over to the family into which he had been adopted, where, if he would have conformed to savage customs, and have drunk so deep of the waters of forgetfulness as to cease to remember country, connection and friends, he might have remained peaceable, if not happy; but beloved Wyoming, doubly dear from her sorrows, would rise to his slumbers, as it was ever present to his waking hours, and he sighed for liberty and home. He thinks the old Indian and squaw—his savage parents—saw that he could not mingle in spirit with them: for they used constantly to mourn for their lost boy. Just at day-breaking they would set up a pitiful cry—oh! oh! ho!—and at evening, as the sun was going down—oh! oh! ho!—and with all their stoicism their sorrows would not cease. At times, while here, he suffered much from hunger, having only a spoonful of parched corn a day for several weeks. He thought he should have famished; and in the severe winters, his sufferings from cold were extreme; but he shared like the rest of the family, and they evidently meant, after once adopting, to treat him kindly.

More than two weary years were passed in this way, when he got to Niagara, where he was detained, though with less suffering, until restored to liberty by the glorious news of peace and independence. It was on the 29th of June, 1784, before the charming valley again met his sight, after having suffered six years of distressing captivity.

Mr. Carey mentions the fact, stated by others, that Walter Butler, a favourite son of Col. John Butler, was killed by the Americans, near Mud Creek, on returning from one of his excursions against our settlements on the Mohawk. He adds—what before I did not remember to have heard—that one of the Wintermoots was killed at the same time. Butler was shot by a rifle ball through the head, aimed at him from an extraordinary distance.

There was a Joseph Carey and Samuel Carey both killed in the battle, but it does not occur to my recollection whether they were relatives of the Mr. Samuel Carey of whom I now speak. His brother, Nathan Carey, was in the engagement, and fortunately escaped. Their father's name was Eleazer Carey, a name held by one of his descendants, still known and highly respected in the valley.

Though at the advanced age of 79, Mr. Carey enjoys tolerable health; his mind active and his memory sound. Though not rich, he is yet, by the industry and frugality of a long life, comfortable in his declining days, and has the happiness of having sons and daughters settled around him, all well to live, and all respectable—and some in very independent circumstances. His wife, Theresa, was the daughter of Captain Daniel Gore, of whom I have spoken; so that if the morning of life was clouded with sorrow and woe, his evening is calm and serene.*

——"But did you not say there was a Mr. *John Carey*, a brave and faithful soldier in the revolutionary war?"

I did: the brother of him of whom I have been speaking. An old and respected friend, I will give you an account of him at the earliest possible moment. —Do not hurry me. I must not mingle things too much together. In due time you shall hear all; but have patience. I have a great deal to tell. There never was a people who did more, or suffered more—or ever received so little remuneration. It was high time that the wrongs and sufferings of Wyoming should be fully stated, and her neglected and traduced character be vindicated. While I can speak, or hold a pen, she shall not need a tongue or hand to defend her.

* Mr. Samuel Carey died in 1842, and was buried with military honours.

NO. XIII.

COLONEL RANSOM.

GEORGE PALMER RANSOM was a working bee from the beginning. Though scarcely 14, he enlisted in his father's company and marched, on the 1st of January,

1777—the dead of winter—to join Washington's army. Ransom's company consisted of 82 men, and Durkee's was equal, both being full. In September following, the company had 62; but Gaylord, father of C. E. Gaylord; two Sawyers, brothers of the former sheriff Slocum, had died, as had Spencer.—Underwood had a rupture and was discharged. Porter was killed at Millstone—Colton, Worden, Austin, and James Smith had returned or were on furlough. These particulars are adverted to for the purpose of showing beyond doubt, that the two companies of Durkee and Ransom were large—having more than 80 in each. They went by Stroudsburgh and reached Morristown early in the evening.

Thence they marched to Millstone—they were attached to no regiment or Brigade—but were called the Independent Companies and acted as a distinct corps—in the most active and dangerous position, between the lines of the two armies. The enemy was at Brunswick—our men at Millstone, within little more than an hour's march. As might have been expected, they were immediately engaged. The enemy came out in considerable force to forage, and had three or four pieces of cannon. General Philemon Dickerson (brother of John Dickerson, author of the Farmer's Letters), commanded a detachment of New Jersey militia, who, with the two independent companies, attacked the British. A sharp engagement ensued—the enemy were routed; forty-seven wagons and one hundred and thirty horses were taken. In this engagement Justice Porter was cut in two by a cannon ball, and fell dead close by the side of Serj. Thomas Williams. Porter is spoken of by all who knew him, as a remarkably fine fellow. Pleasant of countenance, well formed, extremely active and withal buoyant and gay—a most cheerful companion as well as an excellent soldier. One of the wagons, a trophy of victory, was brought to Wyoming by Capt. Ransom, but with almost everything else was consumed by the fire of the savages. The value of the property taken must have been considerable, as each soldier shared four dollars of the proceeds. Two of the militia were killed and a number of the British. It was a gallant affair; the two companies were commanded by Durkee as the eldest captain. In spring they were ordered to Boundbrook, and placed with other portions of the army under Gen. Lincoln. Just at day, the morning after their arrival, the enemy came upon them by surprise, on three sides. Lincoln's horse was saddled—he mounted—ordered a retreat to a hill about a mile distant. Little execution was done by the fire of the enemy, although they were quite near, and hallooed, "Run, you damn'd rebels, run." If our men knew when to run away, they also knew when to fight—as the regulars well knew, and kept at a respectful distance when we had taken up a suitable position. The summer was sickly; the two companies suffered from the camp distemper. Those also were inoculated for the small-pox who had not previously gone through the disease. The companies were in constant service during the ensuing eventful and severe campaign—wherever there was danger to be met or honour to be won.

They were in the battles of Brandywine and Germantown. At the bombardment of Mud Fort, the companies being stationed at Woodbury, detachments were drafted for duty on the works and sustained the hottest of the enemy's fire. Constant Matthewson, belonging to Ransom's, being with a detachment under the command of Lieut. Spalding, was killed in the fort.

Now the companies were attached to the 1st Connecticut regiment—Lieut. Col. Russell. As, when they first marched, they were kept as a distinct corps, there is reason to believe it was intended to keep them from Wyoming (where, by the resolution of Congress for raising them, they were to be stationed), no longer than the pressing emergency, under which they were called away, demanded; but the pressure of circumstances, superior to all law or contract, compelled the government to keep them below, leaving Wyoming wholly defenceless. They wintered at **Valley Forge.**

Rumours now of the meditated attack of the savages upon Wyoming came down. The officers respectfully but firmly urged on their superiors that the enemy were preparing to strike Wyoming—that there was no force there to defend it—that these companies were raised under a solemn pledge that they should be stationed there for the defence of the inhabitants; and asking to be marched back. But they could not be spared. Some resigned and returned, and the two companies were consolidated into one under the command of Capt. Simon Spalding; and orders given to hasten to the relief of the settlement. Young Ransom was with Capt. Spalding. They marched first to Lancaster—then to Reading, Bethlehem, Nazareth, the Wind-Gap, to Shoup's, four miles from Merwine's, where they were on the 3d of July—the day of the battle. What countless woes might have been averted had they not been ordered away, or permitted sooner to return! The first order was to march in, and take possession of Wilkesbarre fort, as a rallying point; and they advanced to the creek where the gate, this side of Pocono, stands. Meeting the flying inhabitants, who told them, with their force they would do no good, Capt. Spalding sent scouts to see, who returned with news that the whole valley was in possession of the savages. They returned to Stroudsburgh—gave all the assistance in their power to the suffering fugitives, waited for reinforcements, and under the command of Col. Butler, marched in, early in August, to Wyoming.

The battle-ground presented a melancholy spectacle. Most of the bodies were so much decayed they could not be recognized. Mr. Ransom's father was wounded in the thigh, taken prisoner, and carried into Wintermoot's fort, and his head cut off. There was the most tiger-like ferocity exhibited against all who had been into the service from Wyoming, especially the officers. Every species of torture was practised upon them. Such was the state of the bodies that it was impossible then to gather and bury them. In the ring near Perkins' tavern, at Bloody Rock, where the prisoners were murdered, Mr. Ransom counted 27 bodies.

In 1779, when Gen. Sullivan invaded the Indian country, Capt. Spalding's company accompanied him, and Mr. Ransom was at his post. He was in the battle of Newtown, and gives a very interesting account of that memorable invasion. The case of Lieut. Boyd is one of thrilling interest, but our space does not allow of its detail here. We shall recur to that and other incidents hereafter.

In December, 1780, Mr. Ransom was taken prisoner by a party of Butler's Rangers and Indians. Old Mr. Harvey was taken at the same time, with Bullock, Frisby, Cady, and Elisha Harvey, son of the old gentleman.

They were taken to Niagara. On their way they suffered much from cold and hunger; but at Tioga-point they killed a horse, and then faced sumptuously. Next summer the old men were released, young Harvey, Frisby, and Ransom kept prisoners, and sent to Montreal during the summer. In the fall they were removed to Prisoner's Island, where there were 167 American captives.

A sketch, not a biography—an outline is all that my limits permit; but there is one incident, so characteristic of American spirit, and so honourable to the firmness and patriotism of our soldiers, that I beg leave to relate it somewhat at length. "In February, 1781,"—I take Mr. Ransom's own words—"I was in Canada, 45 miles up the St. Lawrence river from Montreal, on an island with about 166 American prisoners. We were guarded by the refugees, or what was called tories, that belonged to Sir John Johnson's 2d regiment. The commanding officer of the guard, on the island, was a young Scotch officer, by the name of MacCalpin, about 18 years of age. The winter was very severe, and a great snow storm came and drifted before the door of the guard, who sent for some of the American prisoners to shovel it away. They refused, saying they were prisoners of war, and he had no right to set them to work for his pleasure. Enraged at this, the officer ordered them into irons, and directed others to take the shovels and go to work; these also refused, and were ironed. So he went on commanding and meeting with resolute disobedience to what they considered a tyrannical order. They had taken up arms and periled their lives to resist British tyranny, and would not now, though prisoners, submit to it. Some were ironed two together—some to a bar four together; thus he kept putting into irons as long as he had hand cuffs left. Among the last who refused, were myself and one Wm. Palmeters. We were then put into an open house, without door, floor, or windows, and directions given that we should have neither victuals, brandy, nor tobacco; but our faithful friends contrived to evade the guard, and we were furnished with all. There we remained all night, suffering extremely from the cold. The next morning MacCalpin came, thinking our spirits were broken, and demanded if we would not shovel snow. One word all answered—'Not by order of a d—d Tory.' He then took us out of that place, and put us in a hut just finished, with a good floor, and we sent for a black man, a good fiddler, for we had two on the island. We then opened our ball, dancing to keep ourselves warm, jigs, hornpipes, four and six handed reels. Where four were ironed to one bar, they could dance the cross-handed, or what we called the York reel. We continued in this merry mood until our Scotch gentleman found the place was too good for us. He then took us out and put us into a loft of one of the huts, which stood so low that a man could stand up only under the centre of the ridge. Here we were kept in extreme suffering two days and nights. In the mean time MacCalpin sent for Charles Grandison, our fiddler, and ordered him to play for his pleasure. The black went, but firmly declared he would not play while his fellow-prisoners were in irons. The officer then ordered a sort of court martial, composed of tories, who of course brought in the poor negro guilty. The sentence of the court was that he should be stripped—tied up, and receive ten lashes on his naked back—which was done. Smarting with the lash, the officer then demanded if he would fiddle as he was ordered. 'No, not while my fellow-prisoners are in irons.' Again he was tied up, and ten lashes laid on, but his firmness was not to be shaken, and the officer sent him to his hut.

"But I left my story to tell about the fiddler. MacCalpin then sent a party of soldiers to bring up some of the prisoners, several of whom were flogged severely; and one, against whom the tories had a particular spite, was tied neck and heels, a rope put round his neck, and he was thus drawn up to the chamber floor and kept until he was almost dead—let down, and then drawn up again. One John Albright, a young continental soldier, was flogged almost to death for being a kind-hearted man speaking his mind freely. But not one American was found to shovel snow.

"We remained here till the 9th day of June, when myself and two others, James Butterfield and John Brown, made our escape from the Island and laid our course for Lake Champlain. The 11th at noon, we came to the lake, and three days after we got to a settlement at Hubbertston, Vermont—the next day to Castleton, to a fort—from that to Pultney, where I had an uncle living. My companions went on to Albany, and there proclaimed the cruelty of the Scotch officer; it was published in the papers—a flag was dispatched to remonstrate against such abuse of our men; and we had the pleasure to hear, not long after, that MacCalpin was tried and broke—the prisoners being called as witnesses against him."

After visiting his relations at Canaan, Litchfield county, Connecticut, of which he was a native, Mr. Ransom returned to Wyoming, and soon after joined his company, attached to Col. Butler's regiment, stationed at West Point, where he remained till honourably discharged, at the close of the war.

From that time to this, Mr. Ransom has resided at Plymouth, upon the beautiful Shawnee flats, perhaps the richest portion of Wyoming. He has been called by the votes of his fellow-citizens to command the regiment, which his knowledge of military tactics well fitted him to manœuvre and discipline. Having served his country during the dark hours of the revolutionary contest long and faithfully, unambitious of office, he has lived, and still lives respected and beloved. Hardships endured while in the service combined with age, have much affected his limbs, so that he helps himself along with two short staves or crutches. He could scarcely dance now, though his heart, I will answer for it, is as light, and his spirit as firm for liberty and his country, as in '81.

He was strongly made, broad chested, and active in early life. He sprang quick and moved fast who got ahead of him then. His life and cheerfulness in the most gloomy hour diffused itself in good humour and spirit, through the whole company. The death of his father—the losses and sacrifices in the Revolutionary contest, for the savages and tories spared nothing of theirs when they swept the valley by fire and sword—left him poor at the close of the war, and imposed the necessity of constant industry. Children and grandchildren, among the most respectable in the valley, are living and growing up around him, and may be proud to claim descent from such ancestors. Without being wealthy, he is yet comfortable in his old age. No one takes a livelier pleasure in beholding the freedom and prosperity of his beloved country, the fruits of his father's and his own toils and sufferings. Rare indeed is the case presented of a son's serving through the whole of the Revolutionary contest, and of his father serving several years and laying down his life in the same noble cause. Verily the services and the blood of the Ransoms have been a portion of that seed from which have sprung up the independence, freedom, and prosperity, which make happy our favoured land. Long may these blessings continue—long may the veteran soldier and patriot live to enjoy them. And may the young men of the present generation take pattern from these noble spirits, and resolve to give everything, even life itself, to defend the glorious cause of Liberty and Law.*

* 1845. Col. Ransom is still in the enjoyment of very tolerable health, except his lameness, though his age is 82. A grandson, George Palmer Steele, has just closed his term of office as sheriff of Luzerne. Capt. Ransom, his father, was born in Canterbury. He and Capt. Durkee had both been in the old French war. Durkee, at the time of his death, was 50, Capt. Ransom 41. Col. Durkee, an older brother, who is frequently spoken of, 1769, and afterwards as colonel of one of the Connecticut regiments, died at Norwich, more than 40 years ago, and was buried with extraordinary display.

NO. XIV.

COL. JOHN JENKINS.

"COL. JOHN JENKINS was a very prominent man for many years in Wyoming. He was the son of *John Jenkins, Esq.*, a respectable magistrate, an accurate surveyor, and an ardent patriot. You have probably seen an account of a town meeting, legally warned, of the inhabitants of Westmoreland, at the beginning of the troubles with England, at which votes were passed, that make the blood thrill through the heart even now, declaring their decided hostility to the unconstitutional measures of the British Parliament—denouncing them as ruinous to American liberty, and pledging themselves to stand by the Continental Congress in the steps taken to vindicate the cause of freedom and their country.* John Jenkins, Esq., had the honour to preside as moderator of the meeting when those glorious resolutions were adopted."

"I have heard of them, but have not seen them. It required good and stout hearts thus early to take so bold a stand. They were patriots, indeed: and for myself, I would rather have those patriotic votes to show, as the work of an ancestor of mine, than the proudest patent of nobility ever granted by a king. His descendants ought to have them beautifully copied, framed, and hung up as a parlour ornament."

"You are right—they should. It would show a just and patriotic pride. The old gentleman took an active part in the transactions of the times until the expulsion of the inhabitants, in 1784, when he removed to Orange county, New York, and there died.

"John Jenkins, the son, of whom I now speak, had been appointed collector of taxes, but that did not exempt him from military duty. In November, 1777, he was on a scouting party up the river, near fifty miles. Mr. York (father of the late Rev. Miner York) was one of his companions. Lemuel Fitch was another; they were ambushed not far from Wyalusing, captured by a party of Indians, and taken to the British lines. I am told there is somewhere in existence a journal of Mr. Jenkins, kept during his captivity, but my searches for it have been unavailing.† An Indian chief of some celebrity was a prisoner to the Americans in Albany, and Col. John Butler sent Mr. Jenkins, under an escort of Indians, to be exchanged for the chief. On the way he suffered exceedingly, and had it not been that a young savage had become warmly attached to him, Mr. Jenkins thought he should have been massacred, and was almost sure he should

* Mrs. Bertha, consort of Col. John Jenkins, died in 1841, aged 84 years. She is several times mentioned in our annals.
† Since found.

have been starved. Ardent and constant in his attachments, as implacable and cruel in his resentments, the savage presents a character in which vice and virtue are strangely mingled and strongly contrasted. The young Indian, amidst rum and riot, for his sake kept himself sober and calm, fed him—protected him: and Mr. Jenkins was prompt, at all times, to do justice to his faithful friend, though, from the cruelties practised here, the savages generally were objects of horror and detestation.

"Arrived at Albany, the chief for whom he was to have been exchanged had just died of small-pox. The Indians insisted on taking Mr. Jenkins back with them. From their conduct and character he felt certain that they would take his life in revenge for that of their chief the moment they were beyond reach of pursuit. He was protected, and found his way home to a cordial welcome from friends and bride, for he had been recently married. After the massacre and expulsion of our people, Mr. Jenkins joined Capt. Spalding's company, and came in with him under the command of Col. Zebulon Butler, having the provisional appointment of lieutenant, subject to confirmation by Congress. When the troops had advanced to the second mountain, within five or six miles of Wilkesbarre, two parties were detached, of ten men each, one under Ensign M. Hollenback, to go down between the mountains and strike the valley opposite Nanticoke falls; the other, under Lieutenant Jenkins, to go northerly and strike the river at Lackawanna. Ensign Hollenback saw a party of savages, who fled to their canoe; a shot from one of his rifles wounded an Indian who sprang into the river, but was buoyed up by his friends till they reached the opposite shore, when he was carried off—whether dead or alive, could not be ascertained. One of our men, bravely, perhaps rashly, swam the river, found marks of blood, took the canoe as a trophy, and returned to his companions. Ensign Hollenback then marched up to Wilkesbarre and met the main body. Lieut. Jenkins, on arriving at the river at Pittston, wheeled to march down. when he encountered a party of the enemy. His orders were prompt—his conduct spirited. At the head of his men he advanced; they fired on the Indians, but their retreat was too rapid. A person with him assured me that the conduct of Jenkins showed that he was of true courage, an undoubted soldier; a character which he sustained throughout the war. Congress confirmed his appointment—issued his commission—and he continued in active service till peace.

"In 1779, when General Sullivan advanced into the Indian country, Lieut. Jenkins was selected, for his activity, zeal, and knowledge of the country, for one of his guides; the arduous and responsible duty he performed in a satisfactory manner. Lieut. Jenkins was in the decisive battle of Newtown, and among the most efficient and useful officers of his grade in that campaign.

"As this is meant as a sketch rather than a biography, you will hardly expect me to trace Mr. Jenkins through the war. He was always at the post of duty, of danger, and of honour; and left the service, at its close, with the reputation of a faithful patriot and good soldier.

"When peace came Mr. Jenkins became an active surveyor, and followed his compass, both in the Genesee country, and on the waters of the Susquehanna. In civil and political affairs he took an active part, and possessed a large share of public confidence. He held various civil and military offices in Luzerne—was commissioner of the county, member of assembly, colonel of militia, &c. When the great division in parties took place, Col. Jenkins zealously espoused the Democratic side—while his distinguished friend and rival, Col. Franklin, took an active part with the Federal party. For many years these two famous champions maintained a prominent lead, and were, in a good measure, the rallying points of the different parties. It was huzza for *Col. Jenkins!* Huzza for *Col. Franklin!* If I had time I would run a parallel between them; but not now. Both were respected—both beloved—both were men of unquestionable public virtue, capacity and patriotism.

"Col. Jenkins died in April, 1827, aged 73. In person he was of middle height, stout, well proportioned, framed for strength, endurance and activity combined; extremely hospitable, remarkably clever; yet grave, almost to austerity, in his looks when in thought or not speaking; but when animated in conversation there was a pleasing expression on his countenance. In conversation he was brief and sententious—sensible and plain. Like Atreus' son,

'He spoke no more than just the thing he ought.'

Col. Jenkins purchased the spot and built his house on the site of the old Wintermoot fort, where he lived many years, and where he died.—But several particulars press upon my mind, and I must speak of the colonel again."

NO. XV.

THE INMAN FAMILY.

"No faction's voice
Called them to the field—
But the pure consecrated love of home."

"Your account of the GORE family surprised—charmed me, and at the same moment made me sad. How dire must have been the necessity that should call so great a number of sons and sons-in-law, of one man, into the battle field. Seven! I should have thought, with all his ardour—with all his patriotism, the heart of the father would have burst with anxiety. The whole upon one cast!—Seven!—It was a fearful, a tremendous hazard. Seven! and five lay corpses on the bloody field at night! It was at once glorious and painful! What devotion to country! What attachment to liberty! What affection for the dear domestic ties of wife, children, parents and home! But I presume there was no other such instance, or anything like it, in the history of that fatal day?"

"It is scarcely to be imagined that any one family could muster more, and few so many; but the *necessity*—the *necessity* (from the two companies being drawn away) was imperious that every one who was left, able to carry a gun, should go out; and then, alas! there were too few. Others were equally spirited, and sent every one who was able, to the field. There was the INMAN family, a name that should be ever dear to Wyoming. Five brothers went to the battle field. Two others, one quite a lad, the other about 19—for there were seven sons—would have gone, but they had not arms. It is an interesting fact in the history of the invasion of Wyoming, that the companies of Durkee and Ransom were obliged to find their own arms. Of course, men of spirit, and regarding themselves as the special defenders of the settlement, they would obtain the best rifles and muskets the country afforded. When called away they took with them their guns, and thus Wyoming was not only left without men, but deprived of their arms; so that, for those who remained, there were not sufficient. There would otherwise have been six or seven of the Inman brothers in the battle; as it was, there were five—the two boys being left at home with their aged parents."

"Come to the point—what was the issue? how many fell? did they all escape? did they all return?"

"Two—Elijah Inman and Israel Inman, fell on the field; two escaped without injury; and the fifth, hotly pursued by the bloody savages, plunged into the river, overheated with exertion, and hid himself under the willows. Poor fellow! he might as well have fallen in the fight; for a cold settled on his lungs, and in a few weeks took him to his grave. Thus three sons perished."

"It was an awful mortality in one family."

"True, but the melancholy tale is not yet ended. I have another scene of woe to paint; but first let me say that they did not fall wholly unavenged. In the flight Rufus Bennett was closely pursued by a savage; both had discharged their pieces, and the Indian was chasing with tomahawk and spear. Richard Inman drew up his rifle, and the Indian fell dead within a few feet of his intended victim.

"With the rest of the settlement, the Inman family fled; but in the hope to put in some winter grain, returned in the fall. They found their farm a scene of desolation. Fire and destruction had done their utmost, and danger they knew lurked around them. Just at the setting in of winter the lads said they heard wild turkies in the neighbouring woods; and Isaac, a young man of 19, took his gun and went out. Shots were heard, and he did not return. Snow immediately after fell. That Indians had been in the neighbourhood was soon known, for other families had suffered; and the only hope was that he was alive, though a prisoner. Spring—which brings forth sweet blossoms—the warbling of birds—and wakens sounds of gladness and of joy, brought grief and woe to the already bruised heart of the poor old father. Isaac, the lost boy, might well have been a favourite. He was tall, straight as an arrow, gay, sprightly, and every way a very pleasing young man.

'Death found strange beauty on his manly brow
And dashed it out.'

"His mangled corpse was found, when the snow melted, in the edge of a little creek that passes through their farm; he had been shot; a war club lay by his side—his light silken hair was yet stained with blood—but I cannot tell it. He had been murdered and scalped with all an Indian's barbarity. So that four of the family fell that year; that is to say—Elijah, David, Israel and Isaac."

"It is a story of singular horror and sadness. That family indeed deserved well of their country. The father in the course of nature must long since have been gathered to our parent earth; but do any of his children, brothers of the fallen patriots, remain? O—I hope so—and in prosperity."

"Your wish is truth. A few miles below Wilkesbarre lives Col. EDWARD INMAN, one of our most respectable and wealthy citizens. He owns one of the noblest farms in the county—part of it the same where his father dwelt, and part added by his own industry, consisting of several hundred acres, embracing a large body of the most productive flats. Plenty crowns his board, and independence cheers the evening of his days."*

"I am rejoiced to hear; and with the poet I can say—

'The joy
With which their children tread the hallowed ground
That holds their venerated bones; the peace
That smiles on all they fought for; and the wealth
That clothes the land they rescued'—

Bring gladness to my heart."

* Elijah Inman, the father, died Feb., 1804, aged 86; Susan Inman, the mother, died 1809, aged 88.

NO. XVI.

MRS. LUCY IVES

WHEN the *Hazleton Travellers* were in a course of publication the writer received a brief letter, but replete with interesting matter, from the lady whose name is at the head of this number. Not choosing to disclose all he had learned, the information was preserved purposely to be first brought out in our history. Her tale was so full of sorrow, so shrouded in deepest woe, we thought to work up the materials into an essay of engrossing interest. Every effort to do so has failed—the heart swelled with emotion—the pen refused to trace a line; and the statement of Mrs. Ives, so touching in its simplicity, and so overwhelming in its dreadful record, we are obliged to give as we received it. Art could not heighten the calamity—fancy would strive in vain to add a single tint to the encrimsoned picture.

"Lucy Williams, now Lucy Ives, says she was at Forty Fort at the time of the battle, a child of ten years old.

APPENDIX

"She had two brothers in the battle, and a brother-in-law. Both her brothers were killed, and her brother-in-law wounded.

"Her father and family went immediately through the swamp; but he soon returned, hoping to secure a part of his harvest, and while endeavouring to do so was killed by the Indians.

"They had lived in Wyoming, at the time of the battle, about five years.

"Mother and children, after father's death, went to Canterbury, their native place, in Connecticut, and did not return till peace.

"Her father had a large stock of cattle, horses and sheep; everything was lost.

"Mother had five children left, Esther, Desire, Martha, Lucy and Darius, dependent on her, and the world to grapple with.

"My father's name was Elihu Williams. My brothers who were killed were named Rufus and Elihu."

We may add that they were highly respectable, but so broken, and having only one son, an infant, at the time of their expulsion, to return and re-establish the family, that the same degree of prosperity which has come to many of the ancient sufferers did not come to them. Would not the justice, as well as the generosity of the government, be exhibited by a grant of land to be divided among those who could make out a case like that of Mrs. Ives?

NO. XVII.

STEPHEN ABBOTT.

"ON the other side of the river, opposite Forty Fort, lives STEPHEN ABBOTT, a respectable and independent farmer. His father, John Abbott, was an early settler in Wyoming. There was one cannon, a four pounder, in the Wilkesbarre fort, and it had been agreed upon that, when certain information came that the enemy was dangerously near, the gun should be fired as a signal. At work on the flats, with his son, a lad eight or nine years old, he heard the terrific sound come booming up. Where, or how near the enemy might be, of course he could not tell; but loosening the oxen from the cart, he hastened to the place of rendezvous. He was in the battle, and fought side by side with his fellows to defend their homes. It makes my heart bleed to recur, as in these sketches I am obliged to do so often, to the retreat of our people. Again and again I aver there was no dishonour in it. I do not believe a braver, or more devoted set of men ever marched forth to battle; but remember, a great part of the fighting men, those fit for war, raised for the defence of Wyoming, were away; defending the country, to be sure—fighting in the thrice glorious cause of liberty and independence, most certainly, but leaving their own homes wholly exposed, so that our little army was made up of such of the settlement as was left, who could carry a gun, however unfit to meet the practised and warlike savage, and the well-trained rangers of the British Butler. Mr. Abbott took his place in the ranks. He had a wife and nine children (the eldest boy being only eleven) depending on his protection, labour and care. If a man so circumstanced had offered his services to Washington, the general would have said, 'My friend, I admire your spirit and patriotism, but your family cannot dispense with your services without suffering—your duty to them is too imperious to permit you to leave them, even to serve your country.' Such would have been the words of truth and soberness. But the emergency allowed no exemption. In the retreat Mr. Abbott fled to the river at Monockasy Island, waded over to the main branch, and not being able to swim, was aided by a friend and escaped. In the expulsion which followed, taking his family he went down the Susquehanna as far as Sunbury. What could he do? Home—harvest—cattle, all hopes of provision for present and future use were at Wyoming. Like a brave man who meets danger and struggles to overcome it—like a faithful husband and fond father, he looked on his dependent family, and made his resolve. Mr. Abbott returned in hopes to secure a part of his excellent harvest which he left ripening in his fields. I am somewhat more particular in mentioning this, my friend, for I wish, as you take an interest in this matter, to impress this important fact upon your mind—that our people, though sorely struck, though suffering under a most bloody and disastrous defeat, did not lie down idly in despair without an effort to sustain themselves. No: the same indomitable spirit which they had manifested in overcoming previous difficulties, still actuated them. Mr. Abbott came back, determined, if possible, to save from his growing abundance the means of subsistence. He went upon the flats to work with Isaac Williams.

"Mr. Abbott and Mr. Williams were ambushed by the savages, and both murdered and scalped. There is a ravine on the upper part of the plantation of Mr. Hollenback, above Mill creek, where they fell.

"All hope was now extinguished, and Mrs. Abbott, (her maiden name was Alice Fuller,) with a broken heart, set out with her nine children (judge ye how helpless and destitute!) to find their way to Hampton, an eastern town in Connecticut, from whence they had emigrated. Their loss was total. House burnt—barn burnt—harvests all devastated—cattle wholly lost—valuable title papers destroyed—nothing, nothing, saved from the desolating hand of savage ruin and tory vengeance. 'God tempers the wind to the shorn lamb.' They had between two and three hundred miles to travel, through a country where patience and charity had been already nearly exhausted by the great number of applicants for relief. But they were sustained; and, arrived at their native place, the family was separated, and found homes and employment among the neighbouring farmers, where they dwelt for several years, until the boys, grown up to manhood, were able to return, claim the patrimonial lands—again to raise the cottage and the byre, and once more to gather mother and children round the domestic hearth, tasting the charms of independence and the blessings of home."

"An interesting case, most certainly. Besides the deprivation of a father, the direct loss of property must have been considerable—more than a thousand dollars, I should suppose. I confess it appears to me very plain, that the continental Congress, having drawn away the men of war raised for the defence of Wyoming, thereby brought down the enemy on a defenceless place, and were the cause of the sufferings and losses, and that the national government is, therefore, by every consideration of justice and honour, though late postponed, bound to make good to the sufferers the losses sustained—Did you say that Mrs. Abbott, the widow, also returned?"

"Yes—and long occupied the farm where her husband fell. She was afterwards married to a man whose name was known widely as the extent of the settlement; a shrewd man—a great reader—very intelligent—distinguished far and near for the sharpness of his wit, the keenness of his sarcasm, the readiness of his repartees, and the cutting pungency of his satire; withal not unamiable—for in the domestic circle he was kind and clever, and they lived happily together; but his peculiar talent being known, for many years every wit and witling of the country round about thought he must break a lance with him. Constantly assailed—tempted daily 'to the sharp encounter'—armed at all points like the 'fretful porcupine'—cut and thrust, he became expert from practice as he was gifted for that species of warfare, by nature. All the old people, in merry mood, can tell of onslaught and overthrow of many a hapless wight who had the temerity to provoke a shaft from the quiver of old *Mr. Stephen Gardiner.*"

"You began by speaking of Mr. Stephen Abbott. Did he marry before he returned from Connecticut, or did he take a Wyoming girl to wife—a daughter, as he was the son of one of the revolutionary patriots?"

"You shall hear. He married a Searle. (In other parts of our work particulars of that patriotic and suffering family are detailed.) Having resettled on the patrimonial property, a fruitful soil, industry and economy, brought independence in their train. Could you look upon the expelled orphan boy of 1778, pattering along his little footsteps beside his widowed mother, and other orphan children, as they were flying from the savage, and contrast his then seemingly hopeless lot with the picture now presented, you would say, 'It is well.' In a very neat white house himself, his four children living near, each also occupies a white house,

APPENDIX.

which are the abodes of agricultural independence and comfort. Mr. Abbott has a second wife, having intermarried with the daughter of Colonel Denison. Now past 70, the old gentleman enjoys excellent health—the canal passes through his farm, and a coal mine opened near its banks yields him a revenue equal to every reasonable desire. Long may they live to enjoy it.

NO. XVIII.

THE BLACKMAN FAMILY.

I now take pleasure to introduce to you the BLACKMAN family, firm and true in the hour of danger; prompt at the call of duty, and deep sufferers when the overwhelming calamity fell on our people. Major Eleazer Blackman is 73 years of age this month of May. He is the son of Elisha Blackman, who died in Sept., 1804, in Wilkesbarre, aged 87.

I believe I have mentioned to you that companies of old men, out of the trainband, were formed, called "THE REFORMADOES," to defend the forts, and do garrison service, while the younger portion performed the more active duties. Thus the fort in Plymouth was kept by a company, of which old Mr. Bidlack was captain. The fort at Pittston was kept by a company, of which old Mr. Blanchard, father of the late Captain Jeremiah Blanchard, was captain. Jenkins' fort, above Wintermoot's, was commanded by Captain Harding, father of the Hardings slain at Exeter; old Esq. Jenkins was his lieutenant. And at Wilkesbarre the "Reformadoes" were commanded by Wm. Hooker Smith, the Elisha Blackman, of whom I just spoke, being his lieutenant.

"What! were all these forts to be garrisoned? Pray, how were they to be built? Did the Continental Congress build them, or were they erected by the colony of Connecticut?"

Very natural, and very proper questions, my friend. I will tell you. In conversation with Major Eleazer Blackman, who, though only about 13 years old at the time, is yet, from his clear mind and extraordinary memory, very intelligent in respect to all that happened at that early day; he informed me that neither the Continental Congress, nor colony of Connecticut expended a penny in building those forts. The people of Wyoming built them all, in the language of a resolution of the town of Westmoreland, "WITHOUT FEE OR REWARD." He, too young to go out to battle, worked at the fort at Wilkesbarre, drove oxen to haul in timber, dug in the trenches, and laboured constantly until it was finished. This fort stood where the court house now stands, and embraced from a quarter to half an acre. It was square, built by setting yellow pine logs upright in the earth close together, 15 feet high, surrounded by a trench. The corners were so rounded as to flank all sides of the fort. The gate opened towards the river, and they had one double fortified four pounder for defence and as an alarm gun to the settlement.

The court house and jail of Westmoreland were within the limits of the fortification. All the forts were built on the same plan, except, in some cases, there were double rows of logs set on end in the ground, thereby strengthening the defences.

The day preceding the battle Major Blackman's father and two brothers, Elisha and Ichabod, were with the party up at Exeter.

Elisha Blackman, the brother, was 18 at the time of the engagement. The family was from Lebanon in the State of Connecticut, and removed to Wyoming in 1773. He belonged to Capt. Bidlack's company, and when they marched up to battle there were 32 men. Of these only 8 escaped: himself, Serjt. Daniel Downing, Jabez Fish, orderly serjeant, Phineas Spafford, M. Mullen, Samuel Carey, Tom Porter, drummer, and one other; all the rest were slain.

"Four times 8 are 32—so that three-fourths of Capt. Bidlack's company fell. It was a terrible slaughter. Twenty-four out of thirty-two! melancholy indeed!"

You will observe Bidlack's company was near the right, being next to Capt.

Hewitt's. Bidlack was a firm and brave man, and would not retreat although the left was broken and in full flight. True, as was said by his brother, the Rev. B. Bidlack—He died on the field where he stood at the head of his men.

Darius Spafford, brother-in-law of Elisha and Eleazer Blackman, was in the engagement. Two months had not passed away since, in the joy of his youthful heart, he led his bride, Lovina Blackman, to the sacred altar. In the extreme exigency of the case, there was here no exemption as in the Jewish law. The watch fires were kindled on the hills. The gathering brand was lighted. It was "Speed—Malise, speed." Neither the funeral train nor the wedding ceremony afforded exemption. Spafford went like a true-hearted son of Wyoming. The fatal bullet struck him in the shoulder, he fell on the arm of his brother Phineas. "I am mortally hurt," were his last words—"take care of Lovina."

Old Mr. Blackman would not leave the fort. He thought, with Dr. Smith, by remaining they might afford some protection—Eleazer, with his mother and widowed sister, his sister Lucy, and Phineas Spafford, fled with the rest of the affrighted fugitives. The story of their sufferings is the common story of all. A part of the way they kept from famishing by gathering berries. When they came to the German settlement, they were treated with much kindness, were fed, spoken kindly to, and helped on their way. Weary, wayworn and penniless, depending chiefly on charity, they got, in a few weeks, to their former home in Connecticut, where, one and all, they sought a virtuous and honourable independence by labour.

Elisha Blackman, Jr., returned with Capt. Spalding, and aided to defend the settlement and bury the dead. All the property was destroyed, except two cows, which by mere chance were recovered.

The two brothers, Elisha and Eleazer, the former in April, 78—the latter 73 in May—the first in Hanover, the last in Wilkesbarre, each on his own farm, are living in comfortable independence and excellent health, deservedly enjoying, in a good old age, respected by all, the freedom for which they contended and suffered. Long may they continue in the enjoyment of every blessing this world can give. The following anecdote was told by Mrs. B.

Among the Indians who formerly lived in the valley was one known by the name of Anthony Turkey. When the savages removed from Wyoming he went with them, and returned as an enemy at the time of the invasion. With him and the people there had been before a good understanding, and it created some surprise when known that he was with the bloody band who had come on the errand of destruction. It was Turkey who commanded the party that came to Mr. Weeks the Sunday after the battle, and taking the old gentleman's hat, shoved his rocking chair into the street, and sat down and rocked himself. In the invasion of March following, Turkey was here again, and in an engagement on the Kingston flats was shot through the thigh and surrounded by our people. "Surrender, Turkey," said they, "we won't hurt you." Probably conscious of his own cruelties, he defied them, and fought like a tiger-cat to the last. Some of our boys, in malicious sport, took his body, put it into an old canoe, fixed a dead rooster in the bow—fastened a bow and arrow in the dead Indian's hands as if in the act just to fire, put a written "Pass" on his breast "to let the bearer go to his master, King George or the d—l," and launched the canoe into the river. Down it went amid the cheers of men and boys. It so happened that the canoe went clear and came opposite Catawissa, where there was a small settlement. Seeing it drifting, with something in it, a man, eager for the prize, jumped into a boat and pushed off. What was his surprise, as he drew near, to see an Indian, with bow bent and arrow drawn to the head—aimed directly at his breast. He fled quicker than he came, but being a man of resolution pushed off again with his rifle, and found the old warrior just as he had been launched. After towing him in to shore, and a hearty laugh of the people there, he pushed off the canoe, speeding Anthony Turkey to the place of his destination.

NOTE.—Written in 1838. Since, in 1844, Major Eleazer Blackman was gathered to his fathers, aged 79. Thus the esteemed remnant of the ancient people are fast falling around us. The elder brother, Elisha, lives, a hale old man, still an earnest reader of the news, in the possession of all his faculties and the enjoyment of life. He is, it is supposed, one of three survivors who were in the battle.

NO. XIX.

THE STARK FAMILY.

In upper Wilkesbarre, nearly a mile from the Pittston line, northwesterly, or towards the river from the road, there is an ancient family burying-ground, where repose, side by side, Christopher, James and Henry Stark, the father, grandfather and great-grandfather of James and John Stark, Esqs., now residing upon the patrimonial property. It is a remarkable case. James Stark, Esq., aged about 50, can point to the grave of his progenitor *three* generations back.* It is doubted if another instance exists in old Westmoreland, of a person now (1845) half a century old, whose *great*-grandfather was buried here. Christopher must have been a very aged man when, in 1771, he came with his children to the valley. Both he and his son James died before the battle; the former by natural decay, the latter fell a victim to the small-pox when it prevailed in 1777. Two of the name, Aaron and James, are on the town list of inhabitants, 1772. Aaron sold his right to his brother James and removed to another part of the valley.

The family was originally from New England, three brothers having, at an early period, emigrated from England. The glorious old hero of Bennington, who, by capturing the Hessians, broke the power of Burgoyne, was a descendant of one of those brothers, and of course a relative of the Wilkesbarre family. Nor was the patriotic spirit confined to the New Hampshire branch. On the enlistment of the independent companies of Durkee and Ransom, James Stark, son of James and brother of Henry, (whose burial-place we have designated,) joined the army and marched to meet the enemy.

In the battle were three of the name, Daniel, Aaron and James; the latter only escaped, Daniel and Aaron fell. The record shows their courage and devotion to their country's liberty, and that two of them laid down their lives in the sacred cause. A portion of the family, after the war, settled on the Tunkhannock, which is supposed to derive its origin from Daniel. Mr. John D. Stark, of Pittston, is the grandson of Aaron who was slain.

The first, and, for many years, the largest and best frame house in upper Wilkesbarre, belonged to the Stark family. Painted red, more than half a century ago, situate on the first rise from the river, commanding a pleasant prospect of the Susquehanna and the large meadows, it was quite an object, in old times, of curiosity and attraction.

The Wilkesbarre branch retain the homestead, increased by purchase and improved by cultivation. The property has become more valuable than the fondest imaginations of their fathers ever conceived of, by fine deposits of anthracite coal discovered on the land, easy of access, mines being already opened. Moreover, the canal passes more than half a mile through the original plantation.

It may well be a subject of family pride, that the two brothers of whom we speak, James and John, have almost, time out of mind, one or the other, been magistrates in upper Wilkesbarre, dispensing justice among their rural neighbours. To their great credit, be it also recorded, that they have ever discountenanced unnecessary litigation, and been more solicitous to preserve harmony than to multiply fee-bills. It is but a just compliment to James Stark to say, that the neighbourhood and surrounding country are indebted to him for spirited and unwearied exertions to introduce and cultivate every variety of choice fruit, apples, pears, cherries, &c. Much has been done; a great deal has been accomplished. We owe the delicious Sickle pear to his labours. Had his liberal and untiring efforts been properly seconded, Philadelphia would not have boasted finer fruit than Wyoming. We cannot but regard the man who, with industry and care, establishes a nursery—casts about at home and abroad for the finest sorts—engrafting and

---

* Cols. Butler and Denison, the *very first settlers*, have children living not older than James Stark, Esq.

teaching his neighbours to engraft, thus contributing to the general health and pleasure, as a public benefactor.

NO. XX.

NATHAN BEACH, ESQ.

NATHAN BEACH, Esq., of Beach Grove, Salem township, for many years one of the most distinguished citizens of Luzerne, has furnished me with a brief sketch of his life during the war, which we give entire. We may add that Mr. Beach was a magistrate for many years, and for a still longer time postmaster at Beach Grove. Near forty years ago, to wit, in 1807—8, the author and Mr. Beach represented the county of Luzerne in the Assembly, then sitting in Lancaster. Room mates as well as colleagues, a friendly intimacy commenced which has never suffered the slightest interruption. Active, enterprising, having a mind quick to perceive, a memory extraordinarily retentive, and a faculty to communicate with remarkable clearness and spirit the incidents occurring in his eventful life; a more pleasant or instructive companion, in respect to ancient affairs, could rarely be met with. Even now, at the age of 82 (1845), his graphic account of the surrender of Cornwallis, possesses more interest than any we have ever read or heard. Fortune has smiled on his exertions, and the poor exiled boy is now able to ride in his carriage and pair, abounding in wealth, still blessed with health, and buoyant in spirits, esteemed by a large circle of friends and acquaintances.

"In the year 1769 my father removed with his family from the State of New York, to the valley of Wyoming, now Luzerne County, State of Pennsylvania, where he continued to reside within the limits of the said county, until the 4th day of July, 1778, the day after the Wyoming massacre, so called. When the inhabitants, to wit, all those who had escaped the tomahawk and scalping knife, fled in every direction to places of security—about the first of August following I returned with my father and Thomas Dodson, to secure our harvest which we had left in the fields. While we were engaged in securing our harvest as aforesaid, I was taken prisoner by the Indians and tories; made my escape the day following. In the fall of the same year, 1778, my father and family went to live at Fort Jenkins, (Columbia County, Pa.) I was there employed, with others of the citizens, and sent out on scouting parties by Capt. Swany, commander of the fort, and belonging to Col. Hartley's regiment of the Pennsylvania line, continued at said fort until about the first of June, 1779, during which time had a number of skirmishes with the Indians. In May, 1779, the Indians, thirty-five in number, made an attack on some families that lived one mile from the fort, and took three families, twenty-two in number, prisoners. Information having been received at the fort, Ensign Thornbury was sent out by the captain in pursuit of the Indians, with twenty soldiers, myself and three others of the citizens also went, making twenty-four. We came up with them—a sharp engagement took place, which lasted about thirty minutes, during which time we had four men killed and five wounded out of the twenty-four. As we were compelled to retreat to the fort, leaving our dead on the ground, the Indians took their scalps. During our engagement with the Indians the twenty-four prisoners before mentioned made their escape and got safe to the fort. The names of the heads of those families taken prisoners as aforesaid, were Bartlet Ramey, Christopher Forrow and Joseph Dewey; the first named, Bartlet Ramey, was killed by the Indians. Soon after the aforesaid engagement, in June I entered the boat department. Boats having been built at Middletown, Dauphin County, called continental boats, made for the purpose of transporting the baggage, provisions, &c., of Gen. Sullivan's army—which was on its march to destroy the Indian towns in the lake country, in the State of New York, I steered one of those boats to Tioga Point, where we discharged our loading and I returned to Fort Jenkins in August, where I found our family. The Indians still continued to be troublesome; my father thought it

APPENDIX.

advisable to leave the country and go to a place of more safety; we left the Susquehanna, crossed the mountains to Northampton County, in the neighbourhood of Bethlehem; this being in the fall of 1779. In May, 1780, the Indians paid a visit to that country, took and carried away Benjamin Gilbert and family, and several of his neighbours, amounting to eighteen or twenty in all. Said Gilbert was a public Friend, of the society called Quakers. It was then thought expedient to raise a certain number of militia men, and establish a line of blockhouses north of the Blue Mountain, from the Delaware River near Stroudsburg in Northampton county to the river Schuylkill in then Berks, now Schuylkill County, in which service I entered as substitute for Jacob Reedy. In May, 1780, was appointed orderly serjeant in Capt. Conrad Rather's company, in which situation I served that season six months, as follows:—two months under Capt. Rather, two months under Capt. Deal; during this two months the Indians made an attack upon our blockhouse, at which engagement some of the Indians were killed; and two months under Capt. Smeathers. During the winter it was considered unnecessary to continue the service. In May, 1781, the forces were reorganized at the blockhouses, where I served four months. In September of the same year I entered the French service in Philadelphia as wagoner, with Capt. Gosho, wagon master, and was attached to the hospital department; arrived at Yorktown, Virginia, the last of September, about three weeks before the surrender of Lord Cornwallis. I remained with the army in the neighbourhood of Yorktown until June, 1782, at which time the French army left Virginia for Boston, arrived at Providence, State of Rhode Island, about in November; remained there until the first of February, 1783, when the army marched to Boston, and embarked on board of their fleet. I then returned to Philadelphia, Pennsylvania, was discharged, and returned home after an absence of about eighteen months. I was born, says our family register, July, 1763, near a place now called Hudson, on the North River, in the State of New York. Have continued to reside within Luzerne County from September, 1769, to the present time, excepting five years as before stated.

"NATHAN BEACH.

"*September* 3d, 1842."

Mr. Beach related to the writer the following amusing anecdote, showing in what manner the second set of Yankees, confined in the Easton Prison, obtained their discharge.

The captivity of the Yankee party, by Sheriff Jennings of Northampton county, and imprisonment at Easton, has so many laughable circumstances connected with it, that all melancholy impressions are obliterated, and may awaken a smile from all sides of the question. The Wyoming captives found among the inhabitants of Easton a great many friends, whose sympathy for their fate was greater than anger for their fault.

Flip, in those days, was a favourite and fashionable liquor, especially among the New England settlers. Stay, we will delay the narrative only long enough to give the receipt to make it. Put into a quart of beer a tablespoonful of brown sugar, warm it thoroughly by stirring it round with a red hot poker; add from a gill to half a pint of old Antigua rum; grate on half a nutmeg; our grandfathers thought it a capital beverage. Many a liberal-hearted Eastonian was in the habit of visiting the prisoners, furnishing the materials, and partaking of the inspiring draught. The jailor, too, a jovial clever fellow, occasionally sipped a noggin, with his merry charge.

One might think the plan had been concerted. The keeper having closed the evening with an extra mug, lost the power, or the will, to make much resistance. Opening the door to let out some of the visitors, old Mr Beach and his companions pressed it back against him, holding him in durance, till the whole party escaped, and they returned to Wyoming.

At the surrender of Cornwallis, Mr Beach relates that the British marched out, playing 1st, Lord Cornwallis' March—2d, some popular tune in their army, and 3d, God save the King; and stacked arms. The American and French troops advanced playing 1st, Count Rochambeau's March; 2d, Washington's March; and 3d, as they surrounded the stacked arms, Yankee Doodle! On hearing which the British soldiers became almost ungovernably enraged, and could scarcely be restrained from rushing back and seizing their muskets.

And then, said Mr. Beach, was to be seen the most extraordinary sight I ever beheld. The officers of all three armies, in large numbers, on horseback, exchanging courtesies as if they were sworn brothers just met, instead of deadly foes; old acquaintance recognizing and introducing each other to officers to whom they were strangers.

"Grim-visaged war then smoothed his wrinkled front." But an incident occurred, annoying to one of the best officers of the British army. Col. Tarlton was obliged to dismount from a beautiful charger, claimed by a Virginia gentleman, from whom it had been taken.

[Though entirely out of place I cannot repress the curiosity I have to know who were passengers to New York, in the "Bonetta." What an incident to form half a dozen chapters in a romance!]

NO. XXI.

ELISHA HARDING, ESQ.

"HE slept with his fathers," is the simple and beautiful expression of Scripture, when an aged man had closed his earthly pilgrimage. ELISHA HARDING, Esq., of Eaton, has paid the debt of Nature, and gone down to the grave in a good old age, with the universal respect of all who knew him. One of the very few who were left among us who shared in the scenes and sufferings of Wyoming in the Revolutionary war, his departure creates a painful chasm, and compels the remark—"A few, very few years more, and not one will remain who can say—'I was there—I saw the British Butler, his Green Rangers and his savage myrmidons—I saw the scalps of our butchered people, and witnessed the conflagration.'"

Elisha Harding was a native of Colchester, Connecticut, born in 1763, and came with his father to Wyoming in 1770 among the early settlers. Exeter was the place selected for their residence. At the commencement of the Revolutionary troubles, Wintermoot's fort had been erected, and suspicion prevailed that those who controlled it were not friendly to our cause, although their professions were fair. The Jenkinses and the Hardings, the chief Whig families who lived near, thought proper to unite their efforts, and Jenkins' fort was built above Wintermoot's, near the ferry. Young Harding, then a boy too young to lift logs, had yet the true blood flowing in his veins; he could drive oxen; and he worked at the stockade with the spirit of youth and ardour of patriotism. This was in 1777. In November of that year, John Jenkins, Jr., was taken prisoner by the Indians and carried to Niagara. A Mr. York and Lemuel Fitch were taken off at the same time. An old man named Fitzgerald was also made captive. The enemy placed him on a flax-brake, and gave him his choice—to die, or renounce his Whig principles and swear allegiance to King George. The reply is worthy of preservation in letters of gold: "I am an old man—I can continue but a few years at most, and had rather die now, a friend to my country—than have my life spared and be branded with the name of Tory!" He was a noble fellow. And they had the magnanimity to let him go.

The troubles which may be said to have begun with the captivity of Jenkins, now thickened around the settlement. In May, 1778, William Crooks and Asa Budd went up the river and stopped at John Secord's house, where Crooks was shot by the enemy, and Budd escaped. Was not the blood of Crooks the first shed at Wyoming? The people now repaired to the forts for safety. At Jenkins' fort were the family of that name, the head of which was John Jenkins, Esq., a man distinguished in his day by intelligence, zeal for liberty, and extensive influence. In May, 1777, he had been elected a member of Assembly to Connecticut, from Westmoreland. He was the father of the Mr. Jenkins who was a prisoner; and afterwards through the war a brave and active officer. Here were

APPENDIX.

Capt. Stephen Harding, Benjamin, Stukely, and Stephen Harding, Jr., Wm. Martin, James Hadsall, Sr., and Jr., Samuel Morgan, Ichabod Phelps, Miner Robbins, John Gardiner, Daniel Weller, and Daniel Carr, with their women and children.

On the 30th of June the men left the fort and went up the river a few miles to work among their corn; they were ambushed by the savages, and six of them slain. Those who fell were Stukely Harding, and Benjamin Harding, brothers of Elisha; Miner Robbins, James Hadsall, James Hadsall, Jr., and a coloured man named Martin [see note]. The British Butler said our men fought as long as they could stand; when found their bodies were shockingly mangled—full of spear holes—their hands and arms cut as if an attempt had been made to take them prisoners, and they had resisted to the last. Daniel Weller, Daniel Carr and John Gardiner were taken prisoners. Mr. Harding, of whom we write, used to say, that in all his life he never saw a more piteous scene than that of Mr. Gardiner taking leave of his wife and children. After the battle he was allowed to see, and bid them farewell, when he was driven off, led by a halter, loaded almost to crushing with plunder.—He seemed an object of particular spite, probably arising from the revenge of some personal enemy. "Go—go"—was the Indian's command. On the way, a few miles west of Geneva, he became worn out—fell and was given up to the squaws, who put him to death with cruel torture.

The day before the battle, Jenkins' fort capitulated to a detachment under Capt. Caldwell, and young Harding was among the prisoners. As suspected, Wintermoot's fort threw open its gate to the enemy. On the 3d of July in the afternoon about one o'clock, word came up to Jenkins' fort that the Yankees were marching out to battle and all the warriors must go down to Wintermoot's to meet them. The issue is known. The next day Mr. Harding describes the savages, as smoking, sitting about, and with the most stoical indifference, scraping the blood and brains from the scalps of our people, and straining them over little hoops to dry—a most soul-sickening sight. In a day or two Col. Butler, his Rangers, and a party of the Indians left the valley, abandoning the settlement to the tender mercies of the butchers who chose to remain. Among the expelled, he sought his way to Norwich, Connecticut, bound himself to the blacksmith's trade, and despising idleness and dependence, nobly resolved to live above the world and want, by honest industry.

After the war he returned to the beloved waters of the Susquehanna. Whoever dwelt on its banks that did not say—If I forget thee, thou clear and beautiful stream, may my right hand forget its cunning? Whoever left Wyoming, whose soul did not long to return to its romantic hills and lovely plains!

Married, settled, having an admirable farm, and he a first rate farmer, comfort and independence flowed in upon him, crowned his board with plenty, and gave him the means of charitable usefulness, in reward for early toils and present labour.

A man of strong mind and retentive memory, he read much and retained everything worth remembering. Shrewd, sensible, thoroughly understanding human nature, few in his neighbourhood had more influence. A justice under a commission from Gov. Mifflin, he rendered useful services as a magistrate for a long series of years. Of a ready turn of wit, an apt story—an applicable Scripture quotation—a couplet of popular verse, always ready at command, rendered him a prominent and successful advocate in the thousand interesting conflicts of opinion that arise in life. A keen sarcasm—severe retort—an unexpected answer, that would turn the laugh on his opponent, characterized him, but never in bitterness, for he was too benevolent to give unmerited pain. Of old times he loved to converse, and his remarkable memory enabled him to trace with surprising accuracy every event which he witnessed, or heard, during the troubles here. He could describe every house and farm, and name every farmer from the lower to the upper line, living in Exeter before the battle, although but a lad of 12 or 13.

A very worthy—a very clever—a very upright man, he leaves the world respected and regretted. Thick set, not tall, but well knit together he seemed formed for strength and endurance; of an excellent constitution, well preserved by exercise, cheerfulness and temperance, he had known but little sickness. A year ago, 1839, the last time I had the pleasure to see him, his mind seemed in full vigour, and he gave promise of many years of life and enjoyment. In the beginning of August he was struck with apoplexy; mind and body sinking together, he survived the stroke but a short time, and died in the 75th year of his age.

>   "In sober state
> Through the sequester'd vale of mortal life
> The venerable patriarch guileless held
> The tenour of his way; labour prepared
> His simple fare; and temp'rance rul'd his board.
> Tired with his daily toil at early eve
> He sunk to soft repose; gentle and pure
> As breath of evening zephyr; and as sweet
> Were all his slumbers; with the sun he rose
> Alert and vigorous as he, to run
> His destined course: *Virtue and usefulness*—
> Ever marked his path
> ———Along the gentle slope of life's decline
> He bent his gradual way; till full of years
> He dropt like mellow fruit into his grave."

NOTE.—There was not a family in the country more ardently devoted to freedom than the Hardings; or that suffered more.

Those who fell at Exeter, were taken to the burying-ground near Jenkins ferry, where their remains were interred. Elisha Harding, Esq., with pious and patriotic feeling, raised a stone to their memory, with this inscription, "*Sweet be the sleep of those who prefer Death to Slavery.*"

NO. XXII.

THE DANA FAMILY.

NOTWITHSTANDING the story of this patriotic and suffering family is so extensively interwoven in the body of our work, their merits demand some further notice from our pen. ANDERSON DANA, Esq., from Ashford, Windham county, was a lawyer of handsome attainments. Immediately on his removal to Wilkesbarre he took a decided lead in the establishment of free schools, and a Gospel minister. It is a pleasure to trace in the old records the noble impress of his Puritan zeal, on both subjects.—Before the first stump cut on his plantation had begun to decay, his son, Daniel Dana, was placed at school in Lebanon, to prepare himself for a collegiate education at Yale. On his return from the assembly at Hartford, near the close of June, 1778, where, at that most trying period, the people had chosen him to represent them, the enemy having come, Mr. Dana mounted his horse and rode from town to town, arousing, cheering, for the conflict; though by law exempt from militia duty, he hastened to the field and fell.

The death of his son-in-law Stephen Whiton was not less distressing. The young schoolmaster was especially welcome as a suitor, because to a fine person he united pleasing manners, pure morals, and was a scholar. A few weeks only had passed since the celebration of the nuptials, when Whiton, forced by imperious necessity, tore himself from the fond embrace of his sorrowing bride—to return no more.

Mrs. Dana, with a thoughtfulness no where equaled, knowing that as her husband was much engaged in public business, his papers must be valuable, gathered up all she deemed most important, took provisions, and with her widowed daughter, and the younger children, fled. Mr. Anderson Dana, now at the age of 76, residing on the homestead, then a lad of 9, was their chief male protector. Like hundreds of others they sought their way to their former home, in Connecticut, where, while Anderson was put out an apprentice, Daniel was sent to college, and the rest turned their hands to such labour as could best sustain them. The independent spirit exhibited, all unconquerable, is itself a beautiful illustration of the Yankee character. Several months after, Mrs. Whiton was confined with a daughter, who intermarried with Capt. Hezekiah Parsons, for thirty years past one of the most estimable citizens of Wilkesbarre. Smile who may; Mrs. Parsons, if guns are fired suddenly near, is almost thrown into convulsions or fainting, the overwhelming dread, being traced without a doubt, to the alarm suffered by her mother at the time of the battle. If the sorrows of early life are not forgotten, they are assuaged by healing time. Their days have been prosperous, and independence smiles on their declining years. Anderson Dana returned, after a bound service of 10 or 11 years, to recover the patrimonial estate. The father's fondest aspirations never could have reached the degree of wealth and prosperity, which the old plantation exhibits, for not only the canal passes through it, but the rail-road runs near half a mile across it, while, bounded by the main avenue, it is all becoming building lots. Butler and Ross were formerly in advance of Dana, but the Dana property will nearly equal them. But behold that large white building on the upper line of the farm! It is Dana's Academy.

Daniel, as designed by the father, was educated at Yale College. He lived many years in the State of New York, was judge of the court and held other official stations. In advanced age he removed with his children to Ohio, where in 1841, he died aged 80; having lived a life of usefulness, and left a memory without stain or reproach.

The Rev. Sylvester Dana, another son, imbued like his martyred father with a zeal for religion and love of learning, sold his patrimonial right, and obtained a liberal education, with the intent to enter into the Christian ministry. He now resides in Concord, New Hampshire. A few years since Wyoming had the pleasure to welcome him to its now pleasant and peaceful scenes, which he had left abounding in sorrow and clouded with woe.

Eleazer, the youngest son, resides at Owego, New York, where, for forty years past, in an extensive legal practice he has acquired respect, and accumulated a handsome independence.

Five of the grandchildren of the old patriot have been educated at college, making with the two sons named, seven of the family.

Hon. Amasa Dana, of Ithaca, another grandson, has for several terms, represented the district in which he resides in Congress, and his able report at the session of 1843-4, on the reduction of postage, was essentially instrumental in effecting the late reform.

Let those who have no taste for such details turn from them. I own the pleasure it gives me to trace up from the dark and bloody scenes of '78, families of the old sufferers, rising into joyous light, independence and honour.

NO. XXIII.

THE JAMESON FAMILY.

The Jameson family, second to none in respectability, services or sufferings, were among the early inhabitants of Wyoming, having emigrated hither in 1776, from Voluntown, Connecticut. Robert Jameson, the father, was born in 1714, and therefore 62 when he arrived in the valley; but he brought with him a number of sons, men grown, or just entering upon the stage of action. Robert, William, John, Alexander and Joseph. He had one daughter who married Elisha Harvey. A daughter of theirs was married to the Rev. George Lane so long known and beloved in Wyoming. Her husband was taken prisoner by the savages and kept a long time in Canada. Robert and William were in Capt. M'Karachan's company in the battle. Robert fell and William had the lock of his gun shot away, but escaped. The murder of William, near Careytown in the fall of 1778; and of John, in 1782, near the Hanover meeting-house, we have recorded in the body of our work. Thus, of his five sons, three fell victims to the merciless Indians; and the son-in-law was a captive in their hands. Verily this was drinking deep of the cup of woe. John Jameson, the last one slain, had married a daughter of Major Prince Alden, and left two children a son and a daughter; Hannah, a third child was born shortly after his decease, and married Elder Pearce, a distinguished minister of the Methodist Episcopal Church. Polly was married to Jonathan Hunlock; and Samuel, the eldest child, resided at the original farm in Hanover, where he recently died, having sustained the character of an upright and amiable man; for several of the last years of his life, he was a member of the Presbyterian Church. The two other sons of the old gentleman have resided on their beautiful plantation in Salem, adjoining that of N. Beach Esq., having at their command, and hospitably enjoying all the good things, that could make life pass agreeably. Joseph, one of the pleasantest and most intelligent men of our early acquaintance, chose to live a bachelor, the more unaccountable, as his pleasing manners, cheerful disposition, and inexhaustible fund of anecdote, rendered him everywhere an agreeable companion. Alexander was for a great number of years an approved magistrate. He was and is a man of active business habits. These united with a sound judgment led him to the accumulation of wealth to his heart's content. Both these brothers, besides the deep, deep sufferings of their family, were themselves participators in the active scenes of the war and endured hardships that the present inhabitants can form no true conception of. Their mother's maiden name was Dixon, of the family from which the Hon. Mr. Dixon, recent Senator in Congress from Rhode Island, was descended. Their father died in 1786, aged 72. Though far advanced in the vale of years, we cannot but express the hope that their lives may be prolonged to enjoy the blessings won by their worthy labours, and the unsurpassed services and sufferings of their patriotic family.

NO. XXIV.

THE PERKINS' FAMILY.

AMONG the instances of Indian barbarity, the murder of Mr. John Perkins has been narrated. He was from Plainfield, Windham county. On the enlistment of the two independent companies, his eldest son, then an active young man, of about twenty, enrolled his name in the list, and marched to camp under Ransom. Hence the family were objects of especial hatred to the enemy. Aaron Perkins continued in the army, to the close of the war, having given his best days to the service of his country. David Perkins, the next brother, took charge of the family, and by great prudence and industry, kept them together, and not only preserved the plantation, but improved and enlarged it, so that now it is among the most valuable in Kingston. For a great number of years, Mr. Perkins executed the duties of a magistrate to the general acceptance. A son of his held the commission of major in the United States army, and is still in the service. Numbers of his children are well married, and settled around him, or not far distant. The late Mrs. James Hancock, whose amiable character endeared her to all who had the pleasure of her acquaintance, was the daughter of David Perkins. The beautiful farm of Mr. Hancock embracing more than 100 acres of rich alluvial land, contains the lower part of the ancient Indian fort, the upper part, running into the no less valuable plantation of Mr. John Searle, whose grandfather fell in the battle. So that the children, descendants of both those ancient sufferers by savage barbarity, now disport in peaceful triumph on the ruined palace of those haughty and cruel warriors, by whose hands their forefathers fell.

David Perkins, Esq., still lives, in the enjoyment of fine health, and an easy fortune. Aaron, the old soldier, one of the extreme remnant of Ransom and Durkee's men, broken with age and toil, you may yet see, slowly pacing his brother's porch, or in a summer day taking his walk along those beautiful plains. If not enjoying much positive pleasure, he yet seems to suffer no pain. Linger yet, aged veteran! Ye winds blow kindly on him! Beam mildly on his path, thou radiant sun, that saw his father slaughtered! and must have witnessed the gallant soldier in many a noble conflict. Plenty surrounds him. Peace to his declining years! As a most interesting memorial of the past we love to look upon you!

APPENDIX.

Justice prompts me to say that the family of Perkins stands among the foremost on the file of patriotic services and deep sufferings, and is entitled to gratitude and respect.

NO. XXV.

DR. WILLIAM HOOKER SMITH.

The name of this gentleman is several times mentioned in our annals; but it seems proper to add a line or two respecting him. He filled a large space in public estimation at Wyoming, for nearly half a century. A man of great sagacity and tact as well as of an excellent education, his influence was extensively felt and acknowledged. For many years he held the first rank as a physician, and from the numerous cures performed, the old people thought him unequaled. The extraordinary cases of the recovery of Follet and Hagaman, excited wonder: but he was modest, and candid enough to say, that no human means could have availed, beyond the exhibition of a diet at once cool, nourishing and easy of digestion, the patient being kept cheerful and quiet—Nature was the great physician and made the cure. The truth seems to have been, that to great skill in his profession, he united a large share of that capital ingredient—good common sense.

Both the patriotic spirit and activity of Dr. Smith are shown by the fact that, while he was relied on as chief medical attendant, by the settlement, he yet accepted, and exercised the post of captain, commanding in Wilkesbarre, the "old reformadoes," as the aged men were called, who associated to guard the fort. Subsequently when numerous troops were stationed at Wyoming, Dr. Smith was still the principal physician. After the war his enterprise led him to the establishment of mills, at the old forge place, Pittston, where in 1800 he resided.

A daughter married Mr. Isaac Osterhout, and after his decease, Fisher Gay, Esq., of Kingston.* Besides the daughter named, Dr. Smith had a numerous family. William Smith, a third son, is now (1845) living in Windham, Wyoming county, at the advanced age of 85 years. A daughter, Sarah, was married to James Sutton, of Exeter. She died in 1834, aged about 80 years. (Gen. Ross, when the writer began to collect materials for this work, frequently expressed regret at the departure of Mrs. Sutton, whom he represented as having a more perfect knowledge of Wyoming history than any person he ever knew.) But there was another daughter, who was married to Dr. Samuel Gustin, (whose name will be found appended as a witness to the capitulation of Forty Fort.) Dr. Gustin removed to the west, and an only daughter of theirs, who was in the fort at the time of its surrender, married the Rev. Mr. Snowden, father of James Ross Snowden, Esq. The heart leaps more quickly, and the life current flows more kindly, at the mention of his name, when we recollect that the late honoured Speaker of the House of Representatives, and present Treasurer of the State, is the descendant of one of the Wyoming sufferers.

A daughter, Mary, married Mr. Baker, of New York city; Elizabeth married Mr. Bailey, who died in the lake country. Two sons, John and James, resided and died in the State of New York.

Dr. Smith died in the township of Tunkhannock, July 17th, 1815, aged 91 years, having been born in 1724.

His heirs received from Congress, in 1838, an appropriation of $2400 as pay for acting surgeon in the Revolutionary war. For many of these interesting facts we are indebted to the polite attention of Isaac S. Osterhout, Esq., grandson of the deceased patriot. The grant was just in itself, due to the services, and honourable to the memory of Dr. Smith. A very few instances of the kind have occurred.

* Mr. Gay resides near the monument, which is built on his plantation, and it is proper to record, to his honour, that he most liberally presented the ground on which the structure is erected.

A number of cases still remain perfectly clear, and of imperious obligation, which Congress would not refuse to provide for, if the pressure of business would allow them leisure to hear and understand them.

NO. XXVI.

THE SEARLE FAMILY.

——"In reply to your question, I said that Mr. Stephen Abbott married a Searle; Abigail, daughter of William Searle, who was the son of Constant Searle. The last named, (Mrs. Abbott's grandfather,) was in the battle. He was a man advanced in age, having several sons and daughters married, and being the grandfather of a number of children."

"What! old men! grandfathers! were such obliged to go out?"

"They were; the able-bodied men, fit for war, being marched away, created the direful necessity which drew to the battle-field old and young. Mr. Searle was there, and a son of his, Roger Searle, quite a young man; his son-in-law, Capt. Deathic Hewett, commanded the third company raised at Wyoming, by order of Congress, a very short time before the invasion. So there were three of the family in the engagement; and the fourth, (William Searle,) would also have been there, but was at the time confined to the house by a wound received from a rifle-shot while on a scouting party a few days previous to the battle.

"How unsuitable it was that a man like old Mr. Searle should go out, will further appear from the fact that he wore a wig, as was not unusual with aged men in those days. The bloody savages, in their riotous joy, after their victory, made this appendage the source of great merriment. A prisoner (adopted, I have reason to think, after the Indian fashion), was painted and permitted to go down from Wintermoot's to Forty Fort, to take leave of his mother, under a guard. When near the brook that runs by Col. Denison's he saw a group of savages in high glee. On coming near he beheld an Indian on a colt, with a rope for a bridle, having on his head, hind side before, the wig of Mr. Searle. The colt would not go; and one of the wretches pricked him with his spear—he sprang suddenly, the Indian fell on one side, the wig on the other, and the demons raised a yell of delight.

"Mr. Searle, before he went out to battle, took off a pair of silver knee buckles, which he wore—gave them to his family, saying, they might impede his movements;—if he fell, he should not need, and if he returned, he could get them. There was evidently a strong presentiment on his mind—'I go to return no more.'

"The first incident I find myself reluctant to relate—it appears like awakening light thoughts, in the midst of anguish, sorrow, and despair; but it seems proper that those things should be set forth, which make deep impressions of material facts; and I deem it a very important matter, in considering the battle, the defeat, and the present *Claim* of our people—to show that *old men, unfit for war*, by the necessity of the case, were forced into the field against trained, youthful, and expert warriors. The very young also were there. Roger Searle, the son of Constant, a young man of 18 or 19, stood by the side of Wm. Buck, a lad of 14—they fought together, Buck fell, and Searle escaped.

"Wm. Searle, Mrs. Abbott's father, went out through the wilderness with the family, having twelve women and children under his care. I have seen a memorandum kept by him. It runs thus:

"'Battle of Westmoreland July 3, 1778.

"'Capitulation ye 4th.

"'Prisoners obtained liberty to leave the settlement ye 7th.'

"It proceeds to the 25th, when they arrived at their former residence in Stonington, Connecticut.

"On the 13th they got to Fort Penn on the Delaware, and here they received

APPENDIX.

from Col. Stroud, a pass and recommendation, a copy of which may not be unacceptable as a memorial of old times:

"'Permit the bearers, Serjt. WM. SEARLE with twelve women and children, in company with him to pass unmolested to some part of the state of Connecticut, where they may be able by their industry, to obtain an honest living, they being part of the unhappy people, drove off from Wyoming by the Tories and Indians, and are truly stripped and distressed and their circumstances call for the charity of all Christian people; and are especially recommended by me to all persons in authority, civil and military, and to all continental officers and commissaries, to issue provisions and other necessaries for their relief on the road.

"'Given under my hand at Fort Penn.
"'July 14, 1778. JACOB STROUD, Col.'"

Four of the name, to wit, Roger, William, Constant, and Miner Searle, were forty-five years ago among the most intelligent and influential citizens upon the Lackawana; but they all departed in mid-life. Constant, who was in the battle, died at Providence Aug. 4, 1804, aged 45 years. Their descendants retain, or possess, several of the most valuable farms in old Westmoreland, while one at least, whom we could name, from a female branch of the family, is winning his way to distinction in an arduous and honourable profession.

NO. XXVII.

THE GORE FAMILY.

HAVING given you a sketch of the Bidlack family, it seems proper to speak of his lady, MRS. BIDLACK, whose father and brothers were among the most conspicuous actors in the eventful scenes that occurred at Wyoming. Her maiden name was Gore, daughter of Obadiah Gore, Esq.; she was the sister of the late Obadiah Gore, who was for many years an associate judge of the court in Luzerne county. Norwich, in the State of Connecticut, was the place of her birth. Mrs. Bidlack is now (1838) 80 years of age;* but she moves about the house, looking to her domestic concerns with the ease and attention of a woman of forty. In excellent health—with a cheerful flow of spirits, her mind strong and memory clear—to the inquirer after facts in relation to the early history of Wyoming, she is at once a pleasing and valuable instructor.

Of course she must have been about 20 years old at the time of the battle. That day she was in Forty Fort.

Few things have affected me more deeply, in answer to my inquiries into the events that occurred in Wyoming during the war, than the fact of the devotion, heart and soul, of the people here to the cause of liberty and their country. I introduce this remark in no idle or half-meaning spirit; but as a truth justly redounding to their patriotism and honour. It did not seem an unwilling service—the duty performed did not appear to be a grudging compliance with the call of law. Families of half a dozen did not send out one of their number to defend the cause of freedom, while the other five remained at home to plant, to build, to trade, or to make money. The new married man left his bride without claiming the fair exception of the Jewish law. The father, whose first born smiled a persuasive request to stay, left the cradle side, and his dependent infant, with its mother's blessing and consent, given through tears, and he ranged himself in the ranks for battle. Take the instance of the Gore family: The old gentleman was one of the aged men left in Forty Fort, for its defence, while our army marched out to meet the enemy. He was a magistrate under the laws of Connecticut. I have seen his commission, signed in April, 1778, by *John Trumbull*, then governor of that state. His eldest son Obadiah, was a lieutenant in the regular service, at that time under the command of Capt. Weisner, and was on the lines before New York. But in the little band that marched forth on the 3d of July, were his

* Since deceased.

APPENDIX.

sons Samuel Gore, Daniel Gore, Silas Gore, George Gore, Asa Gore. The father in the fort; and five sons marching out to the conflict! nor was this all. John Murfee, who married a daughter of Mr. Gore, (the sister of those five brothers,) was also in the ranks; and Timothy Pearce, another brother-in-law, having ridden all night, came in, and joined our army in the battle field. Thus there were seven in the battle, while an eighth was in service with a regular army; and it proved a most bloody and disastrous day to the family. At sun setting, five of the seven were on the field mangled corpses. Asa and Silas were ensigns, and were slain—George was slain, Murfee was slain. Timothy Pearce held a commission in the regular army, but had hurried in. He also was killed. Lieut. Daniel Gore was near the right wing, and stood a few rods below Wintermoot's Fort, close to the old road that led up through the valley. Stepping into the road, a ball struck him in the arm; tearing it from his shirt he applied a hasty bandage. Just at that moment Capt. Durkee stepped into the road at the same place. "Look out!" said Mr. Gore; "there are some of the savages concealed under yonder heap of logs." At that instant a bullet struck Capt. Durkee in the thigh. When retreat became inevitable, Mr. Gore endeavoured to assist Capt. Durkee from the field, but found it impossible; and Durkee said, "Save yourself, Mr. Gore—my fate is sealed." Lieut. Gore then escaped down the road, and leaping the fence about a mile below, lay couched close under a bunch of bushes. While there, an Indian got over the fence and stood near him. Mr. G. said he could see the white of his eye, and was almost sure he was discovered. A moment after, a yell was raised on the flats below, the Indian drew up his rifle and fired, and instantly ran off in that direction. Though the wave of death seemed to have passed over and spent itself, yet Lieut. Gore remained under cover till dusk, when he heard voices in the road near him. One said to the other, "It has been a hard day for the Yankees." "Yes," replied the other "there has been blood enough shed." He thought one was Col. John Butler, but could not say for certain. After dark Mr. G. found his way to the fort, and met his brother Samuel, the only survivors of the seven. The distress of Mrs. Murfee was very great. She feared her husband had been tortured. When she learned he fell on the field, she was less distressed; and begging her way, among the rest of the fugitives, traversed the wilderness and sought a home in the state from which she had emigrated, having an infant born a few days after her arrival among her former friends.

"What you tell me of a whole family going out to battle, strikes me with surprise. Why did not each family furnish one for the ranks, leaving the others to remain at home?"

"Ah! from that question, it is evident, my friend, you do not yet fully comprehend the situation of the settlement. The men of war—those fit for the arduous duties of the battle field—had almost all been drawn away from Wyoming to Washington's army. Left destitute of their natural defenders, when the enemy came, there was no choice—all who could bear arms were obliged to go. Thus whole families were in the action. And yet the numbers were too few, and the destruction was mournfully excessive. Have you a brother that you love? Can you conceive a father's affection for his sons? What must have been the feelings of Mrs. G.—what the agonizing sorrow of the father, when the tidings came that three of his sons had fallen, and that two of his daughters had become widows! No tongue can tell—no pencil can paint—the sorrows and the sufferings of poor Wyoming; and all undoubtedly occasioned by drawing away the men raised here for its special defence.

The mother of the Gore family survived to see her remaining children highly prosperous. Born in 1720, she lived until 1804, when she died at the house of her son in Sheshequin, aged 84 years.

> ——" If misfortune comes, she brings along
> The bravest virtues. And so many great
> Illustrious spirits have conversed with woe—
> Have in her school been taught—as are enough
> To consecrate distress, and make ambition
> Ev'n wish the frown beyond the smile of fortune."

APPENDIX.

NO. XXVIII.

MRS. YOUNG.

THE papers have already mentioned the decease of Mrs. Young. But the public expect, and it seems fitting, that a more extended notice should be given of one so aged, and whose life was marked by so many vicissitudes. Her maiden name was Phebe Poyner. Her father was a Huguenot, who was compelled to leave France and come to this country, in consequence of persecution for religious opinions. An active and intelligent man, he was a commissary in the old French war. The name of her mother was Eunice Chapman, a native of Colchester, Conn., but married to Mr. Poyner at Sharon, Ninepartners, New York—where the subject of this notice was born, in 1750. Her father died of small-pox at Albany; and her mother married Dr. Joseph Sprague, a widower, who had several children by his first wife. The united families removed to Wyoming in 1770—Mrs. Young being then, of course, 20 years old.

This may be regarded as the date of permanent settlements at Wyoming, 75 years ago. What a change from that day to this? What scenes of joy and woe —of hope, pleasure and sorrow, have marked those years! There were only five white women in Wilkesbarre township when she arrived; Mrs. M'Clure, wife of James M'Clure; Mrs. Sill, wife of Jabez Sill; Mrs. Bennett, grandmother of Rufus Bennett, the brave old soldier, who was in the battle, and still survives; another of the same name, wife of Thomas Bennett, mother of Mrs. Myers, still living, who gives so interesting an account of the entry of the Indians into Forty Fort, and a Mrs. Hickman. At Mill Creek, just above the large merchant mills of Mr. Hollenback, a fort was erected—containing, perhaps, an acre. A ditch was dug around the area—logs, 12 or 14 feet high, split, were placed perpendicularly in double rows, to break joints, so as to enclose it. Loop-holes to fire through with musketry were provided. There was one cannon in the fort, the only one in the settlement, until Sullivan's expedition in '79; but it was useless, except as an alarm gun, having no ball. Within this enclosure the whole settlement was congregated; the men, generally armed, going out to their farms to work during the day, and returning at night. The town plot of the borough had been laid out, but not a house built. It was a sterile plain, covered with pitch pine and scrub oak. Mr. John Abbott (who fell by the hands of the savages, the father of Mr. Stephen Abbott of Jacob's Plains) put up the first house, on the southwest corner of Main and Northampton streets. Mr., afterwards Col. Denison, and Miss Sill, were the first couple married at Wilkesbarre. The wedding took place at a house where the late Col. Wells' house stands. Mrs. M'Clure gave birth to the second child born here—a son. But let us look in upon them. The houses, store and sheds were placed around against the wall of timbers. Matthias Hollenback, then about 20, full of life and enterprise, had just come up the river with a boat load of goods, and opened a store of various articles exceedingly needed.—On the left was the house of Capt. Z. Butler. Next on the right was the building of Dr. Sprague, the physician of the settlement, and who kept a boarding-house. Here Mr. Hollenback and Mr. Denison had their quarters. Capt. Rezin Geer, who fell in the battle, was here.—For bread they used pounded corn; mills there were none; nor a table, nor a chair, nor a bedstead, except the rude manufacture of the hour. Dr. P. would take his horse, with as much wheat as he could carry, and go out to the Delaware to get it ground. A bridle path was the only road, and 70 or 80 miles to mill was no trifling distance. The flour was kept for cakes, and to be used only on extraordinary occasions. But venison and shad were in abundance. All were elate with hope, and the people for a time were never happier.

But sickness came. Zebulon, a son of Capt. Butler, died—two daughters of the Rev. Mr. Johnson; two men, Peregrine Gardiner and Thomas Robinson; then

APPENDIX.

Lazarus Young, a brother of Mrs. Young's husband, was drowned in bringing up mill irons. Soon after, Capt. Butler and Mr. Young, her husband, were taken by the Pennymites and carried to Philadelphia, where they were bailed by friends and permitted to return.

At this time the Indians were numerous around the settlement; some of them, belonging to the Moravian society, very orderly. Among them were Captain Job Gilliway and his wife Comfort. She could sew and do the work of white people. Black Henry and John Lystrom were also of the number; those were friendly and good neighbours. But at the breaking out of the war all left the country, went up the river and joined the Six Nations, to whom they were in a state of vassalage.

About two years the people made their head quarters at the fort; then, becoming numerous, and feeling secure, scattered over the valley.

Dr. Sprague died in Virginia. A son of his fell in the battle. Mrs. Young's husband was up at the Narrows with Colonel Butler on the 1st of July, and was in the battle on the 3d, but escaped.—Mrs. Young was at her house in Hanover, where also were the wife of Col. Denison and her two children, (Col. Lazarus Denison and Betsey, the late Mrs. Shoemaker). These three, with Mrs. Fitch, wife of Sheriff Jonathan Fitch, Mrs. Young and two children, making seven, took a canoe, managed by Levi Vincent, on hearing the dreadful issue and the approach of the enemy, and pushed off into the river, without provisions, to seek safety from the murderous tomahawk. Meeting a boat coming up with stores for Capt. Spalding's company, the sufferings of hunger were relieved, and the distressed fugitives, not knowing the fate of their friends, after a dangerous navigation of 120 miles, landed near Harrisburg, where they were hospitably received and kindly treated. Here they remained until Sullivan's army came to Wyoming and rendered it safe to return.

But we are occupying too much space. As Mrs. Young was the last survivor of those who occupied the fort at Mill Creek, we thought her recollections of those early scenes might not be inappropriate here in conveying information of bygone days—the enterprise, the toil and the sufferings of the pioneers in settling this charming valley.

Mrs. Young was slender and extremely delicately formed. Intelligent, observing, with a retentive memory, great sprightliness and vivacity, and remarkably cheerful, it was delightful to visit her. Young and old, for many years, seemed to take special pleasure in calling and chatting an hour. Of old times her memory was a full and perfect record. For several years she had been blind, and being feeble from great age, had been for a long time confined to the house. Yet a murmur or complaint never escaped her lips. Professing the Christian religion, being a member of the Episcopal Church, and reposing on the merits of a Saviour, her faith was perfect; and hence, in a great measure, that cheerfulness and resignation which rendered the advanced hours of life so serene, and her society so uniformly pleasant. Her mortal remains were gathered to her parent earth at the good old age of 89. She strongly felt, that

> "On a throne of love, where never
> Weeping misery pleads in vain,
> Mercy sits and smiles for ever,
> Soothing grief and healing pain."

And with triumph may have said

> "Thrice welcome death,
> That after many a painful bleeding step,
> Conducts us to our home, and lands us safe
> On the long-wished for shore."

APPENDIX. 49

NO. XXIX

THE DURKEE FAMILY.

MAJOR JOHN DURKEE had been in Col. Lyman's regiment at the taking of the Havana; he is named in our annals as heading a party of the first emigrants in 1769-70. Arrested by Capt. Ogden and sent to Philadelphia, several months imprisonment extinguished his ardour for the settlement of Wyoming, and he returned to Norwich. His name stands on the old records, as one of the original 40 settlers in Kingston. On the breaking out of the Revolutionary war Major Durkee entered zealously into the contest. A paper published Sept., 1774, announces, "On Sunday morning four hundred and sixty-four men, well armed and the greater part mounted on good horses, started for Boston, under the command of Major John Durkee." Subsequently, in a subordinate station, he was with Putnam in the battle of Bunker Hill. Commissioned a colonel of the Connecticut line, on the continental establishment, this "bold Bean-hill man," as he was sometimes called, "accompanied the army to New York, fought at Germantown," and continued to serve with reputation to the close of the arduous struggle. He died in Norwich at his residence on, or near Bean Hill, in 1782, aged 54 years. Military honours were accorded at his funeral, and the display on a similar occasion in that city had never been surpassed. It is evident he left property in Wyoming. Thomas Dyer, Esq., many years afterwards, took out letters at Wilkesbarre, and administered upon his estate.

That Robert Durkee, his brother, received a commission as captain of one of the Independent companies; that, when Congress refused, notwithstanding its solemn pledge to allow the soldiers to return to Wyoming, menaced as it was by impending danger, he, like Ransom, resigned his commission, and hastened home to defend his family; that he entered a volunteer into the battle and fell, is all on record. His residence was in Wilkesbarre on the main avenue, below Gen. Ross's farm. The ancient house is still standing—the property including the old stone wall near where the state road turns off. His widow married Capt. Landon, a respectable citizen of Kingston, and a surveyor. She died Sept. 3d, 1803, aged 65. Amelia Durkee, a daughter, resided on the farm, and in August, 1804, married Philip Weeks (whose family were such terrible sufferers in the battle). Some years afterwards, they moved to Oquago; and so far as our knowledge extends the name in Wyoming has ceased to exist but in remembrance.

NO. XXX.

DR. SILL.

DIED, at Windsor, Connecticut, May 24th, 1845, Dr. ELISHA NOYES SILL, aged 84 years. The middle name is derived from the family of Noyes, long distinguished in Connecticut, residing in Lyme, the birth-place of Dr. Sill. In 1770 he came with his father's family to Wyoming, being then a lad nine years old. They built the second house erected in Wilkesbarre, on the corner now occupied by the dwelling of the late Col. Welles, and here was the first wedding in the valley, the sister of Mr. Sill being married to Mr. Nathan Denison; another sister was afterwards married to Capt. John P. Schott. In 1776 young Sill, then only 15, joined Capt. Durkee's company. The account of the Millstone battle, given by him to the writer (at Hartford, May, 1839) was this: "The two companies which were there alone, were out on parade, before sunrise—we saw the British coming over a rise of ground from towards Brunswick, artillery and infantry. Their numbers being too great, our companies retreated about half a mile. The enemy came out with a train of wagons for flour: we met Gen. Dickinson with the New Jersey Militia.

D

Our troops wheeled, and they returned together, attacked the British, the enemy were defeated, and we took a large number of wagons and horses. Porter of Ransom's company was killed."

Marshall does not mention this gallant affair. Gordon has this imperfect sketch of it.

"The royal troops were confined to the narrow compass of Brunswick and Amboy, both holding an open communication with New York, by water. They could not even stir out to forage but in large parties, which seldom returned without loss. January 20th, 1777, General Dickinson, with about 400 [300] militia and 50 [160] of the Pennsylvania Riflemen, defeated, near Somerset Court House, on Millstone river, a foraging party of the enemy, of equal number, and took 40 wagons and upwards of 100 horses, besides sheep and cattle, which they had collected. The enemy retreated with such precipitation, that he could take only nine prisoners; but they were observed to carry off many dead and wounded in light wagons. The general's behaviour reflected the highest honour on him; for though his troops were all raw, he led them through the river middle deep, and gave the enemy so severe a charge that although supported by three field pieces, they gave way and left their convoy."

Dr. Sill had a brother, named Shadrack, who was with him in the service, and continued after the consolidation in Spalding's company, to the close of the war; but his own youth, and extreme privation, with a severe attack of camp distemper, brought him to the verge of the grave; and he was permitted to return home on furlough. At the time of the invasion, he fled with the exiles; and in October, 1779, removed to Connecticut, prepared himself for the practice of medicine, and, as a physician, as well as in the performance of the common duties of a citizen, lived a life of usefulness and has departed with the respect of all who knew him.

NO. XXXI.

JONATHAN FITCH, ESQ.

JONATHAN FITCH, Esq., for five years high sheriff of Westmoreland county, when jurisdiction passed to Pennsylvania, and the subsequent troubles became serious, removed to Binghamton, N. Y., and gave his name to a stream, near which he made his location. The fact of his passing through the wilderness at the time of the expulsion by the Indians, being the only man to protect a company of an hundred women and children, has been related. He was four times chosen member of Assembly to Hartford or New Haven, so that the two offices of sheriff, and representative to the legislature seem not to have been incompatible.

The writer of the "Binghampton Annals," a work of much interest, thus speaks of him: In the summer of 1789 Jonathan Fitch settled upon the creek that took his name. Mr. F. was from Wyoming and had been sheriff of the county. He was a man of considerable native talent, had mingled much with men of information, and was polished in his manners. He was the first representative to the state legislature from the county of Tioga. Subsequently he was judge of the court.

NO. XXXII.

THE ATHERTONS.

OF the Athertons, there were two branches among the earliest settlers in Wyoming. In the Forty or Kingston list, the names of James and John Atherton are found.

Of the very few names of the settlers in 1762–3, that I have been able to find, that of James Atherton appears as one. They were therefore the real pioneers in this distant settlement, and double sufferers. Undaunted, though his companions fell around him by the merciless tomahawk, he returned. Among those who were slain in the battle, the name of Jabes Atherton is recorded. Their arms essayed with other patriots to defend their country. Their blood enriches its soil, and it is right to record that their descendants are in the full enjoyment of the fruits of their father's enterprise and toil, combined with their own prudence and labour. In passing through Kingston not far above the residence of Col. Denison, looking to the left you may see embosomed in trees in a most romantic situation, a neat dwelling, the farm house of a beautiful plantation. Intermarried with a daughter of the late Gen. Ross, here resides a descendant of one of the early settlers. The farm, extending from the river to the mountain, yields abundance to careful culture, and it is a pleasure to add that it is the seat of intelligence and hospitality.

NO. XXXIII.

BENJAMIN HARVEY.

BENJAMIN HARVEY was esteemed one of the most considerate, prudent men among those who first established themselves in the valley. His name is on the earliest list in the township of Plymouth. He emigrated from Lyme, New London Co., Conn., and was the intimate friend, and frequently the confidential adviser of Col. Butler, they having formerly been neighbours. He was often employed in situations of trust and delicacy, and his opinions were regarded with marked respect.

He had three sons; the oldest, Benjamin, joined the Independent companies in 1776, marched to the lines to join Gen. Washington, and died in the service. Silas, the second son, united with the little band that went out from Forty Fort and fell in the battle. Thus, the stern demands of relentless war had reft from the poor old man his two eldest boys, leaving but one as the stay and solace of his declining years. But the cup of vengeance, the bitter draught of war and woe was not yet exhausted. In December, 1780, the savages made an incursion into the valley, took seven prisoners from Shawnee, the old gentleman himself, and Elisha, his only remaining son, being two of the captives. Their sufferings in that inclement season, bound, loaded and driven several hundred miles through the wilderness to Canada, no pen can describe.

It is wonderful that cold, toil, hunger, and anguish of mind, had not arrested the current of life, and left them a prey to the wolves. They survived, and returned, the old gentleman being earliest released, and Elisha at or near the close of the war. Under the despotic administration of Mr. Justice Patterson, in 1784, Mr. Harvey was cast into prison and treated with special indignity. "Away with him (Samuel Ransom) to the guard house, with old Harvey, another damned rascal."

Elisha intermarried with Rosanna Jameson, of the patriotic Jameson family, and the Rev. George Lane married their daughter. Jameson Harvey, their son, having opened an inexhaustible mine of anthracite in a rocky hill, connected with the farm, and near the canal, has at his command a source of almost boundless wealth. Thus the clouds have dispersed, the sun come out from his hiding, and brightness and prosperity beam on the family which was so long and so deeply shrouded in woe.

NO. XXXIV.

CAPT. TIMOTHY SMITH.

CAPT. TIMOTHY SMITH, or as he is more frequently designated, Timothy Smith, Esq., seems to have been a leading man in the Susquehanna Company, at their meetings in Hartford, before settlements were made in Wyoming. Choosing Kingston for his residence, his name is recorded as one of the "Forty," or earliest settlers. The old Westmoreland records frequently contain his name, and it is evident, that he was an active, thorough business man, commanding confidence and respect. The sobriquet given him by the ancient people shows the estimation in which he was held. Of course all were anxious to induce the legislature of Connecticut to recognize the settlement on the Susquehanna, and extend her jurisdiction and laws therein. Among the agents sent out was Mr. Smith, and to his superior management they ascribed the success of this mission. "Hence," said Mr. John Carey, "the settlers gave him the name of 'old head.'" He was afterwards a member of Assembly to Hartford, and always conducted whatever affairs were entrusted to him, with spirit and prudence; showing that he was a wise and safe counsellor, and an active citizen. His son, who inherited the property, Mr. John Smith, with other excellent properties, was a man of singular benevolence and an admirable nurse of the sick. When, in 1815, the typhus fever prevailed throughout the country, he threw himself in the midst of it, took the disease and died. Dr. John Smith, the grandson, retaining the old homestead, not long since prothonotary of the county, and a respectable physician, does justice to the talent of the public-spirited grandsire, and the excellent social qualities of the father.

NO. XXXV.

GENERAL SPALDING.

Of Capt. Simon Spalding frequently spoken of in our narrative, I have several additional facts and anecdotes, from his son-in-law, Joseph Kingsbury, Esq., so pleasingly related, that I copy from his letter dated Sheshequin, Dec. 2d, 1841.

"Gen. Simon Spalding was a native of Plainfield, Conn.—He was born in 1741, married to Ruth Shepard in 1761, and died the 24th Jan., 1814, aged 73." [I may add, that frequently visiting Sheshequin from 1800 to 1812, I often saw General Spalding. He was a large man, of imposing and pleasing appearance. His merits and services deserve a much more extended memoir; and no one is more capable of doing justice to the subject than Col. Kingsbury.] "He was a captain in the Revolutionary war, and from good testimony, I have no doubt but that he was a brave officer. But Gen. Spalding, as a captain in the war, never had justice done to him. The affair of Bound Brook was a performance of his. He recovered the forage the British had gathered at the time, and took several prisoners. But just as the skirmish was over, and victory secured, an officer of superior rank came up (I forget his name) and to him was the honour of the victory given, when he had no more to do with it than you or I had. General Spalding first discovered this unjust account in Weems's little history of the Revolutionary war, and it mortified the real actor of the scene very much.

"Gen. (then Capt. Spalding) was with Gen. Sullivan in his expedition into the Genessee country. In this tour he discovered, and took a fancy to Sheshequin. On his return to Wyoming he made known his intention to settle at this place. In 1783, in company with his family, and several of his neighbours at Wyoming, with their families, he removed from thence to Sheshequin. They arrived at this place on the 30th day of May. I have heard Gen. Spalding say, that the Indian grass, upon the flats at the time he came here, was as high as his head, when he sat upon a horse. These pioneers set fire to it, and such a fire was never seen before by any one present; it ran from one end of the interval to the other, a distance of about four miles, and no doubt was very destructive to the animals which made their homes in its dense covers.

"When the settlers took possession of Sheshequin, there were a few Indian families resident upon Queen Esther's Flats, and one family on this side of the river, but none of any note among them. These Indians proved very friendly, and the next year mostly moved off to the west.

"Gen. Spalding was a man calculated to gain the love and esteem even of a savage. A better hearted man I was never acquainted with. He had a peculiar tact in pleasing the red skins, and usually, when passing through the place, on treaty business to Philadelphia, he would set some sporting on foot. I remember of hearing it told of a feat performed by a couple of these red skins, at a time when a large company of Indians were on their return from the city of brotherly love. They always made it a point to stop a night with their old friend, who never failed in providing them something to eat. At this time he selected out two long-legged hogs, from a company of half a score or more. He informed the chiefs that these two hogs were a present to them for supper and breakfast, on the following conditions, to wit. The chiefs were to select from their company two young Indians, who were to catch the hogs at fair running, and then they were theirs. This pleased the red skins very much. The young racers were selected, stripped bare to Indian leggins and breechclouts, armed each with a scalping knife. The hogs were turned loose upon the flats, and the sport began. Such ecstasy as the Indians were in, as well as the pale faces present, I expect from the account, does not often happen to any people. The hogs at first were too swift on foot for the two-legged swine in pursuit. Once in a while the red skins would catch the hogs by the tail, but in attempting to stop them, they were generally thrown down, sometimes tumbling heels over head, and sometimes dragged for several rods, till they could hold on no longer; giving loose they were up and at it again. This sport lasted for three-quarters of an hour, when the fiercer brutes finally conquered. A fire was built, the hogs laid on without any dressing, roasted, and eaten with much satisfaction."

NO. XXXVI.

JOSEPH ELLIOTT.

A VETERAN distinguished for extraordinary services and sufferings, claims our attention. He is now, June, 1845, living at Wyalusing, nearly 89 years old, having been born Oct. 10th, 1756. His father died in 1809 aged 97 years, so that the longevity of the family is extraordinary. They emigrated from Stonington to Wyoming in 1776. In 1777 Joseph Elliott was with the detachment of 80 men which ascended to Sheshequin under the command of Col. Dorrance.

At the time of the invasion, he marched out to battle in Capt. Bidlack's company. Pressed by a vas superiority of numbers, his commander slain, he retreated with the rest, and was made prisoner. It was his fate to be dragged to the fatal ring, at Bloody Rock, where the savages, intoxicated with victory and excited by passion to wildest fury, glutted their thirst for blood. A circle was formed, two or three Indians holding or guarding each prisoner while the work of death went forward. Queen Esther raged like a demon. He saw six or seven murdered. A young man, Thomas Fuller, sprang to escape, shook off his guards, but was almost instantly overtaken, and tomahawked. The confusion, the savage yells, the moans of his dying friends, the streams of blood, the scattered brains, for a moment stupefied him. With a ray of returning reason, he saw death almost in a moment certain, and he could but die. With the might of combined courage and despair, he threw off the Indians who held him, and at a spring leaped down the bank, turned off to the right a second, and at a bound cleared a fence, and fled to the river, several of the enemy in full pursuit. He had passed Monockasy Island, and entered the southern branch of the stream, when a bullet struck him in the left shoulder inflicting a grievous wound. Being compelled to steady his wounded arm, dangling by his side, with his right hand, he does not know how he swam the portion of the river, too deep to ford; but found himself on the bank, and took shelter behind a tree a moment to recover breath. His wound bled so profusely that his clothes became a burden, they were so saturated; but he at length arrived at the Wilkesbarre fort, and Dr. Smith afforded his prompt and skillful aid. Among those whom he could remember to have seen butchered, were Jeremiah Ross, Samuel and Joseph Crooker, Stephen Bidlack, and Peter Wheeler.

It will be recollected that in Col. Franklin's account of events the day of the capitulation, Queen Esther headed the Indians, and with insolent pride said, "See here, Col. Denison, I told you I'd bring you more Indians." It is the opinion of Mr. Elliott, that her exasperation of passion was partly owing to this. Several Indian spies had been arrested, and were held prisoners in Forty Fort. Queen Esther had been down from her palace at Sheshequin to obtain their release, which Col. Denison had deemed it proper to refuse. In anger at her disappointment, she probably made the threat, which now she repeated in taunt.

No sooner was Elliott recovered, and his wounded shoulder sufficiently healed, than he entered again upon acceptable services. On Sullivan's advance into the Indian country, a line of expresses, to connect with Wyoming, was established, when Mr. John Carey and Joseph Elliott were selected to perform the duty. And, says Mr. Elliott, "after eighty days' constant service I was taken sick, and cannot tell what should be the cause, unless too often sleeping out in the wet, overdone with fatigue, and being very hungry." Poor fellow! It was cause enough.

But Joseph Elliott was an actor in another trying scene. The making prisoners of all Rosewell Franklin's family by the Indians, is related in the annals of 1782. His account to us of the affair, so far as he was concerned, was this. Several parties were marshalled to pursue the savages. One of these assembled at Mill Creek, numbering nine persons. They chose Thomas Baldwin to be their leader, and himself to be second in command. Making their way up the river with all possible celerity, they were satisfied, when they reached the path on the mountain nearly opposite Frenchtown, that the enemy had not passed. Taking up a position on the hill which was deemed most eligible, being out of provisions, two of the men, expert hunters, went out for venison, when the Indians, thirteen in number, with Mrs. Franklin, her babe, two little girls, and a boy about four years old, as prisoners, were reported by the advanced sentinel to be near. To call in their scattered hunters was of course impossible. There they were seven to thirteen, and it was bravely resolved to give battle. The fire was sharp on both sides. Capt. Baldwin received a rifle ball in the hand which nearly disabled him, but Thomas Baldwin was every inch a soldier, and still exerting himself he led on and cheered his men. How near they were is evident, from the children knowing the voices of our party, and with instinctive sagacity they ran from the Indians, and clung to the knees of their friends. Mrs. Franklin, who had been ordered to sit still, raised her head, on hearing the joyous cry of her children, and the savages instantly shot her. Pressing forward, the Indians were compelled to retreat, leaving two or three of their number dead on the field. The infant was borne off in their flight, and its fate never known. The two little girls and younger boy were, after the burial of their mother, decently as circumstances permitted, brought safely to Wyoming, and restored to the arms of their father. Mr. Franklin had been with another party in eager pursuit, but had failed to find the enemy. Gen. Wm. Ross used to say, the battle for Mr. Franklin's family was one of the best contested in Wyoming.

Peace soon came, and Mr. Elliott was much in the employment of Judge Hollenback, who had the highest confidence in his faithfulness, and the veteran speaks of Judge H. in terms of warm commendation.

A pension of 65 dollars a year, has contributed to render the evening of his days comfortable. Below the middle height, he was well built, and of that cast best shown by experience to be adapted to endure fatigue. June 25th, 1845, when we called on the old gentleman to hear his narrative, he was at work in his garden. In early life Joseph Elliott must have been handsome, for, except the loss of his right eye, he still looks well. His face is round, and lighted up by a benevolent smile. Half his thin hair is still dark, and his manner mild and pleasing. But when he is in full tide, relating the events of battle,—" When the Indians came down on us like so many raging devils," age is forgotten, and he is full of animation. His habits have been simple, his life virtuous, his conduct in war meritorious as fidelity and bravery could render it. He lives universally respected, and it is hoped may enjoy his pension these many coming years. With pleasure we add that his son was, at the last session, a member of Assembly from Bradford county.

APPENDIX.

Israel Skinner, M. D., author of the Revolutionary War in rhyme, seems to have taken from the veteran's lips the account of his escape from the dreadful *Ring*, which we quote.

> "Those who were taken by the Indians there,
> As Joseph Elliott doth to us declare,
> (Who did among the prisoners remain,
> And was one of those appointed to be slain,)
> Were taken to a certain spot of ground,
> And stripped, and in a ring arraigned around,
> As victims of their rage designed to be,
> A sacrifice to savage cruelty.
> A squaw, the Indians did Queen Esther call,
> Was set apart to tomahawk them all.
> This right to her perhaps they did extend,
> To make atonement for some slaughtered friend;
> Elliott says, five or six became a prey,
> In presence of him in his savage way;
> That he himself was in a stupid maze,
> When first he at their cruelties did gaze,
> But being roused in feelings at the sight,
> Bethought to struggle with his utmost might,
> Thinking at worst he could but fall a prey
> To savage vengeance while upon this way.
> Two Indians holding him then quickly were
> By his puissant arm laid prostrate there;
> Then he towards the river pressed his way,
> While missive weapons did around him play
> And many of the savage Indian crew
> Did to the river's margin him pursue—
> But he before their frightful vengeance hied
> And plunged himself beneath the liquid tide,
> And diving on his way as he did flee
> Thereby to shun the savage enmity.
> But while the buzzing bullets dashed around
> In his left shoulder he received a wound,
> Which weakened him so much he thought it best
> When he approached the shore awhile to rest.
> When he had rested, he with all his force
> Leaped from the water and kept on his course;
> When round the place a leaden shower did light
> Which made the liquid billows foam with white;
> Yet notwithstanding those obstructions he
> Sprang up the bank and got behind a tree.
> When he his breath had gained and was revived,
> He urged his way, and to the Fort arrived,
> And there united with his friends again,
> And thus escaped the brutal savage train."

The classical reader, while forming his own opinion whether in poetic charm there is anything equal in Homer or Virgil, will allow us to suggest, that we probably have here a true narration of the facts of this marvellous escape.

NO. XXXVII.

MAJOR EZEKIEL PIERCE.

MAJOR EZEKIEL PIERCE, the father of the Pierce family, was the ready writer of early days, and for a succession of years clerk of the town, the Records being in his hand writing. He had five sons, all grown to manhood, when he removed to Wyoming, in 1771, and must therefore have been advanced towards the decline of life. Their names were Abel, Daniel, John, Timothy and Phineas. When in June 1778, the two Independent companies were consolidated into one under

Capt. Spalding, Timothy and Phineas were commissioned 1st and 2d lieutenants. Timothy was one of the three who rode all night, before the battle, arrived after the troops had marched out, followed, and fell. John also was slain in the engagement. Abel, the father of Mrs. Lord Butler, the writer knew, and remembers with respect and pleasure. He lost a son, Chester, just in the bloom of early manhood, in the civil dissensions that succeeded the Revolutionary war. A daughter Mrs. Hoyt, widow of the late Capt. Daniel Hoyt, of Kingston, still lives, June, 1845.

NO. XXXVIII.

THE FINCH FAMILY.

THREE of the Finch family, John, Daniel, and Benjamin, were killed at the time of the invasion, two in the engagement, one murdered by the Indians, the day previous, near Shoemaker's mill. Our researches have not put us in possession of all the facts, in regard to this suffering family, that we desired.

NO. XXXIX.

THOMAS BROWN.

THE names of Thomas Brown and John Brown are in the list of slain. Thomas, in the retreat, had nearly crossed the river, another person being in company. Overtaken by the enemy he was induced* or forced to return, and on reaching the shore was instantly speared and tomahawked; his companion witnessed the deed but escaped. The particulars of the fall of John we have not learned. Daniel Brown, a brother, was then a lad in Forty Fort. He now resides very independently, near the Wyalusing, a neighbour to the gallant and fortunate Elliott, (who escaped from the fatal ring with Hammond,) having also near him, Mrs. Wells, who was a Ross, and several other of the ancient Wyoming people.

One of the stoccades at Pittston was called Brown's Fort, that family having erected it on their own land. Though not named, it is evidently referred to, in the dispatches of Col. John Butler, as one of the three that capitulated. Several of the descendants of those Revolutionary sufferers still reside on or near the Lackawana.

* I say "induced or forced." The enemy, to make sure of the scalps of their victims, preferred alluring them to the shore, rather than to shoot them in the stream. Promises of life and protection were solemnly made, to be instantly and ruthlessly violated. After peace opened intercourse with Canada, Mr. Hollenback relates that he has seen Indians in their drunken orgies, act over the massacre. Their coaxing the Yankees ashore, and then the murderous struggle, the pleadings for life, "For Jesus Christ's sake," the savage demons would exclaim in broken English, with fiend-like exultation, until, he said, it was almost impossible to keep his hands off them.

NO. XL.

ASA AND JOHN STEVENS.

ASA and JOHN STEVENS are named in the old records, as inhabitants of Wilkesbarre so early as 1772. Rosewell Stevens was one of the patriotic soldiers that entered the service in Ransom's Independent company. Asa Stevens was an officer holding the commission of lieutenant in the militia, and was slain in the battle. Like the Danas they were particularly distinguished by their zeal for the establishment of free schools, and the advancement of learning. This congeniality of sentiment led to the most intimate connection—Mr. Anderson Dana and Sylvester Dana, Esq., marrying sisters of the Stevens family. Removing from Wilkesbarre, Jonathan Stevens, Esq., settled in Braintrim, and afterwards in Bradford county, where, on the organization of that county—having long exercised with intelligence and firmness the duties of a magistrate, he was appointed one of the associate judges. When the author had the pleasure of his acquaintance, thirty years ago, his manners were pleasing—he was intelligent, quick to observe, ready to communicate, and of a most extraordinary memory. His conversation was highly agreeable and instructive.

NO. XLI.

LIEUTENANT JAMES WELLES.

Lieutenant James Welles is on the record of the honoured patriots, who fell in that disastrous battle, which filled Wyoming with lamentation and woe. The family were the earliest settlers in Springfield, on the Wyalusing, from which on danger of the savages becoming imminent, they removed to the more densely settled part of the country in the valley. Resuming the occupation of their property on the restoration of peace, the family became prosperous, and continue among the most respectable and independent inhabitants of that beautiful place, (formerly it will be remembered the residence of the Moravian missionaries and Christian Indians.)

XLII.

COREY AND BULLOCK.

Of the Corey and the Bullock families, no longer residents of Wyoming, we have been able to learn much less than, from their sacrifices and sufferings, could have been wished. Amos and Asa Bullock were killed in the battle. One of the name, probably one of the brothers, who fell, was a lawyer; the father resided at the meadows, six miles on the Easton road, from Wilkesbarre, where the night and day, after the massacre, from the rushing in and departure of the fugitives, images of sorrow and despair, the dreadful uncertainty of the fate of his boys, the scene was inexpressibly distressing. Nathan Bullock, probably the father, was two years afterwards taken by Indians a prisoner to Canada.

Three of the Corey family were among the victims of the rifle and tomahawk; Jenks, Rufus and Anson. The former was one of the original proprietors of Pittston. It may be noted, as extraordinary, that three of the younger branches of the name came by melancholy accident to untimely deaths. One, being shot by a neighbour, mistaken for a deer.—One lumbering some years ago on the Lehigh—the other in the far western country, to which the remains of the family had emigrated. The father died long since in Kingston, and his remains are buried on or near the spot where the tavern stands on the north-east corner at New Troy.

NO. XLIII.

THE CHURCH FAMILY.

The Church family came from Kent, Litchfield county. "An abstract of the second Independent company raised in the town of Westmoreland, commanded by Capt. Samuel Ransom," dated October 7th, 1777, contains the names of Nathaniel Church, John Church and Gideon Church. The present farm on the Kingston flats, opposite Mill Creek, was owned by, and the residence of Gideon, and the property now belongs to his son, Wm. Church. The reader, familiar with old Indian wars, will remember the gallant and successful Captain Church, who was scarcely less distinguished than Mason, the hero of the Pequot conquest. There is no reason to doubt that the families were of the same original stock, that in a very early day emigrated from England.

In the list of slain in the battle, furnished by Colonel Franklin, is the name of Joel Church, who also was the brother of Gideon. With many other Wyoming people, attracted by alluring accounts of the richness of western lands, several of the family removed to Ohio.

NO. XLIV.

CAPTAIN REZIN GERE.

CAPTAIN REZIN GERE commanded the second or upper Wilkesbarre company on the fatal 3d.* He left three sons, the eldest only five years of age, to the care of his widow. Driven with her orphan children from the valley, their house and all their papers were consumed by fire. Too young to know their rights or to return and repossess their farm—the title papers being destroyed—the land of course went into other hands. Captain Jeremiah Gere, a highly respectable citizen of Susquehanna county, recently deceased, was one of the sons. The other brothers not long since visited Wyoming. "We are becoming old and are poor," said they, "our father fell, a commissioned officer, fighting the enemies of liberty and his country—we lost everything, even the land. Is there no redress? Is there no aid to be obtained from the government of the country?" Their case seems one of great hardship. Is there one instance in a hundred in which Congress have granted lands or pensions where the claim was so strong as this?

* He was from Norwich, descended from one of the oldest families of that place. A Mr. Rezin Gere is named in its annals as living an hundred and fifty years ago. Capt Gere was aged 40 years at the time of his death. Stephen Gere, of Brooklyn, Susquehanna county, is the only son now living (June, 1845).

NO. XLV.

PITTSTON.

IN Pittston the leading families, during the Revolutionary war, were the Blanchards, Browns, Careys, Bennetts, Silbeys, Marcys, Benedicts, St. Johns,* Sawyers, not omitting the gallant Cooper. Observe that neat white house on the plain—see that white and tasteful dwelling on the hill—both are occupied by the descendants of Cooper. The Rev. Mr. Benedict was the earliest minister there. Those handsome buildings above Manockasy belong to the Blanchards. Captain Jeremiah Blanchard (the elder) commanded the Pittston company. Unjust censure was cast upon him by some querulous people, because he did not lead his men into battle. The failure to do so arose neither from want of courage nor patriotism. At the head of the valley, the enemy having possession of Wintermoot and Jenkins' Forts, both in sight and only separated from his stoccade by the river, he could not have gone with his men to Forty Fort without leaving the women, children, and everything under his care, to the exasperated fury of the savages.

APPENDIX.

Zebulon and Ebenezer Marcy were brothers. The painful circumstances connected with the flight of the wife of Ebenezer are elsewhere related. The case of the wife of Zebulon was still more distressing. She fled with an infant, six weeks old in her arms, at the same time leading a child two years older. The oldest died in the wilderness, and as there were no means to bury it decently, they covered it with moss and bark as well as they could, and hurried on, leaving its remains to the beasts of prey. The infant daughter, Mrs. Whitmore, formerly Mrs. M'Cord, is now (June, 1845) living in Wyoming county. Zebulon Marcy after the war, established himself on a fine farm, on the Tunkhannock, where he exercised the duties of a magistrate for many years. On the 11th of September, 1834, he closed his eventful life at the advanced age of 90 years.

Pittston, though not the most attractive in reference to soil, of the first five located townships, will probably prove the richest in the valley, from its position, its water power, and unbounded quantities of available anthracite.

* Daniel St. John was the first person murdered after the capitulation. Pronounced by the old people Senshon.

NO. XLVI.

THE GAYLORD FAMILY.

EMIGRATED at an early day to Wyoming, from Norwich. Justus Gaylord commenced a settlement in Springfield, on the Wyalusing, before Indian hostilities began; but was obliged to remove down the river to the more densely populated country.

When the independent companies were raised, two of his sons, Justus and Ambrose, enlisted in that of Captain Ransom, and served during the war. On the restoration of peace, the old gentleman and his son Justus resumed their possessions at Wyalusing; while Ambrose established himself at Braintrim.

Aholiab Buck, captain of the Kingston company, about a year before the battle, had married Miss York, born in Stonington. The (subsequently) Rev. Miner York was her brother. Mrs. Buck was in Forty Fort, having in her arms an infant daughter, a few weeks old, when her husband led his men to the field—no more to return. Their flight, their sorrows, their deep sufferings, so similar to those of hundreds of others, it would seem like repetition to relate. At the conclusion of the war, Justus Gaylord, Jr., and Mrs. Buck were married by the Rev. Mr. Johnson. The author waited upon her, June 25th, 1845, and found the good old lady, now eighty-eight years of age, in fine health and spirits, the profusion of lace upon her cap speaking of habitual fondness for dress, her round, full face, and cheerful smile indicating in early life, remarkable personal beauty. She had walked up a mile to visit Mrs. Taylor, wife of Major John Taylor, the daughter we have spoken of as being on her nursing bosom in July, 1778. Mrs. Gaylord never had but that one child. But Mrs. Taylor has counted seventeen, and near forty grandchildren, besides seven or eight great-great-grandchildren. So that, although the name of Captain Buck is not perpetuated, yet his descendants are now numerous, and "well to live."

In 1806, Justus Gaylord, Jr., was on the ticket for assembly. Luzerne then embraced Wyoming, Susquehanna, and Bradford, except the Tioga district set off to Lycoming. The votes stood

Justus Gaylord, Jr.,   333
Justus Gaylord,   38
                       ———
                       371
Moses Coolbaugh   364

So that if the votes given without the Jr. were added to his list, (his father being a very old man and not a candidate,) he was chosen. But the place had not charm enough to induce the old soldier to contest the election, and Mr. Coolbaugh took the seat. The incident is mentioned to show the respect in which he was held, as well as to show the fact that less than 400 votes chose a member of assembly.

The old gentleman removed with a son to the Ohio, where, at a very advanced age, he died. Justus died May, 1830, aged 73.

Ambrose, who settled in Braintrim, married Eleanor Comstock, daughter of John Comstock, who came from Norwich west farms. Mr. Gaylord died June 12, 1844, and had he lived to November, he would have been 95. His country had not entirely forgotten him, for his old age was cheered by a pension of 80 dollars. His good wife Eleanor, with whom we spent an hour, now (June, 1845,) 82 years of age, appears of perfectly sound mind and memory. She states that her father and two brothers were in the battle, she living in Forty Fort. Her two brothers, Kingsley and Robert, were killed. Her father, exhausted in the flight, threw himself beside a fallen tree. Presently two Indians sprang upon it, intent on those at a distance, and, on stepping down to pursue, bent the bushes so as to brush him. When night came, he found his way to the fort.

Another branch of the name settled in the lower part of Wyoming. The father of the late Charles E. Gaylord, Esq., of Huntington, died while in the service, having been a member of Captain Durkee's company. Lieutenant Aaron Gaylord, one of the officers who fell in the battle, was his brother.

In the queer poem, the American Revolutionary War, in rhyme, I find:

"Next Aaron Gaylord unto death did yield,
With Stoddart Bowen on the tented field."

Dr. Charles Gaylord studied medicine after the war with Dr. Henderson, a distinguished physician of Connecticut, in compliment to whom he gave that name to his son, the present merchant in Plymouth. Dr. Gaylord died in 1839, aged 69 years.

Four, therefore, bore arms for their country, one of whom died in the service, and one fell in battle.

NO. XLVII.

JOSIAH ROGERS

REMOVED with his family to Wyoming, and settled at Plymouth in 1776. After the massacre, with his family he fled, taking his course down the Susquehanna two days' journey; thence across the mountains towards Northampton or Berks. Exhausted by fatigue, and heart-stricken with terror, Mrs. Rogers fainted upon the journey; and notwithstanding the utmost aid was administered their poor means afforded, she died *in the wilderness*, many miles from any human habitation. This was July the 9th, 1778. Husband and children gathered round to look upon the pale face of one who in life they had loved so fondly. It was a scene of inexpressible sorrow. A broken piece of board that lay in the path was used for a spade, and in a hollow where a fallen tree had upturned its roots, a shallow grave was dug, and her remains were buried with all the care and respect their distressed condition would allow. On the board placed over the grave, this inscription was written with a piece of charcoal:

"Here rest the remains of HANNAH, wife of JOSIAH ROGERS, who died while fleeing from the Indians after the massacre at Wyoming."

Frail memorial of reverence and love! yet how slightly more endurable, having reference either to time or eternity, are the costliest monuments that ostentatious pride, or heartfelt grief, have ever erected, to perpetuate what the inexorable law of nature has prescribed shall be forgotten!

The deceased was aged 52 years. Her maiden name was Hannah Ford.

On arriving at the settlement near the Blue Mountain, the same sympathy and kindness were extended to them which the Wyoming people had uniformly experienced from the benevolent Germans. After an exile of some months, the survivors of the family returned to Plymouth, where danger still awaited them.

That the old gentleman was a humourist will be seen from the account given of his hair-breadth escape from Indian captivity or death. His descendant, Dr. Joel J. Rogers, is the narrator.

——"In the spring of 1779, the next year after the massacre, Josiah Rogers, my great-grandfather, having returned, said, 'I will lay my bones in Wyoming.' Indians had not for some time been seen in the valley, and Capt. James Bidlack with Mr. Rogers, started on horseback to go to Plymouth to see, if eligible to remove with their families. After crossing the river some eighty rods below the present bridge, they passed up the road, on the township line, until they were near Toby's creek, where an Indian appeared and rushing towards them from behind the willows, would have seized their bridles. He was instantly followed by others, and the trembling willows then disclosed the cove of the creek above them red with Indians. But a Yankee, though an old man, don't give up, you know, without showing his skill. They were unarmed. but they wheeled their horses suddenly, and made towards the block house on the bank of the river. Capt. Bidlack's saddle having an old girth, which broke, turned and precipitated him to the ground. And now came a race; Bidlack after Rogers! But stepping on a rail, (laid over a slough,) which turned with him, Capt. Bidlack fell and was immediately taken prisoner. Now flew the lead—and now flew my grandfather's old horse, which, as the old gentleman used to say, 'didn't like the smell of an Indian.' One savage, fleet of foot, came very near his horse but did not quite reach him, another was but a few rods behind. He grew quite familiar with the whizzing of balls, but felt no wound.

"The garrison at the block-house, on hearing the firing, advanced to the rescue. The cannon at the Fort in Wilkesbarre, of which the Indians were terribly afraid, was brought to bear, and discharged towards them, arresting their progress. My great-grandfather wore a tight-bodied coat, and an over coat of the same cloth, made of wool-coloured, one part butternut, the other blue, homespun, woven, and dressed, &c. (homespun, you understand). Coming to a new country, he expected to preserve them unsullied for many years, when, alas! on arriving at the block-house, he found the rascals had cut two holes through his over-coat, passing in near the small of the back on one side, coming out eight inches from it on the other, with a rent of a fingers' breadth in his tight-bodied coat. For many years he was compelled to wear, when abroad and at meeting, the evidence of Indian skill in shooting at a mark."

The capture of young Josiah Rogers (with Pike and Van Campen) is related in our annals.

Josiah Rogers lived to the good old age of 96 years, and died in 1815, his wish being accorded "to lay his bones at Wyoming."

The family were highly respectable, and remarkable for their intelligence. Numbers of the name still reside in the lower part of Wyoming.

NO. XLV.

COLONEL ZEBULON BUTLER.

As the biography of Washington is the story of the Revolution, so the life of Col. Zebulon Butler is the History of Wyoming. Almost every letter of our annals bears the impress of his name, and is a record of his deeds. A liberal and natural curiosity would lead to the desire, to learn something of the early life of a man so distinguished—for he was in full manhood when he made his first appearance on the waters of the Susquehanna. A native of Lyme, New London County, Zebulon Butler was born in 1731. From the neat hand-writing and business style of

John Butler, his father, it may be inferred that the education of the parent had not been neglected. It would seem probable that both parents came from England. A bill of exchange drawn in favour of Jacob Hurd, on Mr. Samuel Storke, for £80 sterling, in February, 1746, would show business transactions of some importance abroad. Another paper leads to the conclusion that the sum was part of a legacy to Mr. John Butler's wife, of several hundred pounds. In an old bill,

John Butler to Jacob Hurd

Is charged, cash paid, £190—Gold ear rings,—A gold ring,—Several ounces of silver,—A note of hand for £300, payable six months after date, and cash in full, —With various other charges amounting to £710 10s.

On the breaking out of what is usually called "the Old French War," Zebulon Butler entered the military service of his country, bearing the commission of ensign, in one of the Provincial companies, raised by Connecticut for the crown. On the northern frontier, particularly at Ticonderoga and Crown Point, his ambition was soon gratified, by entering upon a field of stirring and honourable action. So early as 1761, he had attained the rank of captain, and the following year sailed with his company on the memorable expedition to the Havana. In the perils, the glory and the acquisitions of the capture of that important place, Captain Butler shared. Whether his future companions in arms, Captains Durkee and Ransom, served as subordinates in these early campaigns, is not certainly known, but is rendered probable from the fact that both were officers in the Old French War, and the three were in the Wyoming conflicts, early associated in friendship and action together.

Peace was concluded with France, and in 1763, the Provincial troops were disbanded. The emigration of Captain Butler to Wyoming in 1769, and subsequent events, in which he bore a part up to the Revolutionary War, have been fully narrated. Soon after the contest with Great Britain commenced, Captain Butler received the appointment of lieutenant colonel of a regiment in the Connecticut line of the army, and in September, 1778, he "was appointed full colonel to the late Charles Webb's regiment, against the will of Lieutenant Colonel Sherman, who intended to have had the regiment." This extract of a letter from Colonel Thomas Grosvenor, dated 1778, is regarded as important, because it shows the excellent standing and popularity of Colonel Butler, the fall immediately after the massacre, when time sufficient had elapsed for the country and constituted authorities perfectly to ascertain the merits or defects of his conduct on that memorable and trying occasion. When it is recollected that Lieutenant Colonel Sherman, his competitor for the office, was the brother of the distinguished Roger Sherman, and that Colonel Butler was absent while his rival was upon the ground, the commission reflects more than common honour upon the recipient. A brief note to that letter in the hand-writing of Colonel Wyllys, among the most able and excellent leaders in Connecticut, though not very important in the matter contained, is copied because it shows the kind and respectful feelings, at that interesting moment, that prevailed in respect to Colonel B.

"Colonel Wyllys desires his best compliments to Colonel Butler and would have written, but hopes Mr. Gore will give him an account of our present situation, and as Mr. G. sets out in the morning begs the colonel to accept this
From his humble servant
Samuel Wyllys."

After being withdrawn from Wyoming, Colonel Butler served with honour to the close of the contest, and when the army was disbanded, returned to his residence in Wilkesbarre, where he passed the remainder of his life, the prudent but steady supporter of the rights of the settlers, looking confidently to the justice of Pennsylvania to settle the existing controversy by an equitable compromise. Such was the estimation in which he was held that in 1787, on the establishment of Luzerne, he received from the Supreme Executive Council the honourable appointment of lieutenant of the county, which he held until the office was abrogated by the new constitution of 1790.

On the 28th of July, 1795, aged 64 years, this gallant soldier and estimable citizen resigned his breath to God who gave it, and his remains were interred in

APPENDIX.

the graveyard in Wilkesbarre. Among other marks of respect paid to his memory, a monody of a dozen verses was written, one of which was inscribed on his tombstone.

> " Distinguished by his usefulness
> At home and when abroad
> In court, in camp, and in recess
> Protected still by God."

Colonel Butler was thrice married. First to Miss Ellen Lord before his emigration from Connecticut. The fruit of this union was two children. The late Gen. Lord Butler and Mrs. Welles, consort of the late Roswell Welles, Esq., a lawyer of handsome talents and attainments, who in his day, was judge of the court, colonel of a regiment, and several times member of Assembly. One daughter of Judge Welles is living, Mrs. Harriet Cowles, consort of Colonel Cowles, of Farmington, Connecticut. Lord had intermarried with the daughter of Abel Pierce, Esq. Their sons, several of whom are now living, are Pierce, John, Chester, Zebulon and Lord.

Pierce is a farmer on the fine plantation running from the river a few rods above the bridge to the village of Kingston. The Rev. Zebulon Butler is the esteemed pastor of a Presbyterian congregation at Port Gibson, Mississippi. John, Chester and Lord, residing in Wilkesbarre, are amongst its most active business men. Sylvina, the eldest daughter, several years since deceased, was the wife of the Hon. Garrick Mallery. Ruth Ann, the second daughter, is married to the Hon. John N. Conyngham, president judge of this judicial district. Phebe, married to Dr. Donalson, has removed with her husband to Iowa.

The second wife of Colonel Butler was Miss Johnson, daughter of the first Gospel minister of Wyoming. Their union was brief, and a son, the late Captain Zebulon Butler, their only child. Of dark complexion, his black eye, when cheerfully animated, was brilliant and pleasing. This son was handsome, and from his extremely fine form, he was eminently attractive. His step was elastic but firm, his head erect, his carriage noble. It was said he was proud. In command of his company on parade, he looked " every inch a man." Honourable, generous, high-spirited, he seemed to pant for a wider field, and more exciting scenes of action. In rolling the bullet, and other athletic exercises, he had no superior. The writer knew, admired and esteemed him. He was cut off in the prime of life, and his numerous and interesting family are widely scattered: it is hoped prosperously situated.

While on duty at West Point, near the close of the war, Colonel Butler married his third wife, Miss Phebe Haight. Three children, by this marriage, survive. Stuben Butler, Esq., of Wilkesbarre, some time since commissioner of the county, and for many years editor of the Wyoming Herald. Lydia, who intermarried with George Griffin, Esq., of New York. The late Rev. Edmund Griffin, whose accurate and extensive learning, and brilliant talents, gave promise of unusual usefulness and fame, and whose early death was so deeply lamented, was the grandson of Colonel Butler. Mrs. Robinson (whose late husband, Mr. John Robinson, was a direct descendant of the pilgrim minister), is the third child. Their only daughter intermarried with H. B. Wright, Esq., recently Speaker of the House of Assembly. We cannot refrain from the remark, that it is at once curious and pleasing, that two Speakers of the House, and two president judges, have been so intimately connected with the ancient Wyoming sufferers.

The distinguishing traits of Colonel Butler's character were activity, energy, a high sense of honour, a courage moral and professional, that, when duty called, knew no fear.

WYOMING MASSACRE.

The Ballad which follows, composed soon after the battle, has never before, that I can learn, appeared in print. Mr. Joel J. Rogers, to whom I am indebted for this interesting relic of the olden time, says, "Written by Mr. Uriah Terry, of Kingston—so says my father. Copied by Uncle Josiah from a manuscript, Dec. 20, 1785. Sixty years ago." These "uncouth rhymes" which

"Implore the passing tribute of a sigh,"

I cannot doubt will be acceptable to the antiquarian.

1. Kind Heaven, assist the trembling muse,
    While she attempts to tell
   Of poor Wyoming's overthrow,
    By savage sons of hell.

2. One hundred whites, in painted hue,
    Whom Butler there did lead,
   Supported by a barb'rous crew
    Of the fierce savage breed.

3. The last of June the siege began,
    And several days it held,
   While many a brave and valiant man
    Lay slaughtered on the field.

4. Our troops marched out from Forty Fort,
    The third day of July,
   Three hundred strong, they march along,
    The fate of war to try.

5. But oh! alas! three hundred men,
    Is much too small a band,
   To meet eight hundred men complete,
    And make a glorious stand.

6. Four miles they marched from the Fort
    Their enemy to meet,
   Too far indeed did Butler lead,
    To keep a safe retreat.

APPENDIX.

7. And now the fatal hour is come—
    They bravely charge the foe,
  And they with ire, returned the fire,
    Which prov'd our overthrow.

8. Some minutes they sustained the fire,
    But ere they were aware
  They were encompassed all around
    Which prov'd a fatal snare.

9. And then they did attempt to fly,
    But all was now in vain,;
  Their little host—by far the most—
    Was by those Indians slain.

10. And as they fly, for quarters cry;
    Oh hear! indulgent Heav'n!
  Hard to relate—their dreadful fate,
    No quarters must be given.

11. With bitter cries and mournful sighs
    They seek some safe retreat,
  Run here and there, they know not where,
    Till awful death they meet.

12. Their piercing cries salute the skies—
    Mercy is all their cry:
  "Our souls prepare God's grace to share,
    We instantly must die."

13. Some men yet found are flying round
    Sagacious to get clear;
  In vain to fly, their foes too nigh!
    They front they flank and rear.

14. And now the foe hath won the day,
    Methinks their words are these:
  " Ye cursed, rebel, Yankee race,
    Will this your Congress please?"

15. " Your pardons crave, you them shall have,
    Behold them in our hands;
  We'll all agree to set you free,
    By dashing out your brains.

E

16. "And as for you, enlisted crew,
     We'll raise your honours higher:
   Pray turn your eye, where you must lie,
     In yonder burning fire."

17. Then naked in those flames they're cast,
     Too dreadful 'tis to tell,
   Where they must fry, and burn and die,
     While cursed Indians yell.

18. Nor son, nor sire, these tigers spare,—
     The youth, and hoary head,
   Were, by those monsters murdered there,
     And numbered with the dead.

19. Methinks I hear some sprightly youth,
     His mournful state condole:
   " O, that my tender parents knew,
     The anguish of my soul.

20. " But O! there's none to save my life,
     Or heed my dreadful fear;
   I see the tomahawk and knife,
     And the more glittering spear.

21. "When years ago, I dandled was
     Upon my parent's knees,
   I little thought I should be brought
     To feel such pangs as these.

22. "I hoped for many a joyful day,
     I hoped for riches' store—
   These golden dreams are fled away;
     I straight shall be no more.

23. " Farewell, fond mother; late I was,
     Locked up in your embrace;
   Your heart would ache, and even break,
     If you could know my case.

24. " Farewell, indulgent parents dear,
     I must resign my breath;
   I now must die, and here must lie,
     In the cold arms of death.

APPENDIX.

25. "For O! the fatal hour is come,
  I see the bloody knife,—
  The Lord have mercy on my soul!"
  And quick resigned his life.

26. A doleful theme; yet, pensive muse,
  Pursue the doleful theme:
  It is no fancy to delude,
  Nor transitory dream.

27. The Forty Fort was the resort,
  For mother and for child,
  To save them from the cruel rage,
  Of the fierce savage wild.

28. Now, when the news of this defeat,
  Had sounded in our ears,
  You well may know our dreadful woe,
  And our foreboding fears.

29. A doleful sound is whispered round,
  The sun now hides his head;
  The nightly gloom forbodes our doom,
  We all shall soon be dead.

30. How can we bear the dreadful spear,
  The tomahawk and knife?
  And if we run, the awful gun,
  Will rob us of our life.

31. But Heaven! kind Heaven, propitious power!
  His hand we must adore;
  He did assuage the savage rage,
  That they should kill no more.

32. The gloomy night now gone and past,
  The sun returns again,
  The little birds from every bush,
  Seem to lament the slain.

33. With aching hearts and trembling hands
  We walked here and there,
  Till through the northern pines we saw,
  A flag approaching near.

APPENDIX.

34. Some men were chose to meet this flag,
    Our colonel was the chief,
    Who soon returned and in his mouth,
    He brought an olive leaf.

35. This olive leaf was granted life,
    But then we must no more
    Pretend to fight with Britain's king,
    Until the wars are o'er.

36. And now poor Westmoreland is lost,
    Our forts are all resigned,
    Our buildings they are all on fire,—
    What shelter can we find?

37. They did agree in black and white,
    If we'd lay down our arms,
    That all who pleased might quietly
    Remain upon their farms.

38. But O! they've robbed us of our all,
    They've taken all but life,
    And we'll rejoice and bless the Lord,
    If this may end the strife.

39. And now I've told my mournful tale,
    I hope you'll all agree,
    To help our cause and break the jaws
    Of cruel tyranny.

THE WYOMING MONUMENT

APPENDIX.

THE MONUMENT.

> "Death is the worst—a fate that all must try—
> And for our country 'tis a bliss to die:
> The gallant man, though slain in fight he be,
> Yet leaves his nation safe, his children free;
> Entails a debt on all the grateful state—
> His own brave friends shall glory in his fate;
> His wife live honour'd; all his race succeed,
> And late posterity enjoy the deed."
>
> ILIAD, Book, 15, v. 580

Not doubting it will prove a subject of interest to many readers, and perhaps be a matter of useful reference hereafter, we proceed to place on record the measures adopted to procure the erection of a monument over the remains of those patriots who fell in the battle, and the steps which were taken to obtain from Connecticut some mark of recognition and regard in requital for the sufferings of the Wyoming people in her cause.

So early as 1809, 36 years ago, several essays were published intended to awaken public attention to the fitness of erecting a monument over the remains of those who fell in the battle. Among others, it being the second or third written by the author of this work, the following appeared in the Wilkesbarre paper of Nov. 3d of that year.

"THE WYOMING MASSACRE.

" Alas!—the horrors of that bloody scene are still fresh in my recollection. The time that has passed since that fatal day seems only like a dream of the night, and all the circumstances of the battle rise on my memory like the events of yesterday. I behold our little band of warriors, full of ardour, marching forth to the engagement; I see the commander, firm and steady, cheering the soldiers to do their duty like men, worthy of themselves and worthy of their country. I well remember, on the morning of the battle, an old man—God bless his memory, for he was a brave one—who insisted on joining the little band of patriots. He had fought under Wolfe at Quebec, and had approved himself a soldier, but age had unnerved his arm, and the frosts of seventy winters had whitened his locks like the snows that crown the summit of Cotopaxi. Two of his sons had already joined the troops; a younger one of seventeen was preparing to follow. The drum sounded the alarm, the hum of active preparation arose from the camp; the old man's eye beamed with the ardour of the warrior; his soul swelled with the proud hope that he could be useful to his country; he seized his rifle, and vain were the entreaties of his son; his daughter dissuaded him in vain; he rushed to the camp resolved to conquer or to perish. The battle raged on our right. Brandt with his savage myrmidons poured from the thicket that flanked our left wing; vain were all our efforts to bear up against the vast superiority of numbers. Like a torrent from the mountain swelled with ceaseless rain, pouring with irresistible fury on the valley, so poured forth the herds of savages from their coverts on our devoted left, until retreat was hopeless and victory impossible. Fickle fortune smiled for awhile on our right. There the gallant Butler, cool and intrepid, directed the storm. He rode steadily in our front, pressed on the foe, and victory hovered over and fanned him with her pinions. But alas, unsustained, every effort was vain, and the reluctant retreat was forced by a prudent affection for the safety of the troops that were left. Then followed all the fury of savage warfare. Fiends seemed to have joined the engagement. I still hear the savage yell rise and mingle with the groans of the dying. I see the spear gleam dreadful, as it flies and arrests its victim. I saw the old man turn like a wounded panther on the foe; three savages fell by his arm, but a fourth cleft his white locks: he died gloriously. Ruin wide and awful extended o'er the plains. The flames of our habitations rose and threw a lurid light athwart the gloom of the evening. But dreadful was the night that followed. The fearful anxiety of the friends of those who went to battle, the agonizing cries of those who had fallen alive into the hands of the savages, the horrors of the midnight sacrifice, all form a scene that, even at this distant day, the mind cannot contemplate without horror.

"Few only escaped the slaughter. Many were the brave men who fell. Never have I rested in quiet since that day, because no testimonial of respect has been paid to the memory of the slain. Now since it is proposed to raise a monument over them do I rejoice. Our old men will be glad that those who fell in the cause of freedom are not unregarded. Our young men shall gather round the tomb; reflect on the virtues of their fathers; their souls shall catch fire as at the altar—they shall swear a new devotion to liberty, and new fealty to their country. Thus shall the monument do justice to the memory of departed patriots.

"The old shall be gratified; the young shall be inspired—I will give my mite with pleasure. Where is the patriot who will not?"

Subsequently, in March, 1810, an irregular ode, of soul-stirring interest, understood to be from the pen of CHARLES F. WELLS, Esq., was published.

"WARRIORS OF WYOMING.

"O! haughty was the hour,
    The hum, the brave array,
When sallied forth Wyoming's power,
    Upon the battle day.

"But soon, when hemmed by sudden foes,
    They gathered round to fight and die,
O! horrid was the shout that rose,
    And long and deep the dying cry.

"Fierce was the fight of strong despair
    And fierce the savage yell,
And dreadful was the carnage where
    The warriors of Wyoming fell.

"No shouting of victorious pride
    Deceived the brave man's dying breath,
But murder rag'd on every side,
    And heavy blows, and blood and death.

"O, gloomy was the day,
    When the widow'd mother heard
The roar of battle die away,
    And no returning band appear'd.

"No more their burning hamlets gleam,
    Along the narrow heath,
Nor stretching o'er the midnight stream,
    Reflect the fire of death.

"No more their little fort around,
    The warriors of Wyoming throng,
They sleep beneath the frozen ground
    Where the wind howls loud and long.

APPENDIX.

> " And there the pausing traveller finds
>   No grave stone rising nigh,
> Where the tall grass bends and the hollow winds
>   May eddy round and sigh.

> " O, when shall their silent home
>   Its mournful glory gain!
> The vollied roar and muffled drum,
>   In honour of the warrior slain?

> " O, when shall rise, with chisel'd head,
>   The tall stone o'er their burial place.
> Where the winds may sigh for the gallant dead
>   And the dry grass rustle round its base?"

Meetings were held and resolutions adopted favourable to the object, but the people, poor, and indebted for their land, were not able to meet the expense. Nor will this be regarded censurable or strange when it is recollected that the Bunker Hill Monument, located in the richest and most populous part of the Union, has but recently been completed.

Subsequently, irregular and yet inefficient movements were made to the end in view, and much of the granite hewn and drawn to the sacred spot, where (through the instrumentality of an old settler) the long forgotten place of interment had been discovered.

Public attention having in 1839 been awakened to the claims of Wyoming upon Connecticut, a committee was appointed by a meeting of ancient sufferers to repair to Hartford and solicit of the Assembly aid to finish the monument.

Confident in the justice of a much larger claim of right upon Connecticut, the committee, consisting of Gen. Wm. Ross, Capt. Hezekiah Parsons and Charles Miner, all natives of that state, repaired to Hartford. Their petition was presented by Lafayette S. Foster, Esq., one of the representatives from Norwich, and a joint committee of the Senate and House appointed for its consideration. After an eloquent appeal by Isaac Toucey, Esq., a report was made unanimously in favour of the grant of $3000 asked. In the House it was most ably supported by Mr. Foster, assisted by Dr. Woodward and several other gentlemen, but rejected, between sixty and seventy members voting in its favour. Gov. Ellsworth had expressed his individual wishes that something should be given, and the committee, from the favourable impression made, and the mass of interesting matter found at Hartford, returned, entertaining confident expectations that a succeeding Assembly, would grant the prayer of the petition.

In May, 1841, a new memorial was presented to the assembly: Chester Butler, and Henry Pettebone, Esqrs., and Capt. H. Parsons, who were appointed a committee for that purpose, having repaired to Hartford. The grounds of claim are set forth in the following propositions. The facts being undeniable, the public will judge of their weight:

"First. Because Wyoming was settled under the authority of Connecticut, as part of the state, under her charter, in the assertion and defence of her claims west of New York.

"Second. Because Connecticut extended her laws here, claimed jurisdiction, collected taxes, authorized the election of representatives to her assembly, and, indeed, recognized this town to be, what it really was, a part and parcel of the state.

"Thirdly. Because the troops raised in Wyoming in the Revolution were considered as Connecticut troops—credited as part of her line on the Continental establishment—making up part of her quota required by Congress, and rendering efficient and honourable service to the state during the war.

"Fourthly. Because, while these services were thus rendering, and *allegiance* cheerfully accorded, the parent state, from its distance and other causes, could not, and did not, perform its correlative duty of *protection,* and guard Wyoming from the danger that menaced her.

"Fifthly. Because the able-bodied men of the settlement being drawn away in her line of the army—the people being unprotected, the British and savages came down, slaughtered many of her inhabitants—devastated the whole settlement with fire and sword, to the total loss of houses, barns, cattle, and the year's harvest—to the utter ruin of every thing but the naked soil.

"Sixthly. Because, discouraging as the circumstances were, the survivors returned to Wyoming—renewed the settlement, and persevered in maintaining the claims of Connecticut, under her chartered limits, to her western lands.

"Seventhly. Because, in the final adjustment of her land claims, Connecticut retained, or obtained, the Western Reserve in Ohio, embracing 120 miles in longitude west of Pennsylvania, by a degree and two minutes of latitude, containing five millions of acres of land—a territory larger than the whole present limits of the state; of which Reserve, if it belonged originally to Connecticut, Westmoreland or Wyoming, as a part of the state, might reasonably have claimed a share; and if it be regarded as a grant for revolutionary services and sufferings, the claim of Wyoming would be stronger still.

"Eighthly. Because Connecticut appropriated five hundred thousand acres of the Reserve to indemnify the sufferers of Groton, New London, Fairfield, Danbury and New Haven, cut off by the common enemy, and appropriated *nothing* to Westmoreland, the greatest sufferer, and not the least meritorious.

"And ninthly. Because it was owing, in a great degree, to the early, persevering efforts of the Wyoming settlers to sustain the chartered and territorial claims of the state west of New York, that the Western Reserve was finally secured to Connecticut.

"Therefore, be it Resolved, That while we are not disposed to go back into those old claims, however clear and strong in equity and justice we may regard them, yet, as it is undeniable that those who fell in the battle were citizens of Connecticut, fighting in defence of her rights and laws; that they were her own children, most of them natives of the state; and while it is but a reasonable mark of respect that their remains should be gathered and decently interred with suitable sepulchral honours, it seems to us but right that the state should make an appropriation to finish the monument in a plain but neat style, worthy of her justice and of their merits and sufferings. If granted, we will receive the donation with grateful hearts, in full and perfect absolution of all other demands existing, or which might be supposed to exist, against the state on the part of the people of Wyoming."

Without taking the yeas and nays, the House by a large majority voted to grant the $3000 asked for the monument, but the *Senate* did not concur. A further effort was made the succeeding year, when the Hon. C. D. Shoemaker, accompanied by Col. Miller Horton, attended on behalf of the ancient people; but their efforts were unavailing, and there, in relation to Connecticut, the claim for aid rests, except that Erastus Ellsworth, Esq., of Windsor, to his honour be it spoken, sent us a present of *Five* dollars, after the rejection of the petition, expressing his deep sympathy for the Wyoming sufferers, and his respect for the services rendered by them to the state and country.

All the efforts of the Gentlemen having failed, the Ladies formed a "Luzerne Monumental Association;" solicited donations, held fairs, and by superior energy and address, obtained the necessary funds and completed the monument.

The following is a list of the officers of the association: Mrs. C. Butler, President. Mrs. G. M. Hollenback, Mrs. E. Carey, Vice Presidents. Mrs. J. Butler, Mrs. Nicholson, Mrs. Hollenback, Mrs. Lewis, Mrs. Ross, Mrs. Conyngham, Mrs. Beaumont, Mrs. Drake, Mrs. Bennet, Mrs. Carey, Executive Committee. Miss Emily Cist, Treasurer. Miss Gertrude Butler, Secretary. Mrs. Donley, Mrs. L. Butler, Corresponding Committee.

On two marble tablets are engraved the names of those (so far as could be ascertained) who fell, and also those who, having been in the battle, survived, but the list must necessarily be very incomplete. And another tablet contains, from the pen of Edward Mallery, Esq., the following chaste, beautiful, and apposite inscription.

APPENDIX.

"Near this spot was fought,
On the afternoon of Friday, the third day of July, 1778,

THE BATTLE OF WYOMING,

In which a small band of patriot Americans,
chiefly the undisciplined, the youthful, and the aged,
spared, by inefficiency, from the distant ranks of the republic,
led by Col. Zebulon Butler, and Col. Nathan Denison,

With a courage that deserved success,
boldly met and bravely fought,
a combined British, Tory, and Indian force
of thrice their number.

Numerical superiority alone gave success to the invader,
And wide-spread havoc, desolation and ruin
marked his savage and bloody footsteps through the valley.

THIS MONUMENT,

commemorative of these events,
and of the actors in them,
has been erected
over the bones of the slain,
By their descendants, and others, who gratefully appreciated
the services and sacrifices of their patriot ancestors."

A suitable enclosure remains to be erected, which, we trust, will early be accomplished.

INDIAN ELOQUENCE.

Published to illustrate the character of the Iroquois, who held dominion over Wyoming.

PERHAPS we cannot present the reader with a greater orator than GARANGULA; or, as he was called by the French, GRAND GUEULE, though Lahontan, who knew him, wrote it Grangula. He was by nation an Onondaga, and is brought to our notice by the manly and magnanimous speech which he made to a French general, who marched into the country of the Iroquois to subdue them.

In the year 1684, M. De la Barre, Governor-General of Canada, complained to the English at Albany, that the Senecas were infringing upon their rights of trade with some of the other more remote nations. Governor Dungan acquainted the Senecas with the charge made by the French governor. They admitted the fact, but justified their course, alleging that the French supplied their enemies with arms and ammunition, with whom they were then at war. About the same time the French governor raised an army of 1700 men, and made other "mighty preparations" for the final destruction of the Five Nations. But before he had progressed far in his great undertaking, a mortal sickness broke out in his army, which finally caused him to give over his expedition. In the mean time, the Governor of New York was ordered to lay no obstacles in the way of the French expedition. Instead of regarding this order, which was from his master, the Duke of York, he sent interpreters to the Five Nations to encourage them, with offers to assist them.

De la Barre, in hopes to effect something by this expensive undertaking, crossed Lake Ontario, and held a talk with such of the Five Nations as would meet him. To keep up the appearance of power, he made a high-toned speech to GRANGULA, in which he observed, that the nations had often infringed upon the peace; that he wished now for peace; but on the condition that they should make full satisfaction for all the injuries they had done the French, and for the future never to disturb them. That they, the Senecas, Cayugas, Onondagas, Oneidas, and Mohawks, had abused and robbed all their traders, and unless they gave satisfaction he should declare war. That they had conducted the English into their country to get away their trade heretofore, but the past he would overlook, if they would offend no more; yet, if ever the like should happen again, he had express orders from the king, his master, to declare war.

Grangula listened to these words, and many more in the like strain, with that contempt which a real knowledge of the situation of the French army, and the rectitude of his own course, were calculated to inspire; and after walking several times round the circle formed by his people and the French, addressing himself to the governor, seated in his elbow chair, he began as follows:—

"*Yonnondio*, [such was the general name for the French Governors of Canada.] I honour you, and the warriors that are with me likewise honour you. Your interpreter has finished your speech. I now begin mine. My words make haste to reach your ears. Harken to them.

"*Yonnondio.* You must have believed, when you left Quebec, that the sun had burnt up all the forests, which render our country inaccessible to the French, or that the lakes had so far overflown the banks, that they had surrounded our castles, and that it was impossible for us to get out of them; yes, surely you must have dreamt so, and the curiosity of seeing so great a wonder has brought you so far. Now you are undeceived, since that I, and the warriors here present, are come to assure you that the Senecas, Cayugas, Onondagas, Oneidas and Mohawks are yet alive. I thank you, in their name, for bringing back into their country the calumet, which your predecessor received from their hands. It was happy for you that you left under ground that murdering hatchet that had been so often dyed in the blood of the French.

"*Hear, Yonnondio.* I do not sleep; I have my eyes open; and the sun, which enlightens me, discovered to me a great captain at the head of a company of soldiers, who speaks as if he were dreaming. He says, that he only came to the lake to smoke on the great calumet with the Onondagas. But Grangula says, that he sees the contrary; that it was to knock them on the head, if sickness had not weakened the arms of the French. I see *Yonnondio* raving in a camp of sick men, whose lives the Great Spirit has saved by inflicting this sickness on them.

"*Hear, Yonnondio.* Our women had taken their clubs, our children and old men had carried their bows and arrows into the heart of your camp, if our warriors had not disarmed them, and kept them back, when your messenger *Akouossan* came to our castles. It is done, and I have said it.

"*Hear, Yonnondio.* We plundered none of the French but those that carried guns, powder and balls to the Twightwies, and Chictaghicks, because those arms might have cost us our lives. Herein we follow the example of the Jesuits, who break all the kegs of rum brought to our castle, lest the drunken Indians should knock them on the head. Our warriors have not beaver enough to pay for all those arms that they have taken, and our old men are not afraid of the war. This belt preserves my words.

"We carried the English into our lakes, to trade there with the Utawawas and Quatoghies, as the Adirondaks brought the French to our castles, to carry on a trade which the English say is theirs. WE ARE BORN FREE. WE NEITHER DEPEND ON YONNONDIO, NOR CORLEAR, [the English.] WE MAY GO WHERE WE PLEASE, AND CARRY WITH US WHOM WE PLEASE, AND BUY AND SELL WHAT WE PLEASE.* If

---

* This proud declaration of Independence accords with, and sustains the opinions expressed by us in our Indian narrative.

your allies be your slaves, use them as such; command them to receive no other but your people. This belt preserves my words.

"We knocked the Twightwies and Chictaghicks on the head, because they had cut down the trees of peace, which were the limits of our country. They have hunted beaver on our lands. They have acted contrary to the customs of all Indians, for they left none of the beavers alive; they killed both male and female. They brought the Satanas into their country, to take part with them, after they had concerted ill designs against us. We have done less than either the English or French that have usurped the lands of so many Indian nations, and chased them from their own country. This belt preserves my words.

"*Hear, Yonnondio.* What I say is the voice of all the Five Nations. Hear what they answer. Open your ears to what they speak. The Senecas, Cayugas, Onondagas, Oneidas and Mohawks say, that when they buried the hatchet at Cadarackui in the presence of your predecessor, in the middle of the fort, they planted the tree of peace in the same place; to be there carefully preserved, that, in the place of a retreat for soldiers, that fort might be a rendezvous for merchants: that, in place of arms and ammunition of war, beavers and merchandize should only enter there.

"*Hear, Yonnondio.* Take care for the future, that so great a number of soldiers as appear there, do not choke the tree of peace planted in so small a fort. It will be a great loss, if, after it had so easily taken root, you should stop its growth, and prevent its covering your country and ours with its branches. I assure you, in the name of the Five Nations, that our warriors shall dance to the calumet of peace under its leaves; and shall remain quiet on their mats, and shall never dig up the hatchet, till their brother *Yonnondio* or *Corlear* shall either jointly or separately endeavour to attack the country which the Great Spirit has given to our ancestors. This belt preserves my words, and this other, the authority which the Five Nations have given me."

Then addressing himself to the interpreter, he said: "Take courage. You have spirit; speak, explain my words, forget nothing; tell all that your brethren and friends say to *Yonnondio*, your governor, by the mouth of *Grangula*, who loves you, and desires you to accept of this present of beaver, and take part with me in my feast, to which I invite you. This present of beaver is sent to *Yonnondio*, on the part of the Five Nations."

De la Barre was struck with surprise at the wisdom of this chief, and equal chagrin at the plain refutation of his own. He immediately returned to Montreal, and thus finished this inglorious expedition of the French against the Five Nations.

Grangula was at this time a very old man, and from this valuable speech we became acquainted with him—a very Nestor of his nation—whose powers of mind would not suffer in comparison with those of a Roman or a more modern senator. He treated the French with great civility, and feasted them with the best his country would afford, on their departure.—*Drake.*

WYOMING CLAIM ON CONGRESS.

As a matter of historical interest, and because the subject may still be regarded as pending before Congress, this memorial is published, not without the hope that the National Legislature may yet be persuaded to take the case under their favourable consideration.

Memorial to Congress in behalf of Wyoming.

At a meeting held by Public Notice at the house of *Wm. H. Alexander*, in

Wilkesbarre, November 7th, 1837,—of a number of sufferers at Wyoming during the Revolutionary War, their descendants and others:

Gen. WILLIAM ROSS was called to the Chair, and ANDERSON DANA appointed Secretary.

CHESTER BUTLER, Esq., from the Committee appointed at a former meeting for that purpose, reported a memorial to Congress which was adopted; and it was ordered that the same be signed by the Chairman and Secretary, in behalf of the Meeting, and be forwarded for presentation.

To the Honourable, the Senate and House of Representatives of the United States, in Congress assembled:

By order of a public meeting, held at Wilkesbarre, Luzerne county, Pennsylvania, the subscribers present you the following memorial in behalf of the Wyoming sufferers, during the Revolutionary war, their heirs, widows, and legal representatives.

The circumstances of the invasion of the Wyoming settlement by the British and Indians; the battle and massacre; the entire expulsion of the inhabitants; the conflagration of their dwellings, and the devastation of their fields—are presumed to be familiar to all of you. In the annals of that fearful but glorious conflict, not a page recounts a livelier devotion to the cause of liberty, or depicts a bloodier field, deeper woes, or more extensive losses of property. Every historian who has written an account of the Revolutionary war, has told the story of her sufferings. All America and Europe were filled, at the time, with the melancholy details. It is not our purpose to awaken your sympathies; but so much we thought proper to say by way of introduction. We would address facts to your reason, and arguments to your understanding; looking to your deliberate judgments for a favourable response to our petition.

The Wyoming settlements were made under the authority of Connecticut. A town called Westmoreland was erected here, attached to the county of Litchfield, near three hundred miles distant, the laws of Connecticut prevailed. Civil and military officers derived their commissions from that state. Representatives were sent from here to her legislature; and the troops raised in Westmoreland were part of the Connecticut line on the Continental establishment. Several towns of Connecticut were burnt by the enemy: New London, Danbury, Westmoreland, Fairfield, Groton and others, were among the number. Connecticut has made all those towns, except one, full and ample remuneration for their losses. Westmoreland, or Wyoming, alone received nothing. Five hundred thousand acres of land, in the Western Reserve, were granted in 1792 to those towns, valued at 6s. 8d., a French crown, per acre—amounting to between five and six hundred thousand dollars. This was a beneficent act on the part of Connecticut, and will redound in all future time to her honour. Was not the grant also just as well as beneficent? Did not the recipients deserve—were they not entitled to this grant? Was not their claim founded in the principles of eternal equity and everlasting justice? Who ever heard a doubt expressed of the righteousness of their claim? If, then, it was just and equitable that New London, Danbury, Fairfield and those other towns should be indemnified, is it not clear as demonstration, that Westmoreland, or Wyoming—where a heavier sacrifice of life, far deeper personal sufferings, and more extensive losses were sustained, was also entitled to remuneration?

We anticipate here, that honourable members may say—"Your claim is doubtless just.—Standing on its own merits of *services, sufferings* and *losses*, it is a strong claim; and when it is considered relatively to those other towns of Connecticut, provided for, it appears of unquestionable validity. But when your parent state was making so ample provision for others similarly situated, why did you not then apply to her for aid? While we admit the claim just, we cannot see as yet, how the general government can be held liable to make you compensation." To this we would reply with all truth and simplicity:

The reason why no provision was made for Westmoreland is simple and easily told.—About the conclusion of the war, by the decree of Trenton, which settled the long existing controversy in respect to these lands, the jurisdiction over

APPENDIX.

Westmoreland ceased in Connecticut, and was transferred to Pennsylvania. It was not until about ten years after this event that Connecticut so far recovered her resources as to be able to make remuneration to those suffering towns which she indemnified. Being no longer a portion of the state, no provision was made for us, as there doubtless would have been, had Westmoreland continued a component part of Connecticut.

Pennsylvania, with a liberality and public spirit most honourable to her patriotism and justice, has granted ample rewards to officers and soldiers of her line, and to others, whose sufferings and merits in the cause commended them to her consideration. Not having been harmoniously a part of Pennsylvania, but maintaining an attitude of opposition, if not of hostility, during, and indeed for some time after the war, it could not be asked or expected that she would make good the losses, or grant rewards for the sufferings of the Wyoming people. So that, to use a common but expressive phrase, "between two stools we came to the ground." Moreover, the disasters of the war utterly prostrated the people of Wyoming. Most of our natural guardians and protectors were slain, and amongst them many of our chief men; widows and orphans, aged or very young men, destitute and poor, constituted our chief population. The unhappy dispute, since, so satisfactorily adjusted by our present parent and protector, noble and liberal Pennsylvania, still continued, as you doubtless know, to perplex and impoverish us. To obtain "this day our daily bread," occupied the thoughts and exertions of us all, and no application was made to Connecticut to share in the bounty she was liberally dispensing. But we ask your patience while we show, as we are sure we can, that to the general government we have a right fairly to look for aid. The services performed, the sufferings endured, and the losses sustained were all in the public service, for the general cause. They all tended to the great end of accomplishing national independence, which has brought prosperity so unbounded to our beloved country. All the debts founded on contract having been paid, Congress have recently, with just and liberal hand, been meting out to claimants, not *by contract*, but *in equity*, liberal rewards for *services performed, sufferings endured*, or *losses sustained*. In those three particulars, no claim can be stronger than that of Wyoming.

Moreover, there is a strong point which we mean to indicate, but not to argue, which statesmen, familiar with the springs of events, will judge whether it has truth for its foundation. About the close of the war, when the issue was certain, and a great empire of independent and powerful sovereignties was taking rank among the nations, it was deemed of the utmost importance that all dispute about territory and jurisdiction should be put to rest. Powerful states were to be conciliated by the favourable adjustment of their claims. Indemnifications were to be allowed to others. Little would those patriots have deserved the award we all yield their wisdom and sagacity, if they had not adopted proper measures to harmonize conflicting interests, and to consolidate the union. How far the national policy we speak of influenced the various measures and final decision which confirmed to Pennsylvania the whole extent of her chartered limits, and granted to Connecticut an indemnification in Ohio, we need not here demonstrate. Certainly that policy was, in a national point of view, wise—a benefit to Connecticut—a blessing to Pennsylvania; and if, for the common good, it excluded Westmoreland from a participation with other towns indemnified, is it not right that the common purse should afford her such remuneration as may be just?

Again—The old continental Congress passed a resolution, Oct. 10, 1780, in which it was declared, in reference to the unappropriated lands which may be ceded to the United States, "that the necessary and reasonable expenses which any particular state shall have incurred since the commencement of the present war, in subduing the British posts, or *in maintaining forts and garrisons within and for the defence of*, or in acquiring any part of the territory that may be ceded or relinquished to the United States, *shall be reimbursed.*" Although the words of the resolution do not reach us, we do respectfully suggest, that its spirit makes strongly in favour of the Wyoming claim.

During the revolutionary war, Wyoming stood an extreme frontier—an outpost on the borders of the settlements of the savage enemy. To Sunbury, the nearest inhabited place down the Susquehanna, it was sixty miles; through the Great

Swamp it was sixty miles; a pathless wilderness to Bethlehem or Easton. The warlike and bloody Mohawks, Senecas, and others of the Six Nations, occupied all the upper branches of the Susquehanna, and were within a few hours sail of our settlements, which were exposed to constant attacks. Our pathways were ambushed, and midnight gleamed with constant conflagration of our dwellings. Thus exposed we stood as a shield to all the inhabitants below us. In this situation every man might justly be regarded as on duty continually. Every man might have been considered as enlisted for and during the whole war. There was no peace, no security at Wyoming. The husbandman took his hoe in one hand and his rifle in the other, to his cornfield. Several forts were built and garrisons steadily maintained. Such was the case with Jenkins's Fort, Forty Fort, and the fort of Wilkesbarre. This was done by the people, by the militia, by common consent and common exertion.* Three hundred miles from Connecticut, it was vain to ask assistance from her, exerting every nerve as she was for the common defence and for the protection of her extensive and exposed sea board. If states which ceded lands were entitled to be reimbursed for keeping up forts, we submit whether a people situated like those of Wyoming, may not properly ask for reimbursement—since not only themselves, but a wide extent of country below, slept in comparative security through their position and exertions?

But Congress early saw and felt for the extremely exposed situation of Wyoming. On the 23d August, 1776, resolutions were entered into, of which one is in the following words: "That two companies on the continental establishment be raised in the town of Westmoreland, and *stationed in proper places for the defence of said town and parts adjacent,* till further orders of Congress." The Monday following, August 26, " Congress proceeded to the election of sundry officers, when Robert Durkee and Samuel Ransom were chosen captains of the two companies ordered to be raised in Westmoreland ; James Wells and Perrin Ross first Lieutenants; Heman Swift and Matthias Hollenback ensigns of said companies." Thus the general government—the continental Congress, took the special defence of Wyoming into their own hands. They were satisfied, it seems, that the militia, however well organized, were not sufficient for its defence. A regular force was deemed necessary, and orders were issued for raising that force "for the special defence of that town and parts adjacent." By another clause it was provided that the men thus raised should be liable to serve in any part of the United States. This provision, notwithstanding they were raised expressly "*for the defence of the inhabitants,*" &c., was perfectly proper; for if the savages on the upper waters of the Susquehanna should be driven off by a force from Albany or elsewhere, so that the source of impending danger should be removed, there was nothing more proper than that those companies, being no longer needed for the defence of the inhabitants, should be marched elsewhere at the discretion of Congress. Imperious necessity, however, almost immediately induced Congress, without the implied contingency of the proximate enemy being removed, to call their services in another quarter. On the 25th October, 1776, the battle of White Plains was fought, and Washington retreated. November 16, Fort Washington surrendered to the enemy, who immediately pushed his victorious troops in pursuit of the American army, and on the 2d December his excellency retired through Princeton to Trenton, Lord Cornwallis pushing upon his rear. "The army," says Marshall, " at no time during the retreat, exceeded four thousand men, and on reach-

---

* Extract from the Westmoreland records.

At a town-meeting legally warned and held in Westmoreland, Wilkesbarre district, August ye 24th, 1776, Col. Butler was chosen moderator for ye work of' ye day.

Voted, It is the opinion of this meeting that it now becomes necessary for ye inhabitants of this town to erect suitable fort or forts, as a defence against our common enemy.

August 28th, 1776, this meeting is opened and held by adjournment.

Voted, Ye three field officers of ye regiment of this town be appointed as a committee to view the most suitable places for building forts for ye defence of said town, and determine on some particular spot or place or places in each district for the purpose, and mark out the same.

Voted, That the above said committee do recommend it to the people in each part as shall be set off by them to belong to any fort, to proceed forthwith in building said fort, &c. *without either fee or reward from ye said town.*

ing the Delaware was reduced to less than three thousand, of whom not quite one third were militia of New Jersey." "The commander-in-chief found himself at the head of this small band of soldiers, dispirited by their losses and fatigues, retreating almost naked and barefoot in the cold of November and December, before a numerous, well appointed and victorious army."

On the 12th December, Congress passed a resolution setting forth that, "whereas the movements of the enemy have rendered this city (Philadelphia) the seat of war," &c., they resolved to adjourn to meet at Baltimore. The SAME DAY they adopted the following resolution: "Resolved, that the two companies raised in Westmoreland be ordered to join Gen. Washington WITH ALL POSSIBLE EXPEDITION."

Thus within less than four months from the first order to raise these companies, and probably within less than ninety days from their enlistment and organization, the extreme and pressing exigencies of the general cause required that they should be withdrawn from the country they were raised to defend, to aid Washington in resisting the alarming advances of the enemy.

The consequences which followed it required but little sagacity to foresee. Stimulated to revenge by the aid sent from Wyoming to Washington; incited by the consequent weakness of the settlements to attack them; and urged by policy to compel the withdrawal from the commander-in-chief of part of his men, by forcing them home to defend their own firesides—the enemy was not long in planning their attack.

The British having gained possession of Philadelphia, inevitable necessity did not allow his excellency to dispense with the services of the Westmoreland companies, but the reiterated rumours of preparations to attack Wyoming, again engaged the attention of Congress. They saw, felt, and acknowledged its exposed situation; but while the heart was assailed, and the whole force of the country was concentrated for its protection, little aid but encouraging words, could be afforded to the threatened extremities. In March, 1778, about ninety days before the invasion, Congress resolved "That one full company of foot be raised in the town of Westmoreland on the east branch of the Susquehanna for the defence of said town and the settlements on the frontiers, and in the neighbourhood thereof, against the Indians and other enemies of the state; the said companies to be enlisted for one year from the time of their enlistment, unless sooner discharged by Congress." That "*the company find their own arms, accoutrements, clothes and blankets,*" and provision was made that these should be paid for.

Thus a third company was raised in this infant and small settlement, having to clothe and arm themselves, if they could, and an exhausted treasury promised to repay the charge. This company was in the battle, and almost literally annihilated.

On the first of July, 1778, Col. John Butler, of the British army, with 400 men regulars and tories, and with 500 Indian warriors, entered the valley of Wyoming. Rumours of the meditated eruption had preceded them, and pressing solicitations had been sent to head-quarters. A number of the officers of the two companies had returned on furlough. The militia were mustered. Old men and boys took their muskets. Retirement or flight was impossible. There seemed no security but in victory. Unequal as was the conflict, and hopeless in the eye of prudence; the young athletic men fit to bear arms, and raised for their special defence, being absent with the main army; yet the inhabitants, looking to their dependent wives and little ones, took counsel of their courage, and resolved to give the enemy battle. On the third of July, about 400 men under the command of Col. Zebulon Butler, marched out to meet the British and their savage allies; being more than double their numbers. On the right wing the conflict was sharply contested for some time, and the enemy gave way. On the left, out flanked by the savages, the men fought, and fell rapidly, until an order was given to fall back and present a longer front to the enemy; a manœuvre which could not be executed under the destructive fire of the Indian rifles. Confusion ensued—a disastrous retreat followed, and a most cruel massacre consummated the bloody tragedy. We cannot dwell on the battle and the consequent horrors. It would be useless if we could. Brother fell by the side of brother; father and son perished on the same field. More than half our little army were slain; many of the rest were wounded; and the whole settlement—very aged men and helpless children, widows and orphans—were now exposed, without protection, to the tomahawk and scalping knife. In utter confusion and distress they all fled—some in boats down the river, but most on foot through the wilderness. Your imaginations must conceive, for words cannot paint, the unequaled misery of their situation. In the simplicity of truth we will state two instances, those of the chairman and secretary of this meeting.

Perrin and Jeremiah Ross, brothers of the chairman, were in the battle and both fell. Mr. Ross, then a lad, his father being dead, was the only male of the family remaining. His mother, six sisters, the widow of his brother Perrin and her five orphan children fled—such was the terror and confusion—not together, but in three separate parties: two down the river to Harrisburg, and thence to Orange County, New York—two to Nescopeck and thence to Fort Allen—the rest by a more easterly route.

The father of Mr. Dana had then recently returned from Hartford, where he had been a member of the Assembly of Connecticut from the town of Westmoreland. He was in the battle; and Mr. Whiting, a young man who had a few months before married his daughter, was also in the battle. Both were slain. Anderson Dana, our secretary, then a lad of 13, his widowed mother and widowed sister, (the latter in delicate health,) with thirteen others, of whom he was the eldest male, having one pack horse to carry the few things they could hastily gather, set out through the wilderness on foot to join their friends 300 miles distant, in Ashford, Connecticut, from whence they originally came. Death and desolation were behind them; before them hunger, and sorrow, and despair. They were twenty days on their journey, living chiefly on charity. Several women of different parties of fugitives, gave birth to children on their way, who were indeed

" Children of misery baptized in tears."

In the valley the demon of destruction completed his work. Scarcely an inhabitant remained. Every house was rifled and burnt. The sweep was universal—everything was destroyed. The cattle driven away and the harvests laid waste. War and woe never looked upon a scene of such utter sorrow and desolation!

GENTLEMEN—Is it not plain that these disasters and sufferings befel the inhabitants from their exertions in the cause of their country? Is it not manifest that *the withdrawing the two companies* raised for the defence of the people, occasioned the attack, massacre and ruin that followed? And is it not right just now when the public treasury is full, and all the other equitable revolutionary claims have been recognized by Congress, that something should be granted to the Wyoming sufferers, and their heirs! Why should all others receive bounty or justice, and we tenfold sufferers receive nothing? In honour, to the dead, as well as justice to the living, we ask it at your hands. Noble Virginia granted Col. George Rogers Clarke and his regiment, who marched with him to Kaskaskias and St. Vincent, one hundred and fifty thousand acres of land on the Ohio. Should not Wyoming receive as much. The portion of New London must have exceeded one hundred and fifty thousand. Ought not Wyoming to receive as much?

Having no other resting place the survivors were obliged to return, desolate and melancholy as were their homes. The battle field was still strewed with the unburied slain, and their remains, as soon as they could be approached that sultry season, were gathered and buried with affectionate and pious care.

The blood and tears shed at Wyoming were not shed in vain. Perhaps few incidents during the war, produced stronger sensations of horror and pity throughout Europe, than the Wyoming massacre. Perhaps few circumstances had so powerful a tendency to discredit, in public estimation, the arms and efforts of the enemy; or had a stronger influence in arousing the people of the whole civilized world in behalf of the American cause.

After the surrender of Lord Cornwallis, and the war might be regarded as ended, Congress issued a proclamation for a general thanksgiving, calling on all classes to acknowledge the goodness of Almighty God in affording aid to our arms—" in confounding the councils of our enemies, and suffering them to pursue such measures as have contributed to frustrate their own desires and expectations; above all in making their *extreme cruelty* to the inhabitants of these states, when in their power; and their *savage devastations of property*, the very means of cementing our union, and adding vigour to every effort in opposition to them."

Thus, honourable representatives of the states and people, have we stated our case; and we respectfully pray that Congress would appropriate a tract of land equal to that granted by the state of Virginia to Col. George Rogers Clarke's regiment; or in proportion to that granted by Connecticut to New London and her other towns—to be divided by commissioners to be appointed by the President of the United States—to the old Wyoming sufferers, their widows, heirs, and legal representatives.

Signed by order and in behalf of the meeting.

WM. ROSS, Chairman.

ANDERSON DANA, *Secretary*.

COL. HUBLEY'S JOURNAL.

Regarding General Sullivan's expedition to avenge Wyoming, and the remaining Wyoming military force having accompanied him, I deemed it proper to preserve a full account of it. To this end I had obtained a journal of an officer in Maxwell's Jersey Brigade, kept during the march; and another by an officer in Poor's New Hampshire Brigade, intending to insert one or the other in the Appendix. But both having been some years ago published in the newspapers, and the kindness of my friend Mr. JORDAN having placed in my possession the journal of Col. ADAM HUBLEY, of Lancaster county, which, besides coming from a superior officer, and a Pennsylvanian, it is believed will have all the freshness of novelty, I give it the preference. The reader will be struck with the harsh, I had like to have said, unsoldier-like reflection upon the public authorities in Gen. Sullivan's address to his army of August 30th. Nor will he be less surprised at the soldiers being called upon to vote whether they should be put on half allowance of flour. In a country replete to profusion with corn, beans, melons, potatoes and peaches, which the army was destroying, the idea of famine, or even want, seems preposterous. On Saturday the 28th, two days previous to that address, Col Hubley says—"The corn already destroyed by our army is not less than 5000 bushels, upon a moderate calculation, and the quantity yet on the ground, *in this neighbourhood*, is at least the same."*

Besides the journal of Col. Hubley, and those of the Jersey and New Hampshire officers, I have obtained the minutes of a Mr. Newman, who was with Gen. Clinton in his march from the Mohawk to Lake Otsego, and thence to his junction with Sullivan at Tioga point. Throwing a cloudy light on that portion of the army, and containing several curious incidents, I think too valuable to be lost, and regret that our limits do not admit of its publication here.

We have then four journals relating to Sullivan's expedition. Is not the inference fair that it was a common practice in the continental army to keep such journals? Are there not in existence very many such diaries in the hands of descendants of Revolutionary soldiers? This remark is made with the hope that they may be sought out and published, as every incident of the war for independence, which has produced Revolutions so extraordinary throughout the whole civilized world, should be regarded worthy of the most careful preservation.

* "It was estimated 160,000 bushels of corn were destroyed during the expedition."
—*Thatcher.*

F

APPENDIX.

COPY OF LT. COL. ADAM HUBLEY'S JOURNAL

ON THE

WESTERN EXPEDITION AGAINST THE INDIANS,

UNDER THE COMMAND OF

MAJOR GENERAL SULLIVAN, 1779.

BY SIMON STEVENS, LANCASTER, PA., AUG. 9, 1845.

GENERAL ORDERS.

Head Quarters, Easton, May 24, A. D. 1779.

WHEN the army shall be fully assembled the following arrangements are to take place:—

Light corps, commanded by Gen. Hand, to consist of—	Armandt's, Hubley's, Shott's, 6 companies of Rangers, Wm. Butler's battalion, Morgan's corps, and all volunteers who may join the army.
Maxwell's brigade consists of—	Dayton, Shreeve, Ogden, Spencer, forming right of first line.
Poor's brigade consists of—	Cilley, Reed, Scammel, Courtland, and form left of first line.
	Livingston, Dubois, Gainsworth, Olden, and form second line or reserve.

The right of the first line to be covered by 100 men, draughted from Maxwell's brigade, the left to be covered by 100 men detached from Poor's brigade, each flank of the second line to be covered by 50 men detached from Clinton's brigade, the flanking division on the right to consist of Hubley's regiment, and a draught from the line of 100 men, the flanking division on left to consist of the German battalion, and 100 draughted men from the line.

ORDER OF MARCH.

The light corps will advance by the right of companies in files, and keep at least one mile in front. Maxwell's brigade will advance by its right in files, sections, or platoons, as the country will admit. Poor's brigade will advance by its left in the same manner. Clinton's brigade will advance by the right of regiments, in platoons, files, or sections, as the country will admit. All the covering parties and flanking divisions on the right will advance by their left; those on the left of the army will advance by their right. The artillery and pack horses are to march in the centre.

Should the army be attacked in front while on its march, the light corps will

APPENDIX.

immediately form to repulse the enemy, the flanking divisions will endeavour to gain the flanks and rear of the enemy. While the line is forming the pack horses will, in all cases, fall into the position represented on the annexed plan. Should the enemy attack on either flank, the flanking division attacked will form a front, and sustain the attack till reinforced—in which case a part of the light corps is to be immediately detached to gain the enemy's flank and rear, the covering parties of the 2d line move to gain the other flank. Should the enemy attack our rear, the 2d line will face and form a front to the enemy, the covering parties of the first line will move to sustain it, while the flanking division face about and endeavour to gain their flank and rear. Should the light troops be driven back, they will pass through the intervals of the main army, and form in the rear. Should the enemy in an engagement with the army, when formed, endeavour either flank, the covering party will move up to lengthen the line, and so much as may be found necessary from the flanking division will display outwards to prevent the attempt from succeeding. The light corps will have their advance and flank guards at a good distance from their main body. The flanking division will furnish flank guards, and the 2d line a rear guard for the main army.

When we find that the light corps are engaged in front, the front of the pack horses halt, and the rear close up, while the columns move in a proper distance, close and display, which will bring the horses in the position they are on the plan for the order of battle. Should the attack be made on either, in flank or in rear, the horses must be kept in the position they are at the commencement of the attack, unless other orders are then given.

SKETCH NO. 1.

[The trees painted by the Indians, between Owego and Chokunüt, on the head waters of the Susquehanna, with their characters.]

Wyoming, July 30th, 1779.—Wyoming is situated on the east side of the east branch of the Susquehanna, the town consisting of about seventy houses, chiefly log buildings; besides these buildings there are sundry larger ones which were erected by the army for the purpose of receiving stores, &c., a large bake and smoke houses.

There is likewise a small fort erected in the town, with a strong abatta around it, and a small redoubt to shelter the inhabitants in cases of an alarm. This fort is garrisoned by 100 men, draughted from the western army, and put under the command of Col. Zeb'n Butler. I cannot omit taking notice of the poor inhabitants of the town; two-thirds of them are widows and orphans, who, by the vile hands of the savages, have not only deprived some of tender husbands, some of indulgent parents, and others of affectionate friends and acquaintances, besides robbed and plundered of all their furniture and clothing. In short, they are left totally dependent on the public, and are become absolute objects of charity.

The situation of this place is elegant and delightful. It composes an extensive valley, bounded both on the east and west side of the river by large chains of mountains. The valley, a mere garden, of an excellent rich soil, abounding with large timber of all kinds, and through the centre the east branch of the Susquehanna.

NO. 2. A SKETCH OF THE ENCAMPMENT AT WYOMING.

Wyoming, July 31st, 1779.—Agreeable to orders, marched the western army under the command of Major General Sullivan, in the following order, from this place to Tioga.

NO. 3. ORDER OF MARCH.

The army being composed of the following regiments and brigades in following manner, viz.:—

Gen. Hand's brigade, { Hubley, German, Shott, Spalding, } Regiments, { Ind. Corps, } Compose Light Corps.

APPENDIX.

Gen. Maxwell's brigade,
{ Dayton,
Shreeve,
Ogden,
Spencer,
From main body.

Gen. Poor's brigade,
{ Cilley,
Reed,
Scammel,
Courland.

Took up the line of march about one o'clock, P. M., viz.: light corps advanced in front of main body about a mile; vanguard, consisting of twenty-four men, under command of a subaltern, and Poor's brigade, (main body,) followed by pack horses and cattle, after which one complete regiment, taken alternately from Maxwell's and Poor's brigade, (composed the rear guard.)

Observed the country to be much broken and mountainous, wood chiefly low, and composed of pine only. I was struck on this day's march with the ruins of many houses, chiefly built of logs, and uninhabited; though poor, yet happy in their situation, until that horrid engagement, when the British tyrant let loose upon them his emissaries, the savages of the wood, who not only destroyed and laid waste those cottages, but in cool blood massacred and cut off the inhabitants, not even sparing gray locks or helpless infancy.

About 4 o'clock, P. M., arrived at a most beautiful plain, covered with abundance of grass, soil excessively rich, through which run a delightful stream of water, known by the name of Lackawanna; crossed the same, and encamped about one mile on the northern side of it, advanced about one half mile in front of main body; after night fell in with rain—continued until morning.

Distance of march this day, 10 miles.

NO. 4. SKETCH OF THE ENCAMPMENT AT LACKAWANNA.

Sunday, August 1st.—Continued at Lackawanna waiting for the fleet, which, by reason of considerable rapids, was detained until nearly 12 o'clock this day before the van could possibly cross them. In getting through, lost two boats, chief of their cargoes were saved. About 2 o'clock, P. M., the whole arrived opposite our encampment, in consequence of which received orders for a march, struck tents accordingly, and moved about 3 o'clock, P. M. About one mile from the encampment, entered the narrows on the river, first detachment and left column under command of Capt. Burk, to join the right column of light corps, and cross the mountain, which was almost inaccessible, in order to cover the army from falling in an ambuscade. Whilst passing through the defile found passage through exceeding difficult and troublesome, owing to the badness of the path; we passed by a most beautiful cataract called the Spring Falls. To attempt a description of it would be almost presumption. Let this short account thereof suffice. The first or upper fall thereof is nearly ninety feet perpendicular, pouring from a solid rock, ushering forth a most beautiful echo, and is received by a cleft of rocks considerably more projected than the former, from whence it rolls gradually and empties into the Susquehanna. Light corps passed and got through the defile about 6 o'clock, P. M.; arrived about dusk at a place called Quilutimunk, and encamped one mile in front of the place, occupied that night by the main army.

The main army, on account of the difficult passage, marched nearly all night before they reached their encamping ground. Great quantities of baggage being dropped and left lying that night obliged us to continue on this ground. All the preceding day numbers of our pack horses were sent back and employed in bringing on the scattered stores, &c.; distance of march this day about 7 miles: fine clear evening. Quilutimunk is a spot of ground situate on the river; fine, open and clear; quantity, about 1200 acres; soil very rich, timber fine, grass in abundance, and contains several exceedingly fine springs.

APPENDIX. 85

SKETCH OF THE ENCAMPMENT AT QUILUTIMUNK.

Monday, August 2d.—In consequence of the difficult and tedious march the preceding day, the army received orders to continue on the ground this day; in the meantime to provide themselves with five days provision, and getting every other matter in perfect readiness for a march next morning at 6 o'clock. Nothing material happened during our stay on this ground.

Wednesday 3d.—Agreeable to orders took up the line of march at 6 o'clock, A. M. Took the mountains after we assembled—found them exceedingly level for at least six miles. Land tolerable, the timber, viz., pine and white oak, chiefly large. About three miles from Quilutimunk we crossed near another cataract, which descended the mountain in three successive falls, the least of which is equal if not superior to the one already described. Although it is not quite so high, it is much wider, and likewise empties into the Susquehanna, seemingly white as milk. They are commonly known by the name of Buttermilk Falls.

SKETCH OF BUTTERMILK FALLS.

About 12 o'clock we descended the mountains near the river; marched about one mile on flat piece of ground, and arrived at Tunkhannunk, a beautiful stream of water so called, which empties into the Susquehanna; crossed the same, and encamped on the river about 1 o'clock. P. M. Nothing material happened this day excepting a discovery of two Indians by the party on the west side of the river. Indians finding themselves rather near the party were obliged to leave their canoe, and make through the mountains. Party took possession of the canoe, and brought it to their encamping place, for that evening immediately opposite the main army. Distance of march this day, 12 miles.

SKETCH OF TUNKHANNUNK ENCAMPMENT.

Wednesday 4th.—The army was in motion 5 o'clock, A. M., and moved up the river for three miles, chiefly on the beach, close under an almost inaccessible mountain. We then ascended the same with the greatest difficulty, and continued on it for near seven miles. A considerable distance from the river the path along the mountain was exceedingly rough, and carried through several very considerable swamps, in which were large morasses. The land in general thin and broken, abounds in wild deer and other game. We then descended the mountain, and at the foot of it crossed a small creek called Massasppi, immediately where it empties into the river. We then continued up the same until we made Vanderlip's farm, discovered several old Indian encampments; one of them appeared to have been very large.

The land, after crossing Massasppi, was exceedingly fine and rich, the soil very black and well timbered, chiefly with black walnut, which are remarkably large, some not less than six feet over, and excessively high. It is likewise well calculated for making fine and extensive meadows. The main army took post for this night on Vanderlip's farm, and the infantry advanced about one mile higher up, and encamped about 1 o'clock, P. M., on a place known by the name of Williamson's farm. Distance of march this day, 14 miles; fine clear day, very hot.

SKETCH OF THE ENCAMPMENT, VANDERLIP'S AND WILLIAMSON'S FARM.

Thursday 5th.—In consequence of orders issued last evening to march this morning at 5 o'clock, we struck tents and loaded baggage. But the boats being considerably impeded by the rapidness of the water some miles below our encampment, could not reach us, and we were obliged to halt all night. Did not join us until 9 o'clock, A. M., all which time we were obliged to halt. On their arrival the whole army was put in motion, and as more danger on this day's march was apprehended than any before, the following distribution of the army took place, viz.: The right and left columns of the light corps, conducted by Gen. Hand, moved along the top of a very high mountain; main body of light corps, under Col. Hubley's command, with an advance of twenty-four men, moved on the beach several miles on the edge of the water. The main army, followed by the baggage, &c., flanked on their right by four hundred men, who had likewise to take this mountain. Thus we moved for several miles, then arrived in a small valley called Depue's farm; the land very good. Observed and reconnoitered this ground for some distance, it being the place on which Col. Hartley was attacked by the savages last year, on his return from Tioga to Wyoming. The country being fine and open, some loss was sustained on both sides; the savages at last gave way, and Col. Hartley pursued his route to Wyoming without further molestation. Continued our march for about one mile, and formed a junction with the parties on the right flank, ascended a high mountain, and marched for some miles on the same. Land poor, timber but small, chiefly pine, after which descended the mountain nearly one mile in length, and arrived in a fine and large valley, known by the name of Wyalusing. The main army took post at this place, and the infantry advanced about one mile in front of them, and encamped about 2 o'clock, P. M. Clear but very warm day; distance of march this day, 10½ miles.

This valley was formerly called Oldman's farm, occupied by the Indians and white people; together, they had about sixty houses, a considerable Moravian meeting house, and sundry other public buildings; but since the commencement of the present war the whole has been consumed and laid waste, partly by the savages and partly by our own people. The land is extraordinarily calculated chiefly for meadows. The grass at this time is almost beyond description, high and thick, chiefly blue grass, and the soil of the land very rich. The valley contains about 1200 acres of land, bounded on one side by an almost inaccessible mountain, and on the other by the river Susquehanna.

SKETCH OF THE ENCAMPMENT AT WYALUSING.

Friday, August 6th.—The boats not arriving before late this day, the army received orders to continue on the ground. In the meantime to be provided with three days provision, get their arms and accoutrements in perfect order, and be in readiness for a march early to-morrow morning. A sub. and twenty-four men from my regiment reconnoitered vicinity of camp; returned in the evening; made no discoveries. Rain all night.

Saturday 7th.—The heavy rain last night and this morning rendered it utterly impossible to march this day; continued on the ground for further orders.

A captain and thirty men from my regiment reconnoitered vicinity of camp; made no discoveries.

This day received a letter (by express) from his Excellency Gen. Washington, dated Head Quarters, at New Windsor.

Sunday, 8th.—The army moved (in same order as on 5th) this morning at 5 o'clock; crossed Wyalusing creek, and ascended an extensive mountain, the top remarkably level; land poor, and timber small. Arrived about 10 o'clock, A. M., at the north end, and descended the same close on the river side, and continued along the beach for some distance, after which we entered an extensive valley or plain, known by the name of Standing Stone; made a halt here for about half an hour for refreshments. This place derives its name from a large stone standing erect in the river immediately opposite this plain. It is near twenty feet in height, fourteen feet in width, and three feet in depth. This valley abounds in grass, the land exceedingly fine, and produces chiefly white oak, black walnut, and pine timber. After refreshment continued our march along the same valley; land not quite so fine. Arrived about 3 o'clock, P. M., at a small creek called Wescuking; crossed the same, and encamped about one mile beyond it, and immediately on the river.

Four o'clock, P. M.—Since our arrival at this place some of my officers discovered a small Indian encampment, seemingly occupied but a few days since; found near the same a neat canoe, which they brought off. This morning the scout, (of three men,) sent up to Sheshequin some days since, returned without making any discoveries.

General Sullivan, on account of his indisposition, came on in the boat.

APPENDIX.

SKETCH OF STANDING STONE.

SKETCH OF ENCAMPMENT AT WESCUKING.

Monday, August 9th.—The boats not being able to reach Wescuking, the ground on which light corps encamped preceding evening. The main body in consequence thereof took post and encamped at Standing Stone, about three miles below light corps encampment, for protection of the boat.

The light corps, on account of their detached situation from main body the preceding evening, and apprehending some danger, being considerably advanced in the enemy's country, for their greater security, stood under arms from 3 o'clock, A. M., until daylight, where they dismissed, with orders to hold themselves in readiness at a moment's warning. Previous to their dismissal my light infantry was sent out to reconnoitre the vicinity of encampment; returned about 7 o'clock, A. M.—made no discovery.

This morning, 9 o'clock, boats hove in sight, in consequence thereof received orders to strike tents, and be in readiness for a march; main army in the meantime arrived about 10 o'clock; the whole was in motion, marched through a difficult swamp; at north of same crossed a small stream, and ascended a hill; lands poor, and wood but indifferent. About 12 o'clock, P. M., descended the same, and entered a small valley; continued about half mile, when we ascended a very remarkable high mountain, generally known by the name of Break Neck Hill.

This mountain derives its name from the great height, of the difficult and narrow passage, not more than one foot wide, and remarkable precipice which is immediately perpendicular, and not less than 180 feet deep. One mis-step must inevitably carry you from top to bottom without the least hope or chance of recovery. At north end of same entered a mountainous and beautiful valley called Sheshecununk. General Sullivan, with a number of officers, made a halt here at a most beautiful run of water, took a bite of dinner, and proceeded on along the valley, which very particularly struck my attention. Any quantity of meadow may be made here; abounds with all kinds of wood, particularly white oak, hickory, and black walnut; the ground covered with grass and pea wines; the soil in general very rich. About 4 o'clock, P. M., arrived on the bank of the river; the whole encamped in a line on a most beautiful plain; consists chiefly in meadows, the grass remarkably thick and high. On our arrival here made discoveries of some new Indian tracks, places on which fire had just been, and fresh boughs cut, and appeared as if the place had just been occupied a few hours before our arrival. Distance of march this day, 9½ miles.

SKETCH OF ENCAMPMENT AT SHESHECUNUNK.

Tuesday, August 10th.—Set in with rain, and boats not reaching this place before 9 o'clock this morning; army received orders to continue on the ground until further orders. Men drew and cooked two days provisions.

One regiment from each of the brigades attended General Sullivan. The general and field officers of the army whilst they were reconnoitering the river and ground near Tioga branch, about three miles above this place, returned without any discoveries worthy of remark about 4 o'clock, P. M.

Wednesday, August 11th.—Agreeable to orders the army moved this morning at 8 o'clock, A. M., in the usual order. Light corps moved half an hour before the main army, and took post on the banks of the river near the fording place. On the arrival of the main army and boats, Col. Forest drew up his boat at the fording place, and fixed several six pounders on the opposite shore in order to scour the woods and thickets, and prevent any ambuscade from taking place. In the meantime the light corps marched by platoons, linked together, on account of the rapidity of the water, and forded the same, and effected a landing about 9 o'clock; they immediately advanced about one hundred yards from the river, and formed in line of battle, in order to cover the landing of the main army, which was safely effected about 10 o'clock, A. M., after which came on pack horses, cattle, &c., covered by a regiment which composed the rear guard. About half past ten o'clock the whole moved in following order.

APPENDIX.

ORDER OF MARCH UP TIOGA FLATS.

Previous to our arrival on the flats we had to pass about one and a half mile through a dark, difficult swamp, which was covered with weeds and considerable underwood, interspersed with large timber, chiefly buttonwood. We then entered the flats near the place on which Queen Esther's palace stood, and was destroyed by Col. Hartley's detachment last fall. The grass is remarkably thick and high. We continued along the same for about one mile, and arrived at the entrance of Tioga branch into Susquehanna about 1 o'clock; we crossed the same, and landed on a peninsula of land which extends towards Chemung, and is bounded on the east by Susquehanna, and on the west by Tioga branch, and continued up the same for about two miles and a half and encamped. This peninsula is composed of excellent meadow and upland; grass is plenty, and timber of all kinds, and soil in general good; distance of march this day, three miles. Since our arrival a scout of eight men was ordered up to reconnoitre Chemung, and endeavour to make discoveries of the number of savages, and their situation, if possible.

Thursday, August 12th.—Tioga Plain. This being a plain calculated to cover the western army during the expedition to the northern part of it, a garrison for that purpose is to remain until our return. Sundry works for the security of the same are now erecting about two and a half miles distant from where Tioga branch empties into the Susquehanna, and where the two rivers are about 190 yards distance from each other; those works to extend from river to river.

Captain Cummings with his scout (sent out last evening) returned this day 11 o'clock, A. M.; made several discoveries at Chemung; an Indian village twelve miles distance from this place; in consequence of which a council of war sat, and determined an expedition should immediately take place for the reduction of the same. The army (two regiments excepted) received orders to be in readiness for an immediate march. Eight o'clock, P. M., the whole were in motion, and proceeded for Chemung.

SKETCH OF ENCAMPMENT AND WORKS ON TIOGA PLAINS.

August 13th, 1779.—Eight o'clock, P. M., the army having marched last evening in the following order, viz.: Light corps, under command of Gen. Hand, led the van, then followed Gens. Poor and Maxwell's brigades, which formed main body, and corps de reserve, the whole under the immediate command of Maj. Gen. Sullivan. The night being excessively dark, and the want of proper guides, impeded our march, besides which we had several considerable defiles to march through, that we could not possibly reach Chemung till after daylight. The morning being foggy favoured our enterprise. Our pilot, on our arrival, from some disagreeable emotions he felt, could not find the town. We discovered a few huts, which we surrounded, but found them vacated; after about one hour's march we came upon the main town. The following disposition for surprising the same was ordered to take place, viz.: Two regiments, one from the light corps, and one from main body, were ordered to cross the river and prevent the enemy from making their escape that way, should they still hold the town. The remainder of the light corps, viz., two independent companies, and my regiment, under command of Hand, were to make the attack on the town. Gen. Poor was immediately to move up and support the light corps. We moved in this order accordingly, but the savages having probably discovered our scouting party the preceding day, defeated our enterprise by evacuating the village previous to our coming, carrying off with them nearly all their furniture and stock, and leaving an empty village only, which fell an easy conquest about 5 o'clock, A. M. The situation of this village was beautiful; it contained fifty or sixty houses, built of logs and frames, and situate on the banks of Tioga branch, and on a most fertile, beautiful, and extensive plain, the lands chiefly calculated for meadows, and the soil rich.

The army continued for some small space in the town. Gen. Hand, in the meantime, advanced my light infantry company, under Capt. Bush, about one mile beyond the village, on a path which leads to a small Indian habitation, called Newtown. On Capt. Bush's arrival there he discovered fires burning, an Indian dog, which lay asleep, a number of deer skins, some blankets, &c.; he immediately gave information of his discoveries, in consequence of which the remainder part of the light corps, viz.: the two independent companies, and my regiment, under Gen. Hand's command, were ordered to move some miles up the path, and endeavour, if possible, to make some discoveries. We accordingly proceeded on in the following order, viz.: Captain Walker, with twenty-four men, composed the van, the eleventh regiment, under my command, after which the two independent companies, the whole covered on the left by Tioga branch, and on the right by Capt. Bush's infantry company of forty men. In this order we moved somewhat better than a mile beyond this place. The first fires were discovered, when our van was fired upon by a party of savages, who lay concealed on a high hill immediately upon our right, and which Capt. Bush had not yet made. We immediately formed a front with my regiment, pushed up the hill with a degree of intrepidity seldom to be met with, and, under a very severe fire from the savages. Capt. Bush, in the meantime, endeavoured to gain the enemy's rear. They, seeing the determined resolution of our troops, retreated; and, according to custom, previous to our dislodging them, carried off their wounded and dead, by which means they deprived us from coming to the knowledge of their wounded and dead. The ground on the opposite side of the mountain or ridge, on which the action commenced, being composed of swamp or low ground, covered with underwood, &c., favoured their retreat, and prevented our pursuing them, by which means they got off.

Our loss on this occasion, which totally (excepting two) fell on my regiment, was as follows, viz.: two captains, one adjutant, one guide, and eight privates wounded, and one serjeant, one drummer, and four privates killed. Officers' names: Captain Walker, (slight wound,) Captain Carberry, and Adj. Huston, (I fear mortal.)

After gaining the summit of the hill, and dislodging the enemy, we marched by the right of companies in eight columns, and continued along the same until the arrival of General Sullivan. We then halted for some little time, and then returned to the village, which was instantly laid in ashes, and a party detached to cross the river to destroy the corn, beans, &c., of which there were several very extensive fields, and those articles in the greatest perfection. Whilst the troops were engaged in this business, Gens. Poor and Maxwell's brigades were fired upon, lost one man, killed, and several wounded. The whole business being completed, we returned to the ruins of the village, halted some little time, and received orders to return to Tioga Plain, at which place we arrived at 8 o'clock, considerably fatigued. Lest the savages should discover our loss, after leaving the place, I had the dead bodies of my regiment carried along, fixed on horses, and brought to this place for interment. The expedition from the first to last continued twenty-four hours, of which time my regiment was employed, without the least intermission, twenty-three hours; the whole of our march not less than forty miles.

Saturday, August 14*th.*—This morning 10 o'clock, A. M., had the bodies of those brave veterans, who so nobly distinguished themselves, and bravely fell in the action of yesterday, interred with military honours, (firing excepted.) Parson Rogers delivered a small discourse on the occasion.

Was employed greater part of the day in writing to my friends at Lancaster and Philadelphia, which were forwarded the same evening.

Sunday, 15*th.*—Agreeable to orders of yesterday, seven hundred men were ordered to march on the grand parade for inspection, and to be furnished with ammunition and eight days provision, for the purpose of marching up the Susquehanna and meeting General Clinton, who is now on his march to form a junction with this army.

Two o'clock, P. M., a firing was heard on the west side of Tioga branch, immediately opposite our encampment. A number of Indians, under cover of a high mountain, advanced on a large meadow or flat of ground, on which our cattle and horses were grazing. Unfortunately, two men were there to fetch some horses, one of which was killed and scalped, the other slightly wounded, but got clear. One bullock was likewise killed, and several public horses taken off. My regiment was ordered in pursuit of them: we accordingly crossed the branch and

APPENDIX.

ascended the mountain, marched along the summit of the same for upwards of two miles in order to gain their rear; but the enemy having too much start, got clear. After scouring the mountains and valleys near the same, we returned, much fatigued, about 5 o'clock, P. M.

Monday, 16th.—The detachment under General Poor's command, agreeable to orders, moved this day, 1 o'clock, P. M., up the Susquehanna for the purpose of forming a junction with Gen. Clinton.

Several of our out continentals alarmed the camp by firing off several guns about 1 o'clock in the morning, in consequence of which light corps stood under arms. Several patrols were sent out to reconnoitre the front of encampment, returned near day-break, but made no discoveries—alarm proved premature. Gen. Hand, being ordered with the detachment under Gen. Poor, the command of light corps devolved on me during his absence.

Thursday, 17th.—Seven o'clock, P. M., a firing was heard about five hundred yards immediately in front of light corps' encampment. A party of fifty men was immediately detached to endeavour to find out the cause of it; returned at 8 o'clock, P. M.; reported that a party of Indians, eleven in number, had waylaid a few pack horsemen, who were just returning with their horses from pasture; that they had killed and scalped one man, and wounded another; the wounded man got safe to camp, and the corpse of the other was likewise brought in.

An alarm was fired by a continental about 11 o'clock, P. M., but proved false.

Wednesday, 18th.—In order to entrap some of those savages who keep sneaking about the encampment, the following parties ordered out for that purpose, and to be relieved daily by an equal number until we leave this ground, viz.: one subaltern and twenty men on the mountain opposite the encampment; one subaltern and twenty men on the island, about a mile and half above the encampment, on Tioga branch, and one subaltern and twenty men in the woods, about a mile and a half immediately in front of light corps' encampment, with orders to waylay and take every other means to take them.

This day, by particular request of several gentlemen, a discourse was delivered in the Masonic form, by Dr. Rogers, on the death of Captain Davis of the 11th Penn., and Lieutenant Jones of the Delaware regiments, who were, on the 23d of April last, most cruelly and inhumanly massacred and scalped by the savages, emissaries employed by the British king, as they were marching with a detachment for the relief of the garrison at Wyoming.

Those gentlemen were both members of that honourable and ancient Society of Freemen. A number of brethren attended on this occasion in proper form, and the whole was conducted with propriety and harmony. Text preached on this solemn occasion was the first clause in the 7th verse of the 7th chapter of Job, "Remember my life is but wind."

Thursday, 19th.—Nothing remarkable this day.

Friday, 20th.—This day arrived Lieut. Boyd, of Col. Butler's regiment, with accounts of Gen. Clinton's movements on the Susquehanna, and that a junction was formed by him with Gen. Poor's detachment, *Chokoanut*, about thirty-five miles from this place. Rain very heavy chief part of the day.

Saturday, 21st.—The detachments under Gens. Clinton and Poor, on account of the very heavy rain yesterday, did not reach this encampment as was expected.

Sunday, 22d.—This day, 10 o'clock, A. M., Gens. Clinton and Poor's detachments, with about two hundred and twenty boats, passed light corps' encampment for the main army, about one and a half miles in their rear. On their passing, they were saluted with thirteen rounds from the park; the light corps being likewise drawn up, and received them in proper form, with Col. Proctor's music, and drums and fifes beating and playing.

Monday, 23d.—This day a most shocking affair happened, by an accident of a gun, which went off, the ball of which entered a tent in which was Capt. Kimball,

APPENDIX.

of Gen. Poor's brigade, and a lieutenant; the captain was unfortunately killed, and the lieutenant wounded.

Gen. Clinton having formed a junction with the army at this place yesterday, the following alterations in the several brigades were ordered to take place, viz.: Col. Courtland's regiment to be annexed to General Clinton's, Colonel Older to General Poor's, and Colonel Butler's regiment, with Major Parr's corps, to General Hand's brigade.

Tuesday, 24th.—This day employed hands to make bags for the purpose of carrying flour; hands employed all day and night in this business.

Agreeable to orders a signal gun was fired for the whole army to strike tents, 5 o'clock, P. M., and marched some small distance in order to form the line of march. Seven o'clock, P. M., another signal gun was fired for the army to encamp in proper order, and to be in readiness for an immediate march. Col. Butler's regiment, with Major Parr's riflemen, joined light corps, and encamped with them this day, 7 o'clock, P. M.

Colonel Shrieve took command of Fort Sullivan this day agreeable to orders. Flying hospital and stores were moved this day to the garrison.

Wednesday, 25th.—This morning was entirely devoted to packing up and getting every thing in readiness for an immediate march. A heavy rain fell in at 11 o'clock, continued greater part of the day, which prevented our movements.

Thursday, 26th.—The army not being perfectly ready to march at 8 o'clock, A. M., agreeable to yesterday's orders, the signal gun for a march was not fired until 11 o'clock, when the whole took up the line of march in the following order, namely: Light corps, commanded by General Hand, marched in six columns, the right commanded by Colonel Butler, and the left by myself. Major Parr, with the riflemen, dispersed considerably in front of the whole, with orders to reconnoitre all mountains, defiles, and other suspicious places, previous to the arrival of the army, to prevent any surprise or ambuscade from taking place. The pioneers, under command of a captain, subaltern, then followed after, which preceded the park of artillery; then came on the main army, in two columns, in the centre of which moved the pack horses and cattle, the whole flanked on right and left by the flanking divisions, commanded by Colonel Dubois and Colonel Ogden, and rear brought up by General Clinton's brigade; in this position the whole moved to the upper end of Tioga flats, about three miles above Fort Sullivan, where we encamped for this night.

This day disposed of one my horses to Mr. Bond, captain, on account of his indisposition, obtained leave to continue either at Fort Sullivan, or go to Wyoming, until the return of the regiment from the expedition.

Friday, August 27th.—On account of some delays this morning army did not move until half past eight o'clock, A. M. Previous to the march the pioneers, under cover of the rifle corps, were advanced to the first and second defile, or narrows, some miles in front of our encampment, where they were employed in mending and cutting a road for the pack to pass. The army marched in same order of yesterday, the country through which they had to pass being exceedingly mountainous and rough, and the slow movements of the pack considerably impeded the march. About 7 o'clock, P. M., we arrived near the last narrows, at the lower end of Chemung, where we encamped in the following order: Light corps near the entrance of the defile or narrows, and in front of some very extensive corn-fields, some refugee Tories, now acting with the favour of the main army, about one mile in our rear, and immediately fronting the corn-fields. After encamping had an agreeable repast of corn, potatoes, beans, cucumbers, watermelons, squashes, and other vegetables, which were in great plenty, (produced) from the corn-fields already mentioned, and in the greatest perfection: distance of march this day, six miles.

Saturday, August 28th.—Fore part of this day being employed by the general and principal officers of the army in reconnoitering the river and finding out some fording place for the artillery, pack horses, and cattle to cross, to gain Chemung, the defile or narrows mentioned in my yesterday's journal being so excessively narrow, and, indeed, almost impracticable for them to pass.

The following disposition for the marching of the army took place accordingly, namely: The rifle corps, with General Maxwell's brigade, and left flanking division of the army, covering the park, pack horses, and cattle, crossed to the west side of the river, and about one and a half mile above recrossed the same, and formed a junction on the lower end of Chemung flats with the light corps, Generals Poor and Clinton's brigades, and right flanking division of the army, who took their route across an almost inaccessible mountain, on the east side of the river, the bottom of which forms the narrows already mentioned. The summit was gained with the greatest difficulty; on the top of the mountain the lands, which are level and extensive, are exceedingly rich with large timber, chiefly oak, interspersed with underwood and excellent grass. The prospect from this mountain is most beautiful; we had a view of the country of at least twenty miles round; the fine, extensive plains, interspersed with streams of water, made the prospect pleasing and elegant from this mountain. We observed, at some considerable distance, a number of clouds of smoke arising, where we concluded the enemy to be encamped.

Previous to the movement of the army this day, a small party of men were sent across the river in order to destroy some few Indian huts, which were immediately opposite our encampment. Before the business was quite effected they were fired upon by a party of Indians, who, after giving the fire, immediately retreated; the party executed their orders, and all returned unhurt to the army.

The scout sent out last evening to reconnoitre the enemy near Newtown, (an Indian village so called,) returned this day, and reported they discovered a great number of fires, and that they supposed, from the extensive piece of ground covered by the fires, the enemy must be very formidable, and mean to give us battle. They likewise discovered four or five small scouting parties on their way towards this place, it is supposed to reconnoitre our army. Since our arrival here a great quantity of furniture was found by our soldiers which was concealed in the adjacent woods. After forming the junction above mentioned, we took up the line of march, and moved to the upper Chemung town, and encamped about 6 o'clock, P. M., for this night. Distance of march on a straight course, about two miles.

From the great quantities of corn and other vegetables here and in the neighbourhood, it is supposed they intended to establish their principal magazine at this place, which seems to be their chief rendezvous, whenever they intend to go to war; it is the key to the Pennsylvania and New York frontier. The corn already destroyed by our army is not less than 5,000 bushels upon a moderate calculation, and the quantity yet in the ground in this neighbourhood is at least the same, besides which there are vast quantities of beans, potatoes, squashes, pumpkins, &c., which shared the fate of the corn.

Sunday, August 29th.—This morning at 9 o'clock the army moved in the same order of the 26th; the riflemen were well scattered in front of the light corps, who moved with the greatest precision and caution. On our arrival near the ridge on which the action of the 13th commenced with light corps, our van discovered several Indians in front, one of whom gave them a fire, and then fled. We continued our march for about one mile; the rifle corps entered a low marshy ground which seemed well calculated for forming ambuscades; they advanced with great precaution, when several more Indians were discovered, who fired and retreated. Major Parr, from those circumstances, judged it rather dangerous to proceed any further without taking every caution to reconnoitre almost every foot of ground, and ordered one of his men to mount a tree and see if he could make any discoveries; after being some time on the tree he discovered the movements of several Indians, (which were rendered conspicuous by the quantity of paint they had on them,) as they were laying behind an extensive breastwork, which extended at least half a mile, and most artfully covered with green boughs, and trees, having their right flank secured by the river, and their left by a mountain. It was situated on a rising ground—about one hundred yards in front of a difficult stream of water, bounded by the marshy ground already mentioned on our side, and on the other, between it and the breast-works, by an open and clear field. Major Parr immediately gave intelligence to General Hand of his discoveries, who immediately advanced the light corps within about three hundred yards of the enemy's works, and formed in line of battle; the rifle corps, under cover, advanced, and lay under the bank of the creek within one hundred yards of the lines. Gen. Sullivan, having previous notice, arrived with the main army, and ordered the following disposition to take place: The rifle and light corps to continue their position; the left flanking division, under command of Colonel Ogden, to take post on the left flank of the light corps, and General Maxwell's brigade, some distance in the rear, as a corps de reserve, and Colonel Proctor's artillery in front of the centre of the light corps, and immediately opposite the breast-work. A heavy fire ensued between the rifle corps and the enemy, but little damage was done on either side. In the meantime, Generals Poor and Clinton's brigades, with the right flanking division, were ordered to march and gain, if possible, the enemy's flank and rear, whilst the rifle and light corps amused them in front. Col. Proctor had orders to be in readiness with his artillery and attack the lines, first allowing a sufficient space of time to Generals Poor, &c., to gain their intended stations. About 3 o'clock, P. M., the artillery began their attack on the enemy's works; the rifle and light corps in the meantime prepared to advance and charge; but the enemy, finding their situation rather precarious, and our troops determined, left and retreated from their works with the greatest precipitation, leaving behind them a number of blankets, gun covers, and kettles, with corn boiling over the fire. Generals Poor, &c., on account of several difficulties which they had to surmount, could not effect their designs, and the enemy probably having intelligence of their approach, posted a number of troops on the top of a mountain, over which they had to advance. On their arrival near the summit of the same, the enemy gave them a fire, and wounded several officers and soldiers. General Poor pushed on and gave them a fire as they retreated, and killed five of the savages. In the course of the day we took nine scalps, (all savages,) and two prisoners, who were separately examined, and gave the following corresponding account: that the enemy were seven hundred men strong, viz., five hundred savages, and two hundred Tories, with about twenty British troops, commanded by a Seneca chief, the two Butlers, Brandt, and M'Donald.

The infantry pushed on towards Newtown; the main army halted and encamped near the place of action, near which were several extensive fields of corn and other vegetables. About 6 o'clock, P. M., the infantry returned and encamped near the main army.

The prisoners further informed us that the whole of their party had subsisted on corn only for this fortnight past, and that they had no other provisions with them; and that their next place of rendezvous would be at Catharines town, an Indian village about twenty-five miles from this place.

Distance of march (exclusive of counter-marches) this day, about eight miles.

Monday, August 30th.—On account of the great quantities of corn, beans, potatoes, turnips, and other vegetables, in destroying of which the troops were employed, and the rain which set in the after part of the day, obliged us to continue on the ground for this day and night. The troops were likewise employed in drawing eight days provisions, (commencing 1st day of September.) The reason of drawing this great quantity at one time was, (however inconsistent with that economy which is absolutely necessary in our present situation, considering the extensive campaign before us, and the time of consequence it will require to complete it,) the want of pack horses for transporting the same, and in order to expedite this great point in view, are obliged to substitute our soldiery for carrying the same.

From the great and unparalleled neglect of those persons employed for the purpose of supplying the western army with everything necessary to enable them to carry through the important expedition required of them, General Sullivan was at this early period under the disagreeable necessity of issuing the following address to the army, which was communicated by the commanding officers to their corps separately, viz.:

APPENDIX.

GENERAL SULLIVAN'S ADDRESS.

"The commander-in-chief informs the troops that he used every effort to procure proper supplies for the army, and to obtain a sufficient number of horses to transport them, but owing to the inattention of those whose business it was to make the necessary provision, he failed of obtaining such an ample supply as he wished, and greatly fears that the supplies on hand will not, without the greatest prudence, enable him to complete the business of the expedition.

"He therefore requests the several brigadiers and officers commanding corps to take the mind of the troops under their respective commands, whether they will, whilst in this country, which abounds with corn and vegetables of every kind, be content to draw one half of flour, one half of meat and salt a day. And he desires the troops to give their opinions with freedom and as soon as possible.

"Should they generally fall in with the proposal, he promises they shall be paid that part of the rations which is held back at the full value in money.

"He flatters himself that the troops who have discovered so much bravery and firmness will readily consent to fall in with a measure so essentially necessary to accomplish the important purpose of the expedition, to enable them to add to the laurels they have already gained.

"The enemy have subsisted for a number of days on corn only, without either salt, meat, or flour, and the general cannot persuade himself that troops, who so far surpass them in bravery and true valour, will suffer themselves to be outdone in that fortitude and perseverance, which not only distinguishes but dignifies the soldier. He does not mean to continue this through the campaign, but only wishes it to be adopted in those places where vegetables may supply the place of a part of the common ration of meat and flour, which will be much better than without any.

"The troops will please to consider the matter, and give their opinion as soon as possible."

Agreeable to the above address, the army was drawn up, (this evening,) in corps separately, and the same, through their commanding officers, made known to them, and their opinions requested thereupon, when the whole, without a dissenting voice, cheerfully agreed to the request of the general, which they signified by unanimously holding up their hands and giving three cheers.

This remarkable instance of fortitude and virtue cannot but endear those brave troops to all ranks of people, more particularly as it was so generally and cheerfully entered into without a single dissenting voice.

Tuesday, August 31st.—Took up our line of march in usual order at 9 o'clock, A. M.; marched about four miles and a half through a broken and mountainous country, and an almost continuous defile on the east side of Cayuga branch, the west of the same for that distance was an excellent plain, on which large quantities of corn, beans, potatoes, and other vegetables stood, and were destroyed by us the preceding day. We then crossed Cayuga branch, where it forks with a stream of water running east and west, and landed on a most beautiful piece of country remarkably level. On the banks of the same stood a small Indian village, which was immediately destroyed. The soldiers found great quantities of furniture, &c., which was buried, some of which they carried off, and some was destroyed. About 2 o'clock, P. M., we proceeded along the path which leads to Catharines town, (an Indian village,) and leaves the Cayuga branch on its left. About 5 o'clock, P. M., we encamped on a most beautiful plain, interspersed with marshes, well calculated for meadows. Wood chiefly pine, interspersed with hazel brushes, and great quantities of grass; distance of march this day, 10 miles.

Wednesday, September 1st.—About 9 o'clock, P. M., whole army moved in good order, on a level piece of ground. About 11 o'clock, A. M., we entered an extensive hemlock swamp, not less than six miles through; the path through almost impassible, owing to the number of defiles, long ranges of mountains, ravine after ravine, interspersed with thick underwood, &c. The infantry, with the greatest difficulty, got through about half past nine o'clock, P. M. The remainder of the army, with the pack horses, cattle, &c., were chiefly the whole night employed in getting through.

As the infantry were approaching Catharines town we were alarmed by the howling of dogs and other great noise. A few of the riflemen were dispatched in order to reconnoitre the place. In the meantime we formed in two solid columns, at fixed bayonets, with positive orders not a man to fire his gun, but to rush on in case the enemy should make a stand; but the riflemen, who had been sent to reconnoitre the town, returned with the intelligence the enemy had left it. We then immediately altered our position on account of the narrowness of the road, and marched in files through the first part of the town, after which we crossed the creek: in a field immediately opposite, where there stood a number of houses also, where we encamped, and substituted the timber of the houses in room of fire-wood. On our arrival, we found a number of fires burning, which appeared as if they had gone off precipitately. This day's march completed 12 miles.

Thursday, Sept. 2d.—The dismal situation of our pack horses and cattle, of which several were killed by falling into ditches, and several otherwise disabled in getting through this horrid swamp last evening, prevented our march this morning. The fore part of this day was entirely employed in collecting them, which, from their scattered and dispersed situation, was attended with the greatest difficulty.

We this morning found an old squaw who, we suppose, by reason of her advanced age, could not be carried off, and therefore was left to our mercy. On examining her, she informed us that the Indians, on our approach last evening, went off very precipitately; that the women and children had gone off in the morning to take shelter in some mountains, until the army had passed them; that Colonel Butler promised he would send back some warriors, who should conduct them by bye-ways to some place of safety. She further adds, that, previous to the squaws going off, there was great contention with them and the warriors about their going off; the former had determined on staying and submitting to our generosity; the latter opposed it, and informed them that, by such a step, the Americans would be able to bring them to any terms they pleased; whereas, did they go off, they would have it in their power to come to more favourable terms, should a treaty of any kind be offered.

Catharines town is pleasantly situated on a creek, about three miles from Seneca lake; it contained nearly fifty houses, in general, very good—the country near it very excellent. We found several very fine corn-fields, which afforded the greatest plenty of corn, beans, &c., of which, after our fatiguing march, we had an agreeable repast. After getting everything in perfect readiness, we took up our line of march at 7 o'clock this morning. The roads from this place for about one mile were rather difficult and swampy. We then ascended a rising country, which was, in general, level, excepting a few defiles which we had to pass, but were by no reason dangerous or difficult. The lands are rich, abounding with fine, large, and clear timber, chiefly white oak, hickory, walnut, and ash; bounded on the left for about three miles with excellent marsh or meadow ground, after which proceeds the beautiful Seneca lake, which abounds with all kinds of fish, particularly salmon, trout, rock, that which resembles perch, as also sheep-head.

Previous to our leaving this place, the squaw which was taken here, was left, and a hut erected, of which she took possession. A quantity of wood was also gathered and carried to the hut for her use; she was also provided with a quantity of provisions. All these favours had such an effect on her that it drew tears from her savage eyes.

It is about three miles in breadth, and about forty miles in length. Upon the right, though considerably up the country, is another delightful lake, called Kayuga lake; abounds with all kinds of fish also, and is about forty-six miles in length.

We proceeded along this beautiful country about twelve miles, and encamped near a corn-field, on which stood several Indian cabins; bearing between the light corps and main army an advantageous ravine, and bounded on our left by Seneca lake.

Previous to our arrival here the Indians who occupied the cabins already mentioned, probably discovered our approach, pushed off precipitately, leaving their kettles with corn boiling over the fire. During our march this day we discovered several trees with the following characters newly cut on them by those savages commanded by Brandt and the Butlers, and with whom we had the action on the 29th ultimo.

Saturday, Sept. 4th.—On account of the rain this morning the army did not move until 10 o'clock, A. M. We passed through a delightful level country, the soil of which very rich, the timber fine and large, interspersed with hazel bushes, fine grass, and pea vines. On our march we discovered several fires burning, which fully intimated some of the savages were not far off in front of us. We destroyed several fields of corn, and, after a march of thirteen miles, we encamped in the woods, in the front of a very large ravine, and about half a mile from Seneca lake. On account of some difficulties with the pack-horses, &c., the main army did not reach so far as the infantry, and encamped about two miles in their rear.

Sunday, Sept. 5th.—About 9 o'clock this morning the army moved through a country much the same as yesterday. About 12 o'clock we arrived at Canadia, about three miles from the last encampment, where we encamped for this night. Previous to our arrival we entered several corn-fields, and furnished the men with two days allowance of the same. The riflemen, who were advanced, retook a prisoner who was taken last year by the savages on the east branch of the Susquehanna. An Indian, who lay concealed, fired, but without effect on our riflemen, and immediately fled.

On examining this prisoner, he informed us that Brandt, with near a thousand savages, including Butler's Rangers, left this town last Friday, seemingly much frightened and fatigued—that they were pushing for Kanadauaga, an Indian village, where they mean to make a stand and give us battle. He further informs us that exclusive of a considerable number of savages killed and wounded in the action of the 29th, seven Tories were killed; that all their wounded, with some dead, were carried in Canoes up the *Cayuga branch*—that they allow they sustained a very heavy loss in that action.

Canadia is much the finest village we have yet come to. It is situated on a rising ground, in the midst of an extensive apple and peach orchard, within half a mile of Seneca lake; it contains about forty well-finished houses, and every thing about it seems neat and well improved.

Monday, Sept. 6th.—The fore part of the day was entirely employed in hunting up our horses and cattle, a number of which were lost. About 2 o'clock we took up our line of march, and moved about three miles, when we encamped on a beautiful piece of woodland, (interspersed with vast quantities of pea vines, which served for food for our horses,) our rear covered by the lake, our flank by considerable ravines.

On the fourth, whilst on our march, several officers' waiters, who had delayed in the rear, lost the path along which the army moved, and, towards night, found themselves near an Indian village, which had been previously evacuated. They found a quantity of plunder, which they brought off, first putting the town in flames. A captain and a party, on missing, being sent in pursuit, and fell in with them as they were returning to the encamping place occupied by the army the preceding day, and conducted them safe to the army at Canadia.

An express from Tioga, with packets, &c., for the army, arrived this day at head quarters—received several letters from my friends.

Tuesday, Sept. 7th.—At half-past seven o'clock the army moved and arrived at the head of the lake about 2 o'clock, P. M. The country we passed through was exceedingly fine, and chiefly along the water for eight miles and a half.

About 3 o'clock, P. M., the rifle and infantry corps crossed at the mouth of the lake, about knee deep, and not above thirty yards wide. On our arrival on the opposite shore, we immediately entered a dangerous and narrow defile, bounded on the left by the head of Seneca lake, and on our right by a large morass and flooded at intervals, well calculated to form an ambuscade. From every circumstance, both as to intelligence and the great advantage the enemy might have had from its situation, we fairly expected an attack. However, we moved through in files, supported by the two flanking divisions, and gained the other side. The main army then crossed, and took our place. We then moved through a second defile, as difficult as the first, and formed again until the main army possessed themselves of the same ground we had just left. We then marched and passed a third defile, and formed in a corn-field, near a large house, which was beautifully situated on the head of the lake, and generally occupied by Butler, one of the savage leaders.

The light corps, flanked by two flanking divisions, received orders to move and gain the rear of the town. The main army took the path, and marched immediately in front of the same; but the enemy no doubt having previous notice of our movements, had abandoned the town, which we entered about dusk, leaving behind them a number of bear and deer skins, and also a fine white child of about three years old.

This town is called *Kanadasaga*, and appears to be one of their capital settlements; about it is a fine apple orchard and a council-house. There was in the neighbourhood a great quantity of corn, beans, &c., which, after taking great quantities for the use of the army, we totally destroyed; burned the houses, which were in number about fifty, and girdled the apple trees. Distance of march this day, about 12 miles.

Wednesday, Sept. 8th.—This day we lay on our ground; the rifle corps, with several other parties, were detached down the lake to destroy a small village, called *Gaghsiungua*, and a quantity of corn, &c., in this neighbourhood, and the army prepared for a march early to-morrow morning.

Various opinions prevailed between many officers about our proceeding any further on account of our provisions; but General Sullivan, with a number of officers, nobly resolved to encounter every difficulty to execute the important expedition, and determined, notwithstanding the horrid neglect in not furnishing us with provision, horses, &c., sufficient to enable us to carry through the expedition, even to proceed on with the scanty pittance, and accomplish the arduous task of destroying the whole Seneca country.

Thursday, Sept. 9th.—On account of a number of pack horses which had gone astray and could not be found, the army did not march at 6 o'clock agreeable to yesterday's orders. A command of fifty men, under a captain, returned from this place to Tioga to escort the sick and those who were not able to proceed without retarding the march of the army, which is now under the necessity on account of our wants to be as expeditious as possible to complete the expedition; all those pack horses which were lame, or otherwise reduced, likewise returned.

About twelve o'clock the army marched; their first route was over bushy land, interspersed with remarkably wild high grass, and appeared to have been formerly cleared. We then descended into an extensive maple swamp, which was very rich, and well calculated for meadow. After marching seven miles, we came to a creek, known by the name of Flint Creek, which the whole, excepting Clinton's brigade, crossed, and encamped on a plain which had been occupied by the enemy but a few days before for the same purpose. Distance of march, seven miles.

The rifle corps who yesterday went to destroy Gaghsiungua this evening returned. They report it was a fine town, well improved, with a great quantity of corn near the same; likewise, an abundance of beans, water-melons, peaches, and all kinds of vegetables, the whole of which they totally destroyed.

Friday, Sept. 10th.—At 8 o'clock this morning the army took up their line of march in the usual order. Their route, about four miles, continued through the swamp, which, in some places, was miry, and difficult for pack horses, otherwise the foot would not have been much retarded. We then arrived on very fine ground for marching, which, to all appearance, was old cleared fields, as they contained a great quantity of wild grass as high as the horses in many places. The land continued in this manner (alternately having a strip of wood between) for about four miles, when we arrived at a lake, (the name I could not learn,)

G

which appeared to be a mile wide, and six or seven miles in length. We marched half a mile along this lake, and came to the mouth, which we crossed; the water was not knee deep, and about thirty yards over: but it narrowed so fast that, about twenty yards from the mouth, it was not in width more than five, but much deeper. We then moved up a fine country from the lake, and in half a mile came to Kanadalaugua, a beautifully situated town, containing between twenty and thirty houses, well finished, chiefly of hewn plank, which we immediately burned, and proceeded about half a mile on our right, where we found a large field of corn, squashes, beans, &c. At this place we encamped, but were very badly off for water, having none but what we sent half a mile for, and that very bad. The Seneca country, from its extreme flatness, having no good springs, which is extremely disagreeable for a marching army. Distance of march this day, 9 miles.

In this town a dog was hung up, with a string of wampum round his neck, on a tree, curiously decorated and trimmed. On inquiry, I was informed that it was a custom among the savages before they went to war to offer this as a sacrifice to Mars, the God of War, and praying that he might strengthen them. In return for those favours, they promise to present him with the skin for a tobacco pouch.

Saturday, Sept. 11th.—Agreeable to orders we took up our line of march this morning precisely at 6 o'clock. We moved through a thicket and swamp near one mile before we gained the main path. The infantry, on account of this difficult swamp, could not possibly march in the usual order, without being considerably dispersed. We moved along this path for about three miles, after which we ascended a rising ground; the country remarkably fine and rich, covered chiefly with pine, oak, and hickory timber. At intervals we crossed considerable clear fields, with remarkably high, wild grass. About 1 o'clock we descended into a most beautiful valley, within one mile of an Indian village, known by the name of Anyayea, situate on a fine plain, within about half a mile of Anyayea lake, which is but small and very beautiful, and abounds with all kinds of fish. This town contains about twelve houses, chiefly hewn logs. About it are several large corn-fields, and a number of apple and other fruit trees. We encamped about two o'clock for this day, after completing a march of thirteen miles.

Sunday, Sept. 12th.—In order to expedite our march, and prevent the enemy from making off with their effects from Jenese, their capital, and last town in the Seneca country, it was determined a garrison of fifty men, with those soldiers who were not very able to march, should continue at this post, in order to guard our stores, viz., ammunition and flour, until our return.

The rain having set in very heavy this morning, we could not move until about twelve o'clock. We then began our march, but, on account of a defile which we had to cross, could not march in the usual order. After passing the same, we took up our line of march as usual, and ascended a rising piece of ground. After marching about five miles, we came to a lake, which we crossed at the mouth, being about knee deep, and about ten yards over. We then ascended another rising piece of ground, composed of exceedingly fine, rich land, with large oak and hickory timber, and, at intervals, with marsh or swamp, well calculated for meadow ground. After arriving within half a mile of Kanaghsas, a small Indian village, which was previously destined for this day's march, night set in, and the main army being at least a mile in our rear, we received orders to encamp for this night, which was in the woods, and exceedingly ill calculated for that purpose, no water being nearer than half a mile. This day's march completed twelve miles.

After we encamped, Lieutenant Boyd, of the rifle corps, some volunteers, and as many riflemen, made up six and twenty in the whole, were sent up to reconnoitre the town of Jenesse, having for their guide an Onieada Indian, named Hanyost, a chief of that tribe, who has been remarkable for his attachment to this country, having served as a volunteer since the commencement of the war.

Monday, Sept. 13th.—This morning before daylight we left; the general beat, on which the tents were immediately struck, and in half an hour the army marched into the town of Kanaghsas, which contained ten houses, situate on a flat near the head of a small lake. The flat contained a great quantity of corn, and vegetables of all kinds, which were remarkably well tended. At this place we halted to draw provisions, viz., beef, (half allowance,) and to destroy the town, corn, &c.

Four men of Lieutenant Boyd's party this morning returned, bringing information of the town of Gaghsuquilahery (which they took for Jenese) being abandoned. About 12 o'clock we were alarmed by some Indians firing and giving chase to Mr. Lodge and a few men who went forward to survey. They wounded a corporal, who died next day, and chased them until one of our camp sentinels fired on them and stopped their career.

Lieutenant Boyd having retired from the town of Gaghsuquilahery to wait for the arrival of the main army, which was detained longer than he expected, he sent back two men to know the cause; these two men had not gone far before they discovered a few Indians ahead. They then retired and informed Lieutenant Boyd, who immediately, with his party, gave chase, and followed them within about two miles and a half from the main army, where a body of savages, of at least four or five hundred, lay concealed, and probably intended giving the main army (the ground being favourable on their side) a fire, and push off according to custom, who immediately surrounded him and his party. He nobly fought them for some considerable time; but, by their great superiority, he was obliged to attempt a retreat, at the same time loading and firing as his party ran.

The Indians killed, and, in the most inhuman manner, tomahawked and scalped six that were found. Nine of the party have got safe in; but Lieutenant Boyd and Henjost, (the Indian already mentioned,) with seven others, are yet missing, one of whom we know is a prisoner, as one Murphy, a rifleman of the party, who made his escape, saw him in their possession. This Murphy is a noted marksman, and a great soldier, he having killed and scalped that morning, in the town they were at, an Indian, which makes the three and thirtieth man of the enemy he has killed, as is well known to his officers, this war.

There being a swamp or morass totally impassable for our horses, in front of Kanaghsas, the infantry and rifle corps passed over, and ascended the hill, wherein Indians lay, in hopes to come up with them; but they had fled, leaving behind them upwards of one hundred blankets, a great number of hats, and many other things, which we took, and then halted until the main army arrived, they having first been obliged, in order to enable them to move, to throw a hedge over the morass.

The whole then took up their line of march, and proceeded to the town of Gaghsuquilahery, through the finest country I almost ever saw, without exception. Before dusk we arrived within sight of the town. The Indians, having thrown themselves in a wood on the opposite side, the following disposition for an attack was immediately ordered to take place, viz.: The infantry, with the artillery, to push on in front; General Maxwell's brigade, with the left flanking division, to endeavour to gain the enemy's right; General Poor's brigade to move and gain their left; the right flanking division, and two regiments from General Clinton's brigade to move round Poor's right flank; the infantry to rush on in front, supported by the remainder of Clinton's brigade. We then moved forward, and took possession of the town without opposition, the enemy flying before us across a branch of Genese river, through a thicket, where it was impossible for us to follow, we not being acquainted with the country, and night having set in. We received orders to encamp, after making a march of eight and a half miles.

Thursday, Sept. 14*th.*—Previous to our march this morning parties were ordered out to destroy the corn, which they did, plucking and throwing it into the river. About 11 o'clock we took up our line of march and proceeded for Jeneise, the last and capital settlement of the Seneca country; the whole crossed a branch of the Jenise river, and moved through a considerable swamp, and formed on a plain the other side, the most extensive I ever saw, containing not less than six thousand acres of the richest soil that can be conceived, not having a bush standing, but filled with grass considerably higher than a man. We moved up this plain for about three miles in our regular line of march, which was a beautiful sight, as a view of the whole could be had at one look, and then came to Jenise river, which we crossed, being about forty yards over, and near middle deep, and then ascended a rising ground, which afforded a prospect which was so beautiful that, to attempt a comparison, would be doing an injury, as we had a view as far as our eyes could carry us of another plain, besides the one we crossed, through which the Jenise river formed a most beautiful winding, and, at intervals, cataracts, which rolled from the rocks, and emptied into the river.

We then marched on through a rough but rich country, until we arrived at the capital town, which is much the largest we have yet met with in our whole route, and encamped about the same.

At this place we found the body of the brave but unfortunate Lieutenant Boyd, and one rifleman, massacred in the most cruel and barbarous manner that the human mind can possibly conceive; the savages having put them to the most excruciating torments possible, by first plucking their nails from their hands, then spearing, cutting, and whipping them, and mangling their bodies, then cutting off the flesh from their shoulders by pieces, tomahawking and severing their heads from their bodies, and then leaving them a prey to their dogs. We likewise found one house burned, in which, probably, was a scene as cruel as the former.

This evening the remains of Lieutenant Boyd and the rifleman's corpse were interred with military honours. Mr. Boyd's former good character, as a brave soldier, and an honest man, and his behaviour in the skirmish of yesterday (several of the Indians being found dead, and some seen carried off,) must endear him to all friends of mankind. May his fate await those who have been the cause of his. Oh! Britain, behold and blush. Jenise town, the capital of the Seneca nation, is pleasantly situated on a rich and extensive flat, the soil remarkably rich, and great parts well improved with fields of corn, beans, potatoes, and all kinds of vegetables. It contained one hundred and seven well-finished houses.

Wednesday, Sept. 15th.—This morning the whole army, excepting a covering party, were engaged in destroying the corn, beans, potatoes, and other vegetables, which were in quantity immense, and in goodness unequaled by any I ever yet saw. Agreeable to a moderate calculation, there was not less than two hundred acres, the whole of which was pulled and piled up in large heaps, mixed with dry wood, taken from the houses, and consumed to ashes. About 3 o'clock, P. M., the business was finished, and the immediate objects of this expedition completed, viz., the total ruin of the Indian settlements, and the destruction of their crops. The following is a part of the orders issued this day, viz.:

"The commander-in-chief informs this brave and resolute army that the immediate objects of this expedition are accomplished, viz.: total ruin of the Indian settlements, and the destruction of their crops, which were designed for the support of those inhuman barbarians, while they were desolating the American frontiers. He is by no means insensible of the obligations he is under to those brave officers and soldiers whose virtue and fortitude have enabled him to complete the important design of the expedition, and he assures them he will not fail to inform America at large how much they stand indebted to them. The army will this day commence its march for Tioga."

Previous to our leaving Jenise, a woman with a child came in to us, who had been taken prisoner last year near Wyoming, and fortunately made her escape from the savages. She, with her bantling, was almost starved for want of food; she informs us that the Indians have been in great want all last spring—that they subsisted entirely on green corn this summer—that their squaws were fretting prodigiously, and continually teazing their warriors to make peace—that by promises by Butler and his minions, they are fed up with great things that should be done for them—that they seem considerably cast down and frightened; and, in short, she says distress and trouble seem painted on their countenances. Distance of march this day, six miles.

Thursday, Sept. 16th.—After destroying several corn-fields, we took up our line of march about 11 o'clock, A. M., and proceeded towards Kanaghsas. Previous to our arrival there, parties were ordered out to reconnoitre the woods, and gather the bodies of those soldiers who fell in the skirmish of the 13th. Fourteen, including those six mentioned in my journal of the 13th, were found, and buried with military honours. The sight was most shocking, as they were all scalped,

APPENDIX.

tomahawked, and most inhumanly mangled. Amongst those unfortunate men was Hanjost, the volunteer Indian, who fared equally with the rest. About six o'clock we arrived at Kanaghsas, and encamped. We found several corn-fields, which were immediately laid waste. Our march this day, 9 miles.

Friday, Sept. 17th.—About 5 o'clock this morning the general beat, the tents were struck, and the line of march taken up about 6 o'clock. We arrived at Anyeaya about 12 o'clock, being the place our stores, with a garrison, was left. It was not with a little satisfaction that we found everything safe. We were not without our apprehensions about them, on account of the intelligence we were fearful the enemy might have collected from the unfortunate prisoners who fell in their hands on the 13th. We encamped in the same order, and on the same ground as on the 11th inst.

Saturday, Sept. 18th.—This morning about 8 o'clock the army moved; the rear was ordered (before they left the ground) to kill all such horses as were unable to move along, lest they should fall into the enemy's hands. On our route we fell in with several Oneida Indians, (our friends,) who seemed much rejoiced at our great success against the Seneca nations. We arrived about 6 o'clock, P. M., at the east side of the Kanadaugua lake, where we encamped, after completing a march of thirteen miles and a half.

Sunday, Sept. 19th.—The army moved at eight o'clock this morning in the usual order;—excepting a few obstructions they met with passing through several swamps, they marched remarkably steady. On our route we were met by an express from Tioga, who brought a number of letters and papers informing us of Spain declaring war against Great Britain. They also brought us the agreeable intelligence of a good supply for the army having come on to Newtown, (about twenty miles above Tioga,) to meet us. This agreeable intelligence conspired to make us exceedingly happy, as we had not only been a long time entirely in the dark with respect to home news, but the disagreeable reflection of half allowance was entirely dispelled.

We pursued our march until we arrived at Kanadasaga, which was about dusk. When the infantry got up; we encamped on the same ground, and in the same position, as on the 7th, after completing a march of fifteen miles.

Monday, Sept. 20th.—The greater part of this day was employed at head-quarters in holding a council in consequence of the intercession made by some Onieda Indians, (our friends) in favour of the Cayuga tribe, who have been for some time past in alliance with the Senecas, and acted with them, and are now desirous to make peace with us. The council determined no treaty should be held with them, and a command of five hundred infantry, with Major Parr's rifle corps, were immediately detached and sent to Cayuga lake, on which their settlement lay, with orders to lay wait and destroy their towns, corn, &c., and receive none of them but in the characters of prisoners of war. Col. Smith, with two hundred men, was also dispatched down the north side of the Seneca lake in order to finish the destruction of Gausiunque, an Indian village about eight miles below Canadasaga. Colonel Gainsworth, with one hundred men, was likewise detached, and sent to Fort Stanwix for some business, from whence he is to proceed to head-quarters on the north river, and join the main army.

About 4 o'clock, P. M., the army took up their line of march, and moved steadily. About half-past five they reached and crossed the outlet of Seneca lake, and encamped about one mile beyond the same.

Tuesday, Sept. 27th.—The army marched this morning about eight o'clock, and continued moving steadily until we passed Canadia about two miles, where we encamped, near the lake. Previous to our marching this morning, Colonel Dearbourn, with a command of two hundred men, marched to destroy a town on the north side of Cayuga lake. Distance of march this day, 13 miles.

Thursday, Sept. 23d.—About 8 o'clock this morning the army marched, and arrived at Catharines town about 2 o'clock, P. M., where we made a small halt. We found at this place the old Indian squaw who was left here on our march up the country. General Sullivan gave her a considerable supply of flour and meat, for which, with tears in her savage eyes, she expressed a great deal of thanks. During our absence from this place a young squaw came and attended on the old one; but some inhuman villain who passed through killed her. What made this crime still more heinous was, because a manifesto was left with the old squaw positively forbidding any violence or injury should be committed on the women or children of the savages, by virtue of which it appears this young squaw came to this place, which absolutely comes under the virtue of a breach of faith, and the offender ought to be severely punished.

I went to view, in company with a number of gentlemen, a very remarkable fall of water, which is about one mile above this place. Its beauty and elegance surpass almost any thing I ever saw. The fall is not less than two hundred feet. About 3 o'clock the army moved about three miles further, and encamped on a plain at the entrance of the great swamp, after completing a march of thirteen miles and a half.

Friday, Sept. 24th.—This morning precisely at 8 o'clock the army moved, and continued their route through the hemlock swamp mentioned in the 1st inst., meeting with much fewer obstructions than we expected, owing to the very dry weather which we have had for this month past. After passing through the same we came to a fine open country, and soon arrived at Kanawaluhery, where there was a post established with a reinforcement of stores, which was a most pleasing circumstance, as the last was issued, and that at half allowance, at Kanadaraga. On our arrival, the garrison saluted with the discharge of thirteen cannon, which compliment was returned them by the army.

Saturday, Sept. 25th.—In consequence of the accession of the King of Spain to the American alliance, and the generous proceedings of the present Congress in augmenting the subsistence of the officers and men of the army, General Sullivan ordered five head of the best cattle, viz.: one for the use of the officers of each brigade, with five gallons of spirits each, to be delivered to them respectively, thereby giving them an opportunity of testifying their joy on this occasion.

In the evening, the whole was drawn up and fired a feu-de-joie, thirteen cannon being first discharged. The infantry then commenced a running fire through the whole line, which, being repeated a second time, the whole army gave three cheers, viz.: one for the United States of America, one for Congress, and one for our new ally, the King of Spain.

The army being then dismissed, General Hand, with the officers of his brigade, attended by the officers of the park of artillery, repaired to a bowery, erected for that purpose, where the fatted bullock was served up, (dressed in different ways,) the whole seated themselves on the ground around the same, which afforded them a most agreeable repast. The officers being very jovial, and the evening was spent in great mirth and jollity.

After dinner the following toasts were drank, the drums and fifes playing at intervals.

1st. The thirteen states and their sponsors.
2d. The honourable, the American Congress.
3d. General Washington and the American army.
4th. The commander-in-chief of the western expedition.
5th. The American navy.
6th. Our faithful allies, the united houses of Bourbon.
7th. May the American Congress, and all her legislative representatives, be endowed with virtue and wisdom, and may her independence be as firmly established as the pillars of time.
8th. May the citizens of America, and her soldiers, be ever unanimous in the reciprocal support of each other.
9th. May altercations, discord, and every degree of fraud, be totally banished the peaceful shores of America.
10th. May the memory of the brave Lieutenant Boyd, and the soldiers under his command, who were horribly massacred by the inhuman savages, or by their more barbarous and detestable allies, the British and Tories, on the 13th inst., be ever dear to his country.
11th. An honourable peace with America, or perpetual war with her enemies.

APPENDIX.

12th. May the kingdom of Ireland merit a stripe in the American standard.

13th. May the enemies of America be metamorphosed into pack horses, and sent on a western expedition against the Indians.

An express, with dispatches for General Sullivan, from Philadelphia, arrived this morning, by whom I received a packet enclosing the commissions for my officers.

About 11 o'clock, A. M., the command under Colonel Dearbourn, who left us the 21st of June to proceed to Cayuga lake, returned, bringing two squaws prisoners; he having, in his route, destroyed several towns and a great quantity of fine corn.

Monday, Sept. 27th.—The detachment ordered to march yesterday moved this morning up Tioga branch to an Indian village, about twelve miles from this place, with orders to destroy the same.

Coleman and Caldwell, two of my soldiers, who, by some means, lost the regiment at Kanadaugua lake, on the eighteenth, after wandering for seven days in the wilderness, found and joined us at this place. They subsisted, during their absence, on the hearts and livers of two dead horses which they found on the path along which the army had marched.

At dusk this evening, the detachment which marched this morning returned, after destroying a considerable quantity of corn, beans, and other vegetables, sixteen boat loads of which they brought with them for the use of the army; they also burned a small village.

Tuesday, Sept. 28th.—Several commands were ordered out this day, viz., one up and the other down the Tioga branch, for the purpose of destroying corn, &c., of which there was a quantity left on our march towards the Seneca country.

All the lame and sick soldiers of the army were this day ordered to go to Tioga in boats, and the pack horses least able for other duty.

Colonel Butler, with his command, after laying waste and destroying the Cayuga settlements, and corn, &c., of which there was a very great quantity, returned, and joined the army about 10 o'clock this morning.

Wednesday, Sept. 29th.—The army marched this morning about 8 o'clock, and continued moving steady until we passed Chemung about one mile, where we encamped on the same ground, and in the same position, as on the 27th. The two commands ordered out yesterday morning returned, and joined the army at this place about 9 o'clock, P. M., after destroying large quantities of corn, beans, and other vegetables.

Thursday, Sept. 30th.—This morning about 8 o'clock the army moved. About 2 o'clock they arrived at Tioga plains, near Fort Sullivan, where the whole formed in regular line of march, and moved into the garrison in the greatest order, when we were received with military honours, the garrison turning out with presented arms, and a salute of thirteen rounds from their artillery, which complement was returned them from the park of artillery with the army.

Colonel Shrieve, governor of the garrison, had an elegant dinner provided for the general and field officers of the army. We regaled ourselves, and great joy and good humour was visible in every countenance. Colonel Proctor's band, and drums and fifes played in concert the whole time.

Friday, Oct. 1st.—This morning the horses belonging to the officers of the brigade were forwarded to Wyoming. We also sent our cow which we had along with us the whole expedition, and to whom we are under infinite obligations for the great quantity of milk she afforded us, which rendered our situation very comfortable, and was no small addition to our half allowance.

This afternoon Colonel Brewer, General Sullivan's secretary, set off to Congress with the dispatches, which contained a relation of the great success of the expedition.

Saturday, Oct. 2d.—This day the commander-in-chief made an elegant entertainment, and invited all the general and field officers of the army to dine with him.

In the evening, to conclude the mirth of the day, we had an Indian dance. The officers who joined in it putting on vizors, (alias Monetas.) The dance was conducted and led off by a young Sachem of the Oneida tribe, who was next followed by several other Indians, then the whole led off, and, after the Indian custom, danced to the music, which was a rattle, a knife, and a pipe, which the Sachem continued clashing together and singing Indian the whole time. At the end of each, the Indian whoop was set up by the whole.

Sunday, Oct. 3d.—Agreeable to the orders of yesterday, the garrison of Fort Sullivan this day joined their respective corps, and the fort was demolished. The stores and other baggage with the park of artillery were put on board the boats, and every other matter put in perfect readiness to move with the army, on their route to Wyoming, to-morrow morning at 6 o'clock.

The young Sachem, with several Oneida Indians, relatives and friends of the unfortunate Indian Hanjost, who bravely fell with the party under command of the much lamented Lieut. Boyd on the 13th ult., who faithfully acted as guide to the army, left us this day, well pleased, (after bestowing some presents on them,) for their native place, the Oneida country.

The German regiment, which composed a part of the flanking divisions of the army, was this day ordered to join and do duty with the third Pennsylvania brigade, commanded by Gen. Hand.

Monday, Oct. 4th.—This day about 8 o'clock the army took up their line of march. We arrived at Wessaukin about 6 o'clock in the evening, after completing a march of fifteen miles. On account of the rain, marching was rather disagreeable this day.

On my arrival at this place I received a letter, with some newspapers, &c., from his excellency President Read, which contained agreeable news, &c.

Wednesday, Oct. 6th.—About 8 o'clock this morning the whole embarked again, and moved, paying no attention to order down the river.

Thursday, Oct. 7th.—Embarked about 6 o'clock, and kept on steadily until we arrived at Wyoming. About 3 o'clock, P. M., the whole army landed and encamped on the same ground, and in the same order, as on the 30th of July.

Thus, by the perseverance, good conduct, and determined resolution of our commander-in-chief, with the assistance of his council, and the full determination of his troops to execute, have we fully accomplished the great end and intentions of this important expedition; and I flatter myself we fully surpassed the most sanguine expectations of those whose eyes were more immediately looking to us for success.

The glorious achievements we have exhibited in extending our conquests so far, and, at the same time, render them so very complete, will make no inconsiderable balance even in the present politics of America. Its future good consequences I leave to the eloquence of time to declare, which will, in ages hence, celebrate the memory of those brave sons who nobly risked their lives, disdaining every fatigue and hardship, to complete a conquest, the real good effects and advantages of which posterity will particularly enjoy.

Whilst I revere the merit and virtue of the army, I am sorry I am under the necessity of mentioning that there was an unparalleled and unpardonable neglect, (and which ought not to pass with impunity,) in those whose business it was to supply them with a sufficient quantity of necessaries to carry them through the expedition, instead of which not more than twenty-two days flour, and sixteen days meat was on hand when it commenced. And, although the army possessed a degree of virtue, perhaps unparalleled in the annals of history, in undertaking an expedition on half allowance, which was in every instance hazardous and imperious, yet, had we not been favoured with the smiles of Providence, in a continuation of good weather, the half allowance itself would not have enabled us to perform what, from that circumstance, we have.

THE END.

INDEX.

OF

WYOMING,

Compiled by Sarah P. Carr

Index of Names

ABBOTT
  Major ---, 355f, 367
  John, 156, 239-240, 486; A 31-32, 47
  Mrs. John (nee Alice Fuller), 240, A 31, 32
  Stephen, vii; A 31-33, 44, 47
  Mrs. Stephen (nee Abigail Searle), A 31, 44
ABINGTON (Lackawanna Co.), 240, 486
ABRAHAM'S
  Creek, 347, 366, see also Tuttle's Creek
  Plains (Wyoming), 178
ACADIA
  ---, 63
ACKE
  ---, 242
ADAMS
  Andrew, Esq., 190
AINSLEY
  John, 156, 466
ALBANY
  (NY), 48, 68, 69, 74, 90, 91, 92, 93, 94, 95, 99, 101, 200, 216, 320; A 26, 27, 47, 73
ALBRIGHT
  John, A 26
ALDEN
  Ensign Mason Fitch, 173, 382
  Major Prince, 138, 293, 332-333; A 41
ALEXANDER
  Robert, 246, 486
  William H., A 75
ALGONQUIN
  Indians, 18
ALLEGHENY
  Mts., 19, 24
  River, 273
ALLEN
  Chief Justice Andrew, 325
  General Ethan, 387, 388, 389n, 412, 460, 490
  Noah, 136
ALLENSBURG (Bradford Co.), 490
ALLISON
  Sgt. ---, 241
AMBOY (NJ), A 50
ANGEL
  Daniel, 136
  Jeremiah, 112n
ANNAPOLIS (MD), 378
ANTIS
  Sheriff Henry, Esq., 331, 335-36, 341,

ANTIS continued
  Sheriff continued, 346, 348, 349, 372, 382, 389, 449
ANYAYEA
  (NY), A 98, 101
  Lake (NY), A 98
ARMENIA (NY), 57n
ARMSTRONG
  Colonel John, 55, 88, 91, 93, 94, 349, 350-51, 353, 354-55, 356, 357n, 358, 359, 360, 361, 364-68, 410, 411, 422n, 485n
ARNDT
  Jacob, 335, 339
ARNOLD
  Ephraim, 137
  Joseph, 137
  Hon. Welcome, 307, 308, 316, 444, 446
ARTICLES
  of Confederation of the U. S., 72
ASHFORD (CT), 231; A 40, 80
ASHLEY
  Benjamin, 137
ASHMEAD
  Samuel, 457, 463
ASSESSORS
  ("Listers"), 156, 277
ASYLUM (Bradford Co.), 302
ATHENS (Bradford Co.), 391, 481, 490
ATHERTON
  A. ---, 242
  Caleb, 482
  Jabez, 242; A 51
  James Jr., 137, A 50
  John A 50
ATWOOD
  Elijah, 167
AUGUSTA Co. (VA), 182
AURORA (newspaper), A 8
AUSTIN
  ---, A 24
AVERIT
  Josiah, 167
AVERY
  ---, 281
  Christopher, 137, 156, 158, 179, 211, 221, 242, 244, 488
  Elisha, 66, 89, 92, 137
  Palmer, 145
AYERS
  Peter, 138
  Samuel, 293, 300-1, 432
AZILUM

AZILUM continued
  See Asylum (Bradford Co.)
BABCOCK
  Elisha, 137
BACKUS
  Ebenezer, 112n
BADGER
  Samuel, 137
BAILEY
  ---, 348; A 43
  Mrs. --- (nee Elizabeth Smith); A 43
  Benjamin, 295
BAKER
  ---, A 43
  Mrs. --- (nee Mary Smith), A 43
  John, 136, 156
  Widow, 179
BALDWIN
  Ebenezer, 112n
  Gideon, 150, 156
  Capt. Isaac, 156
  Sgt. Thomas, 284, 286, 302; A 54
  Waterman, 355n
BALLIOTT
  Stephen, 407
BALTIMORE (MD), 194; A 79
BARBER
  David, Esq., 167
BARLOW
  Joel, 275n, 389n, 400, 401, 404, 412, 436
BARNES
  Titus, 167
BARRE
  Col. Isaac, 142
BARTLE
  Capt. John, 401
BARTON
  ---, 401
  Rowland, 136
BATES
  Caleb, 150, 156, 333
  Robert, 238
BAY
  John Esq., 401
BEACH
  Nathan, Esq., vii, 123, 138, 286, 306, 401; A 36038, 42
  Zerah, Esq.; 211, 232, 255, 372, 385, 401
  Grove (Nescopeck Twp.) 123, 486
BEAR
  Creek, 263, 417-18
  Swamp, 239n
BEAUMONT
  Mrs. ---, A 72
  Hon. Andrew, 490
BEDFORD
  (Bedford Co.), 490
  Co., 362n
BEERS

BEERS continued
 Jabez, 238, 242
BENEDICT
 A. ---, 242
 Silas, 238
BENNETT
 ---, See Myers,
  Mrs. --- (nee
  Bennett)
 Mrs. ---, 138; A 16,
  47
 Isaac, 137
 Ishmael, 227
 John, Esq., A 16n
 Oliver, 302
 Rufus, vvi, 138,
  A 47
 Mrs. Rufus, vii
 Solomon, A 16
 Stephen, 469n
 Mrs. Stephen (nee
  Gates), 469, 469n
 Thomas, 112n, 137,
  138, 156, 278-279,
  286, 482, 487; A 14,
  47
 Mrs. Thomas, 138; A 47
 Hon. Ziba; A 13
 Mrs. Zibe (nee Slocum),
  252; A 72
BERKS
 Co., 212, 286, 340,
  363n, 364, 367;
  A 37, 60
BETHLEHEM
 (Lehigh Co.), 34, 39,
  40, 41, 44n, 45, 53,
  58; A 25, 37, 78
BIDDLE
 Charles, 437
BIDLACK
 Rev. Benjamin, vii; 201,
  377, 306, 329, 332;
  A 11-12, 34
 Capt. James, Jr.; 220,
  222, 224, 225-26, 242,
  258, 261, 277, 332,
  371; A 11-12, 22, 33-34,
  53
 Capt. James, Sr., 140,
  261, 297, 332, 487;
  A 12, 61
 Stephen, A 54
BIDWELL
 Barnabas, 448
BIGELOW
 David, 167
 John, Jr., 167
BIGFORD
 Sgt. Jeremiah, 225, 242
 Samuel, 242
BIGSBEE
 David, 242
 Elisha, 242
BILES
 Joseph, 146, 392
BINGHAM
 Abisha, 137
 Hezekiah, 157, 466n,
  476

BINGHAMPTON
 Annals, A 50
 (NY) A 50
BLACK
 Walnut Bottom
  (Wyoming Co.), 426
BLACKMAN
 Major Eleazur, vii,
  199; A 33, 34
 Mrs. Eleazur, vii; A
  34
 Elisha, Jr.; vii;
  A 33, 34
 Elisha, Sr., 199, 201,
  A 33-34
 Ichabod, A 33
 Lavina: See Spafford,
  Mrs. Darius
 Lucy, A 34
 Miner S., Esq., viii
BLANCHARD
 ---, A 33
 Capt. Jeremiah, Esq.,
  156, 157, 199, 219,
  220, 227, 231; A 33
 Joseph, 240, 487;
  A 20
BLOODY
 Rock (Queen Esther's)
  232n, A 25, 53
BLOOMING
 Grove (Pike Co.), 155,
  345-46n
BLUE
 Laws (violations of),
  284, 299-300
 Mountain(s), 40, 48, 92,
  101, 106, 188, 239n, 286,
  288; A 37, 60
 Ridge (i.e. Blue Mts.),
  212
BOLIN
 Capt. ---, 366
BOLTON
 Lt. Col. Mason; 254
BOND
 Capt. ---, A 91
 Capt. ---, 266
BOSTON
 (MA), 118, 215; A 11,
  37, 49
 Massacre, 118
BOWEN
 Stoddard, 242, A 60
BOWMAN
 Adam, 284
 Ebenezer, 409, 482;
  A 10, 19
 Jacob, 284
BOYD
 Dr. ---, 27
 Sgt. ---, 215, 234,
  235
 Col. James, 54, 57
 John, 242
 Hon. John, 349, 351,
  353-54, 357n, 359
 Lt. Thomas, 272-73; A 25,
  90, 98-99, 100, 102,
  104

BOZRAH
 Twp. (Wayne Co.),
  466, 490
BRACKENRIDGE
 Hon. Hugh Henry,
  463, 481
BRADDOCK
 Gen. Edward, 43, 44,
  50
BRADFORD
 Peris, 138
 William, 70
 William Jr., 70, 308,
  361-62, 444
 Co., xii, 293, 305, 383,
  483, 484; A 9, 54,
  57, 59
BRADLEY
 Abraham Esq., 480
BRADY
 Capt. ---, 413
BRAINTRIM
 (Wyoming Co.), 490;
  A 57, 59, 60
BRANDER
 of Horses, 277
BRANDYWINE
 (Delaware Co.), 203,
  275n, A 24
BRANT
 Joseph, 187, 222, 233,
  266-67, 270, 354n, 468,
  469, 474; A 10, 69,
  93, 96
BREAKALL
 Martin, 285
BREAK
 Neck Hill (Bradford
  Co.), A 87
BREARLY
 Hon. David, 307, 308,
  317, 444, 446
BRIGGS
 Peris, 137
BRINK
 Henry, 347
BRINKERHOOR
 Garrett: 198
BRISTOL
 (England), 63
BROCKWAY
 ---, 366
BRODHEAD
 Col. John Romeyn, vii,
  254, 256
 Luke, 328
BROOKLYN
 (Susquehanna Co.), A
  58
BROWN
 Daniel, 137, A 56
 James, 150, 157
 John, 242/ A 26, 56
 Robert, Esq., 339-40
 Thomas, 242; A 56
BROWNSON
 Josiah, 167
BRUNSWICK
 (NJ), 202; A 24, 49-50
BRYAN

-2-

Index of Names continued

BRYAN continued
  George, 362n
  Samuel, 362
BRYANT
  Prince, 198
BUCK
  Capt. Aholiab: 167,
    220, 242, A 59
  Mrs. Aholiab (nee
    York) A 59
  Asahel, 161, 193,
    226, 244, 486, 488
  Elijah, 138
  William, 226, A 44
  Lt. William, 156, 157,
    166, 167, 242,
    263, 321; A 13
BUCKS
  Co., 362n, 364, 367;
    A 21
BUDD
  Benjamin, 138
  Joseph, 242
BUEL
  Ezra, 112n, 137
BULLOCK
  Amos, 231, 241,
    242; A 57
  Asa, 231, 241, 242;
    A 57
  Nathan, 231, 241, 289,
    488; A 25, 57
BUNKER
  Hill, Battle of, 165; A 49,
    71
BURGOYNE
  Gen. John, 187, 195,
    200, 209
BURIALS
  (Indian), 26-28
BURK
  (Capt.) ---, A 84
BURROUGHS
  Lt. ---, 190
BUSH
  Capt., ---, A 88-89
  Henry, 242
BUTLER
  Corp., ---, 264
  Chester, Esq., v, A 63,
    71, 76
  Mrs. Chester, A 72
  Gertrude, A 72
  John, A 62, 63
  Mrs. John, A 72
  Col. John, iv, vii,
    28n, 187, 216, 218,
    220, 222-223, 227,
    231-237, 233n, 245,
    247, 253, 258, 270,
    272-273, 284, 289;
    A 5, 14-15, 18n, 23,
    25, 27, 31, 39, 46,
    56, 64, 79, 93, 95,
    96, 97, 100
  Lord, A 63
  Mrs. Lord, A 72
  Gen. Lord, 241, 343,
    379n, 407, 409, 430-
    431, 482; A 6-8, 63

BUTLER continued
  Lydia (See Griffin,
    Mrs. George, Esq.
  Phebe, See Donalson,
    Mrs. ---
  Pierce, A 63
  Col. Richard, 268
  Ruth Ann, See Conyng-
    ham, Mrs. John N.
  Stuben, Esq. A 63
  Sylvina, See Mallery,
    Mrs. Garrick
  Capt. Walter, 236, 254;
    A 23, 93, 96
  William, A 82
  Zebulon, 142
  Col. Zebulon (Sr.), v,
    5ln, 98, 105, 112n,
    120, 123, 128-132, 139,
    142, 149, 154, 155, 156,
    158, 160, 172, 175, 183-
    188, 191, 192, 197, 199,
    203, 211, 217, 218-223,
    227, 232, 239, 240, 241,
    245, 257, 260-264, 260n,
    268, 273, 275n2, 277,
    281, 282, 283, 284, 289,
    294, 295, 326, 331, 332,
    334, 335, 342, 355n, 356,
    362, 374, 375, 376-379,
    382, 385, 387, 394, 401,
    405, 406, 407, 408, 415,
    437, 483, 488; A 5, 7, 20,
    25, 28, 35n, 41, 47, 48,
    51, 61-63, 69, 73, 78n,
    83, 90, 91, 103
  Mrs. Zebulon (Sr.) (née
    Phebe Haight), 331-32;
    A 63
  Mrs. Zebulon (sr.) (née
    Johnson), 142, 296; A
    63
  Mrs. Zebulon (Sr.) (née
    Ellen Lord) A 63
  Rev. Zebulon, A 47, 63
BUTLER'S
  Falls (NY), 474
  Rangers, 233, 237n, 254,
    256; A 38-39
BUTTERFIELD
  James, A 26
BUTTERMILK
  Falls (Wyoming Co.),
    A 85
BUTTONWOOD
  ---, 296
CADY
  Manassah, 289, 488, A
    25
CALDWELL
  --- A, 103
  John, 242
  Capt. William, 218, 222,
    233n, 285; A 39
CALKINS
  Dr. John, 150
CALLENDER
  Robert, 555
CAMERON
  Josiah, 242

CAMMERHOFF
  Bishop John C. F.,
    40
CAMPBELL
  Capt. ---, 295
  Capt. Isaac, 243
  Thomas, iii
CANAAN
  (CT), 369, 370,
    481; A 26
CANADA
  ---, 21, 91, 215,
    248, 266n, 332,
    487; A 25, 41, 51,
    56, 57, 73, 74
CANADIA
  (NY) A 96, 101
CANAJOHARIE
  (NY), 94, 97, 143
CANANDAIGUA
  (NY), 272, 471
CANASSATEGO
  (Indian Chief), 37
CANOY
  Indians, 49
CANTERBURY
  (CT), A 27
CAPOUSE
  Meadows (Lackawanna
    Co.), 122, 140, 154,
    220, 239, 281, 345n,
    See also Providence Twp.
CARBERRY
  Capt. ---, A 89
CAREY
  Comfort, vii
  Mrs. E., A 72
  Eleazer, 137, 233n, A
    23
  Henry, 150
  John, vii, 139, 141,
    174, A 23, 52, 54
  Joseph, A 23
  Nathan, 432; A 23
  Samuel, vii, 226, 233n,
    242, 487, A 21023, 33
  Mrs. Samuel (née Theresa
    Gore) vii, A 23
CAREYTOWN
  ---, 246, 279, 355n,
    381, A 41
CARKHUFF
  vs. Anderson, 463
CARLISLE
  (Cumberland Co.) xiii
CARMAN
  Josiah, 238
CARPENTER
  Benjamin, 408
CARR
  Capt., ---, 246, 486
  Daniel, 217, 238, 487,
    A 39
CARRINGTON
  Jonathan, 136
CARROLL
  ---, 446
CARSON
  John, 483
CARTER

-3-

History of Wyoming County, Pennsylvania

CARTER continued
   ---, 465
CARTIER
   Jacques, 21
CARVAN
   Morgan, 136
CARVER
   David, 167
   Samuel, 167
CARY
   Barnabas, 157
CASS
   Gov. ---, 21, 35n
   Daniel, 138
CASTLETON
   (VT), A 26
CATAWBA
   Indians, 29, 31, 32
   River (SC), 31
CATAWISSA
   (Columbia Co.), 240, 305, A 34
CATHARINE'S
   Town, (NY), A 93, 94, 95
CATLIN
   Putnam, 409, 482; A 19
CAYUGA
   Indians, 18, 19, 22, 29, 49, A 74, 75, 101
   Lake (NY), 30, 271; A 95, 101, 103
   River (NY), A 94, 96
CAZENOVIA
   (NY), 393
CENTRE
   Co., 356n
CHAMBERS
   John, 328
   Stephen, 362
CHAMPLAIN
   Capt., ---, 295
   Samuel de, 21
CHANDLER
   Joseph R., Esq., ix
CHAPMAN
   Asa, 288, 305, 487
   Eunice, See Poyner, Mrs. ---
   Isaac A., iii, xv, 25, 28, 38, 50, 54, 276, 342, 354n, 407
   Nathan, 142, 197, 198n
   Sybil, See Kimble, Mrs. Abel
   Uriah (Jr.), 472
   Uriah (Sr.), 156, 159, 211, 466, 468
CHARLES
   I, King of England, 64
   II, King of England: 65, 71, 76-81, 84-86, 88, 89, 97, 103, 121, 311, 314
   River (MA), 64
CHARLESTON

CHARLESTON continued
   Twp. (Northumberland Co.), 166, 168-69
CHARLEVOIX
   (Historian), 21
CHASE
   John, 490
CHEMUNG
   (NY), A 88, 91-92, 103
   River (NY), xi, 187, 270
CHENANGO
   (NY), 30, 35, 186, 187
   Indians, 49
   River (NY), 449
CHEROKEE
   Indians, 29, 32, 35n, 183
CHESAPEAKE
   Bay, xivn
CHESTER
   (Delaware Co.), 434
   Co., iv, A 21
CHEW
   Hon. Benjamin, 111, 114n
CHICTASHICK
   Indians, A 74, 75
CHIKATAUBUTT
   (Mass. Indian chief), 19-20
CHIMER
   Anthony, 156
CHOATE
   William, 167
CHOCONUT
   (NY), 35, 187, A 83, 90
CHOCTAW
   Indians, 35n
CHRISTIAN
   Indians, 29, 34, 39-41, 43-45, 52, 53, 58, 60, 98
CHRISTIE
   Capt., ---, 330, 332, 333, 346, 347
CHRISTMAN'S
   Tavern, 486
CHURCH
   Elias, 199
   Gideon A 58
   Joel, 242; A 58
   John, A 58
   Nathaniel, A 58
   Samuel, 394
   William, A 58
CHURCHILL
   William (sic), 136
CILLEY
   ---, A 82, 84
CIST
   Emily, A 72
   Jacob, Esq., 27
CLARK
   Benjamin, 286
   Col. George Rogers, 80-81
   John, 138

CLARK continued
   Nathaniel, 167
   Phineas, 156
   Roger, 467
   Capt. William, 167
CLAUSE
   David, 92-95
CALVERACK
   (PA), 490
CLAYTON
   Capt. Asher, 55, 56, 57, 107, 120-132, 170
CLEAVELAND
   Aaron, 394
CLEMSTED
   John, 167
CLINTON
   Sir Henry, 253-54, 256, 302
   Gen. James, 264, 268, 269, 270, 271, 273, 275, A 81, 82, 89, 90, 91, 92, 93, 97, 99
CLYMER
   Daniel, Esq., 340, 437, 443, 483
COAL
   xiii, A 35
COBB
   John, Esq., 466
COBB'S
   Gap (Lackawanna Co.), 122, 345n, 467
COCHECTON
   (NY), 465, 468, 469, 470
COFFRIN
   James, 243
   William, 242
COLCHESTER
   (CT), 380-81, A 38, 47
COLE
   Samuel, 242
COLEMAN
   ---, A 103
   Naniad, 138
COLT
   Abraham, 138
COLTON
   ---, A 24
COLUMBIAD
   ---, 275n
COMMITTEE
   of Correspondence, 166
COMSTOCK
   Eleanor, See Gaylord, Mrs. Ambrose
   Ens. John, 282, A 60
   Kingsley, 242; A 60
   Peter, 138
   Robert, 242, A 60
CONCORD
   (NH), A 41
CONDE
   (McKean Co.), 392, 489
CONGRESS
   of Delegates (1754), 67-68

-4-

Index of Names continued

CONNECTICUT
  Charter, 65-89 passim,
    96, 133-34, 150, 153
  General Assembly,
    See General Assembly
    (CT)
  River, 20, 75
CONNESDICO
  (Indian chief), 183
CONSAWLER
  Emanuel, 156
CONSTABLES
  ---, 156, 276
CONTINENTAL
  Congress, 99, 165,
    166, 168, 169, 171-72,
    176, 179, 182-85, 189,
    190, 192, 193, 194, 202,
    206, 213, 214, 215, 216,
    252, 257, 265n, 274, 275,
    290, 307, 312, 313, 339,
    363; A 27
CONWAY
  Gen. Henry Seymour,
    306
CONYNGHAM
  Hon. John N., vii;
    A 63
  Mrs. John N. (nee Ruth
    Ann Butler), A 63, 72
  Redmond, Esq., viii
  Valley, 232, 287, 487;
    See also Scotch Valley,
    Sugar Loaf
COOK
  William Esq., 170, 173,
    174
COOKE
  Jabez, 137
COOLBAUGH
  Moses, A 59-60
COOPER
  Mrs. ---, vii
  George, 220-21, 223-24,
    230, 429n, A 58
  Thomas, Esq., 453, 455,
    483, A 6, 19
COREY
  Anson, 243, A 57
  Jenks, 137, 243; A 57
  Jonathan, 432
  Rufus, 243, A 57
CORNELIUS
  Anthony, 231n
CORONER
  ---, 395, 404
CORTRIGHT
  (sic), John, 242
CORNWALLIS
  Lord Charles, 201-2,
    306, 307, 397, 442,
    444; A 11, 36, 37,
    78, 80
COSHUTUNK
  (Pike Co.), 70, 122,
    139, 155, 171
COTTERELL
  Sir Charles, 27
COTTON
  Rev. John, 24

COUNCIL
  of Censors, 361-68
COURTLAND
  ---, A 82, 84
COURTRIGHT
  Mrs. ---, 230-31
  Cornelius, Esq., vii,
    26, 58
COURTS
  martial, 285
COVELL
  ---, A 4
COWLES
  Col. ---, A 63
  Mrs. --- (nee Jarriet
    Welles), A 63
COXE
  Tench Esq., 87, 89
CRAIG
  Thomas, 107, 123
CRAIN
  Lt., ---, 296
CRARY
  Oliver, 393
CRAWFORD
  ---, 183
  Maj., ---, 382
CREEK
  Indians, 35n
CRIME
  284-85, 298-301,
    390
CROCKER
  Dr. John, 167
CROGAN
  George Esq., 49
CROOKER
  Joseph, 242, A 54
  Samuel, 242; A 54
CROOKS
  William, 214, 486;
    A 38
CROPS
  (Indians'), 52, 59,
    271; A 81n, 89,
    91-101 passim
  (settlers'), 52, 54, 59,
    164, 216, 245, 288,
    367, 400, 475; A 32, 35
CROWN
  Point (NY), 51n, 105,
    187, A 62
CUMBERLAND
  Co., 362
CUMMINGS
  Capt., ---, A 88
CUNNINGHAM
  (Susquehanna Co.),
    490
DANA
  Hon. Amasa, A 41
  Anderson (Jr.), v, vii,
    A 40, 41, 57, 76,
    80, 81
  Anderson, Esq. (Sr.),
    150, 156, 159, 198n,
    199, 209, 210, 211, 221,
    224, 231, 241, 243, 298,
    488; A 40-41, 80
  Mrs. Anderson (née Stevens),

DANA continued
  Mrs. Anderson continued,
    231, A 40, 57, 80
  Daniel, A 40, 41
  Eleazur, A 41
  Rev. Sylvester, vii, A
    41, 57
  Mrs. Sylvester, Esq. (née
    Stevens), A 57
  Academy, A 41
DANBURY
  (CT), 379, A 72, 76
DARLING
  Jabez, 243
DAVENPORT
  Conrad, 243
DAVIDSON
  Douglass, 159
  Samuel, 362n
DAVIS
  Capt., ---, 264, 487,
    A 90
  Mrs. ---, vii
DAYTON
  ---, A 82, 84
DEAL
  Capt., ---, A 37
DEAN
  Josiah, 138
DEARBORN
  Col. Henry, A 103
DECLARATION
  of Independence, 72,
    188, 209, 413n
DELAWARE
  107, 197, 372, 379n
  & Hudson Canal, 475
  Company, 69-70, 72,
    154, 379n, 380, 393,
    444-45, 481, 490
  Indians, 18, 19, 30-39,
    41, 43, 44n, 46-50,
    52, 53, 57, 58, 59, 59n,
    101
  River, 18, 20, 24, 30,
    36, 39, 67, 70, 71, 72
    74-75, 76, 81, 83, 84,
    85, 87, 88, 106, 112,
    121, 135, 139, 141, 145,
    146, 150, 153, 154, 156,
    159, 171, 172, 194, 259,
    286, 294, 296, 306n, 311,
    345, 346, 363, 373, 374,
    375, 377, 389n, 395, 466,
    468, 470, 471, 473, 489;
    A 37, 44, 47, 79
DE LONG
  John, 137
DEMOCRATIC
  Press (newspaper); A 8
DENISON
  Betsey, See Shoemaker,
    Mrs. Elijah
  George, A 19
  Col. Lazarus, A 48
  Nathan, Esq., 105, 139,
    140, 150, 154, 159,
    161, 166, 192, 197,
    199, 209, 211, 217,
    219, 222-23, 227, 229

-5-

DENISON continued
  Nathan, Esq., continued,
    231, 232, 234-36, 239,
    255, 256, 258, 276, 277,
    282, 288, 289, 298, 311,
    319, 328, 336, 394, 401,
    406, 407, 411, 418, 419,
    482, 488; A 5, 6, 10, 14-
    15, 16, 18, 19, 20, 33,
    35, 44, 51, 54, 73
  Mrs. Nathan (neé Sill),
    140, 288, A 47-49
DENNY
  Henry, 463
DERRICK
  William S., Esq., vii
DETROIT
  (MI), 30, 42
DEVONSHIRE
  (England), 63
DEWEY
  Abel, 486
  Charles, 167
DEWIT
  John, 156
DE WITT
  ---, 376, 423n
DIAL
  Rock, xiin
DICK
  ---, 376
  Archibald T., A 18
  Capt. John, 107, 130-
    32, 170, 326, 336
DICKERSON
  John, A 24
  Philemon, A 24
DICKINSON
  ---, 169
  John, 316, 335-36,
    343-44, 365-67, 399n
  Gen. Philemon, 201-2,
    A 49-50
DINGMAN
  Jacob, 138
DISEASES
  ---, 287, 296, see
    also smallpox, typhus
DIVINE
  James, 243
DIVORCES
  ---, 298
DOCTORS
  ---, 139, 150,
    196, 201, 207,
    263, 287-88, 466,
    471, A 43, 47, 50,
    52, 60
DODSON
  Abigail, 286-87
  Thomas, A 36
DONALSON
  Dr. ---, A 63
  Mrs. --- (neé Phebe
    Butler), A 63
DONLEY
  Mrs., --- A, 72
DORRANCE
  Col. Benjamin, vii, 233,
    482, A 8-10, 12

DORRANCE continued
  Col. Charles, A 10
  Col. George, 199, 217,
    219, 222, 242, 244,
    284-85, 482; A 10-11,
    53
  John, 136, 204-5, 209,
    316, 452; A 10-11
  Rev. John, A 10
  Robert, A 16
  Samuel, 137
DOWNER
  Joshua, 392
DOWNING
  George, 243
  Richard, Jr., 457
DRAKE
  Mrs., ---, A 72
  Nathaniel, 140
  Samuel Gardner, 20, 28n,
    A 75
DRAPER
  Simeon, 112n
  Thomas, 137
  William, 138
DREISBACH
  Simon, 363n
DRESDEN
  (VA), 282
DUANE
  ---, 399n
DUBOIS
  Col. ---, A 82, 91
DUDLEY
  Capt. Gideon, 394,
    406, 423, 426-28, 431
  Joseph, 430, 432
DUNKIN
  James, 136
DUNN
  ---, 295
  Levi, 243
  William, 243
DUNNING
  John, 74, 82
DURKEE
  Major Andrew, 137
  Major John, 105, 112,
    116-119, 123, 138,
    149; A 27n, 49
  Capt. Robert, 112n, 161,
    193, 200, 201, 208,
    213, 215, 221-23, 242,
    258, 283, 296; A 12, 14,
    24, 27n, 29, 35, 42, 46,
    49, 60, 62, 78
DUTCHER
  ---, 243
DYE
  James, 467
DYER
  Col. Eliphalet, 81, 111,
    140, 151, 153, 308,
    310, 391, 444-45, A 19
  Thomas, 140
EARL
  ---, 428-429
  Benjamin, 428, 429n
EASTON
  Joseph, 112n, 167

EASTON continued
  (Northampton Co.), 47,
    49, 50, 52, 53, 71, 109,
    110, 112, 122, 265, 275,
    345, 349, 355, 358n,
    368, 394, 431, 437, 465;
    A 19, 57, 78, 82
  Jail, 108, 122-123, 128,
    325; A 37
EDGAR
  James, 363n
EDWARDS
  Jasper, 467
  Timothy, Esq., 385
ELDER
  Rev. John, viii, 54-56
  Thomas, Esq., viii
ELDERKIN
  Jedediah, 111, 391
  Vine, 108
ELICOT
  Andrew, 421n
ELK
  Co., 490
ELLIOTT
  Joseph, 226, 302; A
    53056
ELLMORE
  Dr., ---, 267
ELLSWORTH
  Erastus, Esq., A 72
  Gov. William Wolcott,
    A 71
ENSIGN
  Samuel, 392
  Widow, 179
ERBE
  Capt. Lawrence, 413-14,
    480
ESPY
  Daniel, 362n
EVANS
  Rev. Dr., ---, 273
  Evan Rice (sic), 483;
    A 19
  Griffith, 416-17
  James, 137
EVELAND
  Frederick, 156
EVERETT
  Hon. Edward, vii
  Jacob, 349, 359n
EWING
  G. W., 249-50
EXETER
  Twp., xi, 154, 155, 217,
    232n, 233n, 237, 486,
    487, 490; A 22, 23, 38,
    39, 40, 43
FAIRFIELD
  Co. (CT), 262, 489; A 72, 76
FARMER'S
  Letters, A 24
FARMINGTON
  (CT), 380, 412, 413n, A 63
FARNHAM
  Joshua, 294
FELL
  Hon. Jesse, 482; A 18
FELLOWS

Index of Names continued

FELLOWS continued
  Ephraim, 137
FENCE
  viewers, 156, 199, 276
FERLIN
  Thomas, 137
FERRIES
  ---, 143, 204, 413
FINCH
  ---, 486, A 14
  Benjamin, 243, A 56
  Daniel, 243, A 56
  John, 243, A 56
  Samuel, vii, 235, 255
FISH
  Elisha, 243
  Jabez, 137, 157, 230, 346; A 33
  Mrs. Jabez, 230
  xiv, 120, 139, 141-42, 290, 344, A 98
FISHING
  Creek (Columbia Co.), 279, 281
FISH'S
  Eddy, 109, 343
FITCH
  Col. Elizur, 97, 98
  Jonathan, 298, 488, A 48, 50
  Mrs. Jonathan, A 48
  Lemuel, 200; A 27, 38
  Samuel, 167
FITCHET
  Cornelius, 243
FITZSIMMONS
  Thomas, 362n
FIVE
  Nations, 20, 22-23, 27-28, 68-69, 98, 99, 236; A 73-75 See also, Six Nations.
FLINT
  Creek, (NY), A 97
FLOODS
  xiii, 27, 143, 342-43, 399-400
FOLLET
  Eliphalet, 156, 243
FOLLETT
  Benjamin, 108
FOLLET (T)
  Frederick, 263, 486
FOOT
  Charles, 167
  Daniel, 166
FORD
  David, 471
  Hannah, See Rogers, Mrs. Josiah
FOREST
  Col. ---, A 87
FORROW
  Christopher, A 36
FORSEMAN
  Hugh Esq., 285, 288, 289, 298, 304, 311, 336, 394

FORSYTH (E)
  Charles, 467, 472
FORSYTHE
  James, 137
FORT
  Allen (Lehigh Co.), 40, 43, 46, 50, 131, 286, 295; A 80
  Augusta (Northumberland Co.), 44, 56, 92, 170, 191, 266, 288, 295, 325, 381, See also Sunbury.
  Brown, 231, A 56
  Dickinson, 318
  Duquesne (Westmoreland Co.), 42, 50, 60, See also Fort Pitt
  Durkee, 109, 110, 112, 115, 116, 122-23, 126-29, 199, 265, 490
  James (Manhattan Is.); 78
  Jenkins, 191, 217, 218, 220, 255, 490; A 33, 38, 39, 58, 78
  Jenkins (Columbia Co.); 191; A 36
  Lillo-pe; 346
  Ogden, 117, 139, 199, 490
  Penn (Monroe Co.), A 44-45
  Pitt (Westmoreland Co.), 50; See also Fort Duquesne
  Stanwix (NY), 97, 98, 99, 100, 101, 489; A 101
  Sullivan (Bradford Co.); A. 91, 103-4
  Ticonderoga (NY), 51n, 105; A 62
  Washington (NY), 193; A 78
  Wintermoot, 217, 490; A 29, 58
  Wyoming, 128, 490
FORTY
  (first settlers), 136-38
  Forst, 120, 140, (154), (178), 191, 214, 217, 218, 220-21, 224, 227, 229, 231, 232, 235, 239, 255, 257, 348, 410, 491; A 10, 13, 14, 30, 31, 43, 44, 45, 47, 51, 54, 56, 58, 59, 60, 64, 67, 78
FOSTER
  ---, A 21
  Lafayette S., A 71
FOXEN
  Thomas, 243
FRANCE
  ---, 42, 46, 60, 63, 66, 67, 275n, 295, 350, 395, 396, 397, 398n
FRANCIS
  Col. Turbot, 99-100, 107,

FRANCIS continued
  Col. Turbot continued, 110, 170
FRANKLIN
  Arnold, 301, 488
  Benjamin, 68, 74
  Billa, 392
  Col. John, vii, viii; 138, 150, 157, 199, 211, 220, 229, 232, 234, 237, 241, 245, 268, 271, 280, 281, 282, 284, 285, 286, 289, 290n, 292, 295, 297, 298, 300, 301-2, 305, 311, 329, 332, 336-37, 339n, 344n, 347, 348, 352, 354n, 355n, 356, 359, 360, 366, 368, 369-72, 379n, 380-81, 382, 385, 386, 387-88, 389, 392, 400, 405, 406, 407, 409, 411-12, 413-16, 417n, 418, 421, 422, 423, 425, 426, 427, 428, 420, 432, 433, 435n, 436-38, 456, 480-82; A 28, 54, 58
  Rosewell, Jr., 301, 488
  Rosewell, Sr., 140, 156, 159, 161, 220, 282, 296, 329, 430, 432, 488; A 54
  Mrs. Rosewell (Sr.) 301-2, 329, 487; A 54
  Widow, 179
FREDERICK
  (town) MD 303
FREELAND'S
  Fort (Northumberland Co.), 266
FREEMAN'S
  Oath, 166, 171, 188, 209, 276
FRENCH
  & Indian Wars, viii, 5ln, 105; A 7, 62
  Azilum; See Asylum (Bradford Co.)
FRENCHTOWN
  A. 54
FRIEDENSHUTTEN
  (Bradford Co.), 59
FRISBEE
  James, 167, 289, 488
  Jonathan, 289, 488; A 25
  Zebulon, 136
FRUIT
  trees, siv, A 16, 35, 96, 97
FRY
  --- (Schoolmaster), 467
FULLER
  Alice, See Abbott, Mrs. John
  Capt. Stephen, 137, 142, 143, 158, 161, 243, 244, 297n, 371

-7-

FULLER continued
  Thomas, 243; A 53
FULMER
  Thomas, 99, 100
GAGE
  Gen. Thomas, 118, 120;
    A 11
GAGHSUQUILAHERY
  (NY) A 99
GALLOP
  William, 112n, 138
GARANGULA
  (Grande Gueule) A
    73-75
GARDINER
  ---, 345
  Peregrine, A 47
  Stephen, 411; A 32
GARDNER
  Christopher, 138
  John, 156, 217,
    238, 486; A 39
GARRETT
  Elisha, 347
  Maj. John, 173, 222,
    242, 244
GATES
  ---, See Bennett, Mrs.
    Stephen
  David, 467
  Nathaniel, 466, 469
GAY
  Fisher Esq., A 43
  Mrs. Fisher, Esq. (nee
    Smith) A 43. See also
    Osterhout, Mrs. Isaac
GAYLORD
  Lt. Aaron, 199, 242,
    A 60
  Mrs. Ambrose (nee
    Eleanor Comstock) A 60
  Charles, 156, 204,; A
    24, 60
  Dr. Charles, A 60
  Charles E. Esq. A 24,
    60
  Henderson, A 60
  Joseph, 136, 149
  Justus Jr., A 59-60
  Mrs. Justus, Jr. (nee
    York), A 59. See also
    Buck, Mrs. Aholiab
    (née York)
  Justus (Sr.), 157; A
    59-60
GEHR
  Baltzer, 363n
GENERAL
  Assembly (Connecticut),
    133, 164, 167, 176,
    177, 178, 185, 190,
    191, 192, 196, 205,
    211, 282-83, 288, 291,
    294, 297, 310, 371,
    372, 384, 387, 394,
    395, 441, 488; A 5, 71
  Assembly (Pennsylvania),
    310-11, 314, 317, 322-
    23, 328, 330, 333-38,
    339-341, 342, 344, 362-

GENERAL continued
  Assembly (Penn.) continued
    64, 367, 374-76, 382,
    389, 407, 436, 439,
    440, 448, 454, 457-58,
    461-62, 485
GENESEE
  River, 259, 272, 302-3,
    329, 423n, 443, 449,
    489; A 28, 52, 99
GEORGE
  I, King of England, 27
  II, King of England,
    68, 70
  III, King of England,
    124, 146, 149, 151,
    162, 255, 274, 307;
    A 34, 38, 68, 90
  William A., 414
GERE
  Capt. Jeremiah, A 58
  Rezin, 220, 242, 244;
    A 47, 58
  Robert, 393
  Stephen, A 58
GERMAIN
  Lord George, 253-54,
    256
GERMANTOWN
  (Bucks Co.), 203, 209,
    263, 275n, A 24, 49
GEROLD
  Duty, 138
GERRY
  Elbridge, 274, 375
GERTRUDE
  of Wyoming, iii
GIBSON
  Ch. Justice John Bannister,
    27
GILBERT
  Benjamin, 286; A 37
GILLAWAY
  Capt. Job, 140, A 48
  Mrs. Job (nee Comfort
    ---), 140, A 48
GNADENHÜTTEN
  (Lehigh Co.), 40-41
GORDON
  John, 167
  William, iv, 235, 245,
    256, 257, 266; A 17,
    50
GORE
  --- See Murfee, Mrs.
    John
  Asa, 241, 242; A 46
  Daniel, xiii, 112n,
    136, 156, 199, 206,
    222, 223, 225, 226,
    241, 242, 244, 343,
    432; A 23, 46
  George, 241, 243; A 46
  John, 346
  Obadiah (Sr.), Esq.,
    105, 112n, 128, 142,
    150, 157, 159, 167, 179,
    192, 199, 211, 231, 241,
    282, 283, 285, 297, 311,
    319, 329, 385, 401, 408,

GORE continued
  Obadiah continued, 457,
    463, 482, 488; A 18,
    45, 46
  Mrs. Obadiah, A 46
  Obadiah (Jr.), 137, 149,
    166, 242, 276; A 45
  Samuel, 241; A 46
  Sarah, 303
  Silas, 136, 156, 162,
    241, 242, 243, 244; A 46
  Theresa; See Carey,
    Mrs Samuel
GOSHEN
  (NY), 266, 466, 475
GOSHO
  Capt., ---, A 37
GOSS
  Comfort, 138
  Nathaniel, 137
  Philip, 136, 246,
    486
GRAND
  Jurors, 157
GRANDISON
  Chales, A 26
GRAY
  Col. Ebenezer, 385, 401
  Samuel, 310, 387, 388,
    391, 401
  Thomas, 136, 144
GREAT
  Bend (Susquehanna Co.),
    187
  Swamp (Monroe Co.), 212,
    221, 469; A 77-78
GREEN
  Job, Jr., 138
  Joseph, 166
  Nathaniel, 166
  Mt. boys, 388n, 389n
GREENE
  Gen. Nathaniel, 307
GREENWICH
  Bay (CT), 75
GRIFFIN
  Mrs. George Esq. (nee Lydia
    Butler), A 63
GRISTMILLS
  ---, 142, 197-98, 286,
    334, 348; A 47, 56
GROSVENOR
  Col. Thomas, A 62
GROTON
  (CT), 143; A 72, 76
GUERNSEY
  Lt. Peter, 167
GUSTIN
  ---, See Snowden Mrs.
    Rev. Dr.
  Dr. Samuel, 231, 255; A
    43
  Mrs. Samuel (nee Smith), A 43
HACKLEIN
  Sheriff ---, 170
  Peter, 125-26, 128
HADDEN
  Abigail, 298
  Simeon, 298
HADSELL

-8-

Index of Names continued

HADSELL continued
  James, Jr., 217, 237,
    486; A 39
  James, Sr., 217, 237,
    486; A 39
HAGEMAN
  ---, 239n, 246, 295,
    486; A 43
HALL
  Basil, A 13n
  Charles, A 19
HALLET
  James, 467
HALSTEAD
  John, 264
HAMBLETON
  Joseph, 211
HAMILTON
  Gov. James, 54, 55, 88,
    90-91, 133
HAMMER
  William, 243
HAMMOND
  Lebbeus, 226, 278,
    279, 281, 286, 289,
    470, 482, 487; A 15, 56
HAMPTON
  (CT), 240; A 32
HANCOCK
  James, A 42
  Mrs. James (née Perkins),
    A 42
HAND
  Edward, 373, 375, 376
  Gen. Edward, 260, 261,
    264, 268, 269n, 270,
    271, 275n, A 82-84,
    88, 89, 90, 91, 93,
    102, 104
HANHAM
  Thomas, 63
HANJOST
  (Oneida Indian), A 98,
    99, 101, 104
HANNA
  William R., 483
HANNAH
  James, 167
HANOVER
  (Dauphin Co.), 106,
    115
  xiiin, xiv; 105, 121,
    140, 150, 154, 155,
    191, 220, 246, 276,
    278, 279, 284, 296,
    301, 305, 386, 410,
    413, 430, 486, 487,
    488, 490; A 20, 21,
    34, 41, 42, 48
HARDING
  Abraham, 156; A 33-38
  Benjamin, 217, 486; A
    39
  Elisha, Esq., vii, 218,
    238, 345n, 354n, 367,
    370; A 38, 39, 40
  John, 217
  Lemuel, 150, 157
  Stephen, Jr., A 39
  Capt. Stephen, Sr., 159,

HARDING continued
  Capt. continued, 199,
    211; A 39
  Stukely, 217, 486; A
    39
HARE
  Lt. ---, 254
HARRIS
  Jonathan, 167
  Peter, 137
HARRISBURG
  (Dauphin Co.), 490,
    A 48, 80
HARROT
  Asher, 136
HART
  Joseph, 362n
  Michael, 355n
HARTFORD
  (CT), 75, 77, 85,
    146, 158, 159, 168,
    178, 190, 196, 197,
    198, 205, 206, 207,
    209, 221, 244, 282,
    283, 288, 297n, 310,
    356n, 380, 381, 382,
    383, 386, 387, 401,
    441, 469; A 20, 40,
    49, 50, 51, 71, 80
  Co. (CT), 247; A 12
HARTLEY
  Col. Thomas, 240, 241,
    245, 246, 259, 261,
    268; A 86, 88
HARTZEL
  Jonas, 335, 339
HARVEY
  ---, See Lane, Mrs.
    George
  Benjamin, Jr., A 51
  Benjamin, Sr., 156,
    175, 289, 332, 432,
    488; A 25, 51
  Elisha, 289, 488; A
    25, 41, 51
  Jameson, A 51
  Silas, 243, A 51
HARVEY'S
  Creek, 172
HARWOOD
  John, (i.e. Ch. Miner),
    477
HASKELL
  Lt. Jonathan, 156, 157,
    467, 468, 469
HASTINGS
  John, 167
HATCH
  Benjamin, 243
HAVANA
  (Cuba), 105; A 49, 62
HAWKINS
  Capt. ---, 266
HAWKSEY
  Zebulon, 136
HAYNES
  Benjamin, 471
  Daniel, 138
HAZLETON
  ---, vi

HAZLETON continued
  Travellers, vi
HEATH
  Thomas, 157, 167
HEBBARD
  Moses, 138
  Moses, Jr., 137
HECKEWELDER
  Rev. John G. E., xv, 17,
    18, 30, 32, 35, 42,
    59, 69
HELLER'S
  (Northampton Co.), 265,
    355
HENDERSON
  ---, 360
  Andrew, 352
HENDRICK
  ---, 91
  Peter (Mohawk Indian),
    91, 92, 93, 94, 95,
    96, 97
HENRY
  IV, King of France, 63
HERKIMER
  Co. (NY), 392-93
HERSHARD
  Herman, 457
HEWIT
  Benjamin Jr., 137
  Gershom, 137
  Thomas, Esq., 349, 351-
    53
HEWITT
  ---, A 14
  Capt. Dethick, 214, 215,
    219, 222, 224, 232, 241,
    242, 467, 469; A 33-34,
    44
HIBBARD
  Ebenezer, 157
  William, 156, 178
  Zipron, 157, 243, A 22
HIBLER
  ---, xiiin
HICKMAN
  ---, 239, 486
  Mrs., ---, 138, 239,
    486; A 47
HICKS
  Gershom, 260
  Levi, 243
HILL
  Charles, 393
  Col. Erastus, vii, A
    13n
  Mrs. Erastus (née Pette-
    bone), A 13n
HILLMAN
  ---, 431
  Joseph, 136
HILTSHEIMER
  Jacob, 457
HINMAN
  Titus, 179, 242
HINSDALE
  Stephen, 138
HIOKATOO
  (Seneca Indian), 29n,
    266

-9-

History of Wyoming County, Pennsylvania

HISTORICAL SOCIETY
 of Pennsylvania, viii, 27, 417
HOCKELAGA
 (Canada) 21, See also Montreal
HOCKSEY
 ---, 240, 486
HOLLENBACK
 George M., vii
 Mrs. Geo. M., A 74
 John, 367, 394
 Ens. Matthias, 142, 193, 212, 227, 231, 239n, 244, 286, 394, 408, 412, 482; A 18, 25, 32, 47, 54, 56, 78
HOLMES
 Rev. Elkanah, 144
HOOKER
 Asahel, 167
 Hezekiah, 167
HOOVER
 Emanuel, 57-58
 Henry, 284
 John, 57-58
HOPKINS
 G. F., 58n
 James, 243
 Noah, 57-58n
 Timothy, 138, 157
HOPSON
 Gurdon, 136
HORTON
 Col. Miller, A 72
HOTCHKISS
 Samuel, 137
HOUGH
 James, 471
HOUSE
 of Commons, 306
HOUSTON
 William Charles, 483; A 19
 William Churchill, Esq. 307, 308, 316, 444, 446
HOWARD
 Nathaniel, 243
HOWE
 Gen. George, 193
HOYT
 Capt. Daniel, A 56
 Mrs. Daniel, (nee Pierce), A 56
HUBBAGE
 Lt., ---, 190
HUBBERTSTON
 (VT), A 26
HUBLEY
 Col. Adam, 264n, 265, 268, A 81, 82, 83, 85
HUDSON
 (NY), A 37
 River, 20, 21, 61, 74-76, 86, 87, 351, 442, 443, 449
HUGUENOTS
 ---, A 47
HULL

HULL continued
 Diah, 137
 Stephen, 137
HUME
 Capt., ---, 190
HUNGERFORD
 Benjamin, 167
 Stephen, 138
HUNLOCK
 Jonathan, A 42
 Mrs. Jonathan (nee Polly Jameson), A 42
HUNT
 August, 160, 161
HUNTER
 Col., ---, 288
 Robert, 136
HUNTINGTON
 Samuel, 391
 Twp., xi, 220, 229, 280, 285, 413, 435n, 490; A 13n, 60
HURD
 Jacob, A 62
HURLBUT
 Christopher, Esq., 120, 276, 432
 John, 432
 Deacon John, 276, 282, 283, 286, 288, 289, 304, 482, 488
 Napthali, 305, 482
 Reuben, 137
 Stephen, 138
 William, Esq., 112n
HUSTON
 Adj., ---, A 89
HUTCHINS
 John, 243
HUTCHINSON
 Samuel, 243
HUTS
 of Mercy, See Gnadenhutten
 of Peace, See Friedenshutten
HYDE
 Col. Ezekiel, 392-93, 490
 Judge Jabez, 482, 490
ILLINOIS
 River, 36n
INDIANS
 origins of 17-19, 22-23, 35-36n
INGERSOLL
 Daniel, 218-19, 227, 228, 276
INMAN
 David, A 30
 Col. Edward, vii, 358n, A 30
 Elijah, 243; A 29
 Isaac, 246; A 30
 Israel, 243, 246; A 29
 Richard, 226; A 29
INMAN'S
 Hill, xiv
INTRUSION
 Law, iii

IRON
 Ore, xiii
IROQUOIS
 Indians, 18, 21, 28, 30, 31, 32, 33-34, 35, 36n, 41, 43, 44n, 46, 48-50, 53, 60; A 73
IRVING
 Washington, iii; 75
IVES
 Mrs. --- (nee Lucy Williams), vii, A 30-31
JACKSON
 Asa, 343
 Samuel, 167, 243
 William, 246, 343, 366
JACOBS
 Plains, 26, 28, 240, 343, 422, A 21, 47
JAMES
 I, King of England, 63
 River (VA), 18
JAMESON
 Alexander, vii, 293, A 41-42
 Hannah, See Pearce, Mrs. ---
 John, 156, 305, 487, A 41
 Joseph, 293, 435; A 41, 42
 Polly, See Hunlock, Mrs. Jonathan
 Robert, 243, A 41
 Samuel, A 41-42
 William, 246, 486; A 41
JEFFERSON
 Thomas, 18, 24, 26, 28, 30, 31, 342, 372, 376
JEMISON
 Mary, 29n
JENKINS
 John, Esq., 164, 190, 195-96, 207, 217, 294, 345, 488; A 27, 33
 Col. John (Jr.), 112n, 146, 156, 158, 159, 161, 165, 166, 200, 218n, 255, 260, 268, 281, 285, 298, 311, 319-322, 327, 335, 336, 356, 368, 387, 388, 389, 392, 401, 423, 430, 432, 482, 487; A 27-29, 38
 Mrs. John (Jr.) Bertha ---, vii, 482, A 27n
 Stephen, 138, 430, 438
JENNINGS
 John, Esq., 106, 107, 108, 110, 111-13, 114, 115, 120, 125, 170, 215; A 37
 Joseph, 243
JEORUM
 Zerubabel, 138
JESUITS
 A 74
JEWEL
 Eliphalet, 136
JOHNSON

-10-

Index of Names continued

JOHNSON continued
---, 151, 153
--- (Mrs. Col. Z. Butler), A 63
Ebenezer, 336, 337, 357n, 359, 376, 379n, 380, 389
Edward, 138
Col. Guy, 379n
Henry, 243
Rev. Jacob: 97, 98, 140, 143-44, 183, 232, 288, 296, 324, 325, 438, 482; A 47, 59, 63
Jehoiada Pitt, 356
Sir John, 187, 217, 270, 275n, A 25
Ovid F., Esq., 143
Solomon, 138, 159, 198n
Sir William, 49, 60-61, 92-93, 95-98
William S., 308, 310, 372, 444-45
JOLLEE
John, 137
JONATHAN
(Indian chief), 94
JONES
Lt. ---, 264, 487; A 90
Hugh, 469
Joseph, Esq., 307, 444
Reuben, 467, 471
William, 253
JORDAN
J., Jr., viii, 56n, 417n, A 81
JUDD
Enoch, 162, 197
Maj. William, 168n, 211, 280, 289, 401, 412n, 413n, 436
JUDEA
Twp. (Lycoming Co.), 166, 167, 168, 169
JUNIATA
River, 47, 300, 301
KANADALAUGUA
(NY), A 98
KANADASAGE
(NY), A 101, 102
KANADIA
(NY), 272; A 101
KANAGHSAS
(NY), A 98-102
KANAWALUHERY
(NY), A 102
KASSON
James, 167
KEELER'S
Ferry (Wyoming Co.), 431
KELLEY
Michael, 487
KELLOG
Daniel, 167
Israel, 167
John, 167

KENNE
Cyrus, 137
KENYON
John, 137
KEY
keepers, 157, 277
KEYS
Timothy, 150, 157, 240, 244, 486
KIBBEN
Benjamin, 167
KIDD
John, 483
KIDDER
Sen. Luther, vii
KILBORN
---, 426-28, 438n
KILLAM
Ephraim, 466, 471-73, 476
Jeptha, 472-74
John, 466
Moses, 474, 476
Moses, Esq., 468n, 474
Silas, 472
Zadock, 466
KIMBALL
Capt., ---, A 90-91
KIMBLE
Abel, 466, 471, 473, 476
Mrs. Abel (nee Sybil Chapman), 468n, 473, 476
Ephraim, 472
Jacob, 466, 471, 476
Lucretia See Woodward, Mrs. ---
Stephen, 470-71
Walter, 466, 472-74
KINDERHOOK
(NY), 189, 245
KING
---, 376, 378
Philip (Nanagansett Indian), 20
KINGSBURY
Col. Joseph Esq., vii, A 52
KINGSLEY
---, 250-51, 487
Nathan, 199, 247, 285, 408, 486
KINGSTON
xiv, 25, 105, 136, 138, 140, 143, 144, 150, 154, 155, 178, 220, 256-58, 261, 263, 278, 284, 287, 303, 342, 346, 347, 349, 367, 386, 410, 430, 486, 490; A 8, 10, 11, 19-20, 42, 43, 49, 51, 52, 56, 58, 59, 63, 64
KINNEY
Joseph, 293
Mrs. Joseph (nee Sarah Spalding), 293
Newcombe, 293n
KIRKLAND

KIRKLAND continued
Rev. Samuel, 69, 98, 100
KITTATINNY
Mts., 40, 52, 297
KNAP
Hezekiah, 137
KNIGHT
Thomas, 137
LACKAWANNE
River, xii, xiii, 122, 239, 240, 269, 422, 429, 467, 490; A 28, 45, 56, 84
LACKAWAXEN
(Wayne Co.), 171, 345, 464
River, 266, 306n, 464-65, 469, 470-71, 474, 475
LACKAWAY
(Wayne Co.), 155, 220, 306n, 345n, 389n, 395, 466
LAKE
Champlain, A 26
Erie, 21
Huron, 21
Ontario, A 74
Superior, 21, 32
LAMPHER
Joshua, 136
LANCASTER
(Lancaster Co.), 48, 215, 481; A 25, 36, 89
Co., 56n, 106, 115, 139, 275n, 362n, 455; A 81
Intelligencer, 249
LANDON
Joshua, 243
Capt. Nathaniel, 112n, 156, 159, 199, 244, 395
LANE
Rev. George, A 41, 51
Mrs. George (nee Harvey), A 41, 51
LARNED
---, 296
George, 296-97
John, 296
LARNER'S
(Monroe Co.), 265, 349, 354-55, 417
LASTLEY
James, 156
LAUREL
Hill, 431
Run, 264
LAWRENCE
Daniel, 243
Gideon, 136
John, 205
Rufus, 156
William, 243
LAWSVILLE
(Susquehanna Co.), 490
LAWYERS
---, 298-99, 482-83, A 18-19

LEACH
---, 239, 486
Capt. Ebenezer, 167
LEADER
Sgt. ---, 285
LEATHER
sealers, 157
LEAVENSWORTH
John, 167
LEBANON
(CT), 190; A 33, 40
LEDLIE
Andrew, 107, 130-33, 170
LEE
---, 372
Asa, 136
John, 138
Joseph, 137
Noah, 138
Stephen, 138
LEE'S
Mills, 305
LEGGETT'S
Gap (Lackawanna Co.),
240, 486
LEHIGH
River, 39, 40, 46,
141, 154, 155, 265,
349n, 394
Water Gap (Northampton
Co.), 40, 121, 286
LE MAISTRE
Capt. ---, 254
LEMMON
---, 260
LEONARD
Jesse, 137
William, 137
LEPARD
Francis, 243
LESTER
---, 329, 486
Edward, 167, 246, 486
LEVENWORTH
Capt., ---, A 13
LEVY
Daniel, 483; A 19
LEWIS
Mrs., --- A 72
Elijah, 138
William, 450, 463
LEXINGTON
Battle of, 165
LINCOLN
Maj. Gen. B., 203,
A 24
LITCHFIELD
Co. (CT), 153, 162,
190, 369, 441; A 26,
57, 76
LITTLE
Castle (NY), 272
Meadow (Wayne Co.),
345n
LLOYD
Peter Z., 335
LOCK
James, 243
LOCUST
Hill, 349, 355, 358

LODGE
---, A 99
(Indian Chief), 183
Dr. George, 433-34, 436
LOGANSPORT
(IN), 249-50
LONDON
Gentleman's Magazine,
A 17
LONDONDERRY
(i.e. Wilkes-Barre),
331, 335
LONG
Island (NY), 20, 76, 77,
86-87, 193, 275n, 471;
A 11
Island Sound (NY), 20
LOOMIS
Elijah, 162
Capt. Thomas, 167
LOOP
Capt. Peter, 394, 401
LORANA
Twp. (McKean Co.), 391,
392, 489
LOTHROP
Cyprian, 137
LOWE
Conrad, 243
Jacob, 243
LUDINGTON
Asa, 112n
LUZERNE
Chevalier de la, 395-
99
(origin of name),
395-97
Co., xii, 107, 265,
303, 305, 383, 389n,
395, 404, 407, 408,
409, 413, 415, 418,
420, 430, 433, 434,
437n, 438, 440, 450,
451, 453, 454, 456-57,
461-62, 479, 480, 481,
482, 483, 484; A 4,
6, 7, 9, 14, 16, 17,
19, 27n, 28, 36, 37,
45, 59, 62, 72, 76
LYCOMING
Co., 455, 481; A 59
LYDIUS
Col. John, 69, 91, 93,
95, 96
LYMAN
Phineas, 103
LYME
(CT), 105; A 49, 51,
61
LYONS
---, 281
LYSTRUM
John, 140; A 48
MC ALLISTER
Richard, 362n
MC CALPIN
---, 25-26
MC CARRICAN
Capt. William, 211, 220,
242, 253, 302; A 20-21,

MC CARRICAN continued
Capt. conatinued,
41
MC CARTEE
C., 243
MC CLEAN
(six) (McClain),
Moses, 318, 324, 330
MC CLURE
James, 138; A 47
Mrs. James, 138, 139,
A 47
Thomas, 138
MC CORD
Mrs. --- (nėe Marcy),
A 59
MC COY
Ephraim, 382n
MC CORMICK
Lt. ---, 413
MC DONALD
Capt. ---, 266, A
93
MC DOWELL
Daniel, 305, 488
John, 106, 140, 141,
305, 363n, A 16
Robert, 368
MC INTIRE
Robert, 243
MC KEAN
Bryant, 469-70
Gov. Joseph Borden:
169, 348n, 359n, 413,
430, 431, 434, 437, 438;
A 8
Gen. Samuel, 305
Mrs. Samuel (nėe McDowal),
305
Co., 391, 489, 490
MC LENE
(sic) James, 362n
MC MAHON
Capt. ---, 285
MACHWIHILUSING
See Wyalusing
MACK
---, 38
MAHONING
(Carvon Co.), 286
MAINE
---, 443
MALLERY
Edward, Esq., A 72
Judge Garrick A 19,
63
Mrs. Garrick (nėe Sylvina
Butler), A 63
MAMARONECK
River (NY), 78, 79,
87
MANAHOAC
Indians, 24
MANHATTAN
(NY), 78
MANVIL
Nicholas, 243
MARCY
Ebenezer, 211, 230;
A 59

-12-

Index of Names continued

MARCY continued
  Mrs. Ebenezer, 230
  Zebulon, 217, 428, 429,
    A 59
MARSHALL
  Job, 243
  Chief Justice John, iii,
    iv, 193, 235, 256n,
    257, 273, 275; A 17, 18,
    50, 78
MARTHA'S
  Vineyard (MA), 86-87
MARTIN
  --- A, 39
  Robert, 328, 335, 349,
    351-53, 356, 357n,
    358n
  William, 167, 486; A
    39
MARVIN
  Daniel, 138
  Capt. David, 149
  Samuel, 136
  Seth, 142, 199
  Uriah, 137
MARYLAND
  ---, 35, 71, 303,
    372, 376
MASON
  Dixon Line, 71-72
MASSACHUSETTS
  ---, 64, 65, 66, 67,
    74
  Bay Colony, 74
  Historical Society,
    20
  Indians, 19-20
MASSASPPI
  Creek (Wyoming Co.),
    A 85
MASSAWAMEE
  Indians, 24, 29
MATTHEWS
  Benjmain, 138
MATTHEWSON
  Constant, 203; A 24
  Nero, 243
MAUCH
  Chunk (Carbon Co.),
    286
  Chunk Company,
    xiiin
MAXFIELD
  Joshua, 137
MAXWELL
  Gen. William, 264, 268,
    270, 271; A 81, 82,
    84, 88, 89, 92, 93, 99
MAY
  James, 137
MEADE
  David, 120, 137, 142,
    161-62, 171, 328, 333,
    335, 349, 351, 356,
    357n, 381-82
MEADVILLE
  (Crawford Co.), 162,
    382
MEDCALF
  Andrew, 137

MEELEMAN
  A., 243
MESHOPPEN
  (Wyoming Co.), 279,
    431
MIAMI
  Indians, 249
MICHAEL
  Capt. ---, 283, 295,
    296, 301
MIDDLETOWN
  (Dauphin Co.), A 36
MIFFLIN
  Thomas, 376
MILES
  Stephen, 138
  Milford (Pike Co.),
    465, 66, 470, 471,
    473, 474, 475
MILL
  Creek, 107, 109, 110,
    115, 116, 126, 139,
    140, 142, 143; A 5,
    32, 47, 48, 54, 58
MILLARD
  Andrew, 243
MILLER
  ---, 336-37
MILLINGTON
  Samuel, 138
MILLSTONE
  River (NJ) 201-2, 208;
    A 5, 24, 49
MINER
  Charles, A 71
  Sarah, v, vi
  William Penn, 17, 477
MINGO
  (Indians), 30, 273
MINISINK
  (NY), 48, 70, 122,
    189, 245, 260n,
    266
  Indians, 49
MINISTERS
  143-44, 164, 296, 304,
    438; A 10, 11-12,
    16n, 41, 58, 63
MISSIONARIES
  32, 33, 34, 38, 40,
    52, 58, See also
    Moravians
MISSISSIPPI
  River, 18, 19, 21, 32,
    36n, 42, 489
MITCHEL
  (sic), John, 138
MOBILE
  River, 29n
MOCK
  Abijah, 137
MOHAWK
  Indians, 18, 19, 20,
    21, 22, 29, 49, 60,
    91, 96, 98; A 74,
    75, 78
  River (NY), 29, 30, 236,
    245, 259, 264, 269;
    23, 81
MOHEGAN

MOHEGAN continued
  Indians, 31, 34, 44n, 49
MONOCKASY
  Is., xi, siv, 222, 224-
    25, 269, 290, 490; A
    5, 31, 53, 58
MONROE
  ---, 376
  Co. (PA), 106
MONTCALM
  Marquis de, 51n
MONTGOMERY
  Joseph, 318, 319, 322,
    323, 324, 325, 327,
    330n, 407
  William, Esq., 318,
    325, 330, 357n, 358n,
    363n, 373, 375, 376
MONTOUR
  Esther, 226, 232-33, 278;
    A 53-55
  Capt. Roladn, 233n, A 22
MONTREAL
  (Canada), 21, 42, 51n;
    A 25, 75, See also
    Hockelaga
MONTROSE
  (Susquehanna Co.), 490
MOORE
  Maj. James, 330, 336,
    348, 349, 359n, 362n
MORAVIANS
  ---, 18, 32, 33, 34, 38,
    40, 44, 52, 59, 140; A 86
  See also missionaries
MORGAN
  Samuel, 138, A 39
MORRIS
  James, 167
  Joseph, 107, 130-32, 170
  Gov. Lewis, 92-97
MORRISON
  Capt. ---, 245-46
MORRISTOWN
  (NJ), 201-2; A 24
MORSE
  Joseph, 137
MOSELY
  Increase, Esq., 112n, 167
MOUNT
  Moses, 279
MUD
  Fort (NJ), 203; A 24
MUHLENBERG
  Frederick, 362
  Peter, Esq., 407, 436
MULLEN
  M., A 33
MUNCY
  ---, 166, 168, 169, 171
MUNSEY
  Indians, 273
MURDOCK
  Daniel, 138
MURFEE
  John, 137, 241, 243;
    A 46
  Mrs. John (nee Gore),
    A 46
MYERS

-13-

MYERS continued
    ---, See Peck, Mrs.
      Rev. ---
    Lt., ---, 276, 287, 487
    Mrs. --- (nee Bennett),
      vii; 138, 221, 234,
      237, 304; A 14-16, 47
    Lt. Lawrence, 286, 303,
      430, 483n
    Thomas, 482
NANTICOKE
    William (Nanticoke Chief),
      187
    xivn, 173, 240, 286,
      305, 347, 386, 486;
      A 20, 21, 28
    Indians, 35, 41, 49
NANTMEL
    (Chester Co.), A 21
NANTUCKET
    Is. (MA), 86-87
NARONDIGWANOK
    (Seneca chief),
      187
NARRAGANSETT
    Bay (RI), 66-67
    Indians, 20
    River (RI), 65-66,
      67, 87
BASH
    Phineas, 149, 157
NAZARETH
    (Northampton Co.),
      A 25
NBIL
    Thomas, 243, 253
NELSON
    Hon. Thomas, 308,
      444
    William, 288
NESBITT
    Abraham, 293
    James, 138, 277, 289,
      408, 482
NESCOPECK
    ---, 171, 232, 246,
      276, 394, 395, 415,
      486, 487, A 80
NEVERSINK
    River (Pike Co.), 474
NEVIL
    John, 463
NEW
    England, 20, 53, 55,
      56, 62, 63, 64, 65,
      69, 76, 91, 98, 99,
      105, 108, 110, 144,
      146, 210, 211, 245,
      363, 368, 380, 383,
      385, 389n, 394, 405,
      459, 478, 490; A 20,
      35, 37
    Hampshire, 20n, 264,
      265, 267, 269, 275n,
      307, 375, 378, 380,
      413, 444; A 35, 41, 81
    Haven, (CT), 75, 78, 85,
      133, 159, 178, 192,
      412n, 441, 488, 489; A
      16, 17, 50, 72

NEW continued
    Jersey, 79, 80, 97,
      193, 201, 217,
      368, 307, 328, 334,
      346, 349, 361n, 372,
      376, 444, 467; A 21,
      24, 79, 81
    London (CT), 150, 178,
      489; A 72, 76, 80, 81
    Co. (CT), A 4, 51, 61
    Netherlands, 75, 80, 83
    Providence, 150
    Troy, A 57
    York City, 74, 77, 118,
      193, 253, 284, 297,
      332, 372, 379n, 421n;
      A 11, 13n, 16n, 38,
      43, 45, 49
    York State, 18, 40, 67,
      68, 70, 76, 78-83, 85,
      87-89, 98, 101, 151,
      176, 188, 189, 196,
      217, 264, 273, 302,
      306n, 311, 329, 359,
      376, 380, 390, 392,
      393, 413, 423, 430, 441-
      443, 447, 449, 460, 465,
      466, 468, 469, 471, 474,
      489; A 27, 36, 37, 41,
      43, 47, 71, 72, 80, 92
NEWBURG
    Letters, 350, 355n
NEWCASTLE
    (DE), 71, 72
NEWMAN
    ---, A 81
    ---, A 81
NEWPORT
    Twp., 276, 490
NEWTOWN
    (NY), 187, 200, 205,
      270, A 25, 28, 88,
      92, 93, 101
NIAGARA
    (NY), 42, 51n, 187,
      189, 190, 200, 212,
      247n, 248, 254, 259,
      278, 281, 284, 286,
      287, 290, 297, 305;
      A 23, 25, 38
NICHOLS
    Col. Richard, 75-76, 78,
      84
    Williams, 409, 483
NICHOLSON
    Mrs. ---, A 72
NINE-
    Mile Run Creek,
      417
NINEPARTNERS
    (NY), A 47
NITSCHMAN
    Martin, 45
NORRIS
    Isacc, 68, 74
NORTH
    American Review,
      21
    Branch (Susquehanna
      River), 167, 183

NORTH continued
    Carolina, 256, 372,
      376
    District, 155
NORTHAMPTON
    St., 143
NORTHMORELAND
    ---, 490
NORTHUMBERLAND
    ---, 29n, 168, 170,
      176, 260, 266, 285,
      328, 331, 334, 335,
      340, 341, 346, 347,
      349, 356, 359n, 363n,
      367, 389, 394, 449,
      A 4, 18
NORTON
    Ebenezer, 137
NORWALK
    (CT), 489
NORWICH
    (CT), 178, 293n, 391-3,
      478; A 27n, 39, 45, 49,
      58n, 59, 60
NUTIMUS
    (Delaware Indian), 47
OAKLEY
    John, 359
OGDEN
    ---, 360
    Capt. Amos, 106, 107-
      20, 122-32, 170, 331n,
      361; A 49, 84, 91, 93
    Nathan, 125-28
OHIO
    59, 250, 443, 473n,
      489; A 41, 58, 60, 72,
      77
    River, 19, 30, 35n, 42,
      59, 69, A 80
OLCOTT
    Thomas, 138
OLDER
    Col. ---, A 91
OLDMAN'S
    Farm (Bradford Co.), A
      86
ONEIDA
    Indians, 18, 19, 22,
      24, 29, 34, 35, 44n,
      49, 98; A 74, 75, 98,
      101, 104
ONONDAGO
    (NY), 24, 30, 32, 34,
      43, 44n, 48, 51, 95,
      140, 183, 186, 259
    Council, 19, 22, 24, 29-
      32, 33-34, 43, 44, 48,
      41, 95, 183, 186, 259
    Indians, 18, 19, 23, 49,
      60, 99, 100; A 22, 73,
      74, 75
ONTARIO
    (ship), 290
OQUAGO
    (NY), xii, 30, 187, 198,
      240, 329; A 49
ORANGE
    Co. (NY), 266, 466, 471,
      474, 475, A 27, 80

Index of Names continued

ORMS
  Jonathan, 136
ORTON
  Samuel, 136
O-SAW-SHE-QUAH
  (Yellow Leaf), 252
OSGOOD
  ---, 443
OSTERHOUT
  Isaac, Sr., 431; A 43
  Mrs. Isaac (nee Smith),
    A 43; See also Gay,
    Mrs. Fisher, Esq.
  Isaac S., Esq., A 43
OSWEGO
  (NY), 42, 60, 183,
    185, 187
  River (NY), 449
OTIS
  J., 243
OTSEGO
  Lake, xi; 269, A 81
OWEGO
  (NY), 30, 35, 187,
    465, 472; A 41, 83
PACKER
  Sen. Asa; xii
PAINE
  David, 391
  John, 161
PALMER
  Abel, 243
  George, 488
  Nathan, 482-83; A 19
PALMETERS
  William, A 25
PALMYRA
  (Pike Co.), 464
PARK (E)
  Capt. Silas, 112n, 138,
    156, 157, 159
PARKE
  Thomas, 299
PARKER
  Amos, 246, 486
  Jonathan, 156, 244
  William, 243
PARKS
  Elias, 137
  Rev. Moses, 467
  Silas, Jr., 467
PARLIAMENT
  ---, 165, 307; A 37
PARR
  Major ---, 264, 268,
    271; A 91, 92, 93,
    101
PARRISH
  Capt. Isaac, 156, 157, 466
  Jasper, 470-71
  Stephen, 471
  Capt. Zebulon, 466,
    468, 470-71
PARSONS
  Major ---, 46
  Capt. Hezekiah, A 40, 71
  Mrs. Hezekiah (née Whiton),
    A 40-41

PARTSCH
  Sister, 45
PATTERSON
  Col. Alexander,
    Esq., 112, 260, 324-
    36, 328-341, 344, 346-
    350n, 352-357n, 359-61,
    366, 368, 381, 386,
    389n, 410, 422n, 452,
    453, 485n, A 10, 51
PAXINOS
  (Shawanese chief), 43-
    44, 60
PAXTON
  (Lancaster Co.), 54, 56n
PASTON'S
  Rangers, 107
PEARCE
  Elder, ---, A 42
  Mrs. --- (née Hannah
    Jameson), A 41-42
PECK
  Rev. ---, A 16n .
  Mrs. Rev. --- (nee
    Myers), A 16n
PELLET
  John, Jr., 466, 472, 476
  John, Sr., 466, 476
PELLETT
  William, 467
PENCE
  ---, 280
PENN
  Richard, 71
  Thomas, 71
  Sir William, 71, 74, 82,
    88, 89, 101, 383, 478
PENNSYLVANIA
  Charter, 65-89, passim 98
  Gazette, 56n
  General Assembly, See
    General Assembly
    (Penna.)
PENNYMITE
  Wars, See Yankee-
    Pennamite Wars
PENSIL
  Henry, 225, 243
PEQUOT
  Wars, 105, A 58
PERKINS
  ---, See Hancock, Mrs.
    James
  Aaron, vii; A 42
  David, Esq., vii; A 42
  John, 137; A 42
  Tavern, A 25
PETERS
  Richard, 68, 74, 95, 96
PETTEBONE
  ---, See Hill, Mrs.
    Erastus
  Capt. Abel, A 13n
  Hon. Henry, A 13, 71
  Col. Jonathan, 112n, A 13n

PETTEBONE continued
  Noah, Jr., 243, A 12-13
  Noah, Sr., A 12
  Noah (III), A 13
  Oliver, A 12-13
  Stephen, 263, 486; A 12-13
PHELPS
  Ichabod, A 39
  Joel, 214
  Noah, 438n
PHILLIPS
  John, 277, 395
PICKERING
  Edward, 420-21, 429
  Col. Timothy, 66, 405-
    9, 411-15, 417n,
    420-432, 436-38, 452n,
    480-83
PIERCE
  ---, See Butler, Mrs.
    Lord
  See Hoyt, Mrs. Daniel
  Abel, Esq., 136, 298,
    342, 347, 401; A 55-56, 63
  Chester, 347; A 56
  Daniel, A 55
  Maj. Ezekiel, 155, 156,
    158, 177, 488; A 55
  John, 243, 487; A 55-56
  Phinease, 215, 221, 284,
    351, 352, 356, 359,
    379n, 380; A 15, 55-56
  Timothy, 157, 215, 241,
    242; A 46, 55-56
PIKE
  ---, 215
  Abraham, 280-81, 286,
    289, 487; A 61
PITKIN
  John, 112n
  William, 79, 89
PITTSBURGH
  (Alleghany Co.), 183,
    273; A 8
PITTSTON
  ---, 105, 142, 150,
    154, 155, 191, 219,
    220, 227, 231, 410,
    421, 429
  Ferry, xii
PLAINFIELD
  (CT), A 42, 52
PLAINS
  School House, 57
PLUNKET
  Col. ---, 168-179,
    188, 318
PLYMOUTH
  ---, 36, 105, 140,
    144, 149, 154-55,
    178, 191, 201, 220,
    230, 246, 261, 278,
    289, 292, 297, 303,
    332, 334, 347, 357n,
    386, 410, 435n, 482,
    486-88, 490; A 11, 12,
    26, 33, 51, 60, 61
  (England), 63
  (MA), 18, 64, 65, 67

-15-

PLYMOUTH continued
  Council (England),
    63-67
POCONO
  Mts., 239n
POETRY
  & History of Wyoming,
    iii, vi
POMEROY
  Ralph, 385, 401
POMETACOM
  See King Philip
    (Narragansett Indian),
    20
POOR
  Gen. ---, 264, 267,
    269-71, 273; A 81,
    82, 84, 88-93, 99
  Robert the Scribe (i.e.
    Ch. Miner), 477
PORT
  Gibson (MS), A 63
PORTER
  Jonah, 167, 202, 204;
    A 24, 50
  Thomas, 167, A 33
POST
  Oliver, 138
  -riders, 198
POTTER
  Hon. (Gen.) James,
    357n, 358n, 363n
  John, Esq., 356n
POUGHKEEPSIE
  (NY), iv
POWELL
  Maj. ---, 263-65,
    487
POWHATTAN
  Indians, 24, 29
POYNER
  ---, A 47
  Mrs. --- (nee Eunice
    Chapman), A 47
  Phebe, See Young,
    Mrs. ---
PREHISTORIC
  settlements, 25-27
PRESTON
  (CT), 288, 392
PRINCETON
  (NJ), 201; A 78
PRISONER'S
  Island (Quebec), A
    25-26
PRITCHARD
  Mary, 299
PROCTOR
  Col. ---, 264, 265,
    267, 269-71; A 90, 93,
    103
PROPRIETARY
  Govt. of PA, 36, 79,
    90, 91, 93-96, 101,
    106-8, 111, 112, 124,
    126-27, 129, 131, 133,
    135, 150, 154, 160,
    162, 164-65, 167-68,
    464, 485n
PROSPECT

PROSPECT continued
  Rock, xiv
PROVIDENCE
  (RI), A 37
  Twp. (Lackawanna Co.),
    xi; 154, 155, 486,
    487, 490, See also
    Capouse Meadows
PULTNEY
  (VT), A 26
PUTNAM
  Maj. Israel, A 49
  See Thunkhannock
QUATOGHY
  Indians, A 74
QUEBEC
  (Canada), 42, 51n,
    A 69, 74
QUEEN
  Esther, See Montour,
    Esther
  Esther's Plantation,
    (Bradford Co.), 176,
    233n, 269; A 52-53,
    88; See also Sheshequin
  Esther's Rock, See Bloody
    Rock (Queen Esther's)
QUILUTIMUNK
  (Lackawanna Co.), A
    84-85
RAMEY
  Bartlett, A 36
RAMSAY
  David, iv, 256n-57;
    A 17
RANSOM
  Lt. ---, 300
  Col. George Palmer,
    vii, 482; A 33, 25-27
  Samuel, 105, 156, 159,
    161, 193, 201, 202,
    203, 204, 208, 213,
    215, 221-22, 242, 244,
    258, 283, 332; A 10,
    12, 24-27, 29, 35, 42,
    49, 56, 59, 62
RATHER
  Capt. Conrad, A 37
RAWLE
  William, 450, 457
READ
  James, 359
  Noah, 138
READING
  (Berks Co.) A 25
RED
  Jacket (Indian chief),
    245n
REED
  Joseph, 70, 308, 444
  Samuel, 352, 360
  Col. William, 267; A 82,
    84
REEDY
  Jacob, A 37
REFORMADOS
  ---, 201, A 33
RENIE
  James, 363n
REYNOLDS

REYNOLDS continued
  Christopher, 243,
    299
  Enoch, 490
  Susannah, 299
RHODE ISLAND
  86, 307, 372, 376,
    444; A 37, 42
RICHARDS
  ---, 77
  Elisha, 159, 243
RICHARDSON
  Lt. ---, 190
RICHMOND
  Va., 256n
ROBBINS
  Miner, 214, 486; A
    39
ROBERTS
  Elias, 136, 243
  Hezekiah, 432
  Jabez, 136
  Jonathan, 457
ROBINSON
  Capt., ---, 318, 326,
    330
  John, A 63
  Thomas, A 47
ROCHAMBEAU
  ---, 397, 399
ROCKWAY
  Enos, 243
ROGERS
  Mrs. ---, 230
  Dr. Joel J., A 61,
    64
  Jonah, 279-81, 286,
    289, 293, 395, 432;
    A 61
  Jose, vii
  Josiah, 261, 432; A
    60-61, 64
  Mrs. Josiah (née Hannah
    Ford), A 60
ROOT
  Jesse, 308, 310, 372,
    444-45
  Jonathan, 166
ROSS
  Mrs. ---, A 72
  James, A 8
  Jeremiah, 199, 241,
    243; A 54, 80
  John, 483; A 19
  Lt. Perrin, 156, 159,
    179, 221, 241, 242,
    244; A 78, 80
  Timothy, 178, 243
  Gen. William, v, vii;
    233n, 355, 412n, 430-31,
    480; A 4-5, 8, 41, 43,
    49, 51, 54, 71, 76,
    80-81
  William Sterling; A 4
ROSS'S
  Hill, xiv, 347
ROSSWELL
  Sir Henry, 64
ROYAL
  Greens (Johnson's), 233

Index of Names continued

RUSH
  Dr. Benjamin, 430
  Judge Jacob, 139, 430, 437, 482; A 6, 18
RUSS
  Abraham, 156
RUSSELL
  Lt. Col. ---, A 24
RUTLEDGE
  Hon. John, 307, 399
ST. CLAIR
  Arthur, 362n
ST. JOHN
  Daniel, 239, 486; A 59
ST. LAWRENCE
  River, 19, 21, 32, 42, A 25
SALEM
  Twp., xi, 220, 229, 413, 467, 486, 490; A 36, 42
SAMBOURNE
  Thomas, 440
SATTERLEE
  Elisha, 392, 415
  John, 360-61
SAVAGE
  Abraham, 136
SAWMILLS
  ---, 142, 468
SAWYERS
  ---, 203-4; A 24
SAYBROOK
  (CT); 159
SCAMMELL
  ---, A 82, 84
SCHOOL
  Committe, 159, 277
SCHOOLS
  52, 57, 143-44, 159, 164, 197; A 8, 21, 41, 57
SCHOTTS
  Capt. John Paul, 265, 268, 271, 283, 285, 288, 310, 311, 314, 335, 382, 389, 394, 401, 419, 430, 436, 483; A 49, 82, 83
  Mrs. John Paul (nee Naomi Sill), 288; A 49
SCHUYLER
  Gen. Philip, 99, 182, 212, 216
SCHUYLKILL
  Co., A 37
  River, 286; A 37
SCIOTA
  River, 30, 36
SCOTCH
  Valley, 287-88, See also Conyngham Valley, Sugar Loaf
SCOTT
  John, Esq., 349
SCOVELL
  Lt. Elisha, 254
SEALERS
  of weights & measures, 157

SEARLE
  Abigail, See Abbott, Mrs. Stephen
  Constant, 220, 238, 241, 243; A 44
  John, 26; A 42
  Miner, A 45
  Roger, 226; A 44
  Sgt. William, 286; A 44, 45
SECORD
  John, 190, 214, 289; A 38
SEELEY
  Abel, 244
  Justice John, 328, 334, 359
SEGARD
  Fr. ---, 36n
SEGUANANTHUA
  (Tuscarora chief), 97, 98
SELECTMEN
  ---, 156, 276
SENECA
  Indians, 18, 19, 22, 24, 29n, 35, 49, 69, 187, 216, 222n, 233n, 266; A 74, 75, 78, 93, 101
  Lake (NY), 30, 271; A 95, 96, 97, 101
SENSEMAN
  Sister, ---, 45
SERGEANT
  Jonathan D., 308, 444
SETTLERS
  list of, 136-38, 166-167
SHAMOKIN
  (Northumberland Co.), 32, 35, 37, 38, 44, 58, 232
SHARON
  (NY), A 47
SHAW
  Abram, 243
  John, 137
  Joseph, 243
SHAWANESE
  Indians, 33, 35n, 38, 43, 44, 47, 48, 49, 60
  Twp., 328
SHAWNEE
  See Plymouth
SHAYS
  Rebellion, 413
SHEBOSH
  ---, 45
SHEOLAH
  (Pike Co.), 155, 296, 346n
SHEPARD
  Ruth, See Spalding, Mrs. Simon
SHEPHERD
  Samuel, 311, 319, 340
SHERIFFS

SHERIFFS continued
  ---, 395, 404, 407
SHERMAN
  Lt. Col. Isaac, 282; A 62
  Hon. Roger, 184, 185, 187, 376
SHERRARD
  Moses, 385
SHESHEQUIN
  (Bradford Co.), 59, 176, 187, 233n, 240, 259, 269, 293, 329; A 52, 53, 54, 86-88; See also Queen Esther's Plantation
SHICKSHINNY
  ---, 287
SHIKELLIMUS
  (Onondago Chief), 29, 35, 44n, 94
SHOEMAKER
  Lt. Benjamin, Jr., 1-6, 137, 225, 242, 482; A 16
  Hon. Charles Denison; A 16-17, 72
  Lt. Elijah, 159, 199, 220, 482; A 16-17
  Mrs. Elijah (nee Betsey Denison), 482; A 16, 48
  Henry, 328
SHOEMAKER'S
  Mills, 486; A 56
  Tavern, A 14
SHRAWDER
  Capt. ---, 318, 326, 330, 331, 346, 347
SHREEVE
  Capt. ---, 270, 273; A 82, 84, 91, 103
SICKLE
  Lawrence, 457
SILL
  --- See, Denison, Mrs. Nathan
  Dr. Elisha Noyes, A 49-50
  Jabez, 137, 143, 157, 177, 289; A 47
  Mrs. Jabez, A 47
  Naomi, See Schotts, Mrs. John Paul
  Shadrach, A 50
SILLIMAN
  Prof. ---, A 14
SIOUX
  Indians, 21
SITGREAVES
  Samuel, 465, 468, 483; A 19
SIX
  Nations, 18, 19, 24, 28, 30-37, 39, 43, 44, 47-51n, 53, 54, 57-60, 68, 69, 90-97, 100-102n, 139, 145, 182-84, 187, 200, 237, 259, 262, 270, 275n, 311, 384, 471; A 48, 78, See also Five Nations
SKINNER

-17-

History of Wyoming County, Pennsylvania

SKINNER continued
 Dr. Israel, A 55
SLATER
 Samuel, 167
SLAUGHTER
 Samuel, 156
SLOCUM
 Ebenezer, 247
 Frances, 247-252, 304, 487
 Giles, 247, 276, 351, 352, 355n, 356
 Isaac, 250
 Jonathan, 247-48, 486, 487
 Mrs. Jonathan, 247-49, 414
 Joseph, vii, 249-252
 Judith, 304
 Nathan, 247
 William, 248, 360-61, 394, 414, 480, 482
SMALL
 Pox, 196, 207, 370; A 28, 35, 47
SMEATHERS
 Capt. ---, 286; A 37
SMILEY
 John, 362n
SMITH
 ---, 377-379
 ---, See Gustin, Mrs. Samuel
 ---, See Gay, Mrs. Fisher, Esq. and Osterhout, Mrs. Isaac
 Rev. Dr. ---, 87, 89
 Abel, 137
 Daniel, 483; A 18
 Elizabeth, See Bailey, Mrs. ---
 Francis, 417n
 Garret, 438n
 James, 137, A 24, 43
 John, A 43
 John (Sr.), 112n, A 52
 Dr. John (Jr.), A 52
 Jonathan, 167, 488
 Lemuel, 138
 Mary, See Baker, Mrs. ---
 Oliver, 137
 Samuel, 362n
 Sarah, See Sutton, Mrs. James
 Capt. Timothy, Esq. 156, 158, 159, 488; A 51
 ("Big") William, 360
 ("Little") William, 360
 William (Jr.), A 43
 Dr. (Capt.), William Hooker, 150, 156, 201, 263, 287, 389, 408, 415; A 33, 43, 54
SNOWDEN
 Rev. ---, A 43
 Mrs. Rev. Dr. --- (nee Smith), A 43
 James, Ross, Esq., A 43

SNYDER
 Simon, A 8
SOLOMON
 Capt. ---, 295
SOLOMON'S
 Creek, xiiin, 121-22
SOMERSET
 Court House (NJ), 201-2; A 50
SOUTH
 Carolina, 29, 31, 372, 376, 442
 Seas, (i.e. Pacific Ocean), 64-67, 74
SPAFFORD
 Darius, 224, 243; A 34
 Mrs. Darius (nee Lavina Blackman), 224; A 34
 Phineas, 224
SPAIGHT
 ---, 376
SPAIN
 A 101-2
SPALDING
 Deliverance, 167
 Sarah, See Kinney, Mrs. Joseph
 Lt. Gen. Simon, 123, 177, 193, 203, 215, 219, 221, 227, 239, 245, 246, 262, 268, 271, 283, 285, 293, 295, 305, 322, 329, 330, 340, 392, 395, 401; A 5, 13, 14, 20, 24, 25, 28, 34, 48, 50, 52-53, 56, 83
 Mrs. Simon (nee Ruth Shepard), A 52
SPENCER
 ---, 204; A 24
 ---, A 82
 James, 244
 Josiah, 244
 Levi, 244
SPRAGUE
 ---, See Young, Mrs. ---
 Eleazer, 244; A 48
 Joseph, 408
 Dr. Joseph, 139; A 5, 47-48
 Mrs. Dr. Joseph, 138; A 47
SPRING
 Falls (Lackawanna Co.), A 84
SPRINGFIELD
 (NJ), 203
 Twp. (Bradford Co.), 490, A 57, 59
SQUIER
 Zachariah, 138
STAGER
 William, 116
STAMFORD
 (CT), 75
STANDING

STANDING continued
 Stone (Bradford Co.), 201, 273; A 86, 87
STANLEY
 Col. Gad, 112n, 401
STANSBURY
 Adonijah, 197-98
STAPLES
 Joseph, 243
 Reuben, 243
STARK
 Aaron, 243, A 35
 Christopher, A 35
 Daniel, 243; A 35
 Henry, A 35
 James (1st), A 35
 James, (2nd), 150, 157, 159, 199, 230; A 35
 James, Esq. (3rd), 27, A 35-36
 John, Esq., A 35
 John D., A 35
 William, 390
STEARNS
 Ebenezer, 136
STEELE
 Sir Richard, 28
STERLING
 John, 137
 (Wayne Co.), 465, 467, 472
STEVENS
 ---, See Dana, Mrs. Anderson
 ---, See Dana, Mrs. Sylvester, Esq.
 Lt. Asa, 156, 162, 200, 242; A 56
 John A 56
 Jonathan, A 57
 Nathan, 360
 Phineas, 138
 Rosewell, A 56
 Rufus, 243
 Simon, A 82
 Thomas, 140
 Uriah, 157
STEVENSON
 James, 244
STEWART
 Capt. Lazarus, 57, 115-116, 119, 120, 124, 125-128, 132, 156, 157, 159, 220, 242, 244; A 20
 Lt. Lazarus, Jr., 242
 William, 150
STOCKS
 157-58
STODDART
 Capt. Thomas, 156, 260n
STODDARTSVILLE
 265, 349n
STODERT
 Benjamin, 277
STOKE
 Twp., 328
STONE
 Ebenezer, 138
 Col. William Leete, iii,

-18-

Index of Names continued

STONE continued
  Col. continued, vi,
    57, 59n, 60, 66,
    222n, 233n, 420n
STONINGTON
  (CT), 105, 159; A 5,
    19, 44, 53
STONY
  Point (NY), 273
STORES
  ---, 139; A 4-6, 21,
    45
STORKE
  Samuel, A 62
STORY
  Samuel, 138
STOWELL
  Jonathan, 162
STRONG
  ---, 467
  Capt. Henry, 136
  Henry R., Esq., viii
  J., 151, 153
  Return, 167
  Capt. Solomon, 190,
    203, 244
STROUD
  Col. Jacob, 286, 335,
    339; A 45
STROUDSBURG
  ---, 106, 141, 230,
    239n, 265, 288, 296,
    305, 345; A 24, 25, 37
STUYVESANT
  Peter, 75
SUGAR
  Loaf, 287, See also
    Conyngham Valley,
    Scotch Valley
SULLIVAN
  Gen. John, 232n, 264-268,
    271-76, 278, 347; A 36,
    47, 52, 54, 81-83, 86-
    89, 93, 94, 97, 101-3
  Co. (NY), 468
SULLIVAN'S
  Expedition, 265-275; A
    81-104
SUNBURY
  (Northumberland Co.), 44,
    92, 112, 168, 169, 191,
    288, 295, 325, 331, 348,
    356-59n, 382; A 19, 31,
    77; See also Fort Augusta
SURVEYORS
  of highways, 156, 276
SUSQUEHANNA
  Company, xin, 68-72, 81,
    89, 90-92, 94, 97, 99,
    101, 103-4, 109, 111,
    112n, 124, 133, 146,
    1513, 161, 382-85, 387-
    393, 400-404, 462, 481
  Co., xii, 383, 482, 484;
    A 9, 59
SUTTON
  James, A 43
  Mrs. James (nee Sarah
    Smith), A 43
  Samuel, 410

SWANY
  Capt. ---, A 36
SWEDE
  Nailer, 243
SWEET
  Samuel, 137
SWETLAND
  Belding, A 20
  Luke, 157, 240, 272,
    487; A 19-20
  William, Esq, vii,
    167; A 13, 20
SWIFT
  Elisha, 156, 157,
    159, 162
  Herman, 193; A 78
  Capt. John, 348n, 349,
    351-52, 355, 360,
    415, 417n
TADAME
  (Delware Chief), 46
TALCOTT
  Gen. Eleazur, 112n,
    310, 387
THE TATTLER
  ---, 28
TAX
  Collectors, 209, 277
TAXES
  ---, 149, 157, 179,
    188, 197, 199, 204-7,
    283, 294-95, 297-298,
    306, 361, 371, 384,
    483-84
TAYLOR
  Mrs. John (nee Buck),
    A 59
  John M., 440, 455; A 59
  Preserved, 137
TEDEUSCUNG
  (Delaware chief), 35, 41,
    46-50, 53, 57, 58, 60,
    62
TEED
  Zophur, 138
TEGOHAGWANDE
  (Onondago chief), 99-
    100
TENNANT
  Caleb, 136
TERRY
  Jonathan, 367
  Parshall, 137, 150
  Uriah, A 64
THAYENDENEGEA
  See Bryant, Joseph
THAYER
  Zephaniah, 136
THEONDINTHA
  (Oneida Indian),
    98-99
THOMAS
  Aaron, 156
  Elias, 137
  Moses, 156
  Richard, 457
THOMPSON
  Charles, 48-49, 373
THORNBURY
  Sgt. ---, 241; A 36

TIOGA
  Co., A 50
  Point (Bradford Co.), xi,
    30, 154, 176, 187, 200,
    215, 217, 268-70, 273,
    275, 280, 286, 329, 481;
    A 25, 36, 81, 83, 86-91,
    96, 97, 100, 103
TISHEKUNK
  (Delaware chief), 47
TITHING
  men, 157, 468
TOBY'S
  Creek, A 61
TORIES
  ---, 233, 255, 257,
    258, 270, 279; A 10,
    25, 36, 38, 45, 73, 91,
    93, 96, 102
TOUCEY
  Isaac, Esq., A 71
TOWANDA
  Creek (Bradford Co.),
    395
TOWN
  Mrs. ---, vii
  Committees, 140
  meetings, 147-150, 155,
    157-160, 165-66, 177-
    79, 189, 190-91, 195-97,
    199, 207, 209, 276-77,
    281-82, 288, 297, 308,
    371, 380, 410-12
  treasurers, 156, 276
TRACEY
  Isaac, 138
TRACY
  Andrew, 393
  Zavan, 156
TRENTON
  (NJ), 47, 70, 101, 102,
    104, 201, 301, 308-11,
    315-16, 374, 375n, 441,
    442, 444, 445, 448; A
    78
  Decree of (1782): 145,
    308, 309, 328, 341, 363,
    368, 379, 411, 440n
    441, 446, 449, 450, 453-
    56, 459-63, 479, 481,
    490; A 76
TREUSDALE
  Mrs. ---, 230
TRIPP
  Isaac, Esq., 108, 150,
    156, 195-96, 199, 240,
    248, 304, 486, 488
  Isaac (Jr.), 240, 487
TRUMBULL
  Gov. Jonathan, 133-34, 151,
    154, 188, 210, 211; A 45
  Twp., 392
TUNKHANNOCK
  (Wyoming Co.), 200, 213,
    214, 286, 289, 424n, 428,
    429, 486, 487, 490; A
    43
  Creek (Wyoming Co.), 280;
    A 35, 59, 85
TURENNE

TURENNE continued
  Twp., (McKean Co.), 489
TURNEY
  Lt. ---, 259
TUSCARORA
  Indians, 18, 28, 49,
    97
TUSTIN
  Col. Benjamin, 474
TUTELOE
  Indians, 49
TUTTLE
  Ichabod, 244, 429
TUTTLE'S
  Creek, 347; See
    also Abraham's Creek
TWIGHTWY
  Indians, A 74-75
TYPHUS
  ---, A 52
ULSTER
  Twp., 490
UNAMY
  Indians, 49
UNITED
  Brethren, See Moravians
  States Gazette, A 8
UPDIKE
  Ludwick, Esq., 385
UPSON
  Asa, 279, 487
USHER
  Twp., 393, 490
UTLEY
  Mrs. ---, 287, 486
  Diah, 287, 486
  Elisha, 247, 486
  John, 247, 486
VALLEY
  Forge (Montgomery Co.),
    A 47
VAN CAMPEN
  Aaron, Esq., 120,
    350n
  Benjamin, 156
  Moses, 279-81, 286,
    289, 487
VANDERLIP
  Frederick, 160; A 85
VANGORDER
  Abraham, 190, 244,
    380
  Philip, 190
VAN GORDON
  Wilhelmus, 347
VANHORN
  vs. Dorrance (1795),
    316, 452; A 10
VANTYNE
  Kill (Pike Co.), 473
VAN WEE
  John, 244
VARNUM
  Capt. Eliab, 466
  Joshua, 466
VERMONT
  ---, 378, 380, 388,
    411, 412, 413, 460,
    490; A 26
VINCENT

VINCENT continued
  Levi, A 48
VIRGINIA
  ---, 18, 24, 29,
    31, 65, 71, 88,
    182, 308, 341, 372,
    376, 444, 446, 448;
    A 18, 37, 38, 48, 80,
    81
VOLUNTOWN
  (CT), A 41
VORCE
  Timothy, 137
WADE
  Nathan, 156
WALES
  Nathaniel, Jr., 391
WALKER
  Capt., ---, A 89
WALKING
  Purchase (1737), 47
WALL
  Henry, 136
WALLWORTH
  Thomas, 136, 167
WALLSWORTH
  John, 138
  William, 137
WALTER
  Aaron, 137
WARD
  ---, 336n
  C. L. Esq., viii
  John, 244
WARNER
  William, 156
WARRIOR'S
  Run, 187
WARTERS
  Joseph, 167
WASHINGTON
  Gen'l, George, 193-94;
    201-3, 208-9, 239,
    259, 260, 274, 478;
    A 79
  D. C., 245n, 256, 341,
    350, 490
WATERMAN
  Flavius, 242
WATSON
  Nathaniel, 136
WAUGH
  Joseph, 167
WAYNE
  Gen. Anthony, 106, 273,
    275n
  Co., 464, 465, 471,
    474, 483, 484
WEEKS
  ---, 238
WEISER
  Conrad, 38-39, 47
WELLES
  Harriet, See Cowles,
    Mrs. ---
WESTERN
  Reserve, 310
WHIPPING
  post, 157-58, 285
WHITON

WHITON continued
  ---, See Parsons, Mrs.
    Hezekiah
WILCOX
  Esen, 244, 487
WILD
  game, xiv, 139; A 85
WILKES
  Barre Gazette, xivn
WILLIAMS
  Darius, A 31
  Desire, A 31
  Elihu (Jr.), A 31
  Elihu (Sr.), A 31
  Mrs. Elihu, A 31
  Esther, A 31
  Lucy, See Ives, Mrs.

  Martha, A 31
  Rufus, A 31
  Thaddeus, 262-63
  Sgt. Thomas, vii, 262-
    63, A 5, 24
WILLIAMSON
  ---, 372, 376
WILSON
  ---, 377, 378, 455
WILSONVILLE
  (Pike Co.), 465, 467,
    469, 472
WINDHAM
  (CT), xivn, 81, 97,
    98, 112n
  Co., 231, 240; A 10,
    40, 42
WOLCOTT
  John, 300-1
  Gov. Oliver, Jr., 88,
    91, 99, 389n, 401,
    412, 413n, 436, 443
WOLFE
  Gen. James, 51n, A 69
WOOD
  Major ---, 475
WOODBURY
  (NJ), A 24
WOODWARD
  Dr. ---, A 71
  Mrs. --- (nee Lucretia
    Kimble), 476
  Enos, 466, 476
  Mrs. Enos (nee Mary ---),
    476
  Hon. George W., 306n, 490
  Warren J., Esq., 306n,
    464
  William, 244
WORDEN
  Capt. William, 199; A
    24
WORK
  ---, 337
WRIGHT
  H. B. Esq., vii; A 63
  Thomas, 440
WYALUSING
  (Bradford Co.), 52, 55-
    56, 58, 59, 69, 186,
    200, 213, 245, 269,
    302, 490; A 22, 27, 53, 86

Index of Names continued

WYALUSING
  Creek (Bradford Co.), 468n, A 10, 56, 57, 59
WYANDOT
  Indians, 21, 30
WYBRANT
  Samuel, 137
WYLLIS
  Col. Samuel, 192; A 62
WYLLYS
  George, 210-11
WYOMING
  (Origin of Name), xv
  Battle of, 217-245, passim, 253-58; A 5, 12, 14-15, 17-18, 22, 25, 29, 31, 44-46, 64-68, 79-80
  Co., xii, A 43, 59
  Herald (newspaper), A 63

WYOMING continued
  Massacre, iv, 224-28; A 13n, 15, 17-18, 25, 39, 53-54, 56n, 64-69, 69-70, 73, 79
  Monument, A 19, 69-73
WYSOX
  (Bradford Co.), 264
YALE
  Enos, 137
  Ozias, 136, 244
  College, 143, 197, A 16, 40, 41
YANKEE
  Doodle (song), A 37
  Pennamite Wars, 103-134, passim, 168-179, 344-369 passim
YARRINGTON
  Abel, 289, 412
YATES
  Hon., ---, 481
YORK

YORK continued
  ---, 200, 487; A 27, 38
  ---, See Buck, Mrs. Aholiab and Gaylord, Mrs. Justus, Jr.
  Rev. Miner, A 27, 59
  Co., 265, 362n
YORKTOWN
  (VS), A 11, 37
YOUNG
  Capt. ---, 777
  Mrs. --- (nee Phebe Poyner), A 47
  Mrs. --- (nee Sprague), 139, 253; A 47-48
  Lazarus, 142; A 48
YUCATAN
  ---, 17
ZEISBERGER
  Rev. David, 52-53, 59
ZINZENDORF
  Count, ---, 38-40

-21-

www.ingramcontent.com/pod-product-compliance
Lightning Source LLC
Chambersburg PA
CBHW052128010526
44113CB00034B/940